An Introduction to Law and Regulation

SECOND EDITION

Contemporary life relies on regulation. The quality and safety of the water we drink, the food we eat and the social media applications we use are all governed by multiple regulatory regimes. Although rooted in law, regulation is a multidisciplinary endeavour. Debates about regulation, particularly in the face of rapid change and the emergence of new 'risks', are now commonplace. Despite extensive scholarship, regulation is often poorly understood, even by policymakers, with unintended and even disastrous consequences. This book offers a critical introduction to core theories, concepts, methods, tools and techniques of regulation, including regulatory policy, instruments, enforcement, compliance, accountability and legitimacy. Weaving extracts from texts drawn from many disciplines with accessible commentary, it introduces this important field to students, scholars and practitioners in a scholarly yet accessible and engaging manner with discussion questions and additional readings for those seeking to deepen their knowledge.

Karen Yeung is the University of Birmingham's first interdisciplinary professor, based at Birmingham Law School and School of Computer Science, following previous appointments at King's College London and the University of Oxford. She is recognised worldwide as a leading scholar in the law and governance of emerging technologies, including the regulation of AI and regulation by algorithm. She is extensively involved in AI policy in Europe and elsewhere, including membership of the EU's High Level Expert Group on AI and supporting the European Network of Equality Bodies (Equinet) and the UK's Equality and Human Rights Commission to prevent and combat AI-enabled discrimination.

Sofia Ranchordás is Professor of Administrative Law at Tilburg University and LUISS (Rome) and an Affiliated Fellow at the Yale Information Society Project. She is a leading scholar in regulation and technology. Ranchordás has earned multiple grants for her work on regulation and vulnerability (e.g., NWO-Vidi, WASP-HS). She has served as a visiting professor at the Universities of Pennsylvania and Virginia. Her advisory work and research on regulation and technological change, experimental regulations and regulatory sandboxes have prompted legislative changes.

Law in Context

Since 1970, the Law in Context series has been at the forefront of a movement to broaden the study of law. The series is a vehicle for the publication of innovative monographs and texts that treat law and legal phenomena critically in their cultural, social, political, technological, environmental and economic contexts. A contextual approach involves treating legal subjects broadly, using materials from other humanities and social sciences, and from any other discipline that helps to explain the operation in practice of the particular legal field or legal phenomena under investigation. It is intended that this orientation is at once more stimulating and more revealing than the bare exposition of legal rules. The series includes original research monographs, coursebooks and textbooks that foreground contextual approaches and methods. The series includes and welcomes books on the study of law in all its contexts, including domestic legal systems, European and international law, transnational and global legal processes, and comparative law.

Books in the Series

Acosta: *The National versus the Foreigner in South America: 200 Years of Migration and Citizenship Law*
Alaattinoğlu: *Grievance Formation, Rights and Remedies*
Ali: *Modern Challenges to Islamic Law*
Alyagon Darr: *Plausible Crime Stories: The Legal History of Sexual Offences in Mandate Palestine*
Anderson, Schum & Twining: *Analysis of Evidence, 2nd Edition*
Ashworth: *Sentencing and Criminal Justice, 6th Edition*
Douglas Barton: *Law and Parenthood*
Baxi, McCrudden & Paliwala: *Law's Ethical, Global and Theoretical Contexts: Essays in Honour of William Twining*
Beecher-Monas: *Evaluating Scientific Evidence: An Interdisciplinary Framework for Intellectual Due Process*
Bell: *French Legal Cultures*

Bercusson: *European Labour Law, 2nd Edition*
Birkinshaw: *European Public Law*
Birkinshaw: *Freedom of Information: The Law, the Practice and the Ideal, 4th Edition*
Blick: *Electrified Democracy: The Internet and the United Kingdom Parliament in History*
Ferri Broderick: *International and European Disability Law and Policy: Text, Cases and Materials*
Goodwin Brownsword *Law and the Technologies of the Twenty-First Century: Text and Materials*
Goudkamp Cane: *Atiyah's Accidents, Compensation and the Law, 9th Edition*
Clarke: *Principles of Property Law*
Kohler Clarke: *Property Law: Commentary and Materials*
Collins: *The Law of Contract, 4th Edition*
Collins, Ewing & McColgan: *Labour Law, 2nd Edition*
Cowan: *Housing Law and Policy*
Cranston: *Making Commercial Law Through Practice 1830–1970*
Cranston: *Legal Foundations of the Welfare State*
Darian-Smith: *Laws and Societies in Global Contexts: Contemporary Approaches*
Dauvergne: *Making People Illegal: What Globalisation Means for Immigration and Law*
David: *Kinship, Law and Politics: An Anatomy of Belonging*
Davies: *Perspectives on Labour Law, 2nd Edition*
Dembour: *Who Believes in Human Rights?: Reflections on the European Convention*
de Sousa Santos,: *Toward a New Legal Common Sense: Law, Globalization, and Emancipation*
Diduck: *Law's Families*
Douglas-Scott: *Brexit, Union, and Disunion: The Evolution of British Constitutional Unsettlement*
Dowdle: *Transnational Law: A Framework for Analysis*
Dupret: *Positive Law from the Muslim World: Jurisprudence, History, Practices*
Emon: *Jurisdictional Exceptionalisms: Islamic Law, International Law, and Parental Child Abduction*
Estella: *Legal Foundations of EU Economic Governance*
Fortin: *Children's Rights and the Developing Law, 3rd Edition*
Garnsey: *The Justice of Visual Art: Creative State-Building in Times of Political Transition*
Garton, Probert & Bean: *Moffat's Trusts Law: Text and Materials, 7th Edition*
Woodman Ghai: *Practising Self-Government: A Comparative Study of Autonomous Regions*
Glover-Thomas: *Reconstructing Mental Health Law and Policy*
Punch Gobert: *Rethinking Corporate Crime*
Goldman: *Globalisation and the Western Legal Tradition: Recurring Patterns of Law and Authority*
Haack: *Evidence Matters: Science, Proof, and Truth in the Law*
Rawlings Harlow: *Law and Administration, 4th Edition*
Harris: *An Introduction to Law, 8th Edition*
Harris, Campbell & Halson: *Remedies in Contract and Tort, 2nd Edition*
Harvey: *Seeking Asylum in the UK: Problems and Prospects*
Herring: *Law and the Relational Self*

McHale Hervey: *European Union Health Law: Themes and Implications*
McHale Hervey: *Health Law and the European Union*
Lee Holder: *Environmental Protection, Law and Policy: Text and Materials, 2nd Edition*
Summers Jackson: *The Internationalisation of Criminal Evidence: Beyond the Common Law and Civil Law Traditions*
Jeutner: *The Reasonable Person: A Legal Biography*
Kostakopoulou: *The Future Governance of Citizenship*
Kreiczer-Levy: *Destabilized Property: Property Law in the Sharing Economy*
Kubal: *Immigration and Refugee Law in Russia: Socio-Legal Perspectives*
Lewis: *Choice and the Legal Order: Rising above Politics*
Likosky: *Law, Infrastructure and Human Rights*
Likosky: *Transnational Legal Processes: Globalisation and Power Disparities*
Lixinski: *Legalized Identities: Cultural Heritage Law and the Shaping of Transitional Justice*
Loughnan: *Self, Others and the State: Relations of Criminal Responsibility*
Lunney: *A History of Australian Tort Law 1901-1945: England's Obedient Servant?*
Webb Maughan: *Lawyering Skills and the Legal Process, 2nd Edition*
McGaughey: *Principles of Enterprise Law*
McGlynn: *Families and the European Union: Law, Politics and Pluralism*
Mertens: *A Philosophical Introduction to Human Rights*
Miller: *An Introduction to German Law and Legal Culture: Text and Materials*
Moffat: *Trusts Law: Text and Materials*
Monti: *EC Competition Law*
Morgan: *Contract Law Minimalism: A Formalist Restatement of Commercial Contract Law*
Morgan Yeung: *An Introduction to Law and Regulation: Text and Materials*
Nash: *British Islam and English Law: A Classical Pluralist Perspective*
Ng: *Political Censorship in British Hong Kong: Freedom of Expression and the Law (1842–1997)*
Davies Nicola: *EU Law Stories: Contextual and Critical Histories of European Jurisprudence*
Norrie: *Crime, Reason and History: A Critical Introduction to Criminal Law, 3rd Edition*
O'Dair: *Legal Ethics: Text and Materials*
Oliver: *Common Values and the Public–Private Divide*
Drewry Oliver: *The Law and Parliament*
Roberts Palmer: *Dispute Processes: ADR and the Primary Forms of Decision-Making, 1st Edition*
Roberts Palmer: *Dispute Processes: ADR and the Primary Forms of Decision-Making, 3rd Edition*
Picciotto: *International Business Taxation*
Pieraccini: *Regulating the Sea: A Socio-Legal Analysis of English Marine Protected Areas*
Probert: *The Changing Legal Regulation of Cohabitation, 1600-2010: From Fornicators to Family, 1600-2010*
Radi: *Rules and Practices of International Investment Law and Arbitration*
Reed: *Internet Law: Text and Materials*
Richardson: *Law, Process and Custody*
Palmer Roberts: *Dispute Processes: ADR and the Primary Forms of Decision-Making, 2nd Edition*
Rowbottom: *Democracy Distorted: Wealth, Influence and Democratic Politics*

Sauter: *Public Services in EU Law*
Black Scott: *Cranston's Consumers and the Law*
Seneviratne: *Ombudsmen: Public Services and Administrative Justice*
Seppänen: *Ideological Conflict and the Rule of Law in Contemporary China: Useful Paradoxes*
Siems: *Comparative Law, 3rd Edition*
Stapleton: *Product Liability*
Stewart: *Gender, Law and Justice in a Global Market*
Tamanaha: *Law as a Means to an End: Threat to the Rule of Law*
Taylor: *Fortin's Children's Rights and the Developing Law, 4th Edition*
Tuori: *Properties of Law: Modern Law and After*
Tomkins Turpin: *British Government and the Constitution: Text and Materials, 7th Edition*
Twining: *General Jurisprudence: Understanding Law from a Global Perspective*
Twining: *Globalisation and Legal Theory*
Twining: *Human Rights, Southern Voices: Francis Deng, Abdullahi An-Na'im, Yash Ghai and Upendra Baxi*
Twining: *Jurist in Context: A Memoir*
Twining: *Karl Llewellyn and the Realist Movement, 2nd Edition*
Twining: *Rethinking Evidence: Exploratory Essays, 2nd Edition*
Miers Twining: *How to Do Things with Rules, 5th Edition*
Wan: *Film and Constitutional Controversy: Visualizing Hong Kong Identity in the Age of 'One Country, Two Systems'*
Ward: *A Critical Introduction to European Law, 3rd Edition*
Ward: *Law, Text, Terror*
Ward: *Shakespeare and Legal Imagination*
Watt: *The Making Sense of Politics, Media, and Law: Rhetorical Performance as Invention, Creation, Production*
Quick Wells: *Lacey, Wells and Quick: Reconstructing Criminal Law: Text and Materials, 4th Edition*
Woodhead: *Caring for Cultural Heritage: An Integrated Approach to Legal and Ethical Initiatives in the United Kingdom*
Yeung Ranchordás: *An Introduction to Law and Regulation: Text and Materials, 2nd edition*
Young: *Turpin and Tomkins' British Government and the Constitution: Text and Materials , 8th Edition*
Zander: *Cases and Materials on the English Legal System, 10th Edition*
Zander: *The Law-Making Process, 6th Edition*

International Journal of Law in Context: A Global Forum for Interdisciplinary Legal Studies

The *International Journal of Law in Context* is the companion journal to the Law in Context book series and provides a forum for interdisciplinary legal studies and offers intellectual space for ground-breaking critical research. It publishes contextual work about law and its relationship with other disciplines including but not limited to science, literature, humanities, philosophy, sociology, psychology, ethics, history and geography. More information about the journal and how to submit an article can be found at http://journals.cambridge.org/ijc

An Introduction to Law and Regulation

Text and Materials

Second Edition

KAREN YEUNG
University of Birmingham

SOFIA RANCHORDÁS
Tilburg University and Luiss Guido Carli

CAMBRIDGE
UNIVERSITY PRESS

CAMBRIDGE
UNIVERSITY PRESS

Shaftesbury Road, Cambridge CB2 8EA, United Kingdom

One Liberty Plaza, 20th Floor, New York, NY 10006, USA

477 Williamstown Road, Port Melbourne, VIC 3207, Australia

314–321, 3rd Floor, Plot 3, Splendor Forum, Jasola District Centre, New Delhi – 110025, India

103 Penang Road, #05-06/07, Visioncrest Commercial, Singapore 238467

Cambridge University Press is part of Cambridge University Press & Assessment, a department of the University of Cambridge.

We share the University's mission to contribute to society through the pursuit of education, learning and research at the highest international levels of excellence.

www.cambridge.org

Information on this title: www.cambridge.org/9781009379014

DOI: 10.1017/9781009379007

When citing this work, please include a reference to the DOI 10.1017/9781009379007

First published 2007
Reprinted 2009
Second edition 2024

A catalogue record for this publication is available from the British Library.

A Cataloging-in-Publication data record for this book is available from the Library of Congress

ISBN 978-1-009-37901-4 Hardback
ISBN 978-1-009-37903-8 Paperback

To my devoted husband, Duncan, and to Erica and Fei, our wonderful daughters

To my best friend, Catalina, for being there

Contents

Foreword

It is with great pleasure that I write the foreword for this long-gestating second edition of *An Introduction to Law and Regulation.* As co-author of the first edition, the immersive journey that Karen and I travelled together many years ago was a highly positive and formative aspect of my early academic career and has remained a defining feature of my scholarly outlook as I continue to follow the trajectory of regulation scholarship and its twists and turns over the decades. Writing now primarily from a vantage point somewhat more orthogonal, it has been a stimulating pleasure to travel this path again in reflecting on change and possibility in the field. In keeping with the mission of the Law in Context series to catalyse the development of new fields of teaching through imaginative textbooks, this new edition – appearing some seventeen years after the first – stands as testimony to the enduring significance of the 'regulatory lens'. Regulation then as now provides a cross-cutting analytical entry point for multiple fields of enquiry at both scholarly and pragmatic levels. Then, as now, it continues to function as a force field for dialogue between economics, law and politics in particular, and to do so in a responsive and adaptable manner that is capable of integrating a range of significant empirical developments across those social spheres. The way in which the preface recounts the pathway between the two editions articulates this ongoing salience and flexibility of the field. And as the preface also notes, the conceptual structure of the first edition has stood the test of time – to an extent that is perhaps surprising given the pressures exerted by polycentric forces as various as war, climate change, shifting geopolitics and global health risks in that time. Those pressures collectively run very deep; they may well be tunnelling cracks in some of the foundational assumptions of regulatory scholarship.

A particular challenge is the shifting tectonics of geopolitical relations between North and South. The preface to this new edition acknowledges the importance of this challenge, and the framing chapter on technology includes pertinent extracts related to digital imperialism. While the reverberations of this may not, at least for some time, seriously disrupt the core features of regulatory scholarship, they are generating significant pressure on the infrastructure of the global economy in terms of overarching frameworks of trade, investment and competition law.

Engaging with these geopolitical dynamics will, in my view, be vital to the future shape of both regulatory scholarship and its adjacent irritants over time. In the 1990s and early 2000s, the regulatory landscape was dominated by a cross-national diffusion of independent regulatory agencies where the emphasis was on apolitical technocratic expertise as a central facet of governing through regulation. Today, we see a cross-sectoral, cross-national variegated network operating under conditions of highly contested legitimacy, where it is institutionally very challenging to pin down where decisions get made, or even when decisions get made.

This second edition skilfully guides the reader through these changes, with the implications mixing continuity and change for readers of regulatory scholarship. Continuous with the insights of the first edition, regulation emerges as a negotiated space of politically charged deliberation over the stakes of rules, carried out in spaces where the regulatory framework and institutions lay down guardrails for that deliberation rather than directly carrying out rule monitoring and enforcement. But since the first edition, the balance of power, at least for certain issues, has shifted away from the state as the guarantor of negotiated deliberative space, and the field is faced with the challenge of grappling much more directly – and less procedurally – with the intrusion of concentrated power – public, private and hybrid – into regulatory state dynamics.

From a substantive perspective, this second edition responds to this challenge of concentrated power through two main avenues: periodic engagement with the implications of the rise of transnational private sector digital economic actors and to a lesser extent with those of climate change. It is useful to briefly speculate here on the potential additional implications of other macro-level geopolitical shifts. The rise of China, for example, with its greater attachment to centralized discretionary state command, is changing the incentives for institutional diffusion, encouraging adaptations of developmental state approaches over the more market-oriented regulatory state. Its governance patterns illustrate an intriguing mix that is more developmental than regulatory: a partial embrace of distributed regulatory governance, especially on issues such as trade and investment, yet continued authoritarian management of the macro-political goals of any of these regulatory regimes. China thus retains a capacity to *selectively reshape* international economic governance.

The rise of China is only one specific example of a rise in authoritarian preferences in governing more generally, including within democracies. These have a dual perverse effect that exposes regulatory state developments to a double undermining. They not only undermine the expertise central to the regulatory state (via the use of arbitrary discretion often driven by populist rationales) but also undercut legitimacy-related *critiques* of the regulatory state that often draw from rationales of democratic participation. And beyond rising authoritarianism, the ongoing salience of *crises* to the development of regulatory state trajectories has increased in scope, scale and regularity: so much so that something of a sense of permanent emergency, or polycrisis, is emerging – or at the very least the invocation of unusual powers to deal with crisis situations is developing a routinization of its own. All these dynamics combine to ensure that 'rules run out', and particularly when populism combines with overtly authoritarian leadership – demonstrated by growing debate on illiberal democracies – then contemporary developments cut deeply against the grain of the regulatory state.

All this said, even if at a macro-political level the regulatory state is increasingly undermined and fragile, yet at the level of detailed governance dynamics within a particular sector, the regulatory state is ever *more* relevant, albeit with more complex, fragmented and distributed institutional outlines. For countervailing pressures continue to steer regulatory dynamics towards rule-based governance. And this second edition very effectively integrates many of the changing institutional settings and forms that depart from the traditional regulatory agency. These include data-driven code, certification codes and standards administered by civil society and non-state actors, as well as an increasing public sector preference for using monetary incentives rather than prescriptive rules. Transgovernmental networks, epistemic communities and transnational advocacy coalitions are also important mechanisms that help to make rules continue to matter, even as their institutional legitimacy and clarity become ever more contested.

Moreover, as the second edition powerfully shows (in the detail of its core chapters on tools, instruments, and patterns of enforcement in particular), digital technology now dominates in ways that cut across both service delivery or provisioning and regulatory oversight. This cross-institutional disruption makes it more likely that increasing swathes of transnational economic life can be governed without the nuanced mix of democratic input and rule of law constraints that the new edition highlights as critical.

At least in the medium term, then, regulatory scholarship as depicted here will remain vital to the ongoing viability of a world under pressure, and this volume will be an indispensable guide. This is demonstrated in part by the enduring nature of the fourfold core of the first edition, which persists in this new edition. Both accounts of the field of regulation move from theories of regulation to instruments and tools, enforcement and compliance and finally to legitimacy and accountability. This structure remains intact, although very significantly extended and explored in greater detail across what are now twelve chapters. There are five particularly interesting facets of this mix of continuity and change.

First is the enduring conceptual and even normative relevance of the public/private binary, notwithstanding abundant evidence of the pressures on that distinction, both conceptual and political, and the much greater practical salience of hybrid facets of regulation since the first edition. While distinct notions of public and private actors, institutions and rationales still structure theories of regulation (Chapter 4) and important contexts of regulatory policy (Chapter 5) and enforcement (Chapter 10), elsewhere hybridity suffuses the book, particularly marking more recent developments in regulatory theories, tools and mechanisms of accountability.

Secondly, it is notable that there is no longer a separate chapter on 'regulation above and beyond the state': perhaps unsurprisingly, the presence of global and transnational dynamics is now pervasive throughout the whole book. That this is now possible is testimony to the useful and adaptive nature of regulatory scholarship in terms of its capacity to capture both transnational and national dynamics of governing within an overarching framework. This is a very useful facet of the field in the context of the shifts in geopolitics alluded to earlier.

Third, the enduring salience of legitimacy and accountability is striking, with these facets of regulation once again closing the book, albeit in this edition integrating the transnational dimension into the chapters as noted above. At the same time, their treatment is more extended, as accountability is now explored through a stand-alone chapter. To my mind this appropriately recognises the sheer complexity of the mechanics of holding parties to account in complex multi-level governance settings that also feature intricate networks of public–private hybrid institutional forms and non-human agents.

This brings to the fore the fifth and most striking feature of the new edition: three entirely new introductory chapters on economics, risk and technology. This change can be read as a meta-commentary on what has shifted since 2007. As globalisation has become pervasive and almost taken-for-granted, as just noted, the need for an explicit conceptual framing for the field as a whole that provides a big-picture lens has become more pronounced. The relentless rise of hybrid public–private institutions and multi-level governance has constrained state capacity and blurred clear lines of responsibility. In this setting, risk analysis and risk management, together with technological innovation, have indeed – as Chapters 2 and 3 outline – emerged as important dual pathways for responsive adaptation to emerging regulatory challenges. They are also frameworks that can bracket, at least in the heat of operational pragmatism, the messy political questions of legitimacy and accountability so long embedded in a web of assumptions now under considerable strain from the wicked problems – digital platform power, climate change, security – that the new edition highlights. Risk and technology therefore provide an adaptive and responsive meta-framework for understanding the changing forms and practices of regulatory institutions both domestically and transnationally.

Yet it is simultaneously fascinating to consider the relative *stability* of the economic theories that inform regulatory thinking. The classic foundational concepts of neoclassical micro-economics, nudged at their edges by more recent behavioural economics, remain staple assumptions that undergird regulatory scholarship as an interdisciplinary field. The new edition appropriately reflects this, while also hinting at other conversations that are bubbling away beyond the borders of regulatory scholarship: most notably on strategies for commons-based governance that take off from Elinor Ostrom's work noted briefly in the opening chapter. The now pervasive nature of multi-level governance as noted above brings with it challenges of coverage and perspective, and the field of regulatory scholarship has, in this book as elsewhere, trained its focus primarily on national and transnational settings. By contrast, until very recently, much commons-based scholarship has focused on city-scale or local civil society developments that tend to fall outside the purview of the national-international-transnational dynamics depicted in these pages. In these more localised settings, a growing appetite to question, both methodologically and substantively, the core economic assumptions that open this edition poses a possible challenge to the foundational trajectory of the regulatory state that we may see more of in future. The geopolitical dynamics adverted to earlier in this foreword may well intensify the challenge.

In conclusion, some of the big questions facing the field of regulatory scholarship lurk at the edges of the core assumptions underpinning both the first and the second edition. Where authoritarian or populist political dynamics reject the paradigms of democratic representation mixed with rule of law constraints, as well as any assumptions that both interventionist states and efficient markets are committed to a particular form of liberal market exchange as a shared consensus of transnational political life, then we are in new territory. Beyond the edges of this consensus lies the need to respond to the ecological limits devastated by the radiating effects of global capitalism, as well as the enduring exclusion of so many people and groups as inequality yawns ever deeper. The scope and depth of these require a systemic response that will at the very least tax or and may well elude the arsenal of the regulatory state and its dynamic emergent forms chronicled in this book. Yet whatever transformations are sought in our macro-political economy in the medium or even short term, the rule-bound complexities of regulatory state governance will continue to proliferate at the sectoral micro-level in ever more technocratic webs of hybrid public–private collaboration. This welcome and impressive second edition is both a charting of how the field of regulatory scholarship has changed, and a guide to navigating its implications in practical terms. It will remain indispensable.

Bronwen Morgan

Preface

The first edition of this book appeared in 2007 at a moment in time that, in retrospect, proved to be significant. In the period that followed, a series of major social transformations began to surface across the globe. Towards the end of 2007, a global financial crisis emerged, resulting in taxpayer-funded bailouts to avert the catastrophic failure of the global financial system. This broadly coincided with the release of Apple's iPhone, paving the way for rapid and now ubiquitous take up of smart devices by those living in high-income countries with well-developed digital infrastructures that sustain high-speed internet over which massive volumes of digital data now automatically and continuously flow. The wholescale liberalisation and opening up of markets that now enables the free circulation of goods, services, money, ideas and people has reshaped the distribution of wealth and power, facilitated by the networked digital transformation that has fueled the unstoppable rise of Big Tech. Meanwhile, addressing the climate crisis has become urgent and impossible to ignore, political instability and rising violence in many regions have prompted unprecedented waves of forced migration, while rates of national economic growth have declined and cash-strapped national governments have reduced public spending on essential services and welfare provision. Just as the proposal for this book was taking shape, the Covid pandemic began to spread across the globe, prompting a variety of state-mandated interventions intended to safeguard the health and safety of entire populations that had previously been beyond the realm of our current experience or perhaps even contemplation. Yet those measures were unequal in their impacts. It soon became apparent that groups that had historically been marginalised and unfairly exploited, particularly ethnic minorities, women with little socio-economic power or position and those with disabilities, were the worst affected and least protected. Growing public concern about systematic injustice and exploitation, which was particularly vivid in response to individual incidents of scandalous abuse (such as the murder of African-American George Floyd by a white police officer in Minneapolis, Minnesota, in 2020 by kneeling on Floyd's neck for almost ten minutes while ignoring his protests that he was unable to breathe) prompted public outcry as people took to the streets in protest under the banner of 'Black Lives Matter'.

These changes have significantly, and in some cases profoundly, altered the political, social, technological and economic context in which contemporary regulatory governance takes place. For the purposes of this book, we define regulatory governance (or more simply 'regulation') as 'intentional, organised attempts to manage or control risk or the behaviours of a different party through the exercise of authority, usually through the use of mechanisms of standard-setting, monitoring and information-gathering and behaviour modification to address a collective tension or problem'. By 2020, it had become painfully apparent that the original edition was outdated and required significant updating, while the interest and importance of regulation have continued to grow and intensify. All of these changes, and no doubt many others, have meant that much conventional wisdom about the theories, approaches, instruments and practices of regulation were called into question. The importance and variety of these changes meant that producing a second edition necessitated a wholesale rewrite. Meanwhile, we had developed further experience and expertise, informed by our research, teaching and encounters with regulatory policymakers. Both of us employed the original edition of this book as a teaching aid, cautioning our students about its limited coverage of recent developments in the contemporary landscape, and complemented it with more up-to-date materials. We have nevertheless retained the definition of regulation provided in the original edition, informed by a cybernetic understanding of regulatory governance as a control system entailing three core functions: the setting of standards, information and gathering to monitor compliance with those standards and some kind of enforcement activity to bring any deviations back into alignment with the stipulated standards. However, we have widened the scope of our inquiry, resulting in systematic changes that operate across the entire book. Accordingly, the second edition differs significantly from the original edition in the following respects.

Firstly, we no longer confine our exploration of regulation above and beyond the state into a single chapter and limit our focus to regulation taking place at the national level. As processes of globalisation have continued to expand and deepen, regulatory governance now relies more extensively on a wider and more varied range of non-state actors. Thus, the influence of globalisation and the role of non-state actors are kept in view throughout the entire volume rather than confined to a single chapter.

Secondly, we have included a new section that offers an introduction to basic concepts and influential fields of scholarship that occupy an important role in the study and practice of regulation. Hence, Part I of the book, entitled 'Foundations', provides an introduction to economics (Chapter 1), to the rise of risk in regulatory governance (Chapter 2) and to technological innovation (Chapter 3).

Thirdly, the number of chapters has doubled. This is an inevitable consequence of expanding the scope of our examination, reflecting growing complexity and associated challenges that arise in developing and implementing regulatory policies and the growth of academic literature devoted to its study.

Fourthly, we have significantly shortened the length of the extracts taken from scholarly literature, seeking to simplify and paraphrase key arguments from those texts to aid accessibility. The ease with which academic papers are now readily available in digital format means that those wishing to read more extensively beyond the short extract provided can do so easily, provided they have a stable internet connection.

Fifthly, we have sought to provide more examples that are intended to make more concrete the abstract concepts and ideas discussed in the text. We do this through the use of 'highlight boxes' in which we offer short case studies or highlight key findings from academic studies of specific events or phenomena that serve to illustrate ideas discussed in the main text.

We have, however, retained the same state-centric conception of law that was taken in the original edition, in which law is understood as a set of authoritative rules backed by the legitimate coercive powers of the state. However, when examining the intersection of law and regulation, we offer a 'legal perspective' that departs from the approach taken in the original edition. In that edition, the role of law was depicted by reference to a heuristic framework that identified two roles for law: one 'facilitative' and the other 'expressive', while invoking two images – law as threat and law as umpire. We no longer adopt this heuristic framework in this revised edition for two reasons. Firstly, because our experience of teaching indicated that students did not find this framework especially helpful and did not engage with it on a sustained basis. Secondly, our encounters with scholarly literature and regulatory policymakers and practitioners highlighted a significant failure to engage with what we might call 'constitutional legitimacy'. Time and again, we found that regulatory policymakers and regulatory scholars (even those with legal training), often regarded law as merely an instrument in the hands of the state or other powerful actors, which could be readily harnessed in the service of regulatory and other objectives. This belief fails to recognise that within modern legal systems, rules are embedded in a larger, dynamic and highly complex system of legal institutions, actors, norms and practices that operate together and have evolved organically over time in a specific place and context.

In reorienting our 'legal perspective' on regulation, the approach taken in this second edition springs from the premise that the law is not just a set of rules people are required to follow. Instead, modern legal systems establish and maintain the foundations for peaceful cooperation between strangers ultimately rooted in respect for the rule of law. In other words, the role of the law is not merely important to regulatory institutions, instruments, policies and practices: it is *foundational.* Although modern legal systems are deeply flawed and imperfect, those who live in communities with strong rule of law systems expect law to safeguard their basic security, fundamental rights, property rights and the stability of their private arrangements and transactions. In so doing, the legal system provides a stable, coherent and transparent foundation that enables people to plan their lives and resolve disputes peacefully in accordance with law. At the same time, within democratic polities, law also constructs and constrains democratic institutions that enable the discussion and articulation of collective choices for and on behalf of the community, endowing those institutions with legitimate authority to impose those choices coercively (see Chapter 11). In recognition of this, modern legal systems also seek to condition and constrain the exercise of this coercive authority in the form of institutional safeguards, including constitutional principles that express and protect values lying at the heart of democratic freedom that cut across political programmes. It is the law's role as a source of constitutional safeguards against the abuse of power that we highlight in examining the law's encounters with regulatory studies, a role that has often been overlooked in regulatory scholarship and in policy debates.

This interpretation is consistent with understanding law as a set of state-backed rules and in acknowledging its role as an instrument of regulatory policy. But the legal system and legal rules offered are more than merely instruments of control: for without the rule of law there is no freedom or security, and, without these, democratic governance is impossible. Yet as major changes to our social, political, technological and economic landscape have occurred in the period since the first edition was published, there is some evidence of a weakening in this basic commitment to the foundational ideals upon which governance through law depends and perhaps also, or perhaps partly a product of, the ability of powerful actors to evade the law's reach.

In short, this second edition has entailed the rewriting of the original edition in its entirety. It therefore differs significantly from the original edition in its scope, content and contours. Nevertheless, we have sought to retain intact the underlying conceptual framework and core analytical constructs through which we seek to introduce novices to the study of regulation in contemporary society. We believe this framework remains a valuable and versatile lens with which to navigate this important and complex field of study and practice and hope that, in this edition, we have made that lens more accessible to a wider range of readers.

Acknowledgements

This book is long overdue. Since the publication of the first edition, major societal changes have continued to sweep across the globe, rendering it increasingly outdated. Yet time and again, it was easy to find excuses to avoid committing to the time, energy and dedicated effort that writing a second edition would invariably entail. Two events finally motivated the authors of the original edition of this book to overcome their resistance and continued procrastination. The first was the award from the UK's Office for Students to support Karen's work in developing teaching materials for an exciting new interdisciplinary degree at the University of Birmingham, which eventually launched in September 2021. That degree was aimed at those with a legal background who wished to learn some data science and acquire a more in-depth knowledge of the challenges associated with regulating emerging technologies that she considered necessary to help them navigate the serious regulatory and governance challenges posed by the meteoric and rapid rise of artificial intelligence (AI). The second was a polite email from our colleague, Sofia Ranchordás, asking whether a second edition was planned so that she might recommend it as required reading for students taking her Administrative Law and Regulation course at the University of Groningen, having recommended the original edition for many years. Her enthusiasm and energy provided the boost that Bronwen and Karen needed to overcome their inertia, inviting her to join as co-author of the second edition. And so began the journey that has resulted in the production of this book.

This book is the product of four years of teamwork and friendship, meeting almost every Tuesday online. At that time, we were a team of three, working collaboratively to read, select and review scholarship, improve drafts and gather feedback. Yet the authorship of this book refers to only two team members. For a number of reasons, Bronwen Morgan was not able to continue participating as originally intended. It is therefore fitting and appropriate that our first and foremost expression of thanks and heartfelt gratitude is to her, co-author of the first edition, for graciously allowing us to carry on the work needed to produce this second edition. Her foundational work and original vision were pivotal to the inception of the first edition of the book. We are deeply grateful to her, not only for the good faith and the trust that she has placed in us in continuing the work needed to complete this book but for entrusting us with the task of seeking to continue the book's legacy while attempting to remain faithful to the vision upon which it was grounded.

While writing this book, we were fortunate to benefit from the assistance of a number of young and talented researchers and colleagues. For their invaluable research assistance, we extend our sincere thanks to Riccardo Piselli, Lily Kennedy, Lucas Haitsma, Rosalind Turkie and Madalina Nicolai. Their diligent efforts have significantly contributed to the substance of this work. Additionally, our appreciation goes to Luna Aristei for her exceptional support throughout the development of this book and, in particular, towards the final submission deadline. The manuscript benefited from the suggestions and comments of a number of scholars. We are immensely thankful for the insightful comments and suggestions provided by Catalina Goanta, Nathalie Smuha, Julie Cohen, Irene Kamara, Claudio Radaelli, Liz Fisher, Mariana Gkliati, Kate Bedford, Volker Stocker, Olha Cherednychenko, Emma Ahmed-Rengers, Laura Holden, Aleks Cavoski, Rotem Medzini, Muireann Quigley, Michael Livermore and Cary Coglianese. Their expertise and thoughtful feedback have been instrumental in refining the arguments and perspectives presented in this book.

Karen is grateful to the Office for Students for providing funding support to enable the appointment of Riccardo Piselli as post-doctoral fellow who collated, analysed and suggested texts for inclusion in this book. She is also indebted to Emma Ahmed-Rengers, not only for helpful feedback on various chapters but also for sharing early drafts with students in the MSc in Responsible Data Science programme at the University of Birmingham to elicit their feedback, which we drew upon to improve subsequent drafts. She is also grateful to colleagues at the Melbourne Law School who made it possible for her to visit regularly as a Melbourne Senior Fellow and Honorary Professor to teach an intensive master's course on Regulatory Policy and Practice until the Covid pandemic struck and brought an abrupt halt to international travel. The insightful and thought-provoking contributions of many former students, most of whom were professional practitioners in some regulatory domain, were an important ongoing source of inspiration. She also expresses her deepest thanks to Bob Lee for his tireless encouragement, wisdom and advice in helping her navigate the challenges of life as a senior academic in a rapidly changing institutional, political and economic context. He very kindly offered to read the entire manuscript over the Christmas 2023 vacation period, but we spared him the ordeal in our desire for closure and completion of the manuscript. Most importantly, she wishes to thank her devoted husband and partner, Duncan, to whom she was engaged when the original edition was published and with whom she has produced and nurtured two daughters, Erica and Fei. Without their warmth, love and patience, this book may never have materialised, particularly given the great many unexpected personal and professional challenges encountered along the way.

Sofia would like to thank her colleague Olha Cherenychenko with whom she developed the course Administrative Law and Regulation at her previous institution, the University of Groningen. She is also grateful to her current employers, Tilburg Law School and Luiss Guido Carli, for the opportunity to teach administrative law and regulation from an interdisciplinary perspective. Sofia is deeply indebted to her loved ones who supported her throughout her academic journey. First and foremost, she is grateful to her mother for all her unconditional support. The last year of this book journey was marked by personal challenges that she would not have been able to overcome without the friendship and love of two persons: her best friend Catalina and her partner Gianluca. Gianluca offered immense support during the final months leading to the completion of the book. She thanks him for his love and patience: *Grazie per essere la melodia, l'armonia e il ritmo della mia vita.*

Both of us are grateful to our editors at Cambridge University Press, Sharon McCann and Gemma Smith, particularly for their assistance with obtaining copyright permissions and for skilfully guiding us through the publication process. We also wish to thank Tom Randall who provided invaluable assistance, particularly in attending to and finalising the contractual details supporting the book's commission. Finally, we wish to thank each other: it has been a pleasure and a privilege to collaborate, to learn from each other and to bear with each other's flaws, foibles and follies in our collective quest to produce what is, we hope, an invaluable resource for all newcomers with an interest in acquiring a deeper, richer and more holistic understanding of regulatory governance and its challenges.

Introduction

What is the first thing you do when you wake up in the morning? Perhaps it goes something like this. You check your phone for the latest social media updates. After scrolling through short videos on TikTok and Instagram selected especially for you, you get up, determined to master your morning routine. You choose a yoghurt with nutritional label 'A', which stands for 'low fat' and 'no added sugar'. However, you notice that the 'best before' date on the carton has passed. On opening, the yoghurt smells and looks fine, but you throw it away, figuring that it's not worth taking unnecessary risks. As you head into the shower, you notice that your shower gel label says 'no microplastics' and that 'this package was made of recyclable plastic'. You take pride in living in an ecologically sustainable manner, doing your bit to address the climate crisis. During your cycle to work, you stop at a red traffic light, even though there is no traffic today. You wonder why a traffic light is sited here, given that it appears to have little impact on improving traffic flow nor does it seem to improve community safety.

Do you ever wonder why social media companies are allowed to target you with personalised videos and advertisements? Or how food labels and certifications are produced and how much they actually affect people's consumption decisions? For example, why would you throw away food after the 'best before' date even though it seems safe to eat? Or why stop at a red light when there's no one else about? If you are concerned about the climate emergency, you might have pondered why there are numerous rules and regulations addressing these issues in great detail, yet governments appear rather reluctant to implement more demanding measures to combat climate change. These questions, and many more, can be understood as questions about regulation.

Contemporary life relies on regulation. The quality and safety of the water we drink, the food we eat, the air we breathe, the social media applications we use, the clothes we wear and the transportation that we rely on are regulated by multiple regulatory regimes. But society does not stand still, and regulation is expected to 'keep pace' with the needs and priorities of the communities it is ostensibly intended to serve. Hence, we routinely encounter debates about whether a given regulatory regime continues to be 'fit for purpose' or requires updating, often prompted by technological change, evolving social norms and greater awareness of forms of harms or other threats and 'risks' that enter public consciousness. As a result, affected stakeholders may call for new laws and regulatory measures where they previously did not exist. It is hardly surprising that academic research concerned with regulation is now a well-established, distinct field of scholarly inquiry. Yet acquiring a clear grasp of the content and contours of this work and the nature of its terrain remains difficult and daunting.

When the first edition of this book was published in 2007, its primary aim was to address this problem. It sought to provide a map to help newcomers navigate the field and obtain a holistic understanding of its core features and its varied, wide-ranging terrain. Almost two decades later, policymakers and academic researchers engaged with specific regulatory policies remain poorly acquainted with the body of scholarship we refer to as 'regulatory governance studies' or more simply 'regulatory studies'. For example, ongoing debates about the regulation of digital technologies, social media content and environmental degradation rarely draw upon insights from this literature. Although the regulation of artificial intelligence (AI), for example, now routinely makes newspaper headlines, accompanied by a proliferation of academic and policy papers, many misunderstandings remain regarding whether and why we should regulate, when, how and by whom. Regulation is ultimately a multi- and interdisciplinary endeavour. Regulatory governance scholarship grows out of many disciplines, variously seeking, for example, to understand human welfare; social norms; human psychology; the nature, magnitude and character of risks; the influence of changes to legal rights and duties and political and institutional cultures and their interaction. This is a complex and challenging ambition, which is arguably more important now than ever. By drawing together material from a range of disciplinary perspectives from the humanities and social sciences, including law and public administration, interleaving them with our accessible commentary, we wish to introduce all newcomers to the study of regulation whatever the source of their curiosity, prior disciplinary background or motivation.

Regulation in Historical Context

The origins of regulatory governance scholarship began in the United States where the phenomenon of regulation has been most extensively studied thanks to its early embrace of the 'independent regulatory agency'. During the late nineteenth century, pressures from rapid industrialism, urbanisation and its economic disruption, all linked to long-distance transportation (particularly the railroad firms and their practices) and interstate commerce, prompted calls for national political leadership and a permanent concentration of government controls. The Sherman Act was passed in 1890 as a response to the nineteenth century 'curse of bigness' that affected a number of economic sectors. This statute prohibited trusts, monopolies and cartels in order to promote economic fairness and competitiveness. The independent regulatory agency became the favoured institutional model for responding to these concerns, forming the basis upon which the Interstate Commerce Commission (1887), the Federal Reserve Board (1913) and the Federal Trade Commission (1914) were established.

During the early 1930s, the number of regulatory agencies grew rapidly as part of 'New Deal' reforms enacted to address the crippling impact of the Great Depression, along with the expansion of the federal administration, reflecting an optimistic belief in their ability to provide for the efficient functioning of economic processes (see Chapters 4 and 5). This set of revolutionary regulatory measures, much like other key moments in the history of regulation that would follow, was the immediate response to the Great Depression, a global economic crisis that prompted the federal government to rethink its position in relation to markets. The Stock Market Crash of 1929 is widely regarded as one of the principal triggers of this crisis. By the early 1970s, regulatory activity and the remit of these regulatory agencies widened as public interest in health, safety, environmental preservation and social inequality spawned a wave of regulatory reform in fields as diverse as motor vehicle safety, product design, air and water pollution, occupational health and safety and many others. However, a few years later, regulatory agencies had fallen out of favour, perceived by many as mired in legalism and bureaucracy (see Chapter 5). The regulatory landscape had become too complex and, in some cases, inefficient and burdensome to those subjected to regulatory oversight. Regulatory requirements were often in conflict. This was accompanied by a general distrust of government intervention in the economy, fuelled by the ideology of neoliberalism rooted in a belief in the superiority of market forces. This gave rise to a strong 'deregulatory' impulse, reflected in a raft of measures introduced by the Reagan Administration (1981–1989) to relieve business from the regulatory burdens and making public administration more responsive to citizen's demands via sensitivity to market forces.

The early emergence, longevity and breadth of authority vested in independent regulatory agencies readily explains why regulation has been well-studied in the US context, tightly linked to the study of US Federal 'administrative law'. In contrast, independent regulatory agencies emerged in the United Kingdom and Europe much later, beginning in the late 1970s and early 1980s. In the United Kingdom, their emergence was precipitated by the privatisation of state-owned enterprise under the Thatcher administration as the institutional vehicle through which government oversight over these industries was retained alongside a raft of other 'quangos' (quasi-autonomous government organisations). At roughly the same time, the drive for internal market integration gathered steam as the European Union matured and the role of the European Commission, its administrative arm, grew in size, stature and authority (see Chapter 11). In the US, British and EU contexts, sustained criticisms have been levelled at a perceived 'democratic deficit' and an associated 'crisis' in accountability arising from allowing unelected bureaucrats to make decisions that affect the wider public in which some gain while others are made worse off (see Chapter 12). In Asia, Africa and South America, the rise of regulation is more recent and has often been driven by the conditions attached to international investment law and economic development loans from the World Bank and International Monetary Fund, the influence of the OECD and other international organisations concerned to foster and promote international trade and the need to comply with EU regulations to gain access to lucrative EU markets. Despite their varied trajectories, each can be understood as specific instantiations of the 'regulatory state'.

The idea of the 'regulatory state' was developed in the 1990s, referring to a particular institutional and policy style as the frontiers of the state were rolled back and the state substantially reduced its involvement in the direct provision of welfare and as an employer or property owner. These transformations did not, however, result in the disappearance of the state but a shift in central function, one from 'rowing' to 'steering' as Osborne and Gaebler's well-chosen metaphor implies. Although the larger economic, political and technological context in which regulatory states operate have changed significantly since then, its central regulatory function remains omnipresent. Despite substantial differences in their particular institutional forms, cultures and practices, what unites these regulatory states is an underlying belief that 'politics' and 'administration' can be separated, the latter being a 'science' that could be entrusted to 'experts' and thus insulated from electoral politics.

A second and related theme that has emerged within regulatory states throughout the world is a growing preoccupation with 'risk' (see Chapter 2). Within academic literature, the regulatory state must now contend with the challenges of the 'risk society', referring to the claim of German sociologist Ulrich Beck that technological advances have produced risks that are industrial in scale and global in their impacts, affecting collective risks that individuals cannot mitigate through unilateral action. Accordingly, the state remains risk protector of last resort, expected to undertake organised attempts to manage risks to collective welfare. Although states often look to scientific experts for guidance, with its promise of political 'neutrality' and objectivity, they soon discover that what counts as a 'risk', and how best to understand its nature or severity, rarely attracts widespread community consensus. The impossibility of escaping politics and the dynamic interplay of power between competing actors, groups and organised interests, constitutes a third feature of regulatory debate. In other words, despite attempts to portray regulatory policy as a mundane, technocratic endeavor, in reality regulators (whether they are public or private bodies) wield tremendous power. Yet this does not necessarily imply that governments always have the stronger hand, capable of intervening in the economy at will and obstructing freedom to innovate. The reality is more complex. Many private parties (e.g., multinationals, Big Tech firms) have considerable political and economic power, strategically seeking to influence regulatory policy, while often undertaking regulatory functions themselves. The regulatory landscape thus comprises a complex and often overlapping web of players, institutions, interests and power dynamics, interacting in larger regulatory networks. This messy reality exacerbates challenges of communication, coordination and control, while making the task of holding those wielding regulatory authority to account even more difficult. For example, during the COVID-19 pandemic, coordination between the World Health Organisation, a global health regulator, with national and local public health authorities was characterised by multiple miscommunications and ineffective coordination producing contradictory information, confusion and the dissemination of inaccurate information. As this book unfolds, we observe a persistent tension between two central commitments: on the one hand, a belief in 'rational' regulatory decision-making and regulation informed by scientific knowledge and expert judgement and, on the other, the recognition that regulatory policies and decisions reflect political judgements about individual and collective rights, interests and duties in which active participation, particularly by those directly affected, is required if those policies and decisions are to be considered democratically legitimate.

What Do We Mean by Regulation?

The academic study of regulation now extends far beyond its original interest in independent regulatory agencies, encompassing a much wider and more diverse range of institutions, actors and activities. As a field of inquiry, the study of regulation has porous, permeable boundaries. The meaning of regulation is itself contested, partly because regulation as a phenomenon is notoriously difficult to define with clarity and precision. At their narrowest, definitions of regulation centre on deliberate attempts by the state to influence the behaviour of others by imposing, establishing, monitoring and enforcing legal rules. At their broadest, regulation is seen as encompassing all forms of social control, whether intentional or not and whether imposed by the state or other social institutions. Sometimes scholars, with different disciplinary training, use different terms to refer to the same thing, other times to refer to very different things. This is especially confusing for newcomers. The focus of our examination is on 'regulation', a shorthand expression that we use to refer to 'regulatory governance'. To clarify our terms and ensure consistent usage, we adopt the following definitions.

Definitions

We define regulation as 'intentional, organised attempts to manage or control risk or the behaviours of a different party through the exercise of authority, usually through the use of mechanisms of standard-setting, monitoring and information-gathering and behaviour modification to address a collective tension or problem'. At the core of this definition of regulation are three features. Firstly, regulation is a *purposive* activity, which intentionally seeks to address some kind of social concern; Secondly, regulation entails the operation of some kind of *control system*, which one can view through the lens of cybernetics comprising three key components. As Christopher Hood and his colleagues (Hood et al. 2001: 23) explain:

> One of the standard ways of understanding regulation . . . is to view it from a cybernetic angle . . .. From such a perspective, any control system in art or nature must by definition contain a minimum of the three components . . .. There must be some capacity for standard-setting, to allow a distinction to be made between more or less preferred states of the system. There must also be some capacity for information-gathering or monitoring to produce knowledge about current or changing states of the system. On top of that must be some capacity for behaviour-modification to change the state of the system.

Thirdly, regulation relies on the exercise of authority. So defined, regulation is a specific form of 'governance', that is, a set of systems, institutions, norms and practices through which social coordination is attempted. By authority, we are not only concerned with formal public authority. As the book unfolds, we encounter many private actors that have informal authority, intentionally attempting to regulate, shape and constrain the behaviour of others (see Chapters 7–9). By referring to 'governance' rather than to 'government', we recognise that the task of governing is not the exclusive preserve of the nation-state but often entails a broader range of non-state actors. As the globalisation of markets has proceeded, the state remains central and important. However, regulation has also become decentred due to the existence of a larger set of networked dynamics that now make up modern systems of regulation. The healthcare sector illustrates this decentralisation, as public health regulation comprises a complex network of public and private regulators at the global (e.g., WHO, International Organization for Standardization), national (e.g., ministries of health) and local (e.g., municipalities) levels. Our definitions may differ from those used by other scholars and from ordinary everyday usage. This definitional pluralism need not be a problem, and many of the terms we use throughout this volume are not terms of art. Rather, this book underlines the need to read scholarly and policy texts with care and attention. We endeavour to highlight potential confusion due to terminological variation, particularly when we introduce extracts from the work of others.

Our Approach

This book offers a 'regulatory perspective' or 'regulatory lens', by curating extracts from a wide and sometimes eclectic body of scholarship that we integrate with our commentary, woven together into a larger conceptual map that develops and draws upon a variety of analytical frames that could be applied to any social and economic domain and within and across any jurisdiction. The extracts we have selected range widely in disciplinary perspective, focus, interest, scope and methods of intellectual inquiry. We reproduce extracts from the original texts (rather than paraphrasing) to capture the different voices, texture and discourse that characterises the field invariably reflecting our own scholarly interests and disciplinary training as legal scholars.

Our motivation in writing this book was partly animated by shared interest in (a) the regulatory implications of the on-going networked digital revolution, (b) a commitment to debunking simplistic and sometimes misleading understandings of the 'law' and law's role in society in discussions about regulatory initiatives, reforms and programmes (including a persistent failure to understand the significance and centrality of rule of law concerns) and (c) a desire to highlight how scholarship from other fields (particularly Science and Technology Studies (STS), economics, management, and humanities) can enrich the study of regulation, even though these scholars may not identify themselves as engaged in the study of regulation. Our approach also reflects our mission and experience as educators. Having taught regulation and public law for many years, we have included texts and examples that, in our experience, help pedagogically to enliven and engage our students. We also include, at times, complex and technical texts because we believe that students, preferably with the assistance of their lecturers, should be able to navigate more advanced texts to equip them to operate in the world beyond the university. Our commentary seeks to offer guidance and reflection on these extracts, highlighting common ground and areas of divergence and sometimes drawing out the wider implications of those similarities and differences in order to help orient and navigate readers.

This book offers an introductory account rather than an in-depth analysis, systematic literature review or an intellectual history of the subject. For those with an interest in learning more about regulation, we list a number of reference books under 'Further Reading'. The vastness of the field inevitably required us to be selective, excluding many significant texts. The resulting 'playlist' that we have curated will not be to everyone's taste. Unfortunately, unlike Spotify or other online platforms, we cannot draw on algorithms to personalise the reading to each reader's taste and disciplinary background. Perhaps technology will enable this in a third edition of the book. For the time being, our goal is to offer a navigation tool that can be a useful starting point for newcomers.

Why a Second Edition?

The number and significance of changes to the social, political and technological context that have swept across the globe since the first edition was published in 2007 have transformed the regulatory landscape, providing us with the impetus to produce this second edition. Five changes are especially salient for regulatory studies.

Firstly, processes of globalisation that have fostered the free flow of goods, services, norms, practices and people across national borders have intensified the interconnectedness of national economies and the proliferation of transnational risks, especially in the wake of the 2008 global financial crisis. As economic and regulatory activity have become increasingly denationalised and deterritorialised, this has stretched social relations across time and space, affecting and altering how governments, people, firms, organisations and institutions interact. Secondly, the range of actors and organisations actively and intentionally involved in regulatory tasks and functions has proliferated and expanded, with growing emphasis on the role of non-governmental or 'private' actors occupying some kind of role of 'quasi-regulatory' role or acting as some kind of 'regulatory intermediary'. Thirdly, the technologies of the Second Machine Age, including advances in artificial intelligence (AI), machine learning and foundation/frontier AI models (including large language models), life science research, advanced materials engineering, and their growing convergence, are frequently portrayed as promising techniques for solving societal 'grand challenges'. However, their real-world effects and implications, including their potential adverse consequences, are shrouded in uncertainty. These promises, and accompanying uncertainty, are particularly acute for 'general-purpose' technologies, allowing them to be weaponised in ways that could cause serious and irreversible harm. Fourthly, the need to address global warming to combat climate change is now recognised as an urgent and existential problem, requiring collective action invariably requiring some form of regulation to tackle it effectively. Finally, the COVID-19 pandemic has served as a stark reminder of the transnational nature of 'risks' to human health and the value of collective 'preparedness', generating acute challenges associated with the need to identify and manage new threats to the health and welfare of populations in light of unstable, incomplete yet evolving scientific knowledge and economic, social, political and legal realities.

Multiple changes in the world of ideas, both within public debate and scholarly reflection, have occurred since the first edition was published. We draw attention to three changes that have, in our view, been particularly influential in the study of regulation and that we have sought to incorporate in writing this second edition. Firstly, the language of 'risk', rather than that of 'market failure' appears to be the dominant framework through which regulatory policy is now conducted. Secondly, greater public attention is now paid to various forms of social inequality, particularly on the basis of race and gender, but also in the distribution of the benefits and burdens of globalisation between high- and low-income countries. Hence, there has been a greater recognition of the need to hear the voices, perspectives and experience of those from low-income countries, alongside the rise of 'post-colonial' perspectives and approaches within humanities and social science scholarship. Third, with the rise of populism and the phenomena of online disinformation and misinformation, societies have become increasingly polarised and more susceptible to distrust regulatory expertise and technical knowledge.

These developments have been reflected in the way real-world regulatory regimes have emerged and evolved at the international, regional, national and local levels, while affecting the content and contours of on-going regulatory debates. A wholesale rewriting of this book was therefore needed to take account of the altered landscape and context in producing a second edition. Yet the core concepts around which the study of regulation has proceeded remain largely intact and we have therefore retained and remained faithful to the original edition's basic conceptual frame and structure. Similarly, our original goal of seeking to 'break down a subject which can be rather daunting to newcomers into digestible and accessible form' (original edition, p. 1) remains unaltered. While we acknowledge the need to include perspectives from authors from low- and middle-income regions, the body of literature from which we draw remains dominated by scholarship from the perspective of Western liberal democratic political cultures. Nevertheless, our regulatory perspective standpoint springs from a foundational commitment to democratic governance: we are not writing for the benefit of authoritarian dictators in search of scholarly insights on how to design and implement regulation to effect their purposes.

Law and Regulation?

In light of the above changes, we have widened the range and diversity of topics and perspectives that we seek to encompass in producing this second edition. Our belief in the vital importance of law's role in regulation has not diminished. On the contrary, our approach seeks to demonstrate that the role of the law is not merely central to regulatory institutions, instruments, policies and practices: it is *foundational.* Since the first edition was published, we have encountered a tendency of regulatory studies scholars to understand the law in simplistic, instrumental terms, with non-lawyers inclined to equate 'the law' with legal rules. This belief is superficial, partial and inadequate. It fails to recognise that within modern legal systems, legal rules are embedded in a larger, dynamic and highly complex system of multiple institutions, actors, norms and practices that operate together and have evolved organically over time in a specific place and context. Thus, our book springs from the premise that the law is not just a set of rules people are required to follow. Modern legal systems establish and maintain the foundations for peaceful cooperation between strangers ultimately rooted in respect for the rule of law.

This book is not an introduction to law. Just as the study of medicine requires many years of dedicated university-level study before medical students are permitted to practice medicine, so too does the study of law entail many years of dedicated study to enable students to acquire a sufficient understanding of the nature, content and contours of the law before they can be admitted to legal practice. Although we firmly believe in the foundational role of law, and share a deeply held commitment to the rule of law and its aspirational ideals, we are not suggesting that contemporary legal systems are perfect or free of flaws. Chief among these shortcomings is the complex, cumbersome and expensive nature of its institutions and processes that render it largely inaccessible to ordinary people. Nevertheless, those who live in communities with strong rule of law systems expect law to safeguard fundamental rights, property rights and the stability of their private arrangements and transactions. In so doing, the legal system provides a stable, coherent and transparent foundation that enables people to plan their lives and resolve disputes peacefully in accordance with law.

Law constructs and constrains democratic institutions that enable the discussion and articulation of collective choices for and on behalf of the community, endowing those institutions with legitimate authority to impose those choices coercively (see Chapter 11). In recognition of this, modern legal systems seek to condition and constrain the exercise of this coercive authority in the form of institutional safeguards, including constitutional principles. These principles give legal expression to values lying at the heart of democratic freedom that cut across political programmes. Legal principles are ultimately rooted in the respect for the individual as a moral and autonomous agent entitled to be treated with dignity and respect. It is the law's role as a source of constitutional safeguards against the abuse of power that we highlight in examining the law's encounters with regulatory studies, a role that has often been overlooked in academic scholarship and in policy debates. For example, we discuss how growing polarisation in politics and the limited regulation of social media has increased the propensity of 'rule of law backsliding' (see Chapter 11). We also mention other instances that highlight the role of regulation in safeguarding public values. These include recent regulatory scandals where food safety was seriously neglected, affecting, for example, the health of babies in China (Chapter 12), the safety of the populations living in the vicinity of Japan's Fukushima nuclear power plant was put at risk and the case of the London's Grenfell tower inferno where seventy-two residents, mainly low-income immigrants died.

Legal practitioners, scholars and law students will have invariably encountered regulation in legal practice and/or their courses of study. Regulation is often present in public law courses as secondary legislation, that is, legally binding rules promulgated by law-making institutions other than Parliament including the executive branch of government. These include traditional executive bodies (e.g., ministers, state secretaries, the mayor) but also an array of independent regulators that often arise in the study of Administrative Law. In the United States, federal regulators may be the primary focus of administrative law courses while in many civil law countries, independent regulators are likely to be considered (along with other public regulators), yet these courses may focus more generally on public authorities at the national and local level. For law students, this book will demonstrate that regulation is not limited to the study of public law conventionally understood. Those who have studied banking and financial law, energy law, telecommunications law or health law may in fact be studying regulation, even though they might be focused on the substantive content of specific regulations, rather than engaging more deeply and broadly with questions concerning why these regulations were adopted, what alternatives were available and whether they are legitimate.

Structure and Overview

This book is organised into three parts. Part I, entitled 'Foundations' is intended to provide short introductory guides (or 'primers') to central concepts and analytical approaches upon which the contemporary study of regulation and governance frequently draws. Comprising three chapters, this part aims to help those who find it difficult to navigate the field due to its multi-disciplinary character. Readers may wish to dip into one or more of these chapters, depending upon their existing knowledge or interest in the relevant subject, or may prefer to skip them altogether and proceed directly to Part II. Chapter 1 introduces key concepts of economics and regulatory economics, referring to a branch of social sciences concerned with how society chooses to employ its scarce resources (e.g., money, raw materials, time) to produce goods and services. This chapter offers a brief discussion of economic concepts that have shaped regulation. Some readers might consider the discussion rather technical but this is necessary to reflect insights from leading microeconomics scholarship. Chapter 2 introduces the general concept of 'risk' to help readers understand how the concept of risk is employed in regulatory debates, literature and policies, and to recognise that the risk literature is vast and varied, viewed through many disciplinary lenses. It touches upon various perspectives (contrasting 'technical' quantitative approaches with sociological critiques) introducing challenges associated with claimed 'phases' of risk identification, risk assessment and risk management and the 'riskification' of everything. Chapter 3 introduces a variety of academic literatures across the humanities, law and the social sciences that offer insights on understanding technological change that have direct relevance to the challenges of regulating new and emerging technology yet remain largely fragmented and siloed rather than integrated into a single, readily identifiable scholarly field.

Part II, entitled 'Design, Dynamics and Implementation' is concerned with the 'what, why, whether, and how' of the regulatory endeavour, including the design and architecture of regulatory frameworks. It seeks to introduce readers to core concepts concerning the principal theories of regulation, regulatory policy (e.g., cost-benefit analysis) and the modalities, instruments and techniques that are employed for the purpose of setting of regulatory standards and the ways in which enforcement and compliance is undertaken. It consists of six chapters, which comprise Chapters 4–10.

Chapter 4 offers responses to the question 'why regulate?' and 'why do regulatory regimes emerge in a particular form'? by examining 'theories of regulation'. These theories refer to a set of propositions or hypotheses about why regulation emerges, which actors contribute to that emergence and typical patterns of interaction between regulatory actors. We cover theories that reflect several disciplinary approaches, classifying these theories into four kinds: public interest, private interest theories, systems institutionalist approaches and 'hybrid' theories. For teaching purposes, our discussion of public interest and private interest theories assumes that public and private actors can be distinguished, equating public actors with state actors. Institutionalist and hybrid theories take a more nuanced approach, recognising that the lines between public and private actors are blurred in practice due to plural sources of authority through which regulatory regimes operate, while often blending multiple theoretical approaches.

Chapter 5 examines 'Regulatory Policy' by addressing various questions that arise in considering 'whether' and 'how' to regulate. It focuses on the methodologies of public regulators, that is, authorities established by nation-states or those established by agreement between states in accordance with public international law (for example, those that have some responsibility at the global level for the regulation of specific sectors such as health, transportation, media and entertainment, energy and financial markets). This chapter also focuses on regulation in its narrowest sense: secondary legislation or legislative acts issued by authorities that are part of the executive branch. Although public regulators are frequently influenced by special interest groups (which we discuss in Chapter 4), they often face budgetary, legal and policy requirements that circumscribe how such decisions should be taken. Hence, a range of various 'methods' have been established to provide a more structured framework for evaluating proposed regulatory measures, including cost-benefit analysis, regulatory impact assessments and the use of consultations, all of which are explored in this chapter.

Chapters 6 and 7 are concerned with instruments, tools and modalities of control through which attempts are made to influence the behaviour of others in pursuit of its pre-specified goals. Although multiple tools and techniques can be employed to influence, control and coordinate the behaviour of others, they have been classified in many ways. Chapter 6 classifies regulatory tools according to the underlying technique or 'modality' of control or source of influence, examining five such modalities in turn: command, competition, communication, consensus and code (or 'architecture'). In Chapter 7, our examination builds upon this five-fold classification scheme by exploring a variety of 'hybrid' techniques, referring to an amalgam of mechanisms, sometimes drawing on multiple sources of regulatory influence, including various non-state intermediaries, rather than relying exclusively on the regulatory capacities of the state. Given that public regulators must also make choices about which instruments to adopt for specific purposes in any given context, a variety of issues that bear upon instrument choice are also considered. The chapter closes with a brief overview of various kinds of 'experimental regulation', including regulatory sandboxes.

Chapter 8 examines regulatory rules, beginning with an examination of written rules. It underlines the inescapability of interpretive uncertainty and considers ways in which that uncertainty can be addressed, including varying the precision of rules, how they are specified, the publication of interpretive 'guidance' (sometimes called 'soft law') and the delegation of detailed standard-setting to 'technical experts'. We also consider problems associated with rule avoidance behaviour and difficulties that arise in identifying whether a particular rule should apply to any given set of facts or circumstances and if so how. It also briefly considers how the embedding of standards into algorithmic code rather than linguistic text may appear to solve problems associated with interpretive uncertainty, while, in reality, it merely shifts those problems to another part of the rule application process.

Chapter 9 explores regulatory compliance, enforcement and certification. It analyses the vital role of enforcement action and how rules aimed at influencing human and institutional behaviour are translated into social reality. It draws attention to the human interaction that takes place during encounters with regulatory enforcement officials and regulators. We discuss how 'risk-based' approaches to regulation can be understood and operationalised. It then touches upon the investigatory powers of public regulators, and the nature, purpose and variety of regulatory sanctions. Finally, it examines the role of 'private' bodies and other 'regulatory intermediaries' in certifying that a regulatee's activities complies with regulatory standards that purport to offer consumers, as primary beneficiaries, 'assurance' of the quality of the resulting outputs.

Chapter 10 provides an overview of the role and functions of private enforcement within regulatory regimes and the availability of redress. It draws attention to different 'models of legal responsibility' upon which regulatory regimes rely in allocating and distributing legal rights and duties between regulatees and regulatory beneficiaries. This chapter is the most legally-focused chapter in the volume, selectively highlighting several features of the institutional and enforcement context in which regulation occurs. Examples are private litigation, collective redress mechanisms, the role of courts as authoritative and final interpreters of the law and 'alternative' avenues for redress.

Part III of the book, entitled 'Evaluation' comprises Chapters 11 and 12, which investigate the legitimacy and accountability of regulatory actors. Our primary concern in Chapter 11 is with 'regulatory legitimacy', a term employed in the regulatory governance literature. To understand what regulatory legitimacy entails, however, we need to acquire a basic understanding of legitimacy, which takes up the first part of this chapter. The concept of legitimacy has been extensively studied by scholars from various academic disciplines, including political theory, legal theory, political science, sociology and management studies. The resulting body of scholarship has, however, tended to remain in disciplinary siloes, making the study of legitimacy difficult to navigate. Chapter 11 offers first an exploration of different legitimacy claims that justify why individuals recognise an authority and its rules as legitimate. The chapter then moves to key debates on regulatory legitimacy.

Chapter 12 discusses accountability in regulation. Accountability is part of a family of concepts that relate to the exercise of power and its abuses. It construes the relationship between regulators and regulatees according to principal-agent theory and explains how accountability can be an important mechanism for requiring answerability, ensuring that agents (regulators) do not drift from the interests of regulatees. The chapter explains that accountability consists of four elements: (i) a duty to explain, (ii) exposure to scrutiny, (iii) a potential 'sanction' or a consequence of some kind and (iv) the possibility of being subject to independent review. We explore these elements through the complexities of interdisciplinary debates on transparency, algorithmic accountability, privatisation, and multi-actor regulation and the accountability deficits that often arise when 'everyone is accountable but no one really is'.

The book closes with a short Conclusion.

FURTHER READING

Baldwin, R., Cave, M., and Lodge, M. (eds.). (2010). *The Oxford Handbook of Regulation*. Oxford University Press.

(2012). *Understanding Regulation: Theory, Strategy, and Practice*. Oxford University Press.

Baldwin, R., Scott, C., and Hood, C. (1998). (eds.). *A Reader on Regulation*. Oxford University Press.

Bardach, E., and Kagan, R. A. (1982). *Going by the Book: The Problem of Regulatory Unreasonableness*. Temple University Press.

Braithwaite, J., and Drahos, P. (2000). *Global Business Regulation*. Cambridge University Press.

Breyer, S. (1982). *Regulation and Its Reform*. Harvard University Press.

Croley, S. P. (2007). *Regulation and Public Interests: The Possibility of Good Regulatory Government*. Princeton University Press.

Drahos, P. (ed.). (2017). *Regulatory Theory: Foundations and Applications*. ANU Press.

Ford, C. (2017). *Innovation and the State: Finance, Regulation, and Justice*. Cambridge University Press.

Haines, F. (2011). *The Paradox of Regulation: What Regulation Can Achieve and What It Cannot*. Edward Elgar.

Harlow, C., and Rawlings, R. (2021). *Law and Administration*. Cambridge University Press.

Huber, G. A. (2007). The Craft of Bureaucratic Neutrality: Interests and Influence in Governmental Regulation of Occupational Safety. Cambridge University Press.

Hutter, B. M. (2001). *Regulation and Risk: Occupational Health and Safety on the Railways*. Oxford University Press.

Jordana, J., and Levi-Faur, D. (eds.). (2011). *The Politics of Regulation in the Age of Governance*. Edward Elgar.

Levi-Faur, D. (2011). *Handbook on the Politics of Regulation*. Edward Elgar.

Lobel, O. (2004). 'The Renew Deal: The Fall of Regulation and the Rise of Governance in Contemporary Legal Thought'. *Minnesota Law Review*, 663.

Lodge, M., and Wegrich, K. (2012). *Managing Regulation: Regulatory Analysis, Politics and Policy*. Palgrave.

Majone, G. (1996). *Regulating Europe*. Routledge.

Mattli, M., and Woods, N. (2009). *The Politics of Global Regulation*. Princeton University Press.

Moran, M. (2003). *The British Regulatory State: High Modernism and Hyper Innovation*. Oxford University Press.

Ogus, A. I. (1994). *Regulation: Legal Form and Economic Theory*. Oxford University Press.

Prosser, T. (2010). *The Regulatory Enterprise*. Oxford University Press.

Scott, C. (ed.). (2003). *Regulation*. Routledge.

Sparrow, M., (2000). *The Regulatory Craft*. Brookings Press.

Vibert, F. (2014). *The New Regulatory Space*. Edward Elgar.

1

Introduction to Economics

Introduction

Everyone knows something about economics, and that includes you. Perhaps you first encountered economics as a child, seeking parents' generosity for that initial pocket money. Their advice to manage it wisely revealed the reality that your desires often surpassed the available funds and the rising price of your favourite snack. After a while, you asked for a 'raise'. Your parents blamed inflation but promised you nonetheless additional funds provided that you would work harder and aim for admission to a prestigious university. Undeterred by the university's low acceptance rate and high tuition fees, you decided to go for it. However, you soon discovered disparities in information accessibility. Wealthier peers had enrolled in preparatory courses, an option your parents couldn't afford. You wondered why regulations weren't in place to ensure equal access to university admission information for students from all socio-economic backgrounds. While most countries grant citizens a fundamental right to education, the regulation of higher education access varies greatly, with significant economic implications. This example, which may resonate with some readers, seeks to impart key concepts in economics and regulatory economics. Economics, a branch of the social sciences, examines how societies allocate scarce resources (such as money, raw materials and time) to produce goods and services.

The field of economics attempts to represent reality through the use of models and concepts, which involve abstraction to simplify complex phenomena. As Varian (2009) explains, economists are typically guided by the optimisation principle, which states that economic agents typically choose what is best for them, and by the equilibrium principle, which posits that prices will adjust until demand and supply are equal. Economics studies thus the production, distribution and growth of production and social welfare. It is a discipline with multiple subfields (e.g., public economics, industrial economics, financial economics, health economics and, more recently, the economics of happiness) using a wide range of methods (e.g., cost-benefit analysis, experiments, econometric analysis, game theory).

You may have heard of the distinction between microeconomics and macroeconomics: 'microeconomics focuses on the behavior of individual economic units (consumers, firms, workers, investors) as well as the markets that these units comprise' (Pindyck and Rubinfeld 2018) and thus deals with how individuals and businesses manage their resources (e.g., how to best spend their pocket money). Macroeconomics takes a broader view and studies entire economies, trade, general economic performance and trends at national and international level such as the GDP, employment, inflation or aspects such as the wider economic benefits of higher education and its impact on economic growth.

Microeconomic concepts and tools underpin the most important conventional explanations of why we (need to) regulate (e.g., ensure all students have access to the same information regarding university admission) and how regulators and regulatees interact. For instance, regulation is traditionally justified by the need to correct states of asymmetric information between market actors. An illustration of information asymmetry occurs in the context of consumers seeking to purchase a second-hand vehicle from a seller, be it a professional car dealer or a private owner. In this scenario, buyers possess considerably less information about the vehicle's condition, such as its maintenance history and any past accidents, compared to sellers. Sellers may sometimes choose to withhold certain information or provide inaccurate details to potential buyers, who may not have the resources to verify the accuracy of the information provided. There are several ways to address information asymmetry and ensure fairness for all parties involved. Consumer protection regulations, for instance, require car sellers to disclose certain information to consumers and prohibit false statements and other deceptive practices.

Economics is central to understanding the vocabulary of regulation, the justifications offered in support of the need to regulate (see Chapter 4), the methodologies used to evaluate the costs, benefits and the overall impact of regulatory interventions in society and markets (see Chapter 5) and the challenges of holding regulators accountable for their actions when they misrepresent the public or private interests they were meant to protect (see Chapter 11). This chapter familiarises the novice reader with key concepts of microeconomics that will be used throughout the book. This introduction does not seek to offer a primer on economics, which is a complex science that cannot be reduced to one book chapter. Instead, it provides an accessible, high-level introduction to a number of important economic concepts that scholars and students of regulation may regularly encounter in the field of regulatory studies. The concepts might be at times technical as the chapter follows the terminology used in well-known economics literature.

This chapter is divided in three sections:

(i) Section 1.1 introduces **rational choice theory** and explains central economic concepts such as utility, efficiency and market failures;
(ii) Section 1.2 offers an introduction to **transaction cost economics**, introducing the Coase theorem, the concept of transaction costs and the principal-agent model;

(iii) Section 1.3 highlights some of the central contributions of **behavioural economics** to regulation.

1.1 Basic Concepts: Rational Choice, Efficiency and Market Failures

As Cooter and Ulen explain in the extract below, economics is based on a set of central assumptions. The first assumption is that all individuals seek to maximise their 'utility'. Utility is typically defined as the numerical score representing the satisfaction that a consumer gets from consuming a given good or service. For example, while some individuals will be happy buying a new item of clothing, others will be happier using the same amount of money to go out for a meal. We all have own personal concepts of utility that reflect our preferences and we will thus act individually in a rational way within these preference frameworks. Although firms are generally expected to prioritise profit maximisation, owners, shareholders or other stakeholders may choose to define additional goals. For instance, a chocolate company may invest in corporate social responsibility efforts, such as ensuring fair wages and prices for cocoa farmers.

1.1.1 Rational Choice Theory, Equilibrium and Efficiency

The maximisation of utility is considered a rational choice. Rational choice theory forms the primary framework of neoclassical economics, which is a foundational approach developed in the late nineteenth century that expanded in the early 1900s. Cooter and Ulen explain below that this framework relies on three central assumptions: first, individuals are self-interested and rational actors who make decisions to maximise their utility; second, even though every individual is self-interested and wishes to maximise their own utility, markets tend toward equilibrium through the adjustments of price and demand; third, economic agents pursue efficiency.

The rational choice theory assumes that individuals, often implicitly, make decisions based on the rational and accurate calculation of their costs and benefits. This calculation does not necessarily translate into monetary terms; it can be an intuitive assessment. For example, you might spend an afternoon helping a friend with their homework instead of playing sport because you wish to invest in your friendship. In regulation, this calculation can be complex, as Chapter 5 explains, as it may require regulators to assess not only the benefits of regulation but also its costs to all relevant stakeholders. Costs may also be challenging to measure, for instance, when innovation incentives may be (unduly) distorted. Since each regulatory intervention will have a cost to someone, economic concepts are essential to help us understand how to model the aims of regulation and evaluate costs and benefits.

Equilibrium is a central concept in economics and it occurs when economics forces (demand and supply) are balanced. Market equilibrium occurs when the quantity of goods and services produced equals the quantity demanded by consumers. The result of market equilibrium is a stable price. The extract below refers to general equilibrium, which goes beyond individual markets to encompass the entire economy. While the concept of general equilibrium is important when introducing the novice reader to neoclassical economics, it does not account for the dynamism and innovation in certain regulated markets such as telecommunications and energy. In reality, regulatory analysis also considers dynamic competition and other novel approaches to address the complexities of these fast-changing sectors (see Chapter 3 on technological change).

The pursuit of efficiency is the third central assumption discussed in the extract. Microeconomics books typically define economic efficiency as 'the maximization of aggregate consumer and producer surplus'. There are, however, many different types of efficiency. Cooter and Ulen discuss two concepts of efficiency: *productive efficiency*, which implies that a given bundle of services is created at the lowest possible cost. There is productive efficiency when we are able to minimise the use of resources to produce a given output. There is productive inefficiency when productive resources are not efficiently used and the production is carried out at high costs. The extract also refers to allocative efficiency or Pareto efficiency, which describes a situation where 'scarce resources are used in a way in which they will benefit society as a whole to the greatest extent possible' (Haucap and Schwalbe 2011). Pareto efficiency is widely used in economics analysis. This state is achieved when it is not possible to improve the welfare of an individual by re-allocating resources without simultaneously reducing that of another.

Cooter, R., and Ulen, T. (2011). *Law and Economics*, 6th ed. Addison-Wesley.

12–14

Economists usually assume that each economic actor maximizes something: Consumers maximize utility (that is, happiness or satisfaction), firms maximize profits, politicians maximize votes, bureaucracies maximize revenues, charities maximize social welfare, and so forth. Economists often say that models assuming maximizing behavior work because most people are rational, and rationality requires maximization.

One conception of rationality holds that a rational actor can rank alternatives according to the extent that they give her what she wants. In practice, the alternatives available to the actor are constrained .... A rational consumer should choose the best alternative that the constraints allow .... Choosing the best alternative that the constraints allow can be described mathematically as maximizing .... [T]he rational consumer ranks alternatives according to the extent that they give her what she wants. Consequently, better alternatives can be associated with larger numbers. Economists call this association a 'utility function', about which we shall say more in the following sections. Furthermore, the constraint on choice can usually be expressed mathematically as a 'feasibility constraint'. Choosing the best alternative that the constraints allow corresponds to maximizing the utility function subject to the feasibility constraint. So, the

> consumer who goes shopping is said to maximize utility subject to her budget constraint.
>
> Turning to the second fundamental concept, there is no habit of thought so deeply ingrained among economists as the urge to characterize each social phenomenon as an equilibrium in the interaction of maximizing actors. An equilibrium is a pattern of interaction that persists unless disturbed by outside forces. Economists usually assume that interactions tend toward an equilibrium, regardless of whether they occur in markets, elections, clubs, games, teams, corporations, or marriages.
>
> There is a vital connection between maximization and equilibrium in microeconomic theory. We characterize the behavior of every individual or group as maximizing something. Maximizing behavior tends to push these individuals and groups toward a point of rest, an equilibrium. They certainly do not intend for an equilibrium to result; instead, they simply try to maximize whatever it is that interests them. Nonetheless, the interaction of maximizing agents usually results in an equilibrium ....
>
> Turning to the third fundamental concept, economists have several **distinct definitions of efficiency**. A production process is said to be productively efficient if either of two conditions holds:
>
> 1. It is not possible to produce the same amount of output using a lower-cost combination of inputs, or
> 2. It is not possible to produce more output using the same combination of inputs.
>
> Consider a firm that uses labor and machinery to produce a consumer good called a 'widget'. Suppose that the firm currently produces 100 widgets per week using 10 workers and 15 machines. The firm is productively efficient if
>
> 1. it is not possible to produce 100 widgets per week by using 10 workers and fewer than 15 machines, or by using 15 machines and fewer than 10 workers, or
> 2. it is not possible to produce more than 100 widgets per week from the combination of 10 workers and 15 machines.
>
> The other kind of efficiency, called Pareto efficiency after its inventor or sometimes referred to as **allocative efficiency**, concerns the satisfaction of individual preferences. A particular situation is said to be Pareto or allocatively efficient if it is impossible to change it so as to make at least one person better off (in his own estimation) without making another person worse off (again, in his own estimation).

Productive and allocative efficiency are mostly applied, as analytical constructs, to static contexts, that is, situations where conditions remain unchanged over a specified period. However, in reality, our economies change over time and sectors such as the digital services sector are particularly dynamic. Therefore, conditions such as demand and supply do not remain constant. Also consumer preferences change over time (think, for example, of fashion and how that shapes our garment preferences). The concept of dynamic efficiency moves beyond a specific point in time (such as the present), and instead, it analyzes the behaviour of firms over an extended period of time, say, two years. This concept is important in the realm of investments, where a focus on maximising social welfare over time is essential. Consider a scenario where a pharmaceutical firm invests fifty million dollars today into research to find a new medicine for curing diabetes. In the short term, its costs will increase and this firm will appear as productively inefficient. However, ten years later, the firm is likely to recoup this investment. As Haucap and Schwalbe (2011: 6) explain:

> it is not important that welfare is at maximum at every single point in time but rather that it is maximized throughout the relevant period. Dynamic inefficiency is thus the result of inadequate investment and innovation incentives.

These economic concepts of efficiency do not always guide us in understanding how to distribute welfare across different individuals, that is, to ensure that welfare (e.g., money) is not concentrated in the hands of a few households. This is why in regulation we consider a welfare function as a means of aggregating consumer utilities along with other concepts of efficiency.

Kaldor-Hicks efficiency, highlighted in the extract below, has been particularly influential in regulation. This concept is used not only to justify regulation but also to decide whether or not to regulate through cost-benefit analyses (see Chapter 5). Kaldor Hicks is defined by the compensation principle: efficiency occurs when those who benefit from a given intervention could, in theory, compensate those who are adversely affected, resulting in a potential Pareto improvement. This type of efficiency aims to assess changes in the welfare of society as a whole, assuming interpersonal compensation is possible. Social welfare is viewed as the sum of consumer and producer surplus.

The Kaldor-Hicks test has been criticised because it separates efficiency and equity and it ignores distributional impacts. The trade-off between distribution and efficiency is crucial in economics. Often efficiency is considered as a first step and then redistribution measures can be introduced to yield more equitable market outcomes (e.g., paying a lump sum subsidy to individuals in need). As the extract explains, Kaldor-Hicks efficiency is likely to disfavour local communities in low-income countries and deepen global inequality because it is based on a willingness-to-pay metrics which was defined primarily in the United States without regard for global differences.

Cook E. (2022). 'Efficiently Unequal: The Global Rise of Kaldor-Hicks Neoliberalism'. *Global Intellectual History*, 9(1–2), 247–269, doi:10.1080/23801883.2022.2062423.

In 2006, the Panamanian government was debating whether it should move forward with four major hydroelectric projects surrounding the Changuinola-Teribe watershed, an area inhabited mostly by the indigenous communities of

Ngobe and Naso. To assist in this crucial decision, an American NGO by the name of Conservation Strategy Fund (CSF) was brought on by private investors and public representatives to conduct a cost–benefit analysis . . ..

The CSF deemed the project worthwhile because it added together all the monetized costs and benefits and found that the benefits outweighed the costs. Yet a closer, disaggregated look at their analysis reveals that things were hardly so cut and dry since there were clear winners and losers. The biggest winners by far would be the bankers financing the project, who would receive a return of $193 million . . .. The biggest losers, on the other hand, were the thousands of people who made up the Naso and Ngöbe indigenous communities who had lived along the soon-to-be-extinct rivers for generations. Attempting to put a price tag on the social dislocation, community erasure, cultural destruction and loss of autonomy which would take place if these communities were forced to relocate is impossible, and CSF did not even try to do so. Yet they nevertheless went on to price the damage done to the indigenous at a rather paltry $56 million by narrowly calculating only the losses they would incur by no longer having free access to the natural resources in the area – as if this was all that the indigenous people had lost. Luckily for the bankers and the energy corporation, this relatively low figure only put a small dent in the aggregated cost–benefit analysis. Corporate profits still outweighed indigenous losses, and so – accordingly to the logic of cost–benefit analysis which only looks at the size of the pie and not how it is sliced – the project was deemed economically efficient . . ..

[E]conomists and cost–benefit practitioners define[d here] an efficient outcome as one in which the overall amount of monetized wealth increases in the aggregate, regardless of who *actually* receives these monetary gains – or losses. Since wealthy (mostly foreign) investors would, in the example of the Panamanian hydro project, gain more than the local indigenous people would (supposedly) lose, the project was deemed – in accordance with the teachings of modern, neoclassical economics – efficient and – therefore – worthwhile.

This definition of economic efficiency is widely known today as 'Kaldor-Hicks efficiency'. It was first established in the late 1930s by two economists in Great Britain, Nicolas Kaldor and John Hicks. After being critiqued and marginalized for almost forty years, the Kaldor-Hicks criterion roared back in 1970s America – just as neoliberalism was taking off – as the dominant tool for determining if a given policy, regulation, decision or law should be given a green light or not . . ..

If the winners of a new policy can compensate the losers so that the latter are not harmed by the policy change and yet the winners are still – even after deducting the compensation to the losers – better off than they were before, Kaldor argued, then this serves as proof that the aggregate economic pie has gotten larger and, therefore, the policy is economically efficient and should be endorsed by economists.

Yet, and this is key, at the end of the passage Kaldor makes plain that this crucial compensation test – the heart of the Kaldor-Hicks criterion – is *strictly hypothetical* and under no circumstances should economists recommend whether or not the winners should, in fact, actually compensate the losers or not.

If productive, allocative and dynamic efficiency is not achieved in a market, there is a market failure.

1.1.2 Market Failures

Economics' starting point was, for a long time, a situation of 'perfect competition' where market actors can freely enter and exit the market, possessing perfect information about supply and demand. In this ideal scenario, there is no consideration for economies of scale, a situation in which you can double the output of production for less than the double of the investment or cost. In the case of a single product, economies of scale entail decreasing average costs. In a scenario of perfect competition, a firm would know exactly how much to produce and how much the consumer would be willing to pay for it. If regulators' sole goal were to pursue economic efficiency and if markets operated as described, then competitive markets should be better left alone. In reality, however, competition is often imperfect due to various factors such as market failures.

Market failure is defined as 'a situation in which an unregulated competitive market is inefficient because prices fail to provide proper signals to consumers and producers' (Pindyck and Rubinfeld 2018). Economic literature has identified four central causes for market failures: (i) imperfect competition with the existence of a natural monopoly as an extreme case, (ii) externalities, (iii) asymmetric information distribution which can result in moral hazard and adverse selection, (iv) public goods. Regulatory intervention is traditionally justified in these situations as it may lead to economic improvements.

1.1.2.1 Imperfect Competition and Monopolies

As the extract explains, monopolies – a market characterised by a single seller and numerous buyers – are the first source of market failures. Monopolists may exploit their dominant position by exerting control over prices and establishing profit-maximising prices for their products and services, deviating from what would typically prevail in a competitive market. A monopolist tends to produce less than would occur in a competitive market and sets a price higher than the competitive market price.

While pure monopolies are uncommon in our daily lives, instances of temporary monopolies persist, often created by intellectual property rights such as patents and copyrights. These rights exclude competition under the premise of incentivising research and development or fostering innovation. In various markets, such as energy and telecommunications, only a limited number of firms engage in competition, creating situations akin to monopolistic conditions.

A monopsony represents the opposite phenomenon, that is, a market with many sellers but only one buyer. Contrary to a competitive buyer, a monopsonist will pay a price that depends on the quantity that it purchases. While instances of pure monopsonies are rare, many markets exhibit monopsonist behaviour when large buyers dominate the acquisition of production inputs. Monopoly and monopsony are two types of market power or the ability of a seller or buyer to affect the price of a good or service. In both cases, regulation such as competition laws seek to regulate the prices charged by monopolists or paid by monopsonists and ensure they do not abuse their market power.

As the extract explains, sometimes it is not possible to replace certain monopolies. This is the case of natural monopolies, a specific type of monopoly that exists if a single firm can produce the entire output of the market (the relevant demand) at a cost that is lower than it would be if there were several other firms. Economists refer to this as 'cost subadditivity', which might be due to large fixed costs and small marginal costs. Natural monopolies are common in public utilities such as gas, telecommunications, railways or electricity. The technology required to distribute natural gas can exhibit characteristics of a natural monopoly because it requires large investments. There are high fixed costs associated with building and maintaining the necessary infrastructure, namely the pipelines and distribution networks. However, once these pipelines are operating, the cost of providing more gas to an additional number of households is very limited. Regulatory measures are often implemented to mitigate the potential negative effects of monopoly power (e.g., excessive prices) and guarantee a balance between efficiency and consumer welfare. Even though regulation may be needed to discipline natural monopoly firms, there are, nonetheless, cases where natural monopolies can be contested and thus some form of competition may exist.

Viscusi, K., Harrington, J., and Vernon J. (2005). *Economics of Regulation and Antitrust*, 4th ed. MIT Press.

3–6

If we existed in world that functioned in accordance with the perfect competition paradigm, there would be little need for [regulation]. All markets would consist of a large number of sellers of a product, and consumers would be fully informed of the product's implications. Moreover, there would be no externalities present in this idealized economy, as all effects would be internalized by the buyers and sellers of a particular product.

Unfortunately, economic reality seldom adheres very closely to the textbook model of perfect competition. Many industries are dominated by a small number of firms. In some instances, principally the public utilities, there may even be a monopoly. Consumers who use hazardous products and workers who accept risky employment may not fully understand the consequences of their actions. There are also widespread externalities that affect the air we breathe, the water we drink, and the viability of the planet for future generations ....

The major concern with monopoly and similar kinds of concentration is not that being big is necessarily undesirable. However, because of the control over the price exerted by a monopoly, there are economic efficiency losses to society. Product quality and diversity may also be affected ....

> Recent research has greatly changed how we think about monopolies. For example, one major consideration is not simply how big a firm currently is and what its current market influence is, but rather the extent to which there is a possible entry from a competitor. If firms fear the prospect of such entry, which has been characterized through the theory of contestable markets, then the behavior of a monopolist will be influenced in a manner that will promote more responsible behavior.
>
> One of the reasons concentrated industries emerge is that some firms may have exclusive rights to some invention or may have been responsible for a technological change that has transformed the industry. Coca-Cola and Pepsi Cola are much more successful soft drinks than their generic counterparts because of their perceived superior taste. If their formulas were public and could be generally replicated, then their market influence would wane considerably . . .
>
> **Economic Regulation**
>
> In many contexts where natural monopolies have emerged, for reasons of economic efficiency it is desirable to have a monopolistic market structure. Nevertheless, these economic giants must be tamed so that they will not charge excessive prices. We do not wish to incur all of the efficiency and equity problems that arise as a result of a monopoly. Prominent examples include public utilities. It does not make sense to have a large number of small firms providing households with electricity, providing public transportation systems . . .. However, we also do not wish to give single firms free reign in these markets because the interests of a monopoly will not best advance the interests of society as a whole.

1.1.2.2 Externalities

Externalities are the second source of market failure. 'Physical' externalities occur when the actions of consumers or producers result in costs and benefits that are not 'internalised', that is, they are not reflected in the cost and benefit of products and are not considered by the economic agent causing them. Consequently, market outcomes are distorted and inefficient. As Haucap and Schwalbe explain, these costs and benefits are 'external' to the market in a way that they are not reflected in market prices. Externalities can be positive or negative. For example, the production of chemicals or clothing may cause air and water pollution, which – in the absence of relevant laws and regulations – cause negative externalities. Without regulation, producers of these industries do not have an incentive to strive for optimal levels of pollution. An example of a positive externality is the investment in research and development (R&D). When it produces new knowledge, other firms may draw on them to produce other goods, even though they did not contribute to this initial investment. Also positive externalities may require regulatory intervention (e.g., patents): when there is little reward for investing in R&D, the market may underfund it.

> **Haucap, J., and Schwalbe, U. (2011).** 'Economic Principles of State Aid Control'. DICE Discussion Paper No. 17, 7, https://d-nb.info/1012494764/34.
>
> External effects are thus a matter of damaging or favouring otherwise uninvolved third parties. External effects are a direct result of ill-defined or definable and enforceable rights of disposal so that there is no compensation for the damage or favouritism. Negative external effects are best known from environmental policy. For example, harmful emissions that occur during a production process can cause damage to the residents' health or may require other companies to install costly filter systems. If the persons suffering from environmental pollution do not have assertive ownership rights of the 'good' environment, it will not be possible for them to prevent the causal agent from emitting pollutant emissions or to charge the causal agent with the costs for the environmental pollution (external costs). This lack of inclusion of external costs in the market-based pricing mechanism (lack of internalization) results in excessive pollution. An example of such negative external effects are the CO2 emissions that occur in the course of power production (especially coal and gas-fired power plants), as long as external effects are not internalized through taxes or tradable certificates.

1.1.2.3 Asymmetric Information

Information problems, namely the asymmetric distribution of information between market sides (supply and demand), are important causes of market failure. We should distinguish between incomplete and imperfect information: incomplete information exists when an economic agent does not have enough information about a transaction. This occurs typically before an economic transaction takes place. Imperfect information refers more generally to situations where information is not accurate or symmetrically distributed. Both concepts highlight the complexities of making decisions under conditions of information asymmetry. Consequently, the better-informed side of the market may exploit its position opportunistically, leading to inefficient market outcomes. In such cases, the necessity for regulation arises to correct these information imbalances and ensure fair and efficient market functioning. Haucap and Schwalbe (2011: 9–10) illustrate this cause for market failure with the consumer credit market:

> The suppliers of credits do not have full knowledge of the exact default risk of each credit consumer. Consequently, they will adjust their interest on credits (the price of the credit) to the estimated average default risk. Consumers with low individual default risk (so-called good risks) will view this price as too high and choose not to borrow money. Consumers with above-average risks (so-called bad risks) benefit from what they perceive as comparatively cheap prices. The systematic crowding out of the good risks by the bad (negative selection) can in extreme cases lead to market failure, as utilizing transactions remain absent.

> With respect to the raising of capital for small and medium-sized enterprises in particular, it is assumed that significant information asymmetries exist, which can cause market failure. For both venture capital markets and private granting of credit by banks, it is estimated that the suppliers of capital systematically overestimate the default risk of credits to this group and therefore set the price for raising capital too high. As a result, raising capital is made more difficult for small and medium-sized enterprises in comparison to larger companies, so that they suffer significant competitive disadvantages. In order to compensate for these competitive disadvantages, the public sector often grants concessional credits to small and medium-sized businesses. Due to the selective nature of this preferential treatment, these credits have state aid character. Therefore, prior to state intervention (e.g., through a favourable granting of credit), it should always be examined whether or not protective measures emerge on the market itself that can prevent market failure. Possible protective measures are thereby an effective screening or signalling, which reduce the dangers of moral hazard and adverse selection.

Adverse selection and moral hazard are both concepts related to information asymmetry in transactions. Adverse selection may take place when one party in a transaction has more information than the other and takes advantage of this information to make decisions that negatively impact the less-informed party. This often happens before the transaction takes place.

The insurance industry, which tends to be highly regulated, provides insights into how adverse selection occurs and why regulation may be needed. Many of us become ill and have accidents that can affect our capacity to work. Insurance is important to guarantee that we are assisted when in need and high costs are covered. However, not everyone will voluntarily purchase insurance. Instead, those who are more likely to become ill will buy insurance and the healthiest among us may prefer to be optimistic and 'hope for the best'. In some countries, the costs of health insurance vary depending on the individual's risk to become ill such as the existence of pre-existing health conditions. In other countries, no such price discrimination exists and healthcare costs are calculated in proportion to one's income. This can generate an adverse selection problem if an insurance company only has consumers who are likely to become ill. As Varian explains, this is a well-known scenario that arises when products of different qualities are sold at a single price because buyers or sellers are not sufficiently informed to determine the true quality at the time of the purchase. That is, too much of the low-quality product and too little of the high-quality product would be sold in the marketplace. When all individuals purchase insurance, there is a social gain since the pooling of many individuals' risks reduces the total risk. In other words, when many healthy individuals purchase health insurance (and not only the ones with health preconditions), there is a better distribution of risk.

The extract also discusses moral hazard, which arises when one party, after entering into a transaction, has an incentive to take risks or behave in a way that the other party cannot fully anticipate or control. This occurs when economic actors have an incentive to expose themselves to a risk because they do not bear the full consequences of the negative effects of their actions (see also Chapter 12).

Varian, H. R. (2009). *Intermediate Microeconomic: A Modern Approach*, 8th ed. W. W. Norton & Company.

722–724

Adverse Selection

Suppose that an insurance company wants to offer insurance for bicycle theft. They do a careful market survey and find that the incident of theft varies widely across communities. In some areas there is a high probability that a bicycle will be stolen, and in other areas thefts are quite rare. Suppose that the insurance company decides to offer the insurance based on the average theft rate. What do you think will happen?

Answer: the insurance company is likely to go broke quickly! Think about it. Who is going to buy the insurance at the average rate? Not the people in the safe communities – they don't need much insurance anyway. Instead the people in the communities with a high incidence of theft will want the insurance – they're the ones who need it. But this means that the insurance claims will mostly be made by the consumers who live in the high-risk areas. Rates based on the average probability of theft will be a misleading indication of the actual experience of claims filed with the insurance company. The insurance company will not get an unbiased selection of customers; rather they will get an adverse selection. In fact the term 'adverse selection' was first used in the insurance industry to describe just this sort of problem.

It follows that in order to break even the insurance company must base their rates on the 'worst-case' forecasts and that consumers with a low, but not negligible, risk of bicycle theft will be unwilling to purchase the resulting high-priced insurance . . ..

Moral Hazard

Consider the bicycle-theft insurance market again and suppose for simplicity that all of the consumers live in areas with identical probabilities of theft, so that there is no problem of adverse selection. On the other hand, the probability of theft may be affected by the actions taken by the bicycle owners.

For example, if the bicycle owners don't bother to lock their bikes or use only a flimsy lock, the bicycle is much more likely to be stolen than if they use a secure lock. Similar examples arise in other sorts of insurance. In the case of health insurance, for example, the consumers are less likely to need the insurance if they take actions associated with a healthy lifestyle . . ..

When it sets its rates the insurance company has to take into account the incentives that the consumers have to take an appropriate amount of care. If no insurance is available consumers have an incentive to take the maximum possible amount of care. If it is impossible to buy bicycle-theft insurance, then all bicyclists would use large expensive locks. In this case the individual bears the full cost of his actions and accordingly he wants to 'invest' in taking care until the marginal benefit from more care just equals the marginal cost of doing so.

But if a consumer can purchase bicycle insurance, then the cost inflicted on the individual of having his bicycle stolen is much less. After all, if the bicycle is stolen then the person simply has to report it to the insurance company and he will get insurance money to replace it. In the extreme case, where the insurance company completely reimburses the individual for the theft of his bicycle, the individual has no incentive to take care at all. This lack of incentive to take care is called moral hazard.

Note the tradeoff involved: too little insurance means that people bear a lot of risk, too much insurance means that people will take inadequate care. If the amount of care is observable, then there is no problem. The insurance company can base its rates on the amount of care taken. In real life it is common for insurance companies to give different rates to businesses that have a fire sprinkler system in their building, or to charge smokers different rates than nonsmokers for health insurance. In these cases the insurance firm attempts to discriminate among users depending on the choices they have made that influence the probability of damage.

But insurance companies can't observe all the relevant actions of those they insure. Therefore we will have the tradeoff described above: full insurance means too little care will be undertaken because the individuals don't face the full costs of their actions. What does this imply about the types of insurance contracts that will be offered? In general, the insurance companies will not want to offer the consumers 'complete' insurance. They will always want the consumer to face some part of the risk. This is why most insurance policies include a 'deductible', an amount that the insured party has to pay in any claim.

Besides the regulatory instruments (see Chapters 6–8), there are also various ways through which economic agents address the problem of asymmetric information. For instance, market signaling is a process through which sellers send signals to buyers conveying information about product quality. A dealer of second-hand cars may, for example, offer a one-year warranty to signal that the car is not 'a lemon'.

1.1.2.4 Public Goods

Public goods have two main characteristics: they are non-rivalrous and non-exclusive in their consumption. Non-rivalry can be detected if for any given level of production, the marginal cost of providing it to an additional consumer is zero. For most goods that are provided by private firms, the marginal cost of production is positive, even when it is small. There are cases though where additional consumers of public goods do not add to the cost. For example, once a highway is built and there is no congestion, additional cars driving on it cost zero. Also, virtual goods such as software and information content on the Internet are non-rival in consumption.

Public goods are also non-exclusive, that is, people – including consumers who are unwilling to pay for these goods – cannot de facto be excluded from their consumption. Public goods are thus commodities or services that are available to the whole collectively. National defense is an example of a non-exclusive good because once a country has invested in its national defense, all citizens can be protected.

Recently, the risk of depletion of public goods taking the form of 'common pool resources', such as the oceans and clean air, have sparked considerable interest. Oceans were traditionally regarded non-excludable and non-rivalrous. However, overgrazing also exists in the form of overfishing. Hardin (1968) famously coined this phenomenon as the 'tragedy of the commons' employing the metaphor of a grazing commons, a pasture that was open to all and from which no-one could be excluded. Each herder receives a direct benefit from grazing their animals on the commons but only bears a share of the cost resulting from overgrazing. Accordingly, each herder, acting rationally, will graze as many animals as possible, without regard to the degradation thereby caused.

The tragedy of the commons flows from unlimited access to public goods, prompting Hardin to suggest the privatisation of these goods as well as central government regulation to introduce an element of excludability. Examples are fisheries quotas, government ownership and the restriction of access through auctions of special licenses.

Nobel prize winner Elinor Ostrom partly challenged Hardin's perspective, demonstrating first that incentive structures are more varied and multifaceted than conventional analysis suggested and, second, that the excludability of the commons is more complex than Hardin had argued. It depends, among other factors, on the enforceability of rules and property rights. Factors such as whether the resource is stationary (e.g., a forest) or mobile (e.g., river fisheries), and whether it is challenging to monitor (e.g., ground water), affect the management strategies adopted by communities. Through extensive global case studies on local commons management, Ostrom demonstrated how resource-user communities have, organically and spontaneously, developed effective exclusion methods without relying on external regulation.

Despite Ostrom's legacy, Hardin's arguments advocating for regulation in preventing the tragedy of the commons still hold merit.

1.1.3 Economic Regulation and Social Regulation

The correction of market failures calls for specific types of regulation. The extract below distinguishes between two types of regulation: economic and social regulation. It defines economic regulation as 'government-imposed restrictions on firm decisions over price, quantity, and entry and exit'. While regulation is nowadays no longer limited to state-issued regulations, most economic regulatory interventions on price, entry and exit requirements are issued by public regulators. Economic regulation may also regulate entry of certain professions in order to remedy information problems and guarantee standardised minimum levels of qualification (e.g., professional licenses for medical doctors, see also Chapter 9).

Since the 1970s, regulation has expanded to the social realm as society recognised that markets and their regulation did not suffice to ensure a set of minima such as clean water, a safe working environment, and a healthy environment. As the extract mentions, growing awareness for the effects of climate change have reinforced the tendency to adopt more social regulation. Social regulation addresses various market failures, including negative externalities affecting the environment, health and safety. Examples of social regulation encompass mandates such as wearing protective gear on construction sites.

Viscusi, W., Kip, V., Harrington, J. M., Harrington Jr., J. E. (2005). *Economics of Regulation and Antitrust*, 4th ed. MIT Press.

357–358

Economic regulation typically refers to government-imposed restrictions on firm decisions over price, quantity, and entry and exit. Economic regulation is to be contrasted with social regulation . . ..

Although economic regulation can encompass restrictions on a wide array of firm decisions, the three key decision variables controlled by regulation are price, quantity, and the number of firms. Less frequently controlled variables include product quality, advertising, and investment

Control of Price

Price regulation may specify a particular price that firms must charge, or may instead restrict firms to setting price within some range. If the concern of the government is with a regulated monopolist setting price too high, regulation is apt to specify a maximum price that can be charged . . ..

Control of Quantity

Restrictions on the quantity of a product or a service that is sold may be used either with or without price regulation. From the 1930s up until around 1970s, many oil-producing states, among them Texas and Oklahoma, placed maximum production limits on crude oil production. Although quantity was controlled by the state, price was determined nationally or globally (though obviously these quantity controls influenced the market price . . ..

Control of Entry and Exit

[T]he two critical variables that regulators have controlled are price and the number of firms, the latter through restrictions on entry and exit . . .. Entry may be regulated at several levels. First, entry by new firms may be controlled, as is typically done in the regulation of several public utilities . . .. In addition to controlling entry by new firms, a regulatory agency may also control entry by existing regulated firms .... The former case is exemplified by the airline and trucking regulation. Their respective regulatory agencies made it very difficult for an existing firm to enter a geographic market already served by another regulated firm ....

A basis for exit regulation is that regulation strives to have services provided to a wider set of consumers than would be true in a free market. Attaining this goal may entail regulated firms serving unprofitable markets, which creates a need for regulations that forbid a regulated firm from abandoning a market without regulatory approval ....

Control of Other Variables

A regulatory agency may specify minimum standards for reliability of a service. If an electric utility has regular blackouts, the regulatory agency is likely to intervene and require an increase in capacity in order to improve service reliability ....

Social Regulation

[E]nvironmental and other social regulations have become an increasingly prominent part of the regulatory mix .... [T]he recent emergence of concerns such as global climate change has increased the extent of this form of regulation. There is little doubt that actual market failures exist in the context of social regulation. In many cases, such as air pollution, no markets exist at all for the commodity being produced, and there is no market-based compensation of the victims of pollution. Markets could never suffice in instances such as this.

Economic and social regulation often coexist and are used together to address different market failures.

1.2 Transaction Economics

Transaction economics, developed mainly by Williamson (1975, 1979), studies the costs of transactions within an economic system, explaining that transaction costs are pervasive and exist in every economic transaction. Williamson defined this concept as the costs incurred in the process of planning, executing and enforcing an exchange or transaction, including information search and acquisition, negotiation and contracting, monitoring and enforcement and the costs of adapting to unforeseen circumstances. The starting point for studying transaction costs is, nonetheless, Coase (1937).

In 'The Nature of the Firm', Coase (1937) highlighted that firms emerge when the cost of coordinating through the market (transaction costs) surpasses the cost of coordinating within a hierarchical structure (the firm). Later, in 'The Problem of Social Cost' (1960), Coase developed his Theorem, asserting that, under specific conditions, private parties can autonomously negotiate and achieve efficient resolutions to externalities without requiring government intervention, provided well-defined property rights exist. In essence, the Coase Theorem challenges the notion that complete competitive markets are the sole path to efficiency. Rather, it posits that in cases of market inefficiency, individuals can, under certain conditions, arrange and negotiate their way towards efficiency. Coase argued that, with well-defined property rights and minimal transaction costs – those incurred during exchanges like buying or selling – parties have the capacity to negotiate an economically efficient allocation of externalities, regardless of the initial assignment of property rights.

As explained in the extract, the Coase Theorem has regulatory implications, asserting that, in many instances, private bargaining may be preferable to regulatory intervention (see also Chapter 4).

Pacces, A. M., and Van den Bergh, Roger J. (2012). 'An Introduction to the Law and Economics of Regulation in Pacces'. In A. M. and R. J. Van den Bergh (eds.), 'Regulation and Economics' in *Encyclopedia of Law and Economics*, 2nd ed. Elgar, 1–22.

5–6

Traditionally, in economics, [market failures] are considered sufficient ground for legal intervention. However, since Coase (1960), this logic has been put into question. The sense of Coase's critique to the neoclassical … treatment of market failures is threefold. First, in a frictionless world, market failures would be self-correcting only on condition that property rights are well specified and contracts are enforceable at no cost. This is the famous Coase Theorem that holds in a world of zero transaction costs. The second point is that, when transaction costs are positive as it happens to be the case in most of the real world, legal devices other than regulation may score better in achieving the efficient outcome. Liability, which in some situations is the best way to cope with negative externalities, is the most prominent alternative. The third issue is that regulation is not immune from the problem of transaction costs. Inefficiencies in the design and the implementation of corrective measures due to high transaction costs may imply that society will be better off in the absence of regulation.

One important lesson from the Coasean approach to market failures is that the latter are not sufficient to justify regulation. As Ogus (1994) puts it, the case for regulation rests on the association of market failures with private law failures. For instance, it may not be necessary to regulate, beyond what contract law already does, the duty of the more informed party to a contract to inform the counterparty. But such regulation may well be justified when the potential harm of misinformation is diffused and it is unlikely that the threat of civil liability will deter deception, as for instance in the case of adulterated food or securities fraud … .

A second important implication of Coase's approach to regulation is that, in some situations, the cure (regulation) may be worse than the disease (market failure). This depends on the problem of regulatory failure. The causes of regulatory failure are manifold, but at least two stand out. First, regulators do not have sufficient information about individuals' and firms' behaviour which makes it very difficult, if not impossible, for regulation to effectively improve on market outcomes, however flawed the latter may be .... [R]egulation is self-perpetuating exactly because of its unintended consequences. Faced with regulatory failure, uninformed regulators react by adding new regulations rather than by repealing the existing ones that have failed.

While in the real world (almost) all exchanges will have transaction costs, higher transaction costs can be expected when market actors have different interests and when there are many market actors willing to negotiate. This occurs when an individual (the principal or 'the boss') delegates tasks to another one (the agent). For example, principals can be individuals who appoint financial advisors to manage their wealth, acting for and on their behalf. The **principal-agent theory**, as Eisenhardt explains below, helps us grasp what happens when this delegation occurs, how risks are shared, and how conflicts may emerge (see also Chapter 12).

The key assumptions of the principal-agent theory are as follows: first, agents may have different preferences from their principal; second, agents may have different incentives from the principal because their rewards are different; third, agents may have information that is unavailable to the principal (and vice-versa). This last element – information asymmetries – is a central problem that makes it difficult for principals to monitor how agents execute the tasks they were given. These divergences often result in conflicts, which explains the need for regulation at many levels such as monitoring, incentives, risk sharing, information sharing and accountability. In the case of regulation, regulators are the agents of the citizens they serve. However, as Chapters 4 and 12 explain, the alignment of interests between regulators and regulatees is complex and regulators can often fall short of the regulatees' expectations.

Eisenhardt, K. M. (1989). 'Agency Theory: An Assessment and Review'. *The Academy of Management Review*, 14(1), 57–74, https://doi.org/10.2307/258191.

Specifically, agency theory is directed at the ubiquitous agency relationship, in which one party (the principal) delegates work to another (the agent), who performs that work. Agency theory attempts to describe this relationship using the metaphor of a contract. Agency theory is concerned with resolving two problems that can occur in agency relationships. The first is the agency problem that arises when (a) the desires or goals of the principal and agent conflict and (b) it is difficult or expensive for the principal to verify what the agent is actually doing. The problem here is that the principal cannot verify that the agent has behaved appropriately. The second is the problem of risk sharing that arises when the principal and agent have different attitudes toward risk. The problem here is that the principal and the agent may prefer different actions because of the different risk preferences. Because the unit of analysis is the contract governing the relationship between the principal and the agent, the focus of the theory is on determining the most efficient contract governing the principal-

> agent relationship given assumptions about people (e.g., self-interest, bounded rationality, risk aversion), organizations (e.g., goal conflict among members), and information (e.g., information is a commodity which can be purchased). Specifically, the question becomes: Is a behavior-oriented contract (e.g., salaries, hierarchical governance) more efficient than an outcome-oriented contract (e.g., commissions, stock options, transfer of property rights, market governance)? . . . The agency structure is applicable in a variety of settings, ranging from macrolevel issues such as regulatory policy to microlevel dyad phenomena such as blame, impression management, lying, and other expressions of self- interest.

Over the last half century, rational choice theory has been disputed by behavioural economics, as Section 1.3 shows.

1.3 Introduction to Behavioural Economics

Behavioural economics, pioneered by Amos Tversky and Daniel Kahneman, draws primarily on experimental and interdisciplinary studies. Behavioural economics challenges the assumption that individuals always behave rationally and is devoted to studying how consumers actually make choices. This subfield of economics does not seek to replace the standard framework of neoclassical economics. Instead, it extends rational choice and equilibrium models by providing them with more realistic psychological foundations. Behavioural economics studies mental accounting and how people are strongly influenced by how choices are presented to them. The framing of a choice can often result in irrational choices. For instance, consumers may be more likely to pay $250 for a pair of faded or slightly torn jeans of the exact same brand sold in an exclusive store rather than at a thrift store or a vintage clothing platform (e.g., Vinted). While at times this may seem rational, in many cases, this type of decisions will be the result of framing or biases.

1.3.1 Cognitive Biases

Individuals in the real world act very differently from the model of the 'homo economicus', that is, the self-interested individual who makes rational decisions for utility maximisation. Under conditions of uncertainty and conflict, human decision-making is guided instead by framing or, more accurately, heuristics and biases. Humans are thus not as rational as neoclassical economics modelled them. Sunstein, Jolls and Thaler discuss below our limited rationality, controlling emotions (about fairness or other values), and how this justifies irrational choices, mistakes and the use of mental shortcuts. Individuals also have bounded willpower, which translates itself in poor health or financial choices (e.g., preferring chocolate to fruit as a snack).

Cognitive biases are important to understand why regulation is needed (see Chapter 4). To illustrate, *hyperbolic discounting* or present bias is our inclination to choose immediate rewards (e.g., convenient fast-food takeaway) over rewards that come later in the future (e.g., healthy body). This is also known as myopic decisions in neoclassical economics. *Cognitive dissonance* refers to a state of discomfort caused by contradictory beliefs and actions. It explains why humans tend to have a confirmation bias, that is, a tendency to notice, focus on and accept better evidence that fits within their existing beliefs. Cognitive biases often intensify in challenging scarcity circumstances associated with poverty, such as financial instability. These conditions impact cognitive resources and decision-making abilities. Payday loans take advantage of the irrational decisions stemming from this scarcity mindset.

Sunstein, C. R., Jolls C., Thaler, R. H. (1998). 'A Behavioral Approach to Law and Economics'. *Stanford Law Review*, 50, 1471–1550.

1476–1479

How do 'real people' differ from homo economicus? We will describe the differences by stressing three important 'bounds' on human behavior, bounds that draw into question the central ideas of utility maximization, stable preferences, rational expectations, and optimal processing of information. People can be said to display bounded rationality, bounded willpower, and bounded self-interest. All three bounds are well documented in the literature of other social sciences, but they are relatively unexplored in economics (although, as we noted at the outset, this has begun to change). Each of these bounds represents a significant way in which most people depart from the standard eco nomic model . . ..

Bounded Rationality

Bounded rationality, an idea first introduced by Herbert Simon, refers to the obvious fact that human cognitive abilities are not infinite. We have limited computational skills and seriously flawed memories. People can respond sensibly to these failings; thus it might be said that people sometimes respond rationally to their own cognitive limitations, minimizing the sum of decision costs and error costs. To deal with limited memories we make lists. To deal with limited brain power and time we use mental shortcuts and rules of thumb. But even with these remedies, and in some cases because of these remedies, human behavior differs in systematic ways from that predicted by the standard economic model of unbounded rationality. Even when the use of mental shortcuts is rational, it can produce predictable mistakes. The departures from the standard model can be divided into two categories: judgment and decisionmaking. Actual judgments show systematic departures from models of unbiased forecasts, and actual decisions often violate the axioms of expected utility theory.

A major source of differences between actual judgments and unbiased forecasts is the use of rules of thumb. . .such as the availability heuristic – in which the frequency of some event is estimated by judging how easy it is to recall other instances of this type (how "available" such instances are) – lead us to erroneous conclusions. People tend to conclude, for example, that the probability of an event (such as a car accident) is greater if they have recently witnessed an occurrence of that event than if they have not. What is especially important in the work of Kahneman and Tversky is that it shows that shortcuts and rules of thumb are predictable. While the heuristics are useful on average (which explains how they become adopted), they lead to errors in particular circumstances. This means that someone using such a rule of thumb may be behaving rationally in the sense of economizing on thinking time, but such a person will nonetheless make forecasts that are different from those that emerge from the standard rational choice model . . ..

Bounded Willpower
In addition to bounded rationality, people often display bounded willpower. This term refers to the fact that human beings often take actions that they know to be in conflict with their own long-term interests. Most smokers say they would prefer not to smoke, and many pay money to join a program or obtain a drug that will help them quit. As with bounded rationality, many people recognize that they have bounded willpower and take steps to mitigate its effects. They join a pension plan or 'Christmas Club' (a special savings arrangement under which funds can be withdrawn only around the holidays) to prevent undersaving, and they don't keep tempting desserts around the house when trying to diet . . ..

Bounded Self-interest
Self-interest is bounded in a much broader range of settings than conventional economics assumes, and the bound operates in ways different from what the conventional understanding suggests. In many market and bargaining settings (as opposed to nonmarket settings such as bequest decisions), people care about being treated fairly and want to treat others fairly if those others are themselves behaving fairly. As a result of these concerns, the agents in a behavioral economic model are both nicer and (when they are not treated fairly) more spiteful than the agents postulated by neoclassical theory. Formal models have been used to show how people deal with both fairness and unfairness; we will draw on those models here.

1.3.2 Cognitive Biases and Behavioral Design

Regulators have recently started to draw on behavioural insights to justify the need for regulatory interventions that prevent the exploitation of people's cognitive biases by others and protect individuals from their own fallibility (for example, the use of odd pricing such as $0.99). This has inspired paternalistic interventions that interfere with a person's freedom in order to further their own good. Examples of paternalism include regulatory measures that (intend to) protect vulnerable consumers, restrictions on the legal capacity of minors and 'sin taxes' on tobacco and other unhealthy products. In addition to paternalism, nudging and choice architecture (see also Chapters 6 and 7) are other approaches to regulation that seek to understand and correct cognitive systems besides addressing information asymmetries. As Bohnet explains, behavioural insights can also be employed to improve gender equality, namely in hiring. Discrimination is not always done on purpose but it results from implicit biases, stereotypes and how certain professions and sectors are framed. Not everyone is aware of their biases (e.g., bias to hire a candidate who is similar in terms of physical appearance and preferences) and thus regulation can offer valuable corrections.

Bohnet, I. (2016). *What Works: Gender Equality by Design.* Harvard University Press.

1–7

As late as 1970, only 5 percent of musicians performing in the top five orchestras in the United States were women. Today, women compose more than 35 percent of the most acclaimed orchestras, and they play great music. This did not happen by chance. Rather, it required the introduction of blind auditions. The Boston Symphony Orchestra was the first to ask musicians to audition behind a screen, and in the 1970s and 1980s most other major orchestras followed suit. When they did so, usually in preliminary rounds, it raised the likelihood that a female musician would advance by 50 percent and substantially increased the proportion of women hired.

In theory, an orchestra director cares about the sounds coming out of the bassoon, the flute, and the trumpet, not the ethnicity or sex of the person playing the instrument. In practice, the Vienna Philharmonic, for example, admitted its first female player in 1997. Not so long ago. Orchestra directors and selection committees were quite comfortable with all- male, all- white orchestras and likely not aware of their biases. To change this, no great technological feat was required, just awareness, a curtain, and a decision. Or, more precisely, a design decision. A simple curtain doubled the talent pool, creating amazing music and transforming what orchestras look like . . ..

Stereotypes serve as heuristics – rules of thumb – that allow us to process information more easily, but they are often inaccurate. What is worse, stereotypes describing how we believe the world to be often turn into prescriptions for what the world should be. Much psychological research shows that we cannot help but put people (and other observations) into categories. It rarely is a conscious thought process that informs our thinking about demographic groups. Rather, when we learn the sex of a person, gender biases are automatically activated, leading to unintentional and implicit discrimination.

Through behavioral design we can move the needle toward creating equal opportunities for female musicians, for male teachers, and for everyone else . . .. Behavioral design offers an additional instrument for our collective toolbox to promote change; it complements other approaches focusing, for example, on equal rights, education, health, agency, or on policies making work and family compatible.

Conclusion

This chapter offered a primer on the key economic concepts that have shaped the theories, methodologies and instruments of regulation. Neoclassical economics explains and predicts human behaviour under a set of assumptions: first, individuals and firms are rational; second, they strive to maximise their utility or profits; third, they make decisions on the grounds of full and relevant information. We explained different economic concepts such as efficiency and transaction costs, which we will apply in other chapters.

Discussion Questions

1. Discuss the difference between productive efficiency, allocative efficiency and dynamic efficiency.
2. What are the key sources of informational market failures?
3. Explain how the insurance industry addresses the adverse selection and moral hazard problems.
4. Provide common examples from your daily life where you see some of the features of the principal-agent model. How can this model be used to understand the conflicts that arise in these relationships?
5. How do Hardin and Ostrom differ in the way they approach the tragedy of the commons?
6. What is behavioural economics?
7. What sets behavioural economics apart from standard economics analysis?
8. How does poverty affect the ability of individuals to maximise their utility? Can and should regulators correct this suboptimal conduct? (You may wish to return to this question, after having read Chapters 4 and 5).

2

The Rise of Risk in Regulatory Governance

Introduction

We have considered market failure as a justification for regulatory intervention based on welfare economic analysis, which was particularly influential from the 1980s in many OECD countries (especially the United Kingdom and in North America) and was reflected in sweeping market-oriented reforms to public administration. During that period, the language and discourse of risk began to permeate policy discussions, becoming commonplace by the final decade of the twentieth century. Contemporary discussion about public regulatory intervention is now typically framed in terms of a need to prevent or 'manage risks' through control and oversight mechanisms intended to reduce risk to a socially acceptable level without unnecessarily restricting socially beneficial activities.

Several major disasters have brought the rise of risk and practices of 'risk management' into sharper focus. We highlight three. First, in 1984 the deadly leak of Methyl Iso Cyanate (MIC) gas from a Union Carbide pesticide plant in Bhopal, India, killed over 4,000 people, leaving a further 50,000 permanently disabled. The Indian government's official investigation concluded that the accident was caused by inadequate care in the storage of large quantities of MIC; the design, construction and materials chosen; and inadequate systems for monitoring, measuring and detecting dangers and disposing of unstable materials. The tragedy highlighted how transnational corporations effectively 'export' the risks associated with hazardous manufacturing onto low-income communities where domestic safety standards are typically far lower than in their high-income counterparts. Secondly, the meltdown of the Fukushima nuclear plant, triggered by a giant earthquake and tsunami in 2011, caused over 18,000 deaths in Eastern Japan, provoking re-evaluation of the safety of nuclear power worldwide. While some dismiss the catastrophe as a freak, 'one-off' event, reactor accidents have occurred by several orders of magnitude more frequently than official assessments claim (Downer and Ramana 2021). Thirdly, the 2008 global financial crisis highlighted the systematic and pervasive failure of banks and financial regulators to understand and responsibly manage the risks of routinely traded complex financial products. These disasters cast doubt on the adequacy of contemporary practices of risk assessment and risk management, highlighting the vital need for effective and legitimate institutions through which such failures can be anticipated and averted.

This chapter examines the rise of risk in regulatory governance. The literature on risk is vast and varied, so we can only scratch its surface. It aims to introduce some of the most prominent disciplinary approaches to risk associated with the task of 'public risk management'. First, we begin by examining the concept of risk and related ideas, highlighting differences in usage. We offer a working definition of risk. Secondly, we consider 'technical approaches' to risk assessment, emphasising their reliance on quantitative techniques to estimate the probability that a particular event will materialise. Thirdly, we draw selectively on scholarship from several disciplines (including perspectives from the humanities and social sciences), highlighting how academics have sought to explain risk and how different communities identify, evaluate and respond to risk, particularly those considered to be of public concern. These include (a) psychological studies and (b) sociological studies, including the groundbreaking contribution of cultural anthropologist Mary Douglas and the 'risk society' thesis of German sociologist Ulrich Beck. Beck's thesis is a helpful bridge into Section 2.4, which highlights the rise of risk as a regulatory object. We observe how regulatory policy-making concerned with emerging risks has conventionally sought to distinguish between 'risk assessment', on the one hand, and 'risk management', on the other, a distinction that has proven remarkably resilient in practice despite sustained criticism. Section 2.5 briefly explores the principle of precaution as a basis for informing regulatory decision-making, rooted in the well-known adage that it is 'better to be safe than sorry' when we lack sufficient reliable information and the consequences of a failure to act could be potentially catastrophic. Section 2.6 considers the ever-expanding tentacles of risk and risk management discourse reflecting a tendency to speak of any unwanted future in terms of risk, suggesting that the creeping 'riskification' of everything may reflect the widespread embrace of audit cultures and the production of audit trails in response to calls for accountability and legitimacy. A Conclusion provides a summary of the chapter.

2.1 What Do We Mean by 'Risk'?

Our examination begins with terminology. Within discussions about risk and regulation, concepts of 'risk', 'danger' and 'uncertainty' are frequently invoked. Yet each term, and the relationship between them, may be understood in different ways. It may also seem rather puzzling that debates about risk and regulation are of recent origin, although dangers and hazards have always plagued the human condition, which the following extract helps illuminate:

Renn, O. (1998). 'Three Decades of Risk Research: Accomplishments and New Challenges'. *Journal of Risk Research*, 1(1), 49–71, doi: 10.1080/136698798377321.

50–51

The mathematical tools for risk assessment were developed more than a century before actual risk analyses were performed on technical systems. But the *scientific attempt to study risks in society* and to *professionalise risk management agencies* is a rather recent addition .... Several authors claim that systematic studies of risk began with Chauncy Starr's seminal article on risk and voluntariness in 1968. Others date the beginning in the early 1950s when space exploration programmes were designed and probabilistic tools of safety analysis were developed and implemented. Others again associate the first risk assessment studies of chemical or nuclear power plants with the beginning of risk research. Whatever date one chooses, it will be in the post–World War II time period, which justifies ... claiming that we can look back at roughly three decades of systematic and scientific risk research.

What Is the Meaning of the Term 'Risk'?

There is no commonly accepted definition for the term risk – neither in the sciences nor in public understanding. All risk concepts have one element in common, however: the distinction between reality and possibility. If the future were either predetermined or independent of present human activities, the term 'risk' would make no sense. Although this sounds obvious, it contrasts sharply with more fatalistic views of nature and society ...If one's fate is predetermined, there is no need for anticipating future outcomes other than to please one's curiosity, because negative consequences cannot be avoided.

If the distinction between reality and possibility is acknowledged, the term 'risk' is often associated with the possibility that an undesirable state of reality (adverse effects) may occur as a result of natural events or human activities. It may be difficult to determine, however, what characteristics are necessary to label an outcome as 'adverse' rather than 'desirable' or 'tolerable'. In particular, if one intends to include the common use of the term 'risk' in economic theory, both gains and losses need to be subsumed under 'risk'. In addition ... there is a phenomenon such as 'desired risk' (for example in sports activities) that people aspire to reach for experiencing a special thrill .... Inspired by these arguments, I have chosen the following definition. *Risks refer to the possibility that human actions or events lead to consequences that affect aspects of what humans value* [emphasis added].

This definition implies that humans can and will make causal connections between actions (or events). Consequences are viewed from a non-fatalistic viewpoint, and can be altered by either modifying the initiating activity or event or by mitigating the impacts. Risk is therefore both a descriptive and a normative concept. It includes the analysis of cause-effect relationships (which may be scientific, anecdotal, religious or magic) but also carries the implicit message to reduce undesirable effects through appropriate modification of the causes or, though less desirable, mitigation of the consequences.

Three features of Renn's discussion of risk are worth highlighting: (a) the 'scientific' study of risk through the use of mathematical tools to assess risk, (b) its future orientation and (c) because the future is, by definition uncertain, the fact that the event in question is merely a 'possibility' rather than a necessary reality. Yet it is striking that Renn avoids using the term 'danger' in his account of risk, recognising that some risks are desired or at least must be tolerated to pursue some desired state of affairs. In this way, his definition of risk differs from those offered in the extracts below. Although the authors of these extracts also define risks in terms of some future 'possibility', they emphasise the close connection between concepts of risk and danger.

Garland, D. (2003). 'The Rise of Risk'. In R. Ericson and A. Doyle (eds.), *Risk and Morality*. University of Toronto Press, 48–86.

50–53

What Is Risk?

'Risk' has a range of different meanings. In common, everyday usage it refers to 'the possibility of loss, injury, disadvantage of destruction' (Webster's 1971). Sometimes we characterize persons or things as 'risks' when they are prone to create hazards, or as being 'at risk' when they are more than usually vulnerable to being adversely affected by some problem or danger. We also use the word in its active verb form to mean 'to expose to hazard or danger', a usage that reminds us that we sometimes engage rather than evade dangers in the world around us. 'Risk' has also acquired various more technical meanings in probability theory, in insurance contracts, in risk management manuals and ... in sociological theory.

Risk and Danger

In colloquial use, and sometimes even in theoretical texts, 'risk' and 'danger' are often taken to be the same thing, but it is helpful to distinguish the two terms and clarify their distinct meanings. A *danger* is a 'contingent evil' (Webster's), something that is liable to cause harm, injury or adversity of some kind. In contrast, a *risk* is the *possibility* of some such loss or injury. Risk is a measure of *exposure* to danger, of the *likelihood* and the *extent* of loss. So the ideas of risk and danger are closely connected, but clearly distinguishable. 'Danger' (or its synonyms, 'peril' or 'hazard') is the potential for harm that inheres in a thing, a person or a situation. Risk is a measure of that potential's likelihood and extent. Put at its simplest, risks are estimates of the likely impact of dangers.

Dangers and Our Relation to Them

Neither risks nor dangers are simply brute facts in nature to which we have given a proper name, despite our tendency to talk about 'natural hazards' such as floods and lightning. In their central sense, both risks and danger have *relational* meanings. Each term defines a perceived relationship between ourselves and our world. Each involves a vision of what might happen and how it might affect us ....

The balance between humanly produced hazards and naturally occurring ones has shifted towards the former, as our capacity to act upon the world (and upon each other) has increased from the industrial revolution to the present day. A potential for unwanted size effects and dangerous repercussions is a by-product of the extended scope and increased interdependency of human action. The increase in our powers and technological capability brings with it new possibilities for the misuse or faulty deployment of that increased power. Increases in the range of human actions, investments, and interest will tend to increase our exposure to loss, harm, and hazard. Efforts to combat dangers, reduce our exposure, or remedy harmful externalities have tended to lag behind technological and economic innovation. Today we seek to 'design in' safety features that anticipate risk, but for much of human history, damage limitation has been 'retrofitted' after the fact.

Risks and Uncertainty

Potentially dangerous things become 'risks' only when we assess the likelihood that these adverse effects will indeed occur and weigh the harms that they are liable to bring about. Risks are not 'material' things in the nineteenth-century sense of that term. Risks are an *estimation of possible events*. Unlike dangers or hazards, risks never exist outside of our knowledge of them. They are the product of future-oriented human calculations – assessments made by people in the face of an uncertain world and the possibilities that it holds for them.

Risk always exists in the context of uncertainty. Where there is certainty about an event, where we know for certain that it will or will not occur, we do not talk of risks. Risk begins where certain knowledge ends. Claims about risk are, literally, uncertain knowledge claims – impressionistic guesses, informed estimates and probabilistic predictions about a future that can't be fully known. As John Adams puts it, paraphrasing Frank Knight's classic work, *Risk Uncertainty and Profit* 'if you don't know for sure what will happen, but you know the odds, that's *risk*, and if you don't even know the odds, that's uncertainty'. Statements about risk are claims to know something about a future that can only be 'known' in probabilistic terms.

In an important sense then, risk is not a first order 'thing' existing in the world. It is rather a specific way of assessing and categorizing the (hazardous) relationship that these things have to us, to our plans, our interests and our well-being. The number of risks that exist at any time is a function of the number of risk identifications and assessments that human beings make. (Dangers are a different matter.) If we are becoming a 'risk society' as Beck (1992) and others have claimed, then this is in an important sense, a development for which we (or some of us) are directly and actively responsible. If our orientation towards life's dangers were suddenly to shift from active concern to fatalistic acceptance, our world would be no less hazardous but the risk society would disappear.

The idea of an unforeseen hazard makes sense, at least in retrospect – there may be dangers around the corner of which we are unaware, and familiar phenomena may turn out to have a currently unknown potential to do us harm. But there is no such thing as an unforeseen risk, since, properly speaking, something becomes a 'risk' only to the extent that its potential for adverse consequences has been brought to notice and subjected to some kind of estimation, however rough and ready. One might go further, as Adams does, and say that there is no such thing as an *unmanaged* risk, because as soon as a risk is identified, as soon as it is noticed, we tend to take steps to manage or reduce its adverse consequences. '[R]isk perceived is risk acted upon. It changes in the twinkling of an eye as the eye lights upon it' (Adams 1995: p. 30). Risk, risk perception, and risk management are thus interdependent, interactive, and mutually constituting. This mutuality should be reassuring. The modern world may be crammed full of risks and dangers, but it is also populated by practices and institutions designed to identify and manage risks, reduce uncertainty, and cope with danger.

The two preceding accounts of risk converge on a largely shared conception, helping us understand why the concept has risen to prominence in contemporary debates about regulatory governance. Of particular importance is Garland's observations that potentially dangerous things only become 'risks' if and when we become aware of them, even though there are countless things that may be dangerous, which might cause us harm or loss. As Aven and Renn (2010:10) put it, a risk requires a 'mental construction of the uncertainty' and therefore cannot exist independently of the assessor. Hence, a cancer could exist undetected in a person's body, but this is not a 'risk' on their definition, unless and until it relates to a mental construction of a virtual reality expanding into scenarios of what could happen. Accordingly, if regulation is primarily concerned with intentional attempts to direct and control future behaviours and/or outcomes, then the rise of risk in these discussions can be readily understood. For the purposes of this book, we define risks as 'claimed estimates of the likely impact of a pre-specified and typically unwanted event'. This definition emphasises the future-directed nature of risk, and because risks are estimates that are inevitably speculative and uncertain, we refer to them as 'claimed' rather than as observable 'facts' about the world.

2.2 Technical Approaches: Risk as an Object of Scientific Quantification and Assessment

The future orientation of risk entails possibilities that are – by definition – uncertain and hence might, or might not, occur. When compared with Renn's definition, Garland's definition of risk appears to offer more precision because he refers to risk as a 'measure' or 'estimate' of the *likelihood* and the *extent* of that possibility. However, Renn (1998: 51–52) subsequently elaborates on his initial definition thus:

> Since risk refers to a potential of 'real' consequences, it is both a social construction and a representation of reality. Thus the definition of risk contains three elements: outcomes that affect what humans value, possibility of occurrence (uncertainty), and a formula to combine both elements. All presently used approaches to risk provide different conceptualizations of these three elements.

In engineering and the physical sciences, for example, the term 'risk' is taken to be probability times consequences. In psychology, risk is rather seen as a function of subjectively perceived utilities and probabilities of their occurrence. All these definitions can be paraphrased in the following three questions:

- What are undesirable outcomes and who determines what undesirable means?
- How can we specify, qualify or quantify the possibilities of undesirable outcomes?
- How do we aggregate different classes of undesirable outcomes into a common concept that allows comparisons and the setting of priorities?

Allhoff illuminates variation in usage of the term 'risk', even for the same 'risk object' in the extract below. In contemporary political debates, the rise of risk and its universal appeal rests largely in widespread acceptance that risk can be properly understood as an object amenable to scientific quantification, analysis and assessment thereby providing a stable basis for comparison and judgement which can then inform both public and private decision-making about how to respond to risks.

Allhoff, F. (2009). 'Risk, Precaution, and Emerging Technologies'. *Studies in Ethics, Law, and Technology*, 3(2), Article 2., https://doi.org/10.2202/1941-6008.1078.

1–3

In technical discussions, there are various different senses in which 'risk' is used; here I will follow Sven Ove Hansson and discuss four. First, risk can be some unwanted event which may or may not occur. So we could say that environmental impacts are one of the risks of some emerging technology; this is to say that the technology may or may not have these impacts and, furthermore, that the impacts would be negative. Note that both of these features are important for attribution of risk. If the technology definitely had some specific impact, then we would more appropriately call it a consequence of that technology rather than a risk: the uncertainty is one of the features of risk. And, second, the impact needs to be a bad thing for it to be a risk; otherwise we would call it something else, such as a (potential) benefit. These points might be obvious, but should help us in trying to conceptualize risk. Second, risk can be the *cause* of an event which may or may not occur. If we say that some technology carries environmental risks, what we mean is that it either might cause, tends to cause, or will cause negative environmental impacts. This postulation of a causal mechanism is more committed than the first conception of risk.

The third and fourth conceptions of risk are quantitative, as opposed to qualitative. The third conception holds that risk is the probability of an unwanted event which may or may not occur. So imagine that someone asks about the risk is of some technology having a certain environmental impact. An appropriate answer here might be, for example, 10%. The first sense of risk treated the environmental impact itself as the risk, whereas the second treated the technology as the risk (i.e., that which caused the impact). This third conception, though, tells us how likely it is that some impact will be realized. Fourth, and similarly, we could talk about the *expected outcome* of unwanted events. So imagine that there are 100 fish in some river that we are going to purify using nanoparticles. Further imagine that those nanoparticles are toxic to the fish population, and that some of the fish will die through the purification. We do not know which fish will die, but, given various epidemiological studies, we might reasonably issue a projection of 20%. The risk, then, is 20 fish, in the sense that we expect to lose that many fish. On the third sense, we are given the likelihood that something will happen (e.g., as a percentage), whereas the fourth sense gives us an expected outcome (e.g., in terms of some number of units lost). This fourth conception is the standard use of 'risk' in professional risk analysis. In particular, 'risk' often denotes a numerical representation of severity, that is obtained by multiplying the probability of an unwanted even with a measure of its disvalue. . .

Henceforth, it is this fourth conception that I shall be most interested in, though some of the other conceptions will also recur. There are various reasons to focus on this fourth conception; as already mentioned, it is the standard used in risk analysis. One advantage that it has is that it allows us to assess risks quantitatively, which helps make them commensurable with benefits. For example, if we can say that some remediation will lead to an expected loss of 20 fish, this loss can then be compared, somehow, to the benefits of the remediation, such as more long-term benefits for fish, cleaner water for a local township, and so on. On the first conception, the risk would just be 'the loss of fish'. The second conception acknowledges that the remediation will *cause* the loss of fish, and the third conception tells us the likelihood. The fourth conception, though, ties all of these things together, telling us what we can *expect* to happen, given the remediation. And this is why it is the most useful for risk analysis, even if we can speak of risk in the other three senses.

This explanation of the logic underlying technical risk assessment calculations (which form an essential part of the task of 'risk assessment' undertaken by organisations, for example, to demonstrate safe practice), emphasises the notion of *expected value* (or disvalue). However, as Renn points out in the following extract, these 'technical' risk assessments are only possible if there is sufficient statistical data to make meaningful predictions and stability in the underlying causal agents responsible for the negative effects over the predicted time period. They are unsuited for estimating idiosyncratic events, such as terrorist attacks or events produced from interaction between the human, social and technical order.

Renn, O. (1998). 'Three Decades of Risk Research: Accomplishments and New Challenges'. *Journal of Risk Research*, 1(1), 49–71, doi:10.1080/136698798377321.

52–53

[For] insurance companies . . . [t]heir reference point is the expected value, i.e. the relative frequency of an event averaged over time. The undesirable events are confined to physical harm to humans or ecosystems, which can be objectively observed or measured by appropriate scientific methods. An application of this approach may be the prediction of fatalities in car accidents for the coming year. The expected value can be extrapolated from the statistical data about fatal accidents in previous years. This perspective of risk relies on two conditions. First, enough statistical data must be available to make meaningful predictions. Second, the causal agents that are responsible for the negative effects must remain stable over the predicted time period. The resulting risk assessment is reduced to a single dimension representing an average over space, time, and context.

The answers become more complex when the adverse effects cannot be observed as an immediate effect of a causing agent. If we think of environmental risks such as dioxin, benzene or radioactive particles, the link between exposure and effect is often difficult to draw, sometimes not even measurable. In such risk assessments, causal relationships have to be explored and modelled explicitly. Based on toxicological (animal experiments) or epidemiological studies (comparison of a population exposed to a risk agent with a population not exposed to the risk agent), researchers try to identify and quantify the relationship between a potential risk agent (such as dioxin or ionizing radiation) and physical harm observed in humans or other living organisms. Modelling is a necessary step to isolate a causal agent from among several intervening variables. These risk assessments can serve as early warning signals to inform society that a specific substance may cause harm to humans or the environment even if the effects are not obvious to an unskilled observer. In addition, dose-effect investigations help risk managers to define standards in accordance with observed or modelled threshold values. If there is no threshold value as in the case of most carcinogens, risk assessments provide information about the probability of harm depending on the dose.

Another complication is experienced when people face technological risks, i.e. the possibility of technical malfunctions or human errors in handling such machines. As a tool to model such failures and their consequences, experts use probabilistic risk assessments in an attempt to predict the probability of safety failures of complex technological systems even in the absence of sufficient data for the system as a whole. Using fault tree or event tree analyses, the failure probabilities for each component of the system are systematically assessed and then linked to the system structure. All probabilities of such a logical tree are then synthesized in order to model the overall failure rate of the system.

A probabilistic risk assessment provides the same product as the actuarial analysis on which insurance data is based, i.e. an average estimate of how many undesirable events one can expect over time as a result of a human activity or a technological failure. Several problems are associated with this approach to calculate risks of accidents. It has been proven to be difficult to model common mode failures, i.e. the simultaneous breakdown of technical components. Second, human-machine interactions are difficult to predict. They often rely on idiosyncratic events that defy systematic modelling. Other problems arise when social events interact with technological systems, such as terrorist attacks,

> sabotage, social unrest, or breakdown organizational order (for example alcohol-drinking air pilots or drug-taking nuclear power plant operators). Hard data based on statistical trends is usually not available for interactions between the social and the technological system. Most assessments rely on expert judgments for such events or omit them from the analysis. Using expert judgments is still more valid than pure intuition but there is considerable doubt about the predictive power of these models. In spite of these difficulties, probabilistic risk assessments have been specifically valuable to detect deficiencies in complex technical systems and to improve the safety performance of the technical system under consideration. Examples are chemical plants, power plants, or liquid gas installations.
>
> These . . . technical perspectives on risk . . . anticipate potential physical harm to human beings, cultural artifacts or ecosystems average these events over time and space, and use relative frequencies (observed or modelled) as a means to specify probabilities. The normative implication is obvious: since physical harm is perceived as an undesirable effect (at least for most people and society as a whole), technical risk analyses can be used to reveal, avoid, or modify the causes that lead to these unwanted effects. They can also be used to mitigate consequences, if causes are yet unknown, remote from human intervention, or too complex to modify. Their instrumental functions in society are, therefore, oriented to risk sharing and risk reduction, through mitigation of consequences, standard setting, and improvements in the reliability and safety of technological systems. In addition, the data from technical risk analyses are a crucial input for conducting risk-benefit analyses. For this purpose, the physical damage has to be converted in monetary values.

The preceding extract draws attention to challenges arising when assessing risk from a 'technical' perspective, aimed at specifying the probability of an undesirable future event. Although routinely used to inform policy decisions about collective risks, these are contestable, as Jasanoff highlights below.

S. Jasanoff (2016). *The Ethics of Invention.* Harvard University Press, 45ff.

Risk and Foresight

> Risk assessment is a policy instrument, not an end in itself; it typically precedes and informs regulatory measures designed to protect health, safety, and the environment. Like social insurance schemes, regulatory risk assessment builds on the principle that the probability of harm to affected groups can be calculated in advance. Here, however, the object is not to generate enough money to pay individuals for injury and loss (the primary goal for both public and private insurance) but to make sure that the aggregate amount of harm from major technological developments remains within bounds that society finds tolerable. In conducting risk assessment for hazardous technologies, states affirm a very general responsibility to protect the lives and health of citizens against human-made hazards . . . . By assuming the burdens of assessing and mitigating these risks, state-sponsored risk assessment counters at least in principle Ulrich Beck's

charge of organized irresponsibility. It also serves a democratic function. In many nations, administrative procedures require public disclosure of information about technological risks and give interested parties an opportunity to question state and corporate risk experts. Regulatory risk assessment thus provides a window into the inner workings of technology that is not otherwise available in the course of industrial production. It confers on citizens a right to know about some of the invisible risks of modernity.

Framing Risks: A Question of Values

The most basic limitation is that risk assessment frames problems in ways that may not produce optimal results for collective well-being. The American sociologist Erving Goffman popularized the concept of framing in sociology and social theory. Framing is a widely recognized social process through which individuals and groups make sense of previously unorganized experience .... A Martian or a person from a pre-automotive culture, for example, may not know the vernacular meaning of running a red light; you need to be a member of the global driving culture to interpret that action as unlawful. But in the effort to make sense, framing may accentuate biases that are already built into a social system, and this can cause significant ethical problems.

A second drawback of conventional risk assessment is that it ignores risk's systemic and distributive consequences. Challenging Beck's universalizing notion of the risk society, hazardous technologies do not in practice spread randomly or evenly across space and social groups. They tend to cluster in poorer, politically disadvantaged neighborhoods (and, increasingly, in poorer regions of the world), where people have neither the technological expertise nor the connections and clout needed to keep dangerous developments out of their localities.

A third criticism centers on the ways in which conventional risk assessment restricts the range of evidence that enters into the analytic process. Almost by definition, regulators conducting risk assessment are forced to ignore knowledge that does not look like science as it is usually understood, that is, knowledge gained through publication in peer-reviewed journals or produced through authorized expert advisory processes. This means that the knowledge of ordinary citizens, which may be based on long historical experience and repeatedly verified by communal observation, tends to be set aside as subjective or biased, and hence as mere belief rather than reliable evidence.

The fourth, and in some ways most troubling, problem ... is that [risk assessment] leaves little or no space for public deliberation on benefits while a technology is still on the drawing boards or in its infancy, before substantial economic and material investments have made retreat or substantial redesign unthinkable .... Put differently, the risk assessment-risk management paradigm does not allow for early public consideration of alternatives to a designated technological pathway, including choices not to proceed or to proceed only with caution on a slower timetable .... Yet experience suggests that attempts to segregate underlying political values away from technical analyses of risk are often counterproductive and create expensive, intractable controversies.

This extract by a pioneer of Science and Technology Studies (see Chapter 3), highlights problematic yet rarely stated assumptions that result in biased judgements about what 'counts' as a risk, and as relevant 'data and knowledge' in assessing that risk, particularly in regulatory policy-making. Jasanoff invites critical consideration of the way problems are 'framed' in discussions about societal responses to risks. Jasanoff reminds us that the way scientific or technical communities understand risk are a product of a social practices, processes, assumptions and understandings that are uncritically accepted within those communities while highlighting how better-off communities organise to exclude hazardous or other noxious technological facilities from their vicinity. For example, residents of Ithaca, New York mobilised Cornell University scientists to stop a nuclear power plant being built nearby, exemplifying organised efforts by wealthy communities now referred to as the NIMBY ('not in my back yard') syndrome. Conventions upon which risk assessment proceeds are imbued with certain beliefs about how to see and know the world that might not best serve the collective well-being of the community. Jasanoff's critique points to differences between expert judgements about risk and more subjective understandings of how particular individuals perceive risk, a theme taken up by Garland.

Garland, D. (2003). 'The Rise of Risk'. In R. Ericson and A. Doyle (eds.), *Risk and Morality*. University of Toronto Press, 48–86.

56–57.

When people talk of 'objective risk' they mean a risk that has been scientifically established using the best available data and knowledge, as opposed to 'perceived risk' that is based upon merely 'subjective' impressions. Authorities often respond to public anxiety by seeking to ascertain the 'objective' or 'actual' risk of a particular hazard and using this measure in attempts to persuade citizens to alter their attitudes. The space between expert-defined measures of 'objective risk' and the public's 'subjective' impressions is a problematic one, particularly if the conduct of governments or members of the public bears upon the risk in question. Debates about 'actual risk' and its implications for action are a recurring theme – perhaps the central theme – of contemporary politics.

Whether we accept the idea of 'objective' risk and risk measurements depends on whether we think there are any conventions of categorizing and counting that are sufficiently well-established, widespread and uncontested to deserve that name. But even when strong conventions do exist, the notion of 'objectivity' tends to cloud rather than clarify the issues at stake. Like all measurements, risk assessments depend for their validity upon a prior system of categorizations and metrics, which are, in turn, grounded in specific conventions, or institutions, or ways of life. Objective versus subjective risk is a false opposition. The contrast is more often between different conventions for observation, measurement and evaluation. As Fischhoff says 'what is commonly called the conflict between actual and perceived risk is better thought of as the conflict between two sets of risk perceptions: those of ranking scientists performing within their field of expertise and those of everybody else'.

2.3 Psychological, Sociological and Cultural Approaches to Risk

Although technical approaches to risk assessment are common in regulatory policy-making and practice, academic approaches to risk encompass wider perspectives. Two are considered here: (a) studies by cognitive psychologists seeking to understand how individuals perceive to risk and (b) sociological and anthropological studies concerned with understanding how communities and groups identify and respond to risk.

2.3.1 Risk Perception Studies

Differences between 'expert' vs 'lay' understandings and assessments of risk are central to a rich strand of risk perception research, particularly in the form of psychological studies and experiments. Persistent differences between experts and layperson assessments of risks, particularly of natural hazards and those posed by new technologies, such as nuclear power, for example, have been studied by economists and psychologists. These studies are often motivated by belief that, to regulate and manage risks to health and safety, we need to understand how people think about and respond to risks, otherwise attempts to steer public behaviour in specific directions may fail or might even be counter-productive.

Slovic, P. (1987). 'Perception of Risk'. *Science* 236, 280–285, doi:10.1126/science.3563507.

280–285

Risk Perception Research

Psychological research on risk perception ... originated in empirical studies of probability assessment, utility assessment and decision-making processes. A major development in this area has been the discovery of a set of mental strategies, or heuristics, that people employ to make sense out of an uncertain world. Although these rules are valid in some circumstances, in others they lead to large and persistent biases, with serious implications for risk assessment. In particular, laboratory research on basic perceptions and cognitions has shown that difficulties in understanding probabilistic processes, biased media coverage, misleading personal experiences, and the anxieties generated by life's gambles cause uncertainty to be denied, risks to be misjudged (sometimes overestimated and sometimes underestimated), and judgements of fact to be held with unwarranted confidence. Experts' judgements appear to be prone to many of the same biases as those of the general public, particularly when experts are forced to go beyond the limits of available data and rely on intuition.

Research further indicates that disagreements about risk should not be expected to evaporate in the presence of evidence. Strong initial views are resistant to change because they influence the way that subsequent information is interpreted. New evidence appears reliable and informative if it is consistent with one's initial beliefs' contrary evidence tends to be dismissed as unreliable, erroneous and unrepresentative. When people lack strong prior opinions, the opposite situation exists – they are at the mercy of the problem formation. Presenting the same information about risk in different ways (for example, mortality rates as opposed to survival rates) alters people's perspectives and actions.

The Psychometric Paradigm

One broad strategy for studying perceived risk is to develop a taxonomy for hazards that can be used to understand and predict responses to their risks . . ..

The original impetus . . . came from the pioneering effort of Starr to develop a method for weighing technological risks against benefits in order to answer the fundamental question 'How safe is safe enough?' His 'revealed preference' approach assumed that, by trial and error, society has arrived at an 'essential optimum' balance between risks and benefits associated with any activity. One may therefore use historical or current risk and benefit data to reveal patterns of 'acceptable' risk-benefit trade-offs. Examining such data for several industries and activities, Starr concluded that (i) acceptability of risk from an activity is roughly proportional to the third power of the benefits for that activity, and (ii) the public will accept risks from voluntary activities (such as skiing) that are roughly 1000 times as great as it would tolerate from involuntary hazards (such as food preservatives) that provide the same level of benefits.

The merits and deficiencies of Starr's approach have been debated at length . . .. In recent years, numerous other studies . . . have shown that perceived risk is quantifiable and predictable. They have also shown that the concept 'risk' means different things to different people. When experts judge risk, their responses correlate highly with technical estimates of annual fatalities. Lay people can assess annual fatalities if they are asked to (and produce estimates somewhat like the technical estimates). However, their judgements of 'risk' are related more to other hazard characteristics (for example, catastrophic potential, threat to future generations) and, as a result, tend to differ from their own (and experts') estimates of annual fatalities . . ..

Placing Risks in Perspective

Whereas psychometric research implies that risk debates are not merely about risk statistics, some sociological and anthropological research implies that some of these debates may not even be about risk. Risk concerns may provide a rationale for action taken on other grounds or they may be a surrogate for other social or ideological concerns. When this is the case, communication about risk is simply irrelevant to the discussion. Hidden agendas need to be brought to the surface for discussion.

Perhaps the most important message from this research is that there is wisdom as well as error in public attitudes and perceptions. Lay people sometimes lack certain information about hazards. However, their basic conceptualization of risk is much richer than that of experts and reflects legitimate concerns that are typically omitted from expert risk assessments. As a result, risk communication and risk management efforts are destined to fail unless they are structured as a two-way process. Each side, expert and public, has something valid to contribute. Each side must respect the insights and intelligence of the other.

2.3.2 The Social and Cultural Dimensions of Community Responses to Risk

Sociological studies of risk emerged after technical risk assessment methods had become well-established. By the early 1980s, a distinction between expert knowledge and lay knowledge identified in risk perception studies was widely accepted, with the former considered superior to the latter. Sociologists sought to investigate this alleged dichotomy. They observed how conflicts between competing understandings of risks often entailed challenges to the authority of experts while highlighting issues of trust during public risk conflicts, drawing attention to the broader socio-cultural and socio-structural dimensions of perceptions of risk. Their insights helped to explain why, even when the available knowledge seemed clear to technical risk experts, social groups often disagreed on how risks should be managed.

2.3.2.1 Cultural Studies and the Legacy of Mary Douglas

The work of cultural anthropologist Mary Douglas was pivotal in establishing the importance of sociological approaches to risk, furnishing the social sciences with 'one of the most profound and ambitious bodies of social theory ever to emerge from within anthropology' (Perri 2014: 6). Douglas emphasised risk's socio-structural dimensions, revealing how risk controversies result from fundamentally different worldviews rooted in deep cultural beliefs about how a good society should function, rather than a lack of knowledge or understanding. Her work with American political scientist Aaron Wildavsky, in their 1982 book *Risk and Culture*, argued that differences among people in what they feared and how much they feared those things both reflected, and were driven by, their social organisation rather than simply individual psychological differences in bias. The extract below provides a pithy and succinct account of her core thesis:

Zinn, J. O. (2017). 'The Sociology of Risk'. In Odell Korgen (ed.), *The Cambridge Handbook of Sociology*, vol, 2. Cambridge University Press, 129–138, https://doi.org/10.1017/9781316418376.

130–132

Risk and Culture

Mary Douglas's *cultural symbolic* approach to risk challenged the dominant technical, psychological and economics approaches of the time. Her work with Aaron Wildavsky (1982) was a milestone in social science risk theorising . . ..

> [T]heir central argument was that the perceptions of and responses to risk are fundamentally culturally structured. They argued that technical, economic and psychological approaches fail to understand risk conflicts since these are not caused by a lack of comprehension of the facts, as suggested by technicians and cognitive psychologists, but deeply rooted value differences.
>
> Trained as an anthropologist in the 1940s and 1950s ... Douglas aimed to develop a universal theory which would enable an understanding of the different ways in which social entities (such as small groups, organisations or whole societies) perceive and respond to risk.
>
> Douglas's early anthropological work prepared the basis for her later analysis on risk. She argued that social concerns regarding dirt and pollution are less about bacteria, viruses, or pollutants and more about socio-symbolic disorder and the lack of control of a group's boundaries. The control of the body and its margins serves as a symbol for controlling the rules that define a social group. The reality of *danger* becomes important for a social group as a threat to its boundaries, orders and values. Similarly, the modern notion of *risk* in secularised societies serves to protect the boundaries of social groups in modern societies and is therefore *functionally equivalent* to the earlier notions of danger and sin.
>
> On this basis, Douglas argued that risks are fundamentally socially constructed. While dangers are real, how a social community experiences and responds to them is, in her view, a social activity, determined by how a community is organised and the social values it holds. In order to characterise the different ways in which social groups perceive and respond to risk, Douglas introduced the so-called 'grid-group' typology. The typology characterised social groups, first by the extent to which individual identities and cultural outlooks are fixed and predetermined and the amount of control members accept (grid-dimension), and second by the degree of commitment or solidarity individuals exhibit or feel toward a social group (group-dimension). The combination of these two dimensions resulted in four ideal types to be used to characterise empirical, observable worldviews. They reveal that fierce debates about risk can continue even when the scientific knowledge is relatively uncontested, because they are rooted in fundamentally different world-views.
>
> The first ideal-type, *hierarchy*, is characterised by a high predetermination of identities and control and a high degree of commitment to the group, which is typical for organisations such as the military, the Catholic Church, and traditional bureaucracies. Conversely, in markets we find low predetermination and control and relatively little commitment to the group. The second ideal-type is termed *individualism*. Low predetermination and control of individual identity but high degree of commitment and solidarity characterises the third ideal-type, *egalitarianism*, which is typical for grassroots movements and communal groups. The fourth type, *fatalism*, occurs when predetermination of identity and control is high but solidarity and commitment are low, and when people are rather isolated and lack influence and commitment to a social group.
>
> On this basis, Douglas (1990: 15ff) argued that in an *individualist* culture, social concerns focus on the risks associated with the competitive culture of markets,

where the weak and the losers have to carry the blame for their failure. In a *hierarchical* culture, the focus is on social risks and those who deviate from the dominant social norms tend to be blamed for risks. In an *egalitarian* culture, there is the tendency to focus on natural risks and to blame the system and the faction leaders. In the *fatalist* perspective only fate, itself, is blamed. The cultural approach has been used in a variety of studies to explain, for example the different responses of social groups to AIDs, the financial crisis, and climate change.

The cultural approach contributed to an improved understanding of why risk conflicts are difficult to solve when they are based on fundamental differences in world-views or how a society should be organised. It also helps explain why sometimes particular groups are singled out as being responsible for a particular risk even though there is no evidence to support such a view.

Douglas, M. and Wildavsky, A. (1982). *Risk and Culture: An Essay on the Selection of Technological and Environmental Dangers.* University of California Press.

9–10

Questions about acceptable levels of risk can never be answered just by explaining how nature and technology interact. What needs to be explained is how people agree to ignore most of the potential dangers that surround them and interact so as to concentrate only on selected aspects.

Let us try it another way: the key terms in the debate over technology are risk and acceptability. In calculating the probability of danger from technology, one concentrates on the risk that is physically 'out there', in man's intervention in the natural world. In determining what is acceptable, one concentrates on the uncertainty that is 'in here', within a person's mind. Going from 'out there' to 'in here' requires a connection between the dangers of technology and people's perception of those risks. Neither the one approach (that the perils of technology are objectively self-evident) nor the other (that all perceptions are subjective) can connect the two. Only a cultural approach can integrate moral judgments about how to live with empirical judgments about what the world is like.

The value and power of Douglas' insight is vividly captured in the following extract:

Hacking, I. (2003). 'Risk and Dirt'. In R Ericson and A. Doyle (eds.), *Risk and Morality.* University of Toronto Press.

41–42

Test Case: Terrorists

The obvious test case for a bond between pollution and risk portfolios is . . . the fear of terrorists . . .. The successful attacks of 9/11 clearly aimed at (a) American capitalism and commercial hegemony, in the form of its prime symbol, the World Trade Centre, and (b) against American military hegemony in its symbolic representation by the Pentagon. It is not known where the unsuccessful plane-missile was headed, but it presumed that it was aimed at another symbol. But in the immediate reactions we did not hear a word about capitalism, or military might as the target of the attack. No, the target was liberty itself. This despite the fact that the only internal constraints on American liberty have been imposed by the government itself. Fear of terrorists has had unbelievable consequences for civil liberties in North America. Everyone from the US President down announced, within minutes, that the attack was an attack on liberty, which in American language among other good things is code for purity. In contrast, American terrorists terrorizing Americans are not part of anyone's risk portfolio, for they are not pollutants. They are a little embarrassing, because in their demented way they present themselves as defenders of purity. They are on the border, trying to liberate the US, by violent means, from its own self-pollution and impurity . . .. If you read the rhetoric after reading *Risk and Culture*, you will see that although potential loss of life is taken very seriously, what makes these possibilities so monstrous is that such attacks would pollute, contaminate, defile, poison. I am *not* saying that there is no real threat. I am saying that in being made central to a risk portfolio, the threat is transformed into an assault on purity.

2.3.2.2 Ulrich Beck's 'Risk Society' Thesis

Another a major milestone is Ulrich Beck's book *The Risk Society*, published in German in 1986 and in English in 1992. In the following extract, Draper critically reflects on Beck's thesis that we are becoming a 'risk society'. This highlights the value of Beck's assertion that 'communities of threat' now comprise risk and class positions that overlap nationally and internationally, composed partly of both environmental risks and of pre-existing divisions of social class, gender, race and ethnicity.

Draper, E. (1993). 'Risk, Society and Social Theory'. *Contemporary Sociology*, 22(5), 641–644, https://doi.org/10.2307/2074588.

641–642

[Beck] claims that new technologies and their associated risks are creating a new era, an advanced stage of modernity that is 'freeing itself from the contours of the classical industrial society and forging a new form-the (industrial) "risk society"' (p. 9). This is a new stage of development, because the logic of risk production and distribution differs from the logic behind the distribution of wealth, and because modernization risks are now global, posing greater hazards than ever before. Beck goes so far as to argue that although the pervasive hazards of overproduction frequently escape observation, their unintended consequences have become a dominant force in history and society.

Beck's work received a wide audience when it appeared in German after the catastrophe of Chernobyl. His analysis of global hazards struck a responsive chord in a public eager for insight into pressing environmental problems. His pioneering work in *Risk Society* and other books became a catalyst for innovative thinking about risk and society.

> Beck puts forward an intriguing argument: global endangerment is replacing class society and its alliances as an organizing principle. Whereas in earlier class-based societies only the proletariat was victimized, in the emerging worldwide risk society all groups – even business owners and the rich – are threatened. Yet, to conclude from this, as Beck does, that class society is being replaced seems overblown. Toxic waste dumps are seldom found beneath the green estates of the wealthy. Environmental hazards present the greatest threat to the poor and racial minorities. Dangerous goods find more willing buyers within less developed countries and impoverished communities. And while it is true that the makers of defective autos also die in car accidents, they do so less often because they are much more likely to drive safer cars. In general, the costs of hazards are externalized and paid by the public rather than fully absorbed by business.
>
> Although Beck overstates his case by arguing that universal risks have supplanted class-specific risks, he is on the right track: risk society does indeed produce new conflicts of interest and new communities of the endangered (p. 47). He makes the important point, though only in passing, that risk and class positions overlap on a national and an international scale (p. 41). In fact, the 'communities of threat' that he analyzes are formed partly by environmental risks and partly by preexisting divisions of social class, gender, race, and ethnicity. Beck also refers to the risk-society 'phase' of history – his third stage of social change, following premodernity and simple modernity – as 'reflexive modernity'. Using concepts closely aligned with those used in Giddens's (1990) analysis of high modernity, he argues that as modernization progressively releases people from structural constraints, they reflexively construct their own biographies. The decline of church, neighborhood, and social class alliances makes individuals more dependent on the market, but at the same time, crumbling structures of social support push them back toward bonding. His analysis of family and gender relations is thought-provoking but confusing at times, in part because it is not only a description but also a political exhortation: for modernization to advance successfully, people must actively free themselves from the social control mechanisms that frame modern society.
>
> Beck is most insightful when he applies his ideas of reflexive modernity to science and technology issues in the risk society. Building on closely related theories of trust and legitimation in the work of other analysts of late modernity, he maintains that global society suffers from scientists' errors and blindness about risk. He outlines a political project of 'reflexive scientization', in which science is demystified and knowledge claims are demonopolized. Critics of the prevailing irrational and destructive practices of science, he says, can use science's own tools to reconnect it to emancipatory social practice. Science can 'revive enlightenment'.

The notion of 'manufactured risks' arising from new technologies in advanced modernity highlights the need for organized attempts to manage public risks, particularly by the state, and to which we now turn.

2.4 Regulation as Public Risk Management?

The following discussion considers how risk and related concepts are incorporated and directly implicated in contemporary processes of regulatory governance when undertaken by or on behalf of the state. It is necessarily selective, focusing on organised attempts to manage risk by the state, thereby excluding the role of non-state actors, despite their growing importance in regulatory governance. In this context, Julia Black has identified four main roles played by the concept of risk: (a) as an object of regulation, (b) in justifying regulation, (c) in constituting and 'framing' regulatory organisations and regulatory procedures, and in (d) framing accountability relationships (Black 2010: 203–303). The following discussion focuses primarily on the first of these roles, that is, risk as the *object* of regulation, but the other roles she identifies are considered in Chapter 4 (which considers risk as a justification for regulation), Chapter 9 (which considers risk-based regulation) and Chapters 11 and 12 (discussing the use of risk to legitimise regulatory action and frame regulatory procedures and accountability relationships).

As a regulatory object, it is 'public' (or 'collective') risks to human health, safety, the environment and to the stability and security of the global financial system that have been the primary focus of public risk management. In these contexts, a conventional distinction is often drawn between the task of risk assessment and that of risk management, alluded to above, concisely expressed by Renn (1998: 51) thus:

> Risk assessment is the scientific process of defining the components of risk in precise, usually quantitative terms. In technical risk assessments, this means specifying what is at stake, calculating the probabilities for (un)wanted consequences, and aggregating both components by multiplying the probabilities by the magnitude of the effects. Risk management refers to the process of reducing the risks to a level deemed tolerable by society and to assure control, monitoring, and public communication.

This distinction between risk assessment (which is typically portrayed as amenable to quantification via the application of scientific methods) and management (which involves normative and subjective judgements about relative risk-appetites, values and priorities) is often relied upon for various purposes, some of which are examined in Chapters 11 and 12.

2.4.1 Risk as a Regulatory Object

Beck's risk society thesis draws attention to the magnitude, reach and collective nature of the risks produced by industrial modernization, which, he argues, exceed the capacity and power of individuals to avoid or manage acting alone. Accordingly, responsibility for addressing these risks lies, by default, in the hands of the state, which is better equipped to identify and respond to these risks on behalf of the community. In particular, technological advances often prompt the creation of new risk regimes, such as the development of new chemicals, pharmaceuticals, GMOs, transport, stem cell research, nuclear power, even financial engineering, all of which have led to the development of risk regulation regimes. However, the introduction of new risk regimes is not confined to risks arising from new technological developments. For example, a new regime was established in Britain in the mid-1990s to manage risks to health and safety arising from centres offering climbing, watersport, caving and trekking to children under the age of eighteen, even though these activities are neither 'new' nor 'high tech' activities. Yet, as the extracts from Christopher Hood and his colleagues observe, fundamental questions about risk management are easier to ask than to answer, observing considerable institutional variation across states in seeking to manage risks of various kinds.

Hood, C., and Jones, D. J. C. (1996). 'Introduction'. On C. Hood and D. J. C. Jones (eds.), *Accident and Design: Contemporary Debates in Risk Management.* Routledge.

6–7

'So, What Is Risk Management?'

What does it mean to 'manage' risk, given the variety and dimensionality of the phenomenon? It is certainly easier to say what risk management *is supposed to do* – at least in an abstract and formal way – than what it ought to be *for*. Like any other form of management, risk management can be understood as a process involving three basic elements of any control system . . . namely:

- Goal-setting (whether explicit or implicit)
- Information gathering and interpretation
- Action to influence human behaviour, modify physical structures or both

Each of these three elements is linked to fundamental questions about risk management that are easier to ask than answer. Who is to bear what level of risk, who is to benefit from risk-taking, who is to decide, and who is to pay? Where is the line to be drawn between risks to be managed by the state, and those to be managed by individuals, social groups or corporations? What information is needed for 'rational' risk management and how should it be analysed using what 'justice model'? What actions make what difference to risk outcomes? Who evaluates success or failure in risk management and how? Who decides on what should be the desired trade-off between different risks? There is no general consensus on such questions, yet life-or-death risk management does – and must – go on in all societies through some sort of institutional process.

The term 'risk management' means different things to different people . . .. Some adopt a rather restricted technocentric view, building on the technological hazards literature and putting the emphasis on the safe operation of hazardous processes, technological systems and engineered structures. In a business context, the term means financial provision for risks. In politics, it is sometimes used to refer to the handing of issues that may threaten a government's electoral fortunes. In public policy, 'risk management' has been commonly used to refer to an analytical technique for quantifying the estimated risks of a course of action and evaluating those risks against likely benefits. In this book, we have decided to adopt the broadest view in an attempt to encompass all the major senses of risk management, sometimes at the expense of precision. Accordingly, for these purposes, risk management means all regulatory measures (in both public policy and corporate practice) intended to shape the development of and response to risks. Risk management in this sense means a range of related activities for coping with risk, including how risks are identified and assessed and how social interventions to deal with risk are monitored and evaluated .... Formal doctrines of risk management are usually based on two presuppositions: that risk is acceptable only if it is outweighed by demonstrably greater aggregate benefits and (as with total quality management doctrines) there has to be a continuous striving to reduce the level of risk to a point where it is held to be 'tolerable' as 'low as reasonably achievable' or some other criterion of social acceptability. But doctrines of this type rarely refer explicitly to distributional questions (as opposed to aggregated social costs and benefits) or as to whose view of what is 'tolerable' or 'reasonable' is taken as the dominant one.

Hood, C., Rothstein, H. and Baldwin, R. (2001). *The Government of Risk*. Oxford University Press.

5–7

'As well as a 'risk society', we are also said to live in a 'regulatory state'. The idea of the 'regulatory state' is that a new institutional and policy style has emerged, in which government's role as regulator advances while its role as a direct employer or property-owner may decline through privatization and bureaucratic downsizing. The two ideas of 'risk society' and 'regulatory state' could, indeed, be linked in so far as risk and safety is often held to be one of the major drivers of contemporary growth. In turn, development of risk regulation is interpreted by many to reflect broader political and cultural change .... Another interpretation is the link between regulatory development and the social handling of risk is offered by Michael Power (1997: 141). Power sees the development of an 'audit society' in the UK and other states, which responds to risk and regulatory failure by 'greater investment in formal, generalizable systems of control rather than by developing non-standard capabilities for acting on informal sources of intelligence'. The argument is that patterns observable in the financial world, where the most elaborate and formal audit systems are adopted after every collapse to offer greater 'assurance' about system robustness, are developing in many other domains of social life.

Such macroscopic and world-historical perspectives on risk and its management may have their uses. But most of them do not explain, or even describe, variety *within* the putative 'regulatory state', 'risk society' or 'audit society'. Yet casual observation, academic inquiry and official surveys alike indicate substantial variety in the way risks and hazards are handled by the state. We can observe variation both between one state and another and – perhaps even more strikingly – between one domain of risk and another within a single state.

Even across the affluent democracies, with which those writing about 'risk society' and 'regulatory state' are mainly concerned, substantial variation can be observed in the particular risks and hazards that are chosen for regulation and the way regulation works. For instance, after a 1996 campsite tragedy in Spain when 86 tourists died in a flash flood, a study revealed the extent of differences in campsite regulation across EU countries. According to the study, campers in France would find their campsites tightly controlled, with extensive warning systems, and evacuation and contingency plans to deal with gas bottle explosions, avalanches and floods. In contrast, campers in Greece or Ireland would experience minimal and relaxed regimes. Even neighbouring states may take very different approaches to regulating risk. For instance, for a long time Germany had the most draconian system for checking the roadworthiness of cars, while France had none; even now neighbouring France and the Netherlands adopt sharply contrasting policies towards hemp products. Writing a decade or so ago, Kirsten Shrader-Frechette (1991) noted an exact mirror-image in the regulatory systems governing saccharin and cyclamates in neighbouring Canada and the USA, with cyclamates permitted and saccharin banned in Canada, and cyclamates banned and saccharin permitted in the USA. And even where standards are common, enforcement practices can vary sharply among states'.

Indeed, mini-trade wars often stem from differences in risk regulation regimes between states. Well-known examples include the conflict between the EU's 'precautionary approach' to regulating bovine somatotropin (BST) growth hormones used in the production of milk and beef – and the US's more resilient regulatory approach to this type of risk, and the ban on exports of UK beef by the EU during the BSE crisis while the product was permitted for sale within the UK . . ..

Even more striking than these differences between states in handling a given hazard are variations in the ways risk and hazards are handled across policy domains within the same country. Indeed, it often happens that there is a strong international exchange of knowledge, views and cultures within a particular risk domain, such as chemicals, and air and sea transport, but very little cross-domain exchange within states. The result is a policy and intellectual 'archipelago' of risk domains isolated from one another, with very different policy stances across the various domains . . ..

Some of the variations we can observe across risk regulation domains involve different approaches to standard-setting. Some domains, notably road safety, are dominated by a 'cost-benefit-analysis culture' in which the costs of additional safety measures are weighed against probable benefits using explicit value-of-life calculations . . .. Some risk domains are dominated by various 'quantified risk assessment' culture, notably in nuclear power plant safety, in which risks are expressed in elaborate numbers but the costs and benefits of various forms of regulation and management are not. By contrast, other risks are handled by a culture of inter-agency bargaining – for example over who pays, how much and when over the EU Drinking Water Directive – or of wholly qualitative 'seat of the pants' approaches to standard setting, in cases such as the regulation of guns or activity holiday centres.

The design of institutional machinery and boundaries for risk regulation also varies sharply from one domain to another. Some risks and hazards are handled by 'risk bureaucracies', in the sense of state agencies staffed by specialists in risk management, such as fault-tree engineers, toxicologists and risk-benefit analyses dealing in an alphabet soup of risk management jargon like ALARP and NOAEL, with expert monitoring arrangements and dedicated specialist enforcers. Others are regulated by more generalist agencies, self-regulatory agencies, or the law courts and may rely on lay reporting about hazards rather than specialized monitoring. In some cases, one agency or bureaucracy monopolizes an entire risk domain, while in others the domain is divided up among a multiplicity of players for different stages or aspects of the regulatory task, amounting to a control system made up of multiple regimes, or at least sub-regimes'.

Such examples indicate that risk regulation regimes can vary widely even, perhaps especially, within the same 'regulatory state'. To come to grips with such variation, we need to go beyond generalizing perspectives like 'risk society' to a more disaggregated analysis. [A]ccordingly [we] develop the idea of risk regulation 'regimes' to bring out some of the ways in which risk regulation varies from one domain to another and how it can change over time'.

2.4.2 Risk Assessment and the Role of 'Regulatory Science'

We have already seen that 'technical' risk assessments are possible only under certain conditions, reflected in a famous distinction made by Chicago economist Frank Knight between situations of 'risk' and situations of 'uncertainty', the latter referring to circumstances in which we lack sufficient knowledge to make meaningful assessments of risk. It is in the realm of uncertainty that debates about the precautionary principle arise. Before turning to those debates, however, it is worth noting that since the European BSE crisis (involving an outbreak of fatal and incurable 'Mad Cow's disease' in British-raised cattle prompting the EU to ban exports of British beef in March 1996 which lasted ten years), within the EU the process of risk assessment in regulatory governance is conventionally distinguished from that of 'risk management'. This distinction is based on a belief that risk assessment can be appropriately undertaken by and through the application of scientific methods by suitably qualified experts, while the management of those risks should be appropriately allocated to the political realm because they necessarily entail highly subjective judgements about which risks, and how much risk, the community is prepared to tolerate. Despite its appeal as a means for 'depoliticising' contentious matters about potential hazards, such separation is not straightforward and, as Everson and Vos observe in the following extract, can result in inappropriate attempts to assess risk even when there is insufficient evidence in order to make meaningful quantitative assessments of this kind. STS scholars, including David Demortain (extracted below), have coined the term 'regulatory science' to describe these activities, which are important in regulatory policy-making yet often the locus of political contestation despite their allegedly 'scientific' credentials, resonating with concerns expressed by Sheila Jasanoff extracted in Section 2.2.

Everson, M., and Vos, E. I. L. (2009). 'The Scientification of Politics and the Politicisation of Science'. In M. Everson and E. Vos (eds.), *Uncertain Risks Regulated*. Routledge/Taylor & Francis Group, 1–17.

3–4

In the light of evident shortcomings within the bureaucratic response to the BSE crisis, one important line of reform involved the separation of risk assessment and risk management at the EU and national level. Science and the responsibility for scientific advice were displaced from the traditional executive framework into independent bodies. Regulatory provision was made to ensure that risk assessment and management would be institutionally independent from one another both at European and at Member State level, thus reproducing the international concept of risk analysis pursued within the Codex Alimentarius Commission.

This new regulatory philosophy whereby, wherever it is possible, hazard potential is formulated as a quantifiable risk with reference to technical and scientific criteria alone, has found immediate institutional approval in the creation of independent scientific/ technical bodies such as the European Food Safety Authority (EFSA) at European level and the British Food Standards Agency (FSA), the French Agence Française de Sécurité Sanitaire des Aliments (AFFSA) and the Dutch Voedsel- en Warenautoriteit (VWA) at national level. By the same token, clear responsibility for the risk management function, or the final decision on the acceptability of risk, was given to traditional executive bodies such as the European Commission at European level and national administrations within the Member States.

Within this emergent regulatory philosophy of the rationalisation of risk assessment and management functions, growing reliance on technical and scientific criteria for the framing of the risk problem and the mode of combating risk interestingly also extends to constellations of scientific uncertainty and to the overcoming of uncertain risk. In other words, even in cases where science cannot adequately quantify risk, or situations in which there are scientifically unverified suspicions about the existence of hazard, rationalising regulatory strategies may yet prevail. Typically, 'uncertain risks' concern particular instances of suspected possible hazards, which are usually associated with complex causalities, large-scale, long term and trans-border processes, and which are usually difficult to control. Equally typically, these uncertain risks not only reveal the limits of science but also unveil their political character as a wider public perceives that such hazards could impact negatively upon society and therefore demand that some action be taken by political actors.

Demortain, D. (2017). 'Expertise, Regulatory Science and the Evaluation of Technology and Risk: Introduction to the Special Issue'. *Minerva*, 55, 139–159, https://doi.org/10.1007/s11024-017-9325-1.

140–149

'Regulating technologies, innovations and risks is an activity that, as much as scientific research, needs proof and evidence. As new technologies and products have appeared along the 20th century, regulatory bodies have been created to look over their safety, quality, efficacy, reliability or accessibility. Medicines, foods, chemical products, biological innovations but also aircraft, ships or financial products are affected by this evolution. The regulatory organisations that control these technologies and markets ... are inevitably knowledge-intensive. They are organised to gather and treat information, they maintain large databases, execute or order experiments and tests, set standards for these tests and their implementation.

This knowledge-intensity stems, initially, from the complexity, uncertainty or ambiguity of technological properties and effects. Knowledge is indispensable to deal with the task of regulating technologies and markets. It stems, secondly, from the cultural legitimacy of scientific knowledge in contemporary societies, the fields of practice from which these norms emerge ....

The power of regulatory agencies, in many ways, equates with and is measured by the credibility of the knowledge they produce. Knowledge is a primary resource for these organisations to assert their legitimacy, as the authority and credibility of the scientific experts and professionals that they recruit or consult through advisory committees. Much of what experts do in or for regulatory agencies concern the interpretation of regulatory science. Regulatory science covers the testing of technologies and their risks and the interpretation of test results in a mixed industrial, bureaucratic and academic environment to legitimize the adoption of policy measures (marketing authorisation, labelling, withdrawal, definition of thresholds for exposure, use conditions ...). In regulatory science, dedicated tests, measurements and all sorts of quantitative information are used to try and prove that a technology may or may not be authorised, that a component is hazardous and therefore should be banned, or explicitly labelled, or that use and exposure to the technology should be limited. Relevant examples include clinical trials and the licensing of medicines; toxicological risk assessment and authorisation of chemicals; technology assessment and pollution control technologies; fault tree analysis for nuclear reactor design; life-cycle analysis for elements of new transportation systems and so on ....

These forms of knowledge perform regulatory intervention. By their every content and form, and given the socio-technical protocols and networks that support them, they enable the making of public legally binding decisions about technologies, or invoked to justify not intervening, letting technologies reach the market or stay in use.

Regulatory science is *not* a new subject in the social sciences, particularly in the field of research on expertise and use of science by regulatory agencies for instance, or in the field of STS [but] it seems timely and relevant to bring [the subject] back in, in light of the newer issues on regulation of innovation, regulatory failure and public problematics of industry bias, regulatory capture and expert conflicts of interest. Given the centrality of regulatory science, the enormous decisions and stakes it commends, it becomes crucial to ask where its standards come from and gain credibility, but also, what valuations of technology and appreciation of their risks or benefits do they embed? Who controls these standards? . . .

Regulatory science became an issue in the 1970s and early 1980s, when lawyers and public administration scholars started to worry about the conditions in which more and more scientific knowledge was channelled into the processes of risk and innovation regulation. The science that was used, and how it informed decisions by regulatory agencies, was the site of intense debates and controversies as concerns the political and institutional factors that led to the possible distortions or 'misuse' of science, and the legitimacy of regulatory agencies to shape this knowledge. The study of the use of science in policy-making by public administration scholars has also shown that the shaping of an expertise based on external consultations with scientists or academic professionals is full of dilemmas for administrations . . ..

The notion of regulatory science emerged after or alongside other notions to capture the dilemmas of producing scientific-looking knowledge in politicized environments . . .. Regulatory science . . . denotes a practice of knowledge production and claim-making that does not adhere to the modes of knowledge validation that prevail in established scientific disciplines. It is a kind of scientific practice that is subject to constant negotiation of criteria of facticity and truth; one in which the deconstruction of claims is systematic, and that leaves nearly no site of scientific authority unaffected . . ..

There is an intimate relation between the supposedly scientific activities of measuring, assessing or testing objectified phenomena such as the risks or benefits of a technology, and the legitimacy of deciding on its fate, of structuring a market for it. Regulatory science, as an activity of testing, evaluating and monitoring technologies and their effects, entrenches a particular definition of the regulatory object . . .. Regulatory science is the science that operates within the framework of these legal and technical references for what the product is and what problems these products may pose. It generates information within this framework. It institutionalizes this framework further, and brings credibility and veracity to the references it is founded on. Standards for what and how to analyze in products and technology also embed regulatory strategies and concepts, and particular decision options. By prescribing the production of certain information and not others, regulatory science enables certain regulatory strategies, and discourages others. To use an example, again, founding the evaluation of genetically modified organisms on a concept of 'substantial equivalence' and on a methodology of comparative chemical analysis, is biased towards positive decision of authorizations of these very products, since such chemical analysis rarely finds differences and concerns about potential hazards. As a regulatory-scientific method, it embeds a preference for a light-touch approach, and seems to ease positive market authorization decisions.

Regulatory science is broadly speaking a form of gate-keeping, but its specific criteria, methods and representations of the product and of the risks matter, for they give rise to the possibility to apply certain regulatory options and strategies.

> Regulatory science, in turn, is constitutive of actors of regulatory systems. It is constitutive of a scientific and expert personnel, first: those that can claim with credibility to be able to operate the scientific methods in question, or to have founded them. Behind each regulatory regime stands a dominant disciplinary cadre of expert, which develops the regulatory science framework prevailing in the area, creating a mutually constitutive link between experts, as people, and objects and ways of testing them . . ..
>
> Much of what constitutes an effectively functioning regulatory *regime* thus takes shape at the same time as *standards* for what needs to be analyzed and known. Questioning the emergence of these knowledge standards, their institutionalization, the networks within which they are negotiated, the cadres of scientists and professionals that make them credible, represents a potentially rich field of inquiry about science, knowledge and regulation.

Debates about climate change policies and regulations have grown in prominence in recent decades. Climate change sceptics have doubted the evidence of climate change. Box 2.1 offers a brief glimpse of this debate and the politics of uncertainty.

2.5 Uncertainty, the Precautionary Principle and Public Action

To understand the precautionary principle, it is helpful to bear four matters in mind. First, debate about the principle is often portrayed as a debate between 'sound science', on the one hand, and 'democracy', on the other. But this simplistic framing belies a proper understanding of the principle and what it is intended to do. Secondly, there is no single, definitive precautionary principle. At least sixteen different versions have been identified, suggesting that it may be preferable to speak of a 'precautionary approach' whose basic message is that measures against a possible hazard can be legitimately taken even if the available evidence does not suffice to treat the existence of that hazard as a scientifically established fact. Thirdly, the precautionary principle purports to offer guidance to decision-makers faced with uncertain potential hazards encapsulated in ancient oral traditions of indigenous peoples across the world, reflected in the adage 'better safe than sorry'. However, in some jurisdictions, the precautionary principle is legally binding. For example, it is enshrined in Art 191 of the Treaty of the Functioning of the European Union and has acquired particular importance and prominence in EU case law. However, its legal status is a matter of intense contestation in public international law, including international trade disputes in which the competing 'regulatory risk cultures' of the EU and United States have directly conflicted. We briefly consider the precautionary principle as a guide to collective decision-making in the context of potential threats to the community, rather than as a binding legal principle. Fourthly, the critical 'gateway' to the principle arises only in particular epistemic conditions: that is, when uncertainty and lack of

Box 2.1 Climate Change, Climate Science and the Politics of Uncertainty

In US congressional hearings in 1988 climate scientist James Hansen declared that, based on his analysis of the available evidence, the earth was warming due to the greenhouse effect. Although scientists had been investigating the possibility that the increased atmospheric concentrations of greenhouse gases (GHG) caused by burning fossil fuels might alter the global climate for decades, many still did not by then regard the evidence as sufficient to assert this causal relationship with confidence. Hansen's evidence received considerable media attention. Some scientists criticised Hansen for being unduly confident in his view, even though most climatologists thought he was probably right. For Hansen, the most socially responsible approach was to alert the public to extreme weather events to facilitate policy interventions. Other climate scientists took a different view.

In their book, *Merchants of Doubt*, historians Naomi Oreskes and Erik Conway examine efforts by a group of scientists who tried to promote doubt about a series of environmental and public health threats during the closing decades of the twentieth century, including renowned physicists. The group launched a right-wing think tank The Marshall Institute, which played a leading role in the late 1980s in discouraging then President George H. W. Bush from taking action to address climate change. Oreskes and Conway report that these conservative physicists engaged in highly questionable activities, challenging the reputation and integrity of individual climate scientists who argued that the evidence in favour of GHG-induced global warning was sufficiently compelling to justify policy intervention. The authors posit that the key factor for this group of scientists was their devoted commitment to free-market capitalism, having been deeply influenced by the Cold War and their hatred of communism. As a result, they saw environmental regulations as a new threat to capitalism comparable to the earlier threat of communism, and sought to do everything in their power to challenge scientific evidence that seemed to promote government regulation.

Sources

Elliot, Kevin C. (2017). *A Tapestry of Values.* Oxford University Press.
Oreskes, Naomi, and Conway, Erik (2012). *Merchants of Doubt.* Bloomsbury Paperbacks.

knowledge and understanding about a potential threat precludes meaningful scientific risk assessment.

It was precisely this situation that arose in late December 2020, when news of a deadly and highly contagious airborne virus (which later became known as COVID-19) begin to emerge from China, triggering the global COVID pandemic. At that time, some states pursued a precautionary approach: acting early, swiftly and decisively to close borders and impose restrictions on freedom of movement coupled with intensive efforts devoted to contact-tracing and supporting affected individuals to self-isolate despite the paucity of information and scientific data then available. Others, such as the United Kingdom, adopted a more conventional risk-based 'wait and see' approach. It soon became devastatingly clear that nations that pursued a precautionary strategy fared much better, while the latter produced massive losses: both in human lives and economic havoc wreaked by the prolonged lockdowns later needed to stem the accelerating spread of the virus and the strain placed on hospitals, healthcare services and the essential frontline health and care workers. Justification for the precautionary principle can be based on moral and/or pragmatic grounds (Sandin et al. 2012). In the following extract, Allhoff examines the structure of the precautionary principle, seeking to elicit a common structure gleaned from its well-known yet different formulations.

Allhoff, F. (2009). 'Risk, Precaution and Emerging Technologies'. *Studies in Ethics, Law, and Technology*, 3(2), Article 2 https://doi.org/10.2202/1941-6008.1078.

12–16

It is worth acknowledging that much of the discussion regarding precautionary principles takes place in environmental contexts. The reason, as should become clear, is that the environment is an especially complex system; this complexity then gives rise to a lot of uncertainty regarding risks . . . any intervention into a well-functioning and complex system can have profound (and often negative) consequences. By definition, complex systems have many parts that fit together in complicated ways. Affecting either the parts or the relationships among them can have implications for the other parts and their interactions. Furthermore, feedback cycles can multiply these effects. And, finally, complex systems are the most epistemically intractable. In such systems, we are almost certain to have limited knowledge about their proper functioning and, therefore, knowledge about how some intervention will affect that functionality. As in the case of the Australian rabbits, small perturbations can be disastrous. The environment is obviously one such system, but there are others. Perhaps most analogous is the human body, on which many emerging technologies bear (e.g., genetic technologies, nanomedicine, and so on). Human enhancement continues to receive much attention and is another realm in which complex systems carry novel challenges. The present point, though, is just to establish the particular risks that complex systems offer, given our limited knowledge about them. As intimated and exemplified above, many precautionary approaches derive in environmental contexts for exactly this reason. Now we have seen the motivation for precautionary principles: to recognize the potential for dramatic and irreversible damage in complex systems and to appreciate the limited epistemic situations in which we are likely to find ourselves in regards to those systems. With this in mind, let us return to our discussion of the logical structure of precautionary approaches.

In doing this, let us consider work done by Neil Manson. Manson develops an account of precautionary principles by first looking to see what sorts of generic features they share; he then considers what relationship those features have to each other. In doing so, he does not presuppose that there is a single and general precautionary approach, as those features might have different relationships (or even be different) in different formulations. Nevertheless, he thinks that there is at least something that the different formulations must have in common in order for them to be plausibly considered precautionary principles. Manson argues that given some activity, which may have some effect on the environment, a precautionary principle must indicate some remedy. I think this sounds right, though a couple comments are worth making. Note the use of 'may', which bears emphasis. Central to all precautionary approaches is the notion of uncertainty: if we knew what the consequences were, then we could just see whether the net effect was positive or negative. Even if we had known probabilities for the consequences, we could formulate an expected outcome . . .. But, if we have unknown probabilities or unknown outcomes, everything becomes more complicated; I used these unknowns to motivate the idea of precaution in the first place. So it is critical to precautionary approaches that there be unknowns, as is reflected by 'may' above; other weak modal language, like 'possible', would also be appropriate, though see further discussion below. Second, Manson frames his discussion explicitly in terms of the environment, but I think that it generalizes beyond that context; as mentioned above, there are other contexts in which we have the same salient features, and my discussion will apply to those contexts as well. In what follows, I will offer the discussion at this more general level.

In addition to this acknowledgment of activities, effects, and remedies, Manson then argues that all precautionary principles must share a three-part structure. The first part is the damage condition, which specifies some characteristics of the effect in virtue of which the precautionary approach is warranted. The second part is the knowledge condition, which specifies the state of scientific knowledge regarding the relationship between the activity and the effect. Finally, the third part specifies the remedy, which is the course of action that decision-makers should take vis-à-vis the activity. Putting this all together, all precautionary principles must share this structure: if the activity meets the damage condition and if the link between the activity and the effect meets the knowledge condition, then decision-makers ought to effect the remedy. This is a very general structure, leaving many possibilities for particular precautionary principles. For example, consider the damage conditions, which could characterize the relevant effects in any of the following ways, among others: serious, harmful, catastrophic, irreversible, destructive of something irreplaceable, reducing or eliminating biodiversity, violating the rights of future generations, and so on. Knowledge conditions could invoke parameters like: possible, suspected, indicated by precedent, reasonable to think, not certainly ruled out, not reasonably ruled out, etc. And remedies could be: bans, moratoria, postponements, research into alternatives, attempts to reduce uncertainty, attempts to mitigate the damage conditions, and so on.

So, for example, we could say that if some effect is serious and possible given some activity, then we ought not to perform that activity. The damage conditions do not always scale in a simple way (i.e., in terms of increasing damage) but, to the extent that they do, as the damages become greater, then we might require improved epistemic status before avoiding the remedy. For example, imagine that the damages could be either 'serious' or 'catastrophic', the latter obviously being worse. And then imagine that knowledge conditions could be 'possible' or 'not certainly ruled out'. If catastrophic harms are possible, then we

> might trigger the remedy more readily than we would were the harms to be merely serious. Since 'not certainly ruled out' carries a higher epistemic threshold than 'possible' (i.e., it requires us to have greater knowledge), we should apply that knowledge condition more readily to the catastrophic damages than to the serious ones, all else being equal.
>
> But all else does not have to be equal: rather than adjusting the knowledge condition as the effects become more negative, we could also adjust the remedy. Keeping the knowledge condition the same, then, again think of whether the effects proffer serious or catastrophic harms. As the harms become more substantial, then the remedy can simply become more restrictive. For example, we could say that, if the harms are serious, then the activity should be postponed. Alternatively, we could say that, if the harms are catastrophic, then the activity should be banned. This is not to say that, in either case would the harms necessarily be realized – because of the uncertain relationship between the activities and the effects – just that, all else equal, the remedy should be sensitive to the damage condition. All this is to say (and somewhat contrary to Manson's presentation) that these three conditions are not completely interchangeable, but rather should be interrelated to each other such that the above comparative desiderata attain. Given two different harms, which should be adjusted, the knowledge condition or the remedy? It depends. In some cases, our situation might be fairly hard to improve, so we might then adjust the remedies as the harms look more severe. In others, it might be the case that the remedies are hard to move (e.g., for legislative reasons), so we might then adjust the knowledge condition . . ..
>
> First, note that the knowledge condition effectively amounts to a burden of proof issue between the would-be practitioners of the activity and its opponents. As his condition becomes more stringent proponents of the activity have more work to do in terms of ruling out some negative effect of their activity. For example, and perhaps counter-intuitively, 'possible' is more stringent than 'likely' in the sense that it is easier to rule out some effect being likely than its being possible; we might be able to show that it is not likely that our nanoparticles will have some negative effect on the environment without being able to show that such an effect is impossible. Whether we are willing to proceed with some activity given a possible effect rather than a likely effect, as suggested above, probably has to do with what that effect is, as well as whatever other recourses are available to us vis-à-vis remedies. Second, the remedies postulated by precautionary principles are quite commonly bans on the corresponding activities, though this hardly need be the case; above, we saw a wide range of other available remedies. Bans might make particular sense as the effects become worse, but it bears emphasis that the precautionary approach is not committed in this way.

Manson's general framework (referred to by Allhoff) offers a helpful guide in navigating different formulations of the precautionary principle, drawing attention to three common elements: a damage condition, a knowledge condition and a remedy. Manson highlights variation across each of these conditions and how those conditions relate to each other in the face of changing circumstances. What is lacking from the above extract, however, is a discussion of the role of public participation and democracy, which we consider in Chapter 11's discussion of regulatory legitimacy. A significance source of disagreement about the precautionary principle can be rooted in differences about the principle's primary role in social policy-making. For example, in the context of mounting a compelling defence against criticisms levelled at the precautionary principle, Andy Stirling claims (2016: 653) 'precaution is more important as an epistemic and deliberative process, than as a supposedly self-sufficient "decision rule"'.

However, an investigation of these and other debates about the precautionary principle is beyond the scope of our inquiry.

2.6 The Riskification of Everything?

Throughout our discussion of public risk management, we have not paid close attention to the relevant 'risk object', although we have noted in passing threats posed by emerging technologies, whether from nuclear failure, genetically modified organisms or potential terrorists. Debates about the appropriate role of risk assessment and the precautionary principle have been primarily concerned with threats to human health, safety and the environment. For example, Hood, Rothstein and Baldwin (2001) critically examine nine specific risk regulation 'regimes' across the UK, including attacks by dangerous dogs outside the home, cancer from emissions of benzene, and adverse health effects from exposure to pesticide residues in food and in drinking water. What is common to each of the relevant risk objects, which they subject to examination, is that 'risk' is defined specifically as 'potential adverse consequences to health' (Hood, Rothstein and Baldwin (2001: 1) and from which financial and business risks are expressly excluded (n. 1). So understood, the potential role for the application of scientific methods to attempt to assess the magnitude and probability of such risks can be readily understood. Yet risk objects may have extended to other concerns, including risks to financial system stability, particularly following the 2008 Global Financial Crisis (see Chapter 4).

The expansion of risk discourse to matters beyond well-accepted, conventional understandings of risk as potential harm to human health, safety and the environment has extended to concerns about potential threats to normative values and constructs, including 'privacy risks' and wider 'risks to fundamental rights', particularly in the context of EU data protection legislation and, more recently, the EU's AI Act. This expansion of the range of 'risk objects' beyond concerns for health and safety reflects increasing fluidity in the way in which 'risk objects' are described and understood in public risk management discourse. But once the object of risk refers to a social construct that lacks clear, determinate and readily observable boundaries, such as that of 'privacy', for example, it is no longer possible to apply conventional scientific methods to assess and quantify the likelihood and magnitude of the risk, as is the case for noxious substances, carcinogens or the like. Although we see in Chapter 4 how human rights concerns and other 'moral boundary markers' are invoked by those advocating for regulation (including prohibition) of emerging technologies, notions of 'risk' and the precise, calculative logic with which they are conventionally associated, seem rather unlikely bedfellows. This tension is examined in the following extract focused on the notion of a 'risk to fundamental rights'.

Yeung, K., and Bygrave, L. A. (2022). 'Demystifying the Modernized European Data Protection Regime: Cross-disciplinary Insights from Legal and Regulatory Governance Scholarship'. *Regulation & Governance*, 16(1), 137–155, https://doi.org/10.1111/rego.12401.

144–146

The protection of fundamental rights as one of the European data protection regime's animating policy objectives can be traced back to its historical origins and the emergence of information communication technologies (ICTs). When the regime's foundations were established, there was growing concern that the emergence and spread of ICTs and associated data processing posed potential threats to individual freedom and autonomy informed by experiences of totalitarianism (such as the Nazi regime's use of state record-keeping systems to identify Jews and other 'undesirables') and fictional dystopias (such as Orwell's *Nineteen Eighty Four*), thus helping to infuse the European data protection framework with a distinctive fundamental rights character.

While personal computing, the emergence of the internet and the widespread availability and take up of smart connected devices has become so commonplace that contemporary life without the efficiency and convenience of the networked digital economy has become almost unthinkable, their undeniable benefits can obscure the ways in which these technologies threaten to erode the social foundations upon which democratic freedom is rooted. Hence the dangers associated with personal data processing reach beyond a concern for fundamental rights understood in highly individualised terms. Although the protection of privacy has constituted an important dimension in the struggle for informational power between data subjects and those wishing to collect and process their personal data, many other interests – including personal autonomy, integrity, dignity, pluralism and democracy – have also formed an integral part of the rationale and agenda of European data protection law. These interests extend beyond individual goals of self-realisation to the interests of society as a whole, particularly its character as a 'deliberative democracy'. Seen in this light, contemporary data protection law can be understood as analogous to environmental regulation, in seeking to protect the democratic 'commons' – i.e. the moral, democratic and cultural environment, rather than the natural, physical environment. By seeking to safeguard the collective social and cultural foundations which liberal democratic orders presuppose, and without which individual dignity, autonomy and self-development would not be possible, the 'fundamental rights' character and the justification for establishing a general regime of protection specifically concerned with limiting the processing of personal data becomes more apparent and compelling.

The Turn to 'Risk-based' Approaches to Compliance with European Data Protection Law

With this understanding of fundamental rights, we can now examine their relationship with the pronounced emphasis on 'risk' and on risk management techniques introduced by the GDPR as part of the 'accountability' obligations placed on data controllers to demonstrate compliance. This 'risk-based' turn is, as described below, directly tethered to the protection of fundamental rights. Yet the relationship between risk and fundamental rights is poorly theorised in human rights scholarship generally, and largely overlooked by regulatory governance scholars, who have tended to perceive rights in narrow terms, either as side-constraints or as substantive goals of the regulatory endeavour, or as a vehicle through which private actors may vindicate a regulatory regime's underlying policy goals via litigation. Although data protection law scholars have begun to address this relationship in the context of the European data protection regime, this work remains in its infancy and has often been informed by close textual analysis of the GDPR's provisions . . ..

Risk-based approaches to data protection are not new within informational privacy discourse, yet . . . there is strikingly little analysis of what the concept of 'risk' refers to in this context, or unpacking what, exactly, is meant by a 'risk-based' approach to data protection . . .. Particular care is needed, however, due to the slippery and malleable way in which the term 'risk' can be used (and abused). Within conventional risk assessment methodologies (which draw heavily on a family of methods for the calculation of risk based in the statistical sciences), before any risk calculation can be made, it is first necessary to identify the relevant unwanted or adverse event.

Who, then, are the relevant risk-bearers when the term 'risk' is used in the context of European data protection regime? And what are the relevant 'unwanted events' to which the term risk is intended to refer? . . . our concern is to understand the concept of a 'risk to rights and freedoms of natural persons' in light of the place of fundamental rights within the GDPR and the jurisprudential nature of rights themselves and to consider how these might be reconciled with a 'risk-based' approach to data protection.

Risks, Rights, Harms and Wrongs

Assuming that what must be assessed is the risk that a proposed personal data processing operation might violate the fundamental rights of natural persons (and not merely in their role as data subjects whose data is processed by the controller(s) in question), this immediately raises the question of whether the regime's risk-based approach is compatible with the regime's 'fundamental rights character'. Indeed, the very notion of a 'risk' to fundamental rights seems

> problematic, given that the origins of risk assessment lie in statistical evaluation concerned with tangible harms that are directly quantifiable in mathematical terms. Thus, from the perspective of constitutional and human rights scholarship and legal and moral philosophy, speaking in terms of 'risks to rights' is inherently questionable because it potentially misconceives the very nature of rights and rights protection. The language of risk and the methodologies of risk assessment might imply that fundamental rights violations can be quantified and measured in degrees, rather than recognising the status of rights protection as critical moral boundary markers. Although when analysing violations of fundamental rights, it is possible and meaningful to speak of different levels of culpability (e.g. particularly 'egregious' moral wrongs, in which intentional violations are more culpable than unintentional violations), scale (i.e. whether only a few individuals are affected as opposed to whole populations) and magnitude (e.g. reading only one personal letter without permission in contrast to reading 5 years' worth of personal diaries), these variations do not imply that fundamental rights violations can be unproblematically ranked on a sliding scale from trivial to serious. A violation of a fundamental right is a serious moral wrong, tout court. Thus, attempts to evaluate potential violations of fundamental rights in terms of relative 'risk' levels seem to fly in the very face of their jurisprudential structure and philosophical foundations as setting universal moral boundaries for which deviation cannot be countenanced except in narrowly defined circumstances which are necessary and proportionate in a democratic society.

Yeung and Bygrave attempt to reconcile the tension between the jurisprudential nature of fundamental rights by distinguishing conduct that clearly amounts to a violation of rights from conduct that is more 'borderline' in that it falls short of a clear rights violation and thus poses a substantial 'risk' to rights. On this view, assessing whether some activity generates a 'risk' to fundamental rights, and the magnitude of that risk, requires relevant legal expertise concerning the scope and content of fundamental rights and a clear understanding of the nature of the proposed activity. For activities involving personal data collection and algorithmic processing to inform real-world decision-making of the kind now advancing rapidly across many social domains, these assessments also require considerable relevant technical expertise. As the scale and sweep of networked digital transformations and associated datafication continues apace, the various 'risks' and challenges that they pose to fundamental rights and important collective and individual values is likely to intensify. Whether the language and discourse of 'risk' is the most appropriate vehicle for addressing those concerns is debatable. Nonetheless, the appeal of 'risk' framings in relation to regulatory goals other than the protection of health and safety might be explained by the growing clamour for systematic 'assurance', to help foster trust in a novel technology. In other words, the turn to risk discourse may be a product of organizational demands for auditable proof (see Chapter 9).

Conclusion

The concept of 'risk' now occupies a central role in public regulatory policy-making and practice. This chapter demonstrates that the concept itself, and the way various 'risks' are identified, characterised, evaluated and purportedly 'managed' is complex and contested. It has explored central concepts that arise in contemporary discussions about risk, including some ideas that are understood as guiding principles or accorded legal status (such as, for example, the so-called precautionary principle). Practices and techniques of risk identification, quantification and management are now routinely employed in contemporary regulatory governance, as the language and discourse of risk has become deeply entrenched in public and policy discussions about collective threats, dangers and unwanted future events that our governing institutions are expected to identify, manage and mitigate.

Discussion Questions

1. What is the difference between the concept of risk and the concept of danger? Given that life in the Middle Ages was fraught with dangers, why did those living during that period have no concept of risk?
2. In what way can the Bhopal and Fukushima disasters be understood in terms of a failure to manage the risks associated with particular activities? Who bears responsibility for those failures?
3. What does a technical risk assessment seek to assess? Why is technical risk assessment necessarily probabilistic? Under what conditions, if any, is it possible to generate a quantitative risk assessment?
4. Why have technical risk assessments been criticised? Given the acknowledged limitations of technical risk assessments, might they nevertheless serve a useful social purpose and if so, in what way are they useful and to whom?
5. What do risk perception researchers seek to investigate? What insights arise from risk perception research studies that may be of direct relevance to regulatory governance and why?
6. What do 'sociological' approaches to the study of risk seek to investigate? Can you explain why the work of Mary Douglas is so important to understanding how societies respond to risk? What was Ulrich Beck's 'risk society' thesis? Do you find it convincing? Why or why not? How do the two theories relate to each other?
7. How useful is 'risk' as a regulatory object for the purpose of understanding regulation and to assist regulators in decision-making?
8. Why is a distinction between the task of 'risk assessment' and that of 'risk management' often drawn in contemporary regulatory policy? Why has that distinction been persistently criticised?

9. What is 'regulatory science' and in what way does it differ from conventional science as practised in university research laboratories?
10. Is there such a thing as 'the' precautionary principle? When, if at all, is it appropriate for public decision-makers to have recourse to the precautionary principle?

3

Technological Innovation

Introduction

When we were university students, we spent many hours in university libraries, locating dusty leather-bond volumes to find the prescribed readings before taking handwritten notes. Many of these volumes are now obsolete and outdated. Today, academic papers are available online and instantly accessible via the Internet. More than likely, university students now rely on internet search engines and more advanced artificial intelligence (AI) tools that employ Large Language Models (LLM) that appear to generate answers to complex questions when prompted, drawing on multiple sources of information. (We still recommend prioritising academic databases and your brain, given that LLMs are prone to 'fabrication' and hallucinations.) When one such tool, known as ChatGPT, was launched in 2022, many schools and universities prohibited students from using it, legitimately fearing that students would commit fraud and plagiarism, bypassing important learning processes undermining the validity of university assessments. Emergency meetings were convened, new training courses were devised and lecturers were tasked with 'testing assignments on ChatGPT' to identify fraud. The Italian Data Protection Authority, concerned about the privacy implications of this system, sought to ban its use, but its attempts were largely unsuccessful and short-lived. Did you know that the knowledge-rich leather bound volumes that we consulted as university students once engendered similar fears? In 1751, when Diderot and D'Alembert published the first volume of *Encyclopédie*, their aim of compiling and disseminating knowledge met with controversy, for it was perceived as challenging traditional authorities, including religious and political establishments. Never before had knowledge been presented in this manner. Later, encyclopaedias became mainstream. As we write these words, many universities that once considered banning ChatGPT are now teaching lecturers and students how to use it more effectively.

Technological innovation, be it an encyclopaedia in 1751 or ChatGPT in 2024, can profoundly affect human societies, for good and for ill. As the twenty-first century unfolds, the dizzying pace of social change prompted by advances in science and technology is a source of excitement, fear and, above all, serious uncertainty. Regulators everywhere are now grappling with challenges associated with regulating artificially intelligent systems (or AI) which the OECD defines as a 'machine-based system that, for explicit or implicit objectives, infers, from the input it receives, how to generate outputs such as predictions, content, recommendations, or decisions that [can] influence physical or virtual environments'. Different AI systems vary in their levels of autonomy and adaptiveness after deployment'.[1] As academics who investigate some of the social implications of the on-going digital transformation (including AI systems) and the regulatory challenges they provoke, we are troubled that, in their discussion of these challenges, regulators and many legal scholars appear to lack awareness of a wide-ranging body of scholarship in social sciences and humanities that investigate the intersection between technological innovation and society. Accordingly, the primary aim of this chapter is to introduce readers to this body of work, animated by three aims: (1) to emphasise the importance of attending to what is genuinely new about technological innovations, highlighting points of continuity and discontinuity between on-going contemporary technological changes and historical experience; (2) to highlight how technological innovation, and the new capabilities and functions thereby enabled, can profoundly alter how power is produced, distributed and exercised; and (3) to examine distinctive regulatory challenges which technological change often provokes. The body of literature from which we draw is vast and varied, and we do not purport to offer a comprehensive overview. Instead, this chapter seeks to bring together a selection of material about some of the most important topics, ranging from the politics of artefacts, algorithmic bias and discrimination, digital colonialism, digital platforms as powerful intermediaries and the challenge for regulation in 'keeping pace' with technological change.

Although the term 'technology' can be understood very broadly to include 'techniques' of organisation, bureaucracy or even the law itself (Bennet Moses 2007), the chapter defines technology as 'both material and immaterial artefacts and processes which are created by the application of mental and/or physical effort in order to achieve some value or evolution in the state of relevant behaviour or practice. Hence, technology is taken to include tools, machines, products, or processes that may be used to solve real-world problems or to improve the status quo' (Brownsword, Scotford and Yeung 2016). We begin by considering the way in which familiar frames and narratives have surrounded the emergence of new technologies throughout history. In Section 3.2, we consider the 'First Machine Age', highlighting the way in which the industrial revolution threatened the jobs and livelihoods of certain groups,

[1] OECD (2024). *Explanatory Memorandum on the Updated OECD Definition of an AI System.* OECD Artificial Intelligence Papers No. 8. Available at www.oecd-ilibrary.org/docserver/623da898-en.pdf?expires=1716205080&id=id&accname=guest&checksum=765B500CB68C09AA8E65F00FEBC6D1CD. The EU AI Act, Article 3(1) defines an 'AI system' in similar terms.

resulting in major changes in the organisation of labour and the distribution of power in society and the economy. In Section 3.3, we consider the 'Second Machine Age', ushered in by the networked digital revolution, emphasising the novel technological capabilities and functions that networked digital systems enable and how they have combined with innovations in business models that have enabled the rise of the digital platform and the platform economy, which relies on real-time 'tracking' of individuals across time and space upon which their services rely. We also highlight the adverse unintended effects associated with technological change, another familiar dynamic that surrounds the emergence of new technologies. In Section 3.4, we consider the way in which scholars have sought to understand the relationship between technology and society, in addition to normative insights provided by philosophers of technology. Section 3.5 considers the inherent 'politics' of technology, while Section 3.6 provides a glimpse of the voluminous management studies literature concerned with understanding and fostering technological innovation. Section 3.7 briefly touches upon 'responsible research and innovation' and associated ideas concerned with more intentional, up-stream regulatory approaches aimed at shaping the trajectory of technological change. Section 3.8 considers the law's response to technological change before the chapter concludes.

3.1 Technological Change Throughout History

While claims of 'novelty' are frequently invoked to describe technological innovations, narratives of hope, horror and hubris have always been familiar responses to new technological inventions, reflected in literary works, popular media and ancient mythology.

> **Brownsword, R., Scotford, E., and Yeung, K. (2016).** 'Law, Regulation and Technology: The Field, Frame, and Focal Questions.' In R. Brownsword, E. Scotford and K. Yeung (eds.), *The Oxford Handbook of the Law and Regulation of Technology*. Oxford University Press, 3–38.
>
> 32
>
> [T]echnological disruption – and the hopes and anxieties that accompany such change – is nothing new. Several of the best known literary works of the 19th and 20th centuries evoke hopes and fears surrounding technological advances, including *Brave New World*, which brilliantly demonstrates the attractions and horrors of pursuing a Utopian future by engineering the human mind and body (Huxley 1932); *Nineteen Eighty Four*, with its stark depiction of the dystopian consequences of pervasive, ubiquitous surveillance (Orwell 1949); and before that, *Frankenstein*, which evokes deep-seated anxieties at the prospect of the rogue scientist and the consequences of technology run amok (Shelley 1818).

The narratives of hope and horror associated with technological creativity and human hubris that recur in contemporary and historical literature can be traced back to classical mythology. For example, the authors of the preceding extract draw parallels between contemporary debate concerning the use of geoengineering to address climate change and the insights of Ancient Greek mythology involving Phaethon, who was reluctantly allowed by his father the Sun God Helios to take the reins of the Chariot sun. But Phaethon was then destroyed by Zeus in order to save planet earth from destruction as Phaethon quickly lost control of the sun-chariot, setting the earth ablaze. These well-established and recurring narratives are also called 'sociotechnical imaginaries', a term coined by Jasanoff and Kim, which serves as a conceptual vehicle for examining the under-theorised relationship between science and technology to political power.

> **Jasanoff, S., and Kim, S. H. (2009).** 'Containing the Atom: Sociotechnical Imaginaries and Nuclear Power in the United States and South Korea'. *Minerva*, 47, 119–146.
>
> 120–122
>
> We define national socio-technological imaginaries as 'collectively imagined forms of social life and social order reflected in the design and fulfilment of nation-specific scientific and/or technological projects'. Imaginaries, in this sense ... describe attainable futures and prescribe futures that states believe ought to be attained. In the 2008 US presidential campaign, for example, Barack Obama repeatedly referred to the Apollo mission – shorthand for the claimed US capacity to plan and execute superhuman technological feats – as the inspiration for a massive program to achieve energy self-sufficiency in ten years. Such visions, and the policies built upon them, have the power to influence technological design, channel public expenditures, and justify the inclusion or exclusion of citizens with respect to the benefits of technological progress .... Imaginaries ... are not the same as policy agendas. They are less explicit, less issue-specific, less goal-directed, less politically accountable, and less instrumental; they reside in the reservoir of norms and discourses, metaphors and cultural meanings out of which actors build their policy preferences .... [Imaginaries] project visions of what is good, desirable, and worth attaining for a political community; they articulate feasible futures. Conversely, imaginaries also warn against risks or hazards that might accompany innovation if it is pushed too hard or too fast. In activating collective consciousness, imaginaries help create the political will or public resolve to attain them.

By considering the historical experience associated with the Industrial Revolution (or 'First Machine Age') provoked by the development and take-up of the steam engine alongside contemporary debates arising concerning the on-going networked digital revolution (or 'Second Machine Age'), familiar narratives and themes can be identified and to which we now turn.

3.2 The First Machine Age: The Industrial Revolution

The capacity of networked digital technologies, combined with advances in cloud computing, machine learning and sensing technologies, have facilitated the automation of tasks that were previously believed to require human intelligence and could not therefore be automated. Today, the risk of unemployment from technological innovation is not only faced by manual labourers, but also by lawyers, journalists, radiologists and accountants, for example. Accordingly, many fear that the latest wave of automated systems will precipitate large-scale unemployment. Concerns of this kind loomed large during the Industrial Revolution as production processes were industrialised, scaled up by many orders of magnitude, provoking wholesale shifts in the distribution of power, the organisation of labour, rapid urbanisation and bolstering economic production, with sweeping impacts on the distribution of economic wealth. As Frey emphasises in the following extract, social groups have different interests and incentives, affecting their view of the desirability (or otherwise) of these inventions. Those who stand to lose from the adoption of technological inventions are likely to resist them, while those who stand to gain are more likely to accept and embrace them. Thus, even if technological change can be expected to generate a net positive impact on society for future generations, resistance to technological change may be especially severe when technology affects negatively people's livelihoods. Frey refers to the Luddites, a group of British weavers opposed to industrialisation and the job displacement it created, a term that is still used in contemporary parlance to refer to those averse to the adoption of a new technology.

Frey, Carl B. (2019). *The Technological Trap: Capital, Labor, and Power in the Age of Automation.* Princeton University Press.

ix–xii

Future historians may wonder why we failed to learn from the past. Historically, when large swaths of the population have found their livelihoods threatened by machines, technological progress has brought fierce opposition. We are now living through another episode of labor replacing progress, and resistance is seemingly looming . . ..

Is this not just like the Industrial Revolution in England? . . . Didn't machines displace jobs then as well? . . .

The long-term economic benefits of the Industrial Revolution . . . are uncontested. Before 1750, per capita income in the world doubled every 6,000 years; since then, it has doubled every 50 years. But the industrialization process itself was a different matter. While economic historians are still debating whether the pains inflicted on the workforce by the Industrial Revolution were worth it, for later generations they surely were. Yet many contemporary laborers, who saw their livelihoods vanish as their skills became obsolete, would just as surely have been better off had the industrial world never arrived. As the mechanized factory displaced the domestic system, traditional middle income jobs dried up, the labor share of income fell, profits surged, and income disparities skyrocketed. Sound familiar? Indeed, so far our age of automation largely mirrors the early days of industrialization in economic terms. It took over half

> a century until average people saw the benefits of the Industrial Revolution trickle down . . ..
>
> Attitudes toward technological progress are shaped by how people's incomes are affected by it. Economists think about progress in terms of enabling and replacing technologies. The telescope, whose invention allowed astronomers to gaze at the moons of Jupiter, did not displace laborers in large numbers – instead, it enabled us to perform new and previously unimaginable tasks . . ..
>
> [I]t stands to reason that when technologies take the form of capital that replaces workers, they are more likely to be resisted. The spread of every technology is a decision, and if some people stand to lose their jobs as a consequence, adoption will not be frictionless. Progress is not inevitable and for some it is not even desirable. Though it is often taken as a given, there is no fundamental reason why technological ingenuity should always be allowed to thrive. The historical record, as we shall see, shows that technology's acceptance depends on whether those affected by it stand to gain from it. Episodes of job-replacing technological change have regularly brought social unrest and, at times, a backlash against technology itself. In this regard, the age of automation, which took off with the computer revolution in the 1980s, resembles the Industrial Revolution, when the mechanized factory replaced middle-income artisans in large numbers. Now, as then, middle-income jobs have been taken over by machines, forcing many people into lower-paying jobs or causing them to drop out of the workforce altogether . . ..
>
> During the Industrial Revolution, the Luddites and other groups did what they could to stop the spread of labor-replacing technologies, but they were unsuccessful, as they lacked political clout. In fact, as we shall see, one of the reasons why the Industrial Revolution first happened in Britain is that for the first time, political power was with those who stood to gain from mechanization . . .. [F]or most of history, the politics of progress were such that the ruling classes had little to gain and much to lose from the introduction of labor replacing technology. They rightly feared that angry workers might rebel against the government. In the seventeenth century, for example, the craft guilds had become a force of growing political power in Europe, and they vehemently resisted technologies that threatened their livelihoods. And fearing social unrest, European governments typically sided with the guilds. Consequently, economic incentives to invest in labor saving technology were few. And because mechanization would put the incomes of parts of the population at risk, prompting social unrest and possibly a challenge to the political status quo, the ruling classes did their best to restrict it. One reason economic growth was stagnant for millennia is that the world was caught in a technology trap, in which labor-replacing technology was consistently and vigorously resisted for fear of its destabilizing force. Could countries in the industrial West experience a return of the technology trap in the twenty-first century? While it may seem unlikely, it certainly looks more likely [at the time of writing].

The reception of technological innovation in society may change over time, and the pattern referred to by Frey, in which an initial period of resistance to technological change eventually gives way, is not uncommon. Although these dynamics are difficult to predict, the role of economic structures, incentives and the interplay of political forces are essential to understanding them.

3.3 The Second Machine Age

While the First Machine Age introduced mass production methods undertaken in factories powered by the steam engine, the Second Machine Age refers to the on-going transformation arising from the embrace of networked digital technologies, particularly AI. The Internet and the development of Web 2.0, which allows for user-generated content and interactivity and the rise of digital platforms as powerful social and business intermediaries, have been central to its emergence. To comprehend the nature, significance and scale of these transformative impacts, it is important to understand the novel affordances and capabilities of the technologies themselves. At the heart of the digital revolution are networked computers that rely on algorithms and big data, as well as tiny, cheap-to-produce sensors increasingly embedded into everyday items (e.g., microphones, cameras, wearables) that capture, collect and process data in real time. Networked devices (including smartphones) communicate concurrently in real time with other devices operating across the globe, enabling simultaneous online interaction through messaging, social media apps and real-time video, and have become ubiquitous in modern industrial economies. These devices have rapidly transformed how people interact and engage in day-to-day activities, including the way we work, shop, relax, learn, date and travel while precipitating the 'data deluge' arising from the 'digital breadcrumbs' found in the data traces generated from daily interactions between people and networked devices.

3.3.1 Platforms, Networks and the 'Platform Economy'

During the First Machine Age, the capacity to manufacture goods at scale within factories vastly reduced the costs associated with the production of a single item, radically enhancing manufacturing efficiency. In a similar fashion, the advent of networked digital technologies combined with the ubiquity and widespread take up of smart devices by individuals for everyday use has powered the emergence of the digital platform and the so-called platform economy, facilitating the ability of buyers and sellers to connect in a simple, convenient manner in real time, as Orly Lobel explains in the following extract.

Lobel, O. (2016). 'The Law of the Platform'. *Minnesota Law Review*, 101, 88–167.

88–107

The web is the ultimate matchmaker, capitalizer, and economizer. New digital technologies are turning everything into an available resource: services,

> products, spaces, connections, and knowledge, all of which would otherwise be collecting dust. It's been called 'the sharing economy' . . . 'the peer-to-peer economy' (P-2-P) . . . 'the on-demand economy', 'the App economy', 'the access economy' . . . 'the gig economy', and also, 'the Uberization of everything'. [N]one completely captures the entire scope of the paradigmatic shift in the ways we produce, consume, work, finance, and learn . . .. A new wave of start-ups, relying on digital platform technology, are connecting people and transforming behavior and relationships outside of the digital world, tapping into underutilized human, social, and real capital. This new economy dramatically extends the lifecycle of products, shortens time of use, and exponentially expands connectivity and access . . ..
>
> [T]he platform economy is easier to explain by way of function: a platform company is launched as an online intermediary between buyers and sellers of goods and services – the ancient role of the middleman – enhanced with the modern power afforded by cloud computing, algorithmic matching, pervasive wireless Internet access, scaled user-networks, and near universal customer ownership of smartphones and tablets. While earlier companies such as eBay and Amazon have served as a model for new platform companies, those companies mainly focused on retail of goods as well as online connectivity. More recently, the new wave of digital companies is based on the logic of multi-sided markets that disrupt traditional offline interactions by reshaping the ways individuals transact . . ..
>
> Platform companies adamantly endeavor to be defined first and foremost by what they are not. These companies are not selling the thing itself: the service, the product, the content. Rather, they are selling access to the software, the matching algorithms, and a digital system of reputation and trust between their users. In turn, the platform breaks down traditional industry categorizations and, as a result, presents a challenge when labeling the nature of the business by creating an ambiguous relationship between the provider and user; employer and employee; and owner and consumer . . ..
>
> [The platform economy is ruled by a set of principles which] include the shift from ownership to access.. the monetization of excess, the reduction of overhead, and the extension of the life cycle of products. These principles also include the dynamic use of pricing algorithms and rating data.

The above extract reveals how the networked digital technologies have fuelled the emergence of the 'platform economy', allowing digital platforms to act as powerful intermediaries that connect individuals seeking quite specific kinds of service to those wishing to offer them, whether in the form of rides, temporary accommodation, household help and other small tasks. Hence, digital platforms now include not only the Big Tech companies, which rose to prominence by scaling in the early days of the networked age, such as Alphabet (Google), Apple, Microsoft, Amazon and Meta (Facebook, Instagram, WhatsApp), that provide a wide range of digital services at both the enterprise level (such as cloud services, organizational software solutions and so froth) and consumer level (such as search, shopping, media and entertainment) those and those who rely on the core capabilities they provide in order to provide intermediary services to facilitate the matching of suppliers and potential customers such as Airbnb, TaskRabbit, Etsy, Booking.com and Ebay. Both kinds of platforms, including their practices, operations and implications, are now the subject of extensive scholarly critique while generating significant (and on-going) regulatory challenges (e.g., liability, accountability, safety). To address some of these, the EU has recently enacted a significant legislative reform, including the Digital Markets Act and the Digital Services Act, although analysis of these reforms is beyond the scope of this volume.

Despite their apparent novelty, digital intermediaries have historical antecedents, as Cohen observes in the extract below. She also draws attention to the business models upon which digital platforms rely thanks to the technological affordances of the Internet's networked communications architecture. Cohen reminds us that innovation occurs not only in the form of technological advances, but extends to all other forms of human activity, including forms of organisation, practices and business models. More importantly, it is also vital to bear in mind the underlying incentives and drivers that fuel these dynamics, rooted in the logic of capital accumulation. Multiple forms of innovation have converged to produce profound structural changes, which Cohen highlights below:

Cohen, Julie (2017). 'Law for the Platform Economy'. *UC Davis Law Review*, 51, 133–204.

137–144

No form of economic or social organization is ever wholly new. Pre-existing modes of organization impose their own logics, and path-dependencies matter. It is important to begin by recognizing two important ways in which platforms represent continuity. The intertwined functions that platforms provide – intermediation that provides would-be counterparties with access to one another and techniques for rendering users legible to those seeking to market goods and services to them – have important antecedents in twentieth-century direct marketing and advertising practices . . ..

Reorganization around intermediation and legibility has engendered profound structural changes in the architecture of contemporary networked communication. Platforms emerged at a point of fortuitous technological convergence: new techniques for customer tracking, immersive social design, and data analysis all promised new possibilities for profiting from targeted marketing in an increasingly fragmented media ecosystem. As legibility became a service most effectively and profitably provided at the infrastructural level, however, the demands of the platform business model rapidly began to drive infrastructure design. As a result of that shift, the everyday lives of network users have become increasingly datafied – converted into structured flows of data suitable for continuous collection and analysis at the platform level.

One important technological predicate for the emergence of platforms emerged in the mid-1990s, when researchers at the Netscape Corporation developed the first protocol for identifying visitors to web sites. The protocol, which involved insertion of a small piece of code called a 'cookie' into the user's browser, enabled so-called 'stateful' interactions, such as transactions involving use of a virtual shopping cart. Implemented in 'persistent' form, it also could enable reidentification of those users when they returned to the site later on. The resulting radical democratization of surveillance capability marks a critical inflection point in the pursuit of user legibility. Using cookie technology, anyone with a server connected to the Internet could become a data collector, and cookies also could be served and collected by third parties providing hosting, payment, or marketing services. Willingness to accept at least some kinds of cookies rapidly became an increasingly necessary precondition for transacting online and participating in online communities . . ..

At the same time, a variety of firms – including emerging platform firms, digital advertising specialty firms, and data brokers – were developing new and powerful data analysis capabilities. Those capabilities combined new configurations of information processing hardware capable of sifting, sorting, and interrogating vast quantities of data in very short times with new machine learning techniques for identifying patterns, distilling the patterns into predictions, and continually adjusting the patterns and predictions in response to new data. The result, popularized under the moniker 'Big Data', was a technique for converting voluminous, heterogeneous flows of physical, transactional, and behavioral information about people (or about anything else) into a particular, highly data-intensive type of knowledge. The platform business model emerged as these developments converged with one another and with the demands of capital markets . . ..

The commercial and extractive logics that drove emergence of the platform business model success now impose their own design imperatives, which demand continued evolution of the networked information environment toward ever more pervasive intermediation and datafication. Those imperatives have shaped the emergence of smart mobile devices, wearable computing, and the Internet of things, dictating implementations that emphasize seamless tracking, fine-grained measurement of patterns of behavior and attention, extraction of continuous flows of data, and configuration of data flows into forms best suited to analysis and commercial exploitation. As a result of these interdependent marketplace and infrastructural shifts, commercial information collection has become a nearly continuous condition. Communications networks have gradually been transformed into sensing networks, organized around always-on mobile devices that collect and transmit highly granular streams of structured information via proprietary interfaces and protocols to powerful, proprietary machine learning systems. Put differently, networked media infrastructures have become pervasively platformized . . ..

Platforms represent infrastructure-based strategies for introducing friction into networks. In theory, the twenty-first-century communications infrastructure still known as the Internet is 'open', and for some purposes, that characterization is accurate. For most practical purposes, however, the 'network of networks'

> is becoming a network of platforms; Internet access and use are intermediated from beginning to end.
>
> A network is a mode of organization in which hubs and nodes structure the flows of transactions and interactions. Network organization is not a unique property of digital information and communications networks; rather, as network scientists have shown, such networks simply make visible a latent characteristic of the many human activities that rely on communication and interconnection. Digital information and communications networks do, however, reduce many of the costs and lag times formerly associated with such activities. In addition, participants in networks reap generalized benefits (network externalities) as those networks grow in size and scale, and the relatively low costs of digital interconnection have enabled digital networks to become very large. Infrastructures are shared resources that facilitate downstream production of other goods. Roads and electric power grids, for example, play essential roles as inputs into a variety of downstream goods, as do less tangible resources like linguistic and scientific conventions. Notably, infrastructures may be managed as commons but need not be: some infrastructures, such as the interbank wire transfer system, are club goods financed and controlled by their members; others, such as local electric power suppliers, are managed as utilities and financed based on metered consumption charges; and still others, including facilities for Internet access in most countries, are privately provided but subject to various regulatory obligations. Digital information and communications technologies function both as infrastructures and as networks. As scholars in fields ranging from industrial organization to geography to media and communications studies have shown, the forms of connectivity they provide have reshaped seemingly every area of human activity. Platforms exploit the affordances of network organization and supply infrastructures that facilitate particular types of interactions, but they also represent strategies for bounding networks and privatizing and controlling infrastructures.

Cohen's observations remind us that the Internet lies at the structural foundations of the on-going digital revolution, enabling instant connectivity at scale between people and things in a manner not previously imaginable, leaving few areas of human activity untouched.

3.3.2 Enhanced Capacity for Surveillance, Control and Exploitation?

Growing out of this new and powerful form of interconnectivity made possible by the Internet are new are more subtle yet highly granular forms of 'legibility', a capability that has rapidly found a wide range of valuable uses for those in a position to deploy them: not merely retailers seeking to predictively infer the tastes, preferences and inclinations of their customers but also employers keen to monitor and evaluate the productivity of their workers on an on-going basis. In the following extract, attention is drawn to the way technological affordances and capabilities of digital technologies are more encompassing, instantaneous, interactive and opaque than previous technological systems.

These technologies enable 'algorithmic control', which are more comprehensive, instantaneous, interactive, and opaque than prior forms of 'rational' control, such as direct supervision or bureaucratic control, by removing managers, and human supervision, even further from the scene of work and thus described below as 'contested instruments of control.'

Kellogg, K.. Valentine, M. A., and Christin, A. (2020).'Algorithms at Work: The New Contested Terrain of Control'. *ANNALS*, 14, 366–410, https://doi.org/10.5465/annals.2018.0174.

366–396

Over the past decades, the use of algorithms has transformed how firms and markets operate. We focus in this article on algorithmic technologies, defined in emerging social science usage *as computer-programmed procedures that transform input data into desired outputs in ways that tend to be more encompassing, instantaneous, interactive, and opaque than previous technological systems.* To date, most research in management and economics has emphasized the benefits of using algorithms to improve allocation and coordination in complex markets, facilitate efficient decision-making within firms, and improve organizational learning. These analyses primarily focus on the impact of algorithms in terms of economic value derived from greater efficiency, revenue, and innovation.

First, existing studies have documented how algorithmic technologies can enable individuals to make more accurate decisions than they did before. Some of these improved decision-making processes stem from the finely grained data that organizations are now collecting on how customers engage with products and marketing materials; some stems from computational analyses, such as systems that can improve doctors' interpretation and decision-making about radiologic images, or machine-learning algorithms that can predict customer preferences. In some cases, automated analyses remove humans almost entirely from the decision-making process, such as systems that maintain optimized stock portfolios that outperform human traders . . . .

Second, algorithms now typically provide instantaneous feedback, which relates to the velocity aspect of big data. Given the double ability of digital technologies to automate and produce information, platforms can instantaneously compute, save, and communicate real-time information with workers and managers – including client comments, completion rates, or number of page views . . . .

Third, algorithms can promote interactivity, especially when used in conjunction with algorithmically mediated platforms that provide data from multiple parties . . . .

Last, algorithms can be opaque, for three main reasons: intentional secrecy, required technical literacy, and machine-learning opacity. The data and algorithms used to collect and analyze behavior data are usually proprietary and undisclosed. In addition, given the complexity of the technologies, most workers do not fully grasp what kind of data are being collected about them, how they are being used, or how to contest them.

Finally, in the context of machine learning (e.g., models that perform without using explicit instructions, relying on patterns and inference), algorithms are

> particularly difficult to decipher. According to Burrell, 'When a computer learns and consequently builds its own representation of a classification decision, it does so without regard for human comprehension . . .. The workings of machine learning algorithms can escape full understanding and interpretation by humans, even for those with specialized training, even for computer scientists' . . ..

> This article reviews the interdisciplinary research about algorithms at work to explore how employers are using algorithms for organizational control and how it affects workers. We find that employers may utilize algorithmic control using six main mechanisms, which we call the '6 Rs' – they may use algorithms to direct workers by *restricting* and *recommending*, evaluate workers by *recording* and *rating*, and discipline workers by *replacing* and *rewarding*. Our model suggests four important implications for organization studies. First . . . we draw attention to algorithmic systems as contested instruments of control that allow employers to secure a share of capital from workers' exertions while obscuring their methods for doing so, and to the important outcomes of worker experiences and livelihoods. Second, we demonstrate that algorithmic control can be more comprehensive, instantaneous, interactive, and opaque than prior forms of rational control, and that it can allow for further disintermediation of managers. Whereas technical control leverages technology to limit the need for direct supervision, and bureaucratic control relies on standardized rules and roles for the same purpose, algorithmic control can remove managers (and human supervision in general) even further from the scene of work. Third, employers' use of algorithms in the workplace is sparking the emergence of new forms of work and occupations – algorithmic curation, algorithmic brokerage, and algorithmic articulation – that may not only help employers to implement algorithmic control but also become active areas for worker agency. Finally, workers are engaging in four main forms of algoactivism to resist algorithmic control – individual action, collective platform organizing, discursive framing around algorithmic fairness, accountability and transparency, and legal mobilization around employee privacy, discrimination, worker classification, and data ownership.

It is worth highlighting that although this digital legibility could, in principle, be configured as bi-directional, so that workers might concurrently monitor and track the activities of managers, it is the latter who decide on how these systems are deployed in real-world contexts and thus are well-positioned to resist kind of legibility they impose on less-powerful others. Thus, one of us has described the result as a 'a one-way mirror that allows those looking down to surveil those below, but who lack any realistic prospect of peering into, let alone comprehending, the algorithmic black boxes that increasingly regulate our daily lives' (Yeung 2018: 13).

3.3.3 Impact on Others

The way in which algorithmic control is deployed in real-world settings reflects a familiar dynamic. The history of technology reminds us that the benefits and burdens associated with technological change are unevenly distributed. Technological innovations that offer valuable capabilities are taken up by those in power to enhance and expand their existing economic and political power, reinforcing and reproducing asymmetries in power within existing relationships. Although the Industrial Revolution was characterised by unparalleled increase in production, industrialisation, urbanisation and wealth, it was also accompanied by unsafe and unsanitary labour conditions, the exploitation of children, greater income disparities and major displacement of employees. As Frey explains (above), factory workers accepted these downsides of rapid industrialisation because they lacked the political power to resist. Marxism and the many global political movements in the first half of the twentieth century were in part a reaction to the inequalities created by industrial capitalism.

3.3.3.1 Unintended Adverse Effects

In attempting to grapple with and navigate our present and future encounters with technological change, history reminds us of the need to attend to the ways in which technological innovations may affect how power is produced, distributed and exercised. For example, the forms of algorithmic control that enable managers to track the performance and productivity of workers and to discipline them accordingly has been central to the operation of stock-picking by workers, for example, at online retail giant Amazon, and a source of condemnation and protest by workers. In other words, to the extent that new technological capabilities may enhance power and control, they also generate the potential for oppression, exploitation and dispossession, reflected in the long history of colonialism, enabling workers from low-income countries or under-represented groups in society to be exploited at scale by organisations providing services to high-income countries and beyond. Time and again, history has shown that the impacts of technological innovation on society are decidedly mixed: both good and bad and often unintended, and differentially distributed, as Johnson and Wetmore emphasise in the following extract:

Johnson, D. G., and J. Wetmore (2021). 'Introduction'. In D. G. Johnson and J. Wetmore (eds.), *Technology and Society: Building our Sociotechnical Future*. MIT Press, 1–7

1–2

Technology is a powerful component of the modern world. Its influence can be clearly seen in the fact that many of the iconic accomplishments of modern societies are technological in nature .... Technology has been an important factor shaping the character of human societies and individual lives for millennia, but in looking back over the last century, it is evident that the power of technology to change the way we live is undeniable and awe inspiring. Technologies not only have contributed to broad social and political change but have permeated almost every dimension of daily life in industrialized societies .... The clothes we wear, the banks we put our money into, and the jobs we hold are all impacted or even made possible by global systems that exist only because of the complex technological systems they're built on. We maintain our personal as well as our working relationships through a global communications network. We entertain ourselves by means of digital technologies in which the quality of audio and images improves year after year. In short, a wide range of technologies are now an essential part of our work, play, education, health, finances, child-rearing, and even reproduction. Modern societies have embraced technologies for a variety of reasons, but broadly speaking, new technologies offer new opportunities and the promise of improved lives. Technologies have been used to solve problems that have plagued humanity for centuries, eradicating diseases, harnessing new energy resources, and providing rapid transportation ….

But we must be careful not to confuse technological change with social and human progress. We may be better off in some ways and worse off in others as a result of adopting certain technologies. Technologies rarely, if ever, change the world in a clear, singular way. When we integrate them into our society, they often have far-rippling effects that are not always positive. Economies have been built on the wealth and benefits generated from manufacturing, but many manufacturing techniques degrade our environment and living conditions through the pollutants they produce. Social media has allowed us to share our views with people on the other side of the planet but may also make the measured, thoughtful discourse necessary for democracy more difficult. In addition to what some deem 'side effects', new technologies can also lead to (desirable or undesirable) shifts in power from one group to another …. In some cases, the impacts of new technologies have become perceptible soon after development – like the atomic bombs dropped on Hiroshima and Nagasaki. With other technologies, the implications have manifested more slowly – such as damage to the environment from chemical pesticides and fertilizers generated and accumulated over the past few centuries.

What exactly counts as a 'negative implication' of a technology is up for debate as well because technologies affect different groups of people differently. The benefits may go to some segments of a population while the burdens are borne by other groups. This is the case, for example, with toxic waste disposal plants, which are generally located in poor non-white communities, putting those who live nearby at increased health risk while citizens living farther away reap the benefits. Technologies can reinforce prevailing inequalities, but they can also disrupt status quo arrangements. Think here of how new online news services have put print newspapers out of business or consider how the threat from autonomous vehicles may disempower those who drive vehicles for a living. Thus, while technology must be part of the solution in making a better world, we must also be mindful that simply 'adding' technology would not necessarily create a world we want to live in.

3.3.3.2 Digital Colonialism

Practices of exploitation and dispossession are universal and long standing. Colonialism refers to the combination of territorial, juridical, cultural, linguistic, political, mental/epistemic and/or economic domination of one group of people or groups of people by another (external) group of people (Murrey 2020). Many of us are familiar with critiques to European colonialism, referring to various forms of territorial domination affected by European powers upon non-European people from the late 1400s to the mid- to late 1900s. However, similar critiques have been levelled at practices of domination and exploitation in the contemporary digital economy. 'Data colonialism' has been be defined as 'the decentralised extraction and control of data from citizens with or without their explicit consent through communication networks developed and owned' by third-country companies'. As the following extract explains, these tech companies tend to be based in China or the United States, enabling economic and cultural domination through technological forms of governance. Digital colonialism operates in various ways including the extraction of raw materials to the extent of resource depletion; helping finance armed groups, child soldiers and child labour; and extraction of data and construction of infrastructure by China and the United States under financially attractive conditions without disclosing what happens with data collected through it.

Couldry, N., and Mejias, U. A. (2019). 'Data Colonialism: Rethinking Big Data's Relation to the Contemporary Subject'. *Television & New Media*, 20(4), 336–349. https://doi.org/10.1177/1527476418796632

336–340

[W]hat is missing in the insightful recent accounts of Big Data is a wider frame to make sense of the whole social process under way. That frame is colonialism, used here not as a mere metaphor, nor as an echo or simple continuation of historic forms of territorial colonialism, but to refer to a new form of colonialism distinctive of the twenty-first century: *data colonialism.*

Data colonialism combines the predatory extractive practices of historical colonialism with the abstract quantification methods of computing. Understanding Big Data from the Global South means understanding capitalism's current dependence on this new type of appropriation that works at every point in space where people or things are attached to today's infrastructures of connection . . ..

Data colonialism involves not one pole of colonial power ('the West'), but at least two: the United States and China. This complicates our notion of the geography of the Global South, a concept which until now helped situate resistance and disidentification along geographic divisions between former colonizers and colonized. Instead, the new data colonialism works both externally—on a global scale—and internally on its own home populations. The elites of data colonialism (think of Facebook) benefit from colonization in both dimensions, and North–South, East–West divisions no longer matter in the same way.

The Mechanics of Data Colonialism

The legacy of colonialism from the sixteenth to the twentieth century includes the decimation of millions of native lives and the depletion of vast amounts of natural resources, all for the enrichment of a few. In deploying the concept of data colonialism, our goal is not to make loose analogies to the content or form, let alone the physical violence, of historical colonialism. Instead . . . we seek to explore the parallels with historic colonialism's *function* within the development of economies on a global scale, its normalization of resource appropriation, and its redefinition of social relations so that dispossession came to seem natural.

The Naturalization of Data Capture

Personal data of many sorts is appropriated for ends which are not themselves 'personal'. By personal data we mean data of actual or potential relevance to persons, whether collected from them or from other persons or things. For personal data to be freely available for appropriation, it must first be treated as a natural resource, a resource that is *just there*. Extractive rationalities need to be naturalized or normalized, and, even more fundamentally, the flow of everyday life must be reconfigured and represented in a form that enables its capture *as* data. Jason Moore (2015) argues that capitalism historically depended on the availability of *cheap nature*: natural resources that are abundant, easy to appropriate from their rightful owners, and whose depletion is seen as unproblematic, but whose 'availability to capital' itself had to be constructed through elaborate means of marketization . . ..

The apparent naturalness of data colonialism's appropriations relies also on a large amount of ideological work, just as historic colonialism did . . ..

To accomplish the appropriation of personal data, data colonialism relies on other *extractive rationalities* as well. There is, as many critics have noted (Fuchs 2017; Scholz 2013) – and this is what we share with earlier debates – a social rationality that treats much of the labor that contributes to data extraction as value-less, as 'just sharing'. There is also a practical rationality that frames corporations as the only ones with the power and capacity to process (and thus appropriate) data. Simultaneously, a political rationality operates to position society as the natural beneficiary of corporations' extractive efforts, just as humanity was supposed to benefit from historical colonialism as a 'civilizational' project.

The principal actors in data colonialism can collectively be called the *social quantification sector*, corporations involved in capturing everyday social acts and translating them into quantifiable data which is analyzed and used for the generation of profit. Firms like Amazon, Apple, Facebook, and Google in 'the West', and Baidu, Alibaba, and Tencent in China, are its most well-known players. The social quantification sector includes both big and small hardware and software manufacturers, developers of social media platforms, and firms dedicated to data analysis and brokerage. The latter, a largely unregulated part of the economy, specialize in collecting information from medical, financial, criminal, and other records for categorizing individuals through algorithmic means. Data brokers package and sell those lists to advertisers and other users such as governments and law enforcement agencies.

Yet, in spite of the huge complexity of the social quantification sector, the parallels between the fictions that operationalized the dispossessions of historical colonialism and those that work today to enable data colonialism are striking. Consider the Spanish empire's *Requerimiento*, whose absurdity was first recounted by Bartolomé de las Casas (1951, 58). The purpose of this proclamation, read in Spanish by conquistadors to a non-Spanish speaking audience, was to introduce the natives to the strange new world order they were about to be colonized under, and to demand their simple acceptance (or face extermination, which frequently arrived regardless of compliance). Today, in the era of data colonialism, we are accustomed to similarly incomprehensible documents called Terms of Service, which contain outlandish appropriative claims by corporations. The force of the *Requerimiento* depended on an effective monopoly of physical force. Today's 'muscle' lies in various forms of economic concentration, one of which is the digital platform. Whatever the form of force used, its effect now, as then, is through the discursive act that accompanies it to embed subjects inescapably into relations of colonization.

3.3.3.3 The Geopolitics of Technological Innovation

As AI technologies and systems have become increasingly powerful and pervasive, the geopolitical stakes of national and regional AI advancement have grown in prominence, as depicted in the title of Miailhe's blog post, which also refers to digital colonialism. Miailhe speaks of the 'return of empires', as well as EU regulatory attempts to curb the power of digital empires through regulation and its extraterritorial effect (Bradford 2020, 2023; see Chapter 11).

Miailhe, N. 2018. 'The Geopolitics of Artificial Intelligence: The Return of empires?' *Politique étrangère*, 3 105–117, www.cairn-int.info/journal-politique-etrangere-2018-3-page-105.htm.

110–117

National actors are increasingly aware of the strategic, economic, and military stakes of the development of AI .... In the past 15 months, France, Canada, China, Denmark, the European Commission, Finland, India, Italy, Japan, Mexico, the Scandinavian and Baltic region, Singapore, South Korea, Sweden, Taiwan, the United Arab Emirates, and the United Kingdom have all unveiled strategies for promoting the use and development of AI . . ..

Among the actors who are characterized by their aspiration to global leadership are the United States and China, but also the European Union. Smaller actors such as France, the United Kingdom, and Canada also have an ambitious strategy and are making significant investments in AI. Other countries are specializing in particular aspects of AI, following a niche strategy. India, for example, wants to become an 'AI garage' by specializing in applications specific to developing countries.

Today, the United States and China form a kind of AI duopoly based on the critical dimensions of their markets and their laissez-faire policies regarding personal data protection... In August 2017, the United States launched an investigation against China, accusing it of unfair commercial practices regarding intellectual property, particularly in the area of technology. China's 'Sputnik moment' arrived in March 2016, when South Korean Go champion Lee Sedol was defeated by DeepMind's artificial intelligence program, AlphaGo. In July 2017, Beijing publicized an especially ambitious national strategy aiming to reach a market estimated at $15,700 billion in 2030. It intends to 'become the "primary" center for AI innovation by 2030'.

In line with this policy, closely directed at the highest levels of the state, the Chinese technological ecosystem will pursue an offensive strategy of investments in and reinforcement of AI capabilities .... Since 2016, its 'Belt & Road' initiative for the construction of infrastructures connecting Asia, Africa, and Europe has included a digital component under the 'Digital Belt and Road' program.

Europe has fallen far behind China and the United States in techno-industrial terms. In 2013, a report issued by the French Senate expressed concern, witnessing the Old Continent becoming a 'digital colony'. The situation has not improved over the last five years. The European approach seems to consist in taking advantage of its market of 500 million consumers to provide the foundations of an ethical industrial model of AI, while renegotiating a de facto strategic partnership with the United States. Thus, in April 2018, when the European Commission published its AI strategy, the Swedish Minister for Digital Development declared: 'We can't expect China to do that [to establish ethical norms]. We have to do that. With a democracy and a legal system that works, Europe has to take that as the most important thing. The competition with China, the competition with the US, is of course important. But if we don't create the legal and ethical framework, we will lose anyway.' Europe lags behind in private investment in AI, which ran at approximately €2.4–€3.2 billion in 2016, as compared to €6.5–€9.7 billion in Asia and €12.1–€18.6 billion in North America .... It is difficult, under these conditions, to prevent the purchase of European gems by the American and Chinese giants, as was the case for the British company DeepMind, a pioneer in the field of AI, bought by Google in 2014 for $500 million, or the purchase of Kuka, the prize gem of German robotics, by the Chinese electric household appliance giant Midea in 2016 for $4.5 billion ....

the AI revolution is perceived in Europe – more technophobic than China or the United States – as a wave coming from abroad that threatens its socio-economic model, to be protected against. Driven by dominant industrial actors that have not succeeded in carrying out their own digital transformation, Europeans seek to regulate the revolution of AI (to restrain it) instead of seeking to govern it (to guide it). A universalistic ambition is indeed present here, but it is more conservative than progressive. It results in the search for a European model of AI that ties together the reclamation of sovereignty and the quest for power with respect for human dignity. Balancing these three desiderata will not

> be easy: by regulating from a position of extreme weakness and industrial dependency in relation to the Americans or the Chinese, Europe is likely to block its own rise to power. This is the risk that the General Data Protection Regulation (GDPR) could pose to French and European ambitions for power . . ..
>
> The African continent is practically virginal in terms of digital infrastructures oriented towards AI. The Kenyan government is to date the only one to develop a strategy in this respect. However, Africa has enormous potential for exploring the applications of AI and inventing new business and service models. Chinese investments in Africa have intensified over the last decade, and China is currently the primary trade partner of the African nations, followed by India, France, the United States, and Germany. Africa is probably the continent where cyber-imperialisms are most evident.
>
> Examples of the Chinese industrial presence are numerous there: Transsion Holdings became the first smartphone company in Africa in 2017. ZTE, the Chinese telecommunications giant, provides infrastructure to the Ethiopian government. CloudWalk Technology, a start-up based in Guangzhou, signed an agreement with the Zimbabwean government and will work in particular on facial recognition.
>
> A powerful cyber-colonialist phenomenon is at work here. Still traumatized by the liability of European colonization, Africa, confronted with the combined urgencies of development, demography, and the explosion of social inequalities (with which China is quite familiar), is embarking on a logical but very unequal techno-industrial partnership with China. As the Americans did to Europe after the war, China massively exports its solutions, its technologies, its standards, and the model of company that goes with these to Africa (while also providing massive financing).
>
> Enjoying a free field with respect to the Europeans, the American digital giants are mounting a counterattack. Google, for example, recently opened its first AI research center on the continent in Accra. Moreover, the GAFAMI companies are multiplying startup incubators and support programs for the development of African talent.
>
> AI is an instrument of power right now, and it will be increasingly so as its applications develop, particularly in the military field. However, focusing exclusively on hard power would be a mistake, insofar as AI exercises indirect cultural, commercial, and political influence over its users around the world. This soft power, which especially benefits the American and Chinese digital empires, poses major problems of ethics and governance.

The preceding highlights the way in which national governments may intentionally support and champion technological innovation in specific industries, known in policy terms as 'industrial policy'. These are policies adopted by states to support the growth and technological advancement of specific industries based on a belief that this will boost national productivity and power, thereby serving the national interest. From the viewpoint of international relations scholars, the adoption of national industrial policies can be understood in geopolitical terms, with significant strategic economic and political importance. As Frey observes in the extract below:

Frey, Carl B. (2019). *The Technological Trap: Capital, Labor, and Power in the Age of Automation.* Princeton University Press.

34

It is easy to oversimplify history. However, if there is one predominant factor underlying economic and social change over the past two centuries, it is surely the advancement of technology . . .. Economists estimate that over 80 percent of the income differences between rich and poor countries can be explained by differential rates of technology adoption.

3.4 The Relationship between Technological Change and Society

The preceding extracts have drawn attention to the adverse societal impacts of technological change: not only altering how power is produced, serving as a vivid reminder that the benefits and burdens of technological innovation are differentially distributed amongst groups and communities. We have seen that historical experience of technological change often has direct parallels in contemporary settings when new technologies appear. One common feature invariably associated with the technological innovation is the pervasive uncertainty that it engenders, not only in whether or not the technology will be successfully taken up and employed for useful purposes once released onto the market, the value it is likely to generate for its developers and, perhaps most importantly for regulatory purposes, the kinds of unintended adverse effects that its deployment may create. The nature of the relationship between technological change and society has itself been an object of study and a matter of dispute in academic scholarship, outlined in the following extract:

van de Poel, I. (2020). 'Three Philosophical Perspectives on the Relation between Technology and Society, and How They Affect the Current Debate about Artificial Intelligence'. *Human Affairs*, 30(4), 499–511. https://doi.org/10.1515/humaff-2020-0042.

499–505

I am particularly interested in philosophical thinking about the relation between technology and society, and about that between technological change and social change. Consequently, in this article my focus is on what Mitcham (1994) has called humanities philosophy of technology rather than engineering philosophy of technology. The latter is more interested in issues in engineering practice, like the nature and evolution of technological artifacts, design, and the nature of technological knowledge, while the first focuses more on technology as a social, cultural and historical phenomenon, and its relation to society… the first perspective on technology and society may be characterized by the following two key assumptions:

1. Technology develops autonomously, i.e. according to its own laws, not, or hardly, open to human choice;
2. The impact of technology on society is deterministic

The combination of these assumptions can not only be found among techno-pessimists ... but also among techno-optimists .... The main difference between [them] ... is the values that are associated with technological development and change. For techno-optimists these are positive values like social progress, economic prosperity, freedom and democracy. Techno-pessimists stress negative values like efficiency, instrumentalization, domination of humans, tyranny, alienation, and the end of mankind. Despite these diametrically opposed normative assessments of technological change, they both conceive technological development as an autonomous process that determines societal developments. Consequently, there are few possibilities for human choice in technological development ....

The second perspective on technology stresses the human-made character of technology. Technology is a human construct. Consequently, technologies are shaped by human interests and values, and open to human choice. This view can already be found in some of the works of earlier philosophers of technology like Lewis Mumford (e.g. Mumford, 1934/1963) and Langdon Winner (e.g. Winner, 1977, 1986) .... Although there are, of course, many nuanced differences between thinkers that roughly fit this second perspective ... the following three assumptions are [often] present:

1. Technology is a human product or social construction and, as such, open to human choices;
2. Technology is value-laden, and different products can embed different values, depending on their design;
3. We (can) shape new technologies by our interests and values ....

[I]n this second perspective they tend to talk about technologies in the plural, and to stress that the normative assessment of technologies may be very different from one technology to another. Different technologies have different normative qualities depending on choices made by humans, for example during the design process .... However, the second perspective may also be in danger of overstating the degree to which we can steer or direct technological developments ... a third perspective ... starts from the idea of co-evolution of technology and society .... What sets the third perspective apart from the second, then, is not just or merely a recognition of the co-evolution of technology and society but rather a recognition of what I would like to call the non-malleability of technology, and of the fact that technology brings novelty and, therefore, unforeseen and unintended (social) consequences. With novelty, I mean here that it creates something that did not exist before and that we cannot fully capture beforehand. This novelty is an opportunity; it may, for example lead to new options that help to solve social and moral dilemmas. However, the novelty is also a potential threat in the sense that it may lead to unintended and undesirable risks or side-effects. We can, again, summarize the third perspective in terms of three key assumptions: Technology and society co-evolve; technology does not determine society nor do societal choices fully determine technology:

1. Some aspects of technology development are very hard to change or unmalleable, and are hardly (still) open to human choice;
2. Technology creates novelty and unexpected (and unintended) consequences.

Unlike much of the literature from economics and various sub-strands of political studies that focus on the quest for power and economic advantage associated with scientific and technological advance, scholars from law and applied ethics typically ask critical questions focusing on values and principles that should inform and guide attempts to manage technological change and its impacts. Although various scholars from the philosophy of technology tradition proceed from a belief in 'technological determinism' (see van der Poel extract, above), in which the impact of technological change on society is regarded as an inevitable and unstoppable force, other philosophically inflected writings take a different view. Scholars working within this latter tradition believe that humans and human communities have the power to influence the development of technological change, asking normative questions about what is the 'good' or 'right' thing to do and how should we seek to shape our technologies into our social life and practice in order to live well with our technological inventions. For example, in the extract below, Shannon Vallor considers the implications of the impact of digital automation on human character, focusing on the dangers and likelihood of 'moral deskilling', why these are serious ethical concerns, and considers how they might be addressed. This translates the philosophical thinking about the relation between technology and society and about that between technological change and social change. Vallor's analysis is theoretically anchored in a commitment to 'virtue ethics', a normative philosophical approach that urges people to live a moral life by cultivating virtuous habits. It reflects an Aristotelian view, which understands virtues as cultivated (rather than inborn states of character) requiring skilled and discerning moral judgement joined with a moral motivation and aim that guarantees the goodness of its use.

Vallor. S. (2015). 'Moral Deskilling and Upskilling in a New Machine Age: Reflections on the Ambiguous Future of Character'. *Philosophy & Technology*, 28, 107–124

108–122

[T]his paper focuses on an important aspect of deskilling/upskilling that has yet to be fully articulated in the literature on the social impacts of emerging technologies, namely the potential in many professional and private contexts for an ICT-driven *moral deskilling* of human beings, along with an equally powerful potential for moral reskilling or upskilling . . ..

Why should we care about technology's impact on moral skill development enough to study it? . . . if moral skills are a prerequisite to the cultivation of virtuous character, then we should be greatly concerned about the impact of emerging technologies upon them. But . . . I offer a second reason. Moral skills are *intrinsically valuable* – even when they do not lead to the development of truly exemplary persons of virtue. Consider how many have lamented the skills of artistic handicraft lost to mass manufacture of ready-made objects and the resulting resurgence of interest in 'handmade', 'custom', or 'artisanal' products. I submit that our interest is not only in the economic welfare of the artisan, or the quality of their products, but also in the connection between an artifact and a human whose excellence and skill was responsible for its production. We think that it is *good* that we humans are good at making beautiful and commodious objects for living. Even if machines could produce all such goods for us, it would be sad and regrettable if humans were no longer capable of doing the same. Wouldn't we want to say the same in the case of moral skills? Even if intelligent machines could somehow direct all human interactions to produce the most just, harmonious, and compassionate outcomes possible, *we would be diminished as creatures* were we utterly helpless to act justly and compassionately without their assistance . . ..

Moral skills are thus necessary (while not sufficient) conditions of genuine moral virtue or practical wisdom. Moral virtue assumes the availability of prior opportunities to cultivate, through stable and repeatable practices of the right sort, the prerequisite moral skills. Without them, even a person who sincerely wishes to do well consistently and for its own sake will be incapable of doing so. It follows that if new technological practices disrupt the cultivation of moral skills on a large enough scale, the future of human character may be profoundly affected. For this reason, moral skills are even more crucial than other skillsets to shield from widespread loss and cultural devaluation . . ..

I identify three potential hazards of moral deskilling posed by today's emerging technologies, intended to supply only a representative sample and not an exhaustive list: the risk that military drones and other autonomous weapons systems may engender moral deskilling of soldiers in the use of military force; the risk that new media practices of multitasking may engender deskilling in the realm of moral attention; and the risk that social robotics may engender moral deskilling in practices of human caregiving . . ..

Understanding the ambiguous and open horizon of emerging technologies' impact on moral skills can help us not only to better identify the moral risks and benefits of such technologies in the abstract but also to envision new developmental and design possibilities that concretely realize potential moral benefits of these technologies, while effectively minimizing the losses they might otherwise inflict on our own moral capacities and excellences.

Yet envisioning those developmental and design possibilities is not enough. One could fill a library with all the possibilities for ethical technologies that have been envisioned and never built or sold. Movements that privilege 'values by design' or 'participatory design' are a fine start, but will not take us all the way. What would be required to feed our moral imaginations more reliably into the process of technological development, manufacture, and mass marketing? I assert that what would be needed is a deeper shift of cultural values in technological societies, one that would reflect a new global awareness that humans are technomoral artificers *and* artifacts. We can no longer afford to view technological development as something to be delegated to engineering wizards and marketers, who make tools to be adopted by human consumers; human beings must acquire a sense of collective responsibility for intelligently directing the course of our own technomoral evolution – for consciously using technologies to aid us in becoming the practically wise beings that we want to be, beings who can live the kinds of lives we genuinely want to live. The imagination of the moral self must lead the way for the 'technologies of the self'.

3.5 Politics and Technological Innovation

The sweeping social impacts of the Industrial Revolution demonstrate that to engage in sustained, critical reflection about the real-world impact and likely trajectories of new technology, we must attend to the larger social, economic and political context that inform and interact with their emergence. Accordingly, Johnson and Wetmore suggest that critical inquiries into technology are best framed through the lens of 'sociotechnical systems', thereby bringing people, things, practices, values and meanings into the frame and avoiding the myth of 'neutrality', in recognition that there is no such thing as a 'view from nowhere'.

Johnson, D. G., and Wetmore, J. (2021). 'Introduction'. In D. G. Johnson and J. Wetmore (eds.), *Technology and Society: Building our Sociotechnical Future.* MIT Press.

94–95.

To understand how technologies are developed, what they mean, and how they are used, it is best to focus on what we will call 'sociotechnical systems' – assemblages of things, people, practices and meanings .... To grasp what a sociotechnical system is, it helps to look at an example. Consider the safety air bag in an automobile. It can be seen as a system of sensors, an inflator and a bag, but this tells one very little about why it was created, what it does, or even how it works. The sociotechnical system of an air bag includes the numerous relationships the device has with people and other devices. For instance, the modern air bag is meaningless if not viewed in the context of modern transportation, automobiles, and car collisions. Its purpose cannot be understood without looking at how insurance companies encouraged its development, how government regulation shaped its design, how engineers had certain users in mind when they built it. The air bag can work only when there are automobile manufacturers and distributors, a road system and drivers with certain habits. The device itself is not without meaning, but its purpose, value and implications are best understood in its broader socio-technical context.

3.5.1 The Myth of Technological Neutrality: Artefacts Have Politics

Yet the need to consider the larger socio-technical context in which new technologies are embedded should not blind us to the political choices that have been 'hard-wired' into the technology itself. For nineteenth-century industrialists, the appeal of steam-powered machines was readily identifiable – enabling them to rapidly increase the scale and speed of manufacturing while significantly lowering the cost of labour per unit of production. But the political dimensions of technologies may reach even further than their functional capabilities: they may inhere in the design of the technology itself. The point is vividly demonstrated in the following two extracts.

Winner, L. (1980). 'Do Artifacts Have Politics?' *Daedalus*, 109(1), 121–136.

121–131

In controversies about technology and society, there is no idea more provocative than the notion that technical things have political qualities. At issue is the claim that the machines, structures, and systems of modern material culture can be accurately judged not only for their contributions of efficiency and productivity, not merely for their positive and negative environmental side effects, but also for the ways in which they can embody specific forms of power and authority . . ..

We all know that people have politics, not things. To discover either virtues or evils in aggregates of steel, plastic, transistors, integrated circuits, and chemicals seems just plain wrong, a way of mystifying human artifice and of avoiding the true sources, the human sources of freedom and oppression, justice and injustice. Blaming the hardware appears even more foolish than blaming the victims when it comes to judging conditions of public life. Hence, the stern advice commonly given those who flirt with the notion that technical artifacts have political qualities: What matters is not technology itself, but the social or economic system in which it is embedded. This maxim, which in a number of variations is the central premise of a theory that can be called the social determination of technology, has an obvious wisdom . . ..

Technical Arrangements as Forms of Order

Anyone who has travelled the highways of America and has become used to the normal height of overpasses may well find something a little odd about some of the bridges over the parkways on Long Island, New York. Many of the overpasses are extraordinarily low, having as little as nine feet of clearance at the curb. Even those who happened to notice this structural peculiarity would not be inclined to attach any special meaning to it. In our accustomed way of looking at things like roads and bridges we see the details of form as innocuous, and seldom give them a second thought. It turns out, however, that the two hundred or so low-hanging overpasses on Long Island were deliberately designed to achieve a particular social effect. Robert Moses, the master builder of roads, parks, bridges, and other public works from the 1920s to the 1970s in New York, had these overpasses built to specifications that would discourage the

> presence of buses on his parkways. According to evidence provided by Robert A. Caro in his biography of Moses, the reasons reflect Moses's social-class bias and racial prejudice. Automobile-owning whites of 'upper' and 'comfortable middle' classes, as he called them, would be free to use the parkways for recreation and commuting. Poor people and blacks, who normally used public transit, were kept off the roads because the twelve-foot tall buses could not get through the overpasses. One consequence was to limit access of racial minorities and low-income groups to Jones Beach, Moses's widely acclaimed public park . . ..
>
> Histories of architecture, city planning, and public works contain many examples of physical arrangements that contain explicit or implicit political purposes. One can point to Baron Haussmann's broad Parisian thoroughfares, engineered at Louis Napoleon's direction to prevent any recurrence of street fighting of the kind that took place during the revolution of 1848 . . ..
>
> If we examine social patterns that comprise the environments of technical systems, we find certain devices and systems almost invariably linked to specific ways of organizing power and authority. The important question is: Does this state of affairs derive from an unavoidable social response to intractable proper ties in the things themselves, or is it instead a pattern imposed independently by a governing body, ruling class or some other social or cultural institution to further its own purpose?

The racist design of Long Island's bridges was intentional, aimed at excluding African Americans, the overwhelming majority of whom relied on public buses. But the unfair discriminatory impacts of technological design may not be conscious or intended. In many cases, they arise from underlying biases and assumptions that are deeply embedded in our social structures, norms and attitudes. In the following extract, Criado Pérez highlights the 'invisibility of women' in the development of technology throughout history, producing inequality and injustice in the distribution of benefits and burdens of technological change.

> **Criado Pérez, C. (2019).** *Invisible Women: Data Bias in a World Designed for Men*. Chatto.
>
> 186–191
>
> Men are more likely than women to be involved in a car crash, which means they dominate the numbers of those seriously injured in car accidents. But when a woman is involved in a car crash, she is 47% more likely to be seriously injured than a man, and 71% more likely to be moderately injured, even when researchers control for factors such as height, weight, seat-belt usage, and crash intensity. She is also 17% more likely to die. And it's all to do with how the car is designed – and for whom . . ..
>
> Women tend to sit further forward than men when driving. This is because we are on average shorter. Our legs need to be closer to reach the pedals, and we need to sit more upright to see clearly over the dashboard. This is not, however,

> the 'standard seating position'. Women are 'out of position' drivers. And our wilful deviation from the norm means that we are at greater risk of internal injury on frontal collisions ....
>
> From development initiatives to smartphones, from medical tech to stoves, tools (whether physical or financial) are developed without reference to women's needs, and, as a result these tools are failing them on a grand scale. And this failure affects women's lives on a similarly grand scale: it makes them poorer, it makes them sicker, and, when it comes to cars, it is killing them. Designers may believe they are making products for everyone, but in reality they are mainly making them for men. It's time to start designing women in.

Concerns about unfair discrimination, particularly on the grounds of gender and race, are now commonplace in discussions about power asymmetries associated with technological design and innovation, reflecting belated recognition that technological innovation has long treated the white male body as the universal norm producing systematic and unjust injustice discrimination.

3.6 Management Studies: Understanding and Fostering Innovation

We now turn to the study of technological innovation by scholars from management studies and several economics sub-disciplines who investigate technological innovation, seeking (among other things) to understand why some succeed while others fail. These inquiries, which substantially pre-date the emergence of the Internet, tend to start with firms operating in the market: they proceed on the typically unstated assumption that innovation is inherently desirable and worth pursuing (cf. Chapter 1). Scholars working within this field have examined a wide range of matters associated with technological change, including the innovation pathways and processes, the conditions necessary for technological innovation to emerge, obstacles to market adoption, how new products and processes enter the market or create new markets and the diffusion of novel products and processes throughout society.

Although the term 'disruptive' is often used in common parlance to describe any phenomenon that disturbs the status quo, management scholars have developed a much more precise classification scheme in which 'disruptive' innovation is distinguished from other kinds of innovation, including incremental, breakthrough and, more recently, 'frugal' innovation. Thus 'disruptive innovation' is a term of art coined by Harvard scholar Clayton Christensen. As he explains in the extract below, disruptive innovation is rare. It refers to a process by which a product or service takes root initially in simple applications serving fringe customers at the bottom of a market and then relentlessly acquires market traction, eventually displacing established competitors. The personal computer was once an example of a disruptive innovation that replaced mainframe and mini computers. Unlike disruptive innovation, 'incremental' or 'sustaining' innovations refer to significant improvements and smaller ameliorations of existing products and processes. 'Breakthrough' (or radical) innovation, on the other hand, refers primarily to a significant improvement in existing technology. For example, Zipcar, a car-sharing platform, was an important technological improvement of an existing service that allowed consumers to rent cars more conveniently. Distinguishing between different types of innovation is relevant to regulators as disruptive, and breakthrough innovations may pose greater and more complex regulatory challenges than incremental innovations due to uncertainty concerning their applications and potential adverse impacts.

Christensen, C. M., McDonald, R., Altman, E.J. and Palmer, J. E., (2018). 'Disruptive Innovation: Intellectual History and Directions for Future Research'. *Journal of Management Studies*, 55(7), 1043–1078.

1047–1050

Like other management theories, the theory of disruptive innovation began with an observation that generated a research question. Across industries ranging from computers to retail to steel, leading firms failed to remain dominant in their respective markets ....

To investigate the drivers of this failure, Christensen (1997) first examined the disk-drive industry .... From his study of the disk-drive industry, Christensen (1997) induced an account of disruptive innovation that consisted of three principal components. First, in many industries, the pace of technological progress outstrips customers' demand for higher-performing technologies. As a result, incumbents can overserve the market by producing more advanced, feature-rich products than customers need; doing so leaves a gap at the bottom of the market between customers' needs and the performance provided by firms – a gap that provides an opening for entrants .... Second, for firms, a strategically crucial distinction between different types of innovation – in technology or in business model – can emerge in an industry. Most are sustaining innovations, which improve products and services along dimensions of performance that mainstream customers care about and that markets have historically valued; such innovations enable incumbents to sell more products to their best existing customers at higher margins and higher profitability. The rarer type is a disruptive innovation. When initially introduced, disruptive innovations are inferior to incumbent products on accepted performance dimensions, but they offer a novel mix of attributes that appeals to fringe customer groups, notably those near the bottom of the market. They may be, for instance, smaller, cheaper, more accessible, or more convenient. Finally, the third component of Christensen's model was that existing customers and established profit models constrain established firms' investments in new innovations; thus, investments unattractive to incumbents may be attractive to entrants who lack many (or any) customers and enjoy fewer competing investment opportunities. Consequently, incumbents are typically unmotivated to develop disruptive innovations that promise lower margins, target smaller markets, and introduce inferior products and services that their existing customers cannot use ....

> The initial model of disruptive innovation pinpoints low-end disruptions, in which upstarts enter at the bottom of the market and take hold within an existing value network before moving up-market and attacking incumbents. The steel industry (minimills) and retailing (discount retailers) offer examples of low-end disruptions. By contrast, new-market disruptions occur in completely new value networks whose initial customers have not used the prior generation of products and services; thus, these disruptive entrants compete for customers that would otherwise go without the product or service . . ..
>
> Specifying different categories of disruption has led to a clearer conceptualization of the circumstances that give rise to disruptive innovation. Another important refinement was defining 'disruptiveness' as a relative, not absolute, phenomenon. In other words, a given innovation can be disruptive to one firm but sustaining to another firm. For mail-order and catalogue retailers, the internet was a sustaining innovation since they could use the internet to make more money in the way they were already structured to make money. But it was disruptive relative to in-store retailers that could not leverage the internet to improve their cost structures or business processes . . ..
>
> [T]echnologies and business models go together – disruptive innovations must be evaluated relative to a firm's business model. Such refinements pointed to a related insight: no innovation is inherently disruptive. Firms make strategic choices to position an innovation in a disruptive way – most often by targeting non-consumers in new markets.

Management scholars typically assume that innovation is inherently valuable and tend to assume that technological innovation is directly and causally linked to economic growth and productivity. This assumption has resulted in the acritical support of allegedly innovative companies allowing them to earn large profits and exclude their competition, even when the basis of their success was supported by public funds. Although her argument is not extracted here in full, Mazzucato claims that the evidence supporting these assumptions is limited and equivocal. She therefore advocates that the state should play a more pro-active 'entrepreneurial' role in fostering technological innovation.

Mazzucato, M. (2011). *The Entrepreneurial State.* Demos.

17–54

> Across the globe we are hearing that the state has to be cut back in order to foster a post-crisis recovery, unleashing the power of entrepreneurship and innovation in the private sector. This feeds a perceived contrast that is repeatedly drawn by the media, business and libertarian politicians of a dynamic, innovative, competitive private sector versus a sluggish, bureaucratic, inertial, 'meddling' public sector. So much so that it is virtually accepted by the public as a 'common sense' truth . . ..
>
> The view of the current government – shared by its predecessor – is that the role of the state in spurring innovation is simply to provide the 'conditions for innovation to flourish'. The UK Government states that if it invests in skills

and a strong science base, ensures a strong legal framework within an amenable macroeconomy, and supports entrepreneurial clusters, then the market will do the rest through the incentive of the profit motive . . ..

Lessons from these experiences are important. They force the debate to go beyond the role of the state in stimulating demand, or the role of the state in 'taxpayers' money is potentially misdirected to badly managed firms in the name of progress, distorting incentives as it goes along. Instead it is a case for a targeted, proactive, entrepreneurial state, able to take risks, creating a highly networked system of actors harnessing the best of the private sector for the national good over a medium to long-term horizon. It is the state as catalyst, and lead investor, sparking the initial reaction in a network that will then cause knowledge to spread. The state as creator of the knowledge economy. It cannot be called 'new' industrial policy because it is in fact what has happened, though in a 'hidden way' to prevent a backlash, over the last three decades in the development of the computer industry, the internet, the pharma–biotech industry, and many more including today's nanotech industry. None of these technological revolutions would have occurred without the leading role of the state. It is about admitting that in many cases, it has in fact been the state, not the private sector, that has had the vision for strategic change, daring to think – against all odds – about the 'impossible', creating a new technological opportunity, making the large necessary investments, and enabling a decentralised network of actors to enable the risky research, and to allow the development and commercialisation process to occur in a dynamic way . . ..

Myth-busting ..: R&D Is Not Enough

The literature on the economics of innovation, from different camps, has often assumed a direct causal link between R&D and innovation, and between innovation and economic growth. Yet, surprisingly, there are very few studies which prove that innovation carried out by large or small firms actually increases their growth performance – the macro models on innovation and growth do not seem to have strong empirical 'micro foundations' . . ..

Technological change is a good example of the truly unique situation since R&D investments not only take years to materialise into new products, but most lead to failure. In the pharmaceutical sector, for example, innovation takes up to 17 years from the beginning of an R&D project to the end; it costs about $403 million per drug; and the failure rate is extremely high: only 1 in 10,000 compounds reach market approval phase, a success rate of 0.01 per cent. When successful, often the search for one product leads to the discovery of a completely different one. The process is characterised by serendipity. This of course does not mean that innovation is based on luck. Far from it, it is based on long-term strategies and targeted investments. But the returns from those investments are highly uncertain and thus cannot be understood through rational economic theory (as will be seen below, this is one of the critiques that modern day Schumpeterians make of endogenous growth theory, which models R&D as a game-theoretic choice). Furthermore, the ability of companies to engage in innovation differs greatly and is one of the main reasons that firms

> are so different from each other, and why it is nearly impossible to find firms distributed 'normally' around an 'optimal size firm' (the 'representative' agent), a concept so dear to neoclassical microeconomic theory . . ..
>
> Not all innovations lead to economy-wide growth. This is only true for new products or processes that have an impact on a wide variety of sectors in the economy, as was the case with the rise with electricity and computers. These are what economists call general purpose technologies (GPTs) characterised by three core qualities, pervasive, improvement and innovation spawning:
>
> - They are pervasive in that they spread to many sectors.
> - They get better over time and, hence, should keep lowering the costs of its users.
> - Make it easier to invent and produce new products or processes.

3.7 Towards 'Responsible' Technological Innovation?

The strong normative orientation underpinning philosophy of technology is also shared in a rather different strand of literature, that is arguably more concrete and practical in its focus. This literature, which has proceeded in recent years under the rubric of 'responsible research and innovation' or more simply 'responsible innovation' is oriented towards seeking actively to shape and influence the direction of technological innovation, emphasising the need to embed public participation into processes of scientific research and technological innovation process.

> **Owen, R. and Manpesa, M. (2019).** *Responsible Innovation and Responsible Research and Innovation* in Simon, D., Kuhlman, S., Stamm, J. and Canzler, W. (eds), Handbook on Science and Public Policy. Edward Elgar. 26–48
>
> 27–39
>
> Responsible Innovation (RI) and Responsible Research and Innovation (RRI) are often used interchangeably, and it is easy, but mistaken, to consider them as being the same thing . . ..
>
> The discourse of RI has strong academic roots. This is in contrast with the distinctly EC policy roots associated with the RRI discourse . . . RI emerged at the beginning of the current decade but has historical foundations that go back many decades, and builds on discussions and debates concerning the social responsibility of science that have an equally long history . . ..
>
> Acknowledging the power of innovation to create futures – and associated with these uncertainties and vulnerabilities – RI asks how we can and should meaningfully engage as a society with the futures innovation seeks to create, futures that are being created unintentionally or by design. For example, how the future world of work might be transformed by artificial intelligence and machine learning, or how our future world might be transformed by techniques intentionally aimed at engineering the climate at a planetary scale. But RI goes further, asking how we can build on this engagement to respond and act in

> order for us to collectively take some measure of responsibility for those futures, rather than discount them, or leave them to chance and ourselves to moral luck. This makes RI as much about intended impacts, visions, purposes, political agendas and associated public policies as it does about understanding and responding to emergence, given the inevitable social, ethical, environmental and political entanglements, dilemmas, uncertainties and risks science and innovation present. These are uncertainties and entanglements we must expect to occur to varying degrees but often lack the knowledge and foresight to accurately predict. RI therefore firstly asks what kind of future we want innovation to create, and secondly, given that the future is inherently uncertain and unpredictable, how we should proceed under conditions of ignorance, ambiguity and uncertainty ... RI also acknowledges the important but often narrow focus that current institutional processes of ethical oversight present and the lack of formal and systematic processes for engaging citizens and stakeholders with the purposes, agendas and politics of potentially disruptive science and innovation and their broader impacts on culture and society ....
>
> Responsible Research and Innovation (RRI), like RI, emerged as a discourse at the beginning of the current decade. Unlike RI however, it was from the outset a public policy discourse that emerged from within the European Commission (EC)... Rene von Schomberg, then at the EC Directorate General for Research, was instrumental in initiating RRI as a policy discourse, which rapidly became adopted by the EC's Science in Society programme within the Research Directorate at the time. Leaning on ethics and technology assessment traditions, von Schomberg's first significant RRI contribution (eventually published in 2012) was pivotal in setting out a vision and framing for RRI in its early days. This vision and framing showed distinct similarities with the RI discourse described above. This is clear for example when considering his definition for RRI, which has become by far the most cited:
>
> Responsible Research and Innovation is a transparent, interactive process by which societal actors and innovators become mutually responsive to each other with a view to the (ethical) acceptability, sustainability and societal desirability of the innovation process and its marketable products (in order to allow a proper embedding of scientific and technological advances in our society). (Von Schomberg, 2012, p. 50)
>
> > However, as time went on it became increasingly clear that von Schomberg's original, more holistic vision would succumb to RRI as a policy artefact ... in practice ... has become framed by the EC 'as a package that includes multi-actor and public engagement in research and innovation, enabling easier access to scientific results, the take up of gender and ethics in the research and innovation content and process, and formal and informal science education'.

Owen and Manpesa go on to observe that both discourses advocate a notion of shared responsibilities for the development and consequences of techno-visionary science and innovation, fostering collective responsibility, for example, through continuous embedding of public and stakeholder engagement, but they remain 'fragile and contested'.

3.8 Taming Technological Change through Law?

Different fields of law have also studied technological change. For example, intellectual property law confers legal protection to intellectual creations, such as patents and copyright, while competition law seeks to address concentration of power within markets, including market power created by technological change. The digital revolution has permeated contemporary society so pervasively that different fields of law, ranging from labour law (e.g., work performed through digital platforms such as food-delivery) to property law (e.g., data ownership) are currently grappling with challenges associated with the need to adapt to provide meaningful responses to new kinds of transactions, relationships and configurations of power.

3.8.1 Does the Law Have a 'Pacing' Problem?

Many claim that the law has a 'pacing problem', referring to the alleged inability of the law to 'keep up' with technological change. In the following extracts, three authors offer more nuanced and thoughtful accounts that recognise the law's inherent flexibility and thus capacity to adapt to change. Cristie Ford focuses on the nature of the challenges encountered by law in the face of technological change focusing on problems of fit, visibility and legibility. In a similar vein, Crootof and Ard identify three kinds of legal uncertainties arising from tech-fostered change: whether and how extant law applies, normative uncertainties that arise when the law may be unable to accomplish its aims and institutional design and application uncertainties.

Ford, C.(2022). 'Innovation and Regulatory Agencies'. In M. Maggetti, F. Di Mascio and A. Natalini (eds.), *Research Handbook on Regulatory Authorities*. Edward Elgar. 441–457

445–447

Innovation will affect regulation no matter how it is structured. In its design, regulation constitutes the spaces in which innovation happens. It creates loopholes, opportunities, boundaries, and incentives. Different tradeoffs will make sense in different circumstances . . ..

An innovation (whether to business process, technology, or in finding novel uses for existing products) is concerning, for regulatory purposes, because of its ability to outstrip existing regulatory structures, such that they no longer fit or work properly. As a result, rules may stop operating as intended, perhaps because they are not broad enough to capture new behaviour or phenomena, or because activity has moved away from the formal object with which the regulation is concerned. This leaves regulators potentially focusing on the wrong things. Responding to this and similar innovation-generated problems requires that the regulator be able to recognize that its effectiveness has been compromised, to understand the particulars of how it has been undermined, and to respond to it. This is not a straightforward or easy set of tasks. The nature of the challenge can be broken down into three different kinds of regulatory analytical problems. First, particularly fast-moving innovations can generate information and data problems for regulators. These were present around deep water oil drilling in the Gulf of Mexico between 1995 and 2010, for example, or the explosive growth of the over-the-counter derivatives market for credit default swaps between 2004 and 2007 . . ... Consider, for example, the fact that in 2010, it was British Petroleum itself that had to devise never-before-tried responses – like the 'junk shot' and the 'top kill' – to the terrible and ultra-deep oil leak that followed the explosion of its Deepwater Horizon rig. The regulator was utterly unequipped to manage that disaster, for reasons that prominently included the lack of information they had on the risks that BP was running and the risks of ultra-deep oil drilling in general. Complex systems, characterized by multiple interconnections, can also create unanticipated and outsized reactions, where system effects or multiple small errors' combined effects mutually reinforce each other These are another form of information and data problem.

The second kind of problem that innovation generates for regulation is the visibility problem. One such example is the visibility problem that is created by incremental innovation; like the apocryphal frog in boiling water, one tends not to notice change until it has reached significant levels, and interests and practices have accreted around it . . ..

The third and most profound kind of problem that innovation presents for regulation is the legibility problem. Legibility is the ability to make sense of one's environment, to make reasonable sense-making assumptions, and to draw appropriate analogies between the familiar and the new. Innovation, by its nature, upends categories and undermines assumptions. Consider, for example, how special purpose entities in finance, which according to the traditional legal model of the firm seem to operate on corporate law principles, actually achieve their objectives through the separate legal mechanism of contract.

Crootof, R., and Ard, B. J. (2021). 'Structuring Techlaw'. 34 *Harvard Journal of Las & Technology*, 348–417.

348–377

The legal community constantly grapples with technologies that enable new conduct or facilitate previously rare actions, blur established legal categories, diffuse or centralize capabilities, and expose the limits of existing regulatory institutions . . ..

The conventional approach is to tackle these quandaries by identifying something about a technology or its use that is 'exceptional' and argue that this distinction necessitates new law or even a new legal regime; or, alternatively, that a lack of exceptional characteristics implies that the technology can be adequately governed by extant rules. But while these focused studies are individually useful, the exceptionalist approach fosters siloed and potentially incomplete analyses, masks the repetitive nature of the underlying questions, and thereby results in the regular reinvention of the regulatory wheel. At best, a compartmentalized assessment is a missed opportunity. At worst, it leads to ineffective, counterproductive, or even harmful rules and policy prescriptions . . ..

Shifting our focus from the particular details of any given technology to the legal uncertainties, the fundamental challenge of techlaw is not how to best regulate novel technologies, but rather how to best address familiar forms of legal uncertainty in new sociolegal contexts . . ..

To resolve a legal uncertainty, a legal actor must first identify which kind it is. [We] delineate the three main kinds of tech-fostered legal uncertainties: (1) application uncertainties, which raise the question of whether and how extant law applies; (2) normative uncertainties, which arise when the law is arguably unable to accomplish its aims; and (3) institutional uncertainties, which exist when there are questions about different regulatory entities' relative authority, competence, and legitimacy to apply and update the law. Our focus on legal uncertainty emphasizes that there is nothing particularly special about new technologies and no need to distinguish certain technologies as 'exceptional' or their usage as 'legally disruptive'. Instead, all technologies can raise all three types of legal uncertainties as social circumstances and uses change . . ..

Application uncertainties ask whether and how extant law applies and may manifest as legal gaps or legal overlaps; normative uncertainties ask whether the law can accomplish its aims when it is arguably overinclusive or under-inclusive; and institutional uncertainties ask whether a regulatory entity is equipped to resolve application and normative uncertainties. In short, application uncertainties encourage a focus on what the law is, normative uncertainties invite the question of what the law should be, and institutional uncertainties highlight concerns about who should decide these questions . . ..

The facile but persistent claim that 'law cannot keep up with new technologies' ignores the myriad ways in which law shapes most technological developments and obscures the fact that all new technologies are governed by complex and overlapping tech-neutral background rules. Even if you invent the first thingamabob, you are bound by the rules of commercial law should you try to sell it, and you cannot use it to batter someone without incurring tort liability. Most existing law can be applied to most new technologies most of the time. However, there is often some element of uncertainty, as it may be unclear how the law should apply or which law (if any) is relevant. These 'application uncertainties' – situations where there is some indeterminacy as to whether and how existing law applies to an artifact, actor, or activity – are the most commonly addressed kinds of tech-fostered uncertainties. They highlight both settled law and its outer limits . . ..

Normative Uncertainties

Seemingly reasonable resolutions of application uncertainties may still result in undesirable outcomes when the applicable rule is incapable of accomplishing a desired result, inviting legal actors to reevaluate the rule or regime's underlying purpose. These normative uncertainties may manifest as the law becoming underinclusive, in that it fails to apply to the full range of activity necessary to achieve its purposes, or overinclusive, in that it unnecessarily restricts socially valuable activity.

Institutional Uncertainties

All laws are grounded on assumptions about the state of the world; when a technological development complicates or upends those assumptions, legal actors must evaluate whether and how laws still apply. Institutional uncertainties exist when there are questions about the adequacy and effectiveness of regulatory entities, either singly or in combination, to respond to these application and normative uncertainties. Instead of the substantive legal issues raised by application or normative uncertainties, these uncertainties raise institutional design issues that are simultaneously descriptive and normative: Do the legal actors possess the authority, competence, and legitimacy to resolve the application and normative uncertainties before them? How should questions arising from overlapping institutional jurisdictions be addressed? When is a new institution needed?

One type of institutional uncertainty arises when no existing individual or combination of institutions appears to have the authority, competency, or legitimacy to govern certain artifacts, actors, or activities. The perceived inadequacies of extant institutions may prompt calls for a different regulator – or an entirely new form of regulation.

3.8.2 Temporal Challenges: Whether, When and What?

At the heart of the challenges that law encounters in responding to technological innovation is profound uncertainty: about the likely benefits, opportunities, risks and threats that those technologies may pose, in addition to uncertainty about whether they will be adopted, for what purposes and in which domains. For policy-makers, this generates a series of dilemmas in deciding whether, when and how to respond. One of the most intractable difficulties faced by policy-makers when faced with calls to introduce specific measures to address worries about the adverse impacts associated with new and emerging technologies concerns matters of timing. The so-called Collingridge dilemma referred to in the following extract:

Bennett M., L., and Zalnieriute, M. (2020). 'Law and Technology in the Dimension of Time'. In S. Ranchordás and Y. Roznai (eds.), *Time, Law and Change: An Interdisciplinary Study*. Hart, 303–326.

309

There is much discussion in the literature about the timing of legal interventions, mostly in the context of discussions about the best time to introduce new laws that prohibit, regulate or encourage new activities. Many of these refer to the 'Collingridge dilemma', an articulation of the challenge in regulating in a shifting space. Move too early and there is a risk that new laws will be poorly designed, failing to match the final form that technology takes. Move too late and socio- technical systems are less flexible – the changes needed to comply with new regulation make them very expensive or even impossible. The regulation of the Internet is a good example to illustrate this tension. For instance, laws regulating copying using digital tapes failed to deal with Internet file-sharing and thus became irrelevant, while, by failing to incorporate early cyber-security standards, it is difficult to retro-fit the Internet for security today. As Murray points out, new regulations are influenced by an existing regulatory framework rather than operating from scratch. There is thus path dependence in socio-technical and regulatory states and some regulatory options prove difficult in practice once socio-technical systems have reached particular states of development. The choice of regulatory timing thus ought to be made with awareness of the diffusion pattern of the technology concerned so that there is, for example, greater urgency where technology diffuses exponentially after reaching a critical mass of users.

A further challenge that overlays the temporal dilemma concerns what kind of policy approach is warranted in the face of technological innovation. As Chander observes in the following extract, these responses have been broadly categorised as 'wait-and-see', on the one hand, and a 'precautionary approach'' on the other.

Chander, A.. (2017). 'Future-proofing Law'. *UC Davis Law Review*, 51(1), 1–25.

3–4

When it comes to emerging technologies, should we wait and see or should we regulate in advance? Proponents of the precautionary principle would be more likely to prefer preemptive regulation designed to foresee and forestall potential risks. Proponents of risk-based approaches often prefer to wait-and-see, depending on the particular risks involved. This so-called procrastination principle would have regulators learn from experience before intervening, but as Jonathan Zittrain notes, 'The procrastination principle rests on the assumption that most problems confronting a network can be solved later or by others.' Innovators themselves often prefer 'to ask forgiveness, not permission', but they often recognize the need for regulation to assure the public or even to stymie competition.

However, this is rather crude binary classification obscures considerable variety in the range of available policy responses, particularly given the highly elastic nature of the so-called precautionary principle, which we touched upon in Chapter 2. While engaging in debates about the validity or otherwise of the precautionary principle, the following observations by Andy Stirling, following his careful review of the criticisms made of the precautionary principle, reminds us of the need for robust methods of appraisal, explicit value judgements and enhanced deliberation in when seeking to grapple with the uncertainty associated with technological change:

Stirling, A. (2016). 'Precaution in the Governance of Technology'. In R. Brownsword, E. Scotford and K. Yeung (eds.), *The Oxford Handbook of Law, Regulation and Technology*. Oxford University Press, 645–669

662

In summary there are two important general promises for the regulation of emerging technologies, that are offered in these kinds of emerging frameworks for more precautionary appraisal. These are, first, to help 'broaden out' attention to greater diversities of options, practices and perspectives in policy debates over technology. Secondly, there is the promise of 'opening up' more vibrant, mature and robust policy debates over the implications of different interpretations of uncertainty. Neither of these implies any necessary conflict between precaution and innovation. Nor is there any tension between precaution and science. Understood in terms less coloured by partisan interests, the precautionary principle can thereby be recognised simply to point to a range of practical regulatory tools, through which to better address the unavoidable (if often neglected) challenges of incomplete knowledge. By helping to reduce intensities of regulatory capture, the main contributions of such approaches are to encourage more robust methods in appraisal, make value judgements more explicit, and enhance qualities of deliberation.

Conclusion

This chapter has traversed a broad array of academic literatures, drawing from multiple disciplines across the humanities, law and the social science concerned with technological innovation. We have shown that despite claims of novelty, the reception of new technologies into society often attract familiar concerns and proceed according to a familiar dynamic, drawing parallels with concerns expressed during the First Machine Age, with the unfolding Second Machine Age. These include fears about the impacts of automation arising from the on-going digital revolution on employment and the conditions of workers and the exploitation of citizens, consumers and their data by those in positions of power. Although existing scholarship has remained largely fragmented and siloed, rather than integrated into a single, readily identifiable scholarly field, they contribute to an established, rich and rapidly growing body of literature that is often overlooked in both policy and academic discussions. At the same time, we have highlighted distinctive yet common regulatory challenges which technological change typically provokes.

Discussion Questions

1. What are 'socio-technical imaginaries'? In what way, if any, do they help us reflect critically on the policy challenges posed by technological innovation?

2. Can technological innovation be equated with human 'progress'? Why or why not?
3. How is the relationship between technological change and society best understood? What factors influence whether a particular technological innovation is adopted in practice?
4. Is technology 'neutral'? Why or why not?
5. Why is it helpful to consider:
   (a) the affordances of a technological invention?
   (b) the socio-technical system in which a technological invention operates?
   (c) the political-economic dynamics and structures in which technological adoption occurs?
   (d) the geopolitical context in which technological inventions emerge?
6. What is the difference between 'sustaining' and 'disruptive' innovation, and why is the difference significant?
7. What kind of concerns can be brought within the rubric of technology 'ethics'?
8. What is 'responsible research and innovation'? How do you understand the relationship between responsible research and innovation and ethical perspectives on technological innovation?
9. In what ways, if any, does technological change pose challenges for law in general?
10. Can you identify specific kinds of technological change that have posed specific challenges to a particular area of law, and what is the nature of those challenges?

4

Theories of Regulation

Introduction

In recent decades, the volume of clothing produced worldwide has increased by 400 percent, yet household expenditure on clothing has declined (Barber 2021) due to the emergence of 'fast fashion' manufacturers. These companies offer multiple clothing collections each year, enticing consumers with remarkably low prices. These garments are produced primarily in low- and middle-income countries, where labour and material costs are significantly lower than in the countries where those garments are sold. Fast fashion, heavily promoted on various social media channels, caters to younger generations and enables students to embrace fashion trends affordably. Buying a fast-fashion item is often difficult to resist, even for those aware of their damaging environmental impact. The textile dyeing and other harmful chemicals involved pollutes rivers; the fast-paced turnover of fashion encourages the swift disposal of clothing items, adding to the burden of landfills. While the imperative to address the environmental consequences of fast fashion is evident, the regulatory landscape does not incentivise environmentally sustainable practices within the garment industry. This example encapsulates the theoretical challenges of regulation: On one hand, there is a compelling public interest in safeguarding the environment; on the other, the private interests of consumers, companies and entire industries (e.g., advertising) are served by the rapid turnover of fashion and hence have little appetite for regulatory reform. To complicate matters, the fast-fashion industry operates within complex global supply chains, which means that coordinated global regulatory action would be needed.

In this chapter, we examine a set of theories of regulation that help us to make sense of various regulatory outcomes and dynamics of the kind we observe in relation to fast fashion. A theory of regulation is a set of propositions or hypotheses explaining *why* regulation emerges (in the case of positive/empirical theories) or should emerge (prescriptive/normative theories). These propositions also help explain *which actors* contribute to that emergence, and help to make sense of *patterns of interaction* between regulatory actors and their *outcomes*. We organise theories of regulation into four broad categories

(i) public interest theories, (ii) private interest theories, (iii) institutionalist theories and (iv) hybrid theories. It is important to recognise, however, that their aims and objectives are rather different, depending partly on the underlying disciplinary perspectives from which these theories draw. Accordingly, the extracts draw from legal, economic, sociological and risk regulation scholarship, all of which have helped illuminate why particular dynamics and patterns of regulation emerge.

As we noted in the Introduction, early scholarship defined regulation primarily in terms of state intervention into the economy through the creation and implementation of new laws. Early theories of regulation are often described as 'public interest theories'. These theories define regulation as intentional interventions by a state-based regulator, ideally to promote the general welfare of the community motivated by a desire to serve the public interest. These theories seek normatively and morally to justify *why regulation is needed*. Private interest theories, by contrast, are sceptical of the so-called public interestedness of regulators, recognising that regulation often benefits powerful groups in society rather than those it was ostensibly intended to benefit. They seek to explain *why regulation in fact emerges*, offering a prescriptive account of the political and interest-group dynamics that preceded it. What we call 'institutionalist and hybrid theories' combine various approaches to regulation, typically emphasising the interdependency of state and non-state actors in the pursuit of both public benefit and private gain in contestation about the appropriate scope, content and orientation of regulatory regimes (Chapters 7 and 8).

Our discussion of public interest and private interest theories is predicated on a distinction between 'public' actors, here defined as state actors, and 'private' actors. This assumption is primarily pedagogical, reflecting the approach taken by a large body of influential scholarship. However, our discussion of *institutionalist theories* recognises both that the lines between public and private actors is often blurred and there is greater plurality in the sources of authority through which regulatory regimes are established and operate. *Hybrid theories* illustrate this phenomenon, which can be at least partly attributable to the privatisation of formerly public services and functions and the globalisation of markets. Our discussion proceeds in four parts. We begin with an account of public interest theories of regulation, distinguishing economic understandings of the public interest and those defined in terms of broader, non-economic conceptions of the public interest. Public interest theories contrast rather starkly with the private interest theories of regulation that we discuss in Section 4.2, which includes both the 'Chicago school' and so-called public choice theory. Section 4.3 then selectively considers institutionalist theories of regulation, including systems and network-based theories of regulation, while Section 4.4 offers an overview of hybrid theories that combine elements from public, private and institutionalist theories. The final section concludes.

4.1 Public Interest Theories

Public interest theories are based on the premise that regulation is intended to serve the public interest. They are concerned primarily with the conditions under which regulatory intervention is considered necessary or justified to protect the general welfare. These theories adopt two assumptions: first, that although competitive market forces can generally be expected to serve the public interest, they may need a 'helping hand' in circumstances of market failure (see Chapter 1). Second, public regulators can correct market failures through regulation. Public interest theories of regulation are primarily concerned with the normative foundations that justify regulatory intervention to advance the public interest. However, they may also include prescriptive dimensions that identify *how* the protection of the public interest is best achieved through regulatory intervention. The following discussion distinguishes those normative foundations into two categories: on the one hand, the pursuit of economic efficiency and, on the other, the pursuit of other non-efficiency based goals, including distributive justice, the protection of moral and ethical values and the management of 'risk'.

4.1.1 Economic Approaches

As Shleifer explains, debate about whether regulation, understood as state intervention in the economy, can be justified, has a long history. These debates were primarily discussed through the conceptual lens of welfare economics, proceeding on the premise that the purpose of regulation is to correct market failures, thereby serving the public interest by facilitating 'economic welfare', understood as the efficient use of society's limited resources and the avoidance of waste. Shleifer also highlights the ubiquity of regulation in contemporary life, reminding us that across all parts of the world, regulation has been traditionally justified by the need to address 'market failures' (see Chapter 1).

Shleifer, A. (2010). 'Efficient Regulation'. In D. P. Klesser (ed.), *Regulation vs. Litigation: Perspectives from Economics and Law*. University of Chicago Press, 27–44.

27–28

American and European societies are much richer today than they were 100 years ago, yet they are also vastly more regulated. Today, we work in jobs extensively regulated by the government, from hiring procedures, to working hours and conditions, to rules for joining unions, to dismissal practices. We live in houses and apartment buildings whose construction – from zoning, to use of materials, to fire codes – is heavily regulated. We eat food grown with approved fertilizers and hormones, processed in regulated factories, and sold in licensed outlets with mandatory labels and warnings. Our cars, buses, and airplanes are made, sold, driven, and maintained under heavy government regulation. Our

> children attend schools that teach material authorized by the state, visit doctors following regulated procedures, and play on playgrounds that are certified based on government-mandated safety standards. Government regulation is extensive in all rich and middle income countries. It transcends not only levels of economic development, but also cultures, legal traditions, levels of democratization, and all other factors economists use to explain differences among countries. There is surely a lot of variation across countries, but it pales by comparison with the raw fact of ubiquity. Why is there so much government regulation? . . . Markets fail . . . because of externalities, asymmetric information, and lack of competition, and governments need to regulate them to counter these failures. Regulation is ubiquitous because market failures are.

Besides market failures, government regulation is also needed when private law instruments such as contracts are not sufficient to make the market more efficient. Ogus explains that a justification for regulation arises when both the market and private law instruments fail (see Section 4.2). This means that neither market mechanisms (see Chapter 1) nor contracts between parties were able to address market inefficiencies (e.g., monopoly power producing higher prices or product shortages). As discussed in Chapter 1, private law instruments can help parties allocate rights more efficiently. However, private law instruments are only valid between the signatory parties. In addition, market inefficiencies often affect many third parties yet contract parties lack sufficient incentives to comply with their contractual terms. An example of the former are negative externalities such as pollution. Government regulation is therefore needed to protect the public interest, imposing legal duties on parties that would not typically arise from contracts between private parties and would likely have a stronger deterrence effect (for example, criminal sanctions for serious regulatory infringements, see Chapter 10). In this way, regulation can be understood as the 'necessary exercise of collective power through government in order to cure 'market failures' to protect the public from such evils' (Ogus 2004). According to Ogus, regulation is thus justified because the 'regulatory regime can do what the market cannot' and this underpins virtually all public-interest accounts of regulation.

Ogus, A. (2004). *Regulation: Legal Form and Economic Theory.* Hart.

30–32

> Any attempt to formulate a comprehensive list of public interest goals which may be used to justify regulation would be futile, since what constitutes the 'public interest' will vary according to time, place, and the specific values held by a particular society . . .. [We] . . . construe economic welfare in terms of allocative efficiency, a situation in which resources are put to their most valuable uses . . .. [O]n certain key assumptions, the unrestricted interaction of market forces generates such efficiency. In the real world in many sets of circumstances these assumptions, notably adequate information, competition, and the absence of externalities, are not fulfilled – in short, there is 'market failure'. Many

> instances of market failure are remediable, in theory at least, by private law and thus by instruments which are compatible with the market system in the sense that collective action is not required. But ... private law cannot always provide an effective solution. Where, then, 'market failure' is accompanied by 'private law failure'... there is a prima facie case for regulatory intervention in the public interest. It is important to stress that it is only a prima facie, and not a conclusive, case for such intervention. The reason is that either the regulatory solution may be no more successful in correcting the inefficiencies than the market or private law, or that any efficiency gains to which it does give rise may be outweighed by increased transaction costs of misallocations created in other sectors of the economy. In other words, 'market failure' and 'private law failure' have to be compared with 'regulatory failure'.

Ogus points out that the meaning of public interest is contextual and situated, changing with time, place and circumstances. Welfare economics approaches to the public interest theory define the 'public interest' in terms of the most efficient allocation of scarce resources (allocative efficiency) (see also Chapter 1). In so doing, it is assumed that the pursuit of allocative efficiency reduces economic waste, thereby allowing greater opportunities for people to pursue their own version of the good life, expressed in terms of their capacity to maximise their utility, based on each person's ability to pay.

4.1.2 Non-economic Conceptions of the Public Interest Justifying Regulation

The dominance of welfare economic approaches in public interest theories of regulation has, over time, given way to non-economic or 'political' public interest justifications, oriented towards the pursuit of a variety of collective goods and values other than allocative efficiency. Distributive concerns have underpinned major environmental, safety and health regulatory intervention for more than a century. The following selected extracts cover a range of collective goals and values that have featured in academic scholarship, including the pursuit of distributive justice and the pursuit of other moral and ethical values deemed worthy of social protection. It is worth recognising, however, that many market failures raise distributive justice concerns, which we touch upon in the following examination of the turn to risk-based accounts of regulation.

4.1.2.1 Risk Management

The concept and language of risk is increasingly relied upon to describe the justification for regulatory intervention in terms of public interest theories of regulation. In the following extract, Julia Black observes that although risk is now used to describe the object of regulation (see Chapter 2), how we identify what counts as a 'risk' that warrants regulation has varied since the 1980s. Although 'risk' provides a strong regulatory narrative, this is also true of economics. For example, she points out that the public utility regulators (water, rail, telecommunications and so forth) are typically described as 'economic' regulators, whose role was typically justified in terms of correcting market failures (monopoly, barriers to entry or exit, externalities or principal-agent problems). But she notes that there is fluidity between these characterisations: risk-based justifications can subsume economics if the object of regulation is cast as 'market risk' and the purpose of regulation is framed simply as 'managing the risk of market failure'. At the same time, various 'risks' that are used to justify regulation, such as pollution or environmental risk, are classic examples of negative externalities and couched in the language of welfare economics. Yet Black claims that 'risk' is more unstable than market failure as a foundation for justifying regulation, with neoclassical economics offering a clearer basis for regulators to decide about how and when to regulate. However, risk also opens up opportunities to civil society to participate in regulatory decision-making.

Black, J. (2010). 'The Role of Risk in Regulatory Processes'. In R. Baldwin, M. Cave and M. Lodge (eds.), *The Oxford Handbook of Regulation*. Oxford University Press, 302–348.

306–308

Risk is not just being used to define the object of regulation, it is also being used as a justification for governmental regulation. Concomitantly, therefore, it is being used to determine the boundaries of the state's legitimate intervention in society. Government's role is to manage risk, and it is justified in intervening in society in the pursuit of that objective.

However, as a justification for regulation, risk provides an unstable base. For it poses the question of which risks the state should attempt to manage, through regulation, social welfare provision, or some other means, and which risks should be managed by others . . ..

Risk is thus being used as a justification for regulation but it is not alone. As noted above, economics is usually the main contender for this role. Indeed all the main textbooks on regulation since the early 1980s have used economics to provide the boundaries of the state's legitimate intervention in society, or at least in that part of it which constitutes the market.

The principles of economic liberalism provide a much clearer and, for policy makers, more stable basis on which to base decisions about when and how to regulate than does the notion of risk.

The comparative instability of risk as a justification for regulation has a number of implications. Most critically, its very contestability provides policy makers with a significant challenge, as it opens up debate as to what government should do, how, and why. In an attempt to provide some stability, some foundation on which to base risk regulation, governments and policy makers have tried to devise various 'rules' or principles for how to make decisions about risk. There is as yet no consensus as to what these principles should be, nor how they should operate in particular contexts, however. Moreover, using risk to justify regulation also has significant implications for the engagement of civil society. Just as risk creates instability for policy makers, it creates opportunities for civilians. For the very contestability of risk potentially opens the door to civil society to participate in decision-making, a door which adherence to economic rationales of regulation keeps firmly shut.

As explained below, the regulation of risk is central to the organisation of modern societies. Risk regulation (much like most areas of regulation) is focused on the anticipation and prevention of harms. This implicates the definition of priorities and protocols to follow in case of (natural) disasters and crises. As Hutter and Lloyd-Bostock suggest, regulation is justified by the belief that we are required to control the risks around us. While risk assessments are now frequently employed in support of regulatory proposals, contradictory scientific evidence may sometimes complicate the enactment of risk regulation (see Chapter 2).

Hutter, B., and Lloyd-Bostock, S. (2017). *Regulatory Crisis.* Cambridge University Press.

3–7

We use the term 'risk regulation'. Over the past two decades, regulation and risk management have become increasingly aligned, both conceptually and in practice. Contemporary regulation is dominated by concepts of risk, reflecting social theorists' recognition of the growth of 'risk' as a key organizing concept in modern societies. Concern with risk is concern with anticipation of what could happen, the aim being to avoid or reduce actual harm through anticipation and thus prevention. Increasingly, regulation is explicitly designed and discussed in terms of systematic risk assessment and prioritization . . ..

The emergence of regulation can be seen as an early expression of a key aspect of the 'risk society' thesis, namely the belief that we should be able to manage risks and control the world around us. In its early years, regulation reflected the view that the state could exercise control over the untoward effects of industrialization through the promulgation of laws, together with policing through specialist inspectorates. Since then, successive governments have introduced more and more regulations across an increasing number of areas of economic and social life, ostensibly in the hope that risks can be controlled. Regulators have been invested with the responsibility of enforcing and keeping up to date with these controls, and have also been given a growing technical role in the development of regulations. The fortunes of regulation have been variable, with some periods of great popularity, others of relative inactivity and still others of open criticism. Yet there has undoubtedly been an inexorable growth of regulation, and even during periods of apparent anti-regulation, governments have contributed to this growth through forms of 're-regulation'.

Accompanying these changes has been a shift in the relationship between regulation and disasters/crises. Disasters and crises have become some of the most extreme challenges to risk regulation systems as they may be taken to represent a failure of regulation's core mission to anticipate and manage risks. Increasingly, regulators find themselves in the spotlight as questions are raised about why regulation 'failed', effectively framing them as part of the cause of disasters and crises.

4.1.2.2 Distributive Justice

As distributional inequality has become even more pronounced over the past four decades, it has been accompanied by growing awareness that, although the public interest is served through the efficient allocation of resources, those resources should also be fairly and justly distributed within the community. Theories of distributive justice seek to specify the conditions under which the allocation of resources are considered just or fair. Before implementing new regulatory interventions, contemporary democratic states are increasingly expected to consider these implications on these conditions. Distributive justice is often associated with the principle of equality: in the treatment of persons, the distribution of opportunities and even in concrete outcomes and living standards, although there are a wide range of different ways in which theories of equality and justice are understood and conceptualised and we make no attempt to survey those theories here. It is sufficient for present purposes to note an intimate connection between the promotion of equality in the distribution of resources and the public interest underpinnings of regulatory intervention. Examples include regulations promoting affirmative action in labour law and access to education of historically underrepresented groups (for example, mandated quotas of university admission of scheduled tribes or castes in India who have historically been excluded from participation).

Although traditional regulatory scholarship has justified the need for regulation in economic terms, particularly by addressing market failures, social and distributive justice elements have not received equal attention. Narratives such as that of the meritocratic character of the US higher education system focused on economic concepts and quantifiable measurements while failing to account for historical inequalities. As Sandel explains, the lack of measures to address inequality was historically accepted due to narratives of social mobility and meritocracy (hard work and the 'American dream'). While competitive and allegedly meritocratic access to US universities could in theory help underrepresented groups, in *The Tyranny of Merit*, Sandel (2020) explains how privileged groups are able to use their financial resources to skew the system in their favour. Sandel contrasts this situation with some Northern European countries where social mobility is generally easier. This is explained by decades of egalitarian tax policies and active regulatory intervention in education (e.g., free education and generous support to students in Denmark) and labour sectors.

Sandel, M. (2020). *The Tyranny of Merit.* Farrar, Straus and Giroux.

13–23

In an unequal society, those who land on top want to believe their success is morally justified. In a meritocratic society, this means the winners must believe they have earned their success through their own talent and hard work . . ..

Those admitted [to elite colleges] with sparkling, legitimate credentials take pride in their achievements, and consider that they got in on their own. But this is, in a way, misleading. While it is true that their admission reflects dedication and hard work, it cannot really be said that it is solely their own doing. What about the parents and teachers who helped them on their way? . . . What about the good fortune to live in a society that cultivates and rewards the talents they happen to have? . . .

College admission is not the only occasion for arguments about merit. Debate about who deserves what abound in contemporary politics. On the surface, these debates are about fairness: Does everyone have a truly equal opportunity to compete for desirable goods and social positions?

But our disagreements about merit are not only about fairness. They are also about how we define success and failure, winning and losing – and about the attitude the winners should hold toward those less successful than themselves . . ..

At a time when anger against elites has brought democracy to the brink, the question of merit takes on a special urgency. We need to ask whether the solution to our fractious politics to live more faithfully by the principle of merit, or to seek a common good beyond the sorting and striving . . ..

The Rhetoric of Rising

Americans have long tolerated inequalities of income and wealth, believing that, whatever one's starting point in life, it is possible to rise from rags to riches. This faith in the possibility of upward mobility is at the heart of the American dream.

In line with this faith, mainstream parties and politicians have responded to growing inequality by calling for greater equality of opportunity – retraining workers whose jobs have disappeared due to globalization and technology; improving access to higher education; and removing barriers of race, ethnicity, and gender . . ..

But the rhetoric of rising now rings hollow. In today's economy, it is not easy to rise. Americans born to poor parents tend to stay poor as adults . . .. It is easier to rise from poverty in Canada or Germany, Denmark and other European countries than it is in the United States . . ..

Seventy percent of Americans believe the poor can make it out of poverty on their own, while only 35 percent of Europeans think so. This faith in mobility may explain why the U.S. has a less-generous welfare state than most major European countries.

4.1.2.3 Moral, Ethical Values and Human Rights

Despite the predominance of risk and economics as pre-eminent regulatory narratives, Black rightly points out that 'not all regulation is about risk, not all regulation is about economics, and not all regulation is about either of those things, but about ethical issues, or rights, to name but two', (Black 2010: 305). Throughout history, the 'public interest' – and consequently public-interest regulation – have been defined by moral and religious arguments. An example is the criminalisation of adultery. More recently, the protection of human rights is increasingly portrayed as a universal foundation for the assertion of the morality of individual persons, which justifies the need for regulatory intervention. James Nickel (1987) famously defined human rights as:

> basic moral guarantees that people in all countries and cultures allegedly have simply because they are people. Calling these guarantees 'rights' suggests that they attach to particular individuals who can invoke them, that they are of high priority, and that compliance with them is mandatory rather than discretionary. Human rights are frequently held to be universal in the sense that they exist and are available as standards of justification and criticism whether or not they are recognized and implemented by their legal system or officials of a country.

This definition of human rights focuses on their claimed *universality*, that is, they are a-cultural and a-historical as they are inherent to our human nature and on their *mandatory character*, in that human rights express moral guarantees that are necessary for even a minimal functioning of a good life. It also highlights their dual character: while human rights are moral claims that are universally valid, they might not be accorded explicit recognition as legal entitlements. Human rights serve as moral 'boundary-markers', operating as 'trumps' in political decision-making and regulation, to limit state power and provide guarantees to individuals against unlawful encroachment on their liberty. Human rights mark the boundaries between what is morally desired and which rights should be legally protected. In the extract below, Benhabib also highlights the ubiquity of human rights as a common language that has shaped regulation at the international level. Despite their universal character, human rights will shape national regulations differently given the existence of different legal and cultural traditions and the right to self-government.

> **Benhabib, S. (2008).** 'The Legitimacy of Human Rights'. *Daedalus*, 137(3), 94–104.
>
> 94, 100–104
>
> In recent years, the language of human rights has become ubiquitous around the world, shaping such nascent transnational institutions as the International Criminal Court, and justifying international interventions to halt genocide.
>
> Yet there is wide-ranging disagreement among philosophers and jurists about the nature and scope of supposedly universal human rights. Some argue that

human rights constitute the 'core of a universal thin morality' (Michael Walzer), while others claim that they form 'reasonable conditions of a world-political consensus' (Martha Nussbaum) . . ..

[T]he juridical, constitutional, and common law traditions of each human society, as well as the history of their sedimented interpretations and internal debates, will shape the legal articulation of human rights. For example, while equality before the law is a fundamental principle for all societies observing the rule of law, in many societies, such as Canada, Israel, and India, this is considered quite compatible with special immunities and entitlements that accrue to individuals in virtue of their belonging to different cultural, linguistic, and religious groups. There is, in other words, a legitimate range of variation even in the interpretation and implementation of such a basic right as that of equality before the law . . ..

When states subscribe to various international human rights conventions, a dynamic process is set into motion in civil society and the public sphere. These provisions give rise to a public language of rights articulation and claims-making for all sorts of civil society actors, who range from compliance-monitoring NGOs to women's groups, church groups, advocacy associations, and the like. This new language of public claims-articulation circulates in the unofficial public sphere, and can, and often does, impact further institutional reform and legislation.

Democratic iterations can thus explain how legal cosmopolitanism can be reconciled with the right to self-government of individual polities. In fact, my argument is stronger than this: only in a democratic polity can the varying range in the articulation of rights principles as concrete legal norms be viewed as legitimate. Democratic self-government provides the essential context within which cosmopolitan norms, which articulate moral principles, assume flesh and blood as justiciable claims that the consociates of a polity guarantee to one another. Thus, the diversity of human rights articulation in law is not incompatible with the universalism of human rights declarations. Self-governing peoples engage in creative iterations of abstract cosmopolitan principles . . ..

Basic human rights, although they are based on the moral principle of the communicative freedom of the person, are also legal rights, i.e., rights that require embodiment and instantiation in a specific legal framework. As Ronald Dworkin has observed, human rights straddle that line between morality and justice; they enable us to judge the legitimacy of law. The core content of human rights would form part of any conception of the right to have rights as well: these would include minimally the rights to life; liberty (including to freedom from slavery, serfdom, forced occupation, as well as sexual violence and sexual slavery); some form of personal property; equal freedom of thought (including religion), expression, association, and representation. Furthermore, liberty requires provisions for the 'equal value of liberty' (Rawls) through the guarantee not only of socioeconomic goods – including adequate provisions of basic nourishment, shelter, and education – but also through the right of self-government . . ..

> The discourse of human rights has often been exploited and misused by political moralists; its proper place is to guide the moral politician, be they citizens or leaders. All that we can offer as philosophers is a clarification of what we can regard as legitimate and just in the domain of human rights themselves.

The extract also warns against the misuse of human rights in moral debates. Therefore, drawing on the protection of human rights to justify regulation is often complex. Human rights may be thus more helpfully understood as core boundary markers that set absolute limits to what can and cannot be permitted.

4.1.3 Critiques of Public Interest Theories

Public interest theories of regulation have been criticised on various grounds. Real-world dynamics between regulators and market actors may not produce outcomes aligned with the public interest. That said, these critiques are arguably misplaced, for the aim of public interest theories is not to explain why real-world regulation emerges in a particular form but more modestly to identify whether normative grounds exist to justify regulatory intervention. Unlike public interest theories, private interest theories are *not* primarily concerned with normative justifications for regulation. Rather, as Section 4.2 explains, they are prescriptive accounts that seek to explain the complex dynamics between different market actors, stakeholders and public officials situated in a given socio-economic, political and cultural time and place. They seek to explain, for example, why regulation may fail to pursue the public interest. They do not offer prescriptions on how address to such problems. Private interest theories assume that regulation emerges from the actions of individuals or groups motivated to maximise their self-interest.

4.2 Private Interest Theories of Regulation

Advocates of private interest theories of regulation are typically sceptical about the assumptions made by public interest theorists that regulators are benevolent and motivated to regulate only for the benefit of society as a whole. When regulation serves in practice to promote the public interest, private interest theorists would consider this a coincidental outcome, rather than intentionally produced thanks to the skilful and public-spirited motives and activities of a public regulator. We discuss two different but related varieties of economic private interest theories: (i) the Chicago School of thought, namely through the discussion of regulatory capture and special interest groups and (ii) public choice theories. We discuss first regulatory capture in light of recent scholarly refinements (see Box 4.1 on the Boeing 737 Max airplanes, which were grounded in 2019, following two fatal airplane crashes as an illuminating example of the dynamics of regulatory capture). We then consider public choice theories of regulation that focus on how citizens collectively choose the rules that govern their affairs. On public choice accounts of regulation, the provision of regulation itself is characterised as a 'product' that results from the interplay of forces of supply and demand in the political arena.

4.2.1 The Chicago Economic Theory of Regulation

Private interest theories expect that market actors will attempt to influence regulatory decisions that will serve to benefit their own narrow special interests rather than the collective welfare. These outcomes arise due to either or both 'regulatory failure' and 'regulatory capture'. Regulatory failure arises when the collective costs of regulation outweigh its benefits, while regulatory capture is one important way in which regulatory failure may arise: it occurs when officials within regulatory institutions develop such close relationships with market actors they regulate that they start promoting the narrow interests of this group instead of the public interest of the broader community so that regulatory policies end up serving the interests of the branch of the industry involved rather than the public interest. The term 'regulatory capture' has been variously interpreted by scholars and, as the extract from Carpenter and Moss suggests, requires more nuanced handling. They distinguish between strong and weak capture: in the former case, capture impairs the goal of regulation of pursuing the public interest; in the latter, regulatory capture can be the result of a compromise between regulators and market actors, which may nevertheless serve the public interest.

Carpenter, D., and Moss, D. A. (2014). 'Introduction'. In D. Carpenter and D. A. Moss (eds.), *Preventing Regulatory Capture: Special Interest Influence and How to Limit It*. Cambridge University Press, 1–22.

3–12

[R]egulatory capture is very commonly misdiagnosed and mistreated. Misdiagnosed because the study of regulatory capture, in both academic and policy circles, has grown stale and ever more detached from practice. All too often, observers are quick to see capture as the explanation for almost any regulatory problem, making large-scale inferences about agencies and their cultures without a careful look at the evidence. At the same time, there appears to be a great deal of fatalism – some of it strategic, no doubt – about the impossibility of ameliorating or preventing capture, virtually ensuring that the ailment is mistreated in many cases. Some or even much of this may be the product of highly simplified models – models in which the complete capture of regulators by incumbent firms is all but inevitable . . ..

Degrees of Capture: Strong vs Weak

As a first step, we distinguish between strong capture and weak capture. [To] the extent capture exists, it prevails by degrees rather than by its presence or

> absence. A critical corollary of this argument is that the existence of capture need not translate into a rationale for full-scale dismantling of regulation. Although a sufficiently high level of capture (what we call strong capture) can vitiate the purposes and rationale for regulation, much capture is likely of the weaker form, such that its existence can and does coincide with healthy regulatory functioning. This is not to deny that, where weaker capture exists, it would be better for the polity and the economy to reduce its severity. Yet reducing the severity of capture – or . . . preventing capture – is a far cry from responding to the threat of capture through the wholesale purging of regulation. Strong capture violates the public interest to such an extent that the public would be better served by either (a) no regulation of the activity in question – because the benefits of regulation are outweighed by the costs of capture, or (b) comprehensive replacement of the policy and agency in question. For example, if captured regulation reduced consumer welfare (on net) by completely blocking entry into an industry, this would be a case of strong capture – precisely the sort that Stigler and his disciples saw (and, to some extent, still see) as an inevitable fact of life in regulation, in both developed and developing economies. In Stigler's writings, the existence of capture is enough to reject the public interest theory of regulation altogether. This rejection not only means factually that democracy is not working as advertised, but also that the proper policy response is to weaken or fully remove regulation. It is of course possible that reform of strongly captured regulation would be better than non-regulation, yet for purposes of definition we assume that there might exist a form of capture so robust and incorrigible that it cannot be reformed and hence that abandoning the resulting regulation entirely would best serve the public interest.
>
> *Weak capture*, by contrast, occurs when special interest influence compromises the capacity of regulation to enhance the public interest, but the public is still being served by regulation, relative to the baseline of no regulation. In other words, weak capture prevails when the net social benefits of regulation are diminished as a result of special interest influence, but remain positive overall.
>
> Our priors are that some amount of weak capture may well be fairly ubiquitous . . .. When capture exists, it appears to be empirically limited rather than empirically pervasive. The picture that emerges, therefore, is quite different from the one George Stigler envisioned, in which capture by industry was virtually inevitable and complete. As a result, the optimal policy responses may be quite different as well. When capture is empirically limited, it is much less likely to vitiate the potential benefits of regulation and is more likely, in our terms, to take the form of weak capture than of strong.

Regulatory capture can be explained by standard economic incentives, driving well-intentioned regulators to cater to the interest of the regulatees. Capture might result from information asymmetries between regulators and the firms they are tasked to regulate. Box 4.1 on the regulation of Boeing 737 Max illustrates how this serious case of regulatory capture can have deadly and devastating consequences.

Box 4.1 Regulatory Capture and Boeing 737 Max

In 2018 and 2019 the new Boeing 737 Max crashed twice, killing 346 people. In the United States, the Federal Aviation Authority (FAA) is responsible for certifying the safety of commercial aircrafts such as the 737 Max. The FAA had delegated much of the testing and inspection work to Boeing. Delegation was legally permissible, provided that the FAA monitored Boeing. While this is a common practice in the aviation sector, delegation in this instance can be explained primarily as a result of limited agency resources. For the FAA, however, monitoring of Boeing was challenging due to the aircraft's technical complexity. Boeing reportedly pressured the FAA to grant swift approval to key aspects of the 737 Max, and successfully persuaded the FAA to refrain from classifying aircraft's anti-stall system as 'safety critical'. This system is designed to prevent the airplane from accidentally stalling when airborne. Yet Boeing had concealed internal test data from the FAA that showed that if a pilot took longer than ten seconds to recognise that the system had been erroneously triggered, the consequences would be 'catastrophic'. In addition, the relationship between the FAA and Boeing was one in which top FAA employees were offered significant career incentives to cooperate with Boeing. For example, Ali Bahrami, the FAA head of aviation safety, moved from the FAA to an industry association that advocated for Boeing and then subsequently returned to employment with the FAA. A Brookings report suggests that these employment dynamics (the 'revolving door dynamics'), which are typical of regulatory capture, may have influenced some FAA managers to approve the Boeing 737 Max, endorsing the views of Boeing's management over their own staff engineers on multiple issues.

Sources

Raso, C. (2019). 'Boeing Crisis Illustrates Risks of Delegated Regulatory Authority'. Brookings, www.brookings.edu/articles/boeing-crisis-illustrates-risks-of-delegated-regulatory-authority/.

Shepardson, D. (2023). 'US FAA Tightens Aircraft Certification Oversight after Boeing MAX Crashes'. Reuters (29 November), www.reuters.com/business/aerospace-defense/us-faa-requires-key-flight-control-changes-be-deemed-major-2023-11-28/.

Regulatory capture may also occur in field of environmental protection in which pressure from private interest groups may be intense. This ability of private actors to lobby for regulation in their favour is one of the main criticisms of public interest theories of regulation. This is illustrated by Box 4.2 discussing the case of Roundup, highlighting the pressure exerted by special interest groups in favour of allowing the commercialisation of a product despite its alleged potential carcinogenic components.

4.2.2 Public Choice

Public choice is a private interest theory of regulation that focuses on the study of taxation and public spending. Drawing on principles and concepts from the discipline of economics, public choice theorists characterise regulators as self-interested actors operating in a 'market' for political and regulatory benefits.

Box 4.2 Roundup and Special Interest Groups

Roundup is an herbicide, the world's leading weed killer, produced by Monsanto/Bayer. While several independent studies have found that the primary ingredient (glyphosate) in Roundup may potentially be carcinogenic, Monsanto/Bayer has insisted for years that the product is safe. Regulators throughout the world continue to allow the product to be sold, even though many large retailers have removed it from their shelves. There is mixed evidence on its effects to human health.

In a 2020 report by the EPA, the US federal regulator for environmental protection, concluded there were no risks of concern to human health when glyphosate was used according to the label. The agency's evaluation focused primarily on risks arising from dietary exposure to pure glyphosate, rather than exposure to the Roundup formula. The agency did not place sufficient weight on other toxicology studies done on Roundup. These findings on human health risk were consistent with the conclusions of science reviews by many other countries and other federal agencies. However, the media published information on leaked documents suggesting that Monsanto may have paid experts to support its safety claims, ghost-wrote scientific studies on the safety of Roundup and successfully lobbied regulators at the EPA to keep the agency's own findings – that glyphosate was harmful to humans – under wraps. The EPA continued to partially review the product for two more years. On 23 September 2022, the EPA announced its withdrawal of all remaining portions of the interim review decision for glyphosate and decided that 'pesticide products containing glyphosate continue to remain on the market and can be used according to the product label'.

Until 2021, Monsanto/Bayer had been subject to 125,000 lawsuits linked to the Roundup weed-killer. Settlement payments were estimated at $9.6 billion. Despite the thousands of lawsuits and the existence of contradictory information and studies, EPA deemed glyphosate safe at the time of writing 'when used according to the label'.

Sources

Hakim, D. (2017). 'Monsanto Weed Killer Roundup Faces New Doubts on Safety in Unsealed Documents'. *New York Times* (14 May), www.nytimes.com/2017/03/14/business/monsanto-roundup-safety-lawsuit.html.

EPA (2022). 'EPA Withdraws Glyphosate Interim Decision', US Environmental Protection Agency (23 September), www.epa.gov/pesticides/epa-withdraws-glyphosate-interim-decision.

Croley critically summarises this vision of why regulation emerges: regulation is viewed as a product that is demanded by market actors and supplied by state regulators. When market forces supporting demand are stronger, regulation (the product) will be delivered accordingly so as to favour them. As Croley explains, citizens rarely control their elected officials because they are largely uninformed about the regulatory process and its outcomes, their participation is limited to specific moments (elections, consultations) and they are ultimately a group of individuals with diffuse interests, lacking the strong interests and incentives to collaborate and organise collectively to lobby for a specific regulation. Regulation-seeking groups are better organised, have funding for lobbying regulators and are thus able to better influence the regulatory process.

Croley, S. P. (1998). 'Theories of Regulation: Incorporating the Administrative Process'. *Columbia Law Review*, 98, 1–168.

34–40

The public choice theory of regulation analogizes regulatory decision-making to market decision-making. Specifically, it treats legislative, regulatory, and electoral institutions as an economy in which the relevant actors– including ordinary citizens, legislators, agencies, and organised interest groups most affected by regulatory policies – exchange regulatory 'goods', which are 'demanded' and 'supplied' according to the same basic principles governing the demand and supply of ordinary economic goods. Such regulatory goods include, for example, direct cash subsidies, controls over entry into a market, such as tariffs, controls over the substitutes and complements of economic goods, and price controls. These regulatory goods are demanded by those who stand to gain from them . . .. Regulatory trades take place, then, because they further the (private) economic interests of those on the demand side and the (private) political interests of those on the supply side. The resources necessary to meet suppliers' political needs constitute the 'price' of regulatory goods . . ..

Simply stated, the regulatory interests of the individual voter (or the consumer) are dominated by the regulatory interests of organised subgroups of the citizenry because the latter have incentives to influence regulatory decision-making which the former lacks. The individual voter lacks such incentives given the benefit-cost trade-off of pursuing her regulatory interests: The benefits are low; the costs relatively high . . ..

[C]ollective action barriers constitute the individual voter's main obstacle to organizing to further her regulatory interests; the individual consumer's 'rewards' from her own contribution would be 'negligible' . . .. [F]or reasons deeply rooted in the logic of collective action, most citizens lack any real incentive to try to influence regulatory outcomes.

Thus, while the public choice theory analogises regulatory behavior to market behavior, it also holds that the analogy ultimately breaks down. From the vantage point of ordinary citizens, the crucial differences between regulatory decisions and market decisions are threefold. First, regulatory decisions are 'all-or-nothing' propositions: Whereas in the economic marketplace citizens can decide to patronise airlines or rail lines, or neither, as their individual needs require, a regulatory decision about whether to provide favorable regulation to either affects all citizens, whether they fly, ride the rails, or neither. The scope of regulatory decisions extends across virtually all citizens, who are affected by those decisions at least on the financing side. And once the state makes a decision about which package of regulatory goods to supply, individual voters have no opportunity to 'exit' the regulatory market. Second, regulatory decisions are more permanent than marketplace decisions. Whereas a citizen could elect to fly one week, and then ride a train the next, the collective decision to provide a federal subsidy to the airlines or to the railroads will not be frequently re-examined once made. Finally, regulatory decisions are collective decisions, and,

> as such, must be made simultaneously. Where some decision depends on whether its supporters outnumber its detractors, those supporters and detractors must, at some discrete point and time, be counted.
>
> Because regulatory decisions are, relative to market decisions, infrequent, simultaneous, and global, regulatory outcomes are undisciplined: Individual citizens have little or no occasion for registering their regulatory interests, including their interests against regulatory policies that bring them no benefits .... Because most citizens are largely uninformed about most regulatory decisions, and because they moreover lack incentives to become sufficiently informed to reward legislators who do not shirk, legislators do not – cannot – protect the broad regulatory interests of their constituencies. This is true because organised interest groups – industry groups, occupational groups, and trade associations – who are informed because they have an especially high demand for regulatory goods do monitor legislators, punishing those who consistently fail to provide such goods and rewarding those who provide favorable regulation. Thus interest groups capitalise on the opportunities created by principal-agent slack, made worse by most voters' collective action problems, in order to buy regulatory goods that advantage them ....
>
> Given that the benefits of regulatory goods are higher for organised groups than for individual voters, the former enjoy much more influence – offer higher bids – in regulatory decision-making relative to the latter.
>
> Not that the price of favorable regulation is cheap .... Regulation-seeking groups must front the costs of communicating with politicians and participating in political decision-making, including the costs of consultants, lawyers, and lobbyists ....
>
> [T]he regulatory market works, on the whole, to the advantage of organised groups with narrow interests. Interest groups with the most at stake in a particular regulatory decision, who spend the most to buy that decision, typically see their demand for regulation met by legislators who acquiesce in order to enjoy continued electoral success and the benefits that holding office brings. In the process, ordinary citizens lose, though they rarely feel their loss in any particular case. Nor is the end result purely distributional. The regulatory goods that organised groups obtain often come at a price not worth their costs; concentrated group gains usually 'fall short of the [diffuse] damage to the rest of the community'. Thus are regulatory policies typically inefficient. As regulatory goods are sold to groups representing concentrated interests, the few gain, and the many lose by more.

Early work on public choice viewed the shortcomings of collective action as a justification for minimising the role of government. More recent scholarship focuses on how institutions evolve to address these pitfalls. The most important contribution of public choice is the nuanced understanding of the dynamics between public and private actors. This dynamic also underlies the following subsection on hybrid theories.

4.3 Institutionalist Theories

We now turn to a third group of theories of regulation, which we describe as 'institutionalist' theories, that are something of a grab-bag of mixed approaches. These theories allow for greater institutional complexity, reflecting the permeable and sometimes porous boundaries of any given regulatory regime. They recognise that significant interactions occur between actors in and across the various multi-layered arenas in which regulation occurs. These theories pose challenges to two fundamental premises that have traditionally underpinned both public and private theories of regulation. Firstly, they question the concept of a distinct 'public-private divide', challenging the idea that there is a clear separation between public and private actors and sources of authority. Secondly, these theories question the feasibility of differentiating the pursuit of the 'public interest' from the private interests of specific groups or actors. We consider two broad kinds of approach, which we group together under the headings of 'systems theory' and 'network' theories, respectively. Both of these approaches give considerable prominence to the role of non-state actors, to the transnational contexts of regulatory rule-making and their networked and dynamic nature of interactions that occur between actors in these fora.

4.3.1 Complexity and Systems Theories

What we refer to as 'systems theory' and 'complexity theory' can be understood, at least in part, as scholarly responses to reductionist approaches to the study of regulation that rely on simplifying concepts and abstractions that fail to reflect the complexity of the social world in which we live. Drawing on natural sciences, complexity theory seeks to understand the structure and behaviour of so-called complex systems, highlighting ways in which co-operative interactions of different components and elements within the system may produce 'emergent' behaviour, which may result in unpredictable interactions, outcomes and events. Examples of complex systems include the human immune system, environmental ecologies systems and the dynamics of distributed computing architectures such as the Internet.

For systems theorists, regulatory intervention is best pursued through indirect influence, drawing upon the 'cognitive openness' of social subsystems in order to overcome the limits of their 'normative closure'. This approach is described as 'proceduralisation' in the following extract concerning autopoietic systems. This theory draws on Luhmann's analyses of society's functional systems and it was further developed by Teubner, evolving into a theory of regulation.

Scott, C. (2004). 'Regulation in the Age of Governance: The Rise of the Post-regulatory State'. In J. Jordana and D. Levi-Faur (eds.), *The Politics of Regulation*. Edward Elgar, 145–176.

151–154

For the legal theory of autopoiesis (LTA) the problem of control is a problem of communication. Autopoiesis is a term developed initially in biological sciences, derived from Greek words meaning self-producing, and refers to the idea that law reproduces itself according to its own norms. The problem which the theory addresses is centrally concerned with the difficulties that politics, economy, society and law have in communicating with each other and thus exercising control. Can legislatures create new legal rules and simply expect that they will be translated into laws which are effective in the legal system and which produce the desired changes in behaviour by economic and social actors? The central hypothesis of LTA is that such an expectation would, generally, be far-fetched. LTA provides an explanatory theory for the problems of regulatory control with some ideas as to how such problems might be addressed.

Developing a systems theory perspective associated with the work of Niklas Luhmann LTA perceives the world as consisting of differentiated and autonomous social subsystems. These subsystems – the political, the legal, the social and the economic are the subsystems central to regulation – are said to be cognitively open but normatively and operatively closed. Thus a subsystem is open to 'facts, situations and events of its environment'. This means that no subsystem is immune from the stimulation of its external environment, but such stimulation occurs as disturbance or perturbation. Stimuli are processed according to the normative structure of the subsystem and not the normative structure of the external environment. In the case of the legal system the distinctive character of its differentiation is its adoption of a binary code – in which actions are classified as legal or illegal, lawful or unlawful – to which its operations are oriented.

To take a simple regulatory example, within the political subsystem there may be legislation created which assigns criminal penalties to breaches of rules set down in a regulatory statute. The legislation is the instrument of communication between political and legal subsystems. The legal subsystem, operationalized through a court, receives the legislation on its own terms, processing it according to the wider normative principles of criminal law. The instrumental objectives of the political subsystem in prohibiting the targeted conduct are of no interest within the legal subsystem. The legal norms emphasize principles protective of defendants such as a requirement that intent is proven, that guilt is proved beyond reasonable doubt, and so on. The stringent application of these principles often cuts across the instrumental objectives of a regulatory regime . . ..

The leading exponent of LTA, Gunther Teubner, describes his hypothesis as to the effects of the inherent problems of communications between subsystems in terms of a 'regulatory trilemma'. At its simplest the trilemma describes the three types of problem that can arise in the relationship between law and other subsystems: law may be irrelevant to the other subsystem and of no effect ('mutual indifference'); through creeping legalism law may damage the other system which is to be regulated by inhibiting its capacity for self-reproduction; the self-reproductive capacity of the legal subsystem may be damaged through an 'oversocialisation of law' . . ..

LTA envisions a post-regulatory state in which the legal subsystem relates to other subsystems not through highly specified, or materialized, regulatory law, but rather through working with the grain of the understanding of ordering within other subsystems. Put another way, the successful implementation of regulatory law is dependent on achieving some measure of 'structural coupling'. For Teubner the interesting ways to address the problem do not follow the economic theorists down a deregulatory route emphasizing the control functions of markets, but rather towards more sophisticated, abstract and indirect forms of regulatory intervention, which he describes as 'control of self-regulation', but which is also captured in the concepts 'collaboration', 'reflexive law', 'meta-governance', and 'meta-regulation'. This approach recognizes the 'inner logic' of social systems and sets law the challenge of seeking to steer those social systems. A key aspect of this approach is re-casting the function of law from direct control to proceduralization. Such a shift in regulatory law would not end processes of juridification, but 'would help steer the process into more socially compatible channels'. This modest conception of law's capabilities has led to a concern with targeting the internal management systems of regulated entities in order to secure compliance with regulatory goals.

Thinking about the problem of the relationship between mechanisms of global governance and regulatory law, Teubner himself has invoked ideas of legal pluralism as a complement to LTA. It is, claims Teubner, civil society rather than international governance organizations which is generating effective global regulatory rules, effective in the sense that they are structurally coupled to the economic subsystem to which they apply. The key example he cites is the *lex mercatoria*, the ancient system of legal rules governing economic transactions, but he refers also to the regimes established within multinational enterprises to govern their global affairs. We could think also of international rules governing such matters as sustainability of forests and the protection of the environment from chemical pollution.

The legal theory of autopoiesis highlights important limitations to the use of law as a regulatory instrument, encouraging us to think about the normative structures within other subsystems which might provide the key to control in respect of particular sets of values. The theory suggests a modest role of law in steering or proceduralizing those activities over which control is sought, thus seeking control indirectly.

4.3.2 Networked Theories

The complexity of regulation is also reflected in what we call 'networked approaches' to regulation. These approaches are particularly important in sectors that operate through collaborative and networked relationships. The following extract introduces these networked interactions in healthcare, which is confined to the authors' preliminary reflections on the importance of relying on networked regulation, rather than their discussion of compliance (see Chapter 9). Networks are particularly suitable in complex regulatory contexts, enabling input from different sources of expertise and may help depoliticize the regulatory process.

> **van Erp, J., Wallenburg, I., and Bal, R. (2020).** 'Performance Regulation in a Networked Healthcare System: From Cosmetic to Institutionalized Compliance;. *Public* Administration, 98 (1), 46–61.
>
> 46–48
>
> The introduction of market elements in many Western healthcare systems, as an attempt to enhance performance while reducing costs, has sparked the development of multi-layered governance networks. In these networks, state actors exercise regulatory authority and share regulatory roles with hybrid and non-state actors such as hospitals, insurance companies, professional medical associations, licensing boards and accrediting bodies . . ..
>
> The central question guiding this article is: How did the institutional transition towards a more compliant DRG system take place within the networked governance structure of the Dutch healthcare system, and what role did the public regulator play in this transition? Based on extensive qualitative interviews conducted in 2012 and 2016 with various network participants as well as a survey of medical specialists, our study analyses the mechanisms that underlie the development in medical specialists' attitudes to correct coding and billing – from highly sceptical to more accepting – as well as the rapid institutionalization of compliance practices in hospital organizations . . ..
>
> Complex problems such as healthcare cost management can only be addressed by actors collaborating in networked relationships. Collaborative governance networks are arrays of vertical and horizontally aligned relationships between organizations to achieve regulatory goals that cannot be achieved effectively by a single organization. Network and collaborative governance theories indicate how governments 'take a step back' in order to create room for manoeuvre for different public and private actors operating with some degree of autonomy from central government. Networks mobilize resources and creativity in dealing with complex (regulatory) issues, and may depoliticize by focusing on technical aspects rather than the competing values underlying regulatory goals.

Another example of networked regulation can be found in the regulatory intermediary model (RIT) developed by Abbott, Levi-Faur, Snidal and others. This model offers an analytical framework for understanding the complex interactions between actors in regulatory regimes. Regulatory intermediaries (I) are 'go-between' actors who can be private actors such as for-profit certification companies that grant a safety or nutrition label to a company (regulatee, the target of regulation) (T) seeking approval from a regulator (R). This RIT model is common, for example, in food safety regulation. This model operates through 'regulatory chains', in which each actor in its own way contributes to (or stalls) the regulatory process. The extract describes briefly this model and its shortcomings. Regulatory intermediaries are commonly used to improve the regulator's operational capacity, legitimacy and expertise.

In several regulatory situations, independent intermediaries are required for the sake of effectiveness. This is the case of intermediaries employed for the assessment of the impact of regulations or dispute resolution bodies.

> **Abbott, K. W., Levi-faur, D., and Snidal, D. (2017).** 'Theorizing Regulatory Intermediaries: The RIT Model'. *The ANNALS of the American Academy of Political and Social Science*, 670(1), 14–35, https://doi.org/10.1177/0002716216688272.
>
> 14–15
>
> Regulation is typically conceived as a two-party relationship between a rule-maker or regulator (R) and a rule-taker or target (T). This conception can be represented as R → T, where R is an actor with authority and capability to regulate the target T, whose behavior it seeks to affect. In fact, however, both rulemakers and rule-takers often require various forms of external assistance and resources to accomplish their goals. To this end, they may engage with (or be engaged by) diverse intermediaries (I), which subsequently act on their behalf or in conjunction with them to achieve their regulatory goals. These intermediaries – their interests and functions, successes and failures – stand at the center of our conceptualization of regulatory governance as a three- (or more) party relationship, represented as R → I → T.
>
> Regulatory intermediaries can be private sector actors, such as for-profit certification companies, accounting firms, or credit ratings agencies; civil society groups, such as NGOs; or governmental bodies, such as transgovernmental agency networks or international organizations . . ..
>
> Regulatory intermediaries, and intermediation itself, are often contested and controversial. During the recent financial crisis, private credit ratings agencies – authorized to assess the risk of financial instruments for regulatory purposes, such as bank capital requirements – made exorbitant profits and were widely seen as both having favored private interests and having failed spectacularly . . ..
>
> The principal reason for regulators to incorporate intermediaries into the regulatory process is that intermediaries possess capacities relevant to regulation that regulators themselves lack, or that intermediaries can provide more effectively or at lower cost.

Institutional theories focus on the interaction between public and private actors but they are primarily focused on the pursuit of the public interest. There is considerable variation, however, in their underlying aims and objectives, particularly the regulatory phenomenon that they seek to explain, or to draw attention to. In Section 4.4, we discuss hybrid theories of regulation where we observe not only the collaboration between public and private actors but also the intertwining of public and private interests. These theories justify regulation in different ways and on different grounds: we group them together primarily due to their shared focus on the dynamic interaction between actors and their public interest narrative.

4.4 Hybrid Theories

We now consider 'hybrid' versions of the institutionalist and public interest theories of regulation that focus on policy responses to climate change. These approaches are primarily normative, seeking to address weaknesses in traditional public interest theories. For example, public interest theories have sought to address negative externalities such as pollution, but more recent theories argue for a more comprehensive understanding of environment harms. We also consider hybrid versions of private interest theories that describe how both private, self-interested economic processes and other dynamic interactions between interest groups, such as religious groups advocating from a particular moral standpoint, may support regulation that seeks to pursue the public interest. This is the case of the Baptists and Bootleggers theory, according to which self-interested parties may join forces to support the same regulatory outcome, despite having radically different motivations.

4.4.1 Institutionalist and Public Interest Hybrids

Traditional public interest theories – broadly referred to in the following extract as regulatory governance systems – regard environmental regulation as a response to negative externalities, such as pollution. Parker and Haines suggest that regulation should go beyond this approach and develop a more comprehensive understanding of the human embeddedness within ecological systems. This might include more radically interventionist 'top-down' measures (such as new legal and regulatory norms including criminalisation). The second challenge for ecologically rational regulatory studies is to understand how an ecologically rational approach can be supported from the ground up. This perspective draws on institutionalist views of regulation and is based on recognition of the need to rely on transnational regulation and on networks of actors.

Parker, C., and Haines, F. (2018). 'An Ecological Approach to Regulatory Studies?' *Journal of Law and Society*, 45, 136–155, https://doi.org/10.1111/jols.12083.

136–140

Regulatory studies has to date been mainly occupied with addressing the global social and economic systems crises of contemporary capitalism. Yet capitalism and indeed human development now face the existential challenge of 'abrupt global environmental change' due to anthropogenic pressure. The emerging discipline of earth systems science aims to define a 'safe operating space for human societies to develop and thrive, based on our evolving understanding of the functioning and resilience of the Earth system'. Taking earth systems seriously means recognizing that economics, capitalism, and all human governance mechanisms can only continue to operate within the ecologically safe zone for humans. While environmental regulation and governance in the past might have defined pollution and use limits for specific local waterways or airsheds and sought to limit environmental impact at a local, regional, or even national level, it is now clear that human activity is causing environmental change at a continental and planetary level . . ..

Regulatory governance systems urgently need to adapt to ensure that humanity – including business and government – operate within ecological limits at a planetary scale whilst also still responding to social and economic tensions and crises . . ..

[The] dominant policy approach, instrumentally rational regulation, sees capitalism's impact on the natural world as an 'externality' or market failure. Regulatory tools of a variety of kinds are then proposed to address environmental harms one issue at a time, with care to simultaneously promote competition and support entrepreneurialism. The most prominent alternative is responsively rational regulation, which emphasizes the interconnected nature of social, political, and economic challenges for capitalism and the need for iterated challenge, consultation, and development of regulatory policy and compliance by a plurality of networked public and private actors. Here, environmental responsibility is promoted as taking place through consultation with and in response to environmental NGOs, actors who might be seen to stand for and represent trees, rivers, environments, and animals. It recognizes, indeed hopes, virtuous and rapid change can occur when networked actors recognize that they share the burden of risk or community of fate.

[W]e argue for a . . . shift in regulatory studies scholarship and practice towards a fuller comprehension of our embeddedness as a human species (with all our business, market, legal, political, and social structures) inside ecological systems . . .. Yet much more is needed in recognition of the fact that human flourishing is only possible within ecological (as well as social, economic, and political) systems . . ..

First, an ecologically rational approach to regulation must learn to listen to ecological systems that sustain life and set boundaries to eliminate behaviour inimical to the integrity of life-support systems. This might include radically interventionist 'top-down' measures such as the establishment of legal and regulatory norms against ecocide including the criminalization of further emissions of greenhouse gases into the atmosphere by fossil-fuel companies.

The second challenge for ecologically rational regulatory studies is to understand how an ecologically rational approach can be supported from the ground up. There are already many different ways in which ecological sustainability is being pursued with a plethora of initiatives in food, alternative economic systems, and circular production. How do current regulatory regimes support and inhibit these specific initiatives that have risen to chart a sustainable future? Ecologically rational regulatory studies would ask, first, whether and how these initiatives challenge and transform the dominance of entrenched interests, production systems, and financial flows that are inherently ecologically unsustainable, and what role regulation plays in mediating conflict between the

> sustainable and the unsustainable. But various ecologically sustainable future initiatives may also be in competition with each other. Therefore, ecologically rational regulatory studies should inquire into how contestation between various ecological initiatives are themselves mediated through regulation. We argue that the coexistence of and contestation between different visions of sustainable futures is desirable and indeed generative . . .. [E]cological regulation should not assume that sustainability is monocultural but, rather, the challenge for ecological regulation is in supporting and sustaining a multiplicity of diverse initiatives that interact with one another within planetary boundaries.

In addition to calls for 'ecological regulation', which seeks to have a fuller comprehension of environmental harms, a growing body of literature on the Anthropocene – the time during which humans have had an impact on the earth – has emerged. This strand of scholarship draws on an examination of the magnitude, variety and longevity of human-induced changes, including land surface transformation and changing the composition of the atmosphere, to support a change in our approach to environmental regulation. Since these impacts are global, regulatory interventions increasingly require the action of both public and private actors.

The study of climate change encompasses various approaches to regulation. From a public interest perspective, regulation is justified by the need to reduce the causes and negative effects of climate change and their impact on the planet. However, it is also essential to understand the interests of the private actors who cause pollution as well as the dynamics between private actors and the public actors responsible for the adoption of climate change mitigating measures. In other words, the regulation of climate change is justified by public and private interests, economic and non-economic values, and it requires networks of public and private actors. It should also consider the short-term and long-term risks of harmful activities to the planet, existing and future population and ecosystems. Addressing climate change has the potential to yield long-term advantages for future generations, yet it may also result in substantial immediate costs for present-day societies.

4.4.2 Public and Private Hybrids

The theories of private interest discussed so far assume that each interest group will demand their own regulations and that interests rarely overlap. However, demand for the same regulation may hail from rather different interest groups. The bootlegger and Baptist theory argues that two different interest groups can become united for different reasons. The term 'Baptist' refers to those who are moved by high moral grounds, such as religious convictions. The term 'bootlegger' refers to the groups that are simply driven by the pursuit of economic rents. This theory combines elements of the public interest theory, the capture theory (Stigler) and Peltzman' special interest group and sheds light on important historical and current regulatory debates.

The extract refers to early twentieth-century Prohibition, which hindered the legal distribution and sale of alcoholic beverages. The religious groups that opposed alcohol consumption supported this regulatory intervention; bootleggers who sold alcohol illegally were also very supportive of the regulation, for it enabled them to make additional profits. This theory bears some resemblance with regulatory capture as Baptists and bootleggers tend to act in a similar way: by 'capturing' regulators with public interest appeals to disguise their own private interests. Modern examples of this theory can be found in morally sensitive subjects such as the legalisation of soft drugs (e.g., cannabis), prostitution and abortion.

Yandle, B. (1999). 'Bootleggers and Baptists in Retrospect'. *Regulation*, 22(3), 5–7.

5–7

Here is the essence of the theory: durable social regulation evolves when it is demanded by both of two distinctly different groups. 'Baptists' point to the moral high ground and give vital and vocal endorsement of laudable public benefits promised by a desired regulation. Baptists flourish when their moral message forms a visible foundation for political action. 'Bootleggers' are much less visible but no less vital. Bootleggers, who expect to profit from the very regulatory restrictions desired by Baptists, grease the political machinery with some of their expected proceeds. They are simply in it for the money.

The theory's name draws on colorful tales of states' efforts to regulate alcoholic beverages by banning Sunday sales at legal outlets. Baptists fervently endorsed such actions on moral grounds. Bootleggers tolerated the actions gleefully because their effect was to limit competition. It is worth noting that it is the details of a regulation that usually win the endorsement of bootleggers, not just the broader principle that may matter most to Baptists. Thus, for instance, bootleggers would not support restrictions on the Sunday consumption of alcoholic beverages, although Baptists might. Bootleggers want to limit competition, not intake. Important to the theory is the notion that bootleggers can rely on Baptists to monitor enforcement of the restrictions that benefit bootleggers . . ..

B&B explains how it is possible for public-interest arguments to serve special interests through regulation. The footnote says that rhetoric matters a lot in the world of politics but that neither well-varnished moral prompting nor unvarnished campaign contributions can do the job alone. It takes both.

B&B theory helps to explain how leaders of consumer groups help major pharmaceutical companies-the ones with approved chemical entities-by valiantly supporting a cautious FDA approval process. The theory explains why holders of permits to produce and market EPA-approved insecticides value the efforts of environmental groups who oppose rule changes that facilitate the entry of new, and sometimes less risky, substitutes. Indeed, once the theory is explained, bootleggers and Baptists seem to come out of the woodwork. They are everywhere.

Conclusion

Traditional theories of regulation argued that regulatory intervention is fundamentally explained by the need to correct market failures, that is, imperfections such as information asymmetries between market parties, which the market cannot solve by itself. Traditional theories of public interest assume that regulators are benevolent and make regulatory laws and policies to advance the public interest, often defined in efficiency or welfarist terms. As we shall see, the pursuit of economic efficiency is also manifest in different regulatory decision-making methodologies such as the cost-benefit analysis of regulation (see Chapter 5). This chapter has also considered contemporary and less economically focused approaches to regulation. These perspectives emphasize the pursuit of climate justice, equality, and other moral or ethical concerns as valid grounds for regulatory intervention. We also discussed private interest theories of regulation, which critique and seek to address deficiencies in public interest theories of regulation. Finally, we briefly examined a third category of theories that highlight the complexity of the phenomenon which regulatory intervention seeks to address, drawing attention to the processes through which regulation occurs.

Discussion Questions

1. What are the key premises of the public interest theory of regulation?
2. What are the boundaries of 'public interest' – that is, when is a group representing a 'public interest' as opposed to the interests of its (collective) members? Is the endorsement of group interests by the state a necessary component of a claim to represent the public interest?
3. Overfishing was at the root of traditional studies on the so-called Tragedy of the Commons. Recent research shows that overfishing and the abundance of plastic in oceans are highly problematic for planetary survival. How are fisheries regulated in your jurisdiction? What theory (ies) of regulation ought be used to justify the need for additional regulation?
4. Private interest groups theories describe the influence of powerful groups on regulation.
   a. Could this theory be employed to explain the exploitation of palm oil and the consequent forest depletion in some parts of the world?
   b. Provide arguments in favor and against palm oil exploitation based on institutionalist theories.
5. In March 2023, the Silicon Valley Bank (SVB), an investment bank that financed primarily start-ups in California, collapsed. At least two other smaller banks collapsed in the months that followed. Many financial analysists blamed regulators for this banking failure and feared a new global financial crisis (2008). Conduct some research into the facts that characterise the failure of SVB and its aftermath and discuss whether this is indeed a case of regulatory failure.

5

Regulatory Policy

Introduction

Chapter 4 examined theories justifying regulation. In this chapter, we explore how questions concerning 'whether' to regulate and 'how' to do so can be approached in an 'evidence-based' way. Suppose there has been a surge in construction site accidents, leading to more cases of hospitalised workers with brain damage. Introducing a regulation for improved worker safety may require companies to purchase new equipment for their employees, such as specific types of helmets. However, the new regulation may be ill-advised if the costs for businesses far exceed the safety benefits delivered. This example raises crucial questions about quantifying worker safety and human life. These are dilemmas regularly faced by public regulators and thus central to our analysis in this chapter.

Since World War II, public regulators, facing budget constraints and mounting criticism about a growing number of inconsistent regulations, sought to professionalise the regulatory decision-making process by employing evidence-based methods. The chapter focuses on three methods: cost-benefit analysis (CBA), regulatory impact assessment (RIA) and consultations. Regulators turn to these methods to understand the problem and create an evidence base for a new regulatory proposal. This helps stakeholders comprehend how regulatory decisions are made and what interests were considered. The chapter focuses on the work of public regulators, particularly those typically responsible for specific sectors such as health, transportation, energy and financial markets.

The chapter critically presents these evidence-based methods within their historical context. Section 5.1 discusses the historical background of regulatory policy, an interdisciplinary field focused on regulatory decision-making methods. Section 5.2 focuses on cost-benefit analysis, primarily quantifying the costs and benefits of regulation. Section 5.3 discusses RIAs, considering costs, benefits and overall impact on stakeholders, aiming to improve the 'quality' of regulation. Section 5.4 examines consultations, gathering input from stakeholders to confer additional legitimacy to the regulatory decision-making process.

While the chapter distinguishes between CBA and RIA for pedagogical purposes, in practice, RIA typically encompasses CBA as one of its steps. In the United States, public regulators conduct RIAs, but the academic debate on regulatory decision-making tends to focus on CBA. Worldwide, the OECD has been a primary driver in diffusing regulatory policy.

5.1 Regulatory Policy: Historical Background

We begin with a historical account, tracing the development of regulatory policy against the backdrop of important political and socioeconomic conditions arising during the previous century: (i) the 1930s regulatory reforms in the United States following the Great Depression (the New Deal), (ii) waves of privatisation and deregulation during the 1970s and 1980s as a response to the OPEC oil crisis (Deregulation) and (iii) the global development of regulatory policy and regulatory quality narratives as a reaction to the economic boom of the 1990s.

5.1.1 The New Deal

When US President Franklin Roosevelt took office in 1933 amid the Great Depression, he implemented the 'New Deal' to address the prevailing economic crisis. This comprehensive set of programs and regulations marked a significant regulatory reform impacting various domains including education, employment and financial markets. The New Deal expanded federal regulatory powers, with the Administrative Procedure Act (APA) of 1946 establishing procedures for regulatory agencies. While providing relief programs, the New Deal also reshaped the executive branch's role.

The APA granted regulatory agencies considerable powers with limited executive oversight, leading to a proliferation of regulations without thorough assessments of their necessity, effectiveness and costs. In the following extract, Wiener and Alemanno discuss the emergence of regulatory policy against this historical background. They suggest that, while regulatory intervention is traditionally justified in terms of addressing market failure, the uncoordinated adoption of regulation without oversight allowed room for irrational or unjustified measures. Lack of effective oversight led to regulators being influenced by private interests, and thus often failed to serve the public interest (see Chapter 4).

Wiener, J., and Alemanno, A. (2011). 'Comparing Regulatory Oversight Bodies across the Atlantic: The Office of Information and Regulatory Affairs in the US and the Impact Assessment Board in the EU'. In S. Rose-Ackerman and P. Lindseth (eds.), *Comparative Administrative Law*. Edward Elgar, 309–355.

309–311

> Wherever societies engage in economic activity (which is to say everywhere), demand arises for regulation by the state to curb the undesirable impacts of that activity. In the real world of imperfect markets, regulations can be necessary to correct market failures such as externalities (e.g. health, safety and environmental risks), asymmetric information (e.g. in financial or labor markets), and market power (e.g. entry barriers), as well as correcting other problems such as unfair discrimination. Although regulation can solve such social problems, it can also impose its own problems, including compliance costs, inhibition of innovation, ancillary risks, and rent seeking. Regulators may make mistakes, may choose poorly designed regulations, may neglect social goals other than their own narrow mission . . . may neglect the adverse impacts of their decisions, may aggrandise their own power, or may serve the interests of narrow groups rather than promoting broader public well- being . . ..
>
> Regulators may pursue policies that reduce some risks while introducing new risks or shifting risks to other populations (risk-risk tradeoffs), where regulators are hampered by limited information, bounded decision domains, or the omitted voice of the affected populations . . .. Political scientists and institutional economists have emphasized that in democracies, government decisions are not taken by a single ruler but instead represent a complex aggregation of preferences advocated by specific interest groups and often mediated through contending institutions. Because learning about issues and expressing political voice are costly, the shared general interests of the public at large may go underrepresented while the narrow interests of pressure groups are trumpeted . . .. As a result, wherever states deploy regulation, demand arises for oversight of the regulatory system to reduce the costs and side effects of regulation, promote efficiency in standard- setting and instrument choice, encourage consistency and transparency, ensure accountability, and improve the overall social outcomes of regulation.

By the end of 1970s, the state of the regulatory nation was in disrepair: regulations were poorly written, incoherent, ineffective and imposed high costs on businesses, government and society as a whole. The politicisation of the regulatory process, regulatory inertia and the lack of regulatory oversight were to blame. A new, more rational and efficient approach to regulation was needed.

5.1.2 The 1970s: CBA, Deregulation and Quantification

Jimmy Carter's 1976 US presidential campaign promised regulatory reform and selective deregulation. The Carter Administration (1977–1981) introduced cost-benefit analysis (CBA) to reduce regulatory burdens and increase accountability (see Chapter 12). Agencies used CBA to rationalise regulations rather than resist calls for them. Livermore and Revesz's history of CBA highlights its emergence in 1981 under Executive Order 12,291, directing agencies to perform CBA on major regulations. Supported by technocrats and advocates of smaller government, CBA outlived the Reagan Administration, continued through periods of divided government and saw minimal changes under Clinton. Reagan's significant reform included the Office of Information and Regulatory Affairs (OIRA) and mandated CBA for major rule-makings, continuing its systematic review.

Livermore, M. A., and Revesz, R. L. (2021). *Reviving Rationality: Saving Cost-Benefit Analysis for the Sake of the Environment and Our Health.* Oxford University Press.

18–24

For purposes of controlling regulatory decisions, perhaps the most important institutional innovation within the presidential bureaucracy came at the beginning of the Reagan administration, with the creation of the system of regulatory review overseen by the Office of Information and Regulatory Affairs (OIRA), within the Office of Management and Budget in the White House. OIRA remains relatively obscure and little known among the broader public, but for four decades it has played an extremely important role. Executive Order 12,291, issued by Reagan less than a month after he took office in 1981, required that agencies conduct a cost-benefit analysis of all major rulemakings and submit their proposed rules to OIRA for review. This relatively simple-sounding procedure inserted the White House directly into the regulatory process and established cost-benefit analysis as the substantive standard that was intended to guide agency decision making . . ..

Cabining Political Influence

When President Clinton took office, it was not clear what his election meant for the future of US politics . . ..

One centerpiece of the Clinton approach was his Executive Order 12,866.27 Building on the basic structure of Reagan's Executive Order 12,291, the Clinton Order continued the practice of requiring agencies to conduct cost-benefit analyses of their regulations and subjecting those analyses to OIRA review. However, the Clinton Order did include several substantive and process reforms . . .. [The] Clinton Order included several provisions to make OIRA review more transparent . . ..

The two decades after Clinton's election featured multiple iterations of every possible party alignment in the political branches, with both Democratic and Republican presidents facing both friendly and hostile Congresses. What emerged were two distinctive but also related visions of the regulatory system . . ..

First under President Clinton and then under President Obama, Democratic administrations forged a distinctive identity on regulatory issues. To some degree, the Clinton/Obama approach borrowed some of the regulatory reform ideas that circulated among more moderate Republicans during the 1980s and 1990s – ideas that included the use of cost-benefit analysis to evaluate rules and

> the use of more flexible, market-based instruments to achieve regulatory goals. But the Democratic administrations also had to balance voices from the left on regulatory issues, which tended to be both more focused on using government policy to reduce risks and less concerned with costs imposed on large businesses.
>
> These dynamics between the two parties established a kind of 'Overton Window' on regulatory policies. Named for Joseph P. Overton, who was senior vice president at a free-market think tank in Michigan, the idea of an Overton Window is that there is a certain range of views that are considered acceptable in public discourse, with ideas toward the center of the window forming the basis for policy reforms. For those who find themselves at the fringes of the Overton Window (as Overton himself did), the goal of advocacy is to shift the window so that ideas once considered radical become widely accepted. A recent example of a shift in the Overton Window has occurred on the issues of marriage equality and marijuana legalization: ideas that were once relegated to advocates outside the mainstream have become broadly accepted over the course of the past two decades . . ..
>
> The regulatory Overton Window does not capture the entire spectrum of views but instead reflects the broad consensus among elites within the two political parties. Many Democratic constituencies, such as labor unions and environmentalists, argued that cost-benefit analysis should be abandoned altogether, while libertarians and free-market advocates urged for a radically scaled-back role for government and a reinvigoration of the idea of economic rights. But, in general, these more radical ideas did not succeed in broadly shifting the policy landscape . . ..
>
> With the election of Donald Trump in 2016, the settled dynamics governing administrative governance have broken down. Under Trump, OIRA has largely lost either the desire or ability to effectively perform its oversight role, and cost-benefit analysis has been subject to flagrant manipulation.

CBA was historically presented as a bipartisan economic method to assess the need for new regulatory measures and, thus far, all US presidents have subscribed to it. However, the politics of CBA are nuanced. First, each president changed it slightly and employed it for different political purposes. While in the 1990s, CBA lost its deregulatory nature, more recently, many industries started exerting pressure again on their representatives to deregulate. As a presidential candidate, Donald Trump promised to attend to these requests and upon his election, he drafted a deregulatory agenda attacking existing regulatory tools. Since CBA had become a hindrance to Trump's perception of deregulation, the Trump Administration (2017–2021) also tried to manipulate it. Trump's presidency tried to rely on CBA to target unwelcome regulations in the automotive sector, on hazardous pollutants, energy efficiency and the Clean Power Plan, which aims to reduce greenhouse gas emissions. In the 1990s, a new narrative focused on regulatory quality sought to address some of the shortcomings of CBA.

5.1.3 The 1990s: Regulatory Quality

In the 1990s, the Regulatory Impact Assessment (RIA) emerged as a more comprehensive regulatory appraisal method. Initially focused on identifying the costs of regulatory burdens, RIA evolved from a quantitative emphasis on less regulation to a broader assessment considering non-economic elements, guided by the aim of 'better regulation'. This shift was facilitated by the development of regulatory policy as a multidisciplinary field drawing on insights from various scientific fields, such as economics. High-quality regulatory policy requires regulators to clearly define public problems, like reducing traffic congestion, and use decision-making methods like CBA and RIA to determine whether to regulate.

Since the 1990s, the OECD and the EU have played central roles in promoting 'good' regulatory policy globally. The OECD evaluates national regulatory policies, shares best practices and contributes to the advancement of regulatory policy in member states. The EU's 'Better Regulation' policies, initially responding to perceived over-regulation, aim to promote proportionate and effective regulation, addressing legitimacy concerns. Baldwin explores the meaning of 'better regulation', emphasising a concern for proportionate regulatory intervention.

Baldwin, R. (2010). 'Better Regulation: The Search and The Struggle'. In R. Baldwin, M. Cave and M. Lodge (eds.), *Oxford Handbook of Regulation.* Oxford University Press, 259–278, doi:10.1093/oxfordhb/9780199560219.003.0012.

259–264

What Is Better Regulation?

Towards the end of the last millennium, many national regulators, and their governmental overseers, sought to establish benchmarks for evaluating regulatory quality .... Representative of such efforts were those of the UK's Better Regulation Task Force .... [This] independent advisory body ... published a set of principles of better regulation which were subsequently endorsed by the government .... The principles adopted were that good regulation should be: proportionate; accountable; consistent; transparent; and targeted .... In Australia, the Office of Regulatory Review identified seven qualities of good regulation ... the minimum action necessary to achieve objectives; not unduly prescriptive; accessible, transparent, and accountable; integrated and consistent with other laws; communicated effectively; mindful of compliance burdens; and enforceable ....

At the supra national level, regulatory standards have been published by the World Bank ... and, in the EU (European Union), by the Mandelkern Report of 2002 .... The OECD has also been highly influential in driving forward its programme of better regulation. Good regulation, according to these pronouncements, should: serve clearly identified policy goals and be effective in achieving those goals; have a sound legal and empirical basis; produce benefits that justify costs, considering the distribution of effects across society and taking economic, environmental, and social effects into account; minimise costs and market distortions; promote innovation through market incentives and goal-based approaches; be clear, simple, and practical for users; be consistent with other regulations and policies; and be compatible, as far as possible with competition, trade, and investment-facilitating principles at domestic and international levels (OECD, 2005: 3).

How Can 'Better Regulation' Be Achieved?

Two core messages of the better regulation movement are that regulation can be improved by applying rational approaches to policymaking and that better regulation involves a predisposition to apply informal, low-intervention control styles rather than old-fashioned command methods . . .. What the broad better regulation message delivers, however, is a potential clash between the promotion of more expert, evidence-based regulation and the desire for less intrusive styles of control. The push towards more rational regulation has come through the placing of the Regulatory Impact Assessment (RIA) at the centre of the regulatory improvement process . . .. A typical RIA process involves an assessment of the impact of policy options and sets out the purposes, risks, benefits, and costs of the proposal . . .. RIAs are intended to inform decision-making, not to determine decisions or to substitute for political accountability. The expectation is that the RIA process will encourage better, more rational, regulation by, inter alia, clarifying objectives; identifying the lowest cost ways to achieve objectives; considering alternatives and increasing transparency (see typically: Cabinet Office, 2003) . . ..

The 'better regulation' message . . . emphasises the pursuit of improved regulation by means of a number of linked strategies . . .. Not only are policymakers encouraged to apply RIA processes, but they are urged, inter alia, to cut red tape, reduce regulatory burdens, and structure enforcement policies – notably by adopting risk-based regulatory methods (see, e.g., Hampton, 2005).

Regulatory quality can be contested and varies depending on the audience, constituency, market position and discipline. In the EU, Better Regulation programmes have attempted to respond by offering various principles and toolboxes that seek to provide more substantive guidance to regulators. EU Better Regulation principles rely on various EU Law principles such as subsidiarity, proportionality (Article 5 TEU) and the Charter of Fundamental Rights.

In recent decades, the EU's Better Regulation policy has been taken forward in different ways. Firstly, by the Regulatory Scrutiny Board, established in 2015, as a body comprising European Commission officials and experts that reviews impact assessments and selected evaluations. The second development was the creation of the Fit for Future Platform, a high-level expert group that aims to help the European Commission in its efforts to simplify EU regulations and reduce related unnecessary costs. This platform is part of the Regulatory Fitness and Performance (REFIT) programme, which was established in 2012 to promote EU regulatory efficiency, burden reduction and modernisation. Since the 1990s, the European Commission has devised 'toolboxes' for assessing regulatory quality, drawing not only on RIAs but also on compliance with EU values and law. The better regulation movement has, nonetheless, been primarily focused on regulatory simplification and one-dimensional understanding of the law and how regulation should comply with its fundamental principles.

The history of regulatory policy shows that despite potential critique, regulatory decision-making methods are valuable as they aim to inform and constrain the politics of the regulatory process. They do so by exposing the costs and benefits of a proposed regulation and its overall impact on stakeholders. The following sections provide a more detailed examination of CBA, RIAs and consultations.

5.2 Cost-benefit Analysis

In simple terms, CBA requires a regulator to calculate the costs and benefits of a proposed regulation and issue it only if the benefits exceed the costs. Over the preceding decades, CBA has become deeply entrenched in several jurisdictions either as a regulatory decision-making methodology in its own right or as part of a broader RIA. CBA rests on the premise that new regulations should only be introduced if their benefits will exceed their costs.

CBA's economic rationale is threefold. First, CBA assumes that most costs and benefits can be quantified and compared. Second, it appraises regulations assuming individuals' willingness to exchange income for the positive outcomes of regulation. If a new regulation on water savings costs \$80 billion in the short run, CBA will assess whether individuals would be willing to pay additional taxes for a certain number of years to subsidise the benefits of this new regulation. Third, CBA assumes an uneven distribution of the impact of a proposed regulation. Originally based on the Kaldor-Hicks test (see Chapter 1), CBA initially assumed that those whose welfare will be improved are willing to compensate for the individuals whose welfare is harmed. Current implementations of CBA address distribution in more simplistic terms, focusing on willingness to pay. Nonetheless, distribution of costs and benefits remains difficult to calculate when it occurs over time.

5.2.1 Discounting

CBA relies on estimating various costs of regulation using diverse methods, particularly focusing on discounting to make monetary amounts comparable across time. This process addresses the distribution of costs and benefits over time, acknowledging the impact of time flow on quantifying or monetising costs. Rowell's analysis emphasises the importance of considering the value of time, especially in discussions about the long-term effects of regulations on future generations and climate change. Discounting recognises that some benefits are visible in the short run, while other equally important costs become quantifiable only in the very long run, highlighting the need to account for a distribution of costs throughout time, especially considering the short-term horizons of elected officials. For example, when regulating plastic packages, regulators should balance the short-term benefits of allowing plastics (e.g., low cost, convenience, hygiene) against the long-term costs to the environment (e.g., plastics can take up to several centuries to decompose).

Rowell, A. (2014). 'Time in Cost-Benefit Analysis'. *UC Irvine Law Review*, 4, 1215–1240.

1216–1237

Discounting, or the process of making monetary amounts comparable in time by accounting for the time value of money, is a key aspect of intertemporal valuation in cost-benefit analysis. Discounting policy is important both because of the enormity of its potential impact on final policy decisions, and because it forms a core process allowing quantitative cost-benefit analyses to compare apples to apples, when those apples accrue at different points in time .... In response, agencies and the Office of Management and Budget (OMB) have developed sophisticated (albeit still controversial) methods for discounting future costs and benefits.

Cost-benefit analysis is dependent upon meaningful valuation techniques to support the monetization and comparison of goods, risks, and harms. Meaningful valuations, in turn, must incorporate well-drawn time-signatures to account for the time value of money. The line drawing challenges created by time flow thus poses challenges to monetization for intertemporal valuations in cost-benefit analysis. These challenges relate to discounting, because discounting is the method used to account for the time value of money, once the time signatures of various goods are identified. But the phenomenon of time flow is itself distinguishable from questions of discounting, and should be thought of as providing distinctive puzzles to regulatory analysis in general, and to cost-benefit analysis in particular.

For discounting purposes, agencies must clearly identify whether a cost or benefit will accrue in the present or in the future. Because money has a time value, time indeterminacy – whereby there is no particular time signature attached to a cost or benefit –undermines the analysis' ability to coherently monetize. So unless a regulator knows when a cost or benefit accrues, and how far into the future, she cannot meaningfully discount the impact, which means she cannot meaningfully monetize. For purposes of regulatory cost-benefit analysis, then, it is critical that regulators have a clear idea of what and when impacts will count as occurring in the present and when they will count as occurring in the future. Particularly where there is no clear starting point for the future – a point at which costs and benefits will be treated as occurring in the 'future' and therefore discounted-monetized valuations can be undermined. Unfortunately, our experience of continuous temporal flow makes it challenging to know whether the future should be taken to start tomorrow, next week, next year, or with the next generation ....

> **What Should Be the Starting Point?**
> Fortunately, precisely because the subjective flow of time deprives us of a single natural starting point, there are multiple possible reasonable choices. I suggest that agencies should use a year from initial promulgation of the analysis as their cut-off point – a practice they already use for purposes of discounting, since discounting in whole years is practically easier than using smaller periods. This aligns treatment of future costs and benefits for discounting and non-discounting purposes, and while it is still subject to the moving-target problem, it is an intuitive and reasonable starting point.
>
> What should the endpoint of an analysis be? Sometimes, of course, this will be determined by statute. But often it is not, in which case agencies must choose between many possible end points. One option in such cases would be to adopt a single consistent end point, regardless of context. This is one way to understand Posner's suggestion of ignoring distant-future generations. But some rules (like those affecting climate change) are massive and important, and will have many latent costs and benefits, and others (like small reporting requirement changes) are much smaller, or will be cost-benefit justified in a very short amount of time. This suggests that adopting a single consistent time scope, while beneficial in its simplicity, could be overinclusive for quick and unimportant rules, and underinclusive for slow-moving and important rules. Another approach to managing time scope where there are no statutory restrictions would be to embrace inconsistent time scopes, so long as those scopes were meaningfully tied to some aspect of the underlying rule.

The uneven and sometimes unforeseen distribution of costs between present and future as well as determining the endpoint for this calculation are disputed aspects of CBAs. For example, despite urgent concerns about the impact of human activities on climate change, the legal literature has suggested that CBA has 'almost always proven anti-environmental in practice . . . and in theory'. This is one of the many points of criticism to CBA.

5.2.2 Critique

CBAs are difficult to execute in practice and have been subject to critique. Rose-Ackerman critiques how CBA has been used, including the poor understanding of discounting and the fixation on monetary quantification of non-quantifiable costs (e.g., human life). Rose-Ackerman also reminds us that CBA is a method that aims to inform regulators but which does not replace the final regulatory decision, which may still be captured by private interests (see Chapter 4).

> **Rose-Ackerman, S. (2013).** 'Precaution, Proportionality, and Cost/Benefit Analysis: False Analogies'. *European Journal of Risk Regulation*, 2, 281–286, doi: 10.1017/S1867299X00003469.
>
> 284–285

> CBA is not merely an effort to measure and think about the benefits and harms of a policy. It represents a particular normative commitment, derived from utilitarianism, that puts all costs and benefits on a common scale – usually money, given the lack of a cardinal utility scale. It discounts benefits and costs to the present, adds them up, and picks the level of the policy with highest next benefit. The technique represents a normative commitment to measuring benefits and costs in terms of individual preferences and to comparing across people in terms of their willingness to pay or to accept compensation, measured in monetary terms. It is not a neutral, purely technocratic exercise. The technique is in fundamental tension with the European Commission's description of CBA as 'an aid to decisionmaking, not a substitute for political judgment.' CBA is meant to be a commitment to selecting the option that maximizes net benefits so as to avoid succumbing to partisan political judgments. Furthermore, even if one accepts the underlying premises of cost/benefit analysis, controversy arises over how to discount future benefits and harms, how to account for uncertainty, and how to measure variables – such as, human life and morbidity or the preservation of nature and wildlife – with no obvious market price. Such vexed issues are central to any discussion of whether a policy is more or less 'precautionary' . . .. Cost/benefit analysis draws both on concepts that are at the bedrock of modern economics as a technical discipline and on judgments that cannot be resolved through better techniques developed by clever economists. Rather, these judgments raise fundamental normative questions that cannot be settled by experts. They must be resolved by policymakers taking into account political realities as well as normative concerns.

CBA has long been criticised, for many reasons. First, CBA has been primarily employed as a deregulatory tool in the United States, contributing to the reduction of environmental protections and health and safety safeguards. Second, the performance of CBA in serving its intended purpose has been mixed. It has often failed adequately to assess cost due to miscalculations, technical difficulties and other practical challenges. To illustrate, regulations requiring the wearing of hard hats on construction sites may reduce skull fractures but workers wearing them may behave generally more dangerously because they feel protected. As a result, leg and arm injuries may increase. If behavioral insights (see Chapter 1) are disregarded, CBA may fail to calculate these so-called displacement effects and other hidden costs, including reductions in productivity, expenditure on responding to regulation and distortions in investment. Limitations also arise in appraising benefits due to a lack of relevant data, divergent assessments in valuing intangible impacts, the incommensurability of benefits more generally (e.g., human life, good health) and trade-offs are the most important prominent. Third, CBAs have been employed to confirm rather than to inform regulatory decisions. Fourth, CBA has limited mechanisms to consider the human dimension of regulation and the human challenges of complying with regulation. Despite efforts to 'humanise' CBA and use this method as a pragmatic tool for cataloguing, assessing, reassessing and publicising the human dimension of regulation, problems remain.

CBA has, nonetheless, facilitated the adoption of more progressive regulation when there was sufficient evidence supporting it and thus offering evidence of its effectiveness, despite the initial reluctance of its opponents.

5.2.3 Current Approaches: Climate Change, Race and Inequality

CBA historically neglects racial, gender and long-term climate concerns, with growing recognition that regulatory failures disproportionately impact under-represented groups. For instance, the 2008 Global Financial Crisis disproportionately affected African American borrowers of subprime mortgages, leading to widespread home losses. On his first day in office, President Biden emphasised the importance of CBA while prioritising racial justice, environmental stewardship and equity. This position is aligned with recent critiques against fully quantitative CBA approaches that tend to generate racially biased outcomes by assuming that race does not have an impact on how citizens experience regulation.

Luttrell and Roman-Romero discuss below how CBA contributes to reinforcing racial inequalities.

Luttrell, M., and Roman-Romero, J. (2020). 'Regulatory (In)Justice: Racism and CBA Review'. *Yale Journal on Regulation*, Notice & Comment blog, www.yalejreg.com/nc/regulatory-injustice-racism-and-cba-review-by-melissa-j-luttrell-and-jorge-roman-romero/.

Reliance on CBA to establish regulatory risk thresholds maintains and worsens these racially inequitable disparities. CBA does this: 1) directly, by ignoring – or dramatically undervaluing – equity concerns, even when the statute at issue is meant to reduce disparities; and 2) indirectly, by promoting weak health, safety, and environmental standards, a bias that – in the context of risk regulation – helps to prop up a status quo where racial disparities abound.

CBA is a deeply flawed regulatory decision criterion because it gives no weight to fairness and equity, even when CBA is used to evaluate regulations meant to promote those principles . . ..

The exclusion of distributional weights is crucial because the utility of a reduction in risk (or the utility of 'regulatory relief') depends greatly on the initial position of the individuals experiencing the benefits and losses. In other words, a hundred dollars in 'regulatory relief' that accrues to, say, Mark Zuckerberg does not offer the same utility as a hundred dollars to a family facing food insecurity. Consequently, in CBA, even when dollars are compared to dollars, agencies aren't necessarily making an 'apples to apples' comparison because the methodology fails to accurately capture the utility of both winners and losers and, therefore, one still cannot tell whether total utility has been increased *even after those gains and losses have been monetized.*

The actual utility of a reduction in risk (or the utility of some quantum of 'regulatory relief') depends greatly on the initial position of the individuals

> experiencing the benefits and losses. When *regulatory winners and losers are starting from different positions, a welfare analysis that fails to take this into account is necessarily flawed.*

Gender is another element ignored in regulatory policy. FDA and Canadian health regulations now incorporate diversity requirements in pharmaceutical testing, yet gender differences persist in healthcare, pharmaceutical research and regulation, maintaining the male body as the norm. Reshaping CBA for inequality faces challenges, as features such as discounting may not accurately assess the real costs of climate change, devaluing the future in contrast to current climate change science and policy. To address inequality, racial equity assessments, default equity plans and agency equity audits have been suggested as complements to existing steps within CBA.

5.3 Regulatory Impact Assessment

In OECD countries, RIA serves as a central methodology for appraising public policies and regulations. Similar to CBA, RIA is employed ex ante to evaluate the overall impact of a proposed regulatory intervention and is often mandatory. In the EU, RIA primarily addresses the economic, social and environmental impact of regulation. Despite national variations, RIA includes (i) an economic appraisal of the costs and benefits of a regulatory intervention, considering factors like baseline assessment and the 'do not intervene' option; (ii) a clear identification of the proposed regulation's objectives; (iii) consultation with relevant stakeholders; and (iv) an analysis of alternatives to regulation. RIA encompasses various phases and is a complex method, with this section focusing on selected elements.

In the following extract, Radaelli refers to the quantitative (estimation of costs and benefits) and qualitative dimensions of RIA. The qualitative dimensions include clearly defining the underlying problem that justifies the regulatory intervention, consideration of non-monetary impacts and defining alternatives to the proposed regulation. RIA is not merely the product of an analysis but a process that involves reporting information on how a regulatory problem was defined, who was consulted and with what effects. RIAs are not focused exclusively on reducing costs but seek to offer further transparency to the overall regulatory decision-making process, operating as a 'fire alarm'. Governments can either 'police patrol' bureaucracy through hearings, investigations and other forms of direct monitoring of regulators or 'adopt fire alarms', franchising third parties to monitor regulatory decisions and 'ring the alarm' in case of drift. As the extract mentions, RIA works as a 'fire alarm' because it controls bureaucracy via information-gathering about the proposed regulation and promotes stakeholder participation (see also Chapter 12).

Radaelli, C. (2022). 'Regulatory Impact Assessment (RIA)'. In P. Harris, A. Bitonti, C. S. Fleisher and A. Skorkjær Binderkrantz (eds.), *The Palgrave*

Encyclopedia of Interest Groups, Lobbying and Public Affairs. Palgrave Macmillan, 1122–1129, https://doi.org/10.1007/978-3-030-13895-0_136-1.

1123

Regulatory impact assessment (RIA) is a systematic appraisal of how a proposed rule and/or regulation is likely to affect certain categories of stakeholders and a range of domains such as the environment, gender, and poverty and jobs . . ..

The appraisal may be qualitative (to illustrate: a description, but not an estimation, of how a proposal will trigger effects of an economic sector such as dynamic efficiency), quantitative (e.g., a confidence interval of number of lives saved by an occupational health and safety rule), or monetary. The stakeholders considered may be those directly affected by a policy proposal, a given sector, the business-financial community, foreign investors and trade partners, and the economy as a whole. The depth of the assessment may be limited to the costs of complying with administrative obligations introduced by the proposed rule, or the total compliance cost . . .. Cost–benefit analysis is the core of RIA in countries like the USA but, for example, not in Europe. Within countries, there is vertical variation across subnational institutions depending on devolution and federal arrangements. Horizontally, many countries have dedicated approaches for independent regulators, with guidelines and tests that generally supplement the general guidance for government departments and are suitable for particular sectors, such as the utilities . . ..

RIA is a public document but also and more importantly a process. As process, it includes the essential steps of problem definition, baseline measurement, consultation, the identification of alternative feasible options, the analysis and comparison of options, compliance – enforcement – implementation analysis . . . the final choice of an option based on explicit criteria for decision, and information on how the new regulation will be monitored/evaluated . . ..

Theoretical rationale: RIA as administrative procedure allows stakeholders to observe and be involved in rulemaking *in vivo*. Consultation, notification of the steps leading to new proposals, publication of data, and analyses allow affected stakeholders to observe and respond during the formulation of new proposals. RIA is therefore a 'fire alarm' that can be pulled if and when regulators are making proposals for rules that can negatively affect a pressure group . . .. This theoretical rationale is centered on . . . [the] control of the bureaucracy.

RIA is thus a method that brings evidence into the decision-making process and enables policy learning. It aims to support regulatory decision-making and better regulation. However, those who prepare this evidence are not the decision-makers. The extract highlighted the potential disparity between adoption of RIAs and their implementation on the ground.

5.3.1 RIAs and Better Regulation

Better Regulation policies in the EU have been advanced through various principles and toolboxes. This programme aims not only to improve the quality of regulation but is deeply connected to the principles of EU law and policy. RIA seeks to improve regulatory quality in different ways. First, RIA provides a methodological framework for undertaking a systematic assessment of the economic and non-economic impact of regulation. It requires regulators to define clearly the objectives of regulation, the need for regulatory action, and informs them of the consequences of a regulatory intervention. Second, RIA promotes a set of values familiar to understandings of good governance in democratic political communities, such as transparency, accountability, consistency, targeting and proportionality. The principle of proportionality, one of the cornerstones of EU law, entails that a regulatory intervention should have a legitimate aim and be necessary, adequate and proportionate *stricto sensu*. This principle also encapsulates an efficiency rationale since it requires regulators to pursue optimisation with respect to what is legally and factually possible.

As Radaelli and Meuwese explain, better regulation is 'not just a label', it is a different way of regulating and governing with more information and more control over what regulatory choices are made, who is heard and when. RIA advances better regulation because it mandates an appraisal that would otherwise not happen. It also ensures that alternatives to regulation are considered early on and promotes regulatory legitimacy by involving stakeholders in the process. Although the extract criticises RIA's focus on procedural elements and the avoidance of hard substantive questions, Radaelli and Meuwese argue that RIA remains a useful regulatory decision-making method for stakeholders. RIA is a 'fire alarm' that can be pulled whenever regulators attempt to adopt manifestly inadequate regulations.

Radaelli, C., and Meuwese, A. C. (2010). 'Hard Questions, Hard Solutions: Proceduralisation through Impact Assessment in the EU'. West European Politics, 33, 136–153, doi: 10.1080/01402380903354189.

137–150

Better Regulation is a type of policy that, instead of looking at specific regulatory sectors or stages, takes a 'whole-of-government' approach to the life-cycle of regulation .... It is concerned with the processes through which laws and delegated rule-making are formulated, appraised, and enforced. Impact assessment (IA) is the most popular instrument of Better Regulation – it is used to appraise policy before the formal decision to regulate is taken by the government or a regulatory agency – in our case the European Commission. Other instruments of Better Regulation include rules governing processes of administrative simplification, enforcement and implementation ....

Although the [RIA] framework is all about procedure and avoids as far as possible referring to substance, all individual IAs deal with substance, since they are used to appraise the effects of proposals on a wide range of stakeholders. Some government officers may start challenging impact assessment at the technical level with the aim of establishing control on the formulation of proposals. Pressure groups have already specialised in the generation of

> counter-impact assessments to respond to the Commission's analysis of proposed legislation. The best-known examples can be found in the policy process leading up to the adoption of REACH, the major chemicals regulation that triggered outcries from both the chemicals industry which deemed it too burdensome, and environmental NGOs which thought the regulation did not go far enough. Both sides had prepared their own 'private' IAs, often in cooperation with member states, which were presented as comparable to the 'public' IAs produced by the Commission, thus lending false authority to what were essentially lobby papers. To complicate matters further, private stakeholders were given a seat around the table in an unusual process of revision (or 'renegotiation' according to some) of the original Commission IA . . . .
>
> However, our reading of the evidence on implementation of IA is that there are several ways in which the Commission has been able to fend off the attempts to use the Better Regulation agenda to exercise political control on this bureaucracy . . . . The administrative silos and 'collection of baronies' that beleaguered the Commission at the time of the interviews carried out by Kassim and Menon (2004: 28) have not disappeared, but are less powerful than in the past . . . .
>
> Exactly *because* [RIA] has a rationalistic appeal, its adoption gives the illusion of avoiding decisions on shifting competences, intra- and inter-institutional balance, and how to achieve competitiveness. Possible consequences of this head-in-the-sand strategy include detrimental ones such as symbolic politics and a tick-the-box mentality, but also more positive ones – our findings, indeed, point towards unintended learning.

As the extract suggests, RIAs 'trigger their own politics'. While RIAs may reduce the power of certain interest groups, they may still exert pressure on regulators through other, more sophisticated methods including counter-RIAs, purporting to offer contrary evidence to the foundations of the regulator's RIA.

5.3.2 Critique

In the EU context, RIAs have enhanced the reputation of EU regulation, improving stakeholder perceptions and strengthening the perceived evidence base and legitimacy of EU regulators (see Chapter 11). However, RIA faces criticism for lacking transparency in informing regulatory proposals' development. Furthermore, RIAs remain overly procedural and complex. Also, RIAs fall short of maximising their potential to improve regulatory quality by not consistently encouraging the use of policy mixes that incorporate a broader range of instruments and institutions. In addition, RIA does not align well with a reflexive and dynamic approach to regulation as it does not accompany regulations once they are implemented. Many countries also subject regulations to ex post evaluation mechanisms that reassess the effectiveness of regulation.

5.4 Consultations

Consultation of relevant stakeholders is a crucial step of RIAs: in the United States, the RIA is the object of consultations, while in the EU, consultations are one of the final steps to conclude the RIA process. Consultations serve an important instrumental purpose, advancing the quality of regulation by acquiring relevant information and input from relevant stakeholders about a proposed regulation thus facilitating the transfer and collection of dispersed knowledge. In the EU, consultations have integrated its 'Better Regulation' agenda since 2002. Stakeholder engagement in EU lawmaking (including regulations) is required by Article 11 para. 3 TEU. Consultations also serve an important intrinsic purpose, by giving those potentially affected by a proposed regulation an opportunity to raise concerns within the decision-making process. Consultations can be open to the public or limited to selected stakeholders.

5.4.1 Rationale

The principles of openness, transparency and broad consultation of stakeholders are at the heart of recent 'Better Regulation' policies. The principle of openness in particular requires that consultations are designed in an accessible and understandable way in order to maximise the participation of stakeholders. Recent technological advancements, such as online platforms, have expanded the reach of consultations, enabling ordinary citizens to participate in the rulemaking process. Originally designed for input from functional intermediaries like NGOs and trade associations, consultations have evolved to include direct citizen participation.

However, consultations were not originally designed for broad participation by citizens. Instead, they were crafted to receive public input through functional intermediaries, like NGOs, trade associations and other organised interests, formally representing the various interests affected by a given policy initiative. As the representative nature of these organisations became contested, citizens were invited to have 'their say'. However, in practice, EU participatory channels are not yet conceived so that citizens can impact directly how decisions are made (see Chapter 11).

Chapter 4 discussed how special interest groups seek to influence regulators. Consultations most certainly could come to mind as an influence mechanism, particularly for powerful businesses. The influence of consultations varies, with empirical research (Binderkrantz, Christiansen and Pedersen 2014) showing that the success of business groups in influencing regulators depends on the value of their resources to decision-makers in a specific policy area.

5.4.2 Critique

Consultations have been primarily criticised because of their limited ability to reach out to the general public and gather insights from different stakeholders. As Alemanno points out below, there is no guarantee that the most affected parties will participate in the consultations. Political inequality remains a reality, and in the EU, the quality of the consultation mechanism remains largely at the discretion of the European Commission. It is thus important to understand who participates, why and what is done with stakeholder input. Alemanno's recommends addressing political inequality in consultations through the establishment of an administrative legal procedure for consultations, reaching out to citizens through social media and making consultations less technical and multilingual. Alemanno argues that novel and more equal forms of citizen participation are required to fully democratise consultations (e.g., subsidise citizen lobbies).

> **Alemanno, A. (2020).** 'Levelling the EU Participatory Playing Field: A Legal and Policy Analysis of the Commission's Public Consultations in Light of the Principle of Political Equality'. *European Law Journal*, 26, 114–135, https://doi.org/10.1111/eulj.12371.
>
> 118–126
>
> Public consultations [are] constitutionally stamped as a democratic practice ... [but] the current consultation mechanism provides no guarantee of involvement of affected parties in procedures that concern them .... In these circumstances, the EU Commission remains de facto free in deciding what initiatives are subject to consultation, how to frame those consultations and ultimately what to do with their findings ....
>
> While participation can no longer be assumed to automatically result in increased democratic legitimacy, one has to ask – through empirically informed studies – who actually participates and what the underlying motives for that participation to occur are. The response to consultation typically shows a geographical imbalance, with a gradient of participation between the Member States in the north and western Europe and those in the south and east. It is also characterised by a limited plurality in the interests represented. Studies of EU population of interest representatives found that the participation of different types of interest is not equal. In particular, the consultation process is essentially dominated by corporate representatives, and to a lesser extent by civil society organisations, public authorities and research centres. Apart from a few exceptions, lay citizens are almost absent from the current consultative process. The Commission Better Regulation guidelines acknowledge that data gathered through public consultations does not provide a representative view of the EU population ....
>
> #### Redesigning Public Consultations
>
> *Recommendation no. 1: Establishing a legal framework for EU public participation ....*

> The proposal for a European Law of Administrative Procedure provides an excellent start to overcome current uncertainty [of consultations] and ultimately contribute to ensuring equal opportunities of access and, as a result, the actualisation of the principle of democracy. It foresees inter alia a systematic duty on the EU authority in charge of drafting the act 'to identify and address persons who are likely to be affected by the draft act and invite them to comment' . . ..
>
> *Recommendation no. 2: Implementing political equality by design . . ..*
>
> The current publicity, design, framing, language regime and overall presentation of public consultations act as confounding factors behind the unequal access to consultation for affected individuals.
>
> **Reach out via Social Media**
>
> First, public awareness and overall publicity of the EU Commission 'public' consultations remain modest. Despite the variety of communication channels available today to reach multiple target audiences, the Commission continues to privilege a centralised, and static online platform over other communication channels, such as social media, to reach out. If social media tools have entered – and are now part of – the EU communication policy, their use remains top-down, ineffective and shifting from the policy of multilingualism towards a hegemonic language policy where English dominates. An overhaul of the Commission's strategy in this field would thus be beneficial.
>
> **Multilingualism**
>
> Second, most consultations are made available in a limited number of languages, generally English, French and German. This contradicts the principle of multilingualism that must govern all interactions between the EU institutions and third parties. By now we know that when the survey is made available in all EU official languages, this translates into higher participation. Multilingualism should thus be taken seriously, not least to correct the geographical imbalance in interest representation.
>
> **De-biasing the Framing**
>
> Third, the overall framing of public consultations – typically consisting of a semi-structured survey guiding the responses – is marked by social bias. Despite the self-commitment to employ a 'stakeholder friendly language', most consultation documents and surveys employed by the Commission remain highly technical, to the point of de facto precluding wide participation, thus preventing a 'democratically relevant discussion about goals from taking place'.

The value of consultations depends on who is consulted, on what terms and how the results of consultations are taken into account. Consultations can be both legitimising and de-legitimising, depending on how they are designed, what the role of public regulators is in incentivising participation and how the delivered input is considered in the final decision. If poorly designed, they can greatly de-legitimise regulation. Because consultations are politicised, stakeholder engagement may infuse the regulatory decision-making with the politics it originally sought to control. A combination of expertise and carefully designed stakeholder engagement are recommended as the most legitimacy-enhancing solutions.

Conclusion

Regulatory decision-making methods *do not determine* whether or not to regulate. Rather, CBA, RIA and consultations *inform* regulators so that they can decide whether or not to regulate on the grounds of the best available evidence. These methods have appealed to actors who hold rather different political commitments because they evoke scientific neutrality via their reliance on quantification while enhancing the transparency and accountability of the regulatory decision-making process, particularly through the involvement of stakeholders (see Chapters 11 and 12). In many cases, they seek to reduce complex regulatory issues to appraisal reports. CBA appraises monetary costs and benefits; RIA combines complex quantitative and qualitative methods to deliver an overall assessment of the impact of regulation on relevant stakeholders; and consultations, often as part of a RIA, aim to enhance the legitimacy of regulation by involving different parties in the regulatory process.

These methodologies have been criticised because they are moulded to fit political agendas and confirm regulatory choices rather than challenge them. For example, CBA has been used to justify or oppose climate change. For every RIA that challenges industry interests, there can be a counter-RIA, offering contradictory evidence. Consultations are often drafted in such technical terms that only powerful lobby groups have the means to respond them. While these methods may have generated politics of their own, they have contributed to the improvement of the regulatory decision-making process merely by requiring regulators to explain and justify their proposed decisions.

Discussion Questions

1. From a historical perspective, would you agree that CBA can be regarded as a bipartisan regulatory decision-making methodology?
2. The OECD publishes frequent reports on the regulatory policy of its members (see OECD website). Select a recent (non-European) OECD country report and examine its recent regulatory policy. Are specific historical, social and economic elements considered?
3. In *Atlas of AI* (2021), Kate Crawford discusses the impact of mining of rare earth metals and the depletion of other natural resources for batteries of electric vehicles. At the time of writing, much of the cobalt sourced for car batteries is extracted from mines in the Democratic Republic of the Congo.

Critically reflect on this example and discuss how to design a CBA for the regulation of electric vehicles.

4. Discuss the importance of discounting in the regulation of microplastics and the protection of coral reefs.
5. How should regulatory decision-making methodologies consider the interests of the next generations?
6. How does RIA differ from CBA?
7. Has any recent regulation (decree or similar secondary legislative act) been subject to public consultation in your country or in the EU? Read the questions asked to citizens by the regulators and discuss in a group whether they were suitable to appeal to the general public. If the final report of the consultation is available, identify and qualify the respondents (individuals/businesses/lobby groups) and discuss how the identity of the respondents, and possibly the content of their contributions, may impact the final decision of the regulator.

6

Regulatory Modalities, Instruments and Techniques

Introduction

Chapter 5 examined methods that public regulators may employ to help them decide whether to adopt a particular regulatory proposal. These methods remind us that even if regulatory intervention is clearly needed, public regulators have considerable discretion in deciding *how* best to proceed. For example, when the deadly COVID-19 virus first emerged in late 2019, national governments were under pressure to take action. But what kind of action? Possibilities ranged from public education campaigns (to encourage mask-wearing, keeping a distance from others, etc.) to coercive liberty-restricting measures such as stay-at-home orders, nightly curfews, mandatory quarantine in state-run facilities and the closing of national borders. These decisions required difficult normative choices and trade-offs, frequently attracting criticism and opposition. From a regulatory perspective, the effectiveness of such measures – that is, whether they will 'work' in practice to facilitate the achievement of the designated goal is typically highlighted, yet non-instrumental concerns are also important

This and the next chapter address challenges associated with *how* to regulate. In this chapter, we classify regulatory instruments into five categories based on the underlying mechanisms or 'modality' of control through which they seek to produce the desired response or outcome. The literature is rich and extensive, ploughed by scholars from several disciplines, yielding many approaches to classification. For example, political scientists often distinguish between 'hierarchy, markets and networks' as different macro-sociological approaches to coordinate and allocate resources across society (Thompson 1991). In contrast, scholars of public policy and public administration have distinguished between 'carrots, sticks and sermons' (Bemelmans-Videc et al. 1998). For legal scholars, Lawrence Lessing's fourfold classification of different 'modalities of control', distinguishing between law, markets, social norms and code, is often cited, particularly from those concerned with internet-enabled services (Lessig 2009). Although no classification system is definitive, this pluralism is a strength rather than weakness, by facilitating critical comparison and providing scope for sensitivity to context.

This chapter classifies instruments in accordance with the underlying modality through which behaviour is sought to be controlled, identifying five categories: command, competition, consensus, communication and code (or design). Our terminology may differ from that of other scholars, even when referring to the same or largely similar class of instrument. Classificatory schemes are not watertight, including our own. Accordingly, our taxonomy is a heuristic, offering a useful vantage point for beginning our exploration of the mechanics of regulatory control, focusing on the tools available to public regulators. As we shall see Chapter 7, many instruments have a hybrid character, comprising an amalgam of mechanisms to elicit behavioural change drawing on multiple regulatory capacities, rather than relying exclusively on the state's regulatory capacities.

6.1 Command

Command-based mechanisms for regulating behaviour are familiar and well-known. They typically involve an authoritative body (conventionally a state legislator) promulgating legal rules either prohibiting specified conduct or requiring specified conduct to be taken, underpinned by legal sanctions (either civil or criminal in nature) for violation (see Chapter 9). In this way, the law operates in its classical form – through rule-based coercion – and thus is often referred to as 'classical' regulation or 'command and control' (C&C or CAC) regulation. A succinct account of its attractions and shortcomings is provided in the extract below:

O'Sullivan, K. P. V., and Flannery, D. (2012). 'A Discussion on the Resilience of Command and Control Regulation within Regulatory Behavior Theories'. *Journal of Governance and Regulation*, 1(1), 15–24, https://doi.org/10.22495/jgr_v1_i1_p2.

16

Under command and control (CAC), the regulators fix standards on certain activities (the command) and uses legislation to prohibit the behaviour of the regulated entities which do not conform to these standards (the control). CAC is based on simple cause-effect relations – represented by a linear progression from policy formation to implementation. It creates a stable platform for regulatory participants due to the dependability it creates for the regulator, in terms of operational parameters, and for the regulated entity, in terms of compliance obligations. Its legitimacy is particularly strong in times of crisis where sentiment demands more perspective, intensive and legalistic rules. Latin (1985) describes a number of other strengths to CAC, such as: reduced information and collection costs, greater accountability and legitimacy, enhanced accessibility of decisions to public scrutiny, reduced opportunities for regulatory capture in response to political behaviour, and the increased likelihood that regulations will withstand judicial review. In the German environment sector, the development and enforcement of detailed rules and standards – backed by

> legal sanctions – has been credited with not only increasing the productivity of firms through technology and managerial improvements but with also establishing new markets for firms to exploit. This is consistent with Porter's theory of competitive advantage; where he argues that stringent regulation can facilitate technology innovation in economies, as firms innovate to comply with regulations (Porter 1990).
>
> Many of these arguments have been hotly disputed and by the end of the 1960s governments started to question the suitability of the incumbent regime which was said to be collapsing under its own weight. An array of cost-based arguments have been given against command and control, from its effect of increasing relative prices, creating market inefficiencies, and depressing economic growth. Specifically, many socio-legal scholars have shown that CAC leads to a proliferation of costly rules and overregulation which damages innovation and growth in the economy. This can be explained, in some part, by the high costs of gaining perfect information required to target rules and standards efficiently. CAC is also more resource intensive, as centralising the design, monitoring and enforcement of rules requires significant operational and administrative budgets . . ..
>
> However, Baldwin, Scott and Hood (1998) note that many of the faults presented above are US-centric and are reduced when command and control regulation operates in a enforcement regime which is more flexible, administrative based and less prosecutorial in nature (such as in the UK). Additionally, many of the problems associated with command and control, such as enforcement, are faced by all types of regulatory instruments.

O'Sullivan and Flannery refer to the continued popularity of C&C regulation even with US regulatory policy-makers. They show how the US Federal Communications Commission's (FCC) response to the so-called net neutrality debate during the late 2000s resulted in new laws prohibiting internet service providers from offering less favourable treatment to those who used competitor services. Drawing on each of the three kinds of 'theories of regulation' considered in Chapter 5, O'Sullivan and Flannery (2012: 22) show later in the same article extracted above, that uncertainty surrounding the use of 'alternative' policy instruments (including impacts on costs and the relationships between regulatory stakeholders) can result in the adoption of conventional C&C techniques, despite their well-known shortcomings, concluding that:

> Command and control regulation has a role to play in the optimal regulatory mix, regardless of what the literature postulates, its resilience is testament to this. The practice of annexing regulation to law has many benefits, especially in environments where there is an independent judiciary, strong enforcement practices and a reputation for impartiality. So long as people trust and respect the rule of law, command and control regulation will remain important, in some shape or form.

6.2 Competition

The endurance and popularity of command-based policy instruments reminds us that it is the attractiveness of a particular policy tool *relative* to alternatives that must be considered. Economists trenchantly criticise command-based techniques, ascribing superiority to the operation of competitive market forces that underpin so-called economic instruments. But there are significant uncertainties about the effects and effectiveness of economic instruments, particularly given the challenges of monitoring and enforcement, some of which are highlighted by Ogus in the following extract in his examination of some well-known tools of this kind, including charges, taxes, subsidies and tradeable emission/property rights.

> **Ogus, A. I. (1994).** *Regulation: Legal Form and Economic Theory.* Oxford University Press.
>
> 245–250.
>
> The general disenchantment with ... traditional regulatory forms which has emerged in the last two decades has led to pressure not only to deregulate but also to experiment with other regulatory forms which encourage the desired behaviour by financial incentives rather than by legal compulsion. Such incentives can be either negative (conduct is legally unconstrained but if a firm chooses to act in an undesired way it must pay a charge) or positive (if a firm chooses to act in a desired way it is awarded a subsidy).
>
> Although the idea has recently gained considerable currency as a method of dealing with externalities, particularly those arising from environmental pollution, it is far from new. Governments have sometimes sought to finance and determine the supply of public goods (for example, highways and public broadcasting services) by imposing charges on users. As regards negative externalities, economists have long recognized that the misallocation of resources can be corrected by imposing a tax on the firms responsible, thereby ensuring that the external cost of a product or service is 'internalised' in its price.
>
> Those advocating the use of economic instruments (EIs) have argued that they overcome many of the perceived deficiencies of traditional 'command-and-control' regulation (CAC). First, while CAC often gives rise to a complex and detailed set of centrally formulated standards, EIs can function on the basis of broad target goals, with a reduction of information and administrative costs for both the regulators and the firms. Secondly, the greater freedom conferred by EIs on firms creates incentives for technological development. Thirdly, whereas the enforcement of CAC is subject to considerable uncertainty as regards apprehension, prosecution and the level of sanctions, EIs entail the certain payment of specific sums. Fourthly, negative EIs (i.e. charges) generate funds which can be used to compensate the victims of externalities; CAC regimes rarely allow victims to be compensated ....

2. Forms of Economic Instruments

(a) Charges and Taxes

The most widely used EI form involves the imposition of a charge or tax on individuals or firms. To correct misallocations arising from externalities, the amount set should be equal to the marginal damage which the individual or firm inflicts on others. Because the external cost of the activity is thereby borne by the actor, this should, if the activity takes place within a competitive market, ensure an allocatively efficient level of production and consumption.

From an economic perspective, the principal function of the fiscal instrument is thus to induce a behavioural response. But, of course, taxes are more frequently used simply to produce revenue for general governmental purposes and in such contexts the amounts levied tend to be determined by distributional criteria, notably the ability to pay, rather than by reference to allocational considerations. In consequence, there are difficulties in locating 'genuine' EIs within the mass of fiscal provisions: some instruments may have been intended as revenue taxes, or charges to cover administrative expenditure, but have important incentive effects; others may have been intended as EIs but in practice are dominated by revenue or administrative considerations.

Subject to these difficulties, we may identify three main categories of charges or taxes which have, or may have, important incentive functions, and thus be treated as EIs. They represent interventions at different points in the causal relationship between a given activity and the external costs which it generates . . .

The first is imposed on the use of a product which gives rise to an external cost . . .. [T]he relationship between use of a product and its external cost is inevitably imprecise, and the amount levied may be arbitrary relative to the harm actually caused. This is particularly likely where, as in the case of pollution, the harm varies over time and in relation to the impact of other causes . . ..

The second category . . . attaches to the quality and/or quantity of harmful substances emanating from a given activity; hence, in relation to pollution, it is often called an 'effluent charge'. While evaluation of the external costs may remain highly problematic, the scaling of the payments to the harmfulness of the discharge as it enters the environment allows for a greater focus on the marginal impact of an activity . . ..

Under the third category . . . the amount payable is directly related to the harm caused. Clearly, this approach is feasible only where there is a definite and immediate causal relationship between the activity and the harm and where the latter is easily quantifiable. In practice, therefore, it has been adopted predominantly in situations where specific measures have been taken to eliminate the harm and the tax represents the cost of those measures. Reimbursement of the costs incurred by public authorities in the disposal of waste constitutes a frequently adopted example.

(b) Subsidies

Subsidies represent the symmetrical opposite of charges and taxes: payments are made *to* individuals or firms to induce them to reduce undesirable activity. Economically, they can have the same effect as charges and taxes: if the payment reflects the marginal cost of eliminating the externality, an efficient allocation of resources should ensue. However, a subsidy may encourage output to grow to a larger size than that which would prevail under a perfect-internalising charge and in the long run may therefore generate inefficiency. And, of course, the distributional consequences are profoundly different. A tax on a firm increases its costs of production and also generates revenue which can be used to compensate those adversely affected, while the burden of a subsidy scheme falls on general taxpayers. Moreover, such a scheme may create perverse incentives, for example, by inducing firms to increase externalities in order to attract further subsidies.

For these, as well as political-ideological reasons, there has been a decline in the use of subsidies, most notably in the field of environmental protection, where the 'polluter-pays-principle' has become accepted dogma. Even when subsidies were more generally available, there was a problem, as with taxes, in distinguishing those which were intended to operate as EIs from those designed primarily for redistributional purposes, hence to increase the wealth or income of specific groups of industries or households. Nevertheless, examples can be given of current subsidies used for EI purposes. They may take the form of a grant (or an interest-free loan) to assist in the purchase of a particular product or equipment – e.g. home thermal insulation grants to limit energy consumption – or the preservation of some public good – e.g. wildlife habitats. Compensation may be offered for a loss of profits resulting from a voluntary restriction on the use of harmful products or processes. Finally, subsidies may operate indirectly through a reduction of tax liability; for example, an accelerated depreciation allowance may be granted for capital expenditure on pollution abatement equipment.

(c) Tradeable Emission Rights

An EI much discussed in the context of environmental protection is based on the idea that allocative efficiency can be achieved by allowing pollution rights to be traded. Under a 'pure' form of such a system, a public agency would set an absolute limit to the amounts to be discharged into a given airshed or watershed, derived from its perception of optimal ambient quality, and through an auction process sell rights to emit portions of that total to the firms which bid the highest price for them. Once acquired, the rights would be freely tradeable between firms, so that eventually they would be owned by the firms which would value them the most, because they have the highest costs of pollution abatement. Allocative efficiency will be achieved since the lower-cost abaters will find it cheaper to abate than to acquire the pollution rights.

Economics literature on regulation often equates law with command-based techniques, while techniques that rely on market forces are often discussed as if the law is of little or no relevance. However, this portrayal is misleading.

Firstly, the core mechanism upon which command-based interventions rely ultimately rests on the command of some legitimate authority, backed by credible sanctions. The source of that authority will depend on the nature, structure, purpose and character of the community in which commands are issued: when commands take the form of legally binding rules backed by criminal sanctions for violation promulgated by a national legislature, the law's role occupies centre stage. But within organisations, legitimate authority is typically wielded by managers over their subordinates, to whom they may issue commands backed by sanctions in the form of threats of disciplinary action (and ultimately the threat of the termination of employment) for failure to comply. Even within families, parents exert authority over their children and invariably resort (at least on some occasions) to issuing rules prohibiting or prescribing specific kinds of behaviour on pain of some kind of adverse consequence. Secondly, competition-based tools also rely on the coercive force of law. It is thanks to the law of contract that courts uphold and enforce transactions agreed on the market. In other words, the legal system provides a stable institutional framework, which, at least for communities with a culture of respect for the rule of law, enables economic freedom and guarantees the security of transactions. Nor are the law's coercive demands necessarily avoided by competition-based techniques, some of which (such as taxes and charges) are directly underpinned by coercive legal sanctions operating at a secondary level generating the legal obligation to pay in the event of evasion or non-payment. Even where the obligation to discharge payment arises from a voluntary market transaction between private parties (rather than as liability for a tax or charge due to the state), the law's coercive force may eventually be enlisted to ensure payment.

Bureaucracies are, in essence, bounded communities whose members are constrained by mechanisms put in place by those in authority, including competition-based mechanisms. Such an approach was central to public sector reforms introduced by Thatcher and Reagan in the United Kingdom and the United States, respectively, throughout the 1980s, in which heads of public organisations were incentivised to mimic private sector managerial logic by giving them more discretionary decision-space over operational matters, subject to performance targets. Private sector organisations may also employ competition to incentivise and regulate the behaviour of operational units. In these bureaucratic contexts, the law's influence recedes to the level of permission, providing a stable framework that allows organisations the freedom to arrange their internal affairs as they wish, provided they adhere to legal requirements (and constitutional requirements where applicable) for ensuring external accountability, such as mandatory financial reporting. Yet the contexts in which these mechanisms have been used is reflected in a rather stark disciplinary and sub-disciplinary divide: the study of internal organisation (including the use of 'quasi-markets') within the public sector has typically been the preserve of scholars of government, political science and public lawyers, while mechanisms of internal organisation in the private sector are studied by scholars of management, accounting, finance, economics and (to a lesser extent) corporate law.

6.3 Consensus

A third regulatory modality relies primarily upon consensus and co-operation to regulate behaviour, spanning an exceptionally broad variety of regulatory arrangements. It includes 'self-regulation' through to co-operative partnerships between state and non-state actors that purposefully seek to regulate social behaviour. What unites these approaches, distinguishing them from other classes of instrument, is the mechanism through which behaviour is influenced and constrained: resting primarily on *consent*. The consensual foundations of these arrangements may be derived from the legal support offered by contract law or prevailing social norms within the relevant community.

6.3.1 Self-regulation

Self-regulation is one of the most well-known consensual forms of regulation. It encompasses a wide range of regulatory arrangements that may vary along multiple dimensions, including the level and character of state involvement, their degree of formality, the extent to which some kind of industry body (or 'self-regulatory agency') exerts exclusive or monopoly control over the regulated activity and the level at which behaviour is regulated. Advocates of industry self-regulation claim that industry has superior expertise and informational capacities in comparison with the state and is thus more efficacious. Sceptics, however, point out that such claims are typically invoked for self-serving purposes by members of the so-called elite professions (doctors, lawyers, academics and so forth) to stave off unwanted state intervention (see also Chapter 9). Ogus elaborates on these claims in the following extract:

Ogus, A. (1995). 'Rethinking Self-Regulation'. *Oxford Journal of Legal* Studies, 15, 97–108, https://doi.org/10.1093/ojls/15.1.97. 97–99

I Justifications and Explanations for Self-regulation

What then are the advantages traditionally claimed for self-regulation over public regulation? First, since self-regulatory agencies (hereafter SRAs) can normally command a greater degree of expertise and technical knowledge of practices and innovatory possibilities within the relevant area than independent agencies, information costs for the formulation and interpretation of standards are lower. Secondly, for the same reasons, monitoring and enforcement costs are also reduced, as are the costs to practitioners of dealing with regulators, given that such interaction is likely to be fostered by mutual trust. Thirdly, to the extent that the processes of, and rules issued by, SRAs are less formalized than those of public regulatory regimes, there are savings in the costs (including those attributable to delay) of amending standards. Fourthly, the administrative costs of the regime are normally internalized in the trade or activity which is subject to regulation; in the case of independent, public agencies, they are typically borne by taxpayers.

It would, however, be naive to assume that public interest justifications provide an exclusive explanation for the existence of self-regulatory regimes. Obviously, private interests that are threatened by regulation may gain considerable benefits if they are allowed themselves to formulate and enforce the relevant controls. From the abundant literature on public choice theory which treats legislation as a response to the competing demands of interest groups, there emerges the hypothesis that regulation serves mainly to confer rents (supra-competitive profits) on the regulated firms. If regulatory rule-making remains with the legislature or an independent agency, groups representing such firms have the task of exerting influence on those institutions and diverting them away from public interest goals or other, competing, private interest claims. Of course, delegation of the regulatory powers to SRAs relieves the groups of this task and the relative absence of accountability and external constraints maximizes the possibilities of rent-seeking – 'with self-regulation, regulatory capture is there from the outset'.

II Traditional Criticisms of Self-regulation

Lawyers and economists have been equally scathing in their criticisms of self-regulation. From a legal perspective, it is seen as an example of modern 'corporatism', the acquisition of power by groups which are not accountable to the body politic through the conventional constitutional channels. The capacity of an SRA to make rules governing the activities of an association or profession may itself constitute an abuse if it lacks democratic legitimacy in relation to members of the association or profession. The potential for abuse becomes intolerable if, and to the extent that, the rules affect third parties. Further, if – as often occurs – the SRA's functions cover policy formulation, interpretation of the rules, adjudication and enforcement (including the imposition of sanctions) as well as rule-making, there is a fundamental breach of the separation of powers doctrine. Finally, irrespective of theoretical considerations, SRAs are claimed to have a poor record of enforcing their standards against recalcitrant members.

In line with the rent-seeking hypothesis . . . economists have developed models to predict how firms will benefit from self-regulatory regimes; and numerous studies have been published which purport to validate empirically the prediction. Thus SRAs with exclusive power to issue licences authorizing the practice of a profession or occupation have used that power to restrict entry and thereby to enable incumbent practitioners to earn supra-competitive profits. So also their formulation of ongoing quality standards has enabled them to protect anti-competitive practices: for example, fee regulation and restrictions on advertising which limit price competition; and 'professional ethics' which may serve the well-being of practitioners rather than their clients and mask prohibitions on cost-saving innovation.

> **III The Nature of Self-regulation**
>
> One problem with the traditional criticisms of self-regulation is that they are based on a narrow, stereotyped conception of the phenomenon. There is, in fact, a multitude of institutional arrangements which can properly be described as 'self-regulation' and ... it is wrong to tar them all with the same brush. To appreciate the range of possibilities, it may be helpful to identify some key variables. Take, first, the question of autonomy. There is no clear dichotomy in this respect between 'self-regulation' and 'public regulation', but rather a spectrum containing different degrees of legislative constraints, outsider participation in relation to rule formulation or enforcement (or both), and external control and accountability. Thus, at one extreme, rules may be private to a firm, association or organization; at the other, they may have to be approved by a government minister or some independent public authority. Secondly, the rules or standards issued by the SRA may have varying degrees of legal force: they may be formally binding, codes of practice which presumptively apply unless an alleged offender can show that some alternative conduct was capable of satisfactorily meeting the regulatory goals, or purely voluntary. Thirdly, regimes may differ according to their degree of monopolistic power. They may apply to all those supplying a relevant market; alternatively they may be adopted only by a group of suppliers (or even a single supplier) who compete with others in the market.

As Ogus emphasises, 'self-regulation' encompasses a variety of institutional arrangements. Conventional industry self-regulation entails those involved in the relevant activity agreeing to regulate their own behaviour through some kind of self-regulatory agency (such as an industry or sports association) tasked with promulgating and enforcing a code of conduct governing the behaviour of its members. The power of this body to develop, apply and enforce its code of conduct derives from the agreement of its members in which the ultimate sanction for violation is typically expulsion from membership. The legal force and significance of its depends upon the nature of the commitment between the individual members and the regulatory body, which may be a legally binding contract or much looser and more informal. Critics have persistently criticised industry self-regulation, particularly by professionals (such as doctors, lawyers and engineers) on the basis that it constituted a form of private 'rent-seeking' to protect their own status rather than genuinely serving the public interest (see Chapters 5 and 9), drawing attention to the interests of those excluded from consensual arrangements reached by others. Other self-regulatory regimes may entail some form of state involvement. For example, the state may 'delegate' the task of regulating a particular sector or profession to an industry body or professional association, whilst retaining a residual oversight role, perhaps by imposing periodic reporting requirements on the self-regulatory body while retaining legal power to issue guidance or directions in undertaking its regulatory functions. When the underpinning regulatory arrangements take the form of institutionalised partnerships between the state and industry, they are sometimes described as 'co-regulation' and can be understood as a form of 'hybrid' technique, which we discuss in Chapter 7.

Self-regulation also includes firm-level or corporate 'self-regulation' whereby a single organisation claims to regulate its own conduct in accordance with its own internal rules and policies (see Box 6.1). Such initiatives have proliferated in response to public concerns about the harmful and unethical practices of digital technology firms, prompting many, including the so-called Digital Titans, to formulate and publish statements of their 'ethical principles', publicly proclaiming their intention to operate in accordance with them. Despite their abundant grand statements of principle, these codes typically lack any binding legal status, so that organisations are free to depart from them. Nor are they typically backed by systematic mechanisms to collect information to monitor the firm's adherence to these norms, let alone enforcement mechanisms for sanctioning violation. Accordingly, they do not fall comfortably within this class of instrument for they lack any grounding rooted in consensus (originating from the Latin *consens*, meaning 'agreed') based on agreement, which presupposes at least two parties between whom agreement is reached. Although a single agent can, in principle, make self-binding commitments concerning its future conduct, akin to Ulysses lashing himself to the ship's mast issuing strict orders to his crew not to untie him as the ship sailed past the Sirens so he could safely listen to their song. Yet the success of this 'pre-commitment strategy' turned on Ulysses's inability to free himself from the ship's mast. Accordingly, critics of these voluntary codes decry them as 'ethics washing' – a self-serving public relations exercise to stave off unwelcome forms of legal intervention imposed by law-makers, as private interest theories of regulation have emphasised. As Paul Nemitz (2018: 7) observes:

> In a move of genius, the corporations interested have started to finance multiple initiatives to work on ethics of AI, thus, while pretending best intentions, effectively delaying the debate and work on law for AI.

Consensus also form the underlying foundations for 'networks', which political science scholars often referred to as a mode of governance distinct from markets and hierarchies giving rise to 'governance networks' that rely on negotiated action between interdependent actors that contribute to the production of public governance (Torfing 2012), although a detailed examination is beyond the scope of this book.

6.4 Communication

Regulatory techniques that rely upon *public communication* rest on a belief that members of the regulated community are motivated by rational self-interest and the power of social norms, evident in both public communications campaigns (including mandatory disclosure regimes) and voluntary disclosure and 'transparency' initiatives.

Box 6.1 The Russian Olympic Doping Scandal

Sporting organisations enjoy considerable autonomy in setting and overseeing the rules of sport. Their autonomy is enshrined as a principle in the Olympic Charter, which states that such organisations bear responsibility for ensuring that the principles of good governance are applied. As head of the Olympics movement, the International Olympic Committee (IOC) portrays itself as the leading ethically based sport system governed by principles of non-discrimination, solidarity and fair-play, and the goals of 'Olympianism' include respect for fundamental ethical principles. Yet recent scandals have highlighted systematic failures, including frequent use of performance enhancing drugs ('doping') by members of the Russian Olympic team.

Reports by German investigative journalists identified doping by Russian officials, claiming this was reflected in Russia's success in the 2014 Sochi Winter Olympics (in contrast to its poor performance at the previous Olympics). These reports prompted an independent agency, the World Anti-Doping Authority (WADA) to investigate. WADA monitors the World Anti-Doping Code, to which over 700 sporting organisations have signed up. Legal scholar Professor Richard McLaren, an independent investigator working on behalf of WADA, published his report in 2016. It found that over 1,000 Russians athletes in over 30 sports were involved in state-sponsored doping from 2011 to 2015. WADA recommended that Russia be excluded from the 2014 Rio Olympic Games. Russian authorities aggressively denied any violation. The IOC rejected the Maclaren Report, refusing to act upon it prior to the 2016 summer Olympics in Rio. Instead, the IOC criticised WADA, the anti-doping system and sports governance generally, claiming that it was for the international federations of each sport to determine whether any Russian athletes in their sport should be prevented from participating in Rio.

The IOC was criticised from many quarters for failing to uphold its own ethical rules and responsibilities. The scandal highlighted systematic weaknesses in the regulation and governance of sport worldwide, particularly the failure to take enforcement action in the face of clear evidence of violation. Recent and emerging disclosures of harassment, bullying and sexual assault – including in gymnastics in the United States, women's skiing in Canada and women's sport in Korea. In almost all cases, individuals in positions of authority knew that the conduct of the predators occurred but took no action to stop or prevent it. In many cases, victims had no procedure to report the problems or seek help. In others, sport officials discouraged victims from lodging complaints.

Source

Pound, R. W. (2020). 'The Russian Doping Scandal: Some Reflections on Responsibility in Sport Governance'. *Journal of Olympic Studies*, 1(1), 3–21.

6.4.1 Public Communication Campaigns

Simple communication-based techniques include attempts to persuade and/or educate others to act in a manner intended to facilitate the achievement of regulatory aims by enriching the information available to the targeted audience. They assume that people will make 'better' behavioural choices that serve their self-interest when provided with better information, aligned with the public regulator's objectives. The following extract explains the underlying assumptions and mechanisms through which mandatory disclosure regimes are intended to work, highlighting how communication-based strategies can be employed by non-state actors on a voluntary basis in association with some kind of certification regime as a means for eliciting particular kinds of pro-social behaviours (see Chapters 7 and 9).

Yeung, K. (2005). 'Government by Publicity Management: Sunlight or Spin?'. *Public Law*, 1, 360–383.

367–369

(a) Regulation by Mandatory Disclosure

Rather than attempting to regulate production processes, product composition, quality or price, the state might instead mandate the disclosure of information relating to the composition, its side-effects and/or its process of production, with the aim of facilitating more informed decision-making by citizens in their purchasing and consumption decisions. Such mandatory disclosure regimes may be valuable in responding to 'market failures' arising from circumstances in which the market fails to generate the 'optimal' amount of information ('information deficits'), or in responding to circumstances in which a regulated activity generates external costs ('externalities') which may be efficiently dealt with by informing third parties about the externality to enable them to take steps to avoid it, rather than prohibiting or otherwise restricting the regulated activity. The control mechanism through which mandatory disclosure is designed to work operates in two directions. From the purchasers' perspective, the mandatory disclosure of product information enables them to make more informed decisions concerning the acceptability and desirability of the product. In addition, suppliers may also be expected to adjust their production decisions and processes in the face of mandatory disclosure, not only in response to shifts in purchaser behaviour, but the obligation to disclose certain kinds of information may act as a deterrent against fraud or misrepresentation, reflecting the well-known claim by Louis Brandeis that 'sunlight is the best disinfectant'. Managers naturally have incentives to suppress unfavourable information concerning product quality, so that a scheme in which the disclosure of such information is compelled may be expected to discourage the production of goods and services of such quality. The extent to which any particular scheme of mandatory disclosure relies upon adjustments to purchaser or producer behaviour will vary, depending upon the nature of the risk which the regulatory regime seeks to address, and the kind of information compelled for public disclosure.

Mandatory disclosure regimes may therefore be thought to combine both command and control regulation with market-based mechanisms. To the extent that the state compels disclosure from producers, backed by some form of criminal or civil sanction for non-compliance (possibly supplemented by the conferral of private rights on those who rely on information supplied which fails to meet the mandated standards), mandatory disclosure regimes may be seen as a form of command and control regulation. On the other hand, to the extent that such regimes rely on consumers to decide for themselves whether or not to purchase the product in question, rather than directly controlling the production process or output, they may be seen as a form of 'market-based' form of control, creating a scheme of incentives that may be expected to influence the behaviour of both suppliers and purchasers. In other words, identifying the character of mandatory disclosure regimes serves to highlight the need to approach rigid typologies of regulatory tools and techniques with care, illustrating how particular facets of so-called conventional regulatory techniques of command and control may be creatively combined with market-based techniques to form a potentially valuable hybrid policy instrument.

While economists often favour disclosure-based techniques over what they regard as more interventionist command and control approaches, regarding the former as more responsive to market forces, mandatory disclosure regimes have not been without their own problems. For example, the principle of transparency that may be seen as underpinning disclosure regimes may clash with values of confidentiality and privacy, in circumstances where the latter values may have a plausible claim to priority. Yet appeals to confidentiality may often be invoked by participants in the regulatory process to promote self-serving ends, thereby undermining the effective implementation of regulatory policy objectives. Assessing the overall costs associated with disclosure-based regimes may also be a formidable task, particularly given the difficulties of identifying and quantifying the costs imposed on the regulated entities associated with generating, collating and reporting the information mandated for disclosure, let alone the costs to the authority responsible for administering and enforcing a disclosure regime. In addition, mandatory disclosure systems may, like many other forms of regulation, be unresponsive to the dynamic context in which they operate, locking in behavioural incentives that may become unhelpful, redundant or even counter-productive. Finally, disclosure-based schemes assume that consumers are not only rational decision-makers, who make their purchasing decisions following a reasoned evaluation of product and price information, but that they are capable of accurately understanding and evaluating the information provided. Various empirical studies indicate that the impact of information on individual behaviour is highly context sensitive. For example, in relation to the regulation of financial and investment products, where mandatory disclosure regimes have been a central means of regulation, there is evidence to suggest that the information disclosed may have very little effect on consumer investment decisions, either because they are unaware of the information, fail to appreciate its significance, or choose rationally to disregard such information in their decision-making processes. In other words, regulation by information disclosure assumes that consumers are not only rational decision-makers who make their purchasing decisions based following a reasoned evaluation of the product and price information, but that they are capable of accurately understanding and evaluating the information provided. Yet these assumptions may not accurately reflect the reality of individual behaviour.

(b) Voluntary Disclosure Regimes

Although scholarly analyses of disclosure-based regimes tend to focus on those mandated by the state, such regimes may . . . be 'voluntary' in nature. Within a capitalist economy, producers face powerful incentives voluntarily to disclose information concerning production processes and/or product quality in order to attract purchasers. Rising consumer awareness of the ethical implications of certain production processes has been accompanied by the emergence of voluntary certification systems, or what cynics might describe as 'ethical branding' – in which producers publicly and voluntarily disclose the ethical integrity of their production processes (e.g. tuna fish may be labelled as 'dolphin friendly', cosmetic products labelled as 'not tested on animals', and coffee labelled as compliant with 'fair trade' policies). Whether or not one regards voluntary disclosures of this nature cynically as a mere commercial marketing ploy, or more optimistically as an attempt by individual firms genuinely seeking to 'ratchet up' ethical standards of production in circumstances where multiple producers voluntarily agree to adopt a uniform system through which they endeavour to signal to the consuming public the quality of their product or production processes, such initiatives may be regarded as a regime of voluntary self-regulation by participating producers. The signalling of product quality information may be binary in nature, for example, signifying whether a product meets certain standard specifications, such as the use of the 'FAIRTRADE' logo in conformity with the standards set by the Fairtrade Labelling Organizations International ('FLO'), or might involve a graded quality system, such as the use of 'star' ratings adopted by the Automobile Association ('AA') to indicate the quality of service and facilities offered by approved AA accommodation providers. The information thus disclosed may then be of assistance to consumers in evaluating the quality of the product or service offered and, in this way, the mechanism through which behaviour is influenced operates in a broadly similar fashion to schemes in which suppliers are compelled by law to disclose particular kinds of information.

6.4.2 Voluntary Disclosure and 'Transparency' Initiatives

In the preceding extract, Yeung notes that 'voluntary' disclosure regimes include multi-stakeholder regimes through which applicants may seek 'certification' that their services comply with published 'ethical' or other 'quality' standards, enabling them to publicly portray themselves as a 'certified' producers (see also Chapters 8 and 9). Civil society organisations may also employ communication strategies to elicit behavioural change. For example, NGOs concerned with the exploitation of workers and unsafe working conditions of those in developing countries may engage in concerted communication campaigns to dissuade consumers from buying products from producers known to engage in exploitative labour practices or to encourage the purchase of goods that have been produced in accordance with fair labour standards. What unites these techniques is the intentional attempt to bring social pressure to bear on individual decision-making in an attempt to elicit behavioural change.

Industry-led 'labelling' initiatives also enable firms to signal the 'ethical' credentials of their products or services. The study extracted below examined one such initiative aimed at addressing concerns about the welfare of layer hens in Australian egg production. Based on an analysis of Australian newspaper articles and official policy documents over a twenty-four-year period, it found that, in the absence of a legislative definition, the label 'free range' was interpreted in starkly different ways, ranging from 1,500 hens per hectare (reflected in the voluntary model Code of Practice for the Welfare of Animals), 10,000 hens per hectare (adopted by some Australian supermarkets) and a whopping 50,000 hens per hectare (which the Australian Egg Corporation Limited had certified as 'free range') highlighting political contestation over the meaning of 'free range' as a vehicle for securing animal welfare in egg production.

Parker, C., Carey, R., De Costa, J., and Scrinis, G. (2017). 'Can the Hidden Hand of the Market Be an Effective and Legitimate Regulator? The Case of Animal Welfare under a Labelling for Consumer Choice Policy Approach'. *Regulation & Governance*, 11(4), 368–387. https://doi.org/10.1111/rego.12147.

369–382

Animal welfare for layer hens is a significant issue . . . in 2000, [the] Australian government . . . rejected banning conventional cages. Instead they chose to leave it to industry to label eggs as cage, barn, or free range in order to enable informed choice about hen welfare by consumers in the marketplace. In essence, the animal welfare policy choice was to be left to the 'hidden hand of the market', to adapt Adam Smith's famous metaphor. By 2014, 'free-range' labelled eggs represented up to 40 percent of retail eggs sold in Australia, up from 14.5 percent in 2005 and 8 percent in 2001. Consumers believe that in buying these eggs, they are supporting higher animal welfare, but the meaning and use of this term has become increasingly contentious and has been the topic of ongoing policy debates and initiatives since 2000, as this article will show.

Even when official government policy leaves contentious issues to the market, this does not leave the issue un-regulated. Rather there are always networks of public and private actors who influence and regulate market conduct more or less directly, and more or less effectively or legitimately, regardless of whether government has designed and implemented specific regulatory policy or not. By the same token, even when government does regulate on a specific issue, the shape and impact of that regulation will depend upon how it interacts with a range of other public and private regulation that all seeks influence over the same practices . . . we focus particularly on . . . framing the regulatory agenda and setting objectives. This is because at stake in this case study is the very framing of the issue of the caging of hens in egg production as a regulatory issue, and if so, what sort of issue. Regulatory studies literature often assumes that there is agreement on a substantive policy goal (e.g. less use of cages for hens) and then examines, evaluates, and compares different government, private, and hybrid governance mechanisms for implementing and achieving the goal. The case study in this paper, however, is a situation where the policy goal is at best vague (animal welfare and consumer choice) and in practice hotly contested (ban cages or not). This leaves the issue of animal welfare open to contestation as to what regulatory standards under what type of regulatory agenda would apply . . ..

This paper tracks the interactions between the changing actors, discourses, and regulatory mechanisms mentioned in reported public policy debate about the ethical governance of animal welfare in egg production from 1990 to 2014 . . . by reference to three flashpoints: the decision not to ban conventional cages in 2000; the increasing contestation of the meaning of 'free range' by 2011; and, finally, the rise of consumer regulators in 2014 . . . [we] explain for each flashpoint first which actors interacted and the character of their interaction at each flashpoint; and second, the impact of those interactions on the regulatory capacity of the various actors and regulatory policy . . ..

By 2014, consumer regulators, including the Australian Competition and Consumer Commission (ACCC) and consumer affairs ministers, were rivalling and even eclipsing supermarkets in the public discourse . . . after a series of interventions from 2012 onwards, in 2014 the ACCC successfully established in court that much 'free-range' egg labelling by mainstream large-scale producers was misleading and deceptive to consumers. This was in line with the views of Choice, Green MPs, and animal activists. In 2014, the ACCC took enforcement action for misleading and deceptive conduct against a number of egg producers who had in fact sold 'free-range' labelled eggs produced in intensive large-scale conditions and succeeded in court. Newspapers reported that the ACCC indicated that it planned to prosecute more egg producers and that the supermarket standard of 10,000 hens per hectare was 'not consistent with consumers' understanding of free range'.

By 2014, the supermarkets and the ACCC were both competing to govern the meaning of free range. Both appealed to consumer sentiment in different ways, thus demonstrating the entrenchment of the labelling for consumer choice approach. But neither had sufficient regulatory capacity to dominate the space. The supermarkets sought to co-opt and coordinate consumer and industry understandings of free range, but could not gain legitimacy in the face of consistent consumer and animal activist criticism of the very notion of large-scale 'free range' and ACCC action. ACCC action against misleading and deceptive 'free-range' labelling, on the other hand, could not dominate the space because it was essentially negative. It could say what 'free range' was not. But as a reactive regulatory enforcement agency, the ACCC could not put forward a positive proposal for defining free range and assisting industry to demonstrate legitimacy to consumers and retailers. The result was a stalemate in which no one appeared to have the regulatory capacity to move the debate forward . . ..

Our analysis . . . shows that regulatory policy has shifted from a high conflict debate over whether to regulate production by completely banning battery cages during the 1990s, to a general agreement that regulation should facilitate consumer ability to choose free range to encourage higher animal welfare since

2000. Yet even as agricultural ministries sought to minimize their involvement in regulating on-farm practices and substantive animal welfare practices, citizen and NGO concern about animal welfare in the egg industry still created conflicts and sought to draw in different arms of government – first food authorities (unsuccessfully) and then consumer affairs authorities (with some success) – to ensure fair and meaningful labelling. By 2014, debate had moved from an initiative to improve the welfare of all animals (ban battery cages and require enriched cages) to a contest between industry (supported by agriculture ministries), consumer regulators (supported by consumer and animal advocacy groups), and supermarkets (trying to stake a mediating role for themselves) as to who would set the standard for labelling eggs as 'free range'. At stake was, first, the need to appease consumer sentiment, second, the desire to avoid industry fury and, third, the living conditions of about one fifth of laying hens in the egg industry . . ..

Our regulatory network analysis suggests both potential and difficulties for animal welfare improvements through the market or government regulation.

The limitation is that the market-based consumer choice approach makes political networks opaque and narrows the space for public policy-oriented dialogue. Under the labelling for consumer choice approach, public policy dialogue is no longer about the potential for government regulation of minimum standards for a whole sector in the public interest. Rather, it is concerned with a contest of certification, labelling, and marketing schemes oriented toward certain segments of the market. The policy discourse shifts to what consumers expect. But a policy discourse based on consumer expectation is open to both oversentimentalization (advocates may promote unrealistic ideals of happy free range hens) and manipulation (consumer expectations may be conditioned by whoever can control the most sophisticated marketing and information campaigns, often the supermarkets in Australia). Yet even under a market-based approach, the producers and retailers eventually have to legitimate their preferred definitions of free range by reference to standards and governance systems. The political element of consumer choice – the need for market choices to be underscored by public or private standards that respond to consumer values in some legitimate and overarching way – cannot be avoided.

6.5 Design or 'Code' as Control

Unlike communication-based techniques, 'design-based' techniques can operate without the need for human reason or reflection, seeking to eliminate undesirable behaviour by simply 'designing out' the possibility for its occurrence. Although the use of architecture as a form of control has a long history, it has re-emerged in the regulatory literature in response to the emergence of the Internet and associated processes of digitisation and datafication. For legal scholars, Lessig's observation that cyberspace may be regulated through software code (in opposition to claims that the Internet operated outside the realm of legal rules) has been taken up in more recent debates in response to rapid technological advances. In the extract below, Yeung builds on Lessig's examples, offering a taxonomy of 'design-based' regulatory approaches:

Yeung, K. (2007). 'Towards an Understanding of Regulation by Design'. In R. Brownsword and K. Yeung (eds.), *Regulating Technologies*. Hart, 79–107. 81–82

A Taxonomy of Design-based Instruments

Although Lessig draws upon a wealth of historical examples where architecture has been used to pursue social ends, he refers to them in an undifferentiated fashion. In order to deepen our understanding of these instruments, one useful starting point may be to classify them according to the subject in which the design is embedded (the 'design subject'). The following broad categories are not water-tight, and many typically overlap. Thus, like more traditional policy instruments, any given design-based instrument might be placed in more than one category and instruments could be readily combined.

i. Designing Places and Spaces

When we think about architecture as a means for shaping behaviour, we are typically concerned with how places, spaces and the external environment more generally may be designed to encourage certain behaviours while discouraging others. The Crime Prevention Through Environmental Design (CPTED) approach to urban planning and design begins from the fundamental (and unsurprising) premise that human behaviour is directly influenced by the environment we inhabit. As Lessig demonstrates, the 'code' which constitutes the architecture of the Internet provides a particularly effective means for shaping behaviour in cyberspace, although he also provides a long list of examples involving the use of design for shaping social outcomes in real space: speed bumps on road to reduce traffic speed; railroads and other obstacles to achieve informal segregation between black and white communities; the bridges on Long Island to block buses; building codes to facilitate disabled access; the wide 19th century boulevards of Paris to make it more difficult for revolutionary insurgents to take control of the city, the distance between the White House and the Capitol to make it more difficult for the President and Congress to connect and thereby reduce executive influence over the legislature and similar motivations for the location of constitutional courts in continental Europe.

ii. Designing Products and Processes

But Lessig's illustrations also include cases in which design is embedded into manufactured products or industrial processes in order to alter its social impact or the user's behaviour. He cites several examples, including the technology of cigarettes, security-coded car radios, or spraying marijuana fields with paraquat. Other well-known (and much discussed) examples include digital rights management technology (also called technical protection systems) intended to prevent the unauthorised copying of copyrighted digital material by designing out the possibility for individuals to copy or use such material without authorisation, or car-ignition locking systems which prevent car engines from starting unless all occupants are wearing seatbelts thereby reducing the risk of serious injuries to passengers arising from motor vehicle collisions.

iii. Designing Biological Organisms

All the examples of design-based interventions for achieving social outcomes which Lessig draws upon involve the design of spaces, places or things. So, returning to my earlier example of the ways in which the state might seek to tackle the problem of obesity, it might design public spaces to encourage physical exercise (elevators etc for disabled use only). Town centres might be pedestrianised, allowing vehicular access only to those with mobility impairments. Healthy and low-fat food products might be packaged more attractively, while junk food is packaged in plain, unadorned form to make it appear less appetising and/or clearly labelled with an appropriate 'obesity' warning.

But design-based means can also be extended to the manipulation of biological organisms, from the simplest bacteria through to highly sophisticated life-forms, including plants, animals and, of course – human beings.

Yeung then offers examples of biological forms of design, arguing that we can look 'inside' each instrument class to explore the 'modalities of design', observing that each design-based approach seeks to achieve its specified objectives in different ways, with varying levels of effectiveness. She identifies three, showing how they could help reduce personal injuries and fatalities arising from motor vehicle accidents by (a) encouraging behavioural change (e.g., install speed humps on roads), (b) changing the impact of harm-generating behaviour (e.g., install air-bags inside motor vehicles) or (c) preventing the harm-generating behaviour (e.g., adopt a fully automated smart-transportation system, eliminating single human-driven motor vehicles).

It cannot be assumed, however, that designers can easily 'hard-wire' objects so that they systematically and perfectly elicit the intended behavioural response. The concept of 'affordances' and associated 'scripts' that emerged in science and technology studies (STS) (see also Chapter 3) emphasises the relational nature of the relationship between technological objects and the humans who encounter them in situated social contexts, as explained in the following extract:

Davis, J. L., and Chouinard, J. B. (2016). 'Theorizing Affordances: From Request to Refuse'. *Bulletin of Science, Technology & Society*, 36(4), 241–248, https://doi.org/10.1177/027046761771494. 241–245

Conceptualization: What Is an Affordance?

Affordance first emerged within ecological psychology, defined succinctly as 'what things furnish, for good or ill' (Gibson, 1966, p. 285). Gibson later expanded his definition: The affordances of the environment are what it offers the animal, what it provides or furnishes, either for good or ill .... These affordances have to be measured relative to the animal. (Gibson, 1979, p. 127, italics in original).

A decade later, Norman (1988) proposed an alternate definition, one that emphasized perception and brought the concept into design studies. The term affordance refers to the perceived and actual properties of the thing, primarily those fundamental properties that determine just how the thing could possibly be used. A chair affords ('is for') support and, therefore, affords sitting. A chair can also be carried. (p. 9, italics in original) Norman (1999) went on to distinguish between real and perceived affordances. Real affordances are the functions attached to a given object – what, potentially, that object affords. Perceived affordances are features that are clear to the user . . ..

Mechanisms of Affordance: How Do Artifacts Afford?

Through debates about what affordances are, a second critique has emerged with regard to how affordances work. Empirical studies that identify sets of affordances – that is, the functions an artifact enables and constrains – represent a common but methodologically flawed approach that perpetuates a false binary in which affordances are either present or absent. In contrast, theories that break through the false binary recognize variability in Gibson (1979) and Norman's (1999) germinal formulations, explicating that affordances operate by degrees. For instance, a set of stairs does not just afford climbing, but based on the angle of construction, may facilitate an easy climb, pose challenges to climbing, or be unclimbable entirely. Indeed, variability is key to Evans et al.'s (2017) distinction between features, affordances, and outcomes. A feature is either there or not, and an outcome either obtains or does not, but an affordance necessarily operates through gradations.

The conceptual assumption that affordances vary by degree indicates, in a broad sense, how affordances work. The particularities of this how can be packaged into a suite of interrelated mechanisms. We propose that artifacts request, demand, allow, encourage, discourage, and refuse. Requests and demands refer to bids that the artifact places upon the subject. Encouragement, discouragement, and refusal refer to how the artifact responds to a subject's desired actions. Allow pertains to both bids placed upon on the subject and bids placed upon the artifact. These mechanisms are neither rigid nor exhaustive, but rather serve as analytic pegs that transpose structure onto subject-artifact relationships, which are at once nebulous and identifiably patterned. Indeed, features can rest ambiguously between categories and slip from one category to another. The mechanisms are thus reference points along a gradated continuum . . ..

Conditions of Affordance: Affordances for Whom and under What Circumstances?

A final critique leveraged against affordances theory is its struggle to account for contextual variation. Although both Norman and Gibson constructed affordances as organism-environment relations, such relationality has remained highly conceptual. That is, affordances are largely defined ecologically, but in practice, reduced to a 'homogenous block'. Thus, once we know what affordances are, and how they work, the next question is for whom and under what circumstances?

Affordances operate at the intersection of artifacts, actors, and situations. Though artifacts do have features, the accessibility of those features vary between individual subjects and amid diverse circumstances, fostering an array of possible outcomes. What an artifact requests of one user it may demand of another; what the artifact refuses in one moment, it may later allow. Empirical studies that centralize user and environmental variability demonstrate the structural and relational nature of affordances. The field of digital inequalities research is exemplar in this regard. Important findings demonstrate the ways that access to technology, technological savvy, and social networks affect the likelihood that the features of an artifact will produce (or not produce) a range of results such as technological literacy, access to information, and digitally mediated social connection. These studies are significant for their empirical documentation of the ways that features do not determine outcomes but are instead, mediated through dynamic affordances. In short, the mechanisms of affordances take shape through material and social circumstances.

6.5.1 Regulation by and through Software Algorithms

Recent advances in data-driven technologies, combined with the widespread take-up of smart devices, has enabled novel, scalable yet highly targeted forms of control and coordination. Major expansions in computing power, the volume of digital data produced from the automated tracking of user's online interactions that can, in turn, be parsed by machine learning algorithms to find patterns in correlations that would not otherwise be observable and the availability of cheap cloud storage have led to more advanced forms of behavioural channelling and control. Online environments are enormously fertile, pliable yet opaque settings in which design is now routinely and intentionally used to influence user behaviour. In the extract below, Yeung argues that networked computational systems to coordinate and channel activities between and across multiple individuals and sites can be understood as a novel, powerful and sometimes highly sophisticated form of social coordination, which she terms 'algorithmic regulation'.

Yeung, K. (2018). 'Algorithmic Regulation: A Critical Interrogation'. *Regulation & Governance*, 12(4), 505–523, https://doi.org/10.1111/rego.12158.

506–507

What Is Algorithmic Regulation?

In their broadest sense, algorithms are encoded procedures for solving a problem by transforming input data into a desired output. Although algorithms need not be implemented in software, computers are fundamentally algorithm machines, designed to store and read data, apply mathematical procedures to data in a controlled fashion, and offer new information as the output. Even when confined to software, the term 'algorithm' may be variously understood. Software engineers are likely to adopt a technical understanding of algorithms, referring to the logical series of steps for organising and acting on a body of data to achieve a desired outcome quickly which occurs after the generation of a 'model', i.e. the formalisation of the problem and the goal in computational terms. But social scientists typically use the term as an adjective to describe the *sociotechnical assemblage* which includes, not just algorithms, but also the computational networks in which they function, the people who design and operate them, the data (and users) on which they act, and the institutions that provide these services, all connected to a broader social endeavour and constituting part of a family of authoritative systems for knowledge production. Accordingly, Gillespie suggests that, when describing something as 'algorithmic', our concern is with the insertion of procedure that is produced by, or related to, a socio-technical information system that is intended by its designers to be functionally and ideologically committed to the *computational generation of knowledge.* For him, 'what is central is the commitment to procedure, and the way procedure distances its human operators from both the point of contact with others and the mantle of responsibility for the intervention they make'.

Although computational algorithms include those which encode simple mathematical functions, the excitement surrounding Big Data is largely attributable to sophisticated *machine learning* algorithms, fed by massive (and often unstructured) data sets, that operate computationally and depart from traditional techniques of statistical modelling. Traditional statistical modelling requires the analyst to specify a mathematical function containing selected explanatory variables and, through regression analysis, enables the identification of the goodness of fit between the data and these analytic choices. In contrast, machine learning does not require *a priori* specification of functional relationships between variables. Rather, the algorithms operate by mining the data using various techniques to identify patterns and correlations between the data and which are used to establish a working model of relationships between inputs and outputs. This model is gradually improved by iterative 'learning' that is, by testing its predictions and correcting them when wrong, until it identifies something like what is understood in conventional statistics as a 'line of best fit' to generate a model that provides the strongest predictive relationship between inputs and outputs. Accordingly, this methodological approach is sometimes described as 'letting the data speak'. While conventional statistical regression models worked with 10 or so different variables (such as gender, age, income, occupation, educational level, income and so forth) and perhaps sample sizes of thousands, machine learning algorithms that drive the kind of predictive analytic tools that are now commonly in use are designed to work with hundreds (and sometimes tens of thousands) of variables ('features') and sample sizes of millions or billions.

Algorithmic decision-making refers to the use of algorithmically generated knowledge systems to execute or inform decisions, and which can vary widely in simplicity and sophistication. *Algorithmic regulation* refers to regulatory governance systems that utilize algorithmic decision making. Although the scope and meaning of the term 'regulation' and 'regulatory governance' is contested, I adopt the definition offered by leading regulatory governance

> scholar Julia Black, who defines regulation (or regulatory governance) as intentional attempts to manage risk or alter behaviour in order to achieve some pre-specified goal. Several features of this understanding of regulation are worth highlighting. First, although regulation is widely regarded as a critical task of governments, regulation is also pursued by non-state actors and entities. Just as a public transport authority may regulate vehicle movement to optimise traffic flow, likewise a social media company such as Facebook might regulate the posting and viewing behaviour of users to optimise its financial returns. Secondly, the size of the regulated 'population' is highly variable. It may refer to the intentional actions of one person who adopts some system or strategy to regulate some aspect of her own behaviour (such as an individual who uses a fitness tracking device to help her ensure that she attains a minimum level of daily physical activity) through to regulatory systems that seek to direct and influence the behaviour of a large number of people or entities, such as algorithmic systems employed by digital car-sharing platforms, Uber, to enable drivers to offer motor vehicle transport services to individuals at a pre-specified fee without having had any previous relationship. Thirdly, because regulation is above all an intentional activity directed at achieving a pre-specified goal, any regulatory system must have some kind of system 'director' (or 'regulator') to determine the overarching goal of the regulatory system. Accordingly, I refer to algorithmic regulation as decision-making systems that regulate a domain of activity in order to manage risk or alter behaviour through continual *computational* generation of knowledge from data emitted and directly collected (in real time on a continuous basis) from numerous dynamic components pertaining to the regulated environment in order to identify and, if necessary, automatically refine (or prompt refinement of) the system's operations to attain a pre-specified goal.

Yeung (2018: 509–510) in the same article, then develops a taxonomy of different forms of algorithmic regulation, identifying two alternative forms in which each of the three core components of any cybernetic system can operate notably – in setting standards (fixed or adaptive), information gathering and monitoring (reactive or pre-emptive) and at the level of behavioural change (automated or merely 'recommended' sanctions). Although this produces a taxonomy comprising eight different forms of algorithmic system, she distinguishes between reactive and pre-emptive systems, drawing on various strands of literature to illuminate differences in their underlying logic:

> Taken together, these forms of algorithmic regulation draw upon a modality of control which regulatory governance scholars sometimes refer to as 'architectural' or 'design-based' techniques of control. On this view, algorithmic regulation is simply an application of the use of design for regulatory purposes, building on the logic of the waterlock, devised by the Ancient Egyptians over 3000 years ago to prevent unauthorised entry to a protected space without the need for human intervention. Although simple *reactive algorithmic systems*, such as digital password protection systems, are based on the same logic underpinning primitive control systems, they are of contemporary interest

because digital sensor technology and storage capacity have now become so cheap that it has become *practically feasible* to utilise these systems in order to achieve regulatory policy goals. Hence, Proctor and Gamble's smart soap dispenser, recently installed in some public conveniences in the Philippines which operate by movement sensor technology which triggers an alarm when a user leaves the stall that stops only when the soap-dispensing button is pressed, is not especially novel as an automated control system. Yet these simple algorithmic systems are nevertheless worthy of critical attention because they have become attractive as tools for influencing the behaviour of multiple users, rather than being limited to conventional approach which, in the realm of public hygiene promotion, typically involves displaying a sign in public facilities exhorting users to wash their hands.

Nevertheless, contemporary algorithmic regulation can be distinguished from their simple pre-digital antecedents in two respects. Firstly, complex forms of algorithmic regulation which are configured to optimise a fixed (but reprogrammable) overarching system goal while allowing *variable adaptation* of behavioural standards within the system by utilising machine learning techniques that operate on large multiple sources of data collected from ubiquitous digital sensors that continuously track behaviour, offer a genuinely novel form of design-based control. Secondly, *pre-emptive* algorithmic systems are vastly more powerful than traditional forms of architectural regulation (such as the speed hump or the door lock, for example) because machine learning algorithms, networked communications infrastructure and cloud computing, make it possible to track and intervene in the behaviour of not just a single user, but also an entire population of users across a widely dispersed geographic area, while collecting and analysing population-wide data on an almost instantaneous basis to identify deviations from the system's goal and, increasingly, to predict both individual and population-wide trends that can reveal, and automatically act upon, 'hidden' insight. It is the capacity of these systems to *predict* future action or behaviour based on the algorithmic identification of unexpected correlations within massive data sets that would not be detectable by human cognition (or even ordinary computing techniques) to generate 'actionable insight' that is widely regarded as the 'Holy Grail' of Big Data.

Conclusion

This chapter has surveyed five key 'modalities' of control through which regulatory intervention may be attempted. In practice, however, these modalities are often combined in different ways, which we examine in the following chapter.

Discussion Questions

1. Imagine a situation in which noise from neighbouring properties (including commercial activities) had risen to unacceptably high levels, making it

impossible for you to study during the day and even quite late at night. How could each of the regulatory techniques identified above be employed to respond to this problem?

2. Are there any circumstances or contexts in which one or more regulatory instruments cannot be deployed?
3. How robust are the justifications made in favour of self-regulation?
4. Is self-regulation best explained by public or private interest theories of regulation? What variables and factors might affect your answer?
5. How does 'code' as a regulatory technique affect the role of human agency and normative judgement?
6. Are command-based techniques best understood in opposition to regulatory instruments which are:
   i. competition-based;
   ii. consent-based;
   iii. communication-based; or
   iv. code based?
7. How would you assess the relative 'intrusiveness' of regulatory instrument or technique? Which do you consider to be the least intrusive? The most intrusive?
8. In what ways, if any, does the law contribute to the mechanisms of each regulatory instrument?
9. What features distinguish algorithmic regulation from command-and-control techniques ?

7

Hybrid Instruments and Experimental Regulations

Introduction

In Chapter 6, we examined various regulatory 'modalities' based on a fivefold classification of command, competition, consensus, communication and code (or design). In practice, however, many regulatory instruments are 'hybrids', comprising an amalgam of mechanisms, which we explore in Section 7.1. These hybrids rely on multiple sources of regulatory influence, including a variety of non-state intermediaries, rather than relying exclusively on the state's regulatory capacities. Public regulators must also make choices about which instruments to adopt for specific purposes in any given context, which we examine in Section 7.2. In some cases, public regulators may attempt to experiment with regulations so that, for example, new regulations are initially applied only to a section of the population, which we explore in Section 7.3.

7.1 Hybrid Techniques, Sources of Authority and the Role of Intermediaries

Regulatory instruments often draw upon more than one modality of control, thus displaying a 'hybrid' character. Moreover, the boundaries of each instrument class may overlap, so that any given instrument could be classified in different ways, depending upon the characteristics under examination. Hybrid instruments include so-called new governance techniques, which acquired prominence in EU contexts during the late 1990s, and which advocates claimed offered more flexibility and less formality. Furthermore, as markets have globalised, the capacity of individual states to regulate effectively via unilateral action prompted states to enlist alternative sources of authority in pursuit of their regulatory objectives, leveraging the capacities of private actors, including so-called regulatory intermediaries.

7.1.1 Meta-regulation

The term 'meta-regulation' is often used by regulatory studies scholars to describe regulatory mechanisms that combine conventional command-based regulation with the self-regulatory capacities of regulated firms. Regulated organisations are free to develop their own internal organisational systems provided they can demonstrate to a public regulator that those internal systems comply with legally enforceable standards. In the following extract, Sharon Gilad suggests that, within a regulated organisation, three 'tiers' of operations directed towards regulatory compliance can be identified: (i) core production and operations, (ii) compliance systems and (iii) self-evaluation. Her review of empirical studies of 'process-oriented' approaches to regulation, including meta-regulation, finds that such processes have a 'positive impact on firm's performance' but because those findings are highly varied, existing research is far from conclusive.

> **Gilad, S. (2010).** 'It Runs in the Family: Meta-regulation and Its Siblings'. *Regulation & Governance*, 4(4), 485–506, https://doi.org/10.1111/j.1748-5991.2010.01090.x.
>
> 485–486
>
> Regulators ... are experimenting with regulatory arrangements that allow regulated organizations flexibility to tailor regulation to their individual circumstances, while holding them accountable for the adequacy and efficacy of their internal control systems. Similar trends have been observed in state regulation of health and safety, food safety, financial markets, environmental protection and even airport security. These new forms of regulation were intended to alleviate regulators' limited access to information and expertise, enlist corporate commitment, enhance firms' self-regulatory capacity, and overcome the inherent limitations of prescriptive rules.
>
> These changes to regulatory form have given rise to many labels, including enforced self-regulation, management-based regulation, principles-based regulation, and meta-regulation .... This article argues that these different regulatory configurations belong to a family of 'process-oriented regulation' that mandates and monitors organizations' self-evaluation, design, and management of their first-tier operations (e.g. food processing) and their second-tier governance and controls (e.g. internal quality assurance over food processing).

Gilad describes meta-regulation as a 'dynamic process-oriented regulatory institution' in which 'learning', both by regulators and regulated organisations, is intended to play a central role. She claims that meta-regulation is potentially superior to other forms of process-oriented regulation under conditions of regulatory uncertainty, when the internalisation of regulation is inhibited by widespread and entrenched non-compliance and thwarted by the lack of a stable regulatory agenda, of investment and/or a supportive political environment. However, the experience of meta-regulation in the financial sector, particularly following the 2008 global financial crisis, suggests that the conditions for its success are even more demanding. In the following extract, Julia Black identifies four elements that must be simultaneously present for meta-regulation to succeed, drawing attention to the underlying processes and assumptions that underpin its intended operation and its relative strengths and weaknesses (see also Box 7.1).

Black, J. (2012). 'Paradoxes and Failures: "New Governance" Techniques and the Financial Crisis'. *Modern Law Review*, 75(6), 1037–1063, https://doi.org/10.1111/j.1468-2230.2012.00936.x.

1046–1047

Meta-regulation is fundamentally reliant on the simultaneous presence of four elements: on firms having the appropriate culture to support the compliance systems which are put in place, on having the right incentives to pursue public objectives as well as private profits, and on regulators possessing sufficient skills and industry experience to evaluate firms, and having sufficient courage and political support to challenge them.

In the financial sector, meta-regulation was also adopted as a specific regulatory technique under the capital adequacy rules, where firms were allowed to use their own internal risk models to provide the basis for setting their capital requirements. The key regulatory instrument, referred to globally as Basle II, defined the parameters of the models they were to use, which then had to be approved by the regulators. Their introduction was controversial, and they were demonstrated to have significantly under-estimated the risks to which banks were exposed, and moreover to introduce an unsustainable element of pro-cyclicality into the system (in good economic times, banks had to hold little capital; in recessions, banks have to hold more capital, which can restrict their ability to lend and so to help reinvigorate the macro-economy). Nonetheless, they still have a central role in the global capital regulatory regime, albeit now reinforced by greater capital requirements, some counter-cyclical correction and a leverage ratio under Basle III.

Meta-regulation was also adopted as a broader regulatory philosophy, though not with this moniker, by regulators in the UK, and reliance on senior management was a key part of the substantive dimension of PBR [principles-based regulation] as it operated . . ..

It was also based on the assumption, which the Financial Services Authority (FSA) was not alone in holding, that as it was in the firms' interests to manage its risks well, the regulators could rely on banks' own internal management to ensure this, overseen by effective boards and monitored by shareholders. These assumptions were arguably based on cognitive capture and possibly even regulatory 'rapture' rather than straightforward interest group capture. However they arose, the crisis has shown that these assumptions were deeply flawed.

Regulators, not only in the UK, have now recognised that firms . . . and that their incentives are clearly not well aligned with those of the regulators. Moreover, the crisis demonstrated that regulators were not relying on firms' internal systems and controls as such, but on skilful representations of those systems and controls constructed by those responsible for managing relations

Box 7.1 The 'Safety Case' as Meta-regulation: The Deep Water Horizon Disaster

After the explosion of the Piper Alpha oil platform in the North Sea in 1988, killing 165 men, a formal safety case requirement was adopted for UK offshore drilling. Along with many other British safety-critical industries, UK off-shore drilling adopted a 'reasonable practicability' test for demonstrating that hazards have been controlled effectively. This test dates back to 1949, when a case involving the British National Coal Board established that operators of systems have a legal duty to reduce risk unless the sacrifices (in terms of money, effort, etc.) are grossly disproportionate to the expected benefits. It requires the operator to make conscious, transparent decisions about whether, and what kind of, risk control measures are to be put in place. Risks are regarded as 'tolerable' and legally permissible only if further risk reduction is impracticable or if the associated costs are grossly disproportionate.

In contrast, a prescriptive, reactive regulatory approach to off-shore drilling prevailed when the Deep Water Horizon drilling rig exploded in the Gulf of Mexico in 2010, resulting in the largest environmental disaster in human history, killing eleven employees. This approach placed the legal and moral risk to accommodate changing technology, geology and location on the public regulator, rather than the drilling operator. The official inquiry into the disaster noted that, thanks to technological advances, deep water drilling had become a 'complex, even dazzling enterprise' bringing new risks that neither industry nor government had adequately addressed. Investment in safety, containment and response equipment and practices failed to keep pace, while remarkable financial returns had produced a business culture that had 'succumbed to a false sense of security.'

In the United Kingdom, Norway and Canada, a reactive regulatory approach had, by that time, been replaced by a 'safety case' approach requiring industry to bear responsibility for assessing risks associated with offshore activities and to demonstrate that each facility had the policies, plans and systems in place to manage those risks. Following the Deep Water Horizon disaster, a safety management system (likened to the 'Safety Case' regime used in the North Sea) appears to have been transported from Europe to the Gulf of Mexico. Nevertheless, critics argue that only partial transposition has taken place, falling short of a full-blown safety case approach.

However, a rapid narrative literature review of six safety critical industries in the United Kingdom (automotive, civil-aviation, defence, nuclear, petrochemicals and railways) by Sujan et al. found that although safety-case approaches have been adopted based upon a belief in their perceived superiority, they found there was no systematic empirical evidence that regulation based upon a safety-case approach is more effective than other forms of regulation. Existing evidence comprises largely academic case studies and industrial papers reporting anecdotal evidence, concluding that further empirical evidence is needed to validate specific claims about the effectiveness of safety cases in industry.

Sources

National Commission into the BP Deep Water Horizon Oil Spill and Offshore Drilling (2011). 'Deep Water – The Gulf Oil Disaster and the Future of Off-shore Drilling'. Report to the President, January.

Hopkins, A. (2012). 'Explaining the Safety Case'. Regulatory Institutions Network, Working Paper 87, www.csb.gov/assets/1/7/workingpaper_87.pdf.

Sujan, M. A., Habli, I., Kelly, T. P., Pozzi, S., and Johnson, C. W. (2016). 'Should Healthcare Providers Do Safety Cases? Lessons from a Cross-industry Review of Safety Case Practices'. *Safety Science*, 84, 181–189.

with the regulatory bodies. Management-based regulation was shown to have been myth-based regulation. This is not a new phenomenon. For example, on asking banks to perform stress tests at the height of the crisis, the regulators found that banks did not have the systems, models and information to do so. Although regulators had asked banks to perform stress tests in the past, it became clear that banks had constructed largely fictional models purely for the benefit of the regulators. These really were the 'fantasy documents' that Clarke argues all disaster-management manuals to be. Stress tests had been a way for banks to manage regulators, not to manage themselves ….

What can we take from the FSA's experience in using meta-regulation in the period leading up to the crisis? First, to reiterate, that although the strategy may have weaknesses, reliance on firms' internal management to further the regulatory project is an inevitable element of regulation. Regulatory governance is in significant part a process of an organisation acting on a much larger set of other organisations, all varying widely in their regulatory capacity and organisational complexity. As with risk based regulation, but for different reasons, there is no option to abandon 'meta-regulation' as a regulatory strategy – the fundamental inter-dependence of regulator and regulatee means that reliance is always present, if only implicitly. Regulators cannot be present at all times and in all places – even under command-and-control regimes they have to rely on firms complying with regulation continually, not just when the inspector calls. Meta-regulation does not create this reliance; rather it recognises and converts it from an inevitable fact of regulatory life into a conscious regulatory strategy. Second, that meta-regulation also has a critical point of weakness. In this case, its fundamental weakness is paradoxically the element which is also its potential source of strength: that it relies on firms' processes, systems, controls and internal cultures to work, messy, fragmented and contested though they may be. This is a necessary reliance, but that which is a potential source of strength can also be its Achilles heel.

Meta-regulation can emerge in a bottom-up manner. For example, the following extract refers to a 'transparency tool' developed by an intermediary organisation that was subsequently relied upon by public regulators. The tool is thus a hybrid instrument in that (a) the underlying modality involves both communication (voluntary disclosure) and design (in the form of a publicly accessible database) and (b) the actors involved include a civil society organisation (they describe it as a partnership between two 'quasi-regulatory bodies') with strong industry ties, but maintained by a private consultancy, and subsequently 'adopted' by public regulators as a regulatory instrument. The term 'quasi-regulators' used in the extract below refers to actors who are not formally regulators but nevertheless perform regulatory functions such as, for example, professional organisations and knowledge networks such as the major US credit rating agencies (Moody's and Standard & Poor's).

Avidan, M., Etzion, D., and Gehman, J. (2019). 'Opaque Transparency: How Material Affordances Shape Intermediary Work'. *Regulation & Governance*, 13, 197–219, https://doi.org/10.1111/rego.12217.

198

We chose to study FracFocus, an online chemical registry purporting to inform affected communities and the wider public in the United States (US) and Canada about the environmental and health risks associated with hydraulic fracturing ('fracking'), a suite of practices that have dominated unconventional shale oil and gas extraction over the last decade. FracFocus was launched in the US in 2011 in response to concerns about environmental hazards presumed to be by-products of fracking, such as water consumption and contamination, air pollution, and induced seismicity. FracFocus was established by two quasi-regulatory bodies with strong industry ties and is maintained by a private technology consultancy. In 2012, an equivalent website was established in Canada by the same organizations, with cooperation from the British Columbia Oil and Gas Commission (BCOGC).

Applying Koenig-Archibugi and Macdonald's (2017) extension to the original R–I–T model, we interpreted FracFocus as a regulatory intermediary (I), situated between regulators (R), fracking operators (T), and the public (B) in the US and Canada, and analyzed the dynamics surrounding its relationships with each of these constituents . . . . Our analysis revealed that 22 of 24 US states and two of four Canadian provinces with fracking activity required, permitted, or encouraged disclosure through FracFocus, either solely or in tandem with disclosure through a website operated by the relevant state or provincial regulator. Our analysis also revealed that FracFocus launched just before the first big wave of statutory legislation on fracking disclosure. Although FracFocus was initially conceived as a voluntary tool, it evolved into a de facto statutory disclosure mechanism throughout the US and Canada.

Second, we found that even in states and provinces where FracFocus was not mandated, fracking operators regularly used this website to voluntarily disclose details of their fracking operations, attesting to its overall successful diffusion within the industry.

Third, we explored the effectiveness of FracFocus in providing meaningful information to the public regarding environmental and health risks posed by fracking. To this end, we expanded Weil et al.'s (2006) notion of 'user embeddedness' of disclosure policies into a model comprised of four criteria for assessing information quality: accessibility, granularity, comprehensibility, and timeliness. Using this model, we analyzed the effectiveness of disclosure provided via FracFocus and compared it to the effectiveness of the regulator-operated websites used as the alternative mandatory channel in some jurisdictions. Our overall conclusion was that the information disclosed by FracFocus remained largely unhelpful to citizens, manifesting problems with respect to each of our criteria. In many cases, the information disclosed via regulator-operated websites was more accessible than information disclosed via FracFocus, and was presented at a level of granularity and comprehensibility that better supported public decision-making.

We interpret these findings as showing how a non-official yet formalized intermediary can precede, catalyze, and funnel official regulation in a way that favors industry rather than the public, and we relate this outcome to its material affordances. Our findings also suggest that . . . FracFocus operates essentially as a regulator-in-disguise, blurring the boundaries between the supposedly distinct realms of official regulation and self-regulation, while providing what amounts to 'opaque transparency' for its intended beneficiaries.

Troublingly, the authors found that the information disclosed by FracFocus remained largely unhelpful to citizens, shaping the direction and content of official regulation to favour the fracking industry rather than the public. Their study shows how dynamic interactions within a particular regulatory domain can be examined using a network-based approach (in this case, an embellished 'R-I-T model', which we examined in Chapter 4), generating findings that support private interest theories of regulation while also demonstrating how 'affordances', a concept introduced in Chapter 6, shape regulatory outcomes. It also exemplifies how regulated industries can harness communication techniques to serve self-interested ends while appearing to act in a public-spirited manner. The authors (2018: 198) later explain that 'although FracFocus was initially conceived as a voluntary tool, it evolved into a de facto statutory disclosure mechanism throughout the US and Canada.'

7.1.2 Hybrid Forms of Self-regulation

Self-regulatory 'hybrids' other than meta-regulation are worth noting. For example, Ogus (1995) suggests that some criticisms concerning the monopolistic power of self-regulatory schemes could be addressed by schemes of 'competitive self-regulation' in which self-regulatory agencies could seek state certification or accreditation. In different vein, Medzini (2021) has examined attempts by private firms to enroll the capacities of external third parties to support and improve its compliance activities, focusing on Facebook's enrolling of academics to support its content moderation policies and decisions. Another self-regulatory agency employs contracts by a retailer to regulate those who form part of its product supply chain, examined by Verbruggen in the following extract. These techniques have emerged in response to growing sensitivity by Western consumers to the 'credence attributes' of goods, including fair trade concerns, environmental sustainability and the social and labour conditions of workers.

Verbruggen, P. (2014). 'Regulatory Governance by Contract: The Rise of Regulatory Standards in Commercial Contracts'. *Recht der Werkelijkheid*, 35 (3), 79–100, https://doi.org/10.5553/RdW/138064242014035003005.

79–83

Various scholars have noted that commercial contracts are increasingly important vehicles for the implementation and enforcement of safety, social and sustainability standards in transnational supply chains. While commercial

> contracts have traditionally acted as a principal legal vehicle to facilitate the exchange of commodities between individual entities, they are now increasingly being employed as regulatory instruments of entire transnational supply chains.
>
> Right from the outset, however, it appears that contract law imposes constraints on the use of commercial contracts as a regulatory device. More specifically, the doctrine of 'privity of contract' (*relativé du contrat*) holds that a contract can give rise to rights and duties only for those who are party ('privy') to the contract. This implies that, as a rule, firms can bind their contracting parties only and not the other parties that constitute the supply chain (e.g. second or third-tier suppliers) and parties positioned outside that chain but with an interest in its proper functioning (e.g. consumers, NGOs, workers and other stakeholders). The logic that underpins regulation by contract therefore differs fundamentally from that which underpins (traditional) forms of regulation: regulation operates on the logic that it is binding on the entire group of regulated entities, while contracts in principle only bind those that have agreed to the contract (i.e. the contracting parties) . . . this development was triggered in part by the failure of governments and intergovernmental organisations to adequately address concerns raised by global supply chains, including poor working conditions, child labour, environmental degradation, and unsafe consumer products. In the absence of a legally binding and enforceable public framework applying to these supply chains, firms (Western multinational companies in particular) have developed several strategies to address these concerns and manage the reputational risks involved to their own business operations, their employees, and customers . . ..
>
> By including such regulatory standards in their commercial contracts – and potentially also the monitoring and enforcement mechanisms belonging to those standards – firms seek to impose responsibilities on their business partners for the well-being and protection of third parties, such as local communities, consumers, and workers. From a regulatory perspective, however, if these standards are to be effectively implemented along the entire chain, all firms constituting that chain should be subject to the obligation to comply with the same regulatory standards. This means that not only the seller with whom the firm has a contractual relationship must be under an obligation to comply with the standards, but also the seller's supplier (second tier) and, in turn, that supplier's supplier (third tier), and so on.

For Verbruggen, these contracts are an 'important addition to the existing array of regulatory strategies' yet he acknowledges that their effectiveness is unproven. These, and other strategies adopted by private actors to constrain and influence the behaviour of others, are an active site of academic research, often referred to as 'transnational private regulation' (TPR), 'transnational business governance' and even 'transnational law' (presupposing a much broader and looser understanding of the term 'law' than we adopt throughout this book). This literature examines the rules, practices, processes, strategies and networks created primarily by non-state actors, including private commercial firms, NGOs, trade unions and other civil society actors, comprising technical standard-setters and the like, through which a significant degree of non-state authority is implicated in the performance of regulatory functions, including processes of rule-making, implementation and enforcement that takes place across national borders in many domains. The growth of these regimes is often associated with the inability of nation-states to effectively and legitimately regulate activities occurring globally in the absence of a single centralised 'world' regulator. While some claim that these regimes can overcome the traditional limitations of existing relationships between state regulators and those they regulate, others emphasise the importance of national public enforcement capacities as a precondition for the establishment of private regulatory mechanisms, referring to the nation-state as 'the regulatory gorilla in the closet' (Rees 1996). As the need for broader 'stakeholder accountability' of commercial firms has acquired prominence, national legal systems have begun to legislate to support supply chain regulation, extending and strengthening the sources of authority upon which these mechanisms depend, examined in the extract below.

Gustafsson, M. T., Schilling-Vacaflor, A., and Lenschow, A. (2023). 'The Politics of Supply Chain Regulations: Towards Foreign Corporate Accountability in the Area of Human Rights and the Environment?'. *Regulation & Governance*, 17, 853–869, https://doi.org/10.1111/rego.12526.

853–856

While different private and public measures can contribute to foreign corporate accountability (FCA), more recently, supply chain regulations from the demand-side based on a human rights and environmental due diligence (HREDD) approach have spread . . ..

Indeed, the EU and European member states have taken a pioneering role in this new wave of regulatory innovation. Early supply chain regulations focused predominantly on environmental problems, such as the EU Timber Regulation or the EU Renewable Energy Directive. After the adoption of the United Nations Guiding Principles on Business and Human Rights (UNGPs) in 2011, supply chain regulations that focus on human rights and build on a HREDD approach have emerged or are currently under debate. Examples of such laws are the French Duty of Vigilance law, the Dutch Child Labor act, and the German Supply Chain Due Diligence law. The EU adopted a regulation on conflict minerals and plans to adopt a regulation on deforestation-free products and a directive on corporate sustainability due diligence in the near future. Interestingly, while the UNGPs exclusively focus on human rights due diligence, the inclusion of environmental issues alongside with human rights protection has become more common, reflected in the increasing use of terms such as 'human rights and environmental due diligence' or 'sustainability due diligence'.

The emergence of new supply chain regulations fundamentally challenges and broadens the scope of corporate accountability that previously had a narrow

> focus on accountability toward shareholders and consumers for the own operations of companies. Supply chain regulations push companies to also assess and address the impacts caused by their suppliers and to render account to broader constituencies encompassing public institutions, civil society and affected stakeholders in the Global South. Furthermore, instead of relying on the voluntary actions of companies, supply chain regulations aim to create a level playing field for all corporations, thereby making it more difficult for companies to dissociate from or even take benefits of depredatory practices in their complex supply chains. While new supply chain regulations have widely been interpreted as an important step for hardening corporate accountability, recent studies have criticized their lack of stringency, discussed challenges in the harmonization of policies among EU Members States when implementing EU regulations, the merely symbolic compliance of companies with due diligence obligations, and the often weak enforcement of such regulations . . ..
>
> While earlier EU regulations have aimed to tackle environmental problems associated with the import of specific products such as fish, timber, and biofuels, more recent laws have built on the UNGPs and mainly center on the protection of human rights. Among these laws are some with a rather narrow focus on specific problems or selected human rights, but more recent laws tend to be more comprehensive and cross-sectoral. For instance, the French Duty of Vigilance law and the German Supply Chain Due Diligence law cover all economic sectors and, to differing extent, they include both environmental and human rights issues. Importantly, the EU plans to adopt a regulation on deforestation-free products that covers the 'forest risk commodities' beef, cocoa, coffee, palm oil, soybeans and wood and a cross-sectoral directive on corporate sustainability due diligence. This means that in the near future even EU countries that have not yet adopted HREDD laws will need to supervise the compliance of companies with due diligence requirements and penalize law infringements.

Although not extracted here, the authors observe that supply chain regulations vary in their institutional design, relying on distinct mechanisms through which human rights and environmental norms embodied in supply chain regulations might be enforced and serve as vehicles for securing accountability to a broader range of social stakeholders beyond investors (see Chapter 12). They (2023, 866) conclude:

> The recent proliferation of supply chain regulations is consolidating a new, highly politicized governance landscape in global trade. New laws promise to contribute to regulate global trade and to hold companies into account for the negative externalities of their supply chains. Scholars have argued that such laws represent a trend of bringing the state back in supply chain governance. However, the hardening of FCA is a deeply political process, wherein competing ideas embedded within unequal actor constellations and institutional environments that are not always conducive to sustainability transformation shape the limits of what is achievable.

7.1.3 Algorithmic Reputation and Rating Systems

Hybrid regulatory modalities that combine algorithmic regulation with communication-based techniques have risen to prominence in the form of reputation, ranking and scoring systems. They are commonplace in digital platforms and sometimes employed by public authorities in the form of 'citizen scoring' systems, often to inform a substantive intervention that serves in practice as a sanction albeit not legally characterised as punishment.

7.1.3.1 Reputation and Ranking Systems

Reputation plays an important role in laying the foundations of trust between strangers and is a long-standing object of scholarly inquiry. Market actors have an incentive to maintain their good reputation to attract new customers and keep existing ones. Reputation is a particularly valuable object of regulatory influence, especially in sectors characterised by significant information asymmetries. As Ranchordás explains below, reputation-based instruments are now widely used in the platform economy through which the reputation of service providers is established, maintained or lost through online reviews and ratings that provide information both about professional (e.g., hotel accommodation) and peer-to-peer services (e.g., non-professional Airbnb homes). Although these reputational mechanisms may reduce consumers' search costs, Ranchordás warns of their shortcomings:

Ranchordás, S. (2018). 'Online Reputation and the Regulation of Information Asymmetries in the Platform Economy'. *Critical Analysis of Law*, 5(1), 127–141, https://doi.org/10.33137/cal.v5i1.29508.

128–135

Reputation and word-of-mouth have, for centuries, been regarded as alternatives to formal enforcement mechanisms, as they generate trust and provide a great deal of information to consumers. Relying on reputation is instinctive to humans and it is naturally perceived as a key instrument to promote cooperation . . .. In the last half-century, there has been a revival of interest in the interdisciplinary study of reputation, particularly with the development of the sharing economy and the flowering of user-generated content on platforms like Yelp. One of the key questions that remains unanswered in the literature is whether online ratings and reviews can replace traditional regulation in the management of consumer risks . . ..

Regulators in Europe and the US as well as a strand of legal scholarship have suggested that online reputational mechanisms along with the self-regulatory practices implemented by digital platforms (e.g., background checks) are capable of addressing a number of market failures. The Federal Trade Commission (through its Economic Liberty Task Force) and the European Commission have praised the ability of reputational mechanisms to reduce information asymmetries in the peer-to-peer ('P2P') economy. This position, however, overlooks the shortcomings of online reputational feedback, does not elaborate on the interaction between reputation and traditional regulation, and assumes that the existence of abundant information in the market automatically alleviates the information asymmetries that typically justify state intervention . . ..

Reputational models of informal enforcement can be divided into three categories: (i) reputation for ability; (ii) reputation for integrity; and (iii) reputation for performance. These different types of reputation may be present more in some sectors than in others (e.g., payment platforms will invest in their reputation for integrity) and they may also be cumulative. In the P2P home-sharing sectors [e.g., Airbnb], users providing services try to build a good reputation for friendliness, hospitality, and comfortable accommodation offerings. In the services sectors (e.g., car sharing), platforms ask users to rate service providers on their performance as well as on the safety of the vehicle.

An empirical study conducted by Pew Research in the United States has shown that an overwhelming majority of consumers (82%) read online reviews in order to decide which hotel, restaurant or electronic product to choose. Online reviews are consulted on a regular basis as they are easily accessible, brief, and offer immediate information. Reputational feedback mechanisms reduce search costs and help consumers navigate the vast amount of information published on digital platforms . . .. However, the abundance of online reviews has also meant that consumers bear additional cognitive costs as information becomes more difficult to process. As George Stigler famously explained, consumers will only seek information until the point that search costs equal the value of the information; put another way, a greater number of reviews will not necessary help consumers make a better decision . . ..

While ratings and reviews can be informative and can provide unique insights, reputational mechanisms operate in an obscure way. Platforms often organize comments strategically in order to down-rank negative comments and calculate ratings according to doubtful formulas. Therefore, the existing empirical studies on reputational mechanisms have revealed mixed results on the veracity and trustworthiness of these mechanisms . . ..

[T]he overwhelming majority of reviews are positive. This phenomenon has also been explored in the media, which found that some consumers leave 'five-star reviews' due to feelings of guilt . . .. One of the major shortcomings of online rating and reputational mechanisms resides in this biased and non-expert attitude of reviewers. While the quality control exerted by online reviewers might be continuous and allow for a daily control of the performance of service providers, this evaluation will be done with varying standards of quality, hygiene, and value for money . . ..

Online rating and reputational mechanisms suffer from the same problem as any other type of user-generated content: reviews are unfiltered, directly produced by users, and are often connected to social media profiles. In this context, it is difficult to assess the veracity of the review.

7.1.3.2 Blacklisting and Whitelisting by Algorithmic Classification, Ranking and 'Flagging'

Reputation and rating systems rely on market forces and user self-interest to help monitor and ensure the 'quality' of user-provided services. Digital platforms also retain the power to exclude users from their services, exemplified in the banning of former US president Donald Trump from Twitter (now X) and Facebook following the violent assault by his supporters on the US Capitol Building on 6 January 2021. It is this practical power to impose informal sanctions that public authorities rely on when engaging in 'digital blacklisting'. The socio-technical systems used by US authorities described by Margaret Hu below resonate with the use of 'citizen scoring' systems by UK public authorities (Dencik et al. 2020; Yeung 2023) and the Social Credit System reportedly employed in China (Engleman et al.). What unites them is their reliance on algorithmic regulation combined with some sanction (whether formal or otherwise), opacity concerning their configuration and implementation, with serious rights-violating and/or life-limiting consequences for those affected.

Hu, M. (2015). 'Big Data Blacklisting'. *Florida Law* Review, 7, 1735–1809.

1761–1762

Through big data tools, 'blacklisting' consequences can be imposed by the government absent an actual 'blacklist' or even a 'list' of names. Unlike the manner in which 'blacklisting' practices unfolded in a small data world, an overview of the mechanics of potential big data blacklisting programs demonstrates that the harms of inferential guilt can flow from digitally generated data. Thus, many of the big data blacklisting programs discussed below are not necessarily comprised of a list of individuals who have been placed on a 'blacklist' for government consequences. Rather, these programs utilize big data tools to access and analyze digital data or databases. Once this data is accessed and analyzed, the big data tools can be used deliberately or inadvertently to flag the digitally suspicious. Thus, big data blacklisting programs may, but do not necessarily, draw up a list of individuals for deprivation purposes. The database screening and digital watchlisting systems discussed below show that it is often digitalized data deemed guilty and suspicious that is flagged by the big data tools, and it is not necessarily guilty or suspicious persons who are flagged.

Because many of these programs are classified or semi-classified, it is unclear exactly what digital data or databases, and what statistical analytical methods or algorithmic tools, the government engages to determine how to assess the 'guilt' of those targeted by these big data programs. Yet, these programs may facilitate the assessment of a 'guilty until proven innocent' status … it is important to recognize, however, that the big data technologies (e.g., E-Verify and HAVA) discussed here are simply representative technologies. SAVE/HAVA database screening is not coterminous with the 'No Vote List' per se. The technologies are rapidly evolving …. The specific database screening systems that are deployed today may not be deployed in the future.

Hu describes several digital blacklists used in the United States, including the 'No Work List' (the E-Verify program, an internet-based identity verification system that relies upon database screening protocols jointly operated by the US Department of Homeland Security and the Social Security Administration to determine whether a specific individual may legally work in the United States), the 'No Fly List', maintained by the US federal government prior to the 11 September 2001 terrorist attacks but which subsequently grew to list of over 600 named individuals whom air carriers are directed to deny transport and a 'Selectee List' listing individuals that air carriers were directed to select for additional screening prior to boarding an aircraft and additional luggage screening. Hu (2015) continues:

1776

C. Commonality of Big Data Consequences

The discussion above demonstrates how big data programs operated by the government can assign a heightened suspicion and facilitate inferences of guilt. Heightened suspicion may result from either a data match or a data no-match in a database screening program or digital watchlisting system. Inferences of guilt may appear as labelling an individual as a potential terrorist suspect, a future threat to national security, unlawfully present in the United States, a criminal alien, or as committing identity fraud.

7.2 Instrument Choice

This examination of instruments has demonstrated how various modalities of control can be combined and intentionally harnessed by public regulators to leverage the power, capacities and competence of non-state actors, including regulated organisations themselves, to establish 'hybrid' forms of control. Given the broad array of instruments available, how are policy-makers to choose between them? Costs are clearly an important consideration, including various decision-methods, such as cost-benefit analysis and regulatory impact assessment, examined in Chapter 5. Yet those methods have been criticised for failing to facilitate an evaluation of instruments *relative* to each other. In the following extract, Ogus compares the costs of utilizing command-based techniques with the costs associated with competition-based techniques (which he labels 'economic instruments') to protect the environment from undue pollution.

7.2.1 Relative Costs

Ogus, A. I. (1994). *Regulation*. Oxford University Press.

250–254.

Environmental protection has been the primary area both for the limited existing experience of economic instruments (EIs) and for proposals to adopt them on a more extended basis. In evaluating their merits, and in particular the advantages which they are alleged to possess over command-and-control (CAC) regulation, we shall therefore concentrate on their application to that problem. To reduce the complexity of the comparison, we shall assume that CAC regulation seeks to emulate EIs by using differentiated, rather than uniform, standards. As we have seen elsewhere, uniform standards reduce administrative costs but generate significant allocative inefficiencies by failing to take account of differences in abatement costs.

(a) Information

Regulating pollution by traditional CAC techniques normally involves the agency setting standards which balance the pollution abatement costs to individual firms (PAC) against pollution damage costs (PDC), thus requiring adequate information on both sets of costs. An important advantage claimed for EIs is that, provided the agency can make a reasonable estimate of PDC, it need have no knowledge of PAC. Once a tax has been set so as to reflect the impact on PDC of particular concentrations of pollutant, it is left to individual firms to decide whether it is cheaper to pay the tax or else to abate. Further, the system provides better information for firms on the costs they will incur from pollution: the tax represents a certain sum, whereas what they will have to pay if they contravene a standard depends on such uncertain variables as the enforcement discretion of the agency and the sentencing discretion of the court.

These are powerful arguments, but some qualifications need to be made. First, there is the problem of estimating PDC and thus of setting an appropriate price on discharges. Evaluating environmental harm raises immense difficulties not only because of its geographical and temporal dimensions, but also because of the complex interaction of different polluting sources and such variables as weather and diverse patterns of consumer use. Secondly, without information on PAC, an agency will be unable to predict how much pollution will actually result from a given set of prices and thus how effective those prices will be in relation to the efficiency goal of optimal pollution. To overcome both difficulties, the agency will in practice have to adopt an iterative or 'trial and error' approach: an initial set of prices is established, but these are subsequently modified as their impact is observed and as account is also taken of other variables. The instability of this process will undermine the predictability of the costs imposed on firms, one of the principal benefits claimed for EIs.

Of course, agencies setting standards under a CAC regime face similar difficulties; but the flexibility inherent in negotiating and enforcing individualized standards enables them to adjust to changing conditions in a way that is not possible under a tax system.

(b) Incentives

Since under a tax or subsidy system the cost to a firm of polluting increases proportionately to the pollution, there is an incentive for the firm to abate as much as possible. It will do so up to the point where the marginal abatement cost is equal to the marginal tax (or subsidy) cost, and there is therefore also an incentive to develop cheaper methods of pollution abatement. A tradeable emission rights regime engenders the same incentives: firms which reduce their abatement costs can profitably sell their rights to firms with higher costs.

In this respect, it would appear that EIs are superior to CAC regulation: although a firm will seek to find the cheapest way of meeting a CAC standard, once that standard has been achieved it has no incentive to reduce pollution further. It is true. . .that the standards imposed under some CAC regimes are formulated by reference to the 'best available techniques' not entailing excessive cost', but the agency's perceptions of what is 'best' are unlikely to encourage firms to develop new technologies.

(c) Accidents

A point frequently overlooked in discussions of control instruments is that many cases of serious environmental damage are the result of accidents, rather than deliberate polluting activity. Under CAC regimes, the amount payable by way of penalties can be tailored to reflect the more serious external costs generated by accidents, because it is determined after the accident has occurred. A tax system normally involves an *ex ante* assessment of harm and thus can meet the problem only if the amounts levied reflect the risks of accidental discharges from the individual firm.

As regards industrial health and safety, the contributions levied from firms to finance the compensation payable to victims are in many countries (though not Britain) calculated by reference to the firms' accident record. It is generally acknowledged that the system is effective, at least when applied to firms large enough for the statistical evidence to be reliable. But that very qualification indicates why a tax system cannot create appropriate incentives for avoiding serious pollution accidents. The infrequency of such accidents would render the system arbitrary: the tax would either be too high, for firms with an accident record, or too low, for firms without one.

(d) Enforcement

The assertion that EIs are cheaper than CAC systems in terms of enforcement costs is not easily sustained. Both generally entail the monitoring of discharges. The costs in some individual CAC cases may be high, where protracted negotiation or prosecution follows a detected contravention, but that has to be balanced against the administrative burden of collecting taxes in a larger number of cases and dealing with the proceeds. In justifying its hesitation to adopt EIs more widely, the British government referred to the difficulty and expense of the administrative support which would be required. It has been reported that more than half of the revenue derived from the German system of water effluent charges is absorbed by administrative costs.

(e) Distributional Considerations

One apparently clear advantage of taxes and auctioned tradeable emission rights (but obviously not subsidies) over CAC regulation is that they generate funds which can be used to compensate the victims of pollution. However, the distributional argument for preferring EIs is not so straightforward as may appear. One reason is that the estimation of the distributional consequences of various control instruments is a complex matter: the conditions prevailing in different product, labour, and capital markets as well as the nature of the instruments influence the way in which the ultimate financial burden is shared between shareholders, the labour force, and consumers. Secondly, even if EIs might in theory operate to redistribute resources from (say) the shareholders of polluting firms to householder pollution victims, in practice such transfers are limited. Tax revenues tend to be earmarked, if at all, for government clean-up programmes, and schemes which directly compensate pollution victims are rare.

(f) Empirical Evidence

Although there have been a number of studies of environmental EIs, they provide a far from adequate basis for evaluating the impact of these instruments. One problem is that EIs are generally combined with traditional CAC regimes and it is not possible to isolate the effects of the different approaches. As regards taxes, there is the additional difficulty that the instruments are frequently designed primarily for revenue purposes and the amounts imposed are often significantly lower than would be required for incentive purposes.

Some generalizations have, nevertheless, emerged. The taxes imposed on leaded petrol appear to have had important incentive effects. Effluent charges seem to have made some improvement to water quality, though not to the extent predicted by economists. This is explained on the ground not only that the amounts levied have been too small, but also on the prevalent use of 'grandfather clauses': typically the charges are applied only to new emission sources or to levels of discharges exceeding those current at the time the system is introduced. An exception is the Dutch system, where the charges have been significantly higher and the impact on polluter behaviour significantly greater.

Challenges associated with how to choose between policy tools can be at least partly attributed to knowledge-gaps about them. In the extract below, Capano and Howlett divide these into four clusters of issues:

Capano G, and Howlett, M. (2020). 'The Knowns and Unknowns of Policy Instrument Analysis: Policy Tools and the Current Research Agenda on Policy Mixes'. *SAGE Open*, 10(1),1–13, https://doi.org/10.1177/2158244019900568.

1–3

Based on the most recent reviews of the literature . . . and the combined 50-year experience of the authors in dealing with the subject, . . .four clusters of basic issues in the field. . . still require additional research . . . (a) problems with understanding instrument and mix dynamics, (b) under-examined behavioral issues around policy tools in general and more specifically, (c) measurement and methodological issues, and (d) a variety of issues related to how policy implementation affects tool deployment and use and, subsequently, policy success or failure.

In order to orient ourselves in exploring the academic and policy literature on questions of instrument choice, we can classify it into two groups, those concerned with questions of efficacy, on the one hand, and non-instrumental dimensions of legitimacy, on the other.

7.2.2 Prescriptive Approaches and Tool-Efficacy

A prominent strand of regulatory scholarship appearing between the late 1990s through to the mid 2000s took the form of policy 'prescriptions', comprising strategies their authors claimed would help public regulators identify which instruments were most likely to achieve their desired policy goals efficiently and effectively. This approach is exemplified in the work of Gunningham and Grabosky who develop a set of guiding principles for public regulators, building upon earlier the groundwork laid by Ian Ayres and John Braithwaite (1992) (see Chapter 9). They claim to adopt the standpoint of public policy by asking 'how can we achieve smarter and more effective regulation?' Their policy prescriptions and design principles of general relevance are summarised in the following extract:

> **Gunningham, N., and Sinclair, D. (2017).** 'Smart Regulation'. In P. Drahos (ed.), *Regulatory Theory: Foundations And Applications*, ANU ePress, 133–148, doi:10.22459/RT.02.2017.08.
>
> 133–145
>
> Gunningham et al. (1998) first advocated the concept of 'smart regulation' in a book of that title in 1998. Subsequently, the concept has been refined in various publications by [them]. The term refers to a form of regulatory pluralism that embraces flexible, imaginative and innovative forms of social control. In doing so, it harnesses governments as well as business and third parties. For example, it encompasses self-regulation and co-regulation, using commercial interests and non-governmental organisations (NGOs) (such as peak bodies) as regulatory surrogates, together with improving the effectiveness and efficiency of more conventional forms of direct government regulation. The underlying rationale is that, in the majority of circumstances, the use of multiple rather than single policy instruments, and a broader range of regulatory actors, will produce better regulation. As such, it envisages the implementation of complementary combinations of instruments and participants tailored to meet the imperatives of specific environmental issues . . ..
>
> In terms of its intellectual history, smart regulation evolved in a period in which it had become apparent that neither traditional command-and-control regulation nor the free market provides satisfactory answers to the increasingly complex and serious environmental problems that confront the world. This led to a search for alternatives more capable of addressing the environmental challenge and, in particular, to the exploration of a broader range of policy tools such as economic instruments, self-regulation and information-based strategies. Smart regulation also emerged in a period of comparative state weakness, in

which the dominance of neoliberalism had resulted in the relative emasculation of formerly powerful environmental regulators and in which third parties such as NGOs and business were increasingly filling the 'regulatory space' formerly occupied by the state.

At the heart of smart regulation is a series of regulatory design principles, adherence to which would enable policymakers to take advantage of a number of largely unrecognised opportunities, strategies and techniques for achieving efficient and effective environmental policy. These design principles include:

- The desirability of preferring complementary instrument mixes over single instrument approaches, while avoiding the dangers of 'smorgasbordism' (that is, wrongly assuming that all complementary instruments should be used rather than the minimum number necessary to achieve the desired result).
- The virtues of parsimony: why less interventionist measures should be preferred in the first instance and how to achieve such outcomes.
- The benefits of an escalating response up an instrument pyramid (utilising not only government, but also business and third parties) to build in regulatory responsiveness, to increase dependability of outcomes through instrument sequencing and to provide early warning of instrument failure through the use of triggers.
- Empowering third parties (both commercial and non-commercial) to act as surrogate regulators, thereby achieving not only better environmental outcomes at less cost but also freeing up scarce regulatory resources, which can be redeployed in circumstances where no alternatives to direct government intervention are available.
- Maximising opportunities for win–win outcomes by expanding the boundaries within which such opportunities are available and encouraging business to go 'beyond compliance' within existing legal requirements . . ..

In summary, the preferred role for government under smart regulation is to create the necessary preconditions for second or third parties to assume a greater share of the regulatory burden rather than engaging in direct intervention . . ..

In conclusion, while there has been considerable progress in the development of smart regulation as a theoretical construct, its attempted translation into regulatory policy and practice has been mixed.

7.2.3 Normative Conflict, Organisational Interests, Local Contexts and Political Power

Prescriptive approaches to tool-choice tend to characterise policy-makers as akin to careful restaurant-goers carefully selecting from a menu of options to best suit their tastes and preferences. But there are important political and normative considerations that affect the choice of regulatory instrument, generating tension and conflicts that may elude consensual resolution between stakeholders. The following discussion examines the 'politics' of instrument choice and ideological concerns, suggesting that instruments are not directly substitutable. They show that normative concerns cannot be ignored when choosing between instruments and modalities of control. Yet these are often overlooked or fly beneath the radar due to a failure to recognise that normative conflict is unavoidable, eluding 'win-win solutions'. Moreover, even if one instrument may appear more effective, these concerns might be trumped by political considerations, exemplified in the following extract, uniting interest groups that are normally on opposing sides of political debate, akin to the alliance between 'Baptists and Bootleggers' we encountered in Chapter 4.

7.2.3.1 The Politics of Instrument Choice

We have already noted that competition-based instruments have several attractive qualities. Despite this, policymakers may be reluctant to adopt them for political reasons, as Ogus highlights in his discussion of economic instruments (EIs) in the extract below.

> **Ogus, A. I (1994).** *Regulation*. Oxford University Press.
>
> 255–256
>
> Whatever the merits of EIs, it is not difficult to understand the reluctance of legislatures to use them. In general, as we have seen, in formulating regulatory policy politicians are expected to respond to pressures from both sectional interest groups – notably those representing industry – and ideological interest groups, e.g. environmentalists. Although the influence of the former tends to be stronger than that of the latter, some compromise between the respective demands of the two groups normally emerges. In the present context, however, the environmentalist lobby has combined with the industrial lobby in opposing EIs.
>
> The opposition of environmentalists to EIs can be explained on several grounds. First, they expect governments to respond to the pollution crisis by the adoption of immediate and tough measures. Mandatory CAC standards, cast in a suitably rigorous form, are seen to meet this demand; EIs, which rely on voluntary behaviour and are characterized as 'licences to pollute', are not. Secondly, the use of the criminal law and its institutions stigmatizes pollution; EIs, which involve merely administrative intervention, are morally neutral. Thirdly, the assumption of rational economic behaviour which underpins the arguments for EIs is treated with scepticism. How does economism deal with the crusty general-manager who believes that the old ways of disposing of toxic wastes are the best and that no new-fangled effluent tax is going to change his tried and true practices? Legalism does have a way of dealing with this not-so-uncommon menace to the public health; it takes him to court and threatens to shut his plant down. Fourthly, as regards taxes, governments cannot be trusted to use the proceeds for environmental purposes; and, as regards subsidies, why should taxpayers support polluters?
>
> The political appeal of this last point is overwhelming and certainly sufficient to dampen the demand by polluting industries for subsidies. Industrial opposition

> to tax systems is no less difficult to comprehend. Such systems would seem to require polluting firms to pay twice: they pay not only for the technical equipment necessary to abate pollution, but also for emissions which they are unable to abate. Moreover, the collection of taxes is a matter of administrative routine and difficult to obstruct. The very effectiveness of tax systems in imposing costs therefore makes them much less attractive to polluters than CAC regimes, the enforcement agencies of which can be persuaded not to prosecute. Finally, the influence of the agencies themselves in resisting EIs should not be underestimated. The discretion conferred on them by CAC regimes enables them to enjoy power, prestige, and job satisfaction; administration of a tax system provides little by way of equivalent benefit.

The preceding extract shows how interest groups that may be deeply opposed in their substantive missions may be united in their preference for the same kind of regulatory instrument. Yet disagreement arising from differences in interests, beliefs and normative values are more likely.

Design-based Instruments

Although one attraction of 'code' or 'design-based' instruments is their capacity to compel particular behaviours deemed undesirable, these strategies may be problematic if there is reasonable disagreement about the kind of behaviours should be permissible, highlighted in the following extract:

> **Yeung, K., and Dixon-Woods, M. (2010).** 'Design-based Regulation and Patient Safety: A Regulatory Studies Perspective'. *Social Science & Medicine*, 71, 502–509, https://doi.org/10.1016/j.socscimed.2010.04.017.
>
> 504–505
>
> A commonly used example of the kind of behaviour that could be avoided by action-forcing design is that of 'wrong route' drug administration, often seen as an unambiguous example of egregious patient safety error. Importantly, it typically occurs *unintentionally* – either when an error of planning is made (e.g. someone plans to give a patient a drug through the wrong route, without realising it is the wrong route) or when error of execution is made (someone does not plan to give a patient a drug through the wrong route, but accidentally does so). Thus, both the action and the outcome are unintended – the result of lapses. Administration of vincristine (chemotherapy) via the intrathecal route (the spine), rather than the correct route (a vein) is a classic example of this error, and has very serious (usually fatal) consequences . . ..
>
> Redesigning equipment could mean that it would no longer be possible to connect a normal hypodermic syringe to a spinal device, making it impossible inadvertently to administer the drug intrathecally. It would thus address the fallibilities of individual agents, and promote system-level support for averting error. It is an excellent example of how design could be used to secure better patient safety, and is likely to be welcomed across various stakeholders and interests . . .. But the very simplicity, appeal and likely effectiveness of an action-forcing design solution in the specific context of wrong route drug

administration makes careful appraisal of its more general application to patient safety problems all the more necessary . . ..

The ability of technology to encode values and potentially force them upon their users is especially consequential in the context of healthcare, where definitions of risk, morality and error are often highly contested, and where professional agency has traditionally had an important normative role. Sociological work has repeatedly emphasised the ambiguities and uncertainties inherent in medical work. Bosk's (1979) classic ethnography, for example, identified the 'essentially contested' nature of error; everyone agrees that error is undesirable, but not on whether specific events or actions are errors; 'the grounds for fixing the label "error" to any action are always arguable' (p. 28). More generally, the sociological and anthropological literature on risk has shown that notions of risk are mobilised within particular social, cultural and interactional contexts in many different ways by many different interests. As soon as there is contestation in defining precisely which actions constitute an 'error', who should own the definition and the conditions in which such actions should be prevented, design-based regulation becomes considerably more problematic than might be evident from a superficial examination of the case of wrong route drug administration. Care is therefore needed when using examples where there is full agreement on what constitutes an error and on the need to avoid it, as they may provide a poor basis for designing regulation for less particularist areas . . ..

In many countries, official policy is that any devices designated as single use must not be re-used. The risks of re-use arise from the possibility that previously used devices . . . might not be fully sterilised or performance might be impaired, for example because of damage from the earlier use or from the decontamination process. On this view, any re-use of a single-use device (SUD) would be an error. Amid evidence that re-use is nonetheless widespread, manufacturers' efforts have increasingly turned towards designing single-use devices so that they are effectively auto-disabling and cannot be used again. For example, single use needles can be made to self-blunt once the final vial of blood is drawn, while FemoStop (a device to help seal surgical wounds) has been redesigned by its manufacturers so that its components would be rendered incapable of being re-used if attempts are made to reprocess it.

These technical solutions to a 'safety' problem are far from neutral interventions in an often fraught debate. The re-use of medical devices labelled 'single use only' by manufacturers is highly contentious: there is little consensus on how far re-use constitutes a genuine safety risk for many devices. An alternative to the view that re-use should always be considered an 'error' is that, when appropriate precautions are taken, re-use can very often be justifiable for SUDs where there is very low risk associated with re-use, and further that there are very good environmental and economic reasons for re-use. Research evidence supports the view that re-use of some devices may (subject to various precautions) be safe, or at least that the cost-savings justify the small additional risks. Practitioners may perceive that manufacturers are over-cautious (and self-serving) in their instructions cautioning against re-use. Practitioners may, then, intentionally re-use equipment, even though they intend no harm, especially if re-use prevents waste and allows more patients to benefit from limited resources. Reducing waste, minimising environmental impact, and maximising the number of patients who can be treated may serve the public good, but potentially be contrary to the manufacturers' interests. Only someone acting from bad motives would intentionally administer a drug by the wrong route. But someone who intentionally re-uses a single use medical device might have good motives for doing so. In consequence, practitioners may argue for the role of professional discretion and judgement in determining whether a particular item is fit for re-use, rather than deferring to official rules.

The design of medical devices to prevent re-use exemplifies how artefact design may settle a political an issue 'by fiat' (Winner 1980). Winner argued that artefacts could also be 'inherently political' in that they require or are strongly compatible with particular kinds of political arrangements (see Chapter 3). This 'inherent' politics is reflected in ideological concerns that often influence decisions about instrument choice that cut across legal and constitutional cultures. As we have already noted, the rise of neoliberalism underpinned the drive for deregulation throughout the late 1970s and following decades underpinned public sector reforms to 'roll back the frontiers of the state' in many nations and to reduce burdens on business by reducing and weakening of conventional forms of state-intervention. The reforms initiated during that time left an indelible mark, liberalising markets and paving the way for the triumph of global capitalism. Critics have decried undue reliance on markets, emphasising the value and importance of governance through shared norms and collective values.

Competition-based Instruments

More deeply rooted philosophical objections have also been invoked to challenge faith in markets. In the following extract, Harvard philosopher Michael Sandel asks, 'are there some things that money cannot buy? He answers affirmatively, referring to friendship and the Nobel prize as examples. Trying to buy or hire friends, or to buy a prize, would not work, for attempting to do so would convert them into something else (Sandel 2012: 93). Yet there are other kinds of goods, such as human organs, which could be bought and sold but many believe they should not be. In the following extract, he considers two objections:

Sandel, M. (2012). *What Money Can't Buy.* Penguin Books.

110–114

The fairness objection asks about the inequality that market choices may reflect. The corruption objection asks about the attitudes and norms that market relations may damage or dissolve. Consider kidneys. It's true that money can buy one without ruining its value. But should kidneys be bought and sold? Those who say no typically object on one of two grounds: They argue that such markets prey upon the poor, whose choice to sell their kidneys may not be truly voluntary (the fairness argument). Or they argue that such markets promote a degrading, objectifying view of the human person, as a collection of spare parts (the corruption argument) . . ..

The fairness objection points to the injustice that can arise when people buy and sell things under conditions of inequality or dire economic necessity. According to this objection, market exchanges are not always voluntary as market enthusiasts suggest. A peasant may agree to sell his kidney or cornea to feed his starving family, but his agreement may not really be voluntary. He may be unfairly coerced, in effect, by the necessities of his situation.

The corruption objection is different. It points to the degrading effect of market valuation and exchange on certain goods and practices. According to this objection, certain moral and civic goods are diminished or corrupted if bought and sold. The argument from corruption cannot be met by establishing fair bargaining conditions. It applies under conditions of equality and inequality alike.

The fairness and corruption objections differ in their implications for markets: The fairness argument does not object to marketizing certain goods on the grounds that they are too precious or sacred or priceless; it objects to buying and selling goods against a background of inequality severe enough to create unfair bargaining conditions. It offers no basis for objecting to the commodification of goods (whether ex or kidneys or college admission) in a society whose background conditions are fair.

The corruption argument, by contrast, focuses on the character of the goods themselves and the norms that should govern them. So it cannot be met simply by establishing fair bargaining conditions. Even in a society without unjust differences of power and wealth, there would still be things that money should not buy. This is because markets are not mere mechanisms: they embody certain values. And sometimes, market values crowd out nonmarket norms worth caring about . . ..

A growing body of research confirms what common sense suggests: financial incentives and other market mechanisms can backfire by crowding out nonmarket norms. Sometimes, offering payment for a certain behaviour gets you less of it, not more'.

Sandel offers various real-world examples to support his claims, including an Israeli day-care centre that found that their incidence of late pick-ups doubled when they introduced a fine. Yet twelve weeks later, after abandoning the fining scheme, the new elevated rate of late pick-ups persisted, indicating that the monetary payment had eroded carers' moral obligation to show up on time. (Sandel 2012: 119). Sandel identifies two reasons to hesitate before introducing money into non-market settings:

Social norms (such as civic virtue and public spiritedness) are great bargains. They motivate socially useful behaviour that would otherwise cost a lot to buy. If you had to rely on financial incentives to get communities to accept nuclear

> waste, you'd have to pay a lot more than if you could rely instead on residents' sense of civic obligation . . ..
>
> To view moral and civic norms as simply cost effective motivational tools ignores the intrinsic value of norms. It is not just expensive – it is corrupting. It bypasses persuasion and the kind of consent that arises from deliberating about the risks the facility pose and the larger community's need for it . . ..
>
> A growing body of social psychology offers a possible explanation for this commercialisation effect These studies highlight the difference between intrinsic motivations (such as moral conviction or interest in the task at hand) and external ones (such as money or other tangible rewards). When people are engaged in an activity they consider intrinsically worthwhile, offering them money may weaken their motivation by depreciating or 'crowding out' their intrinsic interest or commitment.
>
> The crowding out phenomenon has big implications for economics. It calls into question the use of market mechanisms and market reasoning in many aspects of social life, including financial incentives to motivate performance in education, health care, the work place, voluntary associations, civic life, and other settings in which intrinsic motivations or moral commitments matter.

Neiman offered a complement to Sandel's critique, written three decades earlier when the ascendancy of neoliberal ideology was taking root. Yet his critique remains salient and powerfully argued, reminding us that value and virtue of citizenship, and the role of coercion for violating collective norms shared by the citizenry, remains important and enduring:

> **Neiman, M. (1980).** 'The Virtues of Heavy Handedness in Government'. *Law & Policy*, 2, 11–34, https://doi.org/10.1111/j.1467-9930.1980.tb00202.x.
>
> 23–25
>
> There seems to be an implicit notion among critics of government coercion that the purpose of law, regulation, and rule-making is merely to influence physical behavior . . . overlook[ing] the act of rule- making as embodying what is viewed as proper, virtuous, just, good, and sacred. While much public policy, regardless of how it is expressed, is often a matter of convenience or a response to pressures by special interests, public policy is also one of the only ways in which secular virtue can be expressed. Focusing entirely on whether administrative regulations, ordinances, and laws are more or less efficient in influencing behavior than are markets, prices, and profit motive tends to underscore the mere directing of behavior as the paramount function of public intervention.
>
> Consequently, tinkering with the calculus of private transactions in order to direct egoistic behavior to public ends ignores the important need to wreak retribution and punishment on those who refuse to satisfy public goals. After all, how can one 'punish' someone who merely refuses publicly offered rewards and payments and continues to behave in ways that contravene publicly expressed goals. To diminish the practice of enforcing rules by punishment and other heavy-handed, even violent, means is to diminish the role of the sacred in

human affairs. And to diminish the sacred is to invite increased difficulty in encouraging individuals to act individually in ways to achieve collective goals and satisfactions . . ..

Once the issue of influencing human beings to behave in particular ways is narrowed so that it becomes one of technique there is then a tendency to obscure the distinction between the application of coercion to discourage undesired behavior and the bestowing of rewards for desired behavior. In a broad sense the two approaches are different in profound ways. When punishing a person, for example, it is claimed that the person had no right to behave as he did and that society, through its designated institutions, considers the punished behavior as improper, immoral, or contemptuous of the popular will, expressed through democratically designed public policies. To pay people so that they behave in desired ways seems, on the other hand, to suggest that it is the right of a person to behave in ways that society may find undesirable, and that the wish of society to elicit other behavior must not be imposed; indeed individuals must be compensated in order for them to change their behavior in a manner consistent with popular will . . ..

Viewing coercion versus noncoercion as only alternative techniques obscures the moral and ethical dimension of human affairs and the role of rule -making and punishment as important sources of a moral consciousness, something that the 'ethics' of economic transactions cannot provide.

Thus the threat of coercion for violating rules of conduct or important social goals is important not simply because it is one way of trying to influence people's behavior, but also because it provides the basis for inflicting retribution on noncomplying individuals. Without allowing for the initial threat, it is far more difficult to impose coercion. But without punishment there is little sense of retribution and 'without retribution we may lose our sense of wrong'. Any system that tries to influence human conduct and does not have a substantial moral and coercive component tends to ignore the evident desire and need of citizens not merely to want to change conduct, but also to punish the wrongdoers . . ..

Any evaluation of the relative merits of coercive and noncoercive approaches should consider what role, if any, a particular approach or method has in the system of punishment and in the satisfaction of at least minimum demands for retribution.

7.2.3.2 Fundamental Rights, Due Process and the Rule of Law

Neiman highlights the communicative, censuring role of legal punishment, trenchantly objecting to those who conceive of law in purely instrumental, behavioural terms, that is, solely as a tool for shaping behaviour. Other legal concerns, often overlooked in regulatory governance scholarship, include the need to ensure respect for human rights, particularly rights to due process (or procedural fairness), the right to equal treatment and values associated with the rule of law (see also Chapter 11 on legitimacy). In the following extract,

Yeung contrasts the ideological attractions of negotiation and bargaining, on the one hand, with rule of law values typically associated with adjudicatory processes, on the other. In the second extract, she draws attention to the way in which algorithmic regulation may undermine rights of due process, right to privacy and data protection and the right to equality of treatment.

Yeung, K. (2004). *Securing Compliance.* Hart. 174, 178–180

In seeking to understand the disagreement concerning the desirability of [collaborative] . . . approaches, we may draw from the voluminous literature that has developed in response to the 'alternative dispute resolution' ('ADR') movement . . ..

As a means of dispute-resolution and form of social ordering, negotiation and bargaining in general are often claimed by ADR advocates to generate a number of other practical benefits when contrasted with formal adjudication. ADR advocates seek to emphasise its informality (implying that it is less alienating and intimidating to ordinary citizens), low cost, width and ease of access, and speed of operation. But in addition to these practical claims, all of which can be regarded as various aspects of the negotiation process that may promote effectiveness in decision-making, lies a further ideological dimension. In particular, it is claimed that because the resolution of disputes through negotiation and bargaining relies primarily on the consent of its participants, who together arrive at a mutually satisfactory outcome, it is more consistent with individual autonomy and freedom than is formal adjudication. Because the latter operates predominantly on the basis of coercion rather than consent, it thus reflects a paternalistic and interventionist state. Modes of resolution that are primarily consent-based are thus claimed to be associated with images of accommodation, conciliation, inclusiveness and participation. Court adjudication, on the other hand, is alleged to be associated with notions of combat, hostility, formality, resistance and exclusion.

Bargaining and the Rule of Law

Enthusiasm for dispute processing by means that do not involve the formal process of law is, however, far from universal . . . [Abel and Auderbach offer] largely political objections . . . essentially grounded in deep-seated scepticism of the ability of methods of alternative dispute resolution to live up to their promises when translated into a world fraught with distributional inequalities.

Both Abel and Auderbach acknowledge, however, that the values to which ADR aspires are nevertheless worthy of allegiance. In this respect, Fiss's arguments 'against settlement' reach further still. To him, '[t]o settle for something means to accept less than some ideal.' Fiss's objections to settlement rest on a particular view of the proper function of adjudication. In his view, the purpose of adjudication is not merely to resolve disputes, but to explicate and give force to the authority of legal rules, to interpret the values upon which they are grounded and to bring reality into accord with them. Thus, when legal disputes are resolved outside the court, this purpose is left wanting. For Fiss, informal non-adjudicative justice is justice denied . . ..

Fiss's objections point to an inherent tension between the use of negotiation and bargaining as a mechanism of decision-making and dispute-resolution and the rule of law, objections which resonate strongly in the critiques of the North American collaborative compliance approaches to regulatory policy implementation . . ..

Because the resolution of disputes through negotiation is shaped by the reciprocal needs and interests of the parties worked out through their bargain, rather than dictated by legal rules, it can be seen as contrary to the rule of law ideal. This is not to say, however, that legal rules have no part to play in the resolution of disputes by negotiation. Rather, participants are claimed to bargain 'in the shadow of the law' so that the outcome ultimately agreed to will be shaped and constrained by the strict legal rights and duties of the parties. But when legal disputes are settled by agreement rather than by adjudication, the resulting agreement need not reflect that which would have resulted from court adjudication through the application of legal rules.

Yeung, K. (2018). 'Algorithmic Regulation: A Critical Interrogation'. *Regulation & Governance*, 12, 505–523, https://doi.org/10.1111/rego.12158.

514–516

Legal Critiques of Algorithmic Power

Legal scholars . . . highlight how algorithmic decision-making systems may antagonise constitutional and democratic values, including risks to informational privacy and other fundamental rights, and to procedural and substantive fairness, which are briefly outlined below.

a) *Informational privacy and fundamental rights*: Among the most prominent legal concerns associated with the algorithmic turn focuses on the right to informational privacy, given the continuous monitoring and collection of personal digital data that many algorithmic systems necessitate. Several scholars have demonstrated how the technique of algorithmic profiling may undermine individual autonomy, self-determination and may risk subverting or antagonize civil and political rights such as the right to freedom from unfair discrimination. Yet because profiling involves inferring a set of characteristics (typically behavioural) about an object of interest, these profiles do not necessarily relate to any specific individual. Rather, they are algorithmic constructions, abstractions of an individual made up of fragments of correlated variables identified from a match between some of her attributes with the profiles inferred from masses of attributes from masses of individuals, which Louise Amoore calls 'data derivatives' (Amoore 2013). In addition, the profiled individual is typically oblivious to how she is being profiled (or indeed that she is being profiled at all), and has no opportunity to understand the basis upon which assessments about her are made. Hence it is practically impossible for any individual to assert a claim of right, to protest that she is 'not like that', or that while she might have been like that in the past, she does not propose to be 'like that' in the future. In other words, concerns about the profiling process may not lend themselves easily to individual rights claiming, given the nature and structure of fundamental rights within contemporary western jurisprudence. While the consequences of inaccurate profiling may be trivial (such as unsuitable product recommendations generated by digital shopping recommendation engines) the same can hardly be said for individuals who are denied the freedom to board an airplane, to be released on bail, or denied access to employment or educational opportunities as a result of these highly opaque decision-making processes.

b) *Due Process*: Other legal concerns highlight the lack of meaningful opportunities for affected individuals to contest algorithmic decisions. Constitutional rights of 'due process' (in the language of American constitutional law) or 'procedural fairness' (in British legal parlance) are intended to ensure that those affected by the decisions of public officials should be given an opportunity to participate in decisions that affect them, and that such decisions should be made in an unbiased manner. While the core principles of Anglo-American administrative law requiring executive discretion to be exercised lawfully, fairly and in accordance with the due process rights of individuals conventionally apply only to the exercise of governmental or public decision-making authority, there is rising anxiety about the freedom of powerful firms to act unilaterally against individuals without giving them an opportunity to contest or challenge such actions. Concerns about hidden bias in decision-making arise in relation to both human and automated forms of decision-making. One advantages of the latter is its capacity for consistency while avoiding the conscious and subconscious biases that invariably affects human decision-making. On the other hand, considerable attention has focused on the extent to which algorithmic decision-making systems may be affected by hidden, unintended biases which may be difficult to detect and which, owing to their capacity to operate on a one-to-many basis, like the Facebook News Feed algorithm, have the capacity to affect many millions of users at a single stroke.

c) *Substantive fairness, equality and distributive justice*: The substantive quality and content of algorithmic decisions has also attracted alarm. Algorithmic decisions may be inaccurate or erroneous. Although algorithmic regulation holds out the prospect of applying objective, mathematically rigorous methods to solve social problems, by drawing on 'raw data' emitted directly from the environment itself, rather than reliant upon the subjective (and therefore fallible) observations and choices of humans, the notion of algorithmic objectivity and infallibility is a widely held myth. Data does not exist 'out there' in some kind of wild, natural state: it must be imagined as data in the first instance, a process which must have an interpretative base. Not only can errors arise in every stage of the process of algorithmic development, from the collection of data and their calibration, the filtering and interpretation of data, the choice of algorithmic technique, the design of the algorithm and the interpretation of algorithmic output, but these processes are inherently subjective. Secondly, algorithmic decision-making processes may render biased judgments, thereby perpetuating discrimination against historically disadvantaged groups. These concerns were identified over 20 years ago by Oscar Gandy who, building on Foucault's work on panopticism, describes how the collection, processing and sharing of information about individuals and groups are used in the marketing and retail industries to coordinate and control access to goods and services (Gandy 1993). Gandy warned that, when used to profile individuals, these technologies are 'discriminatory by design', potentially undermining key aspects of democracy, equality, fairness and distributive justice, yet against which the law offers little protection. Even when considerable care is taken to avoid selection bias, algorithmic systems may unintentionally perpetuate and reinforce historical biases because the feedback loop that these systems rely upon draws on historic data patterns that may replicate themselves in algorithmic system outputs.

7.2.3.3 Constitutional Culture and Institutional Variety

A community's legal, constitutional, institutional and cultural traditions and practices also bear upon instrument choice, discussed by Ogus in the following extract:

Ogus, A (2002) 'Comparing Regulatory Systems: Institutions, Processes and Legal Forms in Industrialised Countries'. Centre on Regulation and Competition. University of Manchester. Working Paper No. 35, https://regulationbodyofknowledge.org/wp-content/uploads/2013/03/Ogus_Comparing_Regulatory_Systems.pdf.

2–3

Comparisons between national systems risk superficiality if no account is taken of the cultural and constitutional context in which the regime is to be found. We may find a strong resemblance between the regimes in two different jurisdictions: for example, similar conditions may be stipulated for the grant of a licence; and similar processes may be laid down. But the functioning of the regulatory system may be strikingly different if, for example, State A has a panoply of process values incorporated into its general administrative law and enforced by an independent judiciary, whereas in State B the matter is simply one of bureaucratic diktat. So also the concrete decisions made may depend not only on the merits of applicants and the use of highly detailed legislative or administrative criteria, but also on the constitutional basis of the system. State A may enshrine a general principle of freedom of economic activity in relation to which the requirement for licensing constitutes a necessarily limited exception; State B may, in contrast, regard the system as simply an instrument facilitating government control of the economy.

Indeed, above and beyond substantive constitutional norms may be other significant aspects to be considered under what may be loosely called 'cultural' variables. Historically, different bureaucratic and regulatory traditions have emerged in different countries relating to the style of rule-making and enforcement. Such traditions may stem from the cultures associated with different legal families (for example, common law; civil law; Scandinavian; Latin American . . .) or operate quite independently of the latter. The report begins, therefore, with

> an attempt to identify how regulation fits into the constitutional and cultural environment . . ..
>
> Constitutions control power and allocate it between different organs of the state, more specifically between legislature, executive and judiciary.

Ogus goes on to explain how variation in constitutional arrangements and traditions, even between Western democratic politics, and variation in regulatory 'styles' or traditions can result in significant differences in how public regulatory authority is allocated, distributed and held in check.

7.3 Experimental Regulation

Thus far, we have said little about the duration and scope of regulatory instruments. While regulation can be amended at any time, most regulations are intended to have a permanent character, universally applicable to all regulatees, and to remain in place for many years. This aids legal certainty and stability, allowing individuals to plan their affairs accordingly, reflecting a central tenet of the rule of law. However, sometimes regulatory measures may be temporary or experimental, that is, of limited duration and scope. Temporary regulations, that is, regulatory instruments with a limited duration, may be needed in times of crises. Examples include regulatory measures adopted during the 2008 Global Financial Crisis to promote financial recovery and temporary regulatory measures adopted to address the public health emergency created by the COVID-19 pandemic (curfews, limited capacity of establishments, vaccination and mask requirements, etc.). Experimental regulation takes various forms but typically involves applying different rules to a group of regulatees with the aim of learning whether these rules are more effective than existing ones. Regulatory sandboxes, depending on their design, are a type of experimental regulation. Regulatory sandboxes recently adopted in the financial and energy sectors offer favourable regulatory conditions to a group of regulatees (e.g., reduced regulatory burdens) to promote innovation in these industries. We briefly consider (a) temporary regulations, including sunset clauses and (b) experimental regulations and regulatory sandboxes.

7.3.1 Temporary Regulations

There are a variety of situations in which temporary regulations may be adopted, including emergencies. Sunset clauses are quite common. These confer a temporary character on a set of regulatory dispositions or a regulation. In principle, these clauses should ensure that certain regulations expire ('sunset') after a certain period. As Ranchordás explains below, sunset clauses have been used for decades, not only to regulate temporary phenomena but also to contribute to the quality of regulation by ensuring that unnecessary regulatory burdens disappear after they have served their purpose or are reassessed after some years. Their introduction in the United States in the 1980s was intended to address obsolete regulation. However, because there were too many sunset clauses to review simultaneously, they were often renewed without an evaluation, producing additional regulatory burdens. Although sunset clauses are now included in the European Commission's 'Better Regulation' toolbox, there is still little evidence that they improve the quality of regulation, with US experience demonstrating that they tend to be easily renewable.

Ranchordás, S. (2015). 'Sunset Clauses and Experimental Regulations: Blessing or Curse for Legal Certainty?'. *Statute Law Review*, 36(1), 28–45, https://doi.org/10.1093/slr/hmu002.

28–32

Sunset clauses determine the expiry of laws on a certain date and are primarily designed to guarantee that the legislator decides on their merits after a determined period . . ..

A sunset clause is a provision that determines the termination of a statute, specific provision, programme, or agency, unless there is solid evidence that the latter should be renewed for another fixed period. Two elements characterize sunset clauses: (i) limited duration; (ii) ex post evaluation. As the word suggests, a sunset clause does not aim at continuity, rather it 'sets the sun' on a provision or entire statute on a specific date, unless there are substantial reasons to believe that the former should be extended for a determined period. This termination or renewal should only occur after an ex post evaluation has taken place. This evaluation looks into the effects of the sunset disposition and verifies whether the objective for which it was enacted has been achieved, or whether the provision should be renewed for a determined period. The renewal of a sunset provision requires an inversion of the burden of proof: the actors requesting it should be able to argue and demonstrate why the sunset clause should be renewed . . ..

Sunset clauses emerged in their current 'format' in the United States in the 1970s as a reaction to the uncontrolled growth of agencies and their powers, excessive bureaucracy and public spending. Between 1976 and 1982, multiple states experienced a 'sunset-clause boom' which aimed to extinguish unnecessary agencies and unnecessary programs . . .. The 'sunset boom' did not however produce the expected results, since evaluations soon became too onerous and automatic renewals took over the review process. In addition, sunset clauses were before long captured by politicians and special interest groups that proposed the inclusion of sunset clauses in bills that otherwise would not obtain sufficient support. This effect was visible in the field of tax law, where sunset clauses were inserted in multiple tax cuts provisions so that lawmakers could reduce the estimation of revenue costs of these laws to the sunset period. By including a sunset clause, politicians could circumvent budgetary constraints and enact laws meant to last under the 'cover' of a temporary provision.

> More recently, sunset clauses have been employed in different countries to fulfil other functions. First, sunset clauses can be employed to update laws which would otherwise become obsolete and terminate laws that are no longer necessary or effective . . ..
>
> [S]unset clauses can also be employed in non-emergency (but still) temporary scenarios. This is the case of the sunset provisions introduced in counter-terrorism laws in numerous countries . . ..
>
> [S]unset clauses have been used as a means to improve the effectiveness of public administration and regulations . . .. This was [already] suggested in 2002 by the Mandelkern Group on Better Regulation that argued that sunsetting regulations could ensure that regulators reassess the underlying regulatory problem and evaluate ex post the regulation. In Germany and in the Netherlands, sunset clauses were also included in the strategy to tackle excessive bureaucracy and reduce the excessive regulatory burdens placed on private actors . . .. In the United Kingdom, the use of sunset clauses is mandatory for secondary legislation 'where there is net burden (or cost) on business or civil society organisations' . . .. The advancement of sunset clauses reflects the idea of 'one in, one out' . . ..
>
> Although sunset clauses have often been inserted in the context of 'better regulation' policies, notably as an instrument to reduce regulatory pressure, there is no evidence that the first is achieving this goal.

7.3.2 Experimental Regulations and Regulatory Sandboxes

Like sunset clauses, experimental regulations are valid for a pre-specified, fixed period. However, their primary motivation is to try out a new regulation, test their effectiveness and, based on the resulting regulatory learning, convert the experimental regulation into a permanent regulatory measure. As Ranchordás explains, experimental regulations introduce rules that typically deviate from existing rules for a fixed period, for a limited group of citizens or territory. While experimental regulations can support various goals, the expected learning depends on the regulation's underlying methodology. Good scientific methods entail ensuring that comparable sample and test groups are considered in the design of an experiment, establishing the adequacy of the intervention, indicating its appropriate duration, and considering a number of relevant variables to determine the internal and external validity of the results. Ranchordás emphasises the need for careful design: even if regulatory experiments cannot be randomised in the same manner as scientific experiments, experimental regulations have been criticised as methodologically flawed in their design, undermining the ability to draw valid conclusions concerning their effectiveness and hence the ability to generalise from them.

Ranchordás, S. (2021). 'Experimental Regulations and Regulatory Sandboxes – Law without Order?'. *Law and Method*, 1–23, doi: 10.5553/REM/.000064.

2–16

The experimental method is deeply rooted in history. Francis Bacon (1561–1626) and Robert Boyle (1627–1691), two well-known early advocates of experimental history, defined experimentalism as the collection and description of existing factual knowledge developed in the arts and crafts. Over the centuries, the experimental method expanded to multiple sciences, including law and policy . . .. The experimental method in law and policy emerged thus to channel power and promote self-governance rather than to improve the quality of regulations. In 1932, Justice Brandeis coined the metaphor 'states-as-laboratories', suggesting that the use of experiments for self-governance purposes could also be combined with the advancement of new policies 'without risk to the rest of the country' (*New State Ice Co. v. Liebmann*). More recently, experiments with laws and policies have been more directly associated with the promotion of technological innovation, the development of novel competition law and market regulation enforcement techniques the construction of alternative scenarios that help institutions design anticipatory policy for uncertain futures, and advance evidence-based lawmaking.

Experimental legal regimes, a broad term employed in this article to refer to all forms of experiments with laws and regulations, normally take the form of a temporary derogation from general rules. It entails that a different legal regime will be applied to a part of the country for a limited period in order to test its effectiveness. For example, in the case of experiments with road traffic legislation, an experimental legal regime could establish that in a set number of highways and for a determined period, drivers could be allowed to exceed the maximum speed limit by 20 km/h during the weekend. Lawmakers could test whether this experimental measure has a positive or negative impact on traffic flow and air quality. These results would then be compared with other roads where drivers were required to comply with the maximum speed limit . . ..

Despite their potential to advance regulatory and economic innovation, experimental legal regimes have been criticized because of their loose methodology, casuistic nature and the limited validity of their results. In addition, existing scholarship has unveiled many other flaws of experimental legal regimes, including their frequent politicization, their premature termination, dissatisfactory evaluations, and the general absence of methodological preoccupations . . ..

In 2019, the French Council of State conducted a thorough research into national and local experimental legal regimes, concluding that most experiments conducted in the previous two decades were characterized by a number of methodological shortcomings. These shortcomings included (i) the definition of contradictory objectives; (ii) ill-defined association of actors and the public concerned by the experiment; (iii) inaccurate construction of the sample; (iv) generalization of the measure tested before its evaluation (Conseil d'Etat, 2019). These methodological shortcomings weakened the results of the underlying legal experiments and could potentially mislead public decision-makers. The

> French Council of State also found that certain legislative actions were incorrectly portrayed as experiments or were used not to gather evidence but rather to support decisions that had already been taken. In some cases, authorities decided to implement the measure before the experiment came to an end. The French Council of State recommended greater care in the design of the experimental legal regimes; in the definition of their duration, the definition of its objectives, and the establishment of their evaluation criteria. This section draws upon these methodological shortcomings to discuss the relationship between methodological shortcomings and the failure to comply with the legal frameworks applicable to experimental regulations . . ..
>
> Experiments can help estimate the effectiveness of different laws and regulations but, as the literature has explained, methodology is key. Lawmakers refer to 'experiments' too loosely, conferring a wrongful scientific sense to temporary laws or simply new measures for which there is no full political compromise at the time of their enactment. These loose experiments rarely comply with any clear set of methodological rules or the rules designed for scientific experiments such as random assignment of measures, the design of representative control and sample groups, and evaluation methods. It is important to highlight that it should not be expected from legal experiments to fully emulate the scientific method. However, an appropriate level of randomization, a clear methodological framework could help ensure the objectivity, effectiveness, validity and legality of experimental legal regimes.

Regulatory sandboxes are a more recent, specific form of experimental regulation. They have been defined as 'a safe testbed for innovation either by allowing for the temporary application of a different regulatory regime to a small group of firms or by offering compliance guidance'. Regulatory sandboxes are both more and less encompassing than experimental regulations: first, not all regulatory sandboxes involve experimental regulatory measures as some do not temporarily derogate from existing rules but simply offer compliance assistance to market actors. Second, regulatory sandboxes involve some element of close collaboration between public and private actors not necessarily present in experimental regulation. Third, regulatory sandboxes are applied to smaller groups of market actors and apply for shorter periods than experimental regulations. While regulatory sandboxes typically last three to six months, experimental regulations may last for several years.

Regulatory sandboxes are widely used in the financial sector to support Fintech regulation. In this context, a group of firms admitted to a regulatory sandbox (cohort) are given a time-limited opportunity to test new financial products without fully complying with regulations that could otherwise make these innovations impossible or more burdensome. The financial regulator hosting the sandbox will oversee the experiment, evaluate it and then assess the results of the sandbox (e.g., whether the novel product can be developed in compliance with general rules, whether the rules that were set aside truly were necessary to protect the consumer). Regulatory sandboxes have been designed in many other sectors such as healthcare, gambling and energy, including the EU's AI Act which invites Member States to establish regulatory sandboxes for AI.

Ranchordás, S. (2021). 'Experimental lawmaking in the EU. Regulatory Sandboxes'. EU Law Live (22 October).

Despite their fast-growing popularity, regulatory sandboxes are still in their infancy. This instrument was originally mentioned in August 2014 in the context of UK's global FinTech policy. The UK Financial Conduct Authority established the first FinTech regulatory sandbox soon after. The first sandboxes ran between 2015 and 2020 and were designed to advance effective competition in the interest of consumers. Regulatory sandboxes emerged in this context as future-proof regulatory instruments which offer flexible tools for uncertain market conditions. In 2020, the UK Financial Conduct Authority initiated a new sandbox (the Digital Sandbox) in order to support innovative firms which are addressing challenges caused by COVID-19.This new sandbox was established as a trial for the creation of potentially more permanent digital testing environments for financial services.

Fintech regulatory sandboxes were regarded as successful at containing the risks of novel financial products within the experimental playground and were rapidly emulated by other sectors. OfGem, UK's energy regulator and later adopter of the sandboxing technique, explained that the appeal of this instrument results from the combination of the flexibility of market-based solutions with a 'robust and responsive regulatory and policy framework that protects and empowers consumers and encourages beneficial innovation' . . ..

While regulatory sandboxes tend to refer to the experimental (and thus temporary) disapplication of existing sandbox tools, derogation from regulatory frameworks or waivers are not the only tools employed in the context of sandboxes. Besides derogations, regulatory sandboxes can also offer participants bespoke guidance, regulatory comfort, and confirmations. Bespoke guidance consists in the provision of guidance and certainty about specific rules in particular situations. This guidance is provided bilaterally to participants solely for the purposes of their trial.

Regulatory comfort is needed when a firm is interested in trying an innovative product or process in a live operating environment, but it is concerned about the potential breach of rules in this context and legal prosecution following this breach. In cases where the firm assesses the risk of non-compliance to be very high, the sandbox could, for the purposes of the trial, provide comfort about what the regulator considers to be compliant behaviour and what its approach to enforcement is. At the resemblance of bespoke guidance, regulatory comfort is provided to the innovator and others involved in the trial . . ..

Participation in regulatory sandboxes is subject to the admission, monitoring, and evaluation of the regulator. It is up to the regulator to select the proposals of the most suitable candidates it wishes to work with in a sandbox to address a

> specific societal or technological challenge. Rules may be set aside or additional help with compliance may be given to the selected parties because there is the assumption that under normal market and regulatory conditions, these market operators would not be able to introduce an innovative product or service into the market. Moreover, regulatory sandboxes provide access to regulatory expertise and a set of tools to facilitate testing of new products that would otherwise not be granted access to markets . . ..
>
> The EU AI Regulation Proposal or, officially, the Artificial Intelligence Act, is the first EU legislative proposal to comprise regulatory sandboxes. These instruments are, at the time of writing, presented in its Title V as 'measures in support innovation'. The proposal does not regulate these regulatory sandboxes in detail as further dispositions will be established in delegated acts. Nevertheless, the proposed Regulation already provides a legal basis for these experiments with a glimpse of some of its potential limits and elements. Title V offers to Member States competent authorities or the European Data Protection Supervisor the possibility to establish 'AI regulatory sandboxes.' These sandboxes 'shall provide a controlled environment that facilitates the development, testing and validation of innovative AI systems for a limited time before their placement on the market or putting into service pursuant to a specific plan'. . .the experiment will be supervised by the competent authorities 'with a view to ensuring compliance with the Regulation.

Although the use of regulatory sandboxes is growing, they have been criticised on various grounds, including their limited scope (small cohorts), self-selection bias (market actors typically apply to participate), limited duration and narrow testing parameters, which raise doubts about their broader contribution of to regulatory learning.

Conclusion

This chapter has focused on three important concerns. Firstly, it has examined 'hybrid' regulatory instruments, which rely upon multiple modalities of control to effect their desired outcomes and/or draw on multiple sources of authority and influence, rather than relying exclusively on the regulatory capacities of the state. Secondly, it has considered a range of matters that affect how public regulators choose from amongst a wide range of regulatory instruments in any given context. Thirdly, it briefly examined various forms of experimental regulation. Chapter 8 continues our exploration of the 'how' of regulatory governance, by examining regulatory rules.

Discussion Questions

1. What are 'hybrid' regulatory techniques, and why have they acquired greater prominence in the last three decades?
2. What is 'meta-regulation' and what are its strengths and shortcomings?

3. Is the use of contractual conditions to specify terms concerning production processes appropriately regarded as a form of self-regulation when used for supply chain management?
4. In what way, if any, is it useful to understand regulatory instruments in terms of their underlying modalities of control and sources of authority?
5. How has the emergence of networked digital technologies facilitated new kinds of hybrid modalities of control? What, if anything, is genuinely novel about these techniques?
6. What factors influence the choice of preferred regulatory instrument in any given context?
7. Are there some things that money cannot buy (see Michael Sandel's extract)? If so, then how (if at all) might that affect the choice of regulatory instrument?
8. What normative values and concerns are implicated by the use of algorithmic regulation and hybrid instruments that incorporate algorithmic regulation?
9. Provide examples of problems or situations in which a temporary regulatory measure may be more effective than a permanent regulation.
10. If there are any ongoing regulatory sandboxes in your jurisdiction, inquire into their design and the adopted regulatory or policy measures.

8

Regulatory Rules

Introduction

This chapter continues our examination of 'how' to regulate by examining regulatory rules. If regulation is understood in cybernetic terms as a control system entailing three components (a standard or rule, a mechanism for gathering information and monitoring the system to identify departures from the standard and a means for bringing the system back into alignment with the standard), this chapter concerns the first of these components. We begin by examining the nature of linguistic rules, highlighting the interpretive uncertainty they invariably generate, and various strategies for seeking to reduce that uncertainty (Section 8.1). We then consider rule avoidance behaviour, including various forms of 'gaming' and other circumvention practices (Section 8.2). Section 8.3 discusses the role of technical standardization, in which the task of specifying detailed rules is largely delegated to industry and which plays a key role in facilitating mass markets and international trade. Section 8.4 examines the inescapable problem of interpretive uncertainty that surrounds the meaning and application of rules, and the role of 'soft law' and regulatory 'conversations' to help flesh out and stabilize their meaning. Interpreting and applying rules to specific factual circumstances raise further challenges, which are considered in Section 8.5, considers the role of regulatory science, RegTech and automated enforcement. The Conclusion highlights the foundational and inescapable tension between rules and discretion which arises within any regulatory regime.

8.1 Rules and Their Limits

8.1.1 The Nature of Rules

Regulatory regimes invariably rely on rules of some kind. Leaving aside design-based forms of regulation in which those rules are encoded into the fabric of artefacts, environments or organisms (See Section 8.5.2), rules are not self-executing. Hence rules' addressees retain the freedom to follow them or not. Consider, for example, frequency with which motorists fail to stop at red light signals. Scholars have devoted considerable attention to the challenges associated with using rules to guide and constrain behaviour. Many of these challenges are rooted in the indeterminate nature of rules, which is itself a product of the inherent indeterminacy of language and the subjective and contingent nature of our understanding of the surrounding factual context. The nature and source of these difficulties are highlighted in the following extract.

Black, J. (1997). *Rules and Regulators*. Oxford University Press, https://doi.org/10.1093/acprof:oso/9780198262947.001.0001.

6–9

The Nature of Rules

The three main problems associated with the use of rules in any context . . . are their tendency to over- or under-inclusiveness, their indeterminacy, and their interpretation. These problems stem from two roots: the nature of rules and the nature of language. Prescriptive rules are anticipatory, generalized abstractions, and when endowed with legal status are distinctive, authoritative forms of communication. They are also linguistic structures: how we understand, interpret, and apply rules depends in part on how we understand and interpret language. In considering the nature and limitations of rules, a legal analysis of the roles which rules are asked to play in a regulatory system needs thus to be coupled to an examination of these linguistic properties.

Inclusiveness

Rules are generalizations: they group together particular instances or attributes of an object or occurrence and abstract or generalize from them to build up a category or definition which then forms the operative basis of the rule. Say, for example, that following a lunch in a restaurant in which my black labrador dog, Rufus, has been particularly disruptive the proprietor wants to make a rule to ensure such disruption does not happen again. She will consider which aspects of the event should form the operative basis of the rule, what the rule should 'bite' on . . .. She could consider banning all black things or all things called Rufus, but . . . she should focus on the fact that Rufus was a dog, and so form a rule, 'no dogs allowed'.

The rule in this example is straightforward, but the process of rule formation is not. In making the generalization, the rule maker is choosing from a range of individual properties which an event or object possesses; in making that choice she searches for the aspect of the particular which is causally relevant to the aim of the rule: the goal which is sought to be achieved or the harm which is sought to be avoided. It is thus the overall aim or purpose of the rule which determines which among a range of generalizations should be chosen as the operative fact or facts for the ensuing rule. However in forming the generalization, which is the operative basis of the rule, only some features of the particular event or object are focused on and are then projected onto future events, beyond the particulars which served as the paradigm or archetype for the formation of the generalization. The generalizations in rules are thus simplifications of complex events, objects or courses of behaviour. Aspects of those events will thus be left out, or 'suppressed' by the generalization. Further, the generalization, being necessarily selective, will also include some properties which will in some circumstances be irrelevant.

Purpose thus interacts with the generalization. The inclusiveness of a rule (or more accurately, its generalization) is a function of the rule's purpose or justification. It is the imperfect match between the rule and its purpose which is represented in the description of rules as over- or under-inclusive. This mismatch can occur for three reasons. First, as noted, the generalization which is the operative basis of the rule inevitably suppresses properties that may subsequently be relevant or includes properties that may in some cases be irrelevant. Secondly, the causal relationship between the event and the harm/goal is likely to be only an approximate one: the generalization bears simply a probable relationship to the harm sought to be avoided or goal sought to be achieved. Thirdly, even if a perfect causal match between the generalization and the aim of the rule could be achieved, future events may develop in such a way that it ceases to be so . . ..

It follows from this that over or under-inclusiveness, although inherent, is likely to be exacerbated in certain circumstances, viz., where the context in which the rule operates is one which is subject to frequent change, where the course of change is unforeseeable, where the range of situations in which the rule will apply is great, and where there is an uncertain causal relationship between the events, objects or behaviour focused on and the harm to be avoided or goal to be achieved . . ..

Legal rules, and particularly regulatory rules, perform social management and instrumental functions. Rules are embodiments of policy decisions, and their success is measured in terms of the extent to which they ensure that the substance of policy is achieved . . ..

Indeterminacy

Rules are also inherently indeterminate. Their indeterminacy arises in part from the nature of language, in part from their anticipatory nature, and in part because they rely on others for their application. Their indeterminacy matters because rules, particularly legal rules, are entrenched, authoritative statements which are meant to guide behaviour, be applied on an indefinite number of occasions, and which have sanctions attached for their breach. It is thus important to know whether this particular occasion is one of those in which the rule should be applied.

The most familiar exponent of the indeterminacy of legal rules is Hart, who described rules as having a 'core' of meaning and a 'penumbra of uncertainty' or 'fringe of vagueness'. The indeterminacy arises not because the meaning of the word is unclear in itself, but because in applying the rule the question would always arise as to whether the general term used in the rule applied to this particular fact situation . . ..

Even if consensus could gradually be built up as to the 'core meaning' of a particular term, the vagaries of future events would mean that there would still be instances 'thrown up by nature or human invention' which would possess only some of the features of the paradigm case or cases but not others . . .. Rules thus have an inherent vagueness which stems not from language but from the prospective generalizations which characterize rules – even if determinant, the limits of human foresight mean that the least vague term may turn out to be vague when applied to a situation unforeseen when the term was defined.

Interpretation

Rules need a sympathetic audience if they are to be interpreted and applied in a way which will further the purpose for which they were formed; rule maker and rule applier are to this extent in a reciprocal relationship. Such a sympathetic interpretation is essentially what those who advocate a purposive approach to interpretation demand. Problems of inclusiveness and determinacy or certainty can be addressed by interpreting the rule in accordance with its underlying aim. By contrast, the purpose of the rule could be defeated if the rule is interpreted literally, if things suppressed by the generalization remain suppressed.

Rules also need an informed audience, one which understands the context of assumptions and practices in which the rule is based, which gave rise to it, and which it is trying to address. As practices change, the application of rules needs to change with them. As we have seen, rules can never be sufficiently explicit to cover every circumstance. Nor can they ever express all the tacit understandings on which the rule is based as to those practices or to the state of the world. A rule 'no dogs allowed' relies on the shared understanding of what a 'dog' is; it does not need to then go on to define 'dog' into its semantic components . . ..

A rule, then, is only as good as its interpretation. To follow Hart again, rules cannot apply themselves, they rely on others for their application. To be applied, rules have to be interpreted . . ..

The problems of interpretation . . . also cover the honest perplexity of those subject to the rule of its application in a particular circumstance, which in turn can affect the certainty of the rule's operation. Given then the centrality of interpretation for the operation of rules, how can the rule maker know how the rule will be interpreted and applied? What is the relationship between rules and their interpretation? The theoretical literature exploring the relationship between rules and interpretation is considerable . . ..

[W]e are not concerned with meaning per se, and whether there is an objectively 'correct' or 'real' meaning, for example. Rather what we are concerned with is how that rule will be interpreted and applied by those it is regulating; not how it should be . . ..

The writing in this area is extensive; however within it the writings of Wittgenstein have been some of the most influential. Wittgenstein was concerned with unreflective rule following, in mathematics or language, and not with legal rules. His theory has nevertheless spawned a considerable debate on

> legal rule following and application. He argued that automatic, unreflective rule following arose from shared judgements in the meaning and application of that rule. If language is to be a means of communication there must be agreement not only in definitions but also . . . in judgements.
>
> Judgements include all the connections we make in our actions between language and the world: between a rule and its application, for example, or between how we have used a term in the past and whether we apply it to a particular new instance. Agreement in judgements arises in turn from shared understandings arising from shared 'forms of life'. The concept of forms of life is cultural; different educations, interests, concerns, human relations or relations to nature constitute distinct forms of life. It includes social contexts, cultures, practices, and training and forms the framework in which our use of language occurs (or our language-game is played, to adopt Wittgenstein's terminology). There are no shared rules without shared patterns of normative actions, and so shared judgements about justifications, criticisms, explanations, descriptions. The interpretation and application of a rule will thus be clear where there is agreement as to the meaning of the rule; agreement in turn comes from shared forms of life.

Drawing on Wittgenstein's analysis, Black draws three lessons that illuminate the nature of legal rules and their interpretation. Firstly, that the 'plain' or 'literal' meaning of a rule refers to the meaning that participants from a specific community would unreflectively assign to it. Evaluative terms normally have a greater range of potentially acceptable interpretations than descriptive ones, particularly those expressed in quantifiable terms (e.g., 'reasonable speed' in comparison with '30 miles per hour'). Secondly, the meaning (and hence application) of a rule is specific to an *interpretive community* so that the 'clarity' of a rule is not an objective matter but specific to a given interpretive community. Thirdly, the notion of an 'interpretive community' offers a theoretical basis for understanding many empirical observations about rule-following and rule interpretation in bureaucratic and regulatory practice. Since it is impossible for a rule-maker to make sufficiently explicit all the tacit assumptions on which the successful application of the rule depend, others will always have scope to adopt interpretations that differ from the rule-maker's intentions. Black also argues that the interpretative approach taken to any given rule is partly a product of the structure of the rule itself, identifying four dimensions along which rules may differ: the substance or scope of a rule, the character or legal status, the sanction attached to a rule and its linguistic structure. The structural form of rules shapes the distribution of discretion or decisional authority within a regulatory system, so that, for example, the use of vague, permissive language can alleviate the likelihood of formalistic interpretations. Colin Diver also considers problems associated with rule formation and interpretation but takes an economic rather than a sociological approach. In the following extract, he considers different ways of formulating rules in light of three desirable qualities: transparency, accessibility and congruence. Given that the uncertainty associated with rule use imposes social costs, the challenge for Diver is to reduce the social costs associated with rule imprecision when designing rules to regulate behavior.

Diver, C. S. (1998). 'The Optimal Precision of Administrative Rules'. In Robert Baldwin, Colin Scott, and Christopher Hood (eds.), *A Reader on Regulation, Oxford Readings in Socio-Legal Studies.* Oxford University Press, 219–269,

https://doi.org/10.1093/acprof:oso/9780198765295.003.0008.

220–224

I. The Concept of Rule Precision

Before we can begin to make useful prescriptions about the precision of administrative rules, we must give the concept some added precision of its own.

A. Three Dimensions of Rules

The success of a rule in effecting its purpose largely depends on the words a draftsman uses to express his intentions. A rational rulemaker will therefore be attentive to the probable effect of his choice of words upon the rule's intended audience. First, he will want to use words with well-defined and universally accepted meanings within the relevant community. I refer to this quality as 'transparency'. Second, the rulemaker will want his rule to be 'accessible' to its intended audience-that is, applicable to concrete situations without excessive difficulty or effort. Finally, of course, a policymaker will care about whether the substantive content of the message communicated in his words produces the desired behavior. The rule should, in other words, be 'congruent' with the underlying policy objective . . ..

Since any criterion for evaluating the 'precision' of administrative rules should include these three values, it would be tempting simply to define as 'precise' a rule that combined the virtues of transparency, accessibility, and congruence. But two formidable obstacles lie in the path of such a venture – measurement and tradeoffs.

B. The Problem of Measurement

We must ask initially how to translate the goals of transparency, accessibility, and congruence into usable criteria for evaluating specific rules. To sketch the dimensions of that task, I offer a simple illustration. Imagine a policymaker who must establish certification criteria for commercial aircraft pilots. One aspect of that task is to define the circumstances under which a pilot, once certified, should no longer be eligible to serve in that capacity. Let us suppose our lawmaker has a rough idea of a policy objective: pilots should retire when the social cost of allowing them to continue, measured as the risk of accidents that they might cause multiplied by their consequences, exceeds the social benefit, measured as the costs avoided by not having to find and train a replacement. But how can the lawmaker capture this idea in a legal standard?

Let us initially offer three alternative verbal formulations for such a rule:

- Model I: No person may pilot a commercial airplane after his sixtieth birthday.
- Model II: No person may pilot a commercial airplane if he poses an unreasonable risk of an accident.
- Model III: No person may pilot a commercial airplane if he falls within one of the following categories. (There follow tables displaying all combinations of values for numerous variables, including years and level of experience, hours of air time logged, age, height, weight, blood pressure, heart rate, eyesight, and other vital signs, that would disqualify a pilot from further eligibility to pilot aircraft.)

Which formulation is most transparent? The answer is easy: Model I. Everyone knows exactly what the words 'sixtieth' and 'birthday' mean. The crucial concept of Model II – 'unreasonable' risk – seems, by contrast, susceptible to widely varying interpretations. Suppose, however, that among the rule's intended audience, the term 'unreasonable risk of accident' had acquired a very special meaning: namely, 'older than 60'. In that case, the two rules would be equally transparent. That contingency, however implausible here, nonetheless reminds us of the danger of judging a rule's transparency without looking beyond its words to its actual impact.

The danger inherent in facial evaluation is even more evident in applying the other two criteria. Is the rule of Model II or Model III more accessible? The former is shorter and more memorable. It also apparently requires only a single judgment-the 'reasonableness' of the risk. That judgment, however, may well rest on a set of subsidiary inquiries as numerous and complex as those encompassed within Model III's more explicit set of tables.

Similarly, our intuition that Model II is more congruent than, say, Model I, may be unreliable. The facial resemblance between Model II and the rulemaker's ultimate objective depends on the unverifiable assumption that 'unreasonable' connotes 'economically inefficient' . . ..

A. An Efficiency Criterion for Rule Precision

Since tradeoffs among values are unavoidable, the morally sensitive rulemaker must reduce those conflicting values to some common denominator. One candidate is the currency of welfare economics – 'social utility'. A social utility-maximizing rulemaker would, for any conceivable set of rule formulations, identify and estimate the social costs and benefits flowing from each, and select the one with the greatest net social benefit. Subject to a constraint on his rulemaking budget or authority, the rulemaker would continue adding to his stock of rules so long as the marginal social benefit of the last increment exceeded its marginal cost.

Diver goes on to argue that evaluating pilot retirement rules across the values of transparency, accessibility and congruence for each of the three models have strengths and shortcomings. Model I, while mechanically applicable, may ground deserving pilots and allow some unfit ones to continue flying. Model II, despite its simplicity, results in varied interpretations. Model III, although objective, faces application challenges. Modifying Model I by allowing exceptions introduces ambiguity in defining exempt pilots. Similarly, enhancing Model II's transparency by detailing components of 'unreasonable risk' raises issues of specificity, diminishing congruence or accessibility. In attempting to decide on which formulation to adopt, Diver (1998: 223–225) argues that:

> Invocation of moral values like fairness, equity, or community offers little promise. Each dimension of regulatory precision implicates important moral principles. Transparent rules help to assure equality by defining when people are 'similarly situated' and divorcing the outcome of an official determination from the decisionmakers. An accessible rule, by contrast, promotes communal and 'dignitary' values by enabling members of its audience to participate in its application to their individual circumstances. Congruence directly fosters the law's substantive moral aims by promoting outcomes in individual cases consistent with those aims.
>
> These principles frequently work at cross-purposes, however, precisely because tradeoffs occur along the three dimensions of precision. A perfectly transparent rule ('no person with a surname ending in a vowel may be a pilot') may assure similar treatment of categorically similar cases, but it may also fail to provide defensible applications. A morally congruent rule ('immorality is prohibited') can be too vague to satisfy the moral imperatives of fair warning and meaningful participation. A perfectly transparent and congruent rule may be so cumbersome as to deprive its audience of fair warning.
>
> **A. An Efficiency Criterion for Rule Precision**
>
> Since tradeoffs among values are unavoidable, the morally sensitive rulemaker must reduce those conflicting values to some common denominator. One candidate is the currency of welfare economics – 'social utility'. A social utility-maximizing rulemaker would, for any conceivable set of rule formulations, identify and estimate the social costs and benefits flowing from each, and select the one with the greatest net social benefit. Subject to a constraint on his rulemaking budget or authority, the rulemaker would continue adding to his stock of rules so long as the marginal social benefit of the last increment exceeded its marginal cost.

Based on his analysis, he concludes that optimal precision varies from rule to rule:

> The degree of precision appropriate to any particular rule depends on a series of variables peculiar to the rule's author, enforcer, and addressee. As a consequence, generalizations about optimal rule precision are inherently suspect.

8.1.2 Rules, Principles and 'Principles-based Regulation' (PBR)

The unavoidable trade-offs associated with drafting rules, particularly the level of detail or 'precision' with which a rule is drafted, resonate with familiar debates within legal scholarship concerning the relative advantages and disadvantages of detailed 'rules', on the one hand, and more broadly framed general 'principles', on the other. Yet the distinction between rules and principles is neither binary nor clear-cut. Instead, as Cristie Ford explains below, they are best understood as located along a spectrum in which the appropriate choice will invariably be a product of the specific priorities, mandate and context in which regulation is intended to operate:

Ford, C. (2010). 'Principles-Based Securities Regulation in the Wake of the Global Financial Crisis'. *McGill Law Journal*, 55, 257–307, https://lawjournal.mcgill.ca/wp-content/uploads/pdf/8421183-Ford.pdf.

263–269

At the theoretical level, the distinction between rules and principles, and their relative advantages and disadvantages, have been quite well canvassed. Generally speaking, rules are considered to have the advantages of being more precise and certain, but the consequent disadvantages of being potentially rigid, reactive, and insensitive to context and therefore inevitably over- or under-inclusive. They may also promote or permit 'loophole behaviour', and be more easily 'gamed' by sophisticated actors. In comparison, principles are more flexible, more sensitive to context, and therefore potentially fairer when applied. On the other hand, principles can be uncertain, unpredictable, and difficult and costly to interpret. Because they allocate substantial decision-making to front-line decision-makers, they can also permit arbitrary conduct and regulatory overreaching . . ..

Rules and principles are also best understood as points on a continuum rather than discrete concepts, and there is a good deal of overlap and convergence among them. Any complex regulatory system will be (and should be) an amalgam of rules and principles . . ..

[S]ettling upon a particular mix between rules and principles requires that choices be made, and public priorities be established. In particular, where these lines are drawn depends on public priorities that the legislator has the mandate to establish. For example, a legislator who is concerned about regulatory overreach or lack of transparency in a particular area would see to it that the regulator had very little discretion (i.e., that expectations are cast as rules rather than principles and are enshrined in a statute) when it comes to such things as access to information, the handling of complaints, or accountability to Parliament. A legislator concerned about individual rights would limit discretion (i.e., would craft rules not principles) regarding hearings, procedural fairness, and participation or consultation rights . . ..

Important external considerations also come into play. For example, how much scope does the legislator want to leave to the interpretation of regulators, courts,

> or tribunals? Where does existing regulatory practice (whether principles-based or rules-based) seem to be well-established, to be working well, and to have created expectations on which stakeholders rely? ... Are some issues particularly important ...? On what specific issues does the political will exist to move decisively away from the status quo? ... All of this requires that policy-makers develop a set of criteria reflecting policy calculations for deciding when to use rules and when to use principles.
>
> Context also matters. An appropriate balance between rules and principles in securities regulation may look quite different from the appropriate balance in other regulatory arenas. The nature of the industry being regulated, the roles of the various players in it, and the risks associated with that area of conduct will inform the regulatory design process. It is relevant that securities regulation is a disclosure-based system that relies heavily on ensuring reasonable access to information as a means for protecting investors. This suggests that congruence is important in this context: core definitions of materiality and disclosure should be broad and principles-based. Preventing fraud and minimizing 'cosmetic' compliance and 'loophole behaviour' are other areas where the over- or under-inclusiveness of rules is particularly problematic. This is the rationale for broad statutory definitions of fraud and commissions' sweeping public interest powers. Financial markets are also complex, fast-moving environments marked by constant product-level innovation. Principles are preferable in this environment when underpinned by effective information-gathering and analytical mechanisms, since detailed rules may only add to complexity and opacity. Principles also make sense where a flexible approach is needed to ensure good corporate conduct – for example, with regard to internal compliance processes, corporate culture, or risk assessment by management. Like the deference accorded to securities commissions under administrative law, principles-based regulation also reflects legislative faith in regulatory expertise, objectivity, fairness, and capacity.

Ford goes on to reflect upon the notion of 'principles-based regulation'. She highlights the importance of attending to the way in which PBR is *implemented*, warning that it may slide into 'bare self-regulation' in the absence of meaningful independent regulatory oversight, engagement and accountability, provoking reflection on the 'role of devolution to industry' in the application of principles-based regulation. Ford (2010: 280–294) explains:

> Principles-based regulation works by devolving the details of regulation to industry, on the assumption that industry has the best information and is in the best position to both assess and bear its own risks. . .Crucially, devolution does not automatically imply weak public oversight. Nevertheless, devolution accompanied by an ideology of self-regulation contributed to insufficient oversight ... [which] allowed banks and investment banks to maintain capital reserves based on their own internal risk-assessment models, with very little scrutiny from regulators.
>
> Regulatory faith in industry actors' competence, if not literally their bona fides, proved to have been misplaced to catastrophic effect. George Soros has charged

that the GFC reflects a 'shocking abdication of responsibility' on the part of regulators. Investment banks and others engaged in originating, structuring, and selling financial products engaged in breathtakingly bad behaviour . . ..

There is also a strong public-choice narrative: banks had little incentive to behave prudently in building tranches of consumer debt-based securities because they sold them to third parties, in a market eager to buy them . . ..

Regulators also seem to have underestimated the degree to which industry actors would try to avoid or circumvent regulatory oversight . . ..

According to the Turner Review [a report commissioned by the Chancellor of the Exchequer in October 2008 to review the causes of the financial crisis and to make recommendations about regulatory changes] the FSA did not fail because it embraced principles-based regulation . . .. Instead, Lord Turner ascribes blame to flaws in FSA philosophy – that is, to a hands-off, market-based regulatory approach that assumed that: markets were generally self-correcting; market discipline could be trusted to contain risk; the primary responsibility for managing risk lay with senior management, not regulators, because senior management had better information; and consumers were best protected through unfettered and transparent markets, not product regulation or direct intervention . . ..

Principles-based regulation is a particular regulatory approach that may or may not be highly interventionist, depending on how it is implemented, even though its effectiveness relies on pulling industry's own experience and information into regulatory expectations. Indeed, some opponents of principles-based regulation are primarily concerned about the possibility that such an approach would allow regulators to overreach, especially in the enforcement context. Whether a principles-based approach amounts to lax regulation, overzealous regulation, or (impossibly) pitch-perfect regulation is a function of how, and how well, it is implemented . . ..

Principles-based regulation as properly understood inevitably requires a robust and capable public role, including meaningful enforcement. Principles-based regulation is not code for a position that promotes allowing industry to do an end run around the regulator . . ..

The GFC represents an important lesson for some new governance scholarship, some of which has not always been particularly interested in how theory plays out in practice. Indeed, the shortfall between the promise of an inspiring theoretical model and its application to real-life regulation makes the problem more (not less) important to solve. What was missing from many aspects of financial regulation, in retrospect, was meaningful accountability . . ..

One of the common arguments in favour of principles-based regulation is that it supports innovation. While this continues to be an important value, more thought needs to go into precisely how it supports innovation, to what point innovation confers net benefits, and to whom those benefits flow. A fundamental risk associated with principles-based regulation is that, in the absence of the (at least putatively) immovable markers that rules represent,

> there will be 'creep' around the meaning of a term. Without regulatory oversight to ensure that terms are interpreted in a reasonable and accountable manner, self-interested actors can be expected to define terms in their own interest.

Ford (2010: 299–300) concludes:

> Principles-based regulation requires considerable regulatory capacity in order to be credible. It requires greater regulatory capacity in terms of numbers, resources, and expertise than has been allocated to it in some of the infamous examples of regulatory failure . . . the failure of Northern Rock in the United Kingdom, and of the SEC's CSE Program in the United States . . ..
>
> Principles-based regulation will not function well if it is purely technocratic, closed, and expertise-based. Technical expertise is not necessarily politically or socially neutral, and expertise-based models can shut down useful discussion. By contrast, principles-based regulation is a system whose evolution depends not on modelling, but on ongoing dialogue with stakeholders based on their real-life experience. Principles-based regulation is actually a different model from that based on technical expertise: it derives its legitimacy from its collaborative, dialogic experience, and it operates on the basis that pragmatic, learning-by-doing experience is a more reliable foundation than abstract theory for regulatory policy development. The quality of the decisions that emerge from its collaborative process, as well as the basic legitimacy of that process, require broad participation. It also matters whether the interpretive community that is engaged in filling in the details around a principles-level regulatory requirement is sufficiently inclusive and diverse. That community must have enough common ground that its constituent parts can speak to each other and a certain degree of trust can exist. At the same time, too much homogeneity limits the range of imaginable possibilities. This calls for a regulatory architecture that specifically builds in opportunities for all key stakeholders to participate.
>
> Adopting PBR does not mean doing away with rules. Rather, it is a particular approach to structuring regulation that includes rules. It gives legislatures the power to set high level regulatory goals and outcomes, and leaves the articulation of processes and details to front line regulators in collaboration with industry itself. Fundamental to principles based regulation is the development of a functional and effective 'interpretative community' that includes industry participants, regulators and other stakeholders in on-going communication around the content of regulatory principles.

8.1.3 Performance or 'Outcome'-based Standards vs 'Process'-based Standards

Closely allied to the notion of Principles-Based Regulation (PBR) is the concept of 'outcome-based' or 'performance based' regulation, although they are not coterminous (see Box 8.1). Outcome-based regulation entails mandating the substantive outcome that the regulated activity must meet, but members of the regulated community are free to determine the means to achieve it. It is often contrasted with 'process-based' or 'technology-based'

Box 8.1 Volkswagen (VW) 'Dieselgate' Scandal

The reliance of performance-based standards on meaningful and effective testing and its vulnerability was vividly demonstrated in the VW Dieselgate scandal. Volkswagen programmed into the on-board software installed in its vehicles the capacity to detect when the vehicle was subject to emissions testing in a laboratory and when in on-road use. During on-road use, the software would automatically re-calibrate to achieve better fuel economy and responsiveness in on-road use, even though this increased emissions well above the legally mandated level, resulting in emissions forty times higher than the mandated maximum limit. It was not until 2015 when a small team of West Virginian academic researchers funded by a grant from a small non-profit organisation (the International Council on Clean Transportation [ICCT]) brought the deception to light. Once the alarm was raised, government regulators initiated the investigations that ultimately led to VW's confession. In the United States, Volkswagen was forced to buy back vehicles or offer effective emissions fixes and also paid almost $3 billion into a fund to help US states cut pollution from road transport. In the EU, more rigorous tests were introduced in 2019.

Rulings by the Court of Justice of the European Union (CJEU) since 2020 have clarified what constitutes an illegal defeat device. Yet, based on extensive testing evidence, the ICCT revealed in 2022 that about 13 million highly polluting diesel vehicles sold from 2009 to 2019 remain on the roads. They identified a further 6 million diesels with 'suspicious' levels of emissions, spanning 200 different models produced by all the major manufacturers, which the ICCT is 'almost certain' were using a software defeat device. Both the ICCT and other environmental charities claim that the proportion of highly polluting vehicles that have been recalled is small, lamenting inadequate transparency over whether repairs are effective, and that few auto manufacturers in Europe have been punished or held to account to deliver effective solutions leaving individual consumers to seek financial compensation via class-action lawsuits.

By 2022, VW had spent more than €30 billion ($33 billion) in legal fees and compensation payments to customers, including $15 billion settlement in the United States. In Europe, compensation payments to consumers have been considerably lower and taken longer to settle because national legal systems in Europe do not easily allow for US-style 'class actions' that allow lawyers to take action on behalf of a whole group of claimants without needing their explicit approval. Yet the scandal has become one of the costliest corporate scandals in history. A fraud trial of the former VW chief executive Martin Winterkorn has been delayed due to his ill health, but eighty-nine court sessions are scheduled through September 2025.

Source

Carrington, D. (2023). 'Dieselgate: Millions of 'Extremely' Polluting Cars Still on Europe's Roads, Says report', *The Guardian*, 22 March, www.theguardian.com/environment/2023/mar/22/dieselgate-millions-of-extremely-polluting-cars-still-on-europes-roads-says-report.

standards, which prescribe how the regulated entity must act comply with regulatory rules. As Spinardi (2019: 523) explains:

> Prescriptive regulation – also known as 'technology-based regulation' – focuses on rules specifying what actions need to be taken to achieve compliance. These

rules are intended to produce a desired level of performance, but in a prescriptive regime the regulator's everyday focus is on checking compliance with the rules and not on measuring, or predicting, performance outcomes .... The alternative approach is performance-based regulation that focuses on outcomes specifying the level of performance that is considered satisfactory.

Outcome-based regulation also became fashionable in the late 1990s early 2000s. It was believed to overcome shortcomings of the 'one-size-fits-all' approach of prescriptive regulation, often aligned with a belief that market-forces facilitate superior outcomes relative to heavy-handed state intervention that infused the prevailing neoliberal de-regulatory agenda. However, as the following two extracts demonstrate, implementing PBR effectively relies crucially on the capacity to evaluate whether the substantive performance standard has been met (or can reliably be expected to be met) in any given case. This generates significant epistemic challenges, including the ability to test, measure and evaluate performance in a manner that reflects real-world experience and the need for appropriate expertise and the need for evaluative judgements in circumstances where in-the-field testing is not morally feasible, some of which are examined in Chapter 9.

In the following extract, Coglianese and Nash consider the behaviour of diesel truck engine manufacturers, which was essentially the same as VW in 'Dieselgate', employing in-vehicle software to 'cheat' emissions limits, resulting in the Environmental Protection Agency's largest ever fine. They draw attention to serious shortcomings of performance-based regulation, arguing that the flexibility offered by performance-based regulation enables regulatees to develop innovative approaches to pass mandated tests while confounding regulators' broader policy objectives.

Coglianese, C., and Nash, J. (2017). 'The Law of the Test: Performance Based Regulation and Diesel-Emissions Control'. *Yale Journal of Regulation*, 33–90, https://scholarship.law.upenn.edu/faculty_scholarship/1712.

44–89

To enforce performance standards, regulators need some way to determine whether regulated targets have met the applicable outcomes. For performance standards, then, the available methods of observation, testing, measurement and monitoring merit attention. . .Methods of assessment can include (1) direct, in-use measurement of actual outputs, whether continuously or at intervals (2) testing under conditions thought to mirror real-world conditions (3) simulations, using mathematical models of relationships among inputs, outputs and various operational constraints ....

These methods of assessment matter.... After all, the extent to which a performance standard works effectively will be a function of ... how accurately and comprehensively the regulator is able to monitor the performance of regulated entities ....

Until the mid-2000s, no feasible method existed to test emissions from heavy-duty diesel engine-powered *vehicles*. Instead, manufacturers had to test *engine* emissions in a laboratory setting with the engine sitting on a block rather than in a vehicle. The inability to test vehicles in use has resulted in important implications for the EPA's performance-based regulation of heavy-duty diesel engine emissions ....

When the EPA subsequently adopted its transient test in 1980, it amounted to a major breakthrough in making the test a much closer approximation to real-world driving conditions. The transient test required manufacturers to test emissions from engines running at a continually changing set of speed/torque conditions ... [but] was still artificial. Manufacturers still measured emissions from engines that ran only for about forty minutes total in a laboratory setting under a defined set of parameters - rather than longer-term monitoring of vehicles in-use. The implications of this testing protocol became increasingly evident after 1998, when the EPA decided to file an enforcement action against the manufacturers of heavy-duty diesel engines, charging them with systematically gaming the agency's performance-based regulatory system ....

[I]n 2000, the EPA announced a major innovation on the horizon: in-use testing. The EPA finalized its in-use testing program in detail in 2005, after in-use testing became possible with the development of 'portable emissions measurement systems' (PEMSs). PEMs are about the size of a large suitcase, mounted inside or outside the cab of a truck. The PEMs available today measure gaseous pollutants .... On-board, in-use testing now makes it possible for the EPA to assess environmental performance over the course of a vehicle's life. According to the program structure, the EPA selects a certain number of diesel engine 'families' to be tested, which comprise about 25% of a manufacturer's fleet in any given year.

Lessons Learned

The history of the EPA's regulation of heavy-duty diesel engine emissions clearly shows that government has actually been quite willing to rely on performance standards for many decades, at least in the automobile emissions context ... the EPA's experience with diesel emissions regulation offers seven counterbalancing lessons ....

1. *Performance standards can sometimes generate problematic 'teaching-to-the-test' responses.* The behaviour of diesel engine manufacturers in the face of regulatory demands reveals an obvious but insufficiently acknowledged problem with performance standards: gaming the system. In the field of education, gaming like this is referred to as 'teaching to the test'. This phenomenon need not be at all malicious or ill intentioned .... Performance standards not only are vulnerable to this problem, but they even seem to invite it ....
2. *Performance standards can sometimes increase, rather than decrease, the cumbersomeness and complexity of environmental regulation* .... The regulatory history of diesel engine regulation reveals that performance standards are not necessarily any panacea for seemingly out-of-control red tape. True, the EPA's performance-based limit gave heavy-duty diesel engine

manufacturers the theoretical flexibility to choose how to reduce NOx emissions. But the agency has also added requirement after requirement to its testing regimen over the years, resulting in a highly prescriptive protocol for how manufacturers must conduct required emissions testing .... Not only did the EPA's standards impose burdensome costs and complexities on the industry but also the EPA itself has hardly found them easy to design. The EPA took decades to refine its testing protocols, and presumably the tests will be refined still further following the Volkswagen scandal ....

3. *Despite their promise of flexibility, performance standards can still sometimes constrain industry choice and opportunities for innovation.* Performance standards' theoretical advantage stems from the discretion they can provide to regulated firms. But in practice, the amount of discretion that a performance standard provides will vary significantly, depending on the meaningful options the standard allows regulated firms to consider .. . ..
4. *Basing a performance standard on a single goal can sometimes lead to undesired outcomes with respect to other goals* .... The paucity of attention to trade-offs in the literature on performance standards is surprising, and particularly worrisome. If government adopts a standard for one goal but ignores other goals, the latter objectives may eventually suffer as industry adapts by securing the mandatory goal at the expense of other goals.
5. *Performance standards eliminate neither conflict nor litigation over environmental policy.* Although some observers have suggested that performance-based regulation will reduce conflict and make environmental policy more collaborative, the experience with the EPA's diesel emissions regulations does not provide much reason to expect any substantial reduction in adversarialism ....
6. *Without effective testing and monitoring, performance standards are destined to fail.* All regulation depends on effective oversight. But since performance standards invite firms to make their own choices, effective testing and monitoring assumes a special significance for this form of regulation ... this case study of diesel engine emissions regulation shows all too well how difficult, if not nearly impossible, it can be for regulators to obtain accurate, relevant information on regulated firms' performance. The EPA's tragic failure to detect Volkswagen's noncompliance twenty years after its experience with diesel truck engine manufacturers only drives this point home. Regulators must remain cognizant that performance on the test very well may not equate to performance in action, especially when regulators test performance in artificial settings, such as a laboratory.
7. *Even when performance standards are implemented fully, and even when firms faithfully comply with them, policy success may still remain elusive.* Performance standards are usually based on an output or outcome that is thought to be a precursor to, or perhaps a proxy for, the ultimate outcome of concern underlying the standards. For that reason, these standards can fail, even when firms fully comply with their letter and spirit, if the link between the outcome specified in a standard and the ultimate outcome of concern prove to be faulty, outdated, or incomplete. Other factors, natural or human, may well contribute to the underlying problem, and these factors may remain

completely unchanged by the regulation. The regulation's design may either fail to target the root cause of the problem or may fail to foreclose other causal pathways that lead to that problem . . ..

Conclusion

Performance standards are clearly not a cure-all. Their success ultimately depends on a regulator's ability to specify performance and then to measure and monitor it accurately, conditions that will not always be met . . .. Although performance standards are sometimes assumed to be 'generally superior' to other approaches, the reality is more complex than previously acknowledged.

Given the strengths and limitations of both principles-based regulation and outcome-based regulation, how do they compare? Cristie Ford considers precisely this question, highlighting the important role of a suitable 'interpretative community' (emphasised in Black's extract, above) and effective and open two-way communication between that community and the regulator:

Ford, C. (2010). 'Principles-Based Securities Regulation in the Wake of the Global Financial Crisis'. *McGill Law Journal*, 55, 1–50.

21–22

[O]utcome orientation has important implications on how regulators approach their task, and understand their mandate. By definition, outcome-oriented regulation accepts that there may be more than one means or process to achieve a regulatory goal. It transfers decision-making about process from regulators to industry. The essential assumption underlying both principles-based and outcome-oriented regulation is that legislators and regulators are in the best position to develop regulatory goals, but may not be in the best position to devise process-based means for achieving those goals. One of the reasons that outcome-oriented regulation is attractive is that it establishes a more direct relationship between regulatory goals and regulatory requirements. Outcome-oriented regulation translates regulatory goals directly and transparently into the outcomes that industry is required to meet. By contrast, process-oriented requirements that are developed by regulators in advance may not be perfectly tailored to regulatory goals, even though regulators possess less contextual information than industry actors do. Process-oriented regulation can also permit market participants to abide by the letter of the law while ignoring its spirit. This is especially the case when it comes to highly complex instruments, or in areas where events are fast-moving and regulators on their own could not hope to keep up with the pace of innovation.

Fundamental to an outcome-oriented system is the existence or development of an 'interpretive community' that collectively develops, on a rolling basis, the detailed content of statutory principles. In order to function transparently and predictably, a principles-based system must build in mechanisms that allow regulators to communicate with industry about their expectations, and that both allow and require industry to speak openly and regularly with regulators about their processes. Communication can take place through a number of channels including official administrative guidance, speeches, 'no action' or 'Dear CEO' letters, compliance audits, comments on industry standards, or specific enforcement actions. Over time, such communication can help develop an interpretive community that understands regulatory expectations, and can usefully interpret regulatory pronouncements about 'reasonableness' or 'effectiveness' in different situations.

Principles-based securities regulation is thus a particular way of structuring regulation, not a decision to do away with rules. Principles-based regulation is based on the conviction that while legislators and statutory drafters have the public legitimacy to establish broad regulatory goals, they are not in the best position to develop detailed guidelines for industry conduct, especially in fast-moving arenas like securities regulation. Those powers are allocated to front-line regulators at the securities commissions whose expertise derives from their proximity to industry and whose accountability derives from the notice-and-comment aspect of their rulemaking powers. Moreover – and this is the crucial point today – even those front-line regulators are limited in their access to information by comparison to the industries they regulate. In order to remain relevant and informed about fast-moving industry practice, to keep regulation sufficiently flexible, and to avoid inhibiting productive innovation, regulators need to establish open and perpetual communication lines with industry. They need to use industry's own good and best practices to add the 'meat' of detail to the 'bones' of their principles-based regulatory expectations.

Described another way, principles-based regulation is a two-tiered approach, in which principles-based legislative drafting provides flexibility, and constantly evolving industry experience and regulatory rules add certainty on a rolling basis. In this formulation, principles-based regulation, as applied, avoids the biggest problems associated with both principles and rules at the level of theory. Moreover, it can produce more effective regulation by ensuring that the party that has access to the best information is the one that provides the detail on any particular issue.

Ford argues that in a principles-based, outcome-oriented system, having an 'interpretive community' is crucial for developing the detailed content of statutory principles (see Section 8.4). Thus, to enhance transparency and predictability, she argues that principles-based systems should include mechanisms allowing regulators to communicate expectations with the industry, whether through administrative guidance, speeches, letters, compliance audits, comments on standards or enforcement actions so that, over time, these communications inform an interpretive community's understanding of regulatory expectations. In other words, principles-based approaches recognise that legislators can set broad goals, but detailed industry guidelines may be better developed by front-line regulators who are close to the industry and with whom they must have ongoing communication to stay informed about fast-paced changes.

8.2 Formalism, Gaming and 'Creative Compliance'

8.2.1 'Playing' the Rules Rather Than Playing by the Rules?

Volkswagen's use of software 'cheat' devices (see Box 8.1) demonstrates that regulatees face powerful incentives to avoid complying with regulatory rules. Detailed, precise standards may offer more specific guidance to regulatees, but they also expand opportunities for circumvention behaviours, including 'creative compliance' and strategic 'gaming' behaviour, discussed in the following two extracts.

McBarnet D., and Whelan, C. (1991). 'The Elusive Spirit of the Law: Formalism and the Struggle for Legal Control'. *Modern Law Review*, 54, 848–873, https://doi.org/10.1111/j.1468-2230.1991.tb01854.x.

848–851

Formalism and the Failure of Legal Control

Formalism implies a narrow approach to legal control – the use of clearly defined, highly administrable rules, an emphasis on uniformity, consistency and predictability, on the legal form of transactions and relationships and on literal interpretation.

Although the term formalism has been used in divergent ways, at its heart 'lies the concept of decision making according to rule,' rule implying here that the language of a rule's formulation – its literal mandate – be followed, even when this ill serves its purpose. Thus, 'to be formalistic . . . is to be governed by the rigidity of a rule's formulation' . . ..

Creative compliance uses formalism to avoid legal control, whether a tax liability or some regulatory obstacle to raising finance, effecting a controversial takeover or securing other corporate, or management, objectives. The combination of specific rules and an emphasis on legal form and literalism can be used artificially, in a manipulative way to circumvent or undermine the purpose of regulation. Using this approach, transactions, relationships or legal forms are constructed in order to avoid the apparent bounds of specific legal rules. In this sense, the detailed rules contribute to the defeat of legal policy. Though creative compliance is not limited to law and accounting, accountants are particularly conscious of its potential to reduce the effectiveness of regulations and to avoid tax. Much of the current impetus for a broad, open approach to professional standard setting stems from concern that a 'mechanistic "cookbook" approach . . . [which] is very precisely drafted . . . will be relatively easy to avoid' .. . .

Creative compliance highlights the limits of formalism as a strategy of legal control. A formalistic approach, which relies upon a 'cookbook' or code of specific and rigid rules and emphasises the legal form of transactions, can 'fail' to control for a variety of reasons. Unless the rules promote the overall purpose of the law, compliance with them and insisting on their literal interpretation or enforcement will not achieve the declared objectives. The letter of the rule may not accord with the spirit in which the law was framed; a literal application of the rules may not produce the desired end, it may be counter-productive; there may be gaps, omissions or loopholes in the rules which undermine their effectiveness. The rules may be out of date and no longer relevant. There may be other problems too. The legal form of a transaction or a relationship may not reflect its legal or its economic or commercial substance. The totality of a transaction or relationship may not be reflected in any individual part. There may be a dynamic adaptation to escape rules. Formalistic regulation may increasingly drift from any relationship with the real world and any chance of effectively controlling it.

All rules can encounter behaviours that may be misaligned with the rule-maker's underlying goals, irrespective of form or legal status. For example, a study by Bevan and Hood on the use of performance targets within the English NHS identified various examples, including a practice by hospitals of removing the wheels from patient trolleys, thereby turning them into 'beds' to meet the maximum prescribed 'trolley wait' times (Bevan and Hood 2006).

8.2.2 Algorithmic Rules: Algorithmic Gaming, Circumvention and Secrecy

Rule avoidance behaviour is not confined to rules in the form of linguistic text. 'Creative compliance' and other 'gaming' strategies can also occur in relation to algorithmically coded rules (see Chapter 6) discussed in the following extract.

Bambauer, J., and Zarsky, T. (2019). 'The Algorithmic Game'. *Notre Dame Law Review*, 94(1), 1–48, https://ndlawreview.org/wp-content/uploads/2018/11/1-Bambauer-Zarksy.pdf.

8–15

[D]iscrimination, as we use the term, is intended to be value neutral … throughout this Article, we assume that algorithms designed to discriminate between subjects are estimating a key characteristic and using proxies that are both legal and ethical to use for decision-making ….

Because discrimination algorithms use proxies to estimate a key characteristic that does not and cannot measure the real thing, there is a gap between the inputs of an algorithm and the true value of the key characteristic. That gap can be intentionally exploited, and when it is, the algorithm is being gamed. Gaming is a purposeful change in order to alter the algorithm's estimates.

To be clear, gaming involves a change in the subject's behavior in order to affect the algorithm's estimate *without causing any change to the key characteristic* that the algorithm is attempting to measure. So, if an algorithm attempts to estimate a subject's health based on food purchases and Fitbit data, and the subject consequently begins to exercise regularly and eat a nutritious diet, those behavioral changes will affect both the algorithm's estimate *and* the subject's actual health. In this case, the algorithm induced a change not only to the subject's behavior but also to the subject's key characteristic (health) and thus the actions do not amount to gaming under our definition. On the other hand, if the subject purchases carrots without eating them and puts his Fitbit on his dog while he watches television, then the subject is engaged in gaming because he is altering his conduct in ways that will not change his overall health.

Gaming Tactics and Countertactics

Given the value-neutral definition of gaming that we provide above, it should be clear that everybody engages in gaming . . .. However, not everybody games the same way. Gaming requires information, time, effort, and resources, so some will be in a better position to game than others. This means that gaming has important distributional effects. Generally speaking, the wealthier and better-educated members of the population will be in a better position to game because they have more resources to learn, discover, and navigate complex rules . . .. Gaming also sometimes requires a lack of moral reservation. For example, some gaming strategies depend on faking the inputs of an algorithm – a polite way of saying that it requires lying.

Gaming strategies can be classified into four basic types.

(i) **Avoidance** is a process by which a person avoids being the subject of an algorithm's model at all. For example, smugglers that avoid routes that are known to have checkpoints and regular law enforcement surveillance aim to avoid criminal investigation and arrest through avoidance.
(ii) **Altered conduct** involves changing behavior with the hope that the new behavior will change the proxies (inputs) that a model is using and recording, thus resulting in a changed estimate. Purchasing carrots without eating them in order to improve health estimates is an example.
(iii) **Altered input** is similar to altered conduct in that the goal is to change an input that the model will use to bias the estimate. However, altered inputs involve manipulating or falsely reporting an input rather than changing conduct in order to manipulate a correctly reported input . . ..
(iv) **Obfuscation** tactics are gaming tactics that are akin to a form of resistance. Finn Brunton and Helen Nissenbaum define obfuscation as 'the deliberate addition of ambiguous, confusing, or misleading information to interfere with surveillance and data collection' and categorize using these tactics as a 'weapon for the informationally weak' (Brunton and Nissenbaum 2015) Often, these measures require cooperation among many individuals. Our examples below will clarify this term further. Obfuscators typically protest the algorithm by confusing or overwhelming it, leading to inaccurate results for both the subject and for others . . ..

In response to gaming (or in anticipation of it), algorithm designers can use one or more countertactics. Most involve changing the estimation model. Algorithm designers can increase the complexity of the model by adding more

> predictive proxy variables or by introducing more randomness so that the incentives and ability to game the algorithm are reduced. They can also design the algorithm to frequently change the model so that either the proxies or the weighting used to apply to each proxy will change over time and be less known or predictable for subjects, and thus more difficult to game .... Algorithm designers also alter the model to rely on more immutable proxies that subjects have less ability to change. These proxies are not limited to the demographic characteristics that dominate equal protection analysis. To the contrary, education, employment, and zip codes are difficult to change, too. And whether they change the model or not, algorithm designers can reduce the transparency of their model so that gamers do not have as much information. Reducing transparency sometimes requires efforts to make it more difficult for interested parties to test (or 'ping') the system to learn its inner workings. Furthermore, those striving to discriminate can do so by gathering more, or differently sourced, data about the same set of proxies. Some of these sources may be more reliable.

The authors argue that from the perspective of values such as autonomy, opportunities for gaming are desirable, allowing those subjected to algorithmic control to resist measurement and judgement while spurring innovation, may adversely affect the system's accuracy, efficiency and distributional fairness.

Although there are several similarities between gaming behaviours around both written rules and algorithmic rules, there are also significant differences. If written rules are to guide behaviour, they must be publicly available and accessible to those they regulate, reflecting a central and well-accepted requirement of the rule of law. This is not true of algorithmic rules. Although deployers of algorithmic systems often claim that algorithmic rules and processes are better kept secret to prevent gaming, these claims are disputed, particularly in the absence of supporting evidence. Another crucial difference concerns the scope for two-way communication between rule-makers and rule-takers. A recurring theme in the preceding extracts is the importance of on-going dialogue and discussion between them if regulatory norms are to promote the policy-maker's intended purpose, given their lack of information and the dynamic nature of real-world environments (Black 1998). Yet this kind of dialogic feedback can be entirely excluded from the configuration of algorithmic regulatory systems. When relied upon in rights-critical contexts by governments to deliver welfare-support, the absence of mechanisms for communication and contestation within systems that rely on algorithmic control to allow mistakes and failures to be properly and swiftly addressed can generate serious injustice at scale (Yeung 2022).

8.3 Standardisation and 'Technical' Standards

The use of precise, detailed rules has also facilitated the emergence of mass markets. In particular, 'technical' standards or specifications have enabled the standardisation of a wide variety of products, services and systems. These standards are typically produced by industry rather than a public regulator (whether legislator or administrative agency), through voluntary collaboration by industry members to develop detailed, precise standards based on their expert knowledge under the auspices of a variety of technical standard-setting bodies, of which ISO, as a global standard-setting body is the largest and arguably the most significant. Although these standards are typically portrayed as dull, intricate 'technical' details best left to experts, we have already observed that the design of artefacts has inescapable political dimensions. As Lawrence Busch puts it 'standards are intimately associated with power' (Busch 2011: 13). Although, historically, compliance with these industry standards is voluntary, public regulators commonly resort to standards as a means for implementing legally binding obligations, particularly as a means for attempting to secure the safety of consumer products. Yet the highly technical nature of these standard-setting fora, the inability of civil society organisations to participate effectively due to the high costs of participation and the lack of transparency concerning the standard-setting process and the resulting standards themselves (which are typically protected by IP rights and thus not available on an open-access basis to the general public) has attracted serious and sustained criticism. The fora in which standard-setting occurs has become an active site of political struggle between nation-states and industry players, intent on shaping standards in a manner that best serves their own interests. As this book goes to press, feverish activity is taking place within and around a number of technical standard setting bodies at the global, European and national level in seeking to establish standards for AI and other technologies that are likely to be integrated into the emerging digital economy. Micklitz explains their origins in the following extract:

Micklitz, H. (2023). 'The Role of Standards in Future EU Digital Policy Legislation'. ANEC/BEUC, Brussels, www.beuc.eu/sites/default/files/publications/BEUC-X-2023-096_The_Role_of_Standards_in_Future_EU_Digital_Policy_Legislation.pdf.

31–32

The leading industrial states established national standardisation organisations in the early years of the twentieth century: the UK in 1901, Germany in 1917, the USA in 1918 and France in 1926. They promoted the foundation of international counterparts, ISO in 1947 and IEC in 1906. Their European counterparts were set up after the foundation of the EEC: CEN in 1961, CENELEC in 1973 and ETSI in 1988. Yet standardisation is at least two thousand years old. The Romans are said to have invented standardisation in the building of their warships. Initially, standardisation was about measuring, making sure that the different bits and pieces which are needed for the same device fit together. The age of industrialisation boosted standardisation. Think of Charlie Chaplin in *Modern Times*. The competent ministries in the rapidly industrialising states were not able to cope with the speed and need of a standardisation production process. However, industries took standardisation into their own hands and – this is crucial – the public authorities in the wider sense began to rely on the expertise enshrined in each and every technical standard. This is worth remembering in terms of designing a new governance structure. Putting technical standards back into the hands of administrations would mean turning the clock back by more than a hundred years. This is undoubtedly not a viable alternative.

Industrialisation went hand in hand with electrification and so went standardisation too. Whenever products were electrified, safety issues were on the agenda. This is visible even today in the bifurcation between the different standardisation organisations, ISO and IEC; CEN and CENELEC and, with the same specialisation at the national level in Germany, DIN and DKE/VDE. However, standardisation did not touch upon product quality. Quality was and should be left – this is the rationale of capitalist production – to the market. However, in the second half of the twentieth century, technical standardisation reached beyond mere measuring techniques and came ever closer to quality by regulating 'design', although in terms of policy the emphasis is laid on performance as process.

The central role of standard-setting bodies in enabling industrialisation and mass production is explained by STS scholar Laurence Busch in the following extract.

Busch, L. (2010). 'Standards, Law, and Governance'. *Journal of Rural Social Sciences*, 25(3), 56–78, https://egrove.olemiss.edu/jrss/vol25/iss3/4.

56–65

Markets have been around since the beginnings of recorded history and perhaps before. People produced various things for their own use. Whatever was left over, despite quality, they attempted to sell in the market if a buyer were available .... Then, much later, after the invention of money, some people determined that they could produce *for the market,* using the money they received to purchase the means of subsistence. To do this, they had to have expectations, however vague, about what a *typical* potential buyer might wish to buy. These expectations were based on everyday knowledge about their community and about those desiring and having the means to purchase a given item. It is this form of market that was central to (the various enactments) of classical liberalism (ie. a market in which producers of a given good produce for the market and prices are set by virtue of their competition). This is the market of Hobbe's 'harmless liberties' (1651), of Locket's *Civil Government* (1690) and especially of [Adam] Smith's *Wealth of Nations* (1776). It is one in which the state provides a legal framework designed to ensure, among other things (1) the enforcement of contracts, (2) a citizenry made up of free laborers, perhaps with some minimal amount of formal education, (3) a good system of transport (to ensure that goods and people can move freely), and (4) prohibition or regulation of monopolies. By the late nineteenth century, the older feudal legal systems in which 'just price' had prevailed had been abandoned ....

> It was not until the mid-nineteenth century that standardisation began to take hold – standardisation that became widely known as the American system. Before then, producing standard parts for anything was simply both too difficult and too costly. Hence manufacturers produced items that looked the same, that functioned in the same way, but that were anything but the same.
>
> Simultaneously, by the mid- to late-nineteenth century a move was afoot to transform markets such that they began to resemble those in the textbooks of economics . . . a series of events took place in industrial nations that transformed the nature of markets. These included *state action* to (1) produce a single currency for each nation, backed by a national bank, (2) ensure the precision and accuracy of weights and measures used in commerce, (3) prohibit or regulate monopolies, and (4) regulate stock markets by establishing clear trading rules. Simultaneously, but largely beyond the power of the state, (5) prices were marked on consumer goods to suppress haggling and speed up the pace of sales, (6) national standards bodies were created, beginning in 1900 with the formation of the British Standards Institution, and (7) mass production of a vast array of intermediate and consumer products became commonplace. By 1900, the enthusiasm for standardization was nearly unbounded. Moreover, it ran across the political spectrum . . . .
>
> By 1930, the advantages of standardization were so well-established that nearly every industrialized nation had a national standards development organization; today nearly every nation on earth has one. Moreover, they are linked together by the International Organisation for Standardization (ISO), thereby ensuring a certain level of standardization globally.

Although not extracted here, Busch observes that prominent American intellectuals were uncomfortable with the growing role of the state accompanying and enabling the drive for standardisation. Many came together after World War II to form the Mont Pelerin Society, including economists F. A. Hayek and Milton Friedman, who were both convinced that the antidote to this oversized role for the state was the market and a return to the principles of classical liberalism, albeit 'with a twist' – in which constitutional principles served to ensure the dominance of the market while limiting the role of the state. Busch (2010: 64–65) continues:

> What eventually came to pass in the performance of the neoliberal model was neither a conspiracy launched by a few economists, nor a perfect enactment of the theories themselves, but a mostly satisfactory performance of the model largely embraced by the owners of financial and corporate capital. Of particular important for our purpose is the is the rise of the new legal framework for international governance consisting of, for example, the World Trade Organisation, the International Monetary Fund, the World Intellectual Property Organisation, and the World Bank. Simultaneously, regional trade organisations began to appear (eg NAFTA, Mercosol, ASEAN) that further limited state power.

> Together these organisations have used international law to significantly limit national sovereignty in the name of free trade. Simultaneously, various leaders in each of the industrialised nations have themselves attempted, with varying degrees of success, to dismantle the welfare state – Reagan in the US, Thatcher in the UK, and more recently (and less successfully) Sarkozy in France. In each instance the assertion has been that the state was itself an impediment to economic growth, the source of many economic problems plaguing the economy, and notoriously inefficient when compared (usually) to an idealised conception of the private firm.
>
> Despite Thatcher and Reagan, arguably the neoliberal perspective(s) remained one contender among several until the collapse of the Soviet Union in 1991. That collapse profoundly affected Western elites. Lacking competition from the Soviets, where was little reason to maintain the welfare state. In particular, owners of financial and industrial capital began to understand that many changes proposed by Hayek and Friedman would have direct financial consequences for them. Put differently, neoliberal theory justified removal of postwar welfare state policies, growth of *freedom to operate* (FTO) in the marketplace, and creation of a nearly global marketplace.
>
> In short, the rise of neoliberalism has involved both the dismantling the rewriting of national laws and the development of new bodies of law that are often international in scope. Still, even as FTO has been welcomed by multinational firms and those firms aspiring to become multinational, it tended toward destabilization even before the recent financial crisis. Put differently, the largest firms have found themselves faced with issues of governance that were largely unforeseen by either management experts or neoliberal theorists. Similarly, NGOs have found it necessary to change their tactics considerably. Standards have been a central feature of that response.

Central to the influence of the standards referred to by Busch are the surrounding networks through which standards propagate, forming the focus of Julie Cohen's attention in the extract below. Cohen draws together common insights on network-and-standards processes within the global regulation of international trade, transnational business regulation and internet governance to argue that 'networked-and-standards'–based governance is an 'emergent category of legal institutions'. Although these fields vary widely, involving different participants and interests and regulated through a variety of institutions whose terms and rules for membership and participation differ considerably, she highlights their resemblance in that

> they are organised as networks, the networks are constituted around standards designed to facilitate and structure flows of economic and communicative activity, and the formulation and administration of those standards reflect the increasing influence of private economic power. (Cohen 2020: 3)

Cohen identifies five features of network-and-standards–based governance that challenge traditional understandings of governance by legal institutions, that is, institutions constrained by the rule of law (understood as adherence to regular procedural rules and associated rule of law values including conformance with principles of public reason, see Chapter 11), although only one of these features is reproduced below:

Cohen, J. (2020). 'Networks, Standards and Networks-and-Standards Based Governance'. In K. Werbach (ed.), *After the Digital Tornado*. Cambridge University Press, 58–80, https://doi.org/10.1017/9781108610018.

75–77

Technocracy and Its Discontents: The Problem of Publicly Available Law

A final distinctive attribute of emergent arrangements for global business governance and global network governance is their highly technocratic character. Some legal scholars who study transnational regulatory processes have worried that those processes lend themselves to capture by elites. It is helpful to understand that tendency as bound up with essential but imperfectly assimilated sociotechnical shifts. The mandated standards around which networked legal institutions are organized exemplify an approach that scholars who study sociotechnical assemblages for financial regulation have called the numericization of governance. They are developed via expert proceedings and encoded in lengthy, highly technical specifications whose implementation requires ongoing supervision by cadres of managerial elites.

The particular expert register in which transnational governance is conducted varies from setting to setting. In the Internet governance context, the language of governance is produced by and for computer scientists and engineers. In world trade governance and transnational financial regulation, the language of governance is predominantly economic and, particularly in financial governance settings, highly quantitative. Environmental and food and drug regulatory processes incorporate technical vernaculars from fields such as climate science, marine ecology, and epidemiology. In other transnational settings, the prevailing vernacular is more generally managerial. For example, detailed operational standards geared to the rhythms of organizational processes and to the benchmarks and reporting conventions used by professional auditors are increasingly common features of transnational environmental and labor regulation. In each case, reliance on technical vernaculars produces both some obvious entry barriers and some less obvious obstacles to broadly democratic policymaking. Even where participation in network governance processes is formally open to all comers, as in the case of the IETF's working groups, the learning curve for those without appropriate technical facility is often steep. Civil society organizations in particular have struggled to attain technical parity with their better-resourced counterparts in the business and technology communities.

Expertise is required, as well, to understand the ways in which methods and analytical commitments that are ostensibly technical also implicate, reflect, reinforce, and sometimes predetermine policy commitments. Disentangling fact from value and understanding the social construction of technology are

> perennial problems in science and technology policy, but network organization under mandated standardization exacerbates them. As substantive policy choices are folded into mandated standards, they become more and more difficult to disentangle, and certain types of especially incommensurable concerns – for example, concerns relating to development of capabilities for human flourishing and protection of fundamental rights – may seem to disappear altogether. A corollary is that, as technocratic oversight of regulatory functions becomes more solidly entrenched, the (explicit or implicit) political commitments of the expert regulators themselves may become more difficult to identify, contest, and dislodge. So, for example, the pathbreaking 'end to end' design of technical protocols for the Internet reflected solid technical judgment about robustness to certain kinds of disruptions and also encoded the generally libertarian commitments of the original Internet pioneers. As a result, although the Internet overall is extraordinarily resistant to disruptions of service, it has proved extraordinarily hospitable to other kinds of threats that exploit networked interconnection. The discourses of risk management and cost-benefit analysis that play increasingly important roles in financial and environmental regulation charge can fail to reckon adequately with certain kinds of large systemic threats.
>
> In the domain of world trade, the leading theoretical models generally have viewed liberalization as an unqualified good and have tended to discount evidence suggesting that it is also important to provide for equitable distribution and domestic capability-building. An important element of the rule-of-law ideal is commitment to publicly accessible rules and publicly accessible reasoning about the justifications for official decisions. From that perspective, network organization under mandated standardization creates a paradox: Effective control of highly informationalized processes requires governance institutions capable of responding in kind, but the very process of optimizing regulatory controls to highly informationalized processes makes governance arrangements more opaque and less accountable to broader global publics.

As both Busch and Cohen observed in the extracts above, the role of expert bodies in setting 'technical standards' within governance frameworks that operate beyond conventional national or international legal frameworks, such as ISO, has grown substantially. Yet as Cohen argues, despite the highly technocratic nature of these standard-setting processes, the resulting standards invariably 'hard-wire' normative policy choices and trade-offs into the standards themselves. This reflects Langdon Winner's (1980) powerful reminder that artefacts are designed with purposes and values in mind, and thus have inescapably political dimensions (see Chapter 3). Although the limited capacity and scope for effective participation by civil society and lay persons in these technical committees might not be intentional and strategic, due to the considerable resource and specialist knowledge required for participation, these standard-setting mechanisms are hospitable vehicles for industry capture (see Box 8.2).

Box 8.2 Case Study: ISO Standards for Tobacco and Tobacco Products

The International Standards Organisation (ISO) was established in 1947 as an international organisation of national standards bodies from over 130 countries, with a mission to 'promote the development of standardisation and related activities in the world with a view to facilitating the international exchange of goods and services, and to developing cooperation in the spheres of intellectual, scientific, technological and economic activity'. An ISO working group produced a technical standard for tobacco and tobacco products and standards (ISO TC/126, established in 1968). An analysis of tobacco industry documents made public as part of the settlement of the Minnesota Tobacco Trial and the Master Settlement Agreement by WHO researchers Bialous and Yach found that the standards developed by ISO/TC 126 are based on the tests and scientific evidence provided by the Cooperation Centre for Scientific Research Relative to Tobacco (CORESTA), a research organisation of industry tobacco chemists with the aim of advancing the interests of the tobacco industry and to pre-empt regulations through the development of its own research and standards. Most of the individuals involved in the work of that ISO/TC 126 were tobacco industry representatives and also members of CORESTA.

Tobacco industry influence is vividly reflected in the ISO standards for the determination of tar and nicotine yield in cigarette smoke, which uses a smoking machine to measure both substances to rank tar and nicotine yields. However, it had been known for decades that this method cannot be used for consumer information or health claims because it does not reflect the tar and nicotine actually delivered to the smoker when inhaled. Yet a 1990 memo by Philip Morris (the world's largest publicly traded tobacco company) recommended that the company seek to promote ISO standard smoking methods worldwide, including in countries that do not traditionally follow ISO standards, to provide maximum latitude for variation in the amount of tar delivery in cigarettes, particularly in countries that mandate the publication of the volume of tar delivery on the cigarette pack. Cigarette design is also used to 'cheat' the smoking machine, such as channel-ventilation bringing additional airflow into the cigarette filter and thus diluting the concentration of cigarette smoke components, yielding an even lower tar reading through the standard smoking machine method while delivering significantly greater amounts of tar when smoked by humans. The authors conclude that the industry is de facto responsible for setting tobacco standard measurement methods, from the testing development to the approval and publication stages. They urge public health authorities to play a larger role in the standard setting arena and that the ISO standard should not be used to justify policies aiming at protecting the public's health.

Source

Bialous, S. A., and Yach, D. (2001). 'Whose Standard Is It, Anyway? How the Tobacco Industry Determines the International Organization for Standardization (ISO) Standards for Tobacco and Tobacco Products'. *Tobacco Control* 10(2), 96–104.

8.4 Stabilising Interpretive Uncertainty

The preceding discussion highlights tensions between detailed rules and open-ended principles. Although detailed rules are often preferred by those required to follow them because they provide more specific guidance, they are especially prone to gaming and circumvention. However, more guidance concerning the meaning of rules can be provided in other ways, including the use of 'soft law'.

8.4.1 Administrative Guidance and 'Soft' Law

When regulatory norms take the form of legislative rules, administrative guidance (sometimes referred to by legal scholars as 'soft law') may be offered, enabling public regulatory agencies to respond quickly and flexibly to changing circumstances. Guidance of this kind is used extensively in practice, although it is not formally binding in legal terms. However, this guidance generate new problems, referred to in the following two extracts concerned with administrative guidance issued in the United States and EU, respectively.

> **Parillo, N. R. (2019).** 'Federal Agency Guidance and the Power to Bind: An Empirical Study of Agencies and Industries'. *Yale Journal on Regulation*, 36, 165–271, www.yalejreg.com/print/federal-agency-guidance-and-the-power-to-bind-an-empirical-study-of-agencies-and-industries/.
>
> 165–169
>
> For individuals and firms regulated by federal agencies, actual regulations are just the beginning of the story. Despite being voluminous and complex, regulations leave numerous important decisions to the agency's discretion or interpretation. Individuals and firms want to know how the agency will use its discretion and how it will read the regulations' ambiguous provisions. And agency officials want individuals and firms to have that knowledge in order to facilitate compliance. So officials provide the public with lots of 'guidance', that is, general statements advising the public on how the agency proposes to exercise discretion or interpret law. Guidance comes in an endless variety of labels and formats, depending on the agency: advisories, circulars, bulletins, memos, interpretive letters, enforcement manuals, fact sheets, FAQs, highlights, you name it. Nobody knows exactly how much guidance there is, because it is not comprehensively collected anywhere, but its page count for any given agency is estimated to dwarf that of actual regulations by a factor of twenty, forty, or even two hundred. Guidance is 'the bread and butter of agency practice', declares a veteran EPA lawyer. 'I cannot imagine a world without guidance', says a former senior FDA official.
>
> Though guidance is a ubiquitous and essential feature of the administrative state, it is also controversial. Full blown regulations that officially bind the agency and the public known as 'legislative rules' can be enacted by an agency only through a costly, time-consuming set of procedures imposed by the Administrative Procedure Act (APA), including notice and comment, in which the parties who will be bound by a policy can participate in its formulation before it is set in stone. By contrast, agencies can issue guidance without any such process, because of the APA's exemptions for 'general statements of policy' and 'interpretative rules', which together cover guidance in all its varieties. Thus guidance can be produced and altered much faster, in higher volume, and with

less accountability than legislative rules can. What justifies this disparity, in the familiar telling, is that guidance, unlike a legislative rule, is not binding on the agency or the public. It is only a suggestion, a mere tentative announcement of Federal Agency Guidance and the Power to Bind the agency's current thinking about what to do in individual adjudicatory or enforcement proceedings, not something the agency will follow in an automatic, ironclad manner as it would a legislative rule. Guidance is supposed to leave space for the agency's case-by-case discretion. If a particular individual or firm wants to do something (or wants the agency to do something) that is different than what the guidance suggests, the agency is supposed to give fair consideration to that alternative approach. If officials treat guidance with this kind of flexibility, it doesn't seem so bad for the agency to be unconstrained in issuing guidance to begin with.

Candone, C. and Coman-Kund, F. (2022). 'Persuasive Rather Than "Binding" EU Soft Law? An Argumentative Perspective on the European Commission's Soft Law Instruments in Times of Crisis'. *The Theory and Practice of Legislation*, 10(1), 22–47, https://doi.org/10.1080/20508840.2022.2033942.

25–26

Problematic EU Soft Law in Times of Crisis

Soft law instruments, in particular those enacted during crisis, are deemed particularly suitable to deal with the complexity and diversity of European affairs in a rapidly changing situation. They are easy to enact, as they do not entail the intricacies of the EU formal decision-making process, which makes the whole adoption procedure much simpler and faster, and in principle they are not subject to the demanding legal protection and scrutiny standards imposed on Union's legally binding acts. Moreover, they are considered to be flexible, in that they leave arguably a great degree of leeway to the Member States, and are easily adapted to changing circumstances, going in the case of the Commission, as far as issuing new such instruments every week during the COVID-19 crisis. In justifying this approach, the Commission routinely argues that the measures adopted by the Member States lead to fragmentation and, therefore, are not efficient, which in turn requires EU level coordination and effective collective action to solve COVID-19-related problems that no Member State can solve on its own.

Notwithstanding the advantages of soft law as part and parcel of Union's 'new modes of governance' arsenal, these instruments also spur tensions and controversy because of their contentious capacity to produce legal and practical effects despite their legally non-binding nature enshrined in Article 288 TFEU.

8.4.2 The Role of Negotiation, Dialogue and Discussion

In both the above extracts, the authors argue that although not legally binding, administrative guidance typically operates *as if* they were 'hard' rules. Within constitutional democratic states, the final authoritative interpretation of legal rules rests with the judiciary when adjudicating a legal dispute brought before a court, reflecting the principle of the separation of powers, intended to safeguard against the dangers of abuse of power that would arise if the power to make rules was vested in the same body that empowered to interpret and apply them (see Chapter 10). Yet the informal, interpretive authority of public agencies is critical to the daily operation of regulatory regimes, rooted in the enforcement discretion they enjoy in order to discharge their legal duties to monitor and implement legislative rules.[1] Interpretive uncertainty concerning the meaning and application of rules also occurs through 'regulatory conversations' between regulators and members of the regulated community, discussed in the extract below.

Black, J. (1998). 'Talking about Regulation'. *Public Law*, 77–105.

77–91

This article is concerned with ... conversations which occur between the regulated and the regulator about rules, their interpretation and appropriate application or waiver in the individual regulatee's circumstances. Such conversations occur in the grey world of regulatory operation and implementation, where law plays a key structuring role but where its operation is a matter of continual interpretation, adjustment, and discussion. The locations for such conversations may vary within the regulatory process and indeed within the regulatory body, but whatever their location they concern the meaning and application of rules. They may be manifested in guidance, waivers, no-action or comfort letters, non-sanctioning of breaches, or the formation of requirements tailored to the individual regulatee's circumstances; they may occur at a fairly high level in the regulatory organisation, or at the relatively low-level and hidden world of enforcement; they may be an implicit part of the regulatory process, or explicitly incorporated into the regulatory structure through the adoption of particular techniques of regulation and rule making.

Conversations ameliorate the limits of rules; they meet the perennial problem of how to resolve the tension between certainty and flexibility; they allow for more general rules to be written which serve as better, because more comprehensible, guides to behaviour, whilst allowing for adjustment to individual circumstances: a form of 'acoustic separation' of law. Conversations have the postmodern credentials of flexibility, communication, responsiveness, and enable individual regulatees to participate in the decision as to the rule's application in their case ....

Conversations ... aid interpretation. As has been well observed, rules do not apply themselves; they need to be interpreted. Interpretation is however a contested exercise. There is no inherent, fixed meaning to rules or to language; the meaning, and hence the application, of a rule is not an objective fact but is

[1] Authority is understood here, as 'non-coercive, content-independent reasons for action' (Raz 1979) (see Chapter 11 for further analysis on authority and legitimacy).

> contingent on the interpretive community reading the rule. The contingency of the application of the rule on the interpretation it receives suggests a particular vulnerability of rules. Rules may receive a number of interpretations and thus be applied in a number of ways. Conversations which involve elaboration of the rule's meaning allow the problem of interpretation to be addressed. They can thus meet the need for certainty in the rule's operation, a need which itself stems from the legal status of rules, and the concomitant rule of law concerns that rules should be able to guide behaviour and allow individuals to plan their lives.

Although not extracted here, Black discusses three settings in which regulatory conversations occur (a) in the course of providing guidance, either formally or informally, to individual regulatees concerning the meaning or application of the rule, including 'no action' letters indicating that the public regulator does not propose to take further enforcement action (even if there is an arguable case to investigate legal violation), (b) during supervised rule-formation, in which regulatees write their own internal rules which are subject to oversight by a public regulator (see Chapter 5) and (c) elaboration, adjustment or waiver by a public regulator in the course of carrying out routine monitoring and enforcement (see Chapter 9). Despite their benefits, Black observes that regulatory conversations generate problems, including antagonism with so-called rule of law values such as requirements that law should be certain, general, open, stable, prospective, transparent, guarantee due process and participation (see Chapter 11). Conversations of this kind may also expose the regulator to charges of 'capture, inconsistency and inequity, emptying the law of any meaningful content, and undermining the regulation and, more particularly, its public interest or social objectives', but as Black observes, they are inevitable.

8.4.3 The 'Liquid' Nature of Informal Interpretive Authority within Transnational Regimes

Interpretive ambiguity and uncertainty also plagues rules established within transnational regulatory regimes that are not rooted primarily in the formal, sovereign authority of nation-states, which need to be addressed. In the following extract, Julia Black argues that these regimes often require individuals or organisations to interpret the rules and help stabilise their interpretation in cases of doubt or contestation. Black develops the notion of 'liquid' authority, contrasting it with the 'solid' authority of public regulators within state-backed regulatory regimes that is grounded in the legal authority of the state. She suggests that any particular exercise of liquid authority is linked to the need for transnational regulators to constantly re-establish and renew their authority in the absence of a formal legal framework and thus are fundamentally linked to legitimacy and strategies of legitimation (see Chapter 11).

Black, J. (2017). 'Says Who?' Liquid Authority and Interpretive Control in Transnational Regulatory Regimes'. *International Theory*, 9(2), 286–310, doi:10.1017/S1752971916000294.

287–295

In the concept of liquid authority, the core conception of authority, as seminally articulated by Raz, as non-coercive, content-independent reasons for action, is retained (Raz 1979). The differentiation of liquid authority from formal legal authority lies in the different sources of authority, which are not grounded in law but in social relations. In finding the source of authority in social relations and a voluntary acceptance of deference, the analysis of liquid authority draws attention to the necessarily fluid, dynamic and ultimately contested bases on which authority is founded when detached from the stabilising structures of the state, hence the metaphor of liquidity to describe it . . ..

Rule-based systems . . . often have individuals or organisations whose role it is to interpret the rules in cases of doubt or contestation in order to stabilise interpretations, either generally or in particular instances . . ..

In the context of a transnational regulatory regime where there is no 'solid' basis for the exercise of interpretive control, the fundamental question is 'on the basis of what authority does this organisation exercise this function?' In the case of the function of interpretation, when exercised in the context of liquid authority, the challenge for the regulator is to answer the question; 'says who?' The exercise of interpretive authority and control in transnational regulatory regimes is a little explored aspect of their operations . . ..

Once the authority of an actor is not based in law but in some other reason for social acceptance, that authority becomes increasingly 'liquid' and potentially contested. As such, the sources of liquid authority resonate strongly with sociological understandings of legitimacy . . . in most writings in law, political science and political theory, legitimacy . . . is associated with a normative acceptance, perhaps even a cognitive acceptance, of the right to govern. It is this sense in which it is used here . . ..

Examining the Exercise of Interpretive Authority in Three Transnational Regulatory Regimes

In any regulatory regime there is a prima facie functional reason to have a clearly identified component which exercises ultimate interpretive control, which is to ensure the coherent and consistent operation of the regime. In order for that control to be recognised as authoritative, ie for people to consider the utterances of that component of the regime as independent reasons for action, it has to be legitimate. In a 'liquid' context, that authority and legitimacy has to be constantly built and renewed. So there is a continually shifting, iterative dynamic between the functional performance of one element of a regulatory regime (interpretation) and the attempts by the regime to establish and stabilise its authority and legitimacy in a changing context. So in this endlessly changing context, do regulatory regimes (and particular components within them) seek to exercise interpretive control, and if so, how? This is a

> deliberately 'sharp' question to pose in what is an apparently endlessly fluid set of regulatory processes where . . . Westphalian state-based notions of authority or legitimacy seem out of place. It is also an empirical question. In exploring that question the article adopts an inductive approach, analysing three contrasting case studies in order to explore the relationship of liquid authority and legitimacy in the performance of the same function, interpretation.

Black then analyses three transnational regulatory regimes with varied operational contexts, institutional positions, and rule types:

1. International Accounting Standards Board (IASB): Founded in 1973 by auditors and professional bodies, it sets accounting standards for the International Financial Reporting Standards (IFRS) Foundation.
2. ISO (International Standards Organisation): A dominant global technical standard-setter, widely referenced by international organizations, the EU, and national governments.
3. Forest Stewardship Council (FSC): Established in 1993, it ensures environmentally sound, socially beneficial and economically viable forest management, competing with other transnational standard setters.

By examining how these regimes exercise interpretive control over their rules, Black (2017: 305–306) identifies differences and similarities, offering the following preliminary observations:

> First, there is a complex interdependency between the legitimacy of the regime as a whole and its functional effectiveness. The function of providing interpretations of rules that apply across the regime is at once an exercise of authority which relies on legitimacy, and is used to constitute that legitimacy by preserving the integrity of the regime through establishing consistency of meaning and application of the rules. Moreover, the manner in which interpretive control is exercised is used to bolster legitimacy claims rooted in constitutionality, internally participative democracy, and expertise and technocratic functionality. In turn, that legitimacy grounds the authority of the regime in the absence of the state. However, liquidity is a differentiated state: some regimes are operating in contexts in which they are more accepted than others, associated in part to the length of time in which they have been in existence and the extent to which their position is contested. ISO is the longest established of the three and is widely accepted as a global technical standard setter, enjoying a quasi-monopoly position in many areas in which it operates as well as the acceptance of many countries' governments. The IASB also has widespread acceptance and now faces only one major competitor – the US – but it had to fight for its institutional position as it grew and in the face of challenges in the immediate wake of the financial crisis. The FSC, in contrast, operates in a context in which it has to compete constantly for regulatory share and is in a continual process of renewing and maintaining its legitimacy and authority in the face of competing legitimacy demands. Thus the authority of each varies in the degree of its 'liquidity' in practice. This in turn seems to have some relation to whether and how they seek to exercise interpretive control over their norms. It is possible to hypothesise, at least, that there is a relationship between the two.

Second, the analysis illustrates the dynamics of a small but significant part of the dense network of regulatory conversations through which such regimes are continually reproduced. It shows that the functional need for a centralised exercise of interpretive control is met by all regimes, but is put under constant pressure as the regimes develop over time. The regimes considered here have responded to the pressures of changes in scale, scope and operational contexts by increasing the density of their institutional structures, introducing central organisational bodies and increasingly formalised processes for providing interpretations. It is notable that rule type is not consistently used as a device to promote consistency of interpretations, and thus to limit the need for the exercise of interpretive control. Moreover, issuing interpretations is a highly strategic function in each case, performed by a central component of the regime acting in accordance with quite formalised procedures which restrict access to those seeking interpretations, and which can become increasingly dense as the functional demands for interpretive consistency increase. As we have seen with ISO, ultimately the demands of scale are such that rule makers strategically target the exercise of the interpretive function to points which they consider most critical to the effective operation of the regime as a whole.

Third, as the regimes or systems grow in scale and scope, and as their institutional position becomes more dominant, greater demands on their legitimacy are made by more legitimacy communities in proportion to the regime's growing influence and claims to authority, to which they have to respond. However, the maintenance of legitimacy and authority is a particular challenge where legitimacy demands compete. For example, the 'logic' of the regime (and on which it may also base its legitimacy) may be one which encourages widespread ownership of the rules through a federated structure, such as the FSC, and in which central control over interpretations may be resisted internally by members. However these internal legitimation demands contrast with those being made by external legitimacy communities, who see consistency as central to the system's functional integrity and thus legitimacy and authority. This contestation renders the exercise of interpretive control more complex in a context where authority is relatively liquid, as the functional need for interpretive control can be in tension with the need to respect the role of others to issue their own, localised interpretations. These competing demands between central control and local autonomy are common in any federated structure, but for those operating in a 'liquid' context, there is no recognised arbiter to resolve them in the form of a constitutional agreement enforced by a court. Instead they have to be resolved by the regime itself, and how it does so will in turn affect the legitimacy it receives from different legitimacy communities, and ultimately its ability to function.

8.5 Interpreting the Facts and Circumstances

Interpretive uncertainty also arises when attempting to apply a rule to a set of facts. It is necessary to understand and interpret the particular facts and circumstances of any given case to identify whether, and if so how, a specific rule applies. Two contexts pose considerable challenges of this kind: first, in evaluating the applicability of regulatory rules to new and emerging technologies and, secondly, when the relevant standards take the form of algorithmic code rather than linguistic text.

8.5.1 Regulatory Science and the Need for Specialist Expertise

So-called regulatory science (see Chapter 2) may include quantitative methods to assess and quantify health and safety risks, including risks posed by new and emerging technologies. The need for specialist scientific knowledge and expertise is particularly acute for outcome-based standards (see Section 8.1.3), as Spinardi highlights in his analysis of fire safety regulation, extracted below. Although fire safety regulations historically took the form of very detailed, prescriptive rules that applied according to building type, Spinardi explains that a new approach called 'Performance Based Design' (PBD) now applies in many jurisdictions requiring engineers to demonstrate performance outcomes for a project. However, Spinardi points out that retrospective measurement of fire safety performance would not be socially acceptable, just as airline reliability cannot be assessed by measuring the number of airlines crashes and fining the carriers after the event, so that prospective performance must be predicted. PBD is touted as addressing dissatisfaction with the perceived 'one-size-fits-all' approach of prescriptive regulation, building on the belief that fundamental fire safety knowledge has progressed sufficiently to enable bespoke fire safety engineering solutions to be designed and assessed. However, Spinardi draws attention to two epistemic challenges associated with this approach, one in relation to the use of computational modelling generally to reliably and accurately forecast safety in real world contexts and the second concerning the lack of expertise on behalf of regulatory authorities to reliably assess safety performance prospectively based on these models:

Spinardi, G. (2019). 'Performance-Based Design, Expertise Asymmetry, and Professionalism: Fire Safety Regulation in the Neoliberal Era'. *Regulation & Governance*, 13, 520–539, https://doi.org/10.1111/rego.12251.

522–531

Regulation of technology raises many issues but perhaps the most fundamental ones hinge on questions of regulatory expertise. Regulation is intended to prevent or limit harmful impacts of technology, but to be effective there must be sufficient understanding of how these impacts occur and how regulations would ameliorate harmful consequences while sustaining technology's benefits.

Regulators thus need to know about the performance of technology. To what extent does a drug cause side effects relative to its benefits? Do genetically modified crops risk contamination of natural species? Are planes safe enough to carry passengers? As MacKenzie (1996) notes, such knowledge of a technology's properties can come from three sources: empirical observation of use or testing; inference from theory; or through communication from trusted experts. In practice, regulatory authorities typically rely on a combination of these sources of knowledge. Evidence is gleaned from usage and testing, with hypotheses, methods of data collection, and analysis shaped by theoretical understanding, and expert advice sought to reach consensus about regulatory action. However, this is far from straightforward because every step involved in learning about the properties of technology requires judgment and negotiation to reach this consensus . . ..

Effective regulation of PBD requires regulators to have expertise in understanding the specific knowledge claims that engineers make about how this performance is achieved.

7. PBD in Operation: Demonstrating Performance

For a PBD fire safety solution to be approved, the regulatory authority should be convinced that the fire safety engineer has demonstrated the required level of performance, whether that is based on equivalence or on first principles derivation from functional requirements. Engineers will typically make their case by quantifying the key properties of the building and its contents and occupants, and then calculating a number of relevant processes with regard to fire and smoke spread, structural response, and human behavior – ideally over a range of appropriate scenarios . . .. This demonstration of performance is typically based on knowledge claims derived from the modelling of phenomena such as fire development, smoke spread, structural response, and evacuation times . . .. [I]t is becoming commonplace to use techniques such as computational fluid dynamics (CFD) to simulate the development and spread of fire and smoke . . ... Engineers can thus design innovative structures that do not comply with prescriptive guidance, and can fine-tune structures to economize on fire protection (which steel requires because it loses strength at temperatures that are typical of many fires). Likewise, a number of different models with varying levels of complexity are used to simulate evacuation behavior. Thus, for some projects, three types of models may be used to make the case for the overall fire safety design.

This use of modelling poses significant challenges for regulators with regard to expertise asymmetry. Not only are building approval regulators unlikely to be up to date with the state-of-the-art fire science that some engineers may draw on, but also they may be unfamiliar with the idiosyncrasies of the various models that embody this science. Most regulators lack the expertise to replicate or even competently interrogate the modelling efforts of fire safety engineers, or to assess the validity of the underlying science or its applicability to the design. This is important because, while the performance of such models for some circumstances has been validated by laboratory tests, they are notoriously dependent on user-competency. Thus Johannson (2014) notes, 'the user has been found to be the most critical link in the chain of simulations' . . ..

Much depends on the initial model choices and assumptions made by the model user, and effective regulation would require regulators who are well versed in the intricacies of the various types of models used for fire and smoke dynamics, structural responses, and evacuation behavior . . .. As Gobeau and Zhou note:

Despite a lack of validation for this application, computational fluid dynamics (CFD) modelling is increasingly used in safety cases as a predictive tool to demonstrate the effectiveness of modern building designs and/or emergency ventilation to control the movement of smoke in the event of a fire . . ..

CFD modelling approaches provide results that looked realistic . . . [but] a comparison of quantitative data; such as the temperature of the hot layer, the depth of the smoke layer along the ceilings, and the rate of propagation of smoke, showed that these key parameters can vary significantly – depending on the modelling approach used.

Expertise Asymmetry or Expertise Deficit?

Effective regulation of PBD fire safety solutions thus appears to depend on the approving authorities having sufficient understanding of the underlying knowledge claims that are often based on simulation model outputs. However, local government personnel, whose role has traditionally been to apply prescriptive guidance that covers all aspects of building design and who rarely have specialist fire safety education, typically conduct day-to-day building regulation. Such approving authorities are thus not well equipped to understand and interrogate the knowledge claims used in PBD fire safety design, and there is particular concern that many regulators lack the expertise to understand the limitations of the modelling tools that are frequently used.

Spinardi goes on to consider whether self-regulation by professional engineers rather than detailed oversight by a public regulator is preferable. He concludes that although one is appropriately sceptical of self-regulation, it would at least acknowledge the issue of expertise asymmetry in PBD by explicitly placing responsibility on the fire safety engineer, reflecting the approach taken by the US Federal Aviation Authority in regulating certification of new aircraft technology. However, he offers two cautions: first, fire safety engineering may not be a sufficiently mature profession to trust its members to be both competent and ethical, and secondly, the intractable challenge of 'knowing' fire safety given that fire safety engineering relies on three diverse disciplines, all involving stochastic processes operating in social contexts that typically do not provide ambiguous guidance as to what 'safety' means. For Spinardi, these challenges are not insurmountable provided that 'appropriate oversight mechanisms are enacted' requiring good governance, good working practices in which fire safety engineering is treated as a 'protected profession' with an appropriate standard of qualifications and experience for accredited members of that profession and supported by legal penalties for those who deviate from professional standards.

8.5.2 The Rise of 'RegTech' and Automated Enforcement

Different challenges arise when algorithmic rules are used to automate regulatory enforcement. The use of networked digital technologies that run on software that encode algorithmic rules into socio-technical systems that operate automatically has become commonplace. Several regulators now employ both automated and semi-automated technologies that allow interconnected systems to communicate and share information with each other via the Internet. These include the take-up of RegTech (regulatory technology) to enhance and streamline regulatory processes, typically employing some kind of automation to help facilitate the information gathering, monitoring and rule-application tasks involved in overseeing compliance with regulatory rules. RegTech is considered particularly useful in complex sectors subject to rapid change, with the most advanced technologies drawing on multiple technologies including machine learning, predictive analytics and blockchain (distributed ledger systems). RegTech has considerable potential to oversee activities involving a high volume of transactions and multiple interactions between regulators and regulatees, which may facilitate risk management, auditing, reporting, compliance and enforcement. The use of 'technological protection mechanisms' (TPM) to protect digital content constitutes an early form of 'RegTech' employed to protect intellectual property (IP) rights. While the allure of these systems is undeniable, their reliance on fully automated, hard-coded rules, thus bypassing of human discretion and debate, can be problematic. We have seen that human interpretation, discussion and judgement is important in addressing interpretive uncertainty concerning their meaning and application of linguistic rules. But when rules are instead coded into algorithms that operate automatically and at scale, this can disrupt the delicate and fragile balance between multiple rights and interests traditionally upheld by modern legal systems rooted in a foundational commitment to the rule of law. The late Ian Kerr, a Canadian lawyer and pioneering law and technology scholar, draws attention to these concerns in his discussion of 'technological protection mechanisms' (TPMs) or 'digital rights management' (DRM) systems, in the extract below:

Kerr, I. R. (2010). 'Digital Locks and the Automation of Virtue. From "Radical Extremism" to "Balanced Copyright"'. In M. Geist (ed.), *Canadian Copyright and the Digital Agenda*. Irwin Law, 247–303

265, 272, 274, 278, 301–302

The best locking systems not only prevent access to interlopers but also grant access to those who have or ought to have permission. This cannot easily be achieved with a typical mechanical lock since it is difficult to ensure that its key-holder always has permission . . .. Whereas the point of a mechanical lock is to guarantee the key-holder automatic entry, the more sophisticated digital locks automate the actual permission with stunning precision . . ..

Shown in their very best light, TPMs can be used to ensure appropriate or authorized permission. However . . . TPMs can go well beyond appropriate or authorized permission. In fact, TPMs can be employed in even more sophisticated DRMs to automate all permissions, shutting down any and every possible course of action except for those pre-selected by the party employing the digital

> lock. While TPMs might be thought of as the building blocks used to restrict access or use, DRMs are designed to manage an entire array of related activities by using various automation and surveillance technologies to identify digital property and those seeking to use it, in order to technologically enforce certain licensing conditions. In so doing, DRM can be used to automate permission systematically ....
>
> The ability to change the ground rules in this way affords tremendous power to those in a position to employ DRM ....
>
> I am concerned about a widespread use of technological constraints – whether in private or public spaces, whether owned or operated by a corporation, a government or an individual – imposed on citizens by property owners who seek total command of their environments. I am concerned because those environments are also our environments. These spaces are crucial to our well-being. They are the playgrounds of our moral development. Yet, digital locks and related techniques allow property owners to eliminate the possibility for moral deliberation about certain kinds of action other-wise possible in these spaces by disabling the world in a way that morally disables the people who populate it. Not by restricting their choices but by automating them – by creating world-altering contrivances that remove people from the realm of moral action altogether, thereby impairing their future moral development ....
>
> The pre-emptive nature of digital locks leaves no room for forgiveness. Instead, digital locks simply disable the property so that it does not permit of any uses other than its pre-programmed use – which likely would not have contemplated and/or could not otherwise accommodate the range of uses that necessity so often demands. As pre-programmed, pre-emptive devices meant to automate permissions, digital locks are not law-abiding. To be sure, they can be programmed to comport with simple legal rules to some extent. And they can be re-programmed if those simple rules are amended. But, generally, these pre-set permissions are unsophisticated and non-negotiable.
>
> It is one thing to program a digital lock to accord with the terms of a contract. It is quite another to program digital locks that delicately balance public and private interests – which is precisely what both the necessity principle and, for that matter, the law of copyright would require.

Kerr raises important concerns about the shortcomings of RegTech. The automation of algorithmic rule enforcement leaves no room for contestation, correction or forgiveness if mistakes occur. These systems may unilaterally alter the balance public and private interests by technological fiat, while side-stepping rule of law values such as transparency, fairness and proportionality as well as the need for flexibility to properly accommodate those whose situation or circumstances are exceptional (Ranchordás 2022).

Conclusion

This chapter has shown that rule-setting is a complex matter. In their familiar linguistic form, rules represent generalised abstractions intended to provide guidance to their addressees. Yet fundamental tensions and trade-offs arise when drafting rules, owing to the inevitability of interpretive uncertainty that surrounds their use. Greater precision in rule-drafting may help reduce this uncertainty but are more likely to become outdated and exacerbate problems of under- or over-inclusion while enhancing opportunities for gaming and circumvention behaviours that undermine the rule's underlying purpose. Although outcome-based standards may provide greater scope for innovation, enabling rule-takers to identify how best to comply with the rule, they presuppose that outcomes can be meaningfully and effectively monitored, measured and enforced while expanding opportunities for cheating. Nor is the use of standards as broad-based 'principles' synonymous with lax enforcement: effective monitoring and oversight remains critical to the success of rules. Practices of gaming and circumvention cannot be eliminated by embedding rules into algorithmic code and can create new dangers and forms of injustice, removing opportunities for two-way communication between rule-maker and rule-taker. Although resort to detailed technical standard-making by experts who belong to a shared interpretive community may appeal to policy-makers, these technocratic processes to not eliminate the need for value-judgements that affect the wider community yet who are unable to effectively participate in them. At the heart of these conundrums lies the double-edged nature of discretion in the hands of public officials, reflecting well-known insights of constitutional jurists A. V. Dicey and K. C. Davis. As administrative law scholar Peter Cane observes:

Cane, P. (2011). *Administrative Law*, 5th ed. Clarendon Press.

140–141

Discretion has advantages and disadvantages. It has the advantage of flexibility: it allows the merits of individual cases to be taken into account. Discretion is concerned with the 'spirit of the law', not its 'letter', and it may allow government policies to be more effectively implemented by giving administrators freedom to adapt their working methods in light of experience. It is useful in new areas of government activity because it enables administrators to deal with novel and perhaps unforeseen circumstances as they arise. On the other hand, discretion may put the citizen at the mercy of the administrator, especially if the administrator is not required to tell the citizen the reason why the discretion was exercised as it was. Discretion also opens the way for inconsistent decisions, and demands a much higher level of care and attention on the part of the decision-maker; discretion is expensive of time and money . . ..

Discretion is often contrasted with rules. Carefully drafted rules, it is argued, can promote certainty and uniformity of result and facilitate retrospective control by giving a standard against which decisions can be judged. Rules may also make the administrative process more efficient by reducing the number of choices administrators have to make in implementing programmes and the time that needs to be spent on individual cases. Rules may also make the administrative process more efficient by reducing the number of choices administrators have to make in implementing programmes and the time that needs to be spent on

> individual cases. Rules can create rights and entitlements for citizens dealing with the administration .... On the other hand, rules are less flexible than discretion: they may make it more difficult to take account of the details of particular cases. Rules may lead to impersonal administration that has little concern for the citizen as an individual.

Although both linguistic and algorithmic rules may be 'gamed' there are important differences between them. Not only are there differences in their transparency and accessibility, but written rules rely crucially on *communication* between regulator and regulated community. We have focused on communications directed at the regulated population at large that apply universally, but written norms also allow more localised 'regulatory conversations' that can help ameliorate problems associated with their use (Black 1998). It is this discretionary authority that is central to our examination of regulatory compliance and enforcement in Chapter 9.

Discussion Questions

1. Can Black's analytical framework for rule interpretation and application accommodate Diver's prescriptions for rule-making?
2. How, if at all, could Diver's rule-making prescriptions be employed to address the phenomenon of 'creative compliance' described by McBarnet and Whelan?
3. What is 'principles-based regulation' and what are its strengths and shortcomings?
4. Are 'performance-based' or 'outcome-based' approaches superior to process-based rules or standards? Why or why not?
5. What is 'creative compliance'? What distinguishes creative compliance from 'cheating'? Is gaming necessarily undesirable? Why or why not?
6. What lessons for standard-setting arise from the VW Dieselgate scandal?
7. In what way are linguistic rules similar to, and different from, algorithmic rules?
8. To what extent can algorithmic rules avoid the problems associated with linguistic rules? To the extent that algorithmic rules succeed in avoiding some of the problems associated with linguistic rules, are they necessarily to be preferred?
9. What is the point and purpose of standardisation and the creation of technical standards?
10. What role, if any, should public regulator and/or civil society organisations play in technical standard-setting bodies?
11. What strategies are available to reduce the interpretive uncertainty associated with linguistic rules?
12. What are the pros and cons of automating the enforcement of rules via software algorithms? Who benefits the most, and who benefits the least from automated enforcement?

9

Regulatory Compliance, Public Enforcement and Private Certification

Introduction

We saw in Chapter 8 that uncertainty in the interpretation and application of regulatory rules cannot be eliminated. In this chapter, we examine issues that arise in relation to compliance with, and enforcement of, regulatory rules. Compliance and enforcement are essential pillars of regulation for they help to secure regulatory effectiveness (see Introduction). Our discussion draws into sharper focus the dynamic, messy and socially contextual nature of regulatory processes and decision-making and their institutional contexts. But what do we mean by enforcement? Within command-and-control regimes, there is a tendency to equate enforcement with the prosecution of offences with legal prohibitions, entailing the formal invocation of the legal process including the imposition of penal sanctions for violating the law. One important contribution of the regulatory compliance and enforcement literature, however, is to highlight the pervasiveness of informal practices throughout the enforcement process. As Hutter (1997: 12–14) points out:

> Compliance is a concept relevant to all forms of enforcement, but the concept is used in a variety of ways in the regulation literature .... A theme running through much regulation literature is that compliance with regulatory legislation should be regarded as much as a process as an event. Regulatory officials may regard compliance both as a matter of instant conformity and an open-ended and long-term process which may take several years to attain. Edelman seeks to shift the emphasis to the process of compliance, especially in view of the belief that compliance is a social and political process that evolves over time .... Many early studies of regulatory enforcement began with the question of how regulators use the law and what they aim to achieve .... It was argued that enforcement of the law did not refer simply to legal action but to a wide array of informal enforcement techniques including education, advice, persuasion and negotiation. These were used by all law enforcement officials, but came into particular prominence in the regulatory arena.

The widespread and extensive use of informal techniques for securing compliance may indicate uncertainty over the objectives or purposes of compliance and enforcement activity. As one of us has observed:

> Throughout the literature concerned with regulatory enforcement, it is typically claimed, rather ambiguously, that the purpose of regulatory enforcement is to 'secure compliance'. But with what must compliance be secured? Regulatory theorists appear to use the phrase not only by reference to compliance with the collective goals underpinning a regulatory scheme, but also by reference to compliance with regulatory standards. The lack of clarity is exacerbated by the tendency of some theorists to use the term interchangeably and inconsistently, sometimes referring to compliance with regulatory standards, but on other occasions referring to compliance with collective goals. The issue is not merely a linguistic, terminological difficulty, for the two reference points, collective goals and regulatory standards, may not necessarily be consistent. So for example, the phenomenon of 'creative compliance', whereby technical compliance with rules may be achieved yet the underlying spirit and purpose of those rules might be simultaneously undermined, is well known. If regulatory standards have been poorly designed, they may fail to influence behaviour in the manner intended, with the result that compliance with regulatory standards may not promote compliance with the scheme's collective goals. And even if standards are well-designed, it is possible to envisage circumstances in which insistence on compliance with standards in situations involving technical or trivial violations could be counter-productive, undermining a general culture of commitment on the part of the regulated community towards the scheme's collective goals. In short, it is possible to distinguish between 'rule compliance' on the one hand and 'substantive compliance' with collective goals on the other, and the two may not always be coextensive.' (Yeung 2004: 11)

For the purposes of this chapter, *compliance activities* refer to decisions, practices or actions taken by a regulatee for the purposes of attempting to comply with a regulatory rule. *Enforcement activities* refer to activities taken by actors involved in overseeing and implementing of regulatory rules to ensure that they are applied in concrete settings, including decisions, practices and actions taken by those with enforcement powers or capacities directed towards ensuring that those subject to regulatory rules comply with them and to address suspected non-compliance with regulatory rules. These include measures taken to monitor, investigate and gather evidence in relation to suspected violations and formal and informal actions directed towards rule-violators, including the application of sanctions.

In this chapter, we examine public enforcement, highlighting the human dimension of regulatory enforcement that forms the focus of a well-developed literature concerned with observing and understanding the dynamic interactions between regulatory enforcement officials and those they regulate in specific contexts. We then consider prescriptive models of enforcement developed by regulatory scholars offering guidance to public enforcement officials in exercising their enforcement powers. In so doing, we highlight how 'risk-based' approaches to regulation have been variously understood and operationalised. Although the idea of risk-based regulation was originally focused on offering guidance to regulatory enforcement officials in prioritising their limited inspection resources, the term is now also used to describe the intentional design of regulatory regimes in which the nature, content and stringency of regulatory requirements vary in proportion to the perceived riskiness of the regulated activity. Regulated activities in which failure or error might have catastrophic consequences, such as nuclear power generation, often require an ex ante approach to regulation, requiring a public official to approve the regulated activity before it can be lawfully undertaken. However, as markets have globalised, these approvals and other compliance verification tasks are sometimes undertaken by 'private' entities and other 'gatekeepers'. These 'certification' services are intended to provide consumers, as the primary beneficiaries of regulatory rules, with 'assurance' regarding the quality of the regulatee's products, services or systems, which we examine in Section 9.6. Enforcement also includes private action taken by those harmed or wronged by those who violate regulatory rules seeking some kind of redress, and is explored in Chapter 10.

9.1 Public Enforcement Action

Problems associated with the interpretation of rules and the circumstances that they govern often surface when attempts are made to enforce those rules in specific real-world settings. Enforcement action is important and indispensable to uphold the rule of law and hold rule-violators legally accountable. Road traffic laws are a familiar example. In the United Kingdom, for example, the driver of a motor vehicle who fails to stop at a red signal may incur three penalty points, in which a driver who builds up twelve or more penalty points within a three-year period may be disqualified from driving. Yet, many of us have observed drivers failing to stop at red signals without incurring any penalty, vividly reminding us that unless some form of 'enforcement action' is taken, the driver will not be held to account for violating the law.

9.1.1 Public Enforcement Discretion: The Human(s) in the (Enforcement) Loop

Just as STS scholars draw attention to the 'practice' of science in specific organisational, political and cultural settings, including regulatory contexts, legal sociologists and socio-legal scholars have drawn attention to the way the law is practiced and implemented 'on the ground' (see also Hertogh's extract in Chapter 10). They share a common belief in the need to investigate and understand both science and law as socially situated practices, particularly the value of empirical observation of the social interactions occurring 'on the street'. The concept of 'street–level bureaucracy' was introduced by Lipsky (1980), referring to frontline civil servants employed by public regulators and their interactions and encounters with regulatees when undertaking their duties and functions. Until then, the focus of observational study in politics and public policy had centred on those occupying formal positions of power:

notably, the elected officials who make policy. Lipsky argued that the true locus of power lay in the bureaucrats, those who turn the policies into actions. This perspective became a formative landmark in thinking about governmental administration and political science more broadly, shifting the focus from elected officials to the everyday bureaucrat. Socio-legal scholars have followed suit, undertaking ethnographic studies of the practices of public enforcement officials when applying regulatory rules, generating a rich body of scholarship emphasising variation in the 'enforcement styles' of public officials and their perceptions of the character, motivations and compliance capabilities of those they regulate. In a study on the conduct of British officials responsible for enforcing environmental regulations, Keith Hawkins (1984) contrasted two major strategies of enforcement: on the one hand, a compliance strategy, which characteristically relies on a conciliatory style of enforcement (preventing harm rather than punishing evil), and a sanctioning strategy, on the other, which is characteristically penal in style (punishing those for breaking a rule and doing harm). Subsequent observational studies of enforcement officials from diverse domains have found considerable variation in enforcement styles and decision-making, demonstrating that compliance is a socially constructed, on-going process. Many of these studies show that the approach taken by enforcement officials is informed by a number of variables, including the legal framework (such as the sanctions at the regulator's disposal); the nature of the interactions between regulator and regulatee; the type of breach; the type of firm; internal bureaucratic leadership; organisation and culture; the personal backgrounds, experiences and attitudes of enforcement officers themselves; and the broad political, economic, social and moral context of the regulation. Particular significance is often ascribed to enforcement officials' perceptions of the nature, disposition, competence and motivations of the regulatee, prompting both enforcement officials and scholars to develop typologies of the regulatory enforcement official. This includes Braithwaite, Grabosky and Walker's (1986) study of Australian regulatory agencies, which identified seven dominant enforcement 'types' (conciliators, benign big guns, diagnostic inspectorates, token enforcers, detached token enforcers and modest enforcers).

9.1.2 How Do Regulatees Understand Compliance?

Observational studies have also shown how different 'types' of regulatees understand and approach regulatory compliance, including the taxonomy developed by Kagan and Scholtz (1984) classifying regulatees into 'amoral calculators', 'political citizens' and the 'organizationally incompetent' (referred to in the extract below). In a slightly different vein, the following study by Fairman and Yapp investigated how small and medium British businesses (SMEs) understand compliance with food safety standards, finding that they regard compliance as an outcome rather than a process.

Fairman, R., and Yapp, C. (2005). 'Enforced Self-Regulation, Prescription, and Conceptions of Compliance within Small Businesses: The Impact of Enforcement'. *Law & Policy*, 27, 491–519, https://doi.org/10.1111/j.1467-9930.2005.00209.x.

494–511

Compliance and non-compliance can be explained by a variety of perspectives. Within economic literature the predominant view sees compliance as a decision motivated by financial arguments or concerns of loss of reputation or status (within rational choice theory). Alternative views see compliance as the consequence of the acceptance or internalization of rules, as the outcome of the learning process, or as a result of organizational management (from an organizational perspective). Kagan and Scholz (1984) combine these perspectives to produce three popularly held 'images' of business corporations and the corresponding theories of non-compliance: 'amoral calculators' (making decisions on risk-benefit criteria); 'political citizens' (choosing not to comply due to disagreements with the rules), or 'organizationally incompetent' (failing to comply because of a lack of good management, systems, or organizational failure) . . ..

2. Conceptions of Compliance

The most interesting finding of this study concerns how SMEs conceptualize compliance. To the majority of SMEs interviewed, compliance meant doing everything they were told to do by an inspector at the last inspection. If all the works were carried out at that time, SMEs believed they were compliant. This was irrespective of the length of time that had passed since the last inspection, changes that had occurred since, and obvious problems of non-compliance (judged by a formal compliance assessment conducted by the interviewer in the premises) . . ..

This understanding of compliance by SMEs may relate to the historically very prescriptive nature of food-safety legislation and enforcement approach taken by inspectors. All the food premises in this study were inspected at least every eighteen months. This close interaction between the enforcer and business may foster reliance on the inspector. SMEs viewed the responsibility of assessing compliance to be the enforcement agency's and not their own:

I am waiting for him (the inspector) to come and put me straight. (Mobile food van)

Most SMEs interviewed were unable to judge their own compliance (as defined by the enforcement agencies) because of a lack of knowledge of the legal requirements . . ..

SMEs believed they were compliant when they had carried out all the works that the inspector required during the regulatory encounter. Therefore, at a fixed point in time when the SME had carried out all the works required by the inspector (assuming the inspector has required all the works required by the law) the SME conception of compliance and a 'formal' concept of compliance

> would be the same. Compliance is, in the mind of the enforcer and in its formal sense, a continual process. Evidence from this study suggests that the conception of compliance by SMEs is static and focussed on a fixed point in time – at the point they carried out the requirements of the inspector. To the enforcer, compliance is a process. To the SMEs in this study, compliance is an outcome. Compliance is achieved once the works required are carried out, and non-compliance will not occur until the time of the next encounter with the enforcer – at the next inspection.
>
> Concepts of compliance and non-compliance are related to harm in the mind of the SME. Experience of the negotiated regulatory encounter has given the SME an accurate picture of enforcement policy: They are aware that formal enforcement action is taken rarely and is only taken when conditions are very poor or the business is non-cooperative. Non-compliance is therefore linked with wilfully causing conditions that cause harm. They do not, however, have any knowledge of enforcement action being taken within their local authority area.
>
> This conception of compliance poses real problems for any requirements that are ongoing, require proactive management, or that are process-based rather than outcome-based. From the qualitative interviews during the case studies, it was clear that the enforced self-regulatory requirement of hazard analysis was often alien to SMEs not only in its language and terminology, but also in its use of systems management. The SMEs in the study did not require systems management – they were too small. To be compliant, SMEs had to adopt systems management approaches. Within their own conception of compliance, the development of the documented system became the outcome they aimed at, rather than the process of implementing and adopting the system.

The perceived burden of compliance and the ability to comply with regulation depend thus on the type and resources of the regulatee. Although large firms have the means to comply with regulations, SMEs typically do not. This difference is particularly relevant when firms are expected to develop their own regulatory standards and internal management systems (see Chapter 7). SMEs often lack the resources or sophistication for implementing and maintaining formal organisational systems that will be the norm in large firms. As Fairman and Yapp (2005: 512–516) show later in their article, SMEs may thus become 'organisationally incompetent':

> Enforced self-regulation has all the features of a regulatory approach that SMEs will find difficult to comply with. It is complex, systems-based, not linked to harm, process-orientated, difficult to judge compliance, and difficult to implement. Where local authorities take educative approaches, compliance with the more prescriptive and the enforced self-regulatory requirements is significantly higher . . ..
>
> **Is Prescription Easier to Comply with Than Enforced Self-Regulation?**
>
> The rationale behind the growth of enforced self-regulation should be questioned. The vast majority of companies (SMEs) find it difficult to comply, not because they are 'amoral calculators' or 'political citizens' in Kagan and Scholz

typology, merely because this regulatory tool *has made them* 'organizationally incompetent'. Enforced self-regulation requires systems management, normally not a feature of small businesses. The tool designed by the regulator forces the enforcer on the ground to attempt to make sense of the requirements with small businesses. Such activity is intensive on time, something that enforcement agencies do not have. The pragmatic response of enforcers is to interpret enforced self-regulation into sets of rules for businesses to follow. Enforced self-regulation therefore fails to live up to two of its objectives – reducing the burden on enforcement agencies, and placing responsibility on businesses.

Although concerns about the 'burdens' imposed on regulated firms and associated compliance costs often loom large in discussions about regulatory rules, Fairman and Yapp's study suggests that small firms may be largely ignorant of the applicable regulatory rules, suggesting that they cannot and do not intentionally attempt to assess the costs of compliance. Yet compliance cost studies, which seek to quantify the costs that regulatory rules place on regulatees in endeavoring to comply, recognise that regulation often imposes disproportionate costs on small businesses relative to large organisations, as indicated in the extract below:

Kitching, J., Hart, M., and Wilson, N. (2015). 'Burden or Benefit? Regulation as a Dynamic Influence on Small Business Performance'. *International Small Business Journal*, 33(2), 130–147, doi: 10.1177/0266242613493454.

131–132

Compliance cost studies quantify the costs of compliance. Businesses, it is argued, face an opportunity cost in diverting scarce resources from value-adding activities towards 'unproductive' compliance. Methods of calculating compliance costs vary with regard to how costs are defined, but usually involve the labour time costs (often monetised) associated with discovering, interpreting and complying with regulations, recording information and reporting to government, and adviser fees. Regulation is argued to raise the substantive, administrative and psychological costs to businesses, deterring start-up, investment and innovation, and ultimately impeding growth. Most studies, though not all, suggest that regulation imposes costs that are regressive, with small businesses suffering disproportionately. Compliance cost studies go beyond perception surveys by highlighting the importance of the financial, time and psychological costs associated with compliance. Like perception surveys, compliance cost studies treat regulation as a static cost burdening small firms. Crucially, however, measuring static costs tells us neither how businesses adapt to regulation in particular ways in particular settings, nor how adaptation influences performance.

9.1.3 Prescriptive Guidance for Public Enforcement Officials

Various scholars have built on the findings of ethnographic studies of enforcement and compliance interactions to develop a set of 'strategic' prescriptions that public regulators are exhorted to adopt. For example, in Chapter 7 we considered the principles of so-called Smart Regulation developed by Gunningham and Sinclair, building on earlier groundwork laid by Ayres and Braithwaite's *Responsive Regulation* (1992). Ayres and Braithwaite drew on a combination of game theory and the findings of observational studies of interactions between public enforcement officials and regulatees to argue for a 'pyramid of enforcement' strategy (see extract by Yeung in Section 9.4.2). They argued that cooperative solutions between enforcement officials and the regulated firm provide the most effective means for securing compliance and should thus constitute the initial approach public enforcement officials adopt when they identify possible non-compliance. For them, only when cooperation is not forthcoming should the regulator adopt a more punitive stance. In that case, the threat of punitive approaches could encourage cooperation between regulated firms and the regulator.

9.2 'Risk-based' Regulation in Enforcement

By the early to mid 2000s, interest in so-called risk-based approaches to enforcement started to acquire considerable steam, particularly after the UK's Hampton Review, which recommended that all regulatory agencies should adopt a risk-based approach to enforcement (Hampton 2005). The phrase 'risk-based regulation' has, however, been used to shape regulatory enforcement in various ways. Care is therefore needed to identify what a specific author means by the phrase. As Julia Black has observed:

Black, J. (2010). 'The Role of Risk in Regulatory Processes'. In Baldwin et al. (eds.), *Oxford Handbook of Regulation*. Oxford Oxford University Press, 302–348.

330

'Risk-based regulation has generally two distinct meanings, which are often conflated. The first refers to the regulation of risks to society: risks to health, safety, the environment, or, less usually, financial well-being. In this respect, 'risk-based' regulation refers to the management of societal risk . . .. The second, emergent meaning of risk-based regulation refers to regulatory or institutional risk: risk to the agency itself that it will not achieve its objectives. For regulators, in this newer sense, risk-based regulation involves the development of decision-making frameworks and procedures to prioritise regulatory activities and the deployment of resources around an assessment of the risks that regulated firms pose to the regulator's objectives. In their narrowest form, risk-based frameworks are used to allocate inspection resources. However, for an increasing number of regulators, risk-based frameworks are being developed to help them structure choices across a range of different types of intervention activities, including education and advice.

9.2.1 Risk-based Regulation as a Guide to Prioritising Enforcement Resources

Risk-based regulation was originally focused on exhorting public regulators to distribute their limited resources more efficiently by strategically targeting their attention on those who pose the 'highest risk' while bearing in mind their exposure to 'institutional risks', described in the extract below:

Rothstein, H. et al. (2006). 'The Risks of Risk-based Regulation: Insights from the Environmental Policy Domain'. *Environment International*, 32(8), 1056–1065, https://doi.org/10.1016/j.envint.2006.06.008.

1057

At its simplest, risk-based regulation can be conceived as allocating resources in proportion to risks to society (such as health, safety or environmental risks), considering both the impacts themselves and the likelihood that they happen, in order to establish appropriate levels of control . . ..

Such strategies are argued to offer a rational method for improving regulatory efficiency by offering 'targeted' and 'proportionate' interventions that maximise the benefits of regulation, whilst ensuring that the burden on the regulated community is commensurate with the risks posed. Risk-based decision-making has been used in a number of domains for many years. These include finance, local road safety measures and occupational health and safety . . ..

Institutions that manage risks to society also face institutional risks in going about their business. For example, enforcement failures, liabilities and damage to reputation can create problems for regulatory decision-making and even threaten the legitimacy of regulatory organisations themselves. If the reputation of a regulator is seriously compromised, that agency may not command the full backing of government or the courts, and may fail to manage its regulated community effectively. Risk-based regulation, therefore, is often additionally conceived as the assessment and management of the bundle of issues usually termed 'business risks' associated with delivering regulatory objectives . . ..

Such institutional risks are an inherent feature of regulation, in so far as they arise from the inevitable complexities, conflicts and puzzles of regulatory activity, which can lead to divergence between expectations and practice. For example, inherent uncertainties, competing priorities, legal and institutional constraints, diversely governable actors and the conflicting demands of stakeholders all could give rise to institutional risks . . .. Greater scrutiny, accountability and control of public and private sector organisations, however, have amplified the institutional risks associated with such problems. For example, the rise of audit and target cultures and increasing external transparency, have put regulators under increasing pressures to account for regulatory activity to the executive, the judiciary and external stakeholders.

Risk-based decision-making provides one way of managing institutional risks by explicitly anticipating those risks within probabilistic calculations of regulatory success and failure . . . risk-based regulation is about defining the limits of what regulation can be expected to achieve. Risk is therefore an attractive concept for regulators because it provides a powerful rationale for regulatory activity and behaviours.

The rise of risk-based regulation across Europe has been driven, at least partly, by the EU's 'Better Regulation' agenda (see Chapter 5) requiring the organisation of regulatory inspections through the lens of risk. Yet a comparative study of regulators in England, Germany, France and the Netherlands, which have all implemented EU requirements that food safety inspections be 'risk-based', found significant differences in how these four EU Member States assess risk, with starkly different implications for what kind of food businesses they need to target to ensure safety within an ostensibly harmonised single market.

Borraz, O. et al. (2022). 'Why Regulators Asses Risk Differently: Regulatory Style, Business Organisation, and the Varied Practice of Risk-based Food Inspections across the EU'. *Regulation & Governance*, 16: 274–292, https://doi.org/10.1111/rego.12320.

289–290

We draw three conclusions from this study.

First, risk concepts have sufficient interpretive flexibility for risk-scoring methods to be constructed in ways that reflect the organization of political economies and nationally specific legal constraints that have long shaped the very enforcement practices reformers seek to standardize. Thus, while risk-scoring can be made to favor operators that belong to professional associations in the well-organized corporatist political economies of Germany and the Netherlands, such memberships carry less value in terms of trustworthiness in the poorly organized pluralist political economies of England and, particularly, France. At the same time, in the juridified regulatory settings of France and Germany, risk-scoring methods are strongly constrained by constitutional and administrative law, while in the less juridified English and Dutch contexts, risk-scoring methods are shaped more by inspectorates' professional preferences and contingent political pressures.

Second, risk-based approaches to regulatory reform are unlikely to make much impact on enforcement practices without more reflection on the assumptions, conceits, and institutional contexts that shape how risk is understood and used by regulators from country to country. As Lascoumes & Le Galès (2007) have argued, policy tools embody particular ideas about the purposes of governance and relationships between 'governors' and 'governed'. Our case shows that risk-based tools are no exception. Instead of challenging regulatory practices, risk-based instruments are sufficiently malleable for inspectorates to codify pre-existing practices in ways that preserve their predilections and institutional commitments. The consequence is that far from stimulating regulatory convergence, risk-based approaches can sustain entirely incompatible and mutually contradictory regulatory practices in different countries. Indeed, if better regulation reformers want to argue risk-based regulation can improve regulatory efficiency, effectiveness, and consistency, then they need to reflect more on what efficiency, effectiveness, and consistency mean in different national contexts. Moreover, the Dutch case suggests that better regulation reforms to slim down and consolidate regulatory agencies in the name of efficiency undermines the evidence-gathering capabilities required for effective targeting of inspections.

> Finally, this paper raises interesting questions for current debates about Europeanisation. Whereas one might expect the Commission to be concerned with regulatory convergence across countries, the case of food safety suggests a greater concern with how closely member states follow their own internal control policies than whether their regulatory practices are externally consistent with each other.

The concept of risk-based regulation has subsequently expanded beyond inspection and enforcement. It is now invoked as a more general rubric to encompass a wider and more varied range of regulatory strategies. For example, the EU's AI Act is described by those involved in its drafting as resting on a 'risk-based' approach (European Commission 2023). Yet the Commission has not defined what this means. Instead, in addition to the notion of 'systemic risk' produced by some 'general purpose AI models', the Act draws attention to four levels of risk that are identified by the AI Act, notably (1) unacceptable risk, (2) high risk, (3) limited risk and (4) minimal or no risk, and that for each of these risk categories, the stringency of applicable regulatory requirements are directly proportional to the level of risk. Thus, practices that fall into the class of 'unacceptable risk' are legally prohibited, those that pose minimal or no risk do not attract regulatory requirements and those identified as 'high risk' attract a reasonably demanding set of regulatory requirements. This understanding of a 'risk-based' approach involves structuring the design, scope and content of regulatory requirements such that they are proportionate to the level of 'risk' associated with the activity in question. Put simply, the more harmful the activity in question, the more stringent and demanding the applicable regulatory standards.

9.2.2 Risk-based Regulatory Enforcement Architectures

In this section, we discuss different public licensing regimes, the growing reliance on predictive enforcement and critiques of risk-based enforcement architectures.

9.2.2.1 Public Licensing Regimes

Many activities that carry a higher risk to the public are regulated via licensing regimes that prohibit the regulated activity from being undertaken unless and until a licence is obtained. For example, those wishing to drive a motor vehicle must first obtain a driver's licence, given that driving is a dangerous activity (to both the driver and to other road users) requiring skill and competence. Public licensing regimes refer to systems that rely on the grant of licenses and permits by a public authority. A permit is a permission to do something that would otherwise be forbidden, while a license is an official document that gives the licence-holder the 'right' to undertake the licensed activity. A license may be permanent or apply for a more limited period of time. Examples are professional licensing for doctors, lawyers, engineers and accountants. There are also environmental licenses for activities that may have significant adverse environmental impacts, such as industrial processes or construction projects. Permits are usually temporary or associated with a specific activity, such as driving a motor vehicle. Public licensing regimes are not unconditional. They can be revoked, for example, if the licence-holder is found guilty of misconduct (e.g., when someone is caught drunk driving several times), serious non-compliance or otherwise generates public safety concerns.

A commitment to 'proportionate' regulation is often invoked to justify the use of ex ante regulatory approaches to the design of regulatory regimes that require prior approval (typically in the form of a permit or licence) by an authorising agency before the activity can be lawfully undertaken (see Chapter 2 on 'entry regulation'). In the EU, in addition to proportionality, public licensing regimes must also comply with a number of general and sector-specific EU law rules and principles. For example, these regimes should not discriminate between economic agents based on their nationality and rules and procedures should be transparent and avoid unduly restricting competition between EU Member States. In addition, an operator established in a different EU Member State should be able to offer services in another without unjustified additional licensing requirements.

As Ogus explains in the following extract, although the costs of administering a licensing regime are high, this may be justified on public interest grounds if performance failure may be 'catastrophic' as is the case for nuclear accidents:

Ogus, A. (2002). 'Regulatory Institutions and Structures'. *Annals of Public and Cooperative Economics*, 73, 627–648, https://doi.org/10.1111/1467-8292.00208.

631

Prior Approval

This regulatory form requires that firms, before lawfully engaging in an activity or supplying a product or service, must first obtain a licence or permit from an authorizing agency; and for such approval they have to satisfy the agency that certain conditions of quality are, or are capable of meeting the requirement of optimal loss abatement. The administrative costs of scrutinizing all applications is very high and to these must be added the opportunity costs arising from any delay before the licence is granted. Moreover, significant welfare losses arise if the system is used for the anti-competitive purpose of creating barriers to entry. The benefit from prior scrutiny must therefore be very large to justify, on public interest grounds, these substantial costs. Two sets of circumstances in which such large benefits are likely to arise may be identified. The first comprises cases (eg nuclear accidents) where the consequences of performance failure maybe so catastrophic, or the social aversion to them so high, that prior scrutiny and prevention is perceived to be preferable to deterrence from the threat of ex post sanctions. In sharp contrast, the second category does not necessarily give rise to large losses in individual cases. The problem, which is particularly acute in relation to the provision of services, is rather that of expressing or measuring a variety of characteristics of performance in a sufficiently succinct and yet comprehensive manner that they can be formulated as enforceable standards. The assessment of a multitude of factors is facilitated by the case-by-case approach adopted in the licensing process.

Ex ante licensing regimes have conventionally been applied to professional occupations typically considered to require advanced levels of training, skill and competence, yet these regimes have come under sustained attacked, as outlined in the extract below:

Svorny, S. (2000). 'Licensing. Market Entry regulation'. In B. Bouckaert and G. De Geest (eds.), *Encyclopedia of Law and Economics*. Vol. III, The Regulation of Contracts. Edward Elgar, 296–328.

297–305

Policy debates about licensure center on justifying entry restrictions and on whether or not the state can assure performance once individuals are granted entry. The identification of qualified personnel is not a sufficient justification for licensure, as this can be accomplished through certification. Certification, or 'voluntary' licensure identifies entities that meet entry standards or standards of performance, but does not restrict the practice of others. Under a system of certification, consumers have access to information about service providers, but they are not constrained from purchasing services from non-certified providers; competition is not limited.

That fact that service providers, trade associations and medical societies actively promote and support licensing has led to the suspicion that licensing benefits these groups at the expense of other providers or consumers. Critics of market entry restrictions note that service providers' earnings rise as competition declines and that consumers are left with fewer options and higher prices. Also at issue is whether information asymmetries or agency costs are strong enough to warrant government intervention. Many believe that in the absence of government intervention, markets would generate sufficient information through reputation and other mechanisms to meet the needs of consumers. Finally, there is the question of whether there is not some other, preferred form of public policy to insure product quality. Potential alternatives include increased civil and criminal penalties and other institutional arrangements which increase the consequences of malfeasance.

In addition to its purported value in reducing agency costs, two other justifications for licensure have withstood the test of time. One age-old justification for licensure is that it provides protection from external effects associated with the purchase of low quality goods and services. This is an externalities argument. The argument is, essentially, that licensure protects society from the side-effects of poor consumption decisions of its individual members. Another traditional defense of licensure is that some people need to be guided by the state in making choices . . ..

> Many observers complain that licensure fosters cartel-like restrictions which raise prices, benefiting professionals at the expense of consumers. The interests of professionals in licensure are seen as primarily self-serving, an attempt to establish monopoly power in an otherwise competitive industry. Scope-of-practice restrictions, which limit paraprofessionals and others from providing services within the bounds of the licensed profession, contribute to the view that licensing rules are anticompetitive. In medical markets, for example, prohibiting nurse practitioners from prescribing drugs or offering treatment without physician supervision is thought to unduly restrict the potential for optimal division of labor and efficiency in resource use . . ..
>
> Where education and training standards are specified, critics lament the lack of opportunity for innovation and the bias toward existing methods of education and training. Why, they ask, should everyone be trained in the same method and with a similar philosophy? In medicine, the lack of competition is seen as hindering the development of alternative treatments that might improve or prolong lives.

9.2.2.2 'Preventive' Approaches to Enforcement

Ex ante regulatory approaches, and the high costs of administering them, are conventionally justified on the basis that 'prevention is better than cure'. These strategies are future-oriented and invariably entail an assessment of risk or danger. For example, to obtain a driver's licence, applicants must undertake a driving test to demonstrate that they can drive competently and safely, based on an assumption that by passing the test, this evidences the applicant is competent to drive without posing an unjustified risk to others (or to themselves). But risk assessments may turn out to be wrong. Following the 9/11 terrorist attacks, preventive approaches to policy interventions grew in popularity, particularly in relation to counter-terrorism measures. Not long after, big data and machine learning approaches to the prediction of future events, which claimed to offer 'more accurate' predictions when compared with conventional statistical risk assessment techniques, became increasingly fashionable across a wide range of domains. In the criminal justice context, for example, there has been considerable interest in seeking to predict, pre-emptively identify and contain 'dangerous' individuals in the name of protecting public safety and security. Yet, as Michael Tonry points out, there have always been unavoidable normative trade-offs associated with seeking to predict and prevent potential threats, and the resulting benefits and burdens of these trade-offs are unevenly and unfairly distributed. Racial discrimination and stigmatisation of underrepresented groups often results from predictive systems, particularly when used in policing and to predict welfare fraud.

Tonry, M. (2019). 'Predictions of Dangerousness in Sentencing: Déjà vu All over Again'. *Crime and Justice*, 48, 439–482.

443–445

> Predictions of dangerousness in our time present the same challenges and raise the same normative and policy issues as they did three decades ago. Eric Holder warned the US Sentencing Commission against using dangerousness predictions when he was attorney general and has repeatedly decried their use since . . .. The development of 'big data' approaches to prediction has attracted the interest of statisticians who have extensively debated trade-offs between technical and ethical issues. Social scientists have been patiently working on development, refinement, and evaluation of correctional prediction instruments since the 1980s.
>
> The normative and policy issues raised by use in sentencing of predictions of dangerousness are back on the table . . .. Reoffending is so common among chronic property, drug, prostitution, and public disorder offenders that use of predictive incapacitation strategies would generate palpably unjust punishments . . ..
>
> A critic might accuse me of being insensitive to the suffering of victims of crimes that would be avoided if their assailants had been incapacitated. I am not. Prevention of foreseeable harms, however, requires trade-offs between interests and costs. There is no cost-free way entirely to prevent many bad things – including crimes, automobile injuries and fatalities, occupational injuries, environmental degradation, and slips in bathtubs – from happening. No one is prepared to forbid use of automobiles, industrial production, or bathing. Instead we try to make activities as safe as they affordably can be while acknowledging their importance. Crime is no different. There would be little violent crime in the community if all males between ages 16 and 30 were locked up; that is not going to happen. Human beings value their liberty and autonomy too much. Incapacitation resulting from predictions of dangerousness diminishes the liberty and autonomy of knowable individual people, disproportionately poor and disadvantaged ones, in exchange for predicted prevention of crimes to hypothetical future victims.
>
> Because the world changes, many predicted crimes may never have happened. Rates of violent crime, for example, declined by two-thirds in the past quarter century. Two-thirds of the crimes that were predicted as grounds for locking people up in 1995 did not happen, but those locked up lost much of their lives as free citizens. The trade-off is thus between punishing specific people much more than they deserve in order, on the basis of predictions that are much more often than not incorrect, to prevent an unknowable number of future crimes. That price, like the costs associated with banning private use of automobiles, is too high. Violent crimes are as much an inevitable fact of life as auto accidents. They are prices we pay for personal freedom.

9.3 Regulatory Investigations and Investigative Powers

Before initiating formal enforcement proceedings against those allegedly in violation of legal rules, a public authority will investigate the facts and circumstances to identify whether there is sufficient evidence to support a prima facie case of suspected violation. To do so, regulatory authorities are typically endowed with coercive powers of information gathering, monitoring and investigation, without which they may be unable to discharge their duty to enforce the law. For example, the European Competition and national competition authorities may conduct unannounced inspections (often called 'dawn raids') on the premises and possessions of undertakings who they suspected may be in violation of competition law. Those subjected to dawn raids are not informed in advance, lest evidence is destroyed before the investigation occurs. The exercise of investigative powers, such as the authority to coercively impose sanctions on individuals who violate the law, involves interferences with the rights and liberties of persons and must therefore be lawful and exercised in accordance with the principles of procedural fairness. When the Commission conducts unannounced inspections, undertakings must cooperate actively in the investigative measures during preliminary enquiries and must hand over any documents when called upon to do so (including documentation and hardware devices that hold and store electronic records) to enable the Commission to obtain evidence of possible competition infringements.

9.4 Regulatory Sanctions

Where regulatory regimes seek to shape and constrain the behaviour of regulatees, their effectiveness will depend on whether they secure the desired behavioural change. Accordingly, the possibility of sanctioning violators is important to deter those who might otherwise be inclined to flout regulatory rules. For present purposes, we define sanctions as the coercive imposition of adverse consequences in response to a violation of a legal rule. In the realm of 'traditional' crimes, we often think of strongly punitive criminal sanctions such as imprisonment, involving substantial deprivations of liberty of the person. In regulatory contexts, however, the sanctions may range from strongly punitive measures (including imprisonment for criminal wrongdoing) to administrative measures that are not (if at all) strongly punitive in their legal form, justification and effects. For example, the revocation of a chemical company's operational license in response to a violation of regulatory requirements may have severe ramifications, resulting in financial distress and perhaps even bankruptcy.

Significant financial penalties may be imposed for violating laws arising under data protection regimes, competition/antitrust, environmental protection and securities regulation, among others. For example, most OECD countries provide for significant financial penalties for infringements of competition law, although their formal legal classification varies. In some jurisdictions (such as the United States and United Kingdom) these sanctions are formally classified as criminal in nature, while in others (such as Australia and the EU) they are formally classified as civil in nature (see

Chapter 10). The range and variety of sanctions available in response to a regulatory violation depends upon the specific regulatory regime and can vary widely across different regimes. Typically, a variety of sanctions are available, so that the exercise of discretionary authority is involved in identifying which sanction to impose and its severity. As every parent knows, deciding on an appropriate sanction to impose on a child for rule-breaking requires attention to several matters, including the nature and severity of the infraction, the purpose the parent seeks to achieve and, for responsible parents at least, a concern to act fairly and proportionately in relation to the child's conduct. Similarly, a variety of concerns must be considered in determining the appropriate regulatory sanction. In the United Kingdom, a review of sanctions available to British regulators was undertaken by an environmental lawyer, Richard Macrory, who made a series of recommendations in 2006, which were taken up in the enactment of the Regulatory Enforcement and Sanctions Act 2008. The following extract is taken from Macrory's reflections on his review:

> **Macrory, R. (2008).** 'New Approaches to Regulatory Sanctions'. *Environmental Law & Management*, 20, 210–214.
>
> To avoid getting lost in a mass of detail, it was necessary to stand back and ask, what is the purpose of penalties? Why are there penalties in a regulatory regime? . . . After reviewing the literature and talking to people I came up with a set of Penalties Principles that should underlie the approach and design of a modern sanctions regime. In brief sanctions should:
>
> - aim to change behaviour
> - aim to eliminate financial gain if applicable
> - be responsive
> - be proportionate
> - restore the harm caused if applicable
> - deter future non-compliance.
>
> The most important are probably the first two. The aim of a sanction in this area is not to punish as such (although a punishment may be necessary in some circumstances), nor is it to create a stigma, but rather to change behaviour and to judge the best way to achieve this. Secondly, since we are dealing largely with businesses engaged in commercial activity and who can make money by non-compliance (rather than say the behaviour of individuals such as litter dropping or smoking in prohibited places), it is very important that the penalty system aims to eliminate any financial gains. This would be only fair to those industries which do comply and would send out the right signals . . ..
>
> Equally important, in every area the regulator is coping with an enormous range of potential offenders. At one extreme are the rogue traders – the 'white van man' for example – and businesses that consciously aim to avoid legal requirements. This does not just apply in environment but in food standards, in health and safety, in building controls and so on. At the other extreme are legitimate businesses which are trying their best. Many trade associations tend to present

> the situation as one where the regulator should just concentrate on the rogue traders since all the rest want to comply. However, it's not quite as simple as that. There is another species in the middle, not 'criminals' who consciously avoid the law, but businesses such as those which inadvertently or through carelessness breach the law. But such a breach may have serious consequences, for instance a water pollution incident which could cause an injury to somebody. It is not possible – public interest will say it is not possible – just to warn that business not to do it again, or even issue a formal caution. And it is circumstances like these that must be addressed . . ..
>
> I looked at the criminal processes and it is clear that criminal law will continue to play an important part in regulation. However, quite rightly, bringing a criminal prosecution is not an easy process. It is designed to cause stigma, ideally on the offender if fined. However, for legitimate businesses that fail to comply with the law, criminal prosecution can be an inappropriate and unwieldy response. Equally, the imposition of a fine may not be the best way to achieve changes in behaviour. One of the concerns is that if there is too much reliance upon the criminal process as a way of dealing with these regulatory offences, the criminal law tends to become devalued. Defence lawyers and even the courts sometimes describe regulatory offences as not criminal 'in the real sense' . . .. My concern is for the company which breaches regulatory requirements through oversight or carelessness, and, yes, makes some money out of it, but has done so by mistake. Does this deserve a criminal conviction? Should this company be subject to the same process? Lastly, and again this is very difficult to quantify, if the criminal process is relied upon too heavily, and because prosecuting somebody is such a major step, there may be what is known as a 'compliance deficit' – in other words it is not possible to deal with all the breaches that should be prosecuted, and breaches that should be sanctioned are not.

In most cases, regulators apply fines and penalties, injunctions, license or permit revocations, compulsory audits and monitoring and may also impose informal sanctions, such as publicizing details of violations by those found in violation (so-called naming and shaming techniques). Macrory goes on to argue that regulators should have a variety of different sanctions at their disposal (beyond criminal fines) in responding to regulatory violations, allowing them greater flexibility to pursue a variety of social purposes when sanctioning regulatory violations, as Yeung explains in the extract below:

> **Yeung, K. (2013).** 'Better Regulation, Administrative Sanctions and Constitutional Values'. Legal Studies, 33(2), 312–339, doi: 10.1111/j.1748-121X.2012.00241.x.
>
> 324–325
>
> While Ayres and Braithwaite's pyramid of enforcement model has been criticized on various grounds, one of its limitations arises from its tendency to overlook the distinct social purposes served by different enforcement tools. In this respect, the Macrory Report provides welcome recognition that there

> are various social goals that regulatory sanctions may properly pursue, including changing the offenders' behaviour, eliminating the gain or benefit arising from non-compliance, restoring the harm caused by non-compliance and deterring future non-compliance. So, in seeking to bring about a change in the offenders' behaviour, regulatory sanctions might seek to bring about the termination of the impugned conduct and prevent specific types of activity, restoration may entail the payment of compensation to those harmed by the offence in order to place the parties affected by the impugned conduct in the position they would have been in had the conduct not occurred, and deterrence of future non-compliance might also entail punishment of offenders for their wrongdoing.
>
> However, identifying the social purposes that any given enforcement tool or sanction may be thought to serve is not always straightforward. Some instruments may serve several purposes whilst the same purpose might be served by several different instruments. Hence enforcement tools are more appropriately characterised in terms of the purpose or purposes for which they are most suited and least suited (or even unsuitable).

The discretion of public enforcement authorities to initiate and maintain legal action against those suspected of violating the law, and to impose sanctions for legal violation, is constrained by constitutional and administrative law. Sanctioning decisions must be made in accordance with the requirements of due process and fair procedure, although identifying what this requires in any given instance typically requires sensitivity to context and circumstances, including the nature, severity and purpose of the sanction. As Yeung (2013: 321) explains in the same article:

> In one sense, procedural fairness refers to an administrative law doctrine more commonly referred to as 'natural justice', comprised of two limbs: decisions by public officials should be made in an unbiased manner; and those affected by such decisions should be given an opportunity to participate in the decisions that affect them. In a broader, constitutional sense, it refers to the values justifying the legal rules of procedure, rather than the specific rules themselves. While procedural fairness can be justified on several grounds, one important justification lies in the importance of accuracy in legal decision making. Because mistakes are unavoidable in the process of legal decision making (due to human frailty and the incompleteness and imperfections of information) we can never be certain that the correct outcome has been reached in all cases. Hence in establishing the requirements of procedural fairness, we must ensure that no person is exposed to an unacceptable risk of a mistaken outcome, and that this risk is distributed fairly among possible victims. The more serious the consequences of mistake, the graver the resulting moral harm. So while there is undoubted moral harm in wrongfully imposing civil liability on a person for breach of contract, the mistaken conviction and punishment of an innocent person for a serious crime generates much graver moral harm.
>
> The demands of procedural fairness therefore vary in relation to the seriousness and gravity of the wrongdoing and the associated sanction: hence the procedural

demands of the criminal law process are much more extensive than those of the civil process. It follows, then, that the requirements of due process in relation to punitive civil sanctions, such as monetary penalties arising under Part III RESA, sit somewhere in the middle-ground: the hybrid quality of such sanctions requires greater procedural protections than those applicable to the paradigm civil process, yet less extensive than those adopted for paradigm criminal wrongdoing. When determining the demands of procedural fairness, the formal label attached to a sanction as civil or criminal is not conclusive, but a matter of substantive characterisation, as the voluminous litigation and case law surrounding Article 6 of the European Convention on Human Rights vividly demonstrates.

9.5 The Role of Litigation via the Courts

The institutional machinery for enforcing regulatory rules varies according to the domain, jurisdiction and legal and constitutional culture in which the violation occurs. Consider, for example, the public enforcement of competition law violations. Within the EU, the European Commission (DG Comp) is principal enforcer of the EU's competition laws with authority to investigate and address anti-competitive practices that affect trade between EU Member States with the power to investigate suspected anticompetitive conduct, to issue prohibition decisions, to impose fines, and to conclude binding agreements with companies. However, this occurs within a system of parallel or coordinated enforcement, in which the Commission serves a coordinating role to ensure that EU competition rules are uniformly applied by national competition authorities, which may conduct parallel investigations. When the European Commission imposes fines, these can be appealed before the General Court of the European Union while fines and other sanctions imposed by national competition authorities are appealed to the competent courts at national level. In contrast, in the United States, both the Federal Trade Commission (FTC) and the US Department of Justice (DOJ Antitrust Division) enforce federal antitrust laws. When the FTC determines that a violation has occurred and imposes a penalty, the affected party may appeal to the US Court of Appeals and, ultimately, to the US Supreme Court. The FTC can also refer evidence of criminal antitrust violations to the DOJ, but only the DOJ can obtain criminal sanctions. The DOJ has sole antitrust jurisdiction over certain industries, including telecommunications, banks, railroads and airlines. State attorneys general may bring federal antitrust suits through 'parens patriae' suits, representing not only individuals residing within their states but also the states themselves. They may enforce both federal and state antitrust laws. In both state and federal jurisdictions, private enforcement actions can be initiated by private litigants seeking compensation for harm arising from alleged violations of competition law and play a crucial role in US antitrust enforcement.

9.6 Private Certifiers and Auditors as Regulatory Intermediaries

Our discussion of licensing regimes has assumed that the task of evaluating licence applications is entrusted to a public authority. However, we have already observed that 'private' governance regimes have proliferated as markets have globalised. These often rely on non-state regulatory intermediaries to evaluate compliance with a set of regulatory rules and thereupon to issue some kind of 'certificate' intended to publicly signify this. A public regulatory regime may mandate that regulated firms acquire certification, which can be undertaken by a private certifier, effectively delegating the role of evaluating compliance with regulatory rules to third parties. Galland explains the origins of the 'certification revolution' in the following extract:

Galland, J.-P. (2017). 'Big Third-party Certifiers and the Construction of Transnational Regulation'. *The Annals of the American Academy of Political and Social Science*, 670(1), 263–279, https://doi.org/10.1177/0002716217694589.

263–265

The markets for goods, be they industrial or the markets for goods, be they industrial or agricultural products, have been regulated by governments at least since the 'invention of the consumer'. In the first three quarters of the twentieth century, governments made rules that mainly addressed their own domestic producers, for the benefit of their own citizens. These rules relied on compulsory regulations, adherence to which was monitored by specialist national (civil service) inspectors (e.g., antifraud or health and safety). Until the 1970s, this market regulation could be described as a two-way interaction between a regulator. For industrial products in the 1970s, a three-way model (R-I-T) was beginning to emerge at the domestic level. From the 1980s, these emerging forms of regulation grew in importance and spread worldwide. Globalization has been accompanied by a proliferation of (international) standards and by the 'certification revolution'. More precisely, most international trade in industrial products is now regulated through a tripartite standard regime (TSR) with three separate phases: standardization, certification, and accreditation.

The general case of the current regulatory regime for international trade in industrial products can be explained using the R-I-T model as follows. Rule makers (Rs), be they nonstate actors or public authorities, set standards or favor the setting of product standards that meet their regulatory goals. So that consumers can trust that the products they buy meet those standards, third-party certifiers (Is) – and accreditation bodies that 'certify the certifiers' – are enlisted as intermediaries to deliver conformity assessment certificates to the regulatory targets, industrial or agricultural producers (Ts). The intended beneficiaries of this whole process are consumers. Within this system, TPCs usually compete for clients, as they are paid by these clients (Ts) to deliver conformity assessment certificates. Accreditation bodies were created to ensure consistency in certification activities and to prevent a possible 'race to the bottom' in audit quality. Within TSRs, accreditation bodies (second level intermediaries) are supposed to check and ensure the competence of third-party certifiers (first-level intermediaries). Although they may be created by Rs, accreditation bodies are independent from Rs, Ts, and their clients (TPCs).

TPCs are positioned between regulators and targets. On one hand, TPCs are appointed or selected by Rs, with the agreement of the accreditor concerned; on the other hand, they have continuous relations with Ts, as their day-to-day work is to monitor the latter's products or industrial processes. This central position generates a tension: the TPCs' duty is to assess targets and ensure that they meet regulators' standards, but TPCs are remunerated not by Rs, but by producers themselves. Moreover, as Rs also wish to keep Ts' compliance costs as low as possible, in the interest of both Ts and consumers, Rs foster competition between TPCs inside specific certification markets. As trade in industrial products is increasingly regulated through TSRs, third party certification activities have undoubtedly been increasing worldwide and in more sectors.

Although third-party certification systems are utilised in many domains and intended to provide 'assurance' that the certified products, services or systems meet specified quality standards, critics question whether these systems provide a valid basis for trust (Busch 2011). Within a larger formalised legal regime that provides for public enforcement, private third parties (including lawyers, accountants and auditors) may nevertheless be appointed by regulatees to provide public assurance of compliance, especially when the latter are required by a public enforcement authority to put third-party oversight requirements in place. These delegates are described by Van Loo below as the 'new gatekeepers' in the following extract:

Van Loo, R. (2020). 'The New Gatekeepers: Private Firms as Public Enforcers'. *Virginia Law Review*, 106, 467–522.

469–493

Over time, policy makers have enlisted a large array of private actors in their quest for optimal regulatory design. Scholarship on the private role in public governance has focused on third-party enforcers whose main function is to provide a support service. Those enforcers include self-regulatory organizations formed by industry and independent auditors mandated by regulators. The corporate law strand of this enforcement literature emphasizes a network of 'gatekeepers', such as lawyers, accountants, and certifiers who guard against compliance and governance failures. For instance, before releasing annual reports a publicly traded company must obtain the signoff of a certified accountant. In these more familiar private enforcement contexts, the private 'cops on the beat' are ancillary actors rather than core market participants . . ..

Policymakers have enlisted a new class of more powerful third-party enforcers: the businesses at the heart of the economy. The ten largest American companies by valuation operate in information technology, finance, oil, and pharmaceuticals. A regulator has put leading firms in each of these industries on notice about their responsibilities for third-party oversight. In addition to the FTC, the Environmental Protection Agency (EPA) – along with the Department of Justice (DOJ) – requires BP Oil and other energy companies to audit offshore oil platform operators for environmental compliance. The Food and Drug Administration (FDA) expects Pfizer and other drug companies to ensure suppliers and third-party labs follow the agency's health and safety guidelines. The Consumer Financial Protection Bureau (CFPB) orders financial institutions, such as American Express, to monitor independent debt collectors and call centers for deceptive practices . . ..

The FDA and Big Pharma

Pharmaceutical companies manufacture drugs but contract with other companies for 'processing, packaging, holding, or testing'. The FDA has the most explicit third-party monitoring expectations of the four case studies. Rulemaking, guidance statements, and warning letters have communicated its policy. One FDA rule states that in every pharmaceutical company there 'shall be a quality control unit . . . responsible for approving or rejecting drug products manufactured, processed, packed, or held under contract by another company'. Monitoring the output is not, however, enough. The company must also directly monitor inputs used by the contractor, including ingredients and materials. After specifying the contractor's internal compliance systems, the manufacturer should conduct audits. Thus, the pharmaceutical company must oversee contractors' organizational processes, inputs and outputs. The FDA places responsibility for third-party activities at the top of the regulated entity. In its formal rules on liability for tainted products, the agency states that it 'regards extramural facilities as an extension of the manufacturer's own facility'. It reiterated this point in its post-inspection warning letters. In other words, the pharmaceutical company is responsible for the third-party contractor's activities as if they were one company. In guidance documents, the agency clarified that it was addressing 'the relationship between owners and contract facilities' . . ..

The FDA does not, however, rely solely on Pfizer to regulate the company's independent contractors. The FDA still routinely inspects and brings enforcement actions directly against those third parties. For instance, in one warning letter to an independent manufacturer, the FDA wrote, 'You and your customer, Pfizer, have a quality agreement regarding the manufacture of drug products. You are responsible for the quality of drugs you produce as a contract facility, regardless of agreements in place . . ..' Pfizer implemented the FDA's organizational advice into its internal processes. It routinely monitors suppliers through audits, inspections, and review of systems. Supplier agreements reflect these review procedures, and when Pfizer recognizes a violation, it can de-list the offender from its list of 'qualified' suppliers or can report violations to the FDA.

Private auditors of various kinds often perform compliance different evaluations. In recent years, 'algorithmic audits' have emerged spontaneously within the digital economy as a response to calls for 'algorithmic accountability'. However, an analysis by a group of UK regulators (the Digital Regulators Cooperation Forum, comprising the UK's Financial Conduct Authority,

Information Commissioners Office, Competition and Markets Authority and OfCom) identifies shortcomings associated with them:

Digital Regulators Cooperation Forum (2022). 'Auditing Algorithms: The Existing Landscape, Role of Regulators and Future Outlook'. Discussion Paper, www.gov.uk/government/publications/findings-from-the-drcf-algorithmic-processing-workstream-spring-2022/auditing-algorithms-the-existing-landscape-role-of-regulators-and-future-outlook.

This nascent audit ecosystem provides a promising foundation; however, work is still needed to ensure that algorithmic processing systems are properly scrutinised. To identify issues with the current landscape and potential solutions, we spoke to stakeholders with expertise in the use of the algorithmic processing systems across academia, industry, the public sector, and civil society . . .. The following sections summarise specific issues raised by stakeholders we spoke to.

Lack of Effective Governance in the Ecosystem

Stakeholders in the AI auditing industry were concerned about the quality of audits in what they perceived as a currently largely unregulated market for auditing. They were concerned that this risked becoming a 'wild west' patchwork where entrants were able to enter the market for algorithm auditing without any assurance of quality . . .. Several stakeholders noted that regulators are unlikely to have the capacity to investigate every instance of alleged harm, and that journalists, academics and other third parties play an important part in scrutinising algorithmic systems . . ..

We also observed that there is a lack of clarity about standards that auditors should be auditing against . . . some stakeholders . . . felt existing standards were often vague and based on general principles, with very few distilled down into anything that can be tested against. This lack of clarity around what good auditing and outcomes look like could act as a disincentive for organisations to pursue internal or external algorithmic auditing. We found that the development of sectoral or domain-specific principles and testable criteria could help to address this lack of clarity. For example, such developments are happening in the health sector. However, establishing such guidance may prove difficult for horizontal regulators who work across sectors and could prove to be less effective than test criteria developed by companies themselves . . ..

Standards bodies are likely to fill some of the gaps left by regulators, yet there are concerns around a lack of transparency over how they are developed and by whom. Standards making is often portrayed as a 'neutral' process led by experts within the specific technical area, yet academic research has revealed that these processes are political. Indeed, given that many technical standards for algorithms will involve value-based choices, some academics have been critical of relying too heavily on standards bodies, which often lack civil society representation and democratic oversight. Moreover, from a geopolitical perspective, the EU, China, and the US have all explicitly stated a desire to take a leading international role in the development of technical standards for algorithms . . ..

Insufficient Access to Systems

We observed that the quality of audit may be compromised if it is not possible for appropriate auditors to obtain sufficient access to algorithmic systems . . ..

Our engagement with stakeholders also revealed a concern that some organisations use 'trade secrets' as a way to block access to systems. Organisations may be more willing to provide access to systems to auditors where the audit is not made public and for the benefit of the organisation only; for external audit that may be provided to the regulator or the public, they may offer only limited access. Nevertheless, where enforcement action is taken against an organisation, regulators have full access to systems . . ..

Finally, a lack of access to effective documentation by the audit client makes audit more challenging to conduct.

Conclusion

This chapter demonstrates that enforcement is essential to facilitate the effectiveness of a regulatory regime. When exercising their discretionary authority to enforce regulatory rules, public enforcers must take a wide range of factors into consideration. We have also observed that the institutional design of regulatory enforcement regimes may vary considerably, highlighting three important features of regulatory architecture around which variation arises and that determine how the regime will be operationalised in practice: (a) ex ante approval or ex post enforcement; (b) the respective roles of private litigants, third party intermediaries and public enforcement authorities; and (c) the availability of sanctions and rights of redress. We have seen that public enforcement entails many, often difficult, tasks and may encompass a wide range of mechanisms, institutions and sanctions that shape and condition the context in which enforcement occurs. Enforcement is a costly and often challenging activity, in which human judgement and discretion remains central, particularly for public enforcement officials with limited resources and enforcement budgets. Yet private actors may also have an important role in helping to secure compliance with regulatory rules, thereby helping to deter and promote legal compliance, while providing those who have suffered harm or wrongdoing arising from the violation of regulatory rules means to seek redress, which we examine in Chapter 10.

Discussion Questions

1. What is compliance? Is compliance best understood as an outcome or process?
2. What are the central challenges of regulatory compliance to SMEs?
3. Identify three public enforcement authorities in your country. What are their main functions?

4. How, if at all, can public regulators assist SMEs in complying with regulatory rules?
5. Investigate the different public licensing regimes applicable to hotels and restaurants in your country. Do these ex ante regimes seem proportionate to the goals they aim to achieve?
6. How do different regulatory enforcement regimes promote deterrence?
7. Choose a regulatory enforcement scandal from your country that caused serious harms to individuals. What was scandalous about this case, and how might such scandals be avoided in future?
8. What is the point and purpose of regulatory sanctions? Why is it considered desirable for public regulators to have a range of different sanctions available?
9. What is the difference between a criminal fine and a civil penalty?
10. Are private certification bodies equivalent to public enforcement authorities? Why or why not?

10

Private Enforcement and Redress

Introduction

In Chapter 9, we examined the public enforcement action and the role of regulatory intermediaries in certification and compliance assurance, which may occur ex ante (i.e., before the regulatee can lawfully engage in the regulated activity) or ex post (i.e., after the regulatee has begun to engage in the regulated activity). However, private enforcement may have an important role: not only in helping to deter regulatory rule violations but also as a means by which those who have suffered some kind of wrong or harm may seek redress. In this chapter, we examine the role and functions of private enforcement within regulatory regimes that provide for ex post enforcement, selectively highlighting several aspects of the institutional and enforcement framework in which regulation takes place. We proceed on the assumption that readers have no significant legal training or expertise; therefore, the chapter begins with a brief examination of the legal rights and duties, civil actions for damages and a basic outline of different 'models' of legal responsibility upon which regulatory regimes rely in allocating and distributing legal rights and duties between regulatees and regulatory beneficiaries (Section 10.1). We then discuss the role and significance of private litigation and the value of 'group' actions, noting their comparatively limited availability in Europe as opposed to the United States (Section 10.2). In Section 10.3, we look more closely at the role and function of courts as authoritative and final interpreters of the law, including the role of judicial review as a means for overseeing the legality of discretionary decisions made by public authorities and we briefly consider alternative and non-judicial channels for redress. Unlike other chapters in this volume, this chapter contains a more extensive discussion of the role of law and legal doctrine, while underlining the importance of the judges, judicial adjudication and the need for certainty and finality in the interpretation of the law and the resolution of disputes. It is important to recognise, however, that this discussion offers a highly selective, brief and simplified account of the role of legal rights, duties and remedies that may be implicated in the violation of regulatory rules rather than offering an in-depth analysis. In addition, it is important to note that rules on enforcement and redress vary depending by jurisdiction, and procedures can be highly regulated. Hence, what we offer here is merely a foundational guide for the study of private enforcement and redress.

10.1 Legal Rights, Duties and Models of Responsibility

In order to understand the significance and limitations of private enforcement of regulatory rules, we need a basic understanding of the nature of legal rights and obligations of persons (both natural and corporate) that constitute an important backdrop against which regulatory regimes operate and through which those regimes are constructed and implemented. Although we observed in Chapter 4 that 'human rights' are an especially important set of moral rights, we also saw that the scope of legal protection accorded to those rights varies depending upon the juridical, constitutional and legal traditions in which they arise. Nevertheless, the distinction between legal and moral rights points to important differences between legal and moral systems for ascribing responsibility. As legal theorist Peter Cane observes, 'law possesses institutional resources that morality lacks', such that '[o]ne of the most important differences between law and morality is that law has much stronger and more highly developed enforcement mechanisms and institutions than morality'(Cane 2002: 12). Thus, although specific conduct might be widely regarded as morally wrongful, it does not necessarily follow that the underlying conduct will entitle the affected person to take legal action seeking some kind of remedy (see also 'standing' below). Whether or not this is possible depends on the legal position of the parties, including whether the affected person can identify and assert a legal 'cause of action' based on the relevant conduct and there is sufficient evidence to prove it before a court.

For example, consider the publication of 'deep fake porn' created through use of AI based face-swapping technologies to generate digital 'deep fake' images in which the face of another person (without their knowledge or consent) has been superimposed onto pornographic videos. Such conduct would be widely regarded as morally wrong. Yet in many jurisdictions, it may be difficult for the victim to point to a criminal offence arising from this conduct or even to assert that their legal rights have been violated and to seek redress through law. Conversely, some activities may constitute legal wrongs, even though we might not typically regard them as morally wrongful, such as unintended interferences with property rights: for example, if I put your phone in my pocket, mistakenly thinking it was mine, then I have violated your legal right to property and, in common law systems, I have committed a legal wrong known as 'trespass to property'. This holds true even if I very shortly thereafter realise my mistake, apologise and return the phone to you. In this example, I may have committed a legal 'wrong' but you have suffered no tangible or substantial harm. For the purposes of identifying whether a person can invoke some kind of legal redress in response to the violation of a rule depends upon whether the activity in question gives the affected person a legal right known in legal parlance as a 'cause of action' against another and whom the courts will hold legally responsible, entitling the affected person to some kind of legal remedy. While a range of evidence, such as expert testimony, relevant documents and witness accounts, may be used to evaluate whether the underlying facts necessary to establish a cause of action can be identified, in practice, significant challenges arise from difficulties in assembling the necessary evidence. However, because the laws of evidence may vary significantly across jurisdictions, the evidential requirements in any given context will be a product of national laws and case law.

In addition, in both civil and common law jurisdictions, less serious harms are often considered unworthy of legal action. The rule 'de minimis non curat lex' or 'the law does not concern itself with trifles' reflects a belief that the legal system does not wish to concern itself with very minor or insignificant disputes. This principle applies in several regulatory fields to set a substantive threshold to justify regulatory enforcement and thus to safeguard the efficient allocation of enforcement resources. For example, in antitrust and competition law, the *de minimis* rule can be invoked to excuse small or inconsequential anticompetitive conduct. For example, if a firm engages in a very minor and non-substantial violation of antitrust laws, it may be deemed inefficient to warrant enforcement action. The meaning of what constitutes 'insignificant' according to this rule varies across fields and jurisdictions.

10.1.1 Civil Actions for Damages

Activities taken by private persons to protect or otherwise vindicate their legal rights seeking some kind of restorative or compensatory remedy following harm or wrongdoing caused by the violation of a regulatory rule can be understood as 'private enforcement' activities, which includes the pursuit of litigation through the courts. These activities serve to uphold the law, providing an institutional vehicle for formally holding rule-violators to account. The kinds of remedies available for violation of a private right of action vary widely, depending on the underlying cause of action. The most familiar private law remedy is an action for damages. For example, in both common and civil law jurisdictions, if one party breaches a contract, the other party can bring an action for damages for breach of contract seeking a financial payment equivalent to the 'loss' suffered by the innocent party arising from the breach. In a similar vein, the common law tort of negligence entitles the plaintiff to an award of damages set at an amount intended to compensate for the harm caused by the defendant's wrong, seeking to put the plaintiff in the position that the plaintiff would have occupied had the wrong not occurred. An award of compensation might also be available for victims of a human rights violation under the European Convention of Human Rights.

However, in English law, the underlying purpose of a damages award for violation of a Convention right is primarily concerned with the defendant's breach of duty to respect those rights rather than the adverse effects on the claimant, so that the amount of damages awarded is usually quite limited.

Depending on the legal system, the source of these 'private' rights of action may rely upon general legal doctrine that are well-established within that legal system, as in the case of general laws of negligence and the law of civil wrongs more generally, or they may be created by specific legislative provision. Common law systems typically rely more on precedent, case law and legal doctrine, while civil law jurisdictions draw primarily on legislation, either at national or transnational level. For example, the EU General Data Protection Regulation confers a set of specific rights on 'data subjects', which they can assert against those who collect and process personal data and, if necessary, invoke the formal legal process to secure compliance by regulatees with their legal duty to act in accordance with the legal enforceable rights of data subjects.

10.1.2 Models of Legal Responsibility

Although it is beyond the scope of this volume to provide a thorough account of the nature, scope and content of private enforcement rights, in making sense of the legal remedies that may be available via private action, it is helpful to acquire a basic understanding of different models of legal responsibility.

10.1.2.1 The Civil and Criminal Paradigms of Legal Responsibility

Within contemporary legal systems, a basic distinction is made between civil and criminal models of responsibility as the basis for legal liability. Although criminal law philosophers have long debated the theoretical and philosophical foundations of criminal punishment, according to the basic paradigm of criminal liability, public censure for violating the criminal law is typically considered central, although in practice the scope and content of many legal duties often depart from this basic paradigm in a number of ways (and which criminal law philosophers have described as 'embarrassing': Lacey 2001). This 'criminal law paradigm' is contrasted with the 'civil law paradigm' of liability, summarised by Yeung in the extract below:

Yeung, K. (2013). 'Better Regulation, Administrative Sanctions and Constitutional Values'. *Legal Studies*, 33, 312–339, https://doi.org/10.1111/j.1748-121X.2012.00241.x.

320

At least four central features are typically associated with the *criminal law paradigm* of liability. First, the imposition of is liability primarily concerned

> with censuring the wrongdoer for activity considered morally blameworthy. Secondly, the sanction for wrongdoing entails serious consequences for the wrongdoer (including restrictions upon, or deprivation of, individual liberty) and carries a significant degree of moral stigma. Thirdly, in response to the seriousness consequences of criminal liability, the 'responsibility' principle is of considerable importance: hence the standard of liability paradigmatically requires proof of culpability (whether intention or recklessness). Finally, the suspected wrongdoer is entitled to a full range of procedural safeguards within the enforcement process.
>
> These four features associated with the criminal law paradigm can be contrasted with those typically associated with the *civil law paradigm* of liability. First, the civil law is primarily concerned to impose obligations of repair on the wrongdoer (compensation and restitution to the victim) rather than condemnation. Secondly, financial liability is incurred towards the victim, not the state. Thirdly, civil liability typically lacks the degree of moral stigma accompanying criminal liability. Finally, the consequences of liability for the wrongdoer are less serious than those associated with the criminal law paradigm, hence proof of culpability is not essential and the procedural rights of the wrongdoer are considerably weaker.

The above extract highlights foundational differences in the social purposes underpinning the criminal and civil liability paradigms. While the primary role of the criminal law is condemnatory, aimed at censuring and punishing the wrongdoer, the role of the civil law is that of repair, aimed at restoring or otherwise compensating the injured party to the position s/he was in prior to the harm-causing event. Accordingly, criminal liability typically requires proof of some kind of moral 'blameworthiness' or culpability (although there are exceptions, particularly in the case of 'strict liability' offences), while civil liability does not. However, this basic distinction between civil and criminal responsibility is not clear-cut. Not only does the design and implementation of contemporary legal systems in practice often blur these distinctions in several ways (which we consider more fully in relation to sanctions below in Section 10.3) it is also possible to identify a wider and more varied range of 'legal models' of responsibility than the civil-criminal binary suggests. Although moral philosophers have tended to focus on the 'agent' whose conduct may be directly linked to the resulting harm or wrong, legal models of responsibility are 'relational' in the sense that they are concerned not only with the position of individuals whose conduct attracts responsibility as moral agents but also with the impact of that conduct on others and society more generally (Cane 2002: 4–5). As Cane observes:

> Responsibility is not just a function of the quality of will manifested in conduct, nor the quality of that conduct. It is also concerned with the interest we all share in security of the person and property, and with the way resources and risks are distributed in society. Responsibility is a relational phenomenon. (Cane 2002: 109)

10.1.2.2 Structuring Legal Relations and Different 'Models' of Legal Responsibility

In allocating legal responsibility for harms and wrongs, legal systems are concerned with striking an appropriate balance of interests between moral agents (D) and moral patients (or 'victims' [V] as they are typically referred to in legal scholarship). In the extract below, Yeung identifies and sketches four broad models of responsibility that be identified in Anglo-American legal systems, notably (1) intention/culpability-based models, (2) risk/negligence-based models, (3) strict responsibility and (4) mandatory insurance schemes. She draws attention to two dimensions along which variation can be identified in each model, reflecting variation in the way in which the law allocates rights and responsibilities between affected parties that may be applied across a range of relational contexts: (1) the 'control' condition, which focuses on the extent to which the agent (D) had a free and voluntary choice concerning whether to undertake the act giving rise to the relevant harm or wrong and thus considered a causally responsible agent and (2) the 'epistemic condition,' concerned with the level and awareness of the agent's knowledge and awareness of the particular facts surrounding the harmful or wrongful consequences of D's conduct.

Yeung, K. (2019). 'A Study of the Implications of Advanced Digital Technologies (including AI Systems) on the Concept of Responsibility within a Human Rights Framework'. Council of Europe, MSI-AUT.

56–61

Intention/Culpability-based Models

Intention/culpability-based models, which constitute the core model of responsibility that underpins the criminal law, focus primarily on the voluntariness of the agent's conduct. They can be interpreted as requiring the satisfaction of two conditions: firstly, the 'control' condition, demonstrating that the agent was causally responsible for the legally proscribed conduct in so far as the agent had a free and voluntary choice concerning whether so to act, and secondly, the 'epistemic condition', requiring proof of 'fault', broadly understood as requiring that the agent had actual knowledge and awareness of the particular facts surrounding the harmful consequences of the agent's conduct, and the agent's action can be understood as based on these facts . . ..

Risk/Negligence-based models

In Anglo-American law, risk/negligence-based models of legal responsibility for tangible harm form the basis of a general duty to take reasonable care to prevent foreseeable risks of harm. These models of responsibility are conventionally applied to determine whether agents are subject to legal obligations of repair towards those who have suffered harm as a result of an agent's failure to discharge this general duty of care. A 'control condition' similar to that which applies to intention/culpability-based models of responsibility also applies to risk/negligence-based models (with some modification), insofar as it must be shown that the agent caused the relevant damage or injury. However, the epistemic condition applicable to risk/negligence-based models is considerably less demanding than those applicable to intention/culpability-based models . . ..

Accordingly, whether or not responsibility based on a risk/negligence model can be ascribed to the human developers of computational agents and systems in circumstances where those systems generate decisions or behaviours that cause harm will depend upon whether that harm was a *reasonably foreseeable consequence* of the computational systems' actions and decisions . . ..

Reasonable foreseeability also plays a role in determining *how* a person is expected to act. The duty of care is discharged if a person acts as an ordinary person exercising reasonable care to avoid foreseeable risks. Hence, reasonable foreseeability operates as the touchstone for determining the relevant 'reference class' for evaluating whether risk-taking activities (such as driving) that may sound in tangible harm to others gives rise to a legal duty of care . . ..

At the same time, identifying whether particular events associated with the operation of a particular technological object is 'reasonably foreseeable' will invariably be a product of our experience and exposure to them. In the emerging phases during which a new technology is being rolled out, expectations of their behaviours (and consequences) will be relatively unsettled and unknown. However, as time passes and we become more accustomed to their patterns of behaviours and action, those behaviours and actions may become more familiar to developers and therefore more likely to be regarded as reasonably foreseeable. Therefore, developers of those technologies should be held responsible for negligently failing to take steps that would have averted the resulting harm and wrongdoing . . ..

Strict Responsibility

The model of legal responsibility applicable to rights violations (including violations of human rights and fundamental freedoms) is that of strict responsibility, or 'strict legal liability' as it is called in Anglo-American legal parlance. On this model, responsibility attaches to the agent *without* proof of fault, so that legal responsibility for rights violations attaches to those who cause them *regardless* of whether the responsible agent engaged in conduct that breached a legally specified standard of conduct, and regardless of whether the conduct was intended or accompanied by any particular mental state. Of the four varieties of strict liability identified by Cane, three are of direct relevance to this study: right-based, outcome-based and activity-based strict liability.

(a) *right-based* strict liability: arises when legal rights are violated such that any violation of the sphere of protection bounded by the right triggers liability. The classic example is trespass to land: by interfering with the land-owners' right to exclusive dominion over the land, all intrusions without the consent of the land-owner constitute unlawful interference even if it the intruder was in no sense blameworthy . . . violations of human rights fall into this category of cases.

(b) *outcome based* strict liability: this form of liability rests on the causation of adverse outcomes (i.e. extrinsic consequences) regardless of fault. Contemporary European product liability laws are based on this model which imposes strict liability on manufacturers for defective products that cause harm to natural persons or property. In relation to advanced digital technologies, questions arise concerning what constitutes a relevant 'defect' .... A similar approach is often applied where the risk of damage is linked to the unpredictability of behaviour of specific risk groups, such as animals. In these cases, liability is attributed to the persons that are considered responsible for supervising the animal, as they are typically regarded as best placed to adopt measures to prevent or reduce the risk of harm.

(c) *activity-based* strict liability arises in connection with a specified activity, such as various 'possession' offences, such as laws which prohibit the possession of guns, knives, illicit substances and so forth. In Anglo-American law, vicarious liability is an important form of activity-based strict liability, where the relevant activity is defined primarily in terms of a relationship with another person, for whose breach of the law the first person is held strictly liable by virtue of that relationship. Vicarious liability applies to the employment relationship, such that an employer will be strictly liable for the unlawful conduct of an employee carried out in the course of his or her duty. Some jurisdictions may adopt a strict liability approach towards those who carry out dangerous activities (e.g. the operator of a nuclear power plant or of an aircraft) or are ultimately responsible for the dangerous activity (e.g. the owner of a vehicle). In such cases, the underlying rationale is that this person has created a risk, and at the same time also derives an economic benefit from this activity.

These various forms of strict liability distribute the risks associated with potentially harmful activity between agents and victims in ways that accord considerable weight to the interests of victims in security of the person and property ....

Mandatory Insurance

Rather than focus on identifying allocating responsibility to potential candidates who can be understood as contributing to for various the harms and wrongs that might arise from the operation of advanced digital technologies, a society might decide instead to prioritise the need to ensure that all those who are harmed by the operation of these technologies should be financially compensated. This may be achieved by instituting some kind of mandatory insurance scheme (which could be established on a 'no-fault' basis), establishing an insurance fund to which all those harmed by the operation of these technologies could have recourse.

Variation in legal models of responsibility described in the preceding extract highlights how each model strikes a different balance between our interest, as agents, in freedom of action and our interest, as victims, in rights and interests in security of person and property. What is missing from the above descriptions of each model, however, is any discussion of (1) the allocation of rights of enforcement, whether to a public enforcement official, a private party or a combination of both and/or (2) the institutional fora and procedural mechanisms in and through which enforcement action may be initiated and maintained.

10.2 Enforcement Rights and Group Actions

Private enforcement actions enable those who have suffered some kind of harm or wrong as a result of regulatory violations to seek some kind of remedy, typically seeking compensation or restitution, for the resulting loss. Although the threat of private damages action may help deter regulatees from violating regulatory rules, collective action problems can often arise with the result that private enforcement action is unlikely. In particular, where conduct giving rise to a regulatory violation affects many people adversely, even if each suffers significant harm, no individual person may be sufficiently motivated to proceed on the basis of recoverable compensation damages, particularly given the costs and risks of litigation and the prospect of free-riding on the successful action of another litigant. In these circumstances, the possibility of 'group claims' (known as 'class actions' in US legal terminology) may have an important enforcement role (see Box 10.1).

10.3 The Role of Judicial Adjudication

Despite institutional variety in the contemporary legal frameworks within which regulatory regimes are established, those against whom a legal penalty, sanction or award of damages has been imposed may appeal to the courts challenging the imposition and/or severity of the penalty or award. The courts are the ultimate arbiters of the law and may be called upon to resolve legal disputes arising from alleged regulatory violations whether instituted by private parties or public enforcement officials. As we have already noted, regulatory disputes surrounding the application of legal standards are often resolved informally through negotiation with public enforcement authorities. Yet the ability of parties to seek a final, authoritative determination from the courts plays a vital role in upholding the rule of law and, ultimately, the legitimacy of the legal and political order. The role of courts and the finality, impartiality and binding nature of judicial determinations in exercising their adjudicative functions distinguishes their role, position and authority from that of the other two branches of government, the executive and the legislature. The distinctiveness and importance of the judicial role is symbolically embodied in the iconography of Justitia, the Roman Goddess of Justice, blindfolded and holding upright a sword in her right hand and a set of scales in her left. This iconography represents a number of important features of the judicial function, including the importance of finality and legal certainty, explained in the extract below:

Box 10.1 Collective Redress in the EU

In the United States, 'class actions', in which a lawsuit that is brought by one or more people on behalf of a group of others who are in a similar situation, have been recognised since *West v Randall* (1820). In that case, Justice Story stated that, 'It is a general rule in equity, that all persons materially interested, either as plaintiffs or defendants in the subject matter of the bill ought to make parties to the suit, however numerous they may be.' However, the availability of collective redress actions throughout EU Member States varies widely, and there is currently no EU-wide scheme. In situations of mass harm, often the only realistic option for consumers is to try and obtain compensation by going to court together and have an expert fight the case on their behalf ('collective redress'). BEUC has been actively advocating for legislative proposals to ensure collective redress is available to as many policy fields as possible, for both material and moral damage, in the areas of financial services, dangerous products and the infringement of consumer rights and contracts in general.

In 2018, the European Commission proposed minimum standards for a collective redress scheme that would have to exist in all EU Member States, but this proposal has not yet been agreed by the European Parliament and Member States. BEUC cites numerous cases in which European consumers have been unable to recover effective compensation because it was impossible to file a collective redress action, either because the existing system was too rigid, the requirements too demanding for consumers to satisfy, or there was no collective redress mechanism in place.

Examples

The Volkswagen emissions scandal (2015): Millions of vehicles were affected by this scandal (Box 8.1) In the United States, Volkswagen quickly settled a class action brought on behalf of affected vehicle owners resulting in substantial damages payments to consumers. In the EU, only four consumer associations (in Belgium, Italy, Spain and Portugal) have taken Volkswagen to court in their respective countries using their national collective redress procedures. The German and Austrian consumer organisations have launched major litigation representing many consumers, but these are not based on collective redress procedures. Together, these cases represent approximately 600,000 European consumers, which is far less than the 8 million affected cars in Europe (See Chapter 8).

Unsafe hip implants (2010): Metal hip implants marketed by various companies were used in several EU countries, including the United Kingdom, Belgium and France from 2003 to 2010. The implants were approved in Europe under the EU Medical Device Directive based on laboratory tests and simulations, but they had not been tested on humans via clinical trials. Many were found to be defective, due to the release of metal particles into the patients' blood and bones, which can cause hypersensitivity leading to pain, effusion and alteration of the surrounding bone. Many patients suffered as a result (approximately 10,000 implants were fitted in the UK, 1,500 in Belgium and 380 in France) but in none of these countries were efficient collective redress procedures available. In July 2010, pressure from the French health authorities forced the producer to withdraw the model from the French market. In Belgium, 1,500 implants were recalled, meaning more frequent checks for affected patients even if the surgeon decided to replace the implant.

Sources

BEUC (2019). 'Why We Need Collective Redress at EU Level', www.beuc.eu.

Osborne, H., Devlin, H. (2018). 'Uncovering the Implants Scandal: The Lack of Transparency Is Shocking'. *The Guardian*, 25 December.

Osborne, H. (2018). 'Firm Pays out to NHS over Defective Hip Replacements'. *The Guardian*, 16 November.

Loughlin, M. (2000). *Sword and the Scales.* Hart.

57

The symbolism of the scales also expresses 'a deep-rooted tendency to see no shades between black and white, to admit no degrees of right and wrong, to allow no distribution of loss and gain among several litigants, to send a party away either victorious or defeated'. When they come to the courts in their quest for justice, litigants certainly expect an answer. This confidence reflects the conviction that a right answer is always to be found to every dispute which arises in law. However novel, complex or ambiguous the issue of contention, the one clear duty of a judge is to provide an answer which will vindicate the apparent rights of one or other of the parties to the litigation . . .. Above all, then, the symbol of the scales is a symbol of order and certainty: the first principles of legal justice is that an answer will be given to all disputes which arise between citizens.

The symbolism reflected in the depiction of Justicia highlights the vital importance of the impartiality and independence in judicial adjudication in the resolution of disputes according to law. At the same time, judges must also be accountable. As Garoupa and Ginsburg explain below, there are various ways of guaranteeing the independence of judges and balancing this independence with judges' accountability. The extract discusses the role of judicial councils that guarantee the accountability of judges, while remaining insulated from politics.

Garoupa, N., and Ginsburg, T. (2009). 'Guarding the Guardians: Judicial Councils and Judicial Independence'. *American Journal of Comparative Law,* 57(1), 103–134

The selection of judges is a central factor in most theories of judicial independence. Judges who are dependent in some way upon the person who appoints them cannot be relied upon to deliver neutral, legitimate, high-quality decisions. While there is near-universal consensus on this as a matter of theory, legal systems have devised a wide range of selection mechanisms in practice, often trying to balance independence with accountability through institutional design. The diversity of systems of judicial selection suggests that there is no consensus on the best manner to guarantee independence. At the same time, there is a trend toward insulating judicial selection from partisan politics. In the United States, this is reflected in the growing scholarly consensus in favor of 'merit selection'. In other countries, it is reflected in the adoption of judicial councils, an international 'best practice' designed to help ensure judicial independence and external accountability . . ..

The Tension between Independence and Accountability

A long and established literature argues that the ideal of judicial independence is a crucial quality of legal systems, and indeed inherent in the notion of judging. Naturally, the ideal is not always met, for it remains the case that in every legal system judges are appointed and employed by the state. It would be unusual indeed if judges did not have a role in implementing social policy, broadly conceived. In democracies, this implies the need for some accountability of judges. While judicial independence is widely studied, accountability has been the subject of much less inquiry. It requires that the judiciary as a whole maintain some level of responsiveness to society, as well as a high level of professionalism and quality on the part of its members . . ..

Judicial Councils in Civil Law and Common Law Systems

Judicial councils are bodies that are designed to insulate the functions of appointment, promotion, and discipline of judges from the partisan political process while ensuring some level of accountability. Judicial councils lie somewhere in between the polar extremes of letting judges manage their own affairs and the alternative of complete political control of appointments, promotion, and discipline. The first model of judicial self-management arguably errs too far on the side of independence, while pure political control may make judges too accountable in the sense that they will consider the preferences of their political principals in the course of deciding specific cases. There are a wide variety of models of councils, in which the composition and competences reflect the concern about the judiciary in a specific context, balancing between demands for accountability and independence.

France established the first High Council of the Judiciary (Conseil Superieur de la Magistrature) in 1946. It was in charge of managing judicial personnel but only a minority of members were themselves magistrates elected directly by fellow judges. Italy's judicial council (Consiglio Superiore della Magistratura), created in 1958, was the first to fully insulate the entire judiciary from political control, a model that has been followed in other judicial reforms . . ..

The French and Italian cases were motivated by a concern about excessive politicization and consequently granted extensive independence to the judicial power. After some time, however, courts became more extensively involved in politics and accountability issues came to the fore . . ..

The motivating concern for adoption of councils in the French-Italian tradition was ensuring independence of the judiciary after periods of undemocratic rule. To entrench judicial independence, most of these countries enshrined the judicial council in their constitution. Independence, however, is a complex and multifaceted phenomenon. Even though judges may be independent from political control, they may become dependent on other forces, such as senior judges in a judicial hierarchy-with just as much potential to distort individual decision-making as more conventional political influence. In civil law countries, in particular, a large proportion of judges are recruited directly from law school using some form of public examination, with no or limited requirements of previous professional experience. This model emphasizes socialization within the ranks of the judicial profession and creates the potential for institutional pressures on judges to decide individual cases in ways that are at odds with their own conscience or reading of the law.

10.4 Judicial Review of Administrative Action

Within regulatory regimes involving a public regulator entrusted with the task of administering regulatory rules, concerns may arise that the public regulator has failed to exercise its decision-making power in accordance with law. For example, an applicant denied a license to carry out the regulatory activity may seek to challenge that decision. In many countries, administrative law requires that before initiating the judicial process to challenge the decision, applicants must first file a statement of objections and request a new decision. If the decision is once again negative, the applicant may then challenge it before a court. An analysis of judicial review is beyond the scope of this volume, and the law on judicial review varies depending on the jurisdiction. Nonetheless, the possibility of judicial review operates as an important institutional safeguard that constrains the exercise of discretionary power by public regulators, and we therefore offer a few brief comments. In particular, there are several important matters that individuals should generally consider when seeking judicial review of a regulatory decision: first, determining the relevant jurisdiction (e.g., civil or administrative court, the location of the court); second, assessing whether the applicant has the right to challenge the decision ('standing'); third, understanding the 'grounds' (or legal bases) for judicial review (e.g., error of law if the applicant disagrees with the applied legal framework, error of fact if the regulator based the decision on incorrect facts); fourth, an awareness of the extent of the court's margin of appreciation (e.g., if the regulator had significant discretion in deciding, courts may typically not substitute their judgement for that of the regulator and will often defer to its expertise).

An important feature of judicial review warranting additional discussion is standing (or 'locus standing', which refers to the entitlement of an applicant to seek judicial review challenging the exercise of discretion by a public authority). While a regulatory decision may be unfavourable to many individuals, only those with standing to seek judicial review may do so. This requires the applicant to demonstrate that they have a sufficient 'interest' recognised by public law to initiate a complaint. An applicant denied a licence by a public authority will clearly meet these criteria, but the extent to which standing will be accorded to those who lack a direct personal interest varies between jurisdictions and is a continuing source of legal controversy. As the extract explains below, in civil law countries such as France, applicants may successfully demonstrate standing if they possess a personal, objective and direct interest, if their rights or interests are affected or if their standing is specified by law or regulations. However, the recent surge in climate litigation provokes questions concerning who has standing to challenge regulatory decisions that adversely impact the environment. While standing criteria vary significantly worldwide, the excerpt below provides insight into how standing in environmental protection may be regulated. It is worth noting that both the French and German administrative law systems have considerable influence globally.

Chevalier, E. (2020). 'Standing before French Administrative Courts and Environmental Protection: Not Specific Enough for an Effective Access to Justice?' *Persona e Amministrazione*, 1, 317–330, https://doi.org/10.14276/2610-9050.2207.

318–323

[F]rom a legal point of view, the intervention of the judge in judicial review (*recours en excès de pouvoir*) depends in particular on the conditions of admissibility of the action, and especially on the definition of standing requirements, and particularly the interest to act (intérêt à agir). These are determined by each legal system, following different national legal traditions . . ..

According to long-established case law, the applicant must show that he has a personal, direct and certain interest in the annulment of the challenged act for its action to be admissible. This requirement is deemed to be satisfied if the applicant demonstrates that there is a link between the contested measure and his personal situation. The interest in bringing action is therefore subject to a broad interpretation. Nevertheless, when applied to environmental litigation, these requirements look particularly restrictive. Indeed, by its very nature, the promotion of the environmental interest is first and foremost that of a collective interest. When initiating judicial review, the individuals do not aim at defending an individual interest, but the protection of a species or other environmental interests, which may be impacted by an administrative act. Obviously, the defence of the environmental interest may be satisfied while defending an individual interest, and then the action would be admissible, the individual situation (and not only the environment or a component of it) is affected by the challenged act, because of geographical proximity or by a neighborhood link. In practice, it is true that such interpretation of individual interest does not prevent the administrative judge from ruling on cases having environmental impact. The success of the movement 'Not In My Back Yard' (or NIMBY) feeds the environmental litigation thanks to the requests brought by individuals . . . paradoxically, it is indeed the existing individual interest that makes it admissible. But the mere defense of environmental interests is never sufficient to declare an individual action admissible . . ..

The conditions of admissibility, as assessed, therefore make it difficult, or even reduce to a bare minimum, the possibilities for an individual to challenge an administrative act impacting the environment or the state of nature. These inadequacies have been partially remedied by the legislative recognition of a presumption of interest to act on behalf of certain associations, which cannot, however, compensate for this restrictive conception as far as individual actions are concerned . . ..

NGOs

Generally speaking, access to justice for associations to challenge the illegality of an administrative act is problematic, either because of a lack of individual interest or a lack of violation of a subjective right. It is precisely one of the achievements of Aarhus convention to impose the contracting states to provide for adequate regime to ensure an effective access to NGOS. The French system differs from the majority of European States since it has for long provided for a specific regime of access to justice for some environmental NGOs. However, this system of presumption does not completely remedy the shortcomings resulting from the limited access to the courts for individuals . . ..

Consequently, legal systems have developed mechanisms of representation. NGOs have emerged as legal representatives or legitimate agents of Nature's interests. In the French system, in a rather pioneer manner, these profits indeed from more relaxed standing rules than individuals and they do not need to pass the 'interest to act' threshold discussed above. Indeed, according to the Law of 10 July 1976, approved NGOs profit from a presumption of standing when bringing a claim for judicial review, which is interpreted widely. The NGOs concerned are those which are approved by a ministerial or [local] decision depending on the geographical scope of its competence.

While an in-depth examination of judicial review is beyond the scope of this volume, the following extract provides a concise overview, including the importance of determining the grounds for judicial review and considering a number of principles that guide it.

Cane, P. (2002). *Responsibility in Law and Morality.* Hart.

268–270.

Judicial Review

The archetypal proceeding for the enforcement of civil law responsibility is the claim for damages by one citizen against another. The archetypal proceeding for the enforcement of public law responsibility is the application by a citizen for judicial review of a decision by a public functionary. The judicial function involved in judicial review is the supervisory function. Oliver describes this function in terms of:

> identifying the limits of the powers of bodies, especially those which interfere with the liberties of individuals or with broad public interests, and laying down the rules for the exercise of decision-making powers . . ..

The grounds of public law responsibility are based on a set of principles of good decision-making. They can be divided roughly into two categories, procedural and substantive. The substantive grounds are traditionally conceptualised in terms of a trichotomous distinction between issues of law, issues of fact, and issues of policy. A decision of a public functionary may attract public law sanctions if it is based on an error of law, an error of fact, or a policy mistake. Policy mistakes are understood in terms of striking a wrong balance between

> competing interests in the subject matter of the decision-making challenged. The procedural category must be understood broadly. The so-called rules of natural justice are designed to avoid conflicts of interest and to secure participation of affected parties in a decision-making process. There are various grounds of judicial review that regulate the basis on which decisions are made. Decision-makers must not 'fetter' their decision-making power by agreeing in advance to make a particular decision. On the other hand, a decision-maker must not act inconsistently by treating like cases differently. A functionary to whom a decision-making power has been allocated must not allow someone else to make the decision either actually or effectively. Decisions must be justiciable in terms of the purposes for which the decision-making power exists, taking account of relevant considerations and ignoring irrelevant ones.
>
> The main function of rules and principles of responsibility under the public law paradigm is to set legal boundaries to the exercise of decision-making powers by public functionaries .... Principles of judicial review also play a part here – self-interested exercise of a public decision-making power would fall foul of the rule that irrelevant considerations must be ignored. But principles of judicial review are more centrally directed against the exercise of public decision-making powers in the interests of particular individuals or groups within society. Rules directed against the pursuit of 'improper purposes', the taking into account of 'irrelevant considerations' and the making of 'unreasonable' decisions, all play a part in securing that in formulating a conception of the public interest, public functionaries do not give undue weight to the interests of particular individuals or groups.

Although Cane notes that a public law remedy may be granted for 'policy mistakes' made by public functionaries, which he describes as mistakes that consist of 'striking a wrong balance between competing interests in the subject matter of the decision-making challenged', it is very rare (at least as a matter of English administrative law) for courts to intervene. In civil law jurisdictions, mistakes made by regulators may be acknowledged, for example, when facts have been wrongly assessed, but courts will often give regulators the opportunity to correct their decisions. Within contemporary constitutions, the exercise of policy judgements typically falls within the discretion of the executive in which accountability for such judgements lies and with ministers of the state who are politically accountable to Parliament. In the realm of administrative law, judges commonly exhibit 'deference' towards the substantive judgments rendered by public officials, reserving heightened scrutiny only in cases of egregious error. The level of 'intensity' applied in scrutinizing these judgments is typically low, particularly when regulatory decisions concern intricate scientific matters requiring technical expertise. However, when the decision under scrutiny pertains to a violation of human rights, this triggers 'strict scrutiny' entailing more rigorous judicial examination in order to safeguard the rights and freedoms of legal subjects against unlawful encroachment by the state.

10.5 'Alternative' and Non-judicial Avenues for Redress

Although, in principle, any person may institute litigation seeking redress from the courts in respect of a violation of their legal rights; in practice, the costs, time and emotional strain involved in litigation means that access to justice is severely limited in practice. Accordingly, only well-resourced individuals and large organisations are typically able to vindicate their rights in court or when the relevant jurisdiction allows for and facilitates group actions (see Section 10.2). Partly in recognition of this, various forms of 'alternative' dispute resolution mechanisms may be available to those seeking redress, including, for example, the role of the Ombud (see 'watchdogs' in Chapter 12) and a variety of other small claims tribunals that may be established, typically concerned with specific kinds of high volume complaints, for example, between landlords and tenants or consumer rights and social security benefits, which are intended to allow for swift, relatively inexpensive and informal means for resolving legal disputes. At the other end of the spectrum are incidents involving catastrophic failures and scandals (such as the US Deep Water Horizon explosion, the UK Grenfell Tower disaster, to name but a few), which may prompt a public inquiry to conduct an independent investigation into review and report on what happened and to make recommendations for reform to prevent future catastrophic failure (see Chapter 12).

Conclusion

This chapter has examined the role of private enforcement in helping secure compliance with regulatory rules and the role of courts in providing the primary legal avenues through which those harmed or wronged by a violation of regulatory rules may seek legal redress. This entailed a brief foray into concepts of legal responsibility, in which the role of criminal responsibility as a vehicle for condemnation and punishment for legal violations is quite different from that of the paradigm of civil legal responsibility, which is concerned primarily with obligations of repair by an actor who has caused harm to another that triggers a legal 'cause of action' upon which the affected person may mount a civil suit seeking some kind of redress. We have seen that although private litigation has the potential to play an important role in helping deter violations of the law, in practice civil litigants face many disincentives to sue, underlying the potential role for 'group' actions. In so doing, we have highlighted the role and function of courts as authoritative and final interpreters of the law, including the role of judicial review as a means for overseeing the legality of discretionary decisions made by public authorities, although 'alternative' and non-judicial channels for redress may play an important role in specific regulatory domains. This and the previous chapters have highlighted variation in the design of the institutional and enforcement architectures in which regulation takes place. This variation, and its significance, is illuminated in the following extract, which draws on the US example of two federal agencies (FDA and SEC), bringing together many of the matters examined in this and Chapter 9.

Issacharoff, S. (2007). 'Regulating after the Fact'. *DePaul Law Review*, 56, 375–388.

378–383

The FDA is the federal agency that most closely resembles the prevailing model of permit-based market entry prevalent in much of Europe and – in less elegant fashion – the rest of the world . . .. The exceptional regulatory reach of the FDA is premised on the notion that market-based solutions, such as loss of reputation, are insufficient in the context of contaminants that carry the potential to do vast harm to the consuming population. The FDA minimizes the potential harm of new pharmaceuticals by requiring manufacturers of drugs to conduct specific tests before the FDA will license them for sale, and by exposing these manufacturers to strict liability. The FDA itself conducts extensive prerelease testing of drugs and monitors their health impact after they are authorized for sale. FDA regulations cover the waterfront of the pharmaceutical market, including preapproval testing, drug manufacturing, labelling, advertising, and post-approval monitoring for adverse drug reactions.

At the other end of the spectrum, we find the SEC, an agency that compels standard forms of disclosure and general corporate organization, but does little to regulate actual business transactions in the highly fluid and volatile securities market. Issuing an offering, or engaging in other forms of securities transactions, is completely unlike bringing a new drug onto the market. There are no laborious testing processes for securities, and there is no federal licensing required before they may issue. Rather, the only question is whether the SEC's reliance on ex post enforcement has justified the charge that it lacks 'meaningful, orderly, and fair regulatory processes'. The SEC takes advantage of its ability to regulate conduct ex post out of a concern that promulgating specific regulations may result in underinclusive standards that are 'susceptible of easy evasion'. Because of the technical issues and rapidly changing substantive context, there are significant administrative benefits to the SEC's approach, including the ability to enlist the private bar as a key participant in enforcing laws against securities fraud. Former SEC Commissioner Harvey Goldschmid emphasized this point: 'Private enforcement is a necessary supplement to the work that the [SEC] does. It is also a safety valve against the potential capture of the agency by industry.' The ex post regulatory model is premised on the idea that parties should be able to internalize the risk of liability-perhaps even for punitive damages-and regulate themselves accordingly.

The extensive literature on the deterrent function of ex post remedies need not be discussed here. The simple point is that ex post remedies require two forms of access: access to the relevant information to establish liability after the fact, and access to an effective enforcement tribunal. Whereas ex ante government regulation sets standards for regulated economic actors to meet, ex post regulation uses the threat of liability to force an internalization of potential damage payments and allows parties to calibrate their anticipatory remedial measures. The key is that both ex ante and ex post review are essential parts of the regulatory model-sometimes operating in tandem, sometimes as substitutes. As Professor Susan Rose-Ackerman explains, relative to after-the-fact enforcement methods, anticipatory statutory regulation utilizes government officials 'to decide individual cases instead of judges and juries; resolves some generic issues in rulemakings not linked to individual cases; uses nonjudicialized procedures to evaluate technocratic information; affects behavior ex ante without waiting for harm to occur, and minimizes the inconsistent and unequal coverage arising from individual adjudication'. Most countries use some mix of ex post and ex ante regulation to control undesirable market conduct. What is not found in developed countries is a complete absence of regulation-a system with neither ex ante entry barriers nor means of enforcing ex post accountability.

Private Enforcement in the ex post World

The SEC provides a perfect example of how enforcement is accomplished even in deregulated markets. Enforcement, if needed, will occur only after allegations of wrongdoing surface. Further, there is no assumption that the SEC itself will be the primary enforcement agent. Indeed, the most sophisticated critical assessments of securities laws turn not on the lack of public enforcement, but on the insufficiency of private enforcement to deter misconduct as a result of complicated incentive structures that make it easier to collect from the firm itself or its insurers than it is to collect from corporate malefactors.

Private enforcement is not a necessary feature of a system of ex post review. One could easily imagine a system of liberalized market entry that is followed by stringent public enforcement of norms of accountability. Under such a system, the SEC could be the exclusive enforcement agency and private rights of action could be eliminated. We reserve the enforcement of the criminal code to public agencies and there is no theoretical reason why the enforcement of civil law particularly in regulated walks of life-could not also be reserved to public agencies. But this would require public agencies to assume markedly different functions than they now have. It is almost inconceivable that the SEC, with its allocation of less than a billion dollars a year, would be able to perform its current functions and serve as an investigator and prosecutor of securities fraud . . ..

In the context of consumer claims, exclusive reliance on ex post governmental enforcement actions is undesirable. The same argument can be extended to broad swaths of our legal system, whether in the securities markets, consumer protection, or products liability. Across these domains, governmental enforcement actions are typically hampered by a lack of resources, a confined jurisdictional authority that may not correspond to the sweep of market-wide harms, a lack of access to local sources of information about perceived harms, the distance of governmental centers from where harms occur, and the political dependence or the risk of political capture of government regulators by politically savvy regulated entities. The basic argument is that decentralized enforcement combining public vigilance with the eagerness of entrepreneurially motivated private actors best protects the public interest.

Discussion Questions

1. What role can private litigation play in regulatory enforcement?
2. Within modern legal systems, what are the respective roles of criminal and civil responsibility?
3. How is legal responsibility different from moral responsibility? Give an example from everyday life where the ascription of moral blame might not be reflected in legal rights and duties?
4. Why might those who are harmed or wronged by a violation of regulatory rules decide not to pursue private action through the courts against the violator? Is the resulting lack of enforcement a matter of public concern? Why or why not?
5. What is the role of courts in regulatory enforcement? How significant is that role?
6. Why do you think legal certainty and finality in legal disputes is important, and what does your answer reveal about the differences between law and morality?
7. Why is judicial independence considered fundamental to the legitimacy of a legal system?
8. How does your country guarantee the independence of the judiciary? Identify the central laws and regulations on the appointment of judges, salaries and other relevant aspects.
9. Consider the following hypothetical problem. As of January next year, the national food and tax regulator has announced that cow's milk will be exempt from value added tax (VAT). However, other non-alcoholic beverages are still subject to this tax at a considerably high rate. A firm that produces oat milk seeks to challenge the regulator's decision. Drawing on the information provided in this chapter, what central elements would the oat milk producer have to consider when deciding to initiate judicial review against the decision?
10. Would it be possible or desirable to rely wholly on private enforcement to enforce regulatory rules? Why or why not?

11

Regulatory Legitimacy

Introduction

Many regulators aspire to control, monitor, co-ordinate and encourage behaviours that society regards as desirable while seeking to discourage and change behaviours that have a negative impact on collective welfare or on other community values or traditions (see Chapter 4). To do so successfully, a regulator must have the capacity to influence others. In earlier chapters, we observed that many regulatory instruments do not rely directly on coercion, whether backed by the authority of the state or otherwise. Why, then, do regulatees comply with regulatory demands? The answer depends at least partly on the legitimacy (or perceived acceptability) of the regulator's power over members of the regulated community.

Consider, for example, parents' attempts to influence and control their children's behaviour. They may employ a wide range of tools: from threats of disciplinary sanctions for violating family rules, to counselling, cajoling and the offering of treats and rewards for 'good' behaviour. For children who have not yet reached adulthood, parental displays of authority are typically regarded as legitimate, grounded in widespread acceptance of the legitimacy of the hierarchical nature of the parent-child relationship. This authority has a flip-side: parents are also considered responsible for many of their children's actions and can be held accountable for their consequences (see Chapter 12's discussion of accountability). In other words, to evaluate whether it is legitimate for one party (e.g., a parent, school, basketball coach) to wield and exercise authority over another (e.g., a child, students), we must consider the *kinds of reasons* that provide the foundation for judgements about the legitimacy of the nature and scope of the relationship through which influence is exerted. When our concern is with regulation, we are typically concerned with organisations and institutions. Contemporary organisations have relationships with various 'stakeholders' in whose eyes the organisation may seek to establish and maintain its legitimacy.

Our primary concern in this chapter is with 'regulatory legitimacy', a term employed in the regulatory governance literature and adjacent fields of social inquiry. To understand what regulatory legitimacy entails, however, we begin in Section 11.1 with the idea of legitimacy more generally. The concept of legitimacy has been extensively studied by scholars from various academic disciplines, including political theory, legal theory, political science, sociology and management studies. To simplify this examination, we limit our consideration to a brief, introductory account of political philosophy and sociological perspectives on the legitimacy of regulatory governance regimes. That said, our inquiry extends beyond the traditional concerns of political philosophy insofar as regulatory legitimacy requires consideration of regulatory institutions that operate beyond the borders of the state, including private and transnational regulatory regimes.

Section 11.1 also examines the wide variety of reasons (or 'legitimacy claims') why those subject to regulatory regimes regard those regimes as legitimate. Some reasons are objective, connected to the normative or theoretical foundations of political consent between the ruler and the ruled (for example, by political representation or the will of the people), while other reasons are subjective, concerned with an individuals' *beliefs* about the regulatory regime (including, for example, a belief in the underlying expertise that informs the regulator's decisions, the regulators' independence and impartiality in decision-making and so forth). Some of these claims carry more weight than others, depending on the relevant and affected community, and some claims may come into conflict. Section 11.2 explores some of the most important debates surrounding regulatory legitimacy, including those associated with regulatory expertise, democratic legitimacy and the role of the rule of law. Contemporary regulators everywhere – but particularly those operating at global level like the WTO or WHO – face challenging questions about their legitimacy and accountability (see Chapter 12). These debates highlight the relational, dynamic and sometimes volatile nature of regulatory legitimacy. In Section 11.3, we discuss how regulators must, like all organisations, establish, nurture and sustain their legitimacy over time and thus often engage intentionally in the quest for 'legitimation', referring to the 'process by which actors strive to create legitimacy', which is inherently social and political (Hurd 2023, see extract below).

11.1 The Concept of Legitimacy

We begin our examination with a brief exploration of the general idea of legitimacy and how it has been approached in academic scholarship. Our aim is to help newcomers to regulatory governance studies acquire a grasp of the general concept of legitimacy to enable them to navigate the scholarly terrain. As we have already indicated, discussions about legitimacy are fundamentally concerned with judgements about the appropriateness of relationships of authority. For example, if we observed a teacher insisting that school pupils should not wear beachwear on a very hot day, we may disagree with the teacher's stance, but we might nevertheless accept that it is legitimate for the teacher to issue such an instruction. Within academic scholarship, the concept of legitimacy has focused on more complex social relations, involving those in positions of power ('rulers') and those they purport to rule over ('the ruled'), evident in the following two short extracts:

> **Hurd, I.,** 'Legitimacy' (Princeton Encyclopedia extract), https://pesd.princeton.edu/node/516.
>
> Legitimacy is commonly defined in political science and sociology as the belief that a rule, institution, or leader has the right to govern. It is a judgment by an individual about the rightfulness of a hierarchy between rule or ruler and its subject and about the subordinate's obligations toward the rule or ruler. When shared by many individuals, legitimacy produces distinctive collective effects in society, including making collective social order more efficient, more consensual, and perhaps more just. Tom Tyler says that if authorities 'are not viewed as legitimate, social regulation is more difficult and costly' (Tyler 2001, 416). This accounts for the interest rulers show in legitimating their rule.
>
> **Hickey, T. (2022).** 'Legitimacy – Not Justice – and the Case for Judicial Review'. *Oxford Journal of Legal Studies*, 42(3), 893–917, https://doi.org/10.1093/ojls/gqac009
>
> 895
>
> Legitimacy has to do not so much with people's relations vis-à-vis one another (at least not with their social and economic relations in that respect), but rather with people's relations with their government or state. Legitimacy is concerned with the right of the state – its political-moral authority – to compel people to comply with laws some of which they will inevitably think unjust. Or it is concerned with what it might take for the state, and for its institutions and laws, to be seen by those subject to them as at least respect and support-worthy.

Both extracts demonstrate that legitimacy is centrally concerned with whether a ruler's purported authority over those they rule is worthy of respect or support. Within political theory, extensive attention has been focused on the legitimacy of a state to rule over its citizens, as Hickey emphasises. He points out that the legitimacy of the state includes its right to 'compel' people to comply with laws, even when they might personally regard those laws as unjust, rooted in the state's 'political-moral authority'. Unlike Hickey, Hurd does not limit his attention to the legitimacy of state power but offers a more general definition that would include relations between states over their citizens but applies more broadly to other regimes of rule and the 'rightfulness' of that rule. Nevertheless, both definitions emphasise that assertions of legitimacy refer to a *judgement* or *belief* about the acceptability of a specific set of relationships of authority that are held collectively by a 'people' over whom rule is asserted, rather than the beliefs or judgements of an individual person. Hurd also observes that questions about the legitimacy between rulers and those they rule has been an important preserve of political theorists, who generally take an objective approach, and that of sociologists, who adopt a more subjective approach:

> **Hurd, I.** 'Legitimacy' (Princeton Encyclopaedia extract), https://pesd.princeton.edu/node/516.
>
> **Historical Evolution**
>
> The subjective approach to legitimacy is grounded in the work of Max Weber, who emphasizes the macro-social consequences of citizens' belief in the legitimacy of their rulers. Weber famously identified three bases for legitimate rule in society (rational-legal, charismatic, and traditional) and argued that the presence of legitimate authority structures the society in such a way that even those who do not share the belief in its legitimacy face incentives to behave as if they did. This he called the 'validity' of the social system. A competing approach to the study of legitimacy begins from the premise that legitimacy depends on a correspondence between a rule and an external moral standard. It strives for an *'objective' model of legitimacy*, based on the strength of the standard itself . . .. The objective approach is inspired by *normative political theory* and seeks to identify normatively acceptable structures of rule; it is not concerned with what people actually *think* of the rule. It therefore has less to say about why people behave the way they do toward sources of authority and more about which sources of authority we *should* respect. The differences between the objective and subjective approaches is evident in their different answers to the question of whether the Nazi government was legitimate or not. To answer that, the subjective approach would need to know whether the citizens in question believed that the government was legitimate: did they believe that it had the right to rule? If so, then the social consequences of legitimacy (i.e. voluntary compliance, lower enforcement costs, etc.) would presumably be present. The objective approach would answer the question by referring to the failure of that government to satisfy the minimum moral requirements it establishes for a government, and so would decide that it was not legitimate regardless of how some people felt about it.

Hurd's extract contrasts basic differences in the focus of political theorists and sociologists in their approach to legitimacy. These differences arise because the interests, preoccupations and general orientation of these two academic disciplines are themselves quite different, although they share an interest in investigating a common social phenomenon. While political theorists have adopted an 'objective' approach to questions of political legitimacy, seeking to interrogate the normative foundations for evaluating the legitimacy of a ruling regime as a matter of moral theory, sociologists have taken a more subjective approach, focused on an empirical investigation of why people subjectively believe in the legitimacy of a ruler to rule over others, rather than whether such attempts to rule are normatively justified. In other words, sociologists are more concerned with the beliefs people hold, rather than whether a ruling regime should, as a matter of normative principle, be deemed as right or just. It is this difference between objective and subjective approaches to which we turn.

11.1.1 Objective Approaches to Legitimacy

Political theorists concerned with understanding the concept of political legitimacy seek to answer the question: why, as a matter of principle, do rulers have the authority to make decisions that affect others (and over others)? As Fabienne Peter explains in the following extract, as a normative construct, political legitimacy refers to some 'benchmark' for political acceptability or 'justification of political authority'. Questions of this kind have been central concerns of several well-known and influential political theorists (including Hobbes, Locke and Rawls) who have sought to identify the conditions under which a political body, particularly the state, is 'legitimate' and thus justified in exerting coercive authority over the citizens rendered subject to its rule. As Peter explains, theorists hold different opinions about a variety of matters pertaining to the political legitimacy of the state, including, for example, whether the exercise of authority by the state generates obligations of political obedience on the part of citizens, the relationship between political legitimacy and justice, and the significance of the consent of the governed in establishing political legitimacy.

Fabienne, P. (2017). 'Political Legitimacy'. In E. N. Zalta (ed.), *The Stanford Encyclopedia of Philosophy*, https://plato.stanford.edu/archives/sum2017/entries/legitimacy.

The normative concept of political legitimacy refers to some benchmark of acceptability or justification of political power or authority and – possibly – obligation. On one view, held by John Rawls (1993) and Ripstein (2004), for example, legitimacy refers, in the first instance, to the justification of coercive political power. Whether a political body such as a state is legitimate and whether citizens have political obligations towards it depends, on this view on whether the coercive political power that the state exercises is justified. On a widely held alternative view, legitimacy is linked to the justification of political authority. On this view, political bodies such as states may be effective, or *de facto*, authorities, without being legitimate. They claim the right to rule and to create obligations to be obeyed, and as long as these claims are met with sufficient acquiescence, they are authoritative. Legitimate authority, on this view, differs from merely effective or *de facto* authority in that it actually holds the right to rule and creates political obligations. On some views, even legitimate authority is not sufficient to create political obligations. The thought is that a political authority (such as a state) may be permitted to issue commands that citizens are not obligated to obey . . ..

There is sometimes a tendency in the literature to equate the normative concept of legitimacy with justice . . .. In [Rawls] view, while justice and legitimacy are related – they draw on the same set of political values – they have different domains and legitimacy makes weaker demands than justice. A state may be legitimate but unjust, but the converse is not possible. Pettit (2012: 130ff) distinguishes more sharply between the two concepts. According to Pettit, a state is just if it imposes a social order that promotes freedom as non-domination for all its citizens. It is legitimate if it imposes a social order in an appropriate way. A state that fails to impose a social order in an appropriate way, however just the social order may be, is illegitimate. Vice versa, a legitimate state may fail to impose a just social order . . ..

The Function of Political Legitimacy

The normative concept of political legitimacy is often seen as related to the justification of authority. The main function of political legitimacy, on this interpretation, is to explain the difference between merely effective or *de facto* authority and legitimate authority.

John Locke put forward such an interpretation of legitimacy. Locke's starting-point is a state of nature in which all individuals are equally free to act within the constraints of natural law and no individual is subject to the will of another. As Rawls (2007: 129) characterizes Locke's understanding of the state of nature, it is 'a state of equal right, all being kings'. Natural law, while manifest in the state of nature, is not sufficiently specific to rule a society and cannot enforce itself when violated, however. The solution to this problem is a social contract that transfers political authority to a civil state that can realize and secure the natural law. According to Locke, and contrary to his predecessor Thomas Hobbes, the social contract thus does not create authority. Political authority is embodied in individuals and pre-exists in the state of nature. The social contract transfers the authority they each enjoy in the state of nature to a particular political body.

While political authority thus pre-exists in the state of nature, legitimacy is a concept that is specific to the civil state. Because the criterion of legitimacy that Locke proposes is historical, however, what counts as legitimate authority remains connected to the state of nature. The legitimacy of political authority in the civil state depends, according to Locke, on whether the transfer of authority has happened in the right way. Whether the transfer has happened in the right way depends on individuals' consent: 'no one can be put out of this estate and subjected to the political power of another without his own consent' (Locke 1980: 52). Anyone who has given their express or tacit consent to the social contract is bound to obey a state's laws (Locke 1980: 63). Locke understands the consent criterion to apply not just to the original institutionalization of a political authority – what Rawls (2007: 124) calls 'originating consent'. It also applies to the ongoing evaluation of the performance of a political regime – Rawls (2007: 124) calls this 'joining consent'.

Although Locke emphasises consent, consent is not, however, sufficient for legitimate authority because an authority that suspends the natural law is necessarily illegitimate . . ..

When is effective or *de facto* authority legitimate? . . . In full, the normal justification thesis says: 'The normal way to establish that a person has authority over another involves showing that the alleged subject is likely to better comply with the reasons which apply to him (other than the alleged authoritative directive) if he accepts the directives of the alleged authority as authoritatively binding and tries to follow them, rather than by trying to follow the reasons which apply to him directly' (Raz 1988: 53) . . ..

Justifying Power and Creating Political Authority

In Hobbes' influential account, political authority is created by the social contract. In the state of nature, everyone's self-preservation is under threat and this makes it rational for all, Hobbes argues, to consent to a covenant that authorizes a sovereign who can guarantee their protection and to transfer their rights to this sovereign – an individual or a group of individuals. When there is no such sovereign, one may be created by a covenant – Hobbes calls this 'sovereignty by institution'. But political authority may also be established by the promise of all to obey a threatening power ('sovereignty by acquisition'; see *Leviathan*, chapter 17). Both manners of creating a sovereign are equally legitimate. And political authority will be legitimate as long as the sovereign ensures the protection of the citizens, as Hobbes believes that the natural right to self-preservation cannot be relinquished. Beyond that, however, there can be no further questions about the legitimacy of the sovereign. In particular, there is no distinction between effective authority and legitimate authority in Hobbes' thought. It might even be argued that Hobbes fails to distinguish between legitimate authority and the mere exercise of power.

Another way in which the relation between legitimacy and the creation of authority may be understood is that the attempt to rule without legitimacy is an attempt to exercise coercive power – not authority. Such a view can be found in Jean-Jacques Rousseau's work. Legitimacy, for Rousseau, justifies the state's exercise of coercive power and creates an obligation to obey. Rousseau contrasts a legitimate social order with a system of rules that is merely the expression of power. Coercive power is primarily a feature of the civil state. While there are some forms of coercive power even in the state of nature – for example the power of parents over their children – Rousseau assumes that harmful coercive power arises primarily in the civil state and that this creates the problem of legitimacy. In the first chapter of the first book of *On the Social Contract* he remarks that while '[m]an is born free', the civil state he observes makes everyone a slave. Rousseau's main question is under what conditions a civil state, which uses coercive power to back up its laws, can be thought of as freeing citizens from this serfdom. Such a state would be legitimate. As he puts it in the opening sentence of the *Social Contract*, 'I want to inquire whether there can be some legitimate and sure rule of administration in the civil order, taking men as they are and laws as they might be.'

11.1.2 Subjective Approaches to Legitimacy

The preceding discussion highlights the objective approach taken by political theorists in seeking to understand the conditions under which the civil state is politically legitimate. Their concern is to identify normative principles or benchmarks against which the legitimacy of a ruling regime can be objectively evaluated. In contrast, sociologists take a subjective approach to questions of legitimacy. The work of sociologist Max Weber is particularly important. Weber argued that the subjective beliefs of the public were of critical importance to understanding social structure and practice because faith in a particular social order produces social regularities that are more stable than those that result from the pursuit of self-interest or from habitual rule-following (Weber 1964: 124). According to Weber, 'the basis of every system of authority, and correspondingly of every kind of willingness to obey, is a *belief*, a belief by virtue of which persons exercising authority are lent prestige' (382). Weber distinguished three 'bases' upon which people may form their beliefs about the legitimacy of authority: because it has been in existence a long time (*tradition*), because they have faith in the *person* of the ruler (*charisma* – see the Box 11.1 for a short study on charisma and authority), or because they trust the *rationality* of the system of rule, whether that system be an organisation (bureaucratic rationality) or legal (legal rationality).

Box 11.1 Charisma as the Basis for Authority: The Case of Ukrainian President Zelensky

Although charismatic authority has not featured in discussions of regulatory legitimacy, it is important in contemporary real-world leadership and authority. Charismatic legitimacy refers loosely to the attractiveness and magnetism that certain personalities seem to be graced with. Even though charisma is personal, it is not inherent to the leader but a 'projection' of the followers onto the leader. Contrary to traditional or divine sources of legitimacy, individuals are not born with the gift of charisma. They build it through engagement strategies with their followers. For Weber, charisma does not coincide with moral virtue. Instead, charisma is unmistakably sociological. Rather than being an inherent property or trait, it arises contextually, 'from collective excitement produced by extraordinary events'.

This is evident in Ukrainian President Zelensky's charismatic leadership. When Russia invaded Ukraine, President Zelensky chose to remain in the besieged capital of Kyiv to lead the Ukrainian resistance. His decision to stay – and to broadcast plucky selfie videos with his team, walking through the heart of government grounds – was widely recognised as an extraordinary display of personal courage. When US President Joe Biden offered US assistance to ferry him out of the country, Zelensky responded like an action-hero film star: 'I need ammunition, not a ride.' Zelensky consolidated his charismatic leadership through his use of social media, speeches at events, engagement with other leaders and military clothing that aimed to convey the clear message that his country was 'at war'.

These events produced 'situational charisma': admiration and faith that cleaves to someone who 'offers, in a time of acute distress, leadership that is perceived as a source and means of salvation from distress'. 'This might be the last time you see me alive', Zelensky would tell reporters. The power of his words, and the obvious gravity of the situation, clearly affected those listening. He became a 'national hero', who could communicate in ways 'that enable . . . him to rise above himself and shine, especially in times of crisis'.

Source

Joosse, P., and Zelinsky, D. (2023). 'Charismatic Mimicry: Innovation and Imitation in the Case of Volodymyr Zelensky'. *Sociological Theory*, 41(3), 201–228, https://doi.org/10.1177/07352751231174436.

Although Weber identified charisma, tradition and rationality as the basis for subjective belief in the legitimacy of the ruling authority, other sociologists have subsequently developed various accounts to make sense of why people form such beliefs. In his discussion of pragmatic legitimacy, Suchman offers a tri-partite classification of legitimacy: pragmatic legitimacy, moral legitimacy and cognitive legitimacy. Brief explanations of each are extracted below.

Suchman, M. C. (1995). 'Managing Legitimacy: Strategic and Institutional Approaches'. *The Academy of Management Review*, 20(3), 571–610.

577–582

All types [of legitimacy] involve a generalized perception or assumption that organisational activities are desirable, proper, or appropriate within some socially constructed system of norms, values, beliefs, and definitions.

Pragmatic legitimacy rests on the self-interested calculations of an organization's most immediate audiences. Often, this immediacy involves direct exchanges between organization and audience; however, it also can involve broader political, economic, or social interdependencies, in which organizational action nonetheless visibly affects the audience's well-being .... Thus, at the simplest level, pragmatic legitimacy boils down to a sort of exchange legitimacy-support for an organizational policy based on that policy's expected value to a particular set of constituents ....

Moral legitimacy reflects a positive normative evaluation of the organization and its activities. Unlike pragmatic legitimacy, moral legitimacy is 'sociotropic' – it rests not on judgments about whether a given activity benefits the evaluator, but rather on judgments about whether the activity is 'the right thing to do'. These judgments, in turn, usually reflect beliefs about whether the activity effectively promotes societal welfare, as defined by the audience's socially constructed value system. Of course, this altruistic grounding does not necessarily render moral legitimacy entirely 'interest-free' ... further, audience perceptions of 'rightness' often unconsciously fuse the good of the evaluator with the good of society as a whole. Nonetheless, at its core, moral legitimacy reflects a prosocial logic that differs fundamentally from narrow self-interest ....

Cognitive Legitimacy ... may involve ... mere acceptance of the organization as necessary or inevitable based on some taken-for-granted cultural account. As Jepperson (1991: 147) noted, such taken-for-grantedness 'is distinct from evaluation: one may subject a pattern to positive, negative, or no evaluation, and in each case (differently) take it for granted'. This observation suggests a third general set of legitimacy dynamics based on cognition rather than on interest or evaluation. Two variants are particularly significant: legitimacy based on comprehensibility and legitimacy based on taken-for-grantedness. Theorists who focus on the role of comprehensibility in legitimation generally portray the social world as a chaotic cognitive environment, in which participants must struggle to arrange their experiences into coherent, understandable accounts. Legitimacy, according to this view, stems mainly from the availability of cultural models that furnish plausible explanations for the organization and its endeavors.

Although Suchman's tripartite classification of the character and source of legitimacy beliefs (i.e., pragmatic, moral and cognitive) differs from Weber's classification (i.e., rational, charismatic and traditional), there is considerable overlap between them (Box 11.2).

While organisational sociologists have focused on people's beliefs in the legitimacy of organisations, sociologists of law have a particular interest in understanding the beliefs people hold about the law underpinning their willingness to comply with the law. In the following extract, socio-legal scholar Marc Hertogh draws on empirical methods to investigate why individuals comply with Dutch traffic laws and whether their perceptions of the legitimacy of these laws vary in relation to personal characteristics, such as a person's level of education, income and gender. According to an earlier series of studies by Tom Tyler, people's beliefs in the law's legitimacy help explain why they comply with law, rather than a person's particular characteristics (e.g., gender,

Box 11.2 Industry Self-regulation: A Case of Pragmatic Legitimacy?

Industry-led schemes of self-regulation (ISR) (see Chapters 7 and 8) have been used to regulate a wide range of issues. Yet they are often criticised for failing to fix the problems that they claim to solve or to generate positive social benefits. For example, scandals concerning mislabelled horsemeat in food supply chains and the fatal collapse of the BSCI-certified Rana Plaza factory in Bangladesh have fed popular scepticism supporting critics' claims that these schemes are tantamount to firms 'marking their own homework'.

Using Suchman's (1995) framework, Frances Bowen argues that the pragmatic legitimacy of ISR based on self-interested calculations can be separated from moral legitimacy based on normative approval. Bowen identifies three core benefits to firms and their immediate stakeholders from these schemes: (1) to maintain strategic control, benefitting participants by enabling them to maintain the ability to respond to social issues on their own terms; (2) to acquire private benefits, by earning or maintaining a sound reputation on social issues, seeking to signal quality or behaviour through participation in industry scheme constituting a form of symbolic participation; (3) to benefit from network effects, which arise when the value generated through the next incremental adopter depends on the number of others who have already adopted. For example, evidence on ecolabels for green buildings, forestry and the apparel industry suggests that the higher the rate of adoption, the more an ISR scheme is recognised as a credible signal of environmental quality and the higher the benefit of adoption to the next incremental adopter.

These benefits can be understood in terms of pragmatic legitimacy based on self-interested calculations of an organisation's most immediate audiences, arising from an exchange-related form of legitimacy based on an organisation's capacity to persuade key stakeholders of its usefulness.

Source

Bowen, F. (2019). 'Marking Their Own Homework: The Pragmatic and Moral Legitimacy of Industry Self-Regulation'. *Journal of Business Ethics*, 156, 257–272. https://doi.org/10.1007/s10551-017-3635-y.

level of education, etc.) or a self-interested fear of sanctions. Hertogh' s results indicate, however, that more nuance is warranted. While those with lower educational backgrounds may be less inclined to regard traffic laws as legitimate; high-income individuals may be more prone to violating them, despite a belief in their legitimacy. Contextual analysis is thus important and caution is needed when attempting to generalise legitimacy perceptions: the type of law or regulation (in the case below, traffic regulation) also influences individuals' legitimacy beliefs in practice. It is important to highlight that, depending on the country and culture, there might be social norms and cultural reasons that justify why individuals comply with traffic rules (e.g., teaching children how to cross the street).

Hertogh, M. (2015). 'What Moves Joe Driver? How Perceptions of Legitimacy Shape Regulatory Compliance among Dutch Traffic Offenders'. *International Journal of Law, Crime and Justice*, 43(2), 214–234.

214–230

Late at night, at a clear intersection with no drivers to be seen on any side, Joe Driver stopped at a stop sign. Why? His stop, after all, delayed his return home, cost him gasoline and denied him some gratification in driving fast. According to Hyde (1983: 386), who first introduced this example, there are several different reasons for Joe's action. These include habit, fear of the police, fear of hitting other (hidden) cars or pedestrians, or simply Joe's idea that stopping at stop signs is in his own best interest. Yet Hyde wonders if there may also be any additional motives for Joe's decision. 'Those who believe that there are call these "legitimacy" ...: [o]ne may adhere to a social order; that is, one may conform to its rules and norms, because one accepts the order as a model or believes it binding.' (Hyde, 1983: 387).

In the Netherlands, the potential relationship between legitimacy and compliance with traffic rules is not only theoretically relevant but also of great practical relevance. In the past two years, most traffic fines went up sharply and in some cases nearly doubled. Dutch traffic fines are now among the highest in Europe. This has led to a wave of public protest .... Also, the police themselves have openly protested against the new traffic fines .... People question the true motives of the Dutch government. Do these high traffic fines really improve traffic safety, as the government claims, or are they just an easy way to make money? ... Are people's (critical) attitudes and opinions about the legitimacy of the Dutch government only words without any real consequences? Or do they also shape the behaviour of Joe and other drivers in the Netherlands? ...

There are basically two positions on legitimacy and compliance: a sceptical and an optimistic position. According to the first position, which is most clearly represented by Hyde, '[l]egitimacy ... is insufficient to result in obedience'(Hyde, 1983: 400). According to the supporters of this position, '*[a]ll* obedience ... stems from a combination of habit, fear of sanctions, and individual conviction that the requested compliance is in the actor's interest'

(Hyde, 1983: 400). Although many social theorists claim that legitimacy is an important motive for compliance, Hyde and others argue that this idea is not supported by empirical evidence . . .. The second position, which is most clearly represented by Tyler (1990), claims the exact opposite . . .. Based on this research, he argues that legitimacy shapes compliance not only in theory, but also in everyday practice.

Discussion: Legitimacy in Context

In general terms, our findings seem to support Tyler's (1990) position that normative motives (including legitimacy) offer a better explanation for regulatory compliance than instrumental motives (like deterrence). . . legitimacy plays an important role in shaping regulatory compliance with Dutch traffic rules. On closer inspection, however, our findings also suggest that there are some important differences between the two types of compliance that were included in this study . . ..

In a recent review of procedural justice studies Tyler (2013: 9) claims: 'Over the last twenty years, research has shown that people obey the law and cooperate with legal authorities primarily if and when they view those authorities as legitimate.' According to Tyler (2013: 22/3), what is 'especially striking' about these results, is that they are true 'irrespective of who the people are'. Contrary to Tyler's 'universalistic' approach, the British political scientist Beetham (1991) has suggested a more 'contextual' approach to legitimacy. According to Beetham (1991: 14): '[l]egitimacy for social scientists is always legitimacy-in-context, rather than absolutely, ideally or abstractly' . . . .

[W]e need to shift our focus of attention from . . . 'Why people obey the law' . . . to 'Why which people obey which law, using which procedure' . . ..

Which People?

When focussing on self-reported compliance, our study largely supports Tyler's general conclusion that personal characteristics are not particularly relevant for legitimacy and compliance. The results from our regression analysis suggest that only two variables related to the social or economic position of traffic offenders (a very low level of education and a non-Dutch background) have a significant (negative) effect on compliance. All other demographic variables (income, low or medium education, age) have no significant effect. Yet when we focus on the level of observed compliance among Dutch traffic offenders, our analysis shows a different result. This time, our regression analysis suggests that their gender, background, level of education, and income are all significant. Most notably, traffic offenders with a high income are more likely to receive more traffic tickets. This holds true for all three categories. Male offenders are also more likely to receive 3 or 4 and 7 or more tickets. Finally, offenders with a medium level of education and offenders with a Dutch background are less likely to receive 7 or more tickets . . ..

In other words, different people react differently to traffic tickets. To some extent (in particular with regard to their personal economic situation), this is

> also reflected in the comments by some of our respondents . . .: People like me with only a minimum income cannot afford a traffic ticket . . ..
>
> It is likely that these and other individual differences will also influence the way in which legitimacy shapes their level of compliance. For example, our findings indicate that the demographic background of Dutch traffic offenders influences their average legitimacy scores. Older respondents display a higher score . . . than younger respondents. Moreover, those offenders with a high level of education and a high income show more 'support for the police . . . than those with fewer qualifications and a low income . . ..
>
> **Which Law?**
>
> Our study of Dutch traffic offenders supports the argument that the perceived legitimacy of laws plays an important role in shaping regulatory compliance. In our study, the legitimacy of traffic laws has a significant and independent effect on self-reported compliance . . .. However, this effect was not found in relation to the observed level of compliance . . .. These findings remind us of the many contextual differences between different laws. In his study, Tyler (1990) focused on the effect of 'the law' in general as if its effects are essentially the same regardless of its substantive content. But what is true for one law may not be true for other laws. After all, 'different substantive areas of law are associated with different perceptions, understandings, and behaviors'.

Hertogh's study found that although people claim that they regard laws as legitimate, direct observation of their behaviour reveals that this may be at variance with their self-reported claims to compliance. In other words, what people claim to believe and do may not reflect what they *actually* do. His study also demonstrates that even when rules are legally binding, it does not necessarily mean that they will be routinely followed and obeyed. Whether they are or not will depend on the willingness of the relevant subjects to comply and this, in turn, is likely to depend upon their beliefs about the legitimacy of the ruling regime and the rules themselves.

11.2 Regulatory Legitimacy

The preceding discussion highlights differences in how scholars have sought to understand the legitimacy of a ruling authority, grounding that legitimacy in a variety of different factors or 'bases'. For example, for many political theorists, the notion of 'consent' between the ruler and rules is of central importance, whereas for sociologists, beliefs resting in tradition, rationality, charisma, self-interest, moral appropriateness and so forth have all been identified as significant. As academic scholarship concerning regulatory governance has developed, questions about the legitimacy of regulatory governance regimes have been among the most significant. We noted in passing that debates throughout Europe centred on independent regulatory agencies that were viewed as 'constitutional anomalies' given that they operated at arms' length from ministerial control, despite having considerable power to decide matters of considerable social and economic import in specific domains. These debates acquired even more salience as the EU became more established and acquired greater spheres of competence over economic and social activity, raising acute questions about its legitimacy to rule.

11.2.1 Expertise as the Basis for Regulatory Legitimacy

Both at the national and EU level, attempts to ground legitimacy have focused primarily around two sources: expert knowledge, on the one hand, and democratic participation, on the other, which co-exist in uneasy tension. Hence, our discussion begins with the influential work of Giandomenico Majone, who argued that economic expertise provides the bases for the legitimacy of 'non-majoritarian institutions' upon which the EU depends and that this reliance on expertise ultimately enhances the EU's democratic credentials by reducing opportunities for political intervention by rent-seeking interest groups. We then offer two short extracts that criticise specific elements of Majone's thesis, before turning to democracy as the basis of legitimacy, again beginning with scholarly attempts to wrestle with concerns about the EU's democratic deficit.

Majone, G. (1996). 'Regulatory Legitimacy'. In G. Majone (ed.), *Regulating Europe*. Routledge, 284–301

284–300.

Regulators wield enormous power, yet they are neither elected nor directly responsible to elected officials. How is their exercise of that power to be controlled? . . .

Independent regulatory bodies, like independent central banks, courts of law, administrative tribunals or the European Commission, belong to the genus 'non-majoritarian institutions', that is, public institutions which, by design, are not directly accountable either to voters or to elected officials. The growing importance of such institutions in all democratic countries shows that for many purposes reliance upon qualities such as expertise, professional discretion, policy consistency, fairness or independence of judgement is considered to be more important than reliance upon direct political accountability . . ..

[R]eliance upon qualities such as expertise, credibility, fairness or independence has always been considered more important than reliance upon direct political accountability – but only for some purposes. The substantive legitimacy of non-majoritarian institutions depends crucially on how precisely those purposes are defined. In essence, this is because accountability by results cannot be enforced when the objectives of an organization are either too vague or too broad. In this section, I argue that the . . . distinction between efficiency and redistribution . . . provides a sound conceptual basis for deciding whether the delegation of policy-making authority to an independent regulatory body has at least *prima facie* legitimacy . . ..

In a democracy, public decisions concerning the redistribution of income and wealth can be taken only by a majority vote since any issue over which there is unavoidable conflict is defeated under a unanimity rule. Redistribution is a zero-sum game since the gain of one group in society is the loss of another group. Efficiency issues, on the other hand, may be thought of as positive-sum games where everybody can gain, provided the right solution is discovered. Hence, such issues could be settled, in principle, by unanimity. The unanimity rule guarantees that the result of collective choice is efficient in the Pareto sense, since anybody adversely affected by the collective decision can veto it.

Naturally, unanimity is practically impossible in a large polity, but there are second-best alternatives. These include various non-majoritarian mechanisms such as consociational strategies, which encourage bargaining among elites of relatively well-organised cleavage segments, supermajorities and, of particular interest in the present context, delegation of problem-solving tasks to independent expert agencies . . .. The main task delegated to regulatory agencies is to correct market failures so as to increase aggregate welfare. It is important to note that the adoption of efficiency as the standard by which the regulators are to be evaluated implies, *inter alia*, that regulatory instruments should not be used for redistributive purposes. Regulatory policies, like all public policies, have redistributive consequences; but for the regulator such consequences should represent potential policy constraints rather than policy objectives. Only a commitment to efficiency, that is, to the maximization of aggregate welfare, and to accountability by results, can substantively legitimise the political independence of regulators. By the same token, decisions involving significant redistribution of resources from one social group to another cannot be legitimately taken by independent experts, but only by elected officials or by administrators directly responsible to elected officials . . ..

I have insisted on the possibility of separating efficiency and redistributive concerns because such a separation is crucial to the substantive legitimacy of regulatory policies. To repeat, the delegation of important policy-making powers to independent institutions is democratically justified only in the sphere of efficiency issues, where reliance on expertise and on a problem-solving style of decision-making is more important than reliance on direct political accountability . . ..

Because of their insulation from partisan politics, their expertise, and their commitment to a problem-solving style of decision-making, independent regulatory bodies and other specialised agencies would seem to be in a better position than government departments to satisfy the new demands of the electorate.

Unlike judges, however, regulators cannot rely on a firm foundation of legitimacy. Regulatory agencies tend to be treated as constitutional anomalies in countries where the delegation of state power to independent institutions is viewed as a serious threat to democracy, parliamentary sovereignty and the hallowed principle that public policy ought to be subject to control only by

> persons directly accountable to the electorate. These traditional principles are used to justify ministerial interference in agency decision-making, and the retention of important regulatory powers by government departments.
>
> Against these attempts to establish political control by means which contradict the very *raison d'etre* of the agencies we must restate [a] central theme: . . . the root problem of regulatory legitimacy in Europe today is not an excess of independence but, on the contrary, the constant threat of politically motivated interference. With greater independence would go greater accountability.
>
> The real question . . . is how agency independence and public accountability can be made complementary and mutually reinforcing rather than antithetical values. Our arguments, and the century-old experience of the American regulatory state, indicate that independence and accountability can be reconciled by a combination of control mechanisms rather than by oversight exercised from any fixed place in the political spectrum: clear and limited statutory objectives to provide unambiguous performance standards; reason-giving, transparency requirements to facilitate judicial review and public participation; due process provisions to ensure fairness among the inevitable winners and losers from regulatory decisions; and professionalism to withstand external interference and reduce the risk of an arbitrary use of agency discretion . . .. [W]hen such a system of multiple controls works properly, no one controls an agency, yet the agency is 'under control'. At that point the problem of regulatory legitimacy will have largely been solved.

The nub of Majone's argument is that regulatory institutions are legitimate when designed and understood as expert-based sites to address market failure, from which redistributive goals are deliberately excluded. His account springs from the premise that regulatory institutions are vulnerable to capture by narrow interest groups, which would result in regulatory decisions that redistribute resources in their favour (see Chapter 4). To avoid these unwanted outcomes, Majone appears to limit here the aims of regulation to the pursuit of economic efficiency, informed by the application of economic knowledge and expertise. The redistributive facets of regulatory policy should be decided by political institutions and majoritarian vote, while reliance on economic expertise to inform the decisions of independent regulatory agencies promotes 'non-majoritarian democracy'. Majone also links the solution for legitimacy deficits of independent regulatory to the debates on independence and accountability, which we delve into in Chapter 12.

Majone was writing during the early 1990s, at the zenith of neoliberalism's influence over contemporary public policy, when economic expertise and the pursuit of economic efficiency dominated policy-making. However, regulatory expertise comes in many varieties besides specialist economic knowledge. As we observed in Chapter 2, 'scientific' knowledge is highly prized within regulatory policy, conventionally enjoying widespread acceptance as impartial and rooted in fact, despite the value judgements and normative premises upon which any form of knowledge invariably rests. The authority of science and the epistemic rigour upon which modern scientific inquiry rests, described in the extract below, plays an important role in the regulation of the different industries such as nuclear energy. Given the catastrophic consequences of nuclear accidents, the validity of the underlying expert probabilistic assessments has great significance. Although scientific knowledge and claims can be an important source of legitimacy when they are credible, in the following extract, John Downer argues that when our concern is with nuclear accidents, calculative assessments offer the veneer of 'mechanical objectivity'. In reality, they may fundamentally lack credibility as they mask deep epistemic uncertainties that defy probabilistic calculation. Nuclear plants are complex systems operating within sophisticated socio-organisational dimensions and stochastic environments. Yet even in the face of previous nuclear accidents, the public narrative accompanying catastrophic disaster remains compelling, while allowing experts to disown their prior risk assessments.

Downer, J. (2014). 'Disowning Fukushima'. *Regulation & Governance*, 8, 287–309.

289–292

Nuclear Probabilism

Th[e] lack of preparedness for nuclear disasters is puzzling, given the recent turn to 'resilience' in policymaking. Western states now invest heavily in planning and preparing for disasters in many spheres – in respect to flooding and terrorism, for instance. So why the neglect in the nuclear sphere?

The answer lies in an institutionally deep-rooted confidence that contingency planning is unnecessary for nuclear disasters. For, as Beck puts it, 'our risk assessment bureaucracies have found ways to deny systemic hazards'. Policymakers treat the risks of nuclear meltdowns as if they are objectively calculable in way that the risks of terrorism are not, and entirely preventable in a way that floods are not. Thus, they defer to expert assurances that nuclear accidents, unlike floods and acts of terror, will not happen, and so need not be prepared for.

Various scholars have noted this institutional disavowal of nuclear disaster, noting that it emerged in the 1960s and 1970s as a response to specific political contingencies. For reasons relating to the Cold War and nuclear weapons, they argue, the West (particularly the US) was committed to nuclear power at the highest levels. Yet official nuclear regulatory studies were threatening the political viability of this commitment by projecting that the potential consequences of an accident could be severe. To circumvent this problem, scholars argue, regulatory agencies, such as the US NRC (then the Atomic Energy Commission), shifted the focus of their studies away from assessments of the *consequences* of a disaster (their primary focus until then) and toward assessments of *likelihood* . . . authorities sought to draw a distinction between 'credible' accidents, which were worthy of political concern, and 'hypothetical' accidents, which were not . . ..

At the heart of this transition was a turn to probabilistic reliability analysis: the creation and adoption of a series of calculative audit tools that offered regulators a means of 'objectively' establishing that nuclear accidents were too improbable to merit serious discussion . . ..

The NRC's 1975 WASH-1400 study of reactor safety is usually regarded as the key document . . . it arrived at its accident probabilities by using models that combined the failure data of generic reactor parts and subsystems to mathematically derive the failure probability of the wider system . . ..

Significant elements of the scientific and engineering community were deeply skeptical of this turn to probabilism . . . Brookhaven National Laboratory, which had overseen previous WASH studies . . . rejected the . . . probabilistic approach to reactor assessments, arguing that 'it would be "charlatanism" to make predictions about probability, and that only 'fringe members of the statistical community' would attempt to do this with the meager data available' . . ..

In 1978, the NRC sponsored an ad hoc Risk Assessment Review Group (RARG), which found in its report that the new safety studies were failing to 'sufficiently emphasize the uncertainties involved' in their findings, with the effect that probabilistic assessment was being 'misused as a vehicle to judge the acceptability of reactor risks' . . ..

For all the recognition of WASH-1400's imperfections, however, its probabilistic approach to risk became entrenched in the mechanics of nuclear regulation. Subsequent NRC safety analyses . . . all adhered to the same underlying premise that the probability of accidents was a fundamentally calculable property. (And all similarly determined that serious accidents were incredibly unlikely.) . . .

Today, probabilism lies at the heart of all nuclear regulatory oversight, with almost every decision being driven by Probabilistic Risk Assessment (PRA), and any qualifications and caveats happening 'offstage' (insofar as they happen at all) . . .. Similar assessments performed on earlier generation reactors like Fukushima have found the risks to be higher, but still nowhere of an order that would justify significant public concern . . ..

The Ideal of Objectivity

Reservations about probabilistic numbers have certainly not disappeared from engineering discourse, even if they have declined in their prominence and prevalence . . ..

This idea – that complex technological properties like risk and reliability should be wholly, objectively, and quantitatively knowable through formal rules and unbending algorithms – [is] the 'Ideal of Mechanical Objectivity' . . . an ideal that characterizes most modern technological discourse, but it is especially prominent in the context of nuclear power. It is easy to imagine why. As US authorities determined in the 1960s, the potential gravity of nuclear accidents begs for declarative assurances and calculative certainty.

On a day-to-day basis this Ideal of Mechanical Objectivity is reflected in the subtext of expert pronouncements about nuclear risk ('The math is the math'; 'It's not an opinion, it's a calculation') . . ..

> **Sociological Misgivings**
>
> Sociologists of knowledge have long recognized that this 'mechanical' notion of technology assessment is idealized, and have worked to highlight its shortcomings . . ..
>
> By far the most prominent approach . . . is Normal Accident Theory (NAT), with its simple but deceptively profound insight that accidents caused by very improbable confluences of events (which no risk calculation could ever anticipate) are 'probable' in systems where there are many opportunities for them to occur . . .. There is another approach to this argument, however, that draws on the sociology of knowledge and Science and Technology Studies (STS) literature. It points to the irreducible epistemological ambiguity of all technological knowledge, and argues that this ambiguity, although manageable in most spheres, becomes crippling in assessments of complex, safety-critical systems that deal with very small probabilities.
>
> These sociological arguments about why nuclear risk calculations must be insufficient are important, especially given that expert authorities are inherently unwilling to undermine their own credibility and self-interest in a sustained way. At the same time, however, they can obscure a more interesting sociological question about why Fukushima (and, indeed, the disaster-punctuated history of nuclear power more broadly) doesn't speak for itself.

11.2.2 Democracy

Some readers may have noticed that our examination of the legitimacy of a regime or rule in Section 11.1 made no reference to its underlying form of government, whether democratic or authoritarian. Yet the question of democratic legitimacy has been front and centre in discussions of regulatory legitimacy, primarily because these accounts have been written by those scholars concerned with regulatory regimes within democratic political orders. Another feature of these analyses is that they are not always explicit about whether their account of regulatory legitimacy is objective or subjective in orientation, and often implicitly blend objective and subjective accounts together. This is particularly true of debate about the legitimacy of the EU regulatory regimes. Although Majone's thesis was directed towards identifying the legitimacy of the European Commission, widely understood as the EU's executive or bureaucratic organ, his analysis can be situated within larger debates about the democratic legitimacy of the EU in light of sustained concerns about the EU's 'democratic deficit'. Scholars of European politics have sought to elaborate on conceptions of democracy that move beyond a simple account of majoritarian voting, as the extract from Schmidt illustrates, drawing on the important work of Fritz Scharpf employing the language of systems theory. The approaches to input, output and throughput legitimacy have been highly influential in regulatory studies.

Schmidt, V. A. (2013). 'Democracy and Legitimacy in the European Union Revisited: Input, Output and "Throughput"'. *Political Studies*, 61, 2–22.

2–5

Fritz Scharpf (1970) . . . divided democratic legitimation into output, judged in terms of the effectiveness of the EU's policy outcomes for the people, and input, judged in terms of the EU's responsiveness to citizen concerns as a result of participation by the people. Missing from this theorization of democratic legitimacy in the EU, this article will argue, is a third normative criterion for evaluation: throughput. Throughput legitimacy builds upon yet another term from systems theory, and is judged in terms of the efficacy, accountability and transparency of the EU's governance processes along with their inclusiveness and openness to consultation with the people . . ..

EU Legitimizing Mechanisms: Output, Input and Throughput

The concepts of output and input legitimacy as applied to the EU have their origins in the work of Scharpf who delineated 'output-oriented' legitimization as centering on the ability of EU institutions to govern effectively for the people and 'input-oriented' legitimization as involving political participation by the people. These normative definitions of legitimacy pick up on Abraham Lincoln's famous dictum about democracy requiring government by the people (political participation), of the people (citizen representation) and for the people (governing effectiveness) at the same time that the input-output terms themselves have been borrowed from systems theories . . .. For Scharpf (1999, pp. 7–21), input legitimacy refers to the participatory quality of the process leading to laws and rules as ensured by the 'majoritarian' institutions of electoral representation.

Output legitimacy is instead concerned with the problem-solving quality of the laws and rules, and has a range of institutional mechanisms to ensure it . . ..

Missing from this systemic theorization of legitimacy is a general theory about the practices that go on in the 'black box' of governance, and constitute what we will call, borrowing again from systems theory, 'throughput' legitimacy . . .. This conceptualization is intended to encompass not only the internal processes and practices of EU governance but also what Schmidt (2006) has previously termed, adding a preposition to Abraham Lincoln's phrase, interest intermediation with the people. 'Throughput' legitimacy concentrates on what goes on inside the 'black box' of EU governance, in the space between the political input and the policy output, which has typically been left blank by political systems theorists. It focuses on the quality of the governance processes of the EU as contributing to a different kind of normative legitimacy from both the performance-oriented legitimacy of output and the participation-oriented legitimacy of input. Throughput is process-oriented, and based on the interactions –institutional and constructive – of all actors engaged in EU governance . . ..

Institutional throughput also encompasses the accountability and transparency of the governance processes . . .. Finally, institutional throughput additionally concerns the quality and quantity of EU governance processes' inclusiveness and the openness of the EU's various institutional bodies to 'civil society'.

The importance of public participation, for example, in consultations has already been noted in Chapter 5. In other words, public consultation can be used not only to improve the quality of regulatory decisions but also to enhance their legitimacy, responding to concerns that, by failing to reflect the views of European citizens, EU regulation lacks legitimacy. Attempts to bolster the democratic credentials of regulatory regimes along the lines suggested by Schmidt offer useful vehicles for analysis and for regulatory design: namely, input legitimacy (referring to the regulator's responsiveness to citizen concerns as a result of participation by the people), output legitimacy (the effectiveness of the EU's regulation outcomes for the people) and throughput legitimacy (referring to the effectiveness, accountability and transparency of the EU's decision-making process, including inclusivity and consultation with those affected). Yet, as Majone's thesis attests, difficulties arise in seeking to reconcile the need for democratic participation with the understandable desire for expert-based regulatory decision-making. In other words, to what extent can the demands of 'technocracy' and democracy be adequately reconciled? In the following extract, Rahman provides an admirably clear account of the perennial tension between legitimacy rooted in expertise, on the one hand, and in democratic participation, on the other, which is inherent in the design and operation of regulatory institutions.

Rahman, K. S. (2011). 'Envisioning the Regulatory State: Technocracy, Democracy and Institutional Experimentation in the 2010 Financial Reform and Oil Spill Statutes'. *Harvard Journal on Legislation*, 18(48), 555–590.

570–585

In light of increasingly complex challenges, from financial crisis to oil drilling technology, the emphasis that technocratic regulation places on expertise seems vital for effective policymaking. Technocracy offers a promise of neutral, objective, rational, and ultimately dependable policy – the very ideal of good governance. Expanding agency authority, expertise, and knowledge offers a way to better respond to social problems while preventing agency capture or ineffectiveness. Yet, these contemporary efforts face the same recurring tensions that have persisted in debates over the regulatory state since its inception.

First, technocratic regulation ultimately cannot resolve either the underlying anxiety of agency legitimacy or the risk of agency capture. Deference to agency expertise seems unavoidable due to the increasing complexity of the social, economic, and technological phenomena subject to regulation, but agency deference is inevitably in tension with values of political accountability and democratic legitimacy. Expanding the autonomy and expertise of agencies may improve their policymaking abilities and the likelihood that policies will be grounded in independent analysis. This effort can to some degree bolster agency legitimacy by grounding agency policy in neutral, expert analysis, but it cannot fully resolve the underlying concerns of democratic accountability . . ..

The second key danger of the technocratic model of regulation: it obscures the reality of the normative disputes underlying seemingly technical policy questions. Research, data, and expertise certainly are valuable tools for improving policymaking. But, as even contemporary defenders of the regulatory state have noted, no regulatory policy can be stripped entirely of its normative commitments . . ..

Third, by limiting the range of political contestability – whether through insulation or technocratic discourse – the technocratic model of regulation undermines its own ability to be responsive to changing conditions and social needs, ironically increasing the risk of ossification, blockage, or misdirected policy. The technocratic model relies largely on its expert officials to generate initiative, adapt to changing conditions and needs, and make the 'right' decisions. To this end, technocratic regulation draws on the public as a source of information to facilitate the authority of the agency. This narrow form of public engagement not only mischaracterizes the normative value of participation in a democracy; it also risks undermining the very practice of participation itself, contributing to a wider demobilization of civic engagement . . ..

These weaknesses of the technocratic model create a fundamental challenge for the modern regulatory state.

Although the importance of democratic participation is undeniable, further difficulties arise when the impact of regulatory policies is felt by third parties yet they lack the opportunity to participate. This is visible at a high level, for example, in relation to Anu Bradford's 'Brussels Effect' whereby EU regulatory policies influence the content of regulatory policy beyond EU borders. Although regulatory influence and legal transplants are not uncommon since regulators regularly draw inspiration from each other, the Brussels Effect does more than inspire regulators outside the EU: it powerfully shapes regulation and extends European values to third parties. As Hadjiyianni points out in the following extract, this creates questions about the extraterritorial legitimacy of EU's power.

Hadjiyianni, I. (2021). 'The European Union as a Global Regulatory Power'. *Oxford Journal of Legal Studies*, 41(1), 243–264.

244–263

Anu Bradford's *The Brussels Effect* demonstrat[es] the impact that a regulatory power like the European Union (EU) can have on the everyday lives of individuals in faraway places. This regulatory influence is evident in relation to a broad range of policy issues, ranging from restrictions on chemicals and hazardous materials to data protection of online users . . ..

As Bradford puts it, 'The EU has become a global regulator not only because of the size of its internal market, but also because it has built an institutional architecture that has converted its market size into a tangible regulatory influence'. According to Bradford, the emergence of the Brussels effect rests on five cumulative elements: (i) a substantial market power; (ii) regulatory capacity, which rests on the ability to promulgate and enforce regulations; (iii) preference for strict standards, which relates to regulatory and consumer ideologies in favour of precautionary regulatory intervention; (iv) inelastic targets, limiting the possibilities for producers to relocate where regulation is less stringent; and finally (v) non-divisibility of standards, swaying the producer/operator towards standardisation rather than customisation of products/services. The latter condition depends on the incentives for non-EU producers to apply EU standards irrespective of the ultimate market because of economic, technical or legal non-divisibility of standards, ie when it is not possible for a company to adjust its practices or product to different markets . . ..

In the absence of state consent for their application to third countries, EU unilateral measures can create mistrust and may lack a legitimate basis for their extraterritorial effects. This is because they challenge conventional bases of legitimacy centred on territorially restrained state sovereignty and the principle of non-interference. In particular, the EU could be perceived as a 'normative empire', which engages in protectionism and exports its own standards. While both the EU and Bradford counter-argue that the Brussels effect does not involve coercive *intention* associated with imperialistic tendencies, this does not alleviate the coercive *effects* of EU unilateral regulation. Even if EU standards could in principle be avoided by not engaging in trade with the EU, given the EU's significant market power, foreign trading partners *de facto* often have to follow EU standards.

When sovereigns are conceived as 'trustees of humanity' consciously acting for the benefit of the international community through unilateral regulation, the legitimacy of their action depends on the extent to which they take into account the interests of third country stakeholders. Similarly, conceiving of EU unilateral measures intentionally designed with extraterritorial reach as a regulatory technique that seeks to strategically fill global regulatory gaps reveals important legitimacy gaps when the decision-making processes for their adoption and implementation do not sufficiently account for third country interests . . ..

Furthermore, EU unilateral regulation designed with extraterritorial reach extends standards to actors that usually do not have a voice in the decision-making process. This can lead to exercise of regulatory power without accountability, representation or participation of affected interests situated outside the EU as the regulating jurisdiction, thus giving rise to a series of 'external legitimacy gaps'. . .. A participation and representation gap is also created because these measures are adopted in the absence of state consent, by a regulating jurisdiction within which third country actors are not usually represented or have a voice in decision-making processes . . .. Overall, when comparing the legitimacy of the Brussels effect with exercises of global regulatory power by other major jurisdictions, the EU legal order is relatively open to third country interests, providing institutionalised opportunities to 'listen' to third country interests, through its impact assessment processes in particular . . ..

As Bradford recognises, harmonisation of standards can have significant benefits, but the question remains as to whether the EU should be making this choice for foreign firms and consumers . . ..

While the inability to resist the EU's global regulatory power might demonstrate the resilience of the Brussels effect, it also demonstrates the importance of the legitimacy concerns and the hegemonic tendencies associated with this

> phenomenon. If a superpower like the United States cannot resist the EU's global regulatory influence, the situation seems grimmer for weaker interests that are often affected by EU power. The exercise of unconstrained global regulatory power can exacerbate the legitimacy gaps when there are insufficient checks in place about *how* the EU exercises such regulatory power so as to guard against abuse and ensure sufficient consideration of third country interests. Looking into the future, the resilience and persistence of the EU's global regulatory power, which according to Bradford may only be challenged by internal EU challenges such as the rise of anti-EU sentiments, does not necessarily ensure its legitimacy.

In asserting that the EU must consider the interests of affected third countries to establish the legitimacy of its actions, Hadjiyianni seems to adopt a nuanced approach to legitimacy, blending both objective and subjective elements. Hadjiyianni's argument is rooted in the 'harm principle', which stipulates that the freedom of agents to engage in actions with adverse 'other-regarding' effects necessitates consent or some legitimising basis. However, the extract grounds this perspective in a normative principle, indicating an objective approach to legitimacy. Conversely, her reference to the potential 'mistrust' arising from unilateral EU action suggests a more subjective concern, addressing the perceived beliefs and attitudes of affected states. In essence, Hadjiyianni's approach implicitly reflects a fusion of objective and subjective standpoints, aligning with the complexity often found in scholarly discussions on regulatory legitimacy.

11.2.3 The Rule of Law

The ideal of 'rule of law' has multiple translations with similar significations (*Rechtsstaat*, *État de droit*). The widely used German term *Rechtsstaat*, for example, refers to a theoretical and ideological trajectory from enlightened absolutism to a self-governed society under law. In the British constitutional tradition, the term 'rule of law' refers primarily a corpus of basic principles and values, that together lend some stability and coherence to the legal order that express a commitment to a scheme of ideas that are 'legally fundamental' (Allan 1994) and which we adopt here. For legal scholars of regulatory governance, rule of law concerns have particular importance: regulatory legitimacy requires that the rule of law is upheld. In civil law countries, scholarship has also emphasised that regulatory legitimacy is grounded on the ability to abide by legal and constitutional principles (e.g., equal treatment, proportionality). Concerns of this kind are rooted in a belief that institutional frameworks and principles are required to constrain the exercise of power by those occupying positions of authority, serving as critical guardrails against the arbitrary exercise of power associated with despotic rule. Hence, it is widely accepted that the rule of law provides a blueprint for institutional design principles that serve as safeguards against the abuse of power, reflected in the two extracts below.

Waldron, Jeremy (2023). 'The Rule of Law'. In E. N. Zalta and U. Nodelman (eds.), *The Stanford Encyclopedia of Philosophy*, https://plato.stanford.edu/archives/fall2023/entries/rule-of-law/.

The Rule of Law is one ideal in an array of values that dominates liberal political morality: others include democracy, human rights, social justice, and economic freedom. The plurality of these values seems to indicate that there are multiple ways in which social and political systems can be evaluated, and these do not necessarily fit tidily together . . ..

The most important demand of the Rule of Law is that people in positions of authority should exercise their power within a constraining framework of well-established public norms rather than in an arbitrary, *ad hoc*, or purely discretionary manner on the basis of their own preferences or ideology. It insists that the government should operate within a framework of law in everything it does, and that it should be accountable through law when there is a suggestion of unauthorized action by those in power.

But the Rule of Law is not just about government. It requires also that citizens should respect and comply with legal norms, even when they disagree with them. When their interests conflict with others' they should accept legal determinations of what their rights and duties are. Also, the law should be the same for everyone, so that no one is above the law, and everyone has access to the law's protection. The requirement of access is particularly important, in two senses. First, law should be epistemically accessible: it should be a body of norms promulgated as public knowledge so that people can study it, internalize it, figure out what it requires of them, and use it as a framework for their plans and expectations and for settling their disputes with others. Secondly, legal institutions and their procedures should be available to ordinary people to uphold their rights, settle their disputes, and protect them against abuses of public and private power. All of this in turn requires the independence of the judiciary, the accountability of government officials, the transparency of public business, and the integrity of legal procedures.

While the concept of the rule of law has evolved over time, Lord Bingham distils its essence into a list of eight principles that may provide a valuable benchmark when attempting to evaluate regulatory legitimacy (Box 11.3).

It is helpful to bear in mind that 'rule of law' serves as an aspirational ideal and is prone to manipulation by those in power for self-serving ends in ways that are contrary to its foundational aspirations. Governance through law ultimately depends on a widespread political culture in which respect for the rule of law is widely held by all the members of a political community, including those in power (Box 11.4).

It is important to note that civil law countries may formulate and seek to protect some rule of law principles through different institutional frameworks, such as the principles of good administration that prevail in EU law and many Member States. In recent decades, the need to ensure that regulation must respect human rights has become increasingly connected to its legitimacy.

Box 11.3 The Rule of Law: Lord Bingham's Eight principles

1. The accessibility of the law: the law must be accessible and so far as possible intelligible, clear and predictable.
2. Law not discretion: questions of legal right and liability should ordinarily be resolved by application of the law and not the exercise of discretion.
3. Equality before the law: the laws of the land should apply equally to all, save to the extent that objective differences justify differentiation.
4. The exercise of power: ministers and public officers at all levels must exercise the powers conferred on them in good faith, fairly, for the purpose for which the powers were conferred, without exceeding the limits of such powers and not unreasonably.
5. Human rights: the law must afford adequate protection of fundamental human rights.
6. Dispute resolution: means must be provided for resolving, without prohibitive cost or inordinate delay, bona fide civil disputes that the parties themselves are unable to resolve.
7. A fair trial: adjudicative procedures provided by the state should be fair
8. The rule of law in the international legal order: the rule of law requires compliance by the state with its obligations in international law as in national law.

Source

House of Lords Select Committee on the Constitution (2023). 9th Report of Session 2022–23 – published 18 January – HL Paper 118, chapter 2, https://publications.parliament.uk/pa/ld5803/ldselect/ldconst/118/11805.htm.

Legal scholars repeatedly emphasise that the rule of law and the protection of human rights are the bedrock of democracy. Yet the rapid growth of wealth and power in the hands of a few extraordinarily wealthy global tech firms and their capacity to employ their technological and economic power for self-serving ends may enable them to evade legal safeguards, undermining basic freedoms of individuals and groups and the very fabric of constitutional democracies. Hence, several legal scholars, including ourselves, believe there is an urgent need to bring the power of private authority rooted in their technological capabilities under law. Paul Nemitz argues that while 'ethics' has an important role in the digital domain, 'no ethics can absolve from the obligation to comply with the law and to respect and support democratic process and all other rules of constitutional democracy'.

Nemitz, P. (2018). 'Constitutional Democracy and Technology in the Age of Artificial Intelligence'. *Philosophical Transactions of the Royal Society* A, 376, 20180089, 1–14,

http://doi.org/10.1098/rsta.2018.0089.

1–10

The triad of human rights, democracy and the rule of law are the core elements of western, liberal constitutions, the 'Trinitarian formula' of our constitutionalist

Box 11.4 Rule of Law Backsliding in the EU: The Case of Poland and Hungary

Rule of law 'backsliding' began in Hungary in 2010 following the election of Fidesz, later followed in Poland by the election of the Polish Law and Justice Party (PiS) government in 2015. In the EU's annual rule-of-law report (2022), which surveys each EU country, the European Commission reports that Hungary and Poland have been stripping their judicial systems of independence and allowing financial corruption to proliferate. In Poland, a series of mechanisms were introduced including a controversial disciplinary mechanism for judges (including the establishment of a Disciplinary Chamber of the Supreme Court), allowing governmental influence over prosecutorial decisions, the relaxation of rules against lobbying members of Parliament and thus facilitating political corruption, a dilution of protections of media pluralism and campaigns by Polish authorities against organisations representing the LGBTQ+ community. In Hungary, other measures have been introduced that undermine the independence of the judiciary (including the exercise of discretion in the appointment of judges, disciplinary measures and the payment of bonuses to judges and court executives), enhancing opportunities for political corruption and reducing the freedom and independence of the media.

The European Commission has responded by instituting a series of measures, including institution of Article 7(1) TEU proceedings (informally referred to as the 'nuclear option' because, in the worst-case scenario, it could strip a member state of voting rights) and commencing infringement procedures against Poland before the European Court of Justice. Although these enforcement measures have hitherto proved inconclusive, more recent threats to withhold EU payments unless rule of law backsliding is satisfactorily addressed are currently considered likely to yield greater cooperation, with recent indicators that both countries signalling a willingness to find a compromise with the European Commission.

A decade of destructive developments in Hungary and Poland has exposed the EU's inability to fully protect its constitutional identity and democratic integrity. Although the European Commission has sought to combat rule of law breaches in the EU, scholars point out that the rule of law can easily be appropriated by politicians. As Bárd and Kazai (2022: 173) observe:

> Autocrats usually do not deny the importance of the rule of law principle because it is considered to be an important element of their political regime's legitimacy. Nevertheless, they do not shy away from giving a perverted meaning to this principle in order to avoid criticism or to justify their decisions. European illiberals are not different. Hungary's and Poland's political leaders regularly relativize the meaning of the rule of law as applied by the EU institutions or explicitly deny that this principle can be given any clear interpretation. They constantly accuse the EU of applying double-standards and criticise it for their disregard for the 'specificities' of the Hungarian and the Polish legal cultures. Last year Hungarian Foreign Minister Péter Szijjártó held a press conference with his Polish counterpart Zbigniew Rau to announce the establishment of a joint comparative law institution to counter the European accusations in an intellectually more sophisticated style.

Sources

Bárd, P., and Kazai, V. Z. (2022). 'Enforcement of a Formal Conception of the Rule of Law as a Potential Way Forward to Address Backsliding: Hungary as a Case Study'. *Hague Journal on the Rule of Law*, 14, 165–193. https://doi.org/10.1007/s40803-022-00182-w.

de La Baume, M. (2020). 'EU Report Renews Hungary, Poland Rule-of-Law Critiques amid Key Negotiations', Politico, 13 July, www.politico.eu/article/commission-unveil-critical-rule-law-report-against-hungary-poland/.

European Commission (2022). '2022 Rule of Law Report, Country Chapter on the Rule of Law Situation in Hungary. Staff Working Document.

European Commission (2022). '2022 Rule of Law Report, Country Chapter on the Rule of Law Situation in Poland'. Staff Working Document.

faith. These principles are the supreme law of the land – all actions of government, legislators and indeed societal reality are measured against them. Given the foreseeable pervasiveness of artificial intelligence (AI) in modern societies, it is legitimate and necessary to ask the question of how this new technology must be shaped to support the maintenance and strengthening of the constitutional 'Trinitarian formula' rather than weakening it . . ..

The principle of rule of law, democracy and human rights by design in AI is necessary because on the one hand the capabilities of AI, based on big data and combined with the pervasiveness of devices and sensors of the Internet of things, will eventually govern core functions of society, reaching from education via health, science and business right into the sphere of law, security and defence, political discourse and democratic decision making. On the other hand, it is also high time to bind new technology to the basic constitutional principles, as the absence of such framing for the Internet economy has already led to a widespread culture of disregard of the law and put democracy in danger, the Facebook Cambridge Analytics scandal being only the latest wake-up call in that respect . . ..

A unique concentration of power in the hands of digital Internet giants which develop artificial intelligence . . ..

The analysis [of the theoretical public benefits of AI] must include the real impacts of new digital technologies and business activities based on the Internet and AI, in particular the activities of the 'Frightful five' shaping our experience with the Internet and digital technologies like AI: Google, Facebook, Microsoft, Apple and Amazon. The pervasiveness of these corporations is thus a reality not only in technical terms, but also with regard to resource attribution and societal matters . . ..

We live in a world which is shaped at least as much by technology as it is by law and democracy. And in the same way that the people shape the law and the law shapes the behaviour of people, we need to get used to – and practice – that the law is shaped by technology and technology is shaped by the law. Any technology has lived with being shaped by the law so far, and it is high time that Silicon Valley and the digital Internet industry also accept this necessity of democracy. At a time when the Internet and AI are becoming all-pervasive, not regulating these all pervasive and often decisive technologies by law would effectively amount to the end of democracy . . ..

The works on ethic rules for technology can be precursors of the law; they can give orientation on the possible content of legal rules. But they cannot replace the law, as they lack democratic legitimacy and the binding nature which allows enforcement with the power of government and the judiciary.

The preceding extract draws attention to the rule of law as an essential requirement for democratic legitimacy by seeking to prevent abuses of authority by the powerful, thereby enabling democratic self-rule rather than autocratic dictatorship, whether by the global tech titans or ruthlessly ambitious politicians who seek to bring about measures that can be described as 'rule of law backsliding' (see Box 11.4).

11.3 Legitimacy Evaluations and the Struggle for (Regulatory) Legitimation

We have seen that there is a wide range of bases or 'claims' to legitimacy that are often asserted in regulatory contexts and that frequently operate in tension. Yet in attempting to evaluate the overall legitimacy of some aspect of regulatory decision, policy or approach, some kind of overarching judgement is implied and unavoidable. The need for legitimacy is rooted in the discretionary power vested in regulators and their need to demonstrate its acceptability. When regulators have a range of possible choices, their decisions may be more difficult to predict and provide greater opportunities for them to abuse their authority. Yet the exercise of discretionary power in the hands of regulatory officials is generally regarded as acceptable and thus legitimate provided that it is subject to the rule of law, for which they are legally accountable (see Chapter 12). Although not extracted below, Baldwin identifies five values that ground the legitimacy claims of administrative officials, rooted in (i) consent (reflected in the existence of a legislative mandate based on the will of the people: an objective legitimacy claim); (ii) systems of control, ensuring that regulatory actors can be held responsible for the adverse impact of their regulation (rule of law, technocracy); (iii) procedural legitimacy or the due consideration of affected parties (input and throughput legitimacy); (iv) expertise or professionals' judgement (input and subjective legitimacy claims); and (v) efficiency and effective achievement of regulatory goals through an optimal deployment of resources (output and subjective legitimacy claims, including pragmatic legitimacy). As Baldwin explains in the following extract, these values form part of a 'discourse of justification' about the legitimacy of governmental administrative processes and decision-making, at least in British and North American settings.

Baldwin, R. (1997). *Rules and Government.* Oxford University Press.

47

How are [legitimacy] claims [of administrative officials] made and how can they be identified? The contention here is that there is a language of justification that invokes certain values. These values are recognized and given meaning according to a discourse of justification (or legitimacy) which attributes relevance to certain forms of argument in discussions of legitimacy and which distinguishes these from other forms of argument. Thus if I were to argue that the Director General of OFTEL should be supported because he wears elegant suits, this argument would be recognized by my listener as not bearing on the issue of legitimacy. Language-users are able to separate legitimacy claims from moral, legal, constitutional, or even aesthetic assertions.

Although Baldwin concedes that each claim is problematic in some respects, he goes on to argue that there is a need to look beyond 'traditional legal values' and that what matters is the cumulative force of more than one legitimacy claim to establish the regime's overall acceptability:

57–58

[Overall], debates concerning governmental processes are unduly confined if conducted with reference solely to what might be called 'traditional legal values'. In order to break out of the straitjacket of the legal paradigm it is necessary to consider the wide range of values being served by governmental processes and it is necessary also to explore the nature of disputes concerning legitimacy. The notion of a discourse of legitimacy makes it possible to explain the role of five rationales for legitimacy claims. The same notion involves a degree of indeterminacy in so far as the weighting of rationales is flexible, but the five rationales can be identified and the values appealed to are not open-ended in nature. The idea of a particular discourse of legitimacy also allows a distinction to be drawn between assessing legitimacy and the assertion of prescriptive political theories. It sees assessing legitimacy as an intermediate level of argument which has significance and offers practical guidance in a way that an immediate appeal to a normative theory of democracy does not.

11.3.1 The Quest for Legitimation

Our discussion of the general concept of legitimacy, and of regulatory legitimacy in particular, has thus far focused on the different kinds of 'claim' or forms of reasoning, invoking the perceived acceptability of the exercise of authority. But as Baldwin emphasises in the preceding extract, 'claims are made in the real world' in which people engage in a 'discourse of justification'. Baldwin thereby draws attention to the messiness, plural perspectives, interests and the reality of the social world. In Section 11.4, we consider the dynamic, intentional processes through which actors, including regulators, engage strategically in various activities aimed at cultivating and maintaining their perceived legitimacy in the eyes of their stakeholders. In so doing, our concern is with strategies and processes of legitimation that, as Ian Hurd explains in the following extract, comprise an inherently social and political process:

Hurd, I. 'Legitimacy'. *Princeton Encyclopedia*, https://pesd.princeton.edu/node/516.

Legitimation is the process by which actors strive to create legitimacy for a rule or ruler. Where legitimacy as a belief is a subjective and an individualistic quality, legitimation is a process that is inherently social and political. Actors and institutions constantly work to legitimize their power, and challengers work to delegitimate it. Legitimation is often done by justifying the existence of rulers or their rules in terms of important normative principles of the society. However, legitimation may also be attempted through payoffs and inducements to subordinates. Material incentives and normative appeals are different strategies for legitimation and their success depends on how the audience responds to them. It is not possible to make a general statement about the efficacy of one or the other as a generic legitimating strategy, nor is it possible to say that legitimacy can only arise by following one or the other.

More recent literature concerned with understanding regulatory legitimation recognise that there are multiple stakeholders (or 'principals', if understood through principal-agent theory) who take a keen interest in what regulators do. On this more nuanced view, what legitimates a regulator is the perception of competence among a variety of 'audiences', in which a regulator is acutely conscious of its reputational status. Moreover, regulatory legitimacy is a moving target rather than a static and stable position fixed for all time, as agencies dynamically interact with, respond to and attempt to shape audience expectation. Because coalitions of audiences 'that matter' are constantly shifting, so too are expectations of regulatory action and behaviour. As the following extract observes, this perspective was first discussed in the United States by Daniel Carpenter who demonstrated how the US Federal Food and Drug Administration was able to secure legitimacy through its reputation. This lens has become highly influential in regulatory studies and its relevance demonstrated empirically with respect to a broad range of agency behaviour across different national regulatory contexts.

Busuioc, M., and Rimkutė, D. (2020). 'The Promise of Bureaucratic Reputation Approaches for the EU Regulatory State'. *Journal of European Public Policy*, 27(8), 1256–1269, doi: 10.1080/13501763.2019.1679227

1258–1262

Bureaucratic reputation is an influential perspective on public organisations that builds on insights from classic scholarship . . .. However, the reputational account has a distinct focus compared to this literature, i.e., it pays particular attention to public organisations' *audiences* . . ..

In this perspective, regulatory authority has both a *formal* (in the act of delegation) as well as an *informal* basis. Regulators expand their formal authority by successfully cultivating, among relevant audiences, a perception of unique capacity to deliver on core tasks. By virtue of this audience-recognised capacity manifest in 'lasting esteem and durable links to social, political and economic organizations . . . that rival and surpass those of politicians', reputed agencies can shift the terms of the formal contract (Carpenter 2001: 354). Audiences can constrain, or even shift principals' preferences, through the political costs that audiences can extract of principals. A reputed agency enjoys deference beyond its formal powers. Correspondingly, failing to successfully cultivate one's reputation can erode the formal (mandated) authority of a regulator.

Not all audiences are equally consequential for an organisation's reputation. Reputation-management requires political astuteness of regulators in selectively responding to, and actively shaping, expectations of audiences 'that matter' – on whose support they depend. Successfully doing so has been shown to have fundamental implications for *de facto* authority and the ability to secure compliance and deference (Carpenter 2010) . . ..

Reputation is an institutional resource for public organisations to achieve authority and legitimacy in governance. EU agencies are especially reliant on other actors to adopt their opinions into binding law (e.g., European Commission) or to implement their decisions (national authorities), often lacking the tools or resources for ('policing') implementation . . ..

From a reputational perspective, however, organisational legitimation is regarded as a product of successful reputation-management for *technical conduct, performative capacities, procedural appropriateness,* and *moral image*. The discourse on the EU regulatory state has prioritised regulators' independent *expertise* – the *technical dimension,* in the language of reputation – as a source of legitimation. In other words, it has emphasised technocratic expertise as *the key criterion for legitimation* above all others. Expertise then provides the means through which EU agencies deliver (e.g., protect us from risks or prevent crises), crucial to their superior performative capacities – *the performative dimension* in the language of reputation.

The *procedural dimension* comes in as well – agencies need to follow clear procedures and due process – but often as a means to safeguard, through process, their primary criterion for legitimation, i.e., independent expert-based policy-making. When it comes to the *moral dimension,* however, EU agencies are to be explicitly unresponsive to political expectations and attempts at influence . . ..

In contrast, reputation literature proposes a more differentiated understanding: it suggests that agencies are exposed to audiences with often *competing expectations* of agency behaviour, outputs, and outcomes. Reputation literature intimates that the standards are in the eyes of the beholder(s) – extending *beyond* formal institutional actors and their expectations, to a variety of different *informal* stakeholders, operating at different levels of governance. Expectations of different groups co-exist and can conflict. Rather than fixed and predetermined, the standards by which regulators are assessed are contested, and assessments vary, depending on audience preferences . . .. As discussed above, what legitimates an organisation is a *perception of competence* among multiple audiences 'that matter'. A reputational lens suggests that *rather than a static prescriptive recipe*, regulatory *legitimacy* is much more of *a moving target* as agencies dynamically interact with, respond to, and attempt to shape audience expectations, and as coalitions of audiences 'that matter' shift, thereby also expectations of regulatory behaviour.

11.3.2 Regulatory Legitimation and Multiple Audiences

The exposure of regulators to multiple audiences and their often competing expectations generates considerable challenges for regulators in attempting to cultivate and sustain their legitimacy. As we explain in Chapter 12, the existence of multiple stakeholders has important implications for the ability to hold regulators accountable for their actions. Yet the need to do so successfully is a matter of considerable importance, particularly for non-state regulators who do not enjoy the democratic imprimatur of the state, as Julia Black explains:

Black, J. (2008). 'Constructing and Contesting Legitimacy and Accountability in Polycentric Regulatory Regime'. *Regulation & Governance* 2(2), 137–164.

148

Reasons for constructing legitimacy

Recognition of regulators' attempts to build legitimacy brings to the fore a key issue which discussion on state-based regulators obscures: an awareness of why regulators need legitimacy and authority. All regulators, but particularly non-state regulators, need legitimacy because it is a critical element in motivating behavioral responses. They require not only that others accept them, but that they will change their behavior because of what of the organizations or standards say. Unlike state based regulators, whose actions are supported by law, non-state regulators cannot necessarily rely on the authority of law to motivate people to behave, or derive their legitimacy from their position in a wider legal order and constitutional settlement. They have to create the motivation for compliance or change in some other way.

Black's observation about the need for legitimacy in order to motivate regulatees to comply with regulatory demands is made in the course of her analysis of the ways in which regulators act strategically in order to actively manage the plurality of demands and claims made upon them by multiple 'legitimacy communities', drawing on Suchman's tri-partite taxonomy of legitimacy. Black (2008: 144–147) continues:

Constructing Legitimacy: The Role of Regulators

It has been implicitly assumed that regulators are passive recipients of these legitimacy evaluations. But regulators, like states or indeed any organization, can play a role in constructing their own legitimacy claims though, absent hegemony, these claims will not necessarily be accepted by all others. Suchman's analysis of how organizations can manage their own legitimacy identifies three main strategies: conforming, manipulating, and informing. Managing their legitimacy encompasses building legitimacy, maintaining it, and repairing it once lost. Organizations can manage their legitimacy by attempting to conform to legitimacy claims that are made on them; they can seek to manipulate them; or they can selectively conform to claims from among their environments, or legitimacy communities, conforming to claims of those that will support them. The form that the strategy takes will vary with the type of legitimacy that is in issue: pragmatic legitimacy (based on self-interested claims of legitimacy communities); moral or normative legitimacy (based on assessments that this is the 'right thing to do') or cognitive legitimacy (based on assumptions that things could not be any other way), and on whether the organization is seeking to build, maintain or repair legitimacy.

Regulators can manage the pragmatic and normative bases of their legitimacy in a number of ways (cognitive legitimacy, by its nature, is far harder to manage strategically). Many state-based regulatory agencies, for example, have developed systems of public consultation, decision-making, and reporting which go well beyond those required by law to enhance their normative legitimacy. Non-state regulators can also seek to manage their legitimacy, both out of self-interest and because they perceive it to be the 'right thing to do': in March and Olsen's terms, out of a logic of consequences and a logic of appropriateness (March & Olsen 1984). Cashore's analysis of the Forest Stewardship Council's (FSC) legitimacy illustrates how the FSC seeks to manage its pragmatic legitimacy by engaging in "brand destroying" activities against those who do not conform (Cashore 2002). Regulators can also seek to develop moral and cognitive legitimacy through, for example, linking themselves to other organizations which are perceived to be legitimate by those whose legitimacy claims they want to meet. The bodies to whom they are linked may also derive enhanced legitimacy from those legitimacy communities that support the regulator seeking the alignment, in systems of mutual legitimacy enhancement or 'legitimacy networks'. For example, a number of the social and environmental accreditation bodies have agreed to ensure that they abide by the Code of Practice developed by the International Social and Economic Accreditation League (ISEAL) on the development, publication and review of standards by member organizations, largely to enhance their credibility (ISEAL Alliance 2004). In turn, ISEAL's legitimacy may be enhanced through its own association with such organizations among certain legitimacy communities. But such a tactic of alignment may not of itself always be successful . . ..

Regulators may thus seek to build legitimacy by conforming to the claims of all or a selective group of legitimacy communities, or by attempting to create new legitimacy beliefs and new legitimacy communities. The important point to note with respect to polycentric regimes is that an organization's legitimacy communities include other participants in the regulatory regime on which the organization relies, or which it would like to enrol in its regulatory processes, as well as those outside it. Social and environmental accreditation regulators, for example, such as the Fair Trade and Labor Organisation (FTLO), rely on pressure groups or NGOs to generate awareness among consumers and in turn generate economic pressures on market actors to conform to those norms, and so have to generate legitimacy among those bodies as well as firms in order to motivate them to act in their support.

Although not extracted here, Black proceeds to investigate the relationship between accountability and legitimacy, emphasising the communicative core at the heart of accountability relations. Black goes on to reflect on the implications of these insights in order to anticipate how regulators are likely to behave when faced with competing legitimacy claims from multiple audiences. Responding to multiple and conflicting claims can be challenging. Regulators may sometimes be able to meet some or even all legitimacy claims as long as they are compatible. What should regulators do when they face incompatible legitimacy claims? Black argues that it is key that these legitimacy claims are accepted by 'one part of their environment, within and outside the regulatory regime'. To conclude, Black (2008: 156–157) hypothesises that regulators are less likely to acquiesce to legitimacy claims, even if the legitimacy gains for that regulator within that particular legitimacy community may be high, where all or some of the following six conditions are present:

(i) the regulator perceives itself to have a low dependency or interconnectedness on that legitimacy community for the performance of its regulatory function;
(ii) where the content of the claims, and the discourse in which they are articulated, is not congruent or consistent with the regulator's, or is only so to a moderate degree;
(iii) where acquiescence with the claims would pose moderate to severe constraints on the ability of the regulator to determine its own structures, goals and activities;
(iv) where the legitimacy community has little means, directly or indirectly, to coerce the regulator to respond;
(v) where the claims being advanced are not widely diffused among others within or outside the regulatory regime;
(vi) and the consequences of acquiescing are uncertain .... A regulator or organisation is more likely to acquiesce to legitimacy claims where it perceives itself to have a relatively high dependence on or interconnectedness with the legitimacy claimant; where the content of the claim and the discourse in which it is expressed is congruent with the organisation; where acquiescence would not pose severe constraints on its discretion; where the claimant can directly or indirectly coerce the regulator; where the claims being advanced are widely diffused; and the consequences of acquiescing are relatively certain.

Conclusion

This examination of regulatory legitimacy has traversed a wide range of scholarly writings. It began with an exploration of the general concept of legitimacy, focusing on the approaches taken by political theorists and sociologists. We have seen that questions of legitimacy can be approached from an objective perspective, concerned with identifying the theoretical foundations upon which the legitimacy of authority should rest. However, questions of legitimacy can be approached from a subjective perspective, concerned with the beliefs that people hold about the acceptability of a regime of rule, whether or not that acceptability is theoretically defensible. What is common to both perspectives, however, is a foundational concern with the *justification* of regulatory authority (whether de jure or de facto) or why regulation is considered acceptable, or likely to be accepted, particularly by those they purport to regulate. Unless they are able to demonstrate the legitimacy of their actions, regulators may find it difficult to elicit compliance with their demands from those they regulate.

Discussion Questions

1. What is the difference between an objective and subjective approach to legitimacy?
2. Can you identify a number of common 'bases' upon which claims to regulatory legitimacy often rest?
3. Why does legitimacy matter to regulators, whether public or private?
4. Discuss whether all public authorities have legitimacy and if so, on what the source(s) of these legitimacy claims are based.
5. Charisma is qualified here as a subjective legitimacy claim that is often separated from morality. Can you identify charismatic leaders throughout history that fit within this separation and discuss what the sources of their charisma were?
6. How does pragmatic legitimacy apply to self-regulation? Conduct a literature review of different domains of activity that self-regulate and explain whether the respective regulators have pragmatic legitimacy and why.
7. Drawing on Hertogh's extract, reflect upon why people comply or do not comply with laws and regulations in your country. Give examples to illustrate your complaints and discuss them from a legitimacy perspective.
8. How do consultations (see Chapter 5) contribute to the democracy legitimacy of regulators?
9. How do expertise and reputation contribute to a regulator's legitimacy?

12

Regulatory Accountability

Introduction

In Chapter 11, we examined the concept of regulatory legitimacy to acquire an understanding of why regulators are regarded as legitimate authorities although they are not directly elected by the people. In this chapter, we examine the relationship between the general public (regulatees) and regulators as a relationship of principals and agents (see also Chapter 1): *principals* (the public) who delegate tasks to *agents* (regulators) who may draw their legitimacy from different sources (e.g., expertise) but may lack incentives to pursue the interests of their principals. This is where accountability enters into the frame. Accountability is about ensuring that those who have been entrusted with a set of tasks – in our case, to regulate – are kept in check.

Accountability is also present in our daily lives. For example, consider a scenario involving a friend who asks you to take care of her dog while she is away on vacation. Your friend is the principal, and you are the agent. When your friend returns and discovers that her dog has lost weight and seems undernourished, she may ask you to explain what happened. Your reply can argue that the dog lost its appetite because it missed its owner, which might be accepted as a reasonable justification. However, if your friend does not believe you, you may have to face the consequences of your poor performance as a dog-sitter. For instance, she may decide to end your friendship. Alternatively, if your friend does not trust your explanation, she might ask a third-party (such as a vet) to provide a professional opinion on the dog's undernourishment. In the context of regulation, accountability is more complex than in this example and has more significant implications. Nevertheless, it also involves the four key elements of accountability: (i) a duty to explain, (ii) exposure to scrutiny, (iii) a potential 'sanction' or a consequence of some kind and (iv) the possibility of being subject to independent review (in our example a vet; in regulation, a 'watchdog,' such as a court of auditors). In our daily lives, as well as in regulation, accountability is crucial in maintaining trust and respect in relationships and ensuring that the actors are acting in the best interests of their principals.

Democratic accountability is a crucial aspect of any democracy. It helps ensure that elected officials are held responsible for their actions. However, independent regulators are often insulated from politics and cannot be held accountable through traditional means such as the ballot box. While they exercise their powers based on their technical expertise (see Chapter 11), this source of legitimacy is contestable. Even for independent regulators, it is important to ensure that they are held accountable for their actions to maintain the integrity of our democratic institutions. This chapter demonstrates that there are many accountability mechanisms employed in regulatory contexts beyond conventional political accountability mechanisms. In the absence of political mechanisms to hold regulators accountable, regulators are subject to a different kind of accountability aimed at ensuring that they fulfil their responsibilities properly and are not abusing their powers. This includes regular reviews of their activities and performance, as well as oversight and monitoring by other institutions, such as courts or independent oversight bodies. In this chapter, our focus is on the notion of 'regulatory accountability' rather than democratic accountability, although the two are closely related.

Regulatory accountability is concerned with both holding regulators accountable for their actions and ensuring that they are acting in the best interests of regulatees (their principals). By guaranteeing that regulators are accountable for their actions, we can maintain trust and respect in the regulatory process and ensure that regulations are being enforced in a legally and socially acceptable way. Ultimately, both democratic and regulatory accountability are critical safeguards, helping to ensure that those who govern us are acting legitimately in our best interests.

In this chapter, we examine various debates surrounding regulatory accountability. The chapter discusses 'how', 'to whom' and 'for what' regulators should be accountable. Accountability is, nonetheless, a complex concept with multiple dimensions, and there is no consensus on its meaning or how regulators should account for their performance. Hence Bovens (2010: 947) explains:

> Accountability is an ever-expanding concept, which 'has come to stand as a general term for any mechanism that makes powerful institutions responsive to their particular publics'. Also, it has prevented much empirical progress in the broad field of accountability studies. Discussions seem to go in circles, as every volume and author tries to redefine accountability in his or her own way. To paraphrase Aaron Wildavsky: 'If accountability is everything, it may be nothing.'

The chapter's starting point is that calls for accountability are always defined in relation to some event, decision or activity and seldom, if ever, established in abstract terms. Instead, accountability is in practice exercised in different ways, appropriate to different circumstances and the nature of actors. The accountability of private regulators is another complex issue that we also consider in this chapter. Private regulators are not accountable to the public in the same way that public regulators are. Instead, they are accountable to their 'stakeholders' – whether shareholders, clients or other affected groups who have a vested interest in their activities. It is thus important to establish clear rules and guidelines for private regulators to ensure that they are responsive to all those affected. In recent decades, the coexistence of multiple accountability forums, the blurring of public and private spheres, reliance on regulatory networks, globalisation and, more recently, the growing use of opaque algorithms by organisations have increased the complexity of questions regarding who is accountable, to whom, for what, and under what circumstances.

The chapter begins with the concept of accountability generally. Section 12.1 unpacks the core elements of accountability as well as the concept's importance. Section 12.2 presents accountability as a matter of answerability, applying it to the regulatory context. To be answerable, regulators should be transparent, justify their actions and allow regulatees to contest them. Section 12.3 discusses current debates on regulatory accountability, including accountability challenges in multi-actor networks, accountability deficits in the context of privatisation and contracting out.

12.1 The Concept of Accountability

Accountability can be understood from two core perspectives: as a source of *moral virtue* of actors in a principal-agent relationship (such as regulators and regulatees) or as a *social mechanism for answerability*, which generates an obligation to explain and to accept the consequences for one's conduct. When accountability is approached as *virtue*, persons and organisations are thought to have an inner responsibility to moral values and public interest norms. They are willing to be responsible, transparent and responsive or to engage in dialog and justification. Accountability exists also as a mechanism that is designed to ensure that agents are brought before a forum to account for their decisions, and/or to answer to any possible charges of misconduct. Our emphasis is on this second perspective.

12.1.1 The Importance of Accountability and its Key Elements

Bovens explains below that accountability is a relational concept that only exists by reference to an individual or group of individuals (the 'forum') to which the agent is accountable and, secondly, that accountability has an informational or communicative dimension. As the extract shows, calls for accountability demand meaningful explanations designed for a specific purpose, forum and provided to a public that is able to understand those explanations. Bovens also views accountability from a principal-agent perspective. Accountability is a conversation between an accountability-giver (the 'agent') and an accountability forum (the 'principal') and not a 'monologue' without consequences. The accountability forum should have the opportunity to discuss the information provided, to ask questions and to judge the agent's performance. In the case of public regulators, the accountability forum is the public.

Accountability, presented in the extract as a *mechanism*, has four central elements: first, the accountability-giver should feel the obligation to inform the accountability forum about a behavior that took place in the context of their relationship; second, the accountability forum should have the opportunity to question the accountability-giver, challenging the accuracy of the information provided; third, the forum should have the ability to judge the conduct of the accountability-giver. Fourth, in case of a negative judgment, the accountability-giver may be subject to negative consequences such as a legal sanction or another form of reprimand.

Accountability is not always given to the same *type* of forum. Depending on who an agent is accountable to, accountability may take different shapes. There are thus different kinds of accountability: *organisational accountability* requires that the agent explain to hierarchical superiors how and why power was used; *political accountability* refers to the obligation of a political agent to justify one's conduct to the agent's political masters (e.g., government ministers before the electorate), a type of accountability that many regulators are directly shielded from when they are established as independent regulators; *legal accountability* focuses on legal scrutiny before a court of law; *professional accountability* entails justifying one's professional or expert judgement before professional colleagues and peers; *administrative accountability* refers to accounts that must be given to third parties such as auditors, courts of auditors and other experts. This distinction is particularly relevant when we discuss algorithmic accountability.

The extract also explores the functions of accountability. By giving an account of one's conduct and allowing the forum to pass judgement on it, accountability may be a cathartic or 'therapeutic' mechanism that can allow the public to understand and come to terms with failings and failures. Accountability can also promote participation in the governance process and, for example, in the case of public regulators to ensure that regulators are appropriately responsive to affected stakeholders and the public at large.

The extract finally introduces a variety of accountability actors that are called upon to monitor and judge the performance of regulators such as courts, the Ombud (or Ombudsman) and courts of auditors.

Bovens, M. (2010). 'Two Concepts of Accountability: Accountability as a Virtue and as a Mechanism'. *West European Politics*, 33(5), 946–967, doi: 10.1080/01402382.2010.486119.

950–956

Accountability as a Mechanism

Historically and semantically, the word 'accountability' is closely related to accounting, in its literal sense of bookkeeping . . ..

[According to a] more traditional, concept of accountability . . . [it is] a notion in which the relation between sovereign and subjects, principal and agents, or, as we shall see, forum and actor, is the defining element.

Staying close to its etymological and historical roots, accountability can also be approached as a specific social relation or mechanism that involves an obligation to explain and justify conduct. This implies a relationship between an actor, the accounter, and a forum, the account-holder, or accountee. Explanations and justifications are not made in a void, but vis-à-vis a significant other. This usually involves not just the provision of information about performance, but also the possibility of debate, of questions by the forum and answers by the actor, and eventually of judgement of the actor by the forum. Judgement also implies the imposition of formal or informal sanctions on the actor in case of malperformance or, for that matter, of rewards in case of adequate performance.

This is what one could also call *passive* accountability because actors are held to account by a forum, *ex post facto*, for their conduct . . ..

The *actor* can be either an individual, for example an official or civil servant, or an organisation, such as a public institution or an agency. The significant other, the *accountability forum*, can be a specific person, such as a superior, a minister, or a journalist, or it can be an institution, such as parliament, a court, or the audit office.

The relationship between the forum and the actor can assume the form of a principal–agent relation: the forum being the principal, for example parliament, which has delegated authority to a minister, the agent, who is held to account for his performance in office. This is often the case with political forms of accountability. However, in many other accountability relations, the forums are not principals of the actors, such as, for example, courts in case of legal accountability, or professional associations in case of professional accountability.

The relationship between the actor and the forum, the actual account giving, usually consists of at least three elements or stages. First of all, before a relation can be qualified as an accountability relation, it is crucial that the actor is, or feels, *obliged to inform the forum about his or her conduct*, by providing various types of data about the performance of tasks, about outcomes, or about procedures. Often, particularly in the case of failures or incidents, this also involves the provision of explanations and justifications. Secondly, there needs to be a possibility for the forum to interrogate the actor and to *question* the adequacy of the information or the legitimacy of the conduct – hence, the close semantic connection between 'accountability' and 'answerability'. Thirdly, the forum may *pass judgement* on the conduct of the actor. It may approve of an annual account, denounce a policy, or publicly condemn the behaviour of an official or an agency. In passing a negative judgement . . . the actor may *face consequences*. These consequences can be highly formalised, such as fines, disciplinary measures, civil remedies or even penal sanctions . . ..

Who should render account? Who is the *actor* required to appear before the forum? In ordinary social relationships amongst citizens, it is usually clear which actor will render an account. This is a far more complicated question to answer when it comes to public organisations. In legal procedures, it is often the organisation as a corporate entity that is required to give an account. This can be called *corporate* or *organisational* accountability .... In most instances of political accountability, it is only the top of the organisation that is called to account externally. This can be called *hierarchical* accountability. A clear example is the political accountability of ministers for civil servants in countries that have a parliamentary system ....

Another question is *why* the actor feels compelled to render account. This relates largely to the nature of the relationship between the actor and the forum, and in particular to the question of why the actor has an obligation to render account. This will subsequently lead to classifications based on the nature of the *obligation*, as for example obligations arising from a hierarchical or principal–agent relationship, a contractual agreement, or obligations which have been voluntarily entered into. This yields a classification based on spatial metaphors: vertical, horizontal, or diagonal accountability.

Why bother about accountability? ...

Accountability as a mechanism is in fact instrumental in achieving accountable governance. Accountability arrangements assure that public officials or public organisations remain on the virtuous path. Therefore, ultimately, accountability as a mechanism is also important because it contributes to the legitimacy of public governance. However, accountability mechanisms may also serve more specific and direct purposes.

First of all, processes of public account giving can have important ritual, purifying functions – they can help to provide public *catharsis*. This is particularly salient in incidental cases of tragedies, fiascos, and failures. Public account giving can help to bring a tragic period to an end, because it can offer a platform for the victims to voice their grievances and for the real or reputed perpetrators to account for themselves and to justify or excuse their conduct ....

Depending on the sort of mechanism involved, passive accountability is also instrumental in achieving various important elements of democratic and 'good' governance. For example, account giving by political executives to political forums, such as elected representatives, political parties, voters, and media, is crucial as a feedback mechanism to establish *popular control* of government ....

Accountability to legal and administrative forums, such as courts, auditors, ombudsmen, inspectorates and controllers, is an important mechanism to *prevent and detect corruption and the abuse of public powers*. Autonomous, or semi-autonomous, accountability forums provide for checks and balances that operate independently from the political process. Good governance arises from a dynamic equilibrium between the various powers of – and increasingly beyond – the state ....

Finally, accountability mechanisms can also serve as a tool to induce *reflection and learning*, as feedback mechanisms that can make and keep governments, agencies and individual officials effective in delivering on their promises.

Beyond the possibility of holding a regulator legally liable for their failures (including the possibility of an award of damages), accountability can be regarded more broadly as a redress mechanism. Drawing on Mashaw's work, Dickinson explains that accountability as redress consists in understanding the full process of accountability within and beyond legal accountability: who is liable or accountable to whom, what they are liable for, through what processes accountability is to be assured, by what standards the putative accountable behaviour is to be judged and what the potential effects are of finding that those standards have been breached. The redress function of accountability is served not only through courts but also through other instruments such as investigation activities such as those conducted by truth commissions, which, following human rights violations, aim to expose the facts, offer conclusions by independent experts to inform the public and promote reparation and conciliation in divided societies.

Dickinson, L. (2011). 'Privatization and Accountability'. *Annual Review Law Sociological Sciences*, 7, 101–120.

103–104

When people speak of accountability, they most commonly are thinking of what we can call accountability as redress: the idea that there is somewhere to go after the fact to punish wrongdoers and 'hold them accountable'. When political scientists or lawyers discuss accountability, they generally refer, either implicitly or explicitly, to this form. Grant & Keohane (2005, p. 29), for example, note the following:

> Accountability, as we use the term, implies that some actors have the right to hold other actors to a set of standards, to judge whether they have fulfilled their responsibilities in light of these standards, and to impose sanctions if they determine that these responsibilities have not been met ....

Administrative law scholar Mashaw (2006, p. 118) also defines accountability in terms of redress. According to Mashaw, accountability includes 'six important things: who is liable or accountable to whom; what they are liable to be called to account for; through what processes accountability is to be assured; by what standards the putative accountable behavior is to be judged; and what the potential effects are of finding that those standards have been breached'. Mashaw's definition gestures to a broad range of mechanisms and processes that various actors may use to implement accountability. But by focusing on judging behavior and an 'effect' or consequence, Mashaw's definition implies a discrete moment of adjudication and some type of sanction.

12.1.2 Accountability as 'Answerability' and as 'Control': Principal-Agent and Stewardship Theories

Bovens' extract focused exclusively on ex post accountability or the obligation of a regulator to 'give an account' for its past conduct. However, as the extract below explains, accountability also has a future-oriented or *preventive* dimension that aims to deter agents from pursuing their own interests in detriment of those of the principal ('shirking') or engaging in corruption. Accountability is thus a mechanism for answerability and a mechanism for control. In its second role, accountability prevents abuse of powers, provides incentives to a good fulfillment of future tasks and creates peer-pressure in terms of performance.

Returning to our opening example: if you did a good job looking after your friend's dog, you may want her to return the favour, by walking your dog when you are at work. You might wish to take measures in advance to improve the likelihood that she will do so and carry out the task in accordance with your wishes. When you take advance measures of this kind, you are addressing a problem called 'shirking', that is, when the agent pursues its own interests rather than the interests of the other (the principal). This problem is central to principal-agent perspectives in regulation, in which regulatory failures may arise if regulators pursue their own policies and interests rather than the interests of the public. Accountability mechanisms reduce the possibilities of 'shirking' or 'drifting'.

On a conventional principal-agent analysis, the principal may adopt various costly ex ante and ex post strategies to reduce or prevent agent's shirking and thus bring the interests of the agent into alignment with those of the principal. First, the principal may 'monitor' the agent closely, to continually 'check-up' on the agent's conduct, to guard against shirking. However, this entails 'monitoring costs' for the principal. Secondly, the principal could reduce the agent's discretion performing the assigned tasks and provide for detailed specifications of the agent's mandate. As the extract explains, the problem is that attempts to reduce these agency costs entail significant transaction costs (see Chapter 1) involved in establishing specific and binding contractual terms. Since contracts are typically not self-enforcing, the principal continues to incur costs as long as the principal-agent relationship lasts. Information asymmetries (see Chapter 1) between principals and agents make this conflict hard to solve. Agency theory considers how principals can effectively ensure that the agent's interests are aligned with that of the principal at the lowest possible cost.

In the extract below, Schillemans and Busuoic discuss the contractual relationship between principal and agent through a series of assumptions that underlie this theory. The assumptions listed in the extract highlight specific aspects relevant to regulatory accountability. As Schillemans and Busuoic explain, principals delegate tasks to agents not only because they may have additional expertise but also to 'shift blame for problematic outcomes' or transfer risk (see Section 12.3.1 below on privatization). While the principal-agent theory has been widely used to simplify accountability issues in regulation, the extract also points out that simplification is simultaneously the greatest strength and weakness of this theory. Given these limitations, recent scholarship has offered theoretical refinements. For example, research shows that principals are not always interested in monitoring agents; many failures result not from shirking or agency drift but rather from forum 'drift' as principal's interests or goals may change over time.

> **Schillemans, T., and Busuioc, M. (2015).** 'Predicting Public Sector Accountability: From Agency Drift to Forum Drift'. *Journal of Public Administration Research and Theory*, 25(1), 191–215, https://doi.org/10.1093/jopart/muu024.
>
> 195–205
>
> The P-A framework essentially portrays a contractual situation, in which the principal is the rightful 'owner' of a job and has chosen to hire a third party to actually carry out the job. The relationship is portrayed as a model of conflict, because the theory assumes from the outset a (level of) goal conflict between the two parties in a contract situation.
>
> The agency problem of the principal essentially is how to effectively tie the agent, given its conflicting interests, to the explicit and implicit terms of their contract. The agency problem is spiced with information asymmetry, moral hazard, and limited political and economic resources to monitor all agents extensively. The principal generally needs a combination of (ex ante and ex post) controls and sanctions to ensure that the agent acts sufficiently according to his will. Implicit in the theory is that necessarily some compromise on control will take place but that this is preferable to alternatives and that the principal is nevertheless better off as a result. Principals are likely to accept *some* level of slack and inefficiency from their agents, given the considerable costs of monitoring and sanctioning . . .. And in some cases, it might be in the principal's interest to limit its control options . . ..
>
> Principal-agent theory has been widely adopted . . .. At the same time, its inherent limitations have also been noted . . ..
>
> The standard expectations for principals and agents in *accountability processes* would be the following:
>
> (1) The principal delegates a task it actually *cares about* to an agent . . .. Sometimes the agent has more resources or superior knowledge, often it is simply more efficient to have another organization carry out the job, and sometimes delegation is a method of creating credible commitment or to safeguard preferences beyond the horizon of an elected official's tenure . . .. Principals may also delegate a task to some other agent in order to shift or avoid the blame for problematic outcomes, as a method of retaining the interesting parts of the job while shifting the tedious parts in a process of bureau shaping to others, or to transfer risks to agents . . ..
>
> (2) The principal source of conflict in principal-agent theory stems from the fact that the agent has (partially) *different objectives and goals* from the principal and is self-centered and opportunistic. This might lead, when uncorrected, to 'bureaucratic/agency drift'. Principals will try to contain agency loss with a combination of *ex ante* and *ex post* controls (such as contract design, screening and selection mechanisms, monitoring and reporting, and additional institutional checks), within the reasonable

confines of limited resources and against the background of a fuller set of priorities and obligations . . ..

(3) The problem of agency drift is further exacerbated by the fact that the agent is understood to be at least at some level autonomous and capable of real agency . . ..

(4) Predictable agents, being rational, self-serving and self-centered, are expected to resist demands for accountability. Rational actors may be expected to nurture the advantages that follow from their superior knowledge and informational advantage and exploit the possibilities offered by the conventional information asymmetry. They will therefore, with some exaggeration, naturally prefer secrecy and they will duck and shy away whenever possible . . ..

(5) Principals, on the other hand, are expected to actually *want* to hold their agents accountable . . ..

However . . . where principal-agent theory would forecast (potential) agency drift, empirical findings rather suggest forum drift: the accountability forum drifting away from agreed upon goals and measures . . .. Research on the behavior of agencies suggest that they often are strongly attached to the job at hand and to their formal and historical task . . .. The principal source of conflict in these and other empirical examples is, thus, not that the agent drifts away from its formal mission and task (but that the principal or the forum does so) . . ..

In conclusion, the central problem of accountability in a principal-agent approach would normally be making the potentially failing agent live up to its role. In the literature described above, however, we find no overarching problem of agency drift. Rather, while there is variation among forums, there are numerous instances of failing forums. Failing in the sense of not caring about the delegated tasks, not wanting to hold their agents accountable, drifting away in preferences from what has been formally instituted, failing to take accountability information seriously and failing to correct and redress the behavior of agents when feasible. What is more, forums were generally found to be satisfied with the existing situation.

The stewardship theory can complement our understanding of accountability challenges. This theory challenges the assumption that a principal-agent relationship is inherently characterised by agency conflicts. The following extract contrasts these two theories. While agency theory focuses on monitoring agents through 'hard' monitoring measures ('keeping the agent on a leash'), stewardship seeks to promote accountability through soft and trust-based measures. The key distinction between these two theories lies in how they conceive human motivation. Agency theory assumes that agents display self-centred behaviour and will only pursue the interests of the principal if they have incentives to do so or extrinsic motivation (e.g., close monitoring, contractual sanctions). Stewardship theory, on the contrary, draws on psychological and sociological analyses of human behaviour and assumes that intrinsic motivation and collectivism can drive an alignment of interests between principals and agents. The steward chooses service above direct self-interest and may be driven by self-realisation, recognition, achievement and respect (internal motivation).

Schillemans, T., and Bjurstrøm, K. H. (2020). 'Trust and Verification: Balancing Agency and Stewardship Theory in the Governance of Agencies'. *International Public Management Journal*, 23(5), 650–676, doi: 10.1080/10967494.2018.1553807.

651–653

Stewardship theory . . . assumes unselfish behaviors from stewards involved in the same supra-individual cause as their principals. The concept of stewardship theory has been embraced by scholars as a contrasting and promising alternative approach in the study of the governance of agencies. In studies of contracting, agency theory is often used to understand why some contracts are 'hard' or 'complete' in the sense that they aim to cover all eventualities, while elements from stewardship theory are used to explain 'soft' or 'relational' contracts that are based on trust and cooperation.

Agency and stewardship theory . . . focus on the relationship between a delegator and a delegatee, which is the central object of analysis in the design of governance regimes. They depart from assumptions about the behavior of individuals and organizations that are then translated into comparably built theories. But, as they are founded on contrasting assumptions, this means that they cover a continuum of possibilities in which concrete forms of governance can be identified . . ..

Stewardship theory was first introduced to the management literature by Davis, Schoorman, and Donaldson (1997a) as a criticism of the postulated selfishness and shirking of agents in much of the literature, which in the public sector may be a 'terrible caricature' (Kelman 1987:81). Similar to agency theory, stewardship theory also analyses how to ensure accountability when a task is delegated from a principal to an executive. Stewardship theory, however, diverges from agency theory in its view on the motivations of agents. Subordinates or executives are assumed to be 'motivated to act in the best interests of their principals' and they prioritize 'pro-organizational, collectivistic behaviours' (Davis, Schoorman, and Donaldson 1997a: 24). The steward simply wants to be a good and loyal steward and will put organizational goals above self-interest.

Stewardship theory views the delegatee as a trustee, more strongly focused on collective goals than on individual goals. If the executive (e.g., a state agency) is not acting opportunistically but shares the same goals as the superior (e.g., a ministry), there will be no reason for the superior not to trust that the executive will fulfill a delegated task without (too much) bureaucratic drift. Stewardship theory seeks to understand the qualities of and conditions for good stewardship. The theory therefore also changes the perspective on the relationship between the principal and the executive. Stewardship theory focuses on how to lay the foundation and foster steward-like behavior . . ..

As Wasserman (2006:961) puts it, stewards are managers who act on behalf of the organization. The difference [between this theory and agency theory] has been summarized as follows:

> Agents, by definition, are given authority by those for whom they act – a contractual relationship. Stewards are entrusted with resources and may act on behalf of individuals with whom there is no direct contractual relationship. Therefore, agents act on behalf of shareholders whereas stewards act on behalf of all stakeholders.

Both agency and stewardship theories conceptualise the relationship between principals and agents (regulatees and regulators) as bilateral. However, this simplification does not consider the multi-actor character of many regulatory networks and the existence of co-regulation and systems of partnerships where principals and agents collaborate closely to regulate and enforce those regulations (see Section 12.3).

In Section 12.2, we explore some of the instruments that can be used to guarantee ex ante control and ex post oversight. Publicity and transparency are used ex post to control for shirking as they ensure that the forum can gather information to understand and challenge the behaviour of agents. Independent reviews conducted by watchdogs offer principals additional scrutiny.

12.2 Transparency and Independent Scrutiny

Explanations and scrutiny are two key elements of accountability. However, transparency is often a pre-requisite to understand the how and why of a decision. Transparency is commonly regarded as necessary to help control agents' behaviour, ensure that principals can monitor their behaviour better and to scrutinize ex post how they exercised their powers. Publicity and transparency are thus essential qualities needed to guarantee accountability. As US Justice Brandeis famously stated, 'sunlight is the best disinfectant'. Transparency literally means that we can see through how a regulator is operating and we can access information that informed its decision-making process. A transparent regulatory process is one where it is possible for outsiders to acquire the information they need to hold a regulator accountable or form an opinion about how well the regulator performed its tasks. However, transparency is not as straightforward as it may seem at first sight. Regulators and regulatees often manage the visibility of transparency undermining accountability. Publicity also differs from transparency as it stems from the regulator itself: the regulator disseminates information on its own initiative or to comply with legislative requirements.

This section first examines different concepts of transparency. It then analyses how, in light of automation, it has become increasingly difficult to provide explanations to non-specialised forums about the functioning the black-box algorithms used to regulate. Third, it considers the importance of the scrutiny conducted by independent bodies such as watchdogs.

12.2.1 Transparency

While accountability is defined as the obligation to account for one's decisions and/or actions to another body or person, transparency is concerned with making those actions and decisions accessable and assessable. Transparency is important to guarantee accountability and can consist of, and operate through, different mechanisms and instruments. Transparency is tightly linked to the communicative dimension of accountability by providing for identification, audit and oversight possibilities. It is also a precondition for, and a product of, the control framework for decision-making processes. Transparency can help address the problem of agency costs by reducing them. Transparency does not necessarily mean, however, that the account giver is adequately communicating with the accountability forum. Instead, many account givers strategically 'manage visibilities' offering transparency without providing explanations nor facilitating accountability. For example, when transparency consists in the publication of complex and imperceptible information, monitoring costs will be too high for principals.

As Flyverbom explains below, transparency is first and foremost a mechanism that helps manage the visibilities within the regulatory process. Transparency means not only providing flows of information but also decisions about disclosure, the translation of information into a format that the forum to whom account is being given understands. Transparency is thus a process of 'meaning making', not in abstract but in relation to a forum.

Flyverbom, M. (2015). 'Sunlight in Cyberspace? On Transparency as a Form of Ordering'. *European Journal of Social Theory*, 18(2), 168–184.

173–174

Transparency revolves around the production and management of visibilities, and these efforts are important features of power and governance. As Otter (2008: 1) points out: '*Who* [can] see *what, whom, when, where*, and *how* ... remains an integral dimension of the everyday operation and experience of power.' Along the same lines, Brighenti (2010: 148) reminds us that: 'The management of visibilities lies at the core of all forms of social control, whether formal or informal. More precisely ... control consists of a purposeful and contextual asymmetrisation and hierarchisation of visibilities.' In this perspective, transparency efforts can be understood as attempts to act on the world by managing possibilities for seeing, knowing and governing. That is, transparency always involves decisions about what to disclose and to whom, but also questions about flows of information and directions of visibility in concrete settings and projects. By differentiating between 'upwards', 'downwards', 'inwards' and 'outwards' forms of transparency, and by adding that these forms of transparency are ultimately about the management of visibilities, we are able to see that transparency always involves choices and divisions – who can observe whom, which activities are opened up and kept closed, and which objects and processes are subjected to transparency standards and which are not? If transparency is

> always managed and multi-directional, we need to conceptualize it in ways that are more attuned to these dynamics. To this end, the concept of translations is central.

Transparency is instrumental to accountability because when information is not accessible, nobody can be held accountable. It is thus a condition for answerability and scrutiny. But there are multiple conceptions of transparency, reflected in different types of transparency with varying degrees of openness. Coglianese and Lehr distinguish between two types of transparency: (i) fishbowl transparency and (ii) reasoned transparency. When regulators provide for fishbowl transparency, they allow regulatees to fully understand how their regulatory decisions were made. This type of transparency includes giving access to internal information by responding to Freedom of Information requests or actively publishing regulatory information. Freedom of information laws are often grounded on constitutional guarantees that establish a 'right-to-know' regarding public data and government-held information. Freedom of information laws allow any citizen to request public information for free or at minimal cost. Besides these laws, fishbowl transparency is also promoted by laws that require openness of records and the active publication of government information. The second type of transparency mentioned by Coglianese and Lehr is 'reasoned transparency', which is required in specific cases, for example, to challenge a regulatory decision in court. The information that is provided should be translated such that it is useful for that specific purpose. These two types of transparency are also connected: without disclosing the facts underlying a certain regulatory decision (fishbowl transparency), it may be impossible to offer reasoned transparency.

Transparency is a public value, a principle of good administration and good governance, and is instrumental to guarantee compliance with the rule of law. However, it is not an absolute principle. Rather, national legislation often specifies limits to transparency for the protection of confidential information, trade secrets, privacy, ongoing investigations and national security.

> **Coglianese, C., and Lehr, D.(2019).** 'Transparency and Algorithmic Governance'. *Administrative Law Review*, 71, 1–56.
>
> 18–21
>
> Transparency is integral to a legitimate government and a fair society. When government is open, officials can be expected to do their jobs better because public accountability presumably inhibits them from advancing their own self-interests at the expense of their duty to produce public value . . ..
>
> Transparency not only deters officials from taking shortcuts and bribes, it also gives other governmental actors – the courts, for example – a basis for their oversight roles. The visibility of governmental institutions also gives other nongovernmental organizations – the media, non-profit advocacy organizations, academic researchers, law firms, and businesses – the opportunity to

> monitor what the government is doing. When private individuals and organizations can learn about what government is doing, they can do a better job of organizing their own affairs by anticipating the establishment of new laws or understanding changes in government programs. Significantly, in a democracy, transparency can also help build an informed citizenry and provide a basis for more meaningful public participation in all facets of governmental decisionmaking . . ..
>
> **Types of Transparency**
>
> *Fishbowl transparency*, as its name suggests, refers to the public's ability to peer inside government and acquire information about what officials are doing. It focuses on public access to information the government holds and information about what the government does. It includes public access to government hearings, records stored in filing cabinets, and materials available on government computers. A series of federal statutes demand that the government provide fishbowl transparency. The Government in the Sunshine Act and the Federal Advisory Committee Act require meetings of multi-member commissions and advisory bodies, respectively, to be open to the public. The Freedom of Information Act (FOIA) requires agencies to provide government documents to members of the public on request. The Administrative Procedure Act (APA) requires agencies to publish notices of new regulations they propose to adopt .... These and other legal requirements help ensure that those who are affected by governmental decisions can monitor what officials are doing and respond on an informed basis. By contrast to fishbowl transparency's emphasis on public access to information about what government is doing, reasoned transparency emphasizes the usefulness of that information – that is, whether government reveals why it took action. Reasoned transparency stresses the importance of government explaining its actions by giving reasons.

As Coglianese and Lehr explain, there are different types of transparency: reasoned transparency entails disclosure of the facts underlying a decision and the reasons offered to justify a certain regulatory decision. In many jurisdictions, regulators are legally required to justify their regulatory decisions by offering explanations. Reasoned transparency is thus closely connected to the duty to explain: reasoned transparency entails revealing the information that is necessary to explain and justify a certain decision.

In 2008, regulators, banks and financial advisors failed to predict the global financial crisis. As Kempeneer (2021) explains, regulators such as national central banks and the European Central Bank (ECB) sought to address this problem by turning to big data to understand bank's financial soundness. However, this shift did not contribute to enhanced transparency since the 'black box' system of the big data assessments does not match existing regulatory perspectives of transparency, which are mostly descriptive and consisting of unilateral data-disclosure. Kempeneer proposes, instead, 'relational transparency', which 'recognises knowledge as something that is created in interaction', promoting joint knowledge production.

Kempeneer, S. (2021). 'A Big Data State of Mind: Epistemological Challenges to Accountability and Transparency in Data-Driven Regulation'. *Government Information Quarterly*, 38, 101578, 1–8, https://doi.org/10.1016/j.giq.2021.101578.

4–6

[The 2008 financial crisis] can be seen as somewhat of a turning point for financial supervision, carrying implications for risk management at large. Supervisors explained how they were left in a tricky situation . . .. Rather than still trying to theoretically understand what might be driving risk, supervisors said they tried to collect as much data as possible, in the hope the data will speak for itself, and nothing will be overlooked . . ..

Regulators conduct a Quality Assurance (QA) process to vet banks' results, relying on all the large amounts of data they collect and (semi-)automated big data tools and techniques. If the results the ECB calculated are similar enough to what the banks submitted, there is a green flag. If there is a minor discrepancy, it is flagged in orange. If there is a large difference between the results, there is a red flag . . ..

[Drawing on interviews], supervisors were said to be overly focused on what came out of their large amounts of data, rather than understanding how banks calculated their results, and where the discrepancy came from. This was very frustrating to respondents in banks. They felt that the QA process acted like a black box; predicting an outcome without necessarily explaining, or justifying, where that outcome comes from . . ..

This obscurity has two dimensions: on the one hand the ECB is not very transparent about their reasoning overall, on the other the ECB uses data-driven models that by nature act as black boxes . . ..

Respondents in banks pointed out that despite the time constraints in the exercise, they tried to reach out to the ECB to better understand where their results came from . . .. Some. . .respondents at the ECB agreed that joint discussions regarding the accuracy and validity of results were helpful . . .. This raises important questions regarding what kind of transparency is useful and necessary in a context of data-driven decision making . . ..

Rather than reducing communication with banks and producing knowledge separately, the ECB could reach out to banks to engage in joint knowledge production . . .. Democratic decision-making should be based on knowledge that, although possibly contested, both parties consider at least valid. Accountability hinges on the justification of the validity of knowledge claims. Moreover, relational transparency would not only improve accountability, but arguably also advance the quality of regulation, as both regulators and regulated entities often have abundant expertise to bring to the table.

12.2.2 The Duty to Explain

Once there is a baseline of transparency that allows for information to be used to give account, the first element of the accountability process is the obligation on the regulator to explain the basis of decisions. This includes not only the final decision itself but also the different steps that led up to this decision. When explaining their thinking process, the regulator should also justify why a certain route was taken when preparing a decision. The duty to explain can be more or less technical depending on the regulatory field and the decision at stake. The obligation to provide information when explaining the decision to stakeholders must be tailored to the regulatory scheme and the public.

With the mounting use of automation, it has become increasingly difficult to understand what reasoned transparency should entail. The extract below sheds some light on three instruments of reasoned transparency: explanations, justifications and contestations. Explanations transfer knowledge, justifications try to convince that a decision is good or was made correctly and contestations aim to show that the decision is bad. These distinctions are important because transparency as such is a limited mechanism of accountability if there are no adequate translations. While 'sunlight' may be 'the best disinfectant', only transparency in the sense of 'sunlight' (for example, providing very large source codes) may be blinding as it allows problems to be hidden in plain sight due to an information overload.

Henin, H., and Le Métayer, D. (2022). 'Beyond Explainability: Justifiability and Contestability of Algorithmic Decision Systems'. *AI & Society*, 37, 1397–1410.

1397–1399

Algorithms are increasingly used to support decision- making. The nature of these Algorithmic Decision Systems (hereinafter 'ADS') varies: some of them rely on machine learning while others do not; some of them involve a form of interaction with human users while others are entirely automatic; some of them are intended for professionals while others are aimed at the general public. Regardless of these differences, ADS are often involved in decisions that can have a significant impact on people: access to credit, employment, medical treatment, judicial sentences, etc. Entrusting ADS to make or to influence such decisions raises a variety of legal, ethical, political, and technical issues .... Broad requirements such as transparency, fairness and accountability are often presented as ways to limit these risks but they are generally ill defined, seldom required by law and difficult to implement

The goal of an explanation is to make it possible for a human being (designer, user, affected person, etc.) to *understand* (a specific outcome or the whole system). For example, an explanation for a bank loan application rejection could be that the number of outstanding loans of the applicant is too high (e.g., greater than a given threshold). This information helps to understand the logic of the [algorithmic decision systems] ....

The goal of a justification is to convince that a decision is good (or adequate, appropriate). A justification of the above loan rejection could be that applications with many outstanding loans have a high probability to lead to credit defaults, which is a risk that the bank wants to reduce. Another justification could be that banking law prohibits granting new loans when the number of outstanding loans of the applicant exceeds a given threshold . . ..

The goal of a contestation is to convince that the decision is bad (or inadequate, inappropriate). A contestation of the above decision could rely on the fact that the applicant has a significant amount of saving.

Account, Accountable, Accountability

According to Reuben Binns (2018), 'a party A is accountable to a party B with respect to its conduct C, if A has an obligation to provide B with some justification for C, and may face some form of sanction if B finds A's justification to be inadequate'. The accounts are the pieces of information that must be provided by the accountable party. We use accountability in the same sense as Binns, and therefore consider that justifications are an essential part of the accounts. Since justifications may not be considered 'adequate' (using Binns' terminology), contestability is also a key requirement for accountability.

Distinguishing Explanations and Justifications

Explanations are transfers of knowledge (from the ADS to the explainee), they are descriptive and intrinsic in the sense that they only depend on the system itself. In contrast, justifications are normative and extrinsic in the sense that they depend on a reference according to which the adequacy or appropriateness of the outcomes can be assessed. Indeed, in order to claim that an outcome is good (or adequate, appropriate) it is necessary to refer to an independent definition of what a good outcome is. In this paper, we use the word 'norm' to denote this external reference, with no legal connotation: a norm can be a legal requirement, but it can also be a corporate objective or an ethical principle for example. In the above example, the first justification is based on a corporate objective (minimization of the risks for the bank) while the second one relies on a legal norm (banking law).

Even if they often support each other, explanations and justifications have different goals and should not be conflated: a user can understand the logic leading to a particular outcome without agreeing on the fact that this outcome is good; vice versa, he/she may want to contest an outcome (being convinced that it is bad) without knowing or understanding the logic behind the algorithm. The distinction between the two notions is best illustrated by Mireille Hildebrandt (2019): 'If the decisions of an automated machine learning application indirectly discriminate on the basis of gender or race they may qualify as prohibited discrimination; explaining why the system so decided may be interesting but will not legally justify the decision. A decision of an automated system should be justifiable independently of how the system came to its conclusion.'

A contestation can be seen as the dual of a justification: its goal is to convince that the decision is bad while the goal of a justification is to convince that the decision is good. They are also dual in the sense that the source (or issuer) of a justification is the operator (or designer) of the ADS whereas the source of a contestation is a user of the ADS or a person affected by its decisions.

> Justifications alone would lead to a unilateral process whereas contestations introduce a dialectic, conversational process.

The second element of accountability is exposure to scrutiny. This entails the requirement to answer questions and allow the process to be made meaningful. Effective scrutiny is a way of counterbalancing the power of the regulators, improving regulatory outcomes and controlling the quality of the regulatory process. There are several scrutiny mechanisms and actors. It can take the form of consultation (see Chapter 5), where response is invited from stakeholders or a process of inquiry initiated by an independent body such as watchdogs.

12.2.3 Independent Oversight: Watchdogs

Independent oversight institutions have become crucial in contemporary democracies, serving as 'watchdogs' that promote accountability, transparency and effectiveness of regulators. The primary goal of watchdogs is to promote transparency, accountability and ethical behaviour by those in positions of power and to ensure that the public is informed and protected against the abuse of public authority. While the term 'watchdogs' can be used in general terms to refer to individuals (e.g., journalists) and organisations that monitor the use of power, this section focuses on watchdogs as independent institutions that oversee regulators. As Wille and Bovens (2020: 185) explain:

> watchdogs are 'statutory agencies that have a primary function of scrutinizing the actions of the public sector and providing reports independent of those scrutinized'. They can do so by providing recommendations, solutions, or by administering sanctions. Ombudsmen, auditors, and anti-corruption agencies are primarily watchdog institutions, courts and parliaments are not.

Well-known watchdogs are Ombud institutions, ethical committees, integrity offices, national courts of auditors and, in the EU, the European Court of Auditors and the European Ombudsman.

Watchdogs investigate performance issues, uncover corruption and report their findings to Parliaments and the public. As the extract explains, these institutions also play an important role in preventing executive abuse by revealing misconduct, corruption and mismanagement. As independent but publicly financed institutions, they promote intra-governmental accountability. That is, they are independent public institutions that hold other public institutions accountable. Moreover, watchdogs do not just highlight the problems in the public sector; they also aim to solve them.

Stuhmcke, A. (2022). 'Government Watchdog Agencies and Administrative Justice'. In M. Hertogh et al. (eds.), *The Oxford Handbook of Administrative Justice*. Oxford University Press, 115–136.

116–117.

> Government watchdog agencies are a global phenomenon. Their role is to render government accountable to the citizen. Defined as an 'institution, person or group of people whose job is to check that [governments] are not doing anything illegal or ignoring people's rights' (Oxford Dictionary 2019), watchdog [s] ... act as administrative mechanisms to 'reconcile the requirements of efficiency and administration and justice to the citizen' (Commonwealth Administrative Review Committee 1971, para 389). To do so they operate across a wide range of government activities to correct poor administration ranging from rudeness to government error through to corruption and other forms of criminal behaviour.
>
> Watchdog agencies come in a multiplicity of forms and resolve a wide range (in both scope and depth) of administrative justice–related issues. The phrase 'watchdog agencies' is used here as an umbrella term to capture the oversight functions of both government and nongovernment agencies, ranging from the courts to industry ombudsman to media including a range of mechanisms such as investigation, review, and inquiry for review of administrative decision-making ....
>
> Statutory watchdog agencies ... include bodies with generalist statutory jurisdiction, such as government ombudsman, through to bodies that have statutory oversight of particular areas of government activity, such as corruption commissions, freedom-of-information agencies, or environmental authorities. They present across legal systems as ombudsman, auditor generals, integrity commissioners, anti-corruption agencies, and commissions of inquiry such as royal commissions. With a mandate to ensure that 'each governmental institution exercises the powers conferred on it in the manner in which it is expected and/or required to do so and the purposes for which those powers were conferred, and for no other purpose' (Spigelman 2004, 726), government watchdog agencies are created to improve government accountability. Universally their shared aim is firstly to safeguard the rights and interests of individuals, and secondly to articulate society's desires as to how government decisions affecting individuals are and should be made ....
>
> The definition of watchdog agencies excludes courts and tribunals. The court system is linked to but separate from watchdog agencies, and the traditional model of administrative law is dominated by the courts as the legitimating mechanism for executive decision-making. However, it is also the case that the reach of courts as a review mechanism to facilitate accountability through judicial review of government decision-making has diminished as the involvement of the executive in lawmaking has increased.

The Ombud, an originally Swedish institution, is an important watchdog that has been transplanted all over the world. As Kirkham (2022) explains, 'the dominant rationale behind the global growth of the ombud institution was a societal need to humanise the bureaucratic systems that implement public power'. The Ombud pursues this goal by handling complaints about government's maladministration through an independent complaint-handling service, conducting investigations into systematic violation of the principles of good administration, rule of law and other legal values and seeking to offer a general quality assurance or incentives to the improvement of public and private services for the benefit of citizens at large. Although the Ombud is most commonly known as a complaint-handler who mediates conflicts between citizens and public regulators and is not allowed to issue sanctions, Erkkilä explains below that the Ombud has also been deployed for additional functions, namely as a guardian of human rights (for example, in South America) and to combat corruption. As the extract explains, the Ombud is also a mediator between regulators and politics who supports the dynamic character of accountability systems.

Erkkilä, T. (2020). *Ombudsman as a Global Institution: Transnational Governance and Accountability*. Palgrave Macmillan.

12–22

In its traditional form, the ombudsman supervises the use of public power and its legality, implying also public administration and government. It operates on the basis of complaints filed by citizens, the public. The ombudsman is not a court, but instead derives its authority from the publicity of its decisions that as such sanction the misuse of power without ruling out the possibility of further legal action. It hence provides an institutional form or site for the public as an 'accountability forum' (Bovens 2005), relying on legal expertise of the ombudsman. Finally, the ombudsman – both an institution and an individual – is also a public figure with a media profile.

Accountability systems also evolve over time and between institutional contexts, where the intra-institutional setting might be decisive in terms of how institutions of accountability function. The institutional changes may be incremental, involving institutions being constantly 'renegotiated' over time (Thelen 2004, 34–35). But as mentioned above, institutional change often implies political conflict, which may manifest itself in various ways in the work of the ombudsman. The ombudsman is also seen as a 'marker of the limits of politics' or as an agent between the fields of law, administration and politics, pointing to its balancing act in maintaining independence while controlling the use of public power . . ..

The institution is often seen as a mediator, an institution of conflict resolution and guardian of human rights. The different types or generations of ombudsmen are now tending to converge conceptually or are 'hybridizing', for example, as classical ombudsman institutions – such as the Finnish Parliamentary Ombudsman . . . are adopting the tasks of human rights institutions, advocates of good governance and even act as mediators alongside their role as legal overseer.

12.3 Contemporary Regulatory Accountability Challenges

We now consider several regulatory accountability challenges discussed in recent academic literature. These include the challenges of holding private regulators and multi-actor networks ('Many Hands Problems') accountable as well as the complexity of giving account to multiple forums or in the context of algorithmic decision-making. The section concludes with a reflection on 'regulatory respect' or the shift from hard and technocratic accountability models to more collaborative and participatory approaches.

12.3.1 Privatisation and Contracting Out

It is not uncommon for scholars to express concern about the weakening of accountability resulting from privatisation and the outsourcing of public tasks. Outsourcing refers to the practice of contracting out specific tasks or services undertaken within the public sector to private firms that perform a certain task on behalf of others. Privatisation involves transferring the ownership and control of public assets or services to private entities. The rationale for both outsourcing and privatisation is to rely on market mechanisms and private sector expertise to reduce costs, raise quality and achieve wider benefits such as greater innovation and improved efficiency.

Advocates of outsourcing often claim that private contractors can be held accountable by private market mechanisms such as competition or electoral politics. However, accountability mechanisms tend to fail in the context of private contracts due to the lack of information about performance, costs and liability allocation. Even though public procurement law aims to promote fair competition among private contracts and offer transparency, public contracts are often underspecified, giving too much discretion to agents and limited oversight opportunities and capabilities to principals. Moreover, the contracting process is typically complex and characterised by limited openness due to the need to protect confidential information. As a result, accountability problems may only be identified too late or never. Minow's example of the controversial outsourcing of military tasks to private contracts illustrates these accountability problems. Minow's critique serves as a critical reminder that private contractors are not bound by the same codes, structures and obligations as public regulators.

Minow, M. (2005). 'Outsourcing Power: How Privatizing Military Efforts Challenges Accountability, Professionalism, and Democracy'. *Boston College Law Review*, 46(5), 989–1026, http://lawdigitalcommons.bc.edu/bclr/.

990–1020

Congressional and media sources charge the Halliburton Company, a Houston-based oil services firm previously headed by Vice President Richard Cheney, with overcharging $61 million worth of gasoline and for charging $186 million for meals not actually served as part of its $10 billion worth of contracts with the Department of Defense . . . to support the U.S. military effort in Iraq . . .. One account indicates that the unaccounted-for charges amount to 43% of the amount the company billed, though that estimate understates the full $5.6 billion of contracts awarded since the start of the Iraq war . . ..

Investigative reports into the abuses at the Abu Ghraib prison identify participation of private contractors as one example of the poor supervision, confused lines of authority, and improper procedures at that site . . ..

Congress adopted bipartisan caps on the number of civil servants employed by the government – but did not limit the number of persons who could be employed through contracts with private companies. For nearly a decade this has allowed policymakers to hide from public view the true size of the government. Many of the functions the government could outsource involve not only commercial activities such as transportation, laundry, and food services, but also planning, policy development, managing weapon systems, and managing the military workforce . . ..

Reliance on private sources for important tasks, such as logistics and maintenance of advanced technological weapons, may in addition relieve the military of developing those capacities internally – to the longterm detriment of military strength. Similarly; depending upon contracts for the leases of trucks and equipment without ensuring appropriate maintenance plans can leave the military vulnerable at crucial movements to failures beyond their control to remedy. If the contractor in turn does not pay subcontractors – as was the case apparently with Halliburton – vendors may grow resentful or even collapse under bankruptcy. Alternatively, the military also may compromise its strength by relying through layers of subcontracts on people it.

Those arguing against the privatisation of prisons, for example, worry that the use of private companies to incarcerate convicted criminals may leave inmates with fewer avenues of redress if prison guards commit abuses. This is precisely the situation described below. On the flip side, other commentators argue that private firms actually provide greater oversight of employees than do government agencies and that religiously motivated workers or volunteers work harder than do civil servants. These examples reflect a concern about the impact of privatisation on accountability, while illustrating that accountability can mean different things depending on the context.

Gunderson, A. (2022). *Captive Market: Accountability and State Prison Privatization*. Oxford University Press.

1–7

[W]hy do states privatize their prisons? Though this question appears simple at first glance, it is much more complex than it appears . . ..

[A]n important incentive to privatize not currently emphasized in the literature is accountability. States' responses to inmate litigation condition the likelihood of privatizing. As the number of people incarcerated grew, so too did the volume of inmate lawsuits facing state governments. Inmates filed lawsuits at ever increasing rates because of growing legal and political concerns, and states were facing a mountain of prison litigation that they had previously never had to handle. Privatizing limits states' legal and political accountability for poor prison conditions. It is in this environment that the modern private prison industry was born . . ..

Private prisons and the role of the market in government service provision has attracted considerable controversy in the scholarly, legal, and public communities. Though there is a surprising dearth of information regarding the public's

> opinion on privatization (see Ramirez, 2021 for one exception), the little evidence that does exist indicates that while citizens support market intervention into benign service areas such as garbage collection and janitorial services, they balk at private companies operating prisons of any kind. Additionally, most Americans seem to agree that the government should not privatize prisons. The public at large is still therefore grappling with the consequences of adopting this policy . . ..
>
> Questions surrounding whether the government is able to delegate such broad authority to a private company or how this delegation squares with the constitution remain at the forefront of debates on prison privatization (Austin and Coventry, 2001). These concerns are largely normative as the federal government has dismissed these challenges as legally inconsequential. A presidential commission released a report on privatization in 1988 and did not consider these accountability concerns to be impediments to prison privatization – the report cites the federal statutes that permit prison privatization and notes no state had yet passed legislation expressly prohibiting privatization of prisons . . ..
>
> An outstanding question centers around the accountability of for-profit corrections companies. Namely, while public managers of prisons are responsible to citizens through the legislative and executive branches, private managers are primarily responsible to their shareholders. A public manager is an employee of the state and can be removed from his post easily. A private manager, however, is beholden to both the government who contracted with them to provide the service and the shareholders of the company by which they are employed. As Laffont and Tirole (1991) point out, employees of private companies suffer from a conflict of interest between the government and their shareholders . . ..
>
> Proponents of prison privatization argue that these concerns can be incorporated into the construction of robust contracts to prevent companies from abusing their informational advantages . . ..
>
> [The] contract is incomplete by its nature since the government cannot fully specify the full spectrum of what must be done in every situation. Additionally, prison contracts can be ineffective at reining in irresponsible behavior on behalf of the companies themselves. Under such conditions, we might expect incentives for the private company to engage in cost-cutting at the expense of quality, whereas a manager of an equivalent public facility cooperates with the government to increase both quality and cost savings

In recent decades, several private actors have gradually assumed greater regulatory roles, particularly in the field of enforcement (see Chapter 10). However, public accountability mechanisms such as transparency obligations and public participation duties do not bind private regulators, which can result in accountability deficits. Kariv-Teitelbaum (2021) acknowledges the value of privatising regulation but also suggests some measures to mitigate the risks of losing accountability when privatising regulation:

> **Kariv-Teitelbaum, Y. (2021).** 'Privatization of Regulation: Promises and Pitfalls'. In A. Dorfman and A. Harel (eds.), *The Cambridge Handbook of*

Privatization. Cambridge University Press, 263–285, doi:10.1017/9781108684330.017.

283

Under certain conditions, [privatization] can complement and reinforce regulatory regimes, while in other situations it may distort regulatory goals. It is therefore essential first to identify which type of entity a regulatory function is privatized to, and to clarify the entity's central motivations and the norms to which it responds. This enables an assessment of when the privatization of regulation may raise concerns, as well as an exploration of how to better design the legal mechanisms that facilitate the privatization process. This is especially relevant in the case of privatizing via delegation, which is often conducted through a formal legal mechanism such as a contract (e.g., outsourcing regulation), franchise or license (e.g., accreditation and certification) or legislative mandate (e.g., industry-based regulators). Further research is required to investigate whether the risks of privatizing regulation can be mitigated by legal mechanisms and limitations, such as: privatizing only easy-to-specify regulatory functions that require narrow discretion; privatizing only peripheral functions that are far from the public regulator's core responsibility; incorporating mandatory duties designed to maintain the public regulators' knowledge and expertise (e.g., mandatory reporting duties, public ownership of databases, etc.); applying public law norms (e.g., mandatory cooling-off periods, an obligation to avoid disproportional infringement of human rights, etc.); or implementing partial public accountability mechanisms (e.g., transparency obligations, public participation duties, etc.).

12.3.2 Many Hands, No Hands, Many Eyes?

Accountability forums can be confronted with multiple potential account givers. It may be challenging to unravel who has contributed to the conduct of an agency, and in what way, and who can be made accountable for specific actions, and to what degree. Dennis Thompson (1980: 905) has called this the problem of 'many hands': 'Because many different officials contribute in many ways to decisions and policies of government, it is difficult even in principle to identify who is morally responsible for political outcomes.' In other words, decisions may cross a number of desks before they are made and implemented. New members of committees add ideas and rules of their own but may no longer work for the institution years later when the effects of poor performance become noticeable. Even when the chain of responsibility was well defined, it could be that the individual who was once responsible no longer works for this body or that the rules have changed in the meantime. Thus, the conduct of an organisation acting as an agent is often the result of the interplay between fatherless traditions and orphaned decisions. The question then arises: who should be held accountable when a decision 'passes many hands'?

Gkliati and Kilpatrick apply the problem of many hands to EU migration policy. The extract connects the problem of the accountability of many actors with other important transparency challenges, namely lack of transparency.

Gkliati, M., and Kilpatrick, J. (2021). 'Crying Wolf Too Many Times: The Impact of the Emergency Narrative on Transparency in FRONTEX Joint Operations'. *Utrecht Law Review*, 17(4), 57–72, https://doi.org/10.36633/ulr.770.

57–63

Whether it is the Lampedusa shipwreck, the Syrian war, terrorism, or Covid-19, the EU migration policy in recent years is heavily crisis-driven. It seems to be in a constant state of emergency, responding spasmodically to perceived threats that change guise, but fit comfortably within a well-designed narrative of securitisation, understood as the political connection of migration to societal dangers, or the political construction of migration as a security issue. Within it, the need for public security vis-à-vis external threats outweighs fundamental rights and the core democratic priority of accountability and oversight of public institutions.

The EU Border and Coast Guard Agency (Frontex) has experienced, since its establishment in 2004, an impressive expansion of its powers and competencies, holding the largest budget amongst all EU agencies. Regrettably, the expansion of its mandate was not coupled with an equivalent enhancement of accountability safeguards, including transparency safeguards. More generally, the lack of transparency has been widely problematised especially in light of the reported involvement of the Agency in human rights violations . . ..

When addressing complex structures, such as the European Border and Coast Guard (EBCG), the attribution of responsibility is not always clear. The multiple actors involved can lead to difficulties in identifying who is responsible for a harmful result, for instance in a case of human rights violations. The political philosopher, Dennis Thompson, describes this as 'the problem of many hands,' a difficulty in pinpointing responsibility.

The problem of many hands, however, is not synonymous with complex organisations and does not always appear when multiple actors are involved. It results from the lack of transparent structures, distinctly defined tasks and responsibilities and gaps in overall openness and transparency. In situations that combine a vague framework, complex structure and lack of transparency, it can become impossible to find one actor that is entirely and independently responsible for the outcome, since the outcome is a collective one. It also becomes practically difficult to distinguish and prove who has contributed, and to what extent, to which particular part of the outcome, and should thus be held responsible for it.

Bovens describes the problem as a practical, but also as a normative one, in highly problematic cases, where the collectivity, with the sum of the actions of its individual members, meets the criteria, but the same cannot be said for all of its individual parts. These are situations where there is no clear division of tasks and formal responsibilities or transparency in the stages of preparation and execution so that the facts, but also the de facto responsibilities, become more or less obvious. This collective outcome can be the case in EBCG operations,

> especially since the clear a priori division of responsibilities and the lack of transparency are long-standing issues.
>
> The problem of many hands functions as a wall behind which actors may hide their own contribution and shift the blame onto other actors involved. This frustrates the attempts to establish accountability and, consequently, the prevention of misconduct in the future. It is, in this sense, a problem of control.
>
> In fact, the problem of many hands is intrinsically connected to blame-shifting, where the actors involved can take advantage of the confusion in tasks and responsibilities in order to deny their responsibility and blame others. The multiplicity of actors can potentially create confusion as to the bearer of responsibility and may result in gaps in the legal accountability and the effective legal protection of those affected by immigration control.
>
> In the case of Frontex, understanding the full range of implications of the command and control structure in practice is undoubtedly constrained by the gaps in transparency . . .. This creates complications regarding the division and allocation of responsibility and inhibits evidence collection. This subsequently creates gaps in accountability, as the different responsibilities can be conflated and hidden behind a veil of secrecy.

The many hands problem is prevalent in regulatory fields with complex networks of actors (see Section 12.3.4).

12.3.3 Multiple Accountabilities

The problem of multiple accountabilities arises when an agent is accountable to multiple forums and is answerable to different stakeholders. This problem affects not only the accountability of regulators but also of regulatees when they are asked to comply with contradictory regulations issued by different regulators. For instance, healthcare regulation embodies autonomous, highly distributed and heterogeneous yet interdependent actors, including healthcare organisations, healthcare workers, professional bodies, patient groups and pharmaceuticals. Regulators must account for multiple regulatees. However, many of these actors may be rivalrous and have conflicting goals. Healthcare stands out simultaneously as a paradigmatic case of the 'many hands' and multiple accountabilities problems with unfortunate consequences for the safety of this sector. In contrast to other regulated sectors (e.g., construction, aviation), healthcare has not experienced a significant improvement in safety throughout the preceding decades arguably due to a failure among healthcare actors, including regulators, to coordinate their actions.

The existence of multiple principals means that agents may be confronted with contradictory instructions and 'blame games'. Multiple accountabilities have been the source of many disasters such as the explosion of the Challenger space in 1983. Aleksovska and Schillemans argue nonetheless that the multiple accountabilities do not necessarily need to be seen in a negative light, as existing studies shows that agents combine different accountability mechanisms to account effectively to multiple forums.

> **Aleksovska, M., and Schillemans, T. (2022).** Dissecting Multiple Accountabilities: A Problem of Multiple Forums or of Conflicting Demands? *Public Administration*, 100(3), 711–736, https://doi.org/10.1111/padm.12763.
>
> Public sector actors are said to operate within webs of accountability. They continuously and simultaneously respond to a multitude of legitimate claims coming from a number of different stakeholders, also referred to as accountability 'forums'. This has been frequently discussed in the literature under the theme of *multiple accountabilities*. The presence of multiple accountabilities, however, is usually seen in a rather negative light. Large-scale tragedies like the space shuttle Challenger disaster, failures of agencies to act consistently, blame games, opportunity costs, and purely symbolic accountability have all been attributed to it. Yet, from the extant literature it remains unclear through which mechanisms multiple accountabilities create these problems, and, thus, how these problems come about . . ..
>
> Other accounts suggest that multiple accountability pressures are accepted as a fact of life by public sector professionals, and that they are often handled in a fairly routinized fashion, using well-developed and tested strategic coping mechanisms. Analyses of the work of executive public managers in the Netherlands and public caseworkers in the United States have found that these actors routinely use the strategies of transparency, anticipation, information gathering, consultations, and building rapport, among others, in their management of multiple accountabilities. Thus, while the multiple accountability pressures might bring some frustrations, they are generally not perceived as insurmountable problems. In addition, scholars have argued that the simultaneous operation of multiple accountabilities has positive effects on the governance regime as a whole, as it enhances the possibilities to hold power to account. Thus, the literature paints a fairly disjointed picture as to the effects and consequences of multiple accountabilities.

The food sector is an example of the existence of multiple accountabilities. The example below illustrates the challenge of holding actors accountable when there is no accountability culture or clear distribution of responsibility (Box 12.1).

12.3.4 Algorithmic Accountability

As regulators and other organisations increasingly rely on automated systems, including systems that incorporate machine learning (or AI), 'algorithmic accountability' has become an important concern. Calls for algorithmic accountability arise from concerns about the opacity and impact of computational systems, and the need to ensure that organisations are held accountable for their impacts on others. However, securing effective algorithmic

Box 12.1 Multiple Accountabilities in the Food Industry: Accountability Challenges in China

In recent years, China has faced several significant food safety scandals. The most notable was the Chinese Milk Scandal of 2008, where melamine was found in baby formula, resulting in 39,965 infants requiring medical attention, 12,892 hospitalisations and 4 fatalities. The incident had far-reaching social implications, triggering a crisis of public trust in the dairy industry. To understand the accountability problems of the Chinese food industry, we need to understand the history of its regulation.

To address the need for preventive health measures, routine health supervision and control of infectious diseases in China, a command-control approach was introduced in 1954. This approach aimed to establish 'food hygiene' and solidify the legal and supervisory standing of health administration nationwide within the framework of the previous command regime. However, this system of public accountability, which was focused on catering and consumption, was unable to keep up with the fast development of the Chinese food industry. Following the first milk scandals, a new multi-sectoral model was adopted in 2004 in order to ensure that different stakeholders assume responsibility for food safety. However, this model did not delineate clearly the boundaries between the different domains of accountability. Consequently, there were many 'power-overlaps and power-vacuums'. Scholarship has pointed out that there is a lack of accountability culture, limited available accountability procedures and limited ways to hold public regulators accountable.

Source

Yang, R., Klasien, H., and Penders, B. (2022). 'Constructing the Accountability of Food Safety as a Public Problem in China: A Document Analysis of Chinese Scholarship, 2008–2018'. *Journal of Chinese Governance*, 7(2), 236–265, doi: 10.1080/23812346.2020.1796160.

accountability can be challenging for at least two reasons: first, limited transparency and complexity characterise 'black-box' algorithmic decisions that make it hard for principals to scrutinise. As Busuoic explains, when complex and opaque algorithms are employed, the ability to provide explanations and make decisions contestable (see above) becomes more limited. Here, providing transparency regarding the potential risks may be insufficient as it does not allow the principals to understand, scrutinise and contest the produced the regulatory decisions. The extract also mentions the limitations of existing regulatory and technological initiatives to explain AI-generated outputs. Second, algorithmic decisions are rarely the product of one algorithm developed by one person or institution but of algorithmic systems that have been produced by many people at many different organisations.

Busuioc, M. (2021). Accountable Artificial Intelligence: Holding Algorithms to Account. *Public Administration Review*, 81, 825–836, https://doi.org/10.1111/puar.13293.

825–831

A proprietary algorithm widely used by US courts to predict recidivism in both bail and sentencing decisions was flagged by *ProPublica* as biased against black defendants; natural language processing (NLP) algorithms for textual analysis can display recurrent gender biases, for instance, associating the word 'doctor' with 'father' and 'nurse' with 'mother' . . .. These are only a few of the growing number of examples of bias encountered in algorithmic systems used not only in private but also public sectors . . ..

[A]s algorithmic systems have become increasingly ubiquitous in the public sector, they raise important concerns about meaningful oversight and accountability and the need to identify and diagnose where the potential for accountability deficits associated with these systems might – first and foremost – lie . . ..

These informational deficits – stemming from algorithms' inherent opacity, complexity, or proprietary nature – have direct implications for the next phase of accountability: *explanation* or *justification*. The ability to explain the *rationale* leading to a particular decisional outcome is key to interrogating and challenging such outcomes. It is this phase that differentiates accountability from transparency or the mere provision of information above: being able to screen, prod, and pry the *logic* behind actions and decisions.

Explainable and Justifiable Algorithms?

Yet explanation is precisely what is especially difficult to achieve due to AI algorithms' inherent operation. This is especially true for deep learning algorithms. These technical challenges are no doubt also due to the fact that traditionally, the main evaluative criteria for algorithm performance have been based on designer-determined metrics such as 'predictive accuracy' rather than model interpretability. However, a growing realization of the need for interpretability – the need to 'provide qualitative understanding between the input variables and the response' (Ribeiro, Singh, and Guestrin 2016, 1136) – is emerging among computer science scholars: 'Understanding the reasons behind predictions . . . is fundamental if one plans to take action based on a prediction, or when choosing whether to deploy a new model' . . ..

As deep learning black-box models continue to be the most successful algorithmic approach, computer science scholars have been working towards rendering such models more understandable. Ongoing potential approaches range from feature visualization techniques – aimed at visualizing the workings of hidden layers of neuron interactions to render internal processes more explicit (e.g., activation atlases by Google and OpenAI) – to interfacing 'black-box' algorithms with 'explainer algorithms', i.e., essentially using algorithms to explain algorithms. 'Explainer algorithms' could conceivably unpack a black-box for instance, by producing a simpler algorithm (say, a decision tree) to explain that black-box. The explainer algorithm effectively re-digests the black-box features into features that are understandable for the human mind . . ..

The discussion above suggests a glaring deficit in algorithm oversight: with black-box algorithms widely used in the public sector and given that such algorithms are not interpretable, domain experts and other public sector users are unlikely to be able to spot biases and unintended consequences of algorithmic performance in the real world. Regulatory efforts too, have fallen behind practice, and in most jurisdictions there is no legal obligation on the industry to rely on interpretable models, or even to explain their algorithms as a prerequisite to commercializing them for public use, even for simpler models. Many algorithms involved in high-stakes public decision-making (e.g., public benefits eligibility) routinely lack for instance, audit trails and meaningful explanations of their outcomes.

GDPR, the EU-wide data protection legislation, does introduce a series of remedies and safeguards on algorithmic decision-making. Yet these protections – and it is much debated whether these amount to a meaningful right of explanation – are restricted to solely automated decisions. In most cases however as noted, high-stakes algorithmic decisions are not fully automated but rather algorithmic outputs serve as decisional aides, falling outside the scope of these protections.

Conclusion

Regulation can be viewed as a principal-agent relationship. Both public and private regulators act as agents of one or different publics (principals) when they regulate. Since regulation is a means to an end rather than an end in itself, it is important to ensure that regulators pursue the interests of their principals. Accountability was presented in this chapter as a mechanism that provides institutional arrangements whereby a regulator accounts to a forum.

Regulators can nonetheless have different accountability holders or forums. While traditional studies on regulatory accountability focused on the principal-agent model, more recent empirical research has demonstrated that account holders are not always invested in the delegation process or do not always stand to lose out when the agents drift from their assigned missions.

Discussion Questions

1. How does the agency theory differ from the stewardship theory?
2. Conduct some research to identify cases where the stewardship theory has been applied to hold regulators accountable.
3. How do accountability mechanisms operate as control measures to prevent abuses of power?
4. Why is accountability a condition for regulatory legitimacy?
5. What does Flyverbom mean by 'management of visibilities' and how does this differ from reasoned transparency that is needed to hold regulatory actors accountable?
6. Identify two regulatory settings that were not mentioned in this chapter, which are characterised by the Problem of Many Hands.

Conclusion

Regulation has become a permanent and enduring feature of the way in which contemporary democratic market economies are governed. There are few spheres of economic activity that are not subject to some form of regulatory oversight and control. Daily news programs rarely pass without some mention of a significant regulatory decision, proposed regulatory reform or allegation of some regulatory failure or scandal. Yet the practice of regulation is far from simple or straightforward. It has spawned a rich and extensive body of scholarly work, requiring familiarity with several disciplines and concepts, including economics, the nature of risk and the relations between technological innovation and society. These concepts were introduced in Part I of the book. When the original edition of this book was first published, its primary aim was to introduce all newcomers to the study of regulation, whatever the source of their curiosity, prior disciplinary background or motivation. This second edition has remained faithful to that original ambition. To this end, we have employed a 'regulatory lens' (set out in Parts II and III of this book) organising the literature around a general conceptual framework supported by a set of analytical constructs that may be applied to the regulation of any social domain, in any democratic jurisdiction, in order to understand and critically evaluate how regulatory governance regimes are designed, practised, implemented and reformed.

More than fifteen years have passed since the original edition of this book was released in 2007. In that year, the first iPhone launched, marking the beginning of the smartphone revolution. Along with many other networked digital applications, these devices have transformed almost every aspect of our lives. The accompanying and on-going digital transformation, fuelling the meteoric rise of Big Tech, has brought myriad benefits and conveniences, including those associated with social media use. These devices have, for example, nurtured increasing political consciousness amongst those who might not otherwise be politically engaged, drawing attention to the urgent and existential threats posed by climate change, the plight of minorities long subject to systemic and structural discrimination, marginalisation, exploitation and exclusion (reflected in the Black Lives Matter movement, #Me Too, the Mahsa Amini protests in Iran) and facilitating the fall from grace of powerful men previously considered untouchable, including acclaimed Hollywood film producer Harvey Weinstein. But the rise of Big Tech has also transformed the distribution of power, raising a host of social, economic, political and legal challenges, which regulators everywhere have belatedly begun to address. These include cybercrime; ransomware attacks; new forms of worker exploitation; exposing teenagers and children with access to smartphones to new forms of harm, resulting yearly in incidents of grooming, scamming and cyberbullying, often with tragic results; and the spread of disinformation, political manipulation and microtargeting, threatening the integrity of democratic elections and undermining epistemic trust. These phenomena appear to have played some role in the outcome of the Brexit referendum, the election of Donald Trump, the 2021 attack by Trump supporters on the Capitol building, and ongoing violent international conflicts in Ukraine and Gaza.

The rise of Big Tech has also benefitted from, and concurrently accelerated, processes of globalisation that were already well underway by 2007. Although globalisation is not a new phenomenon, it has since deepened and widened thanks to the embeddedness of neoliberal ideology, the rapid planetary connectivity the Internet enables, together with extension of complex transnational supply chains. The resulting interdependence between multiple and overlapping systems, as well as a proliferation of non-state actors and organisations involved in the task of regulatory governance, has produced more complex regulatory regimes and greater vulnerabilities to systemic risks. In this respect, the 2008 Global Financial Crisis, the COVID-19 pandemic, the Russian attack on Ukraine and the more recent violence between Hamas and Israel in Gaza, all offer stark reminders. An increasing prominence of risk discourse, including ideas associated with risk assessment and risk management, has accompanied these changes. This has marked a shift in discussions about regulatory intervention in the language of risk and its management, rather than in the language of economics and the need to address market failures.

Although the role of expertise to inform regulatory decision-making has endured, regulators are more inclined to look to expertise, particularly those offering predictions rooted in scientific and other quantitative methods. Experts in data science, machine learning and AI, with their promise of 'more accurate' predictions (relative to conventional statistical analysis) have dethroned economists, who were once the primary 'go to' source of advice for regulators when neoliberalism was on the ascendancy. The globalisation of risk has introduced greater complexity into the task of regulation, demanding more collective and coordinated action by public regulators entailing more systematic and strategic forms of oversight, which has nurtured the proliferation of auditing cultures and systems within and between organisations.

Yet the benefits and burdens of globalisation have been unevenly distributed, exacerbating inequality between rich and poor as a new 'billionaire' class has emerged. Although smartphone technology has contributed significantly to social mobility in several African and Asian middle-income countries such as India, Nigeria and Kenya, the digital divide has not disappeared. Rather, there are now many more and more nuanced digital divides across the globe: those living in remote areas around the world remain deprived of access to basic telecommunications infrastructure or only have access to overpriced internet, while in several African countries, investments in digital infrastructure by wealthier countries bear resemblances to colonialist practices (so-called digital colonialism, see Chapter 3). However, regulation studies has become more sensitive to distributional inequalities, often traceable to entrenched structural discrimination against historically marginalised groups. Intentional attempts to address the sources of distributional inequality and injustice are increasingly recognised as legitimate bases for regulatory intervention. This is a clear departure from an earlier era in which matters of redistribution were largely relegated to the realm of politics. This belated recognition of the importance of equality and inclusion has, however, met with considerable resistance in the ensuring period since 2007, particularly in the face of growing economic hardship or other sources of dissatisfaction, facilitating the turn to populism and the election of extreme right-wing and nationalist governments. We have witnessed the embrace of public policies within self-described democratic states that reflect a 'me first' mentality, challenging the legitimacy of transnational powers such as the European Commission, and fuelling hostility towards immigrants and an unsympathetic attitude towards asylum-seekers seeking protection in ever-expanding numbers in the face of national political instability, uncertainty and violence.

The need for intentional, coordinated action by regulators is, however, arguably most acute and pressing in addressing global warming and the need for urgent reduction in CO2 emissions worldwide. Addressing the climate emergency is a wicked problem. Although communities in many parts of the world turn to electricity-generated vehicles to reduce their carbon footprint, the extractive impact of the expansion of the sourcing of raw materials (lithium, cobalt, nickel, graphite, manganese) primarily through deep earth extraction techniques in Africa and Asia by local workers under unsafe and exploitative conditions, that are needed to produce electric batteries and microchips for computer processes, has been largely overlooked. Similarly, the looming challenge of hazardous waste disposal that electric vehicle batteries generate at the end of their life has been conveniently kicked down the road. Yet lack of sufficient action to tackle the external effects produced by fossil fuel consumption has not prevented states from adopting measures aimed at regulating the impact of activities initiated outside their borders. European regulators are no longer regulating for their own jurisdictions. The global reach of Big Tech firms and their network-enabled practices has prompted European policymakers to design regulations with extra-territorial effects, attempting to ensure that these modern 'digital empires' (Bradford 2020, 2023) comply not only with EU laws (including the EU's General Data

Protection Regulation, Digital Services Act and Digital Markets Act) but also with so-called European values (e.g., respect for human rights, democracy and the rule of law).

In other words, a number of important social, political and technological developments have invariably affected the design, implementation and effectiveness of regulation in the intervening years since the original edition appeared. The regulatory landscape is now considerably more complex than it was before the onset of the Second Machine Age. Perhaps we should not be surprised by the many regulatory failures that occurred in recent decades, but the seriousness of a number of scandalous failures, including VW Dieselgate, the explosion of the Deep Water Horizon oil rig in the Gulf of Mexico and London's Grenfell Tower disaster, suggest that regulatory design, policy and practice is not being undertaken wisely and well, at least in some sectors. In this book, we have attempted to highlight some of the most important regulatory challenges that now arise in this altered landscape, seeking to locate them within their larger political, economic, and societal context. Accordingly, we have brought into the frame scholarship from a number of disciplines in the humanities and social sciences whose authors might not self-identify as regulatory governance scholars. Although these major societal changes have substantially complicated the regulatory endeavour, the basic conceptual framework introduced in the first edition has endured. It continues to provide a valuable analytical frame for understanding, designing, implementing and critically reflecting upon the challenges of regulation and its effectiveness and legitimacy. Despite its superficial appearance as boring, mundane and technocratic, what makes the study of regulation so important and endlessly fascinating, and which we hope we have demonstrated, is that regulation is political 'all the way down'. By this we are not suggesting that regulation is merely politics in disguise. Rather, regulatory decisions require attention to a host of normative values, in light of specific needs and circumstances, which often demand difficult trade-offs between competing values in seeking to steer economic and social activity in directions that better serve the needs and welfare of affected communities and stakeholders. As a field of an interdisciplinary inquiry, which seeks to manage risk, inequality and power imbalances, it is presents a microcosm of contemporary life that is anchored in the stability and protection of the rule of law but capable of adaption to changing social needs and circumstances.

Regulation, at the end of the nineteenth century ensured that trains loaded with coal fuelled the Industrial Revolution. Later, it helped put an end to the exploitation of child labour by industry, but in our altered contemporary conditions, it has hitherto failed to protect children from addictive online content that corrodes their self-esteem and mental health and online grooming and sexual exploitation, while women and girls are increasingly dehumanised by the production of 'deep fake' pornography produced by computer-generated image manipulation techniques. Regulation has not yet put an end to other exploitative practices such as those that allow technological industries to grow thanks to the extraction of minerals in low-income countries. Such practices prosper because current regulatory regimes are failing to protect them. There is still much regulatory work left to do. A substantial gender pay gap remains in most countries, climate change concerns continue to grow, populism is on the rise, and discrimination on the grounds of race, religion, and other grounds is amplified by digital technology. As this second edition goes to press, many serious and enormously difficult regulatory challenges remain. We hope that this book will offer a valuable set of resources that can and will help to address them.

References

Introduction

Beck, U. (1992). *Risk Society: Towards a New Modernity*. Translated by M. Ritter. Sage.

Hood, C., Rothstein, H., and Baldwin, R. (2001). *The Government of Risk: Understanding Risk Regulation Regimes*. Oxford University Press.

Osborne, D., and Gaebler, T. (1994). *Reinventing Government*. Penguin.

Chapter 1 Introduction to Economics

Akerlof, G. A. (1970). 'The Market for "Lemons": Quality Uncertainty and the Market Mechanism'. *Quarterly Journal of Economics*, 84, 488–500.

Baumol, W. J. (1977). 'On the Proper Cost Tests for Natural Monopoly in a Multiproduct Industry'. *The American Economic Review*, 67(5), 809–822.

Baumol, W. J., Panzar, J. C., and Willig, R. D. (1983). 'Contestable Markets: An Uprising in the Theory of Industry Structure: Reply'. *The American Economic Review*, 73(3), 491–496.

Coase, R. H. (1937). 'The Nature of the Firm'. *Economica N.S.*, 4, 386–405. Reprinted in G. J. Stigler and K. E. Boulding (eds.), *Readings in Price Theory*. Richard D. Irwin.

(1960). 'The Problem of Social Cost'. *Journal of Law and Economics*, 3, 1–44.

Hardin, G. (1968). 'The Tragedy of the Commons'. *Science*, 162(3859), 1243–1248. www.jstor.org/stable/1724745.

Mullainathan, S., and Shafir, E. (2013). *Scarcity: Why Having Too Little Means So Much*. Times Books.

Pindyck, R. S., and Rubinfeld, D. L. (2018). *Microeconomics*. 9th ed. Pearson.

Sen, S. C., Nordhaus, W., and Samuelson, P. A. (2019). *Economics* 20th ed. McGrawHill.

Sianesi, B., and Van Reenen, J. (2003). 'The Returns to Education: Macroeconomics'. *Journal of Economic Surveys*, 17(2), 157–200.

Tversky, A., and Kahneman, D. (1982). 'Judgment under Uncertainty: Heuristics and Biases'. In D. Kahneman, P. Slovic and A. Tversky (eds.), *Judgment under Uncertainty*. Cambridge University Press, 3–22.

Varian, H. (2009). *Intermediate Microeconomics: A Modern Approach*. 8th ed. W. W. Norton Company.

Williamson, O. (1975). *Markets and Hierarchies: Analysis and Antitrust Implications*. Free Press.

(1979). 'Transaction Cost Economics: The Governance of Contractual Relations'. *Journal of Law and Economics*, 22, 233–261.

Chapter 2 The Rise of Risk in Regulatory Governance

6, P. (2014). 'Elementary Forms and Their Dynamics: Revisiting Mary Douglas'. *Anthropological Forum*, 24(3), 287–307. DOI:10.1080/00664677.2014.933090.

Aven, T., and Renn, O. (2010). *Risk Management and Governance, Concepts, Guidelines and Applications*. Vol. 16. Springer Science & Business Media.

Black, J. (2010). 'The Role of Risk in Regulatory Processes'. In R. Baldwin, M. Cave and M. Lodge (eds.), *The Oxford Handbook of Regulation*. Oxford University Press, 302–348.

Douglas, M., and Wildavsky, A. B. (1982). *Risk and Culture: An Essay on the Selection of Technical and Environmental Dangers*. University of California Press.

Hood, C., Rothstein, H., and Baldwin, R. (2001). *The Government of Risk: Understanding Risk Regulation Regimes*. Oxford University Press.

Renn, O. (1998). 'Three Decades of Risk Research: Accomplishments and New Challenges'. *Journal of Risk Research*, 1(1), 49–71.

Risk, J. (1995). *Risk*. Routledge.

Sandin, P., Peterson, M., Hansson, S. O., Rudén, C., and Juthe, A. (2012). 'Five Charges against the Precautionary Principle'. In A. Bird and J. Ladyman (eds.), *Arguing about Science*. Routledge, 617–628.

Stirling, A. (2016). 'Precaution in the Governance of Technology'. in R. Brownsword, E. Scotford and K. Yeung (eds.), *The Oxford Handbook on Law, Regulation and Technology*. Oxford University Press.

Chapter 3 Technological Innovation

Bradford, A. (2020). *The Brussels Effect: How the European Union Rules the World*. Oxford University Press.

(2023). *Digital Empires: The Global Battle to Regulate Technology*. Oxford University Press.

Brownsword, R., Scotford, E., and Yeung, K. (2016). 'Law, Regulation and Technology: The Field, Frame, and Focal Questions'. In R. Brownsword, E. Scotford, and K. Yeung (eds.), *The Oxford Handbook of the Law and Regulation of Technology*. Oxford University Press, 3–38.

Moses, L. B. (2007). 'Recurring Dilemmas: The Law's Race to Keep up with Technological Change'. *University of Illinois Journal of Law, Technology and Policy*, 239.

Murrey, A. (2020). 'Colonialism'. In A. Kobayashi (ed.), *International Encyclopedia of Human Geography*. 2nd ed. Elsevier, 315–326. https://doi.org/10.1016/B978-0-08-102295-5.10804-2.

Yeung, K. (2018). 'Algorithmic Regulation: A Critical Interrogation'. *Regulation & Governance*, 12(4), 505–523.

Chapter 4 Theories of Regulation

Ayres, I., and Braithwaite, J. (1991). 'Tripartism: Regulatory Capture and Empowerment'. *Law & Social Inquiry*, 16, 435–496.

Barber, A. (2021). 'Consumed – The Need for Collective Change'. *Colonialism, Climate Change & Consumerism*. Octopus, 98–102.

Becker, G. (1976). 'Toward a More General Theory of Regulation'. *The Journal of Law & Economics*, 19(2), 245–248. www.jstor.org/stable/725165.

Carpenter, D. (2013). *Preventing Regulatory Capture*. Cambridge University Press.

Demsetz, H. (1968). 'Why Regulate Utilities?'. *The Journal of Law & Economics*, 11(1), 55–65. www.jstor.org/stable/724970.

den Hertog, J. A. (2010). 'Review of Economic Theories of Regulation'. Discussion Paper Series, *Tjalling C. Koopmans Research Institute*, 10(18). https://dspace.library.uu.nl/handle/1874/309815.

Downer, J. (2010). 'Trust and Technology: The Social Foundations of Aviation Regulation'. *The British Journal of Sociology*, 61, 83–106.

Gunningham, N., and Johnstone, R. (1999). *Regulating Workplace Safety: Systems and Sanctions*. Oxford University Press.

Levine, M. E., and Forrence, J. L. (1990). 'Regulatory Capture, Public Interest, and the Public Agenda: Toward a Synthesis'. *Journal of Law, Economics, & Organization*, 6, 167–198. www.jstor.org/stable/764987.

Luhmann, N. (2004). *Law as a Social System*. Oxford University Press.

(2013). *Introduction to Systems Theory*. Polity Press.

Nickel, J. W. (1987). *Making Sense of Human Rights: Philosophical Reflections on the Universal Declaration of Human Rights*. University of California Press.

Peltzman, S. (1976). 'Toward a More General Theory of Regulation'. *Journal of Law and Economics*, 19(2), 211–240.

Posner, R. A. (1969). 'Natural Monopoly and Its Regulation'. *Stanford Law Review*, 21 (3), 548–643. https://doi.org/10.2307/1227624.

(1974). 'Theories of Economic Regulation'. *The Bell Journal of Economics and Management Science*, 5(2), 335–358. https://doi.org/10.2307/3003113.

Stigler, G. J. (1971). 'The Theory of Economic Regulation'. *The Bell Journal of Economics and Management Science*, 2(1), 3–21. https://doi.org/10.2307/3003160.

Suraci, O. (2021). 'The Best-dressed Polluter Regulation and Sustainability in the Fashion Industry'. *Hastings Environmental Law Journal*, 27(2), 225–242.

Tollison, R. D. (1988). 'Public Choice and Legislation'. *Virginia Law Review*, 74(2), 339–371. https://doi.org/10.2307/1073146.

van der Heijden, J. (2022). 'The Value of Systems Thinking for and in Regulatory Governance: An Evidence Synthesis'. *SAGE Open*, 12(2). https://doi.org/10.1177/21582440221106172.

Chapter 5 Regulatory Policy

Adler, M. D., and Posner, E. A. (1999). 'Rethinking Cost-Benefit Analysis'. *The Yale Law Journal*, 109(2), 165–247. https://doi.org/10.2307/797489.

Adler, M., and Posner, E. A. (2001). *Cost-Benefit Analysis: Economic, Philosophical, and Legal Perspectives*. Chicago University Press.

(2006). *New Foundations of Cost-Benefit Analysis*. Harvard University Press.

Alberto, A. (2022). 'EU Citizen Participation "in the Union's Democratic Life": A Policy and Legal Analysis, *The EU Political System After the 2019 European Elections*, 23–44. doi:10.1007/978-3-031-12338-2_2.

Alemanno, A. (2015). 'How Much Better Is Better Regulation? Assessing the Impact of the Better Regulation Package on the European Union: A Research Agenda'. *European Journal of Risk Regulation*, 6(3), 344–356. www.jstor.org/stable/24769555.

De Francesco, F., and Radaelli, C. M. (eds.). (2023). *The Elgar Companion to the OECD*. Elgar Companions to International Organisations. Edward Elgar.

Dunlop, C. A., Maggetti, M., Radaelli, C. M., and Russel, D. (2012). 'The Many Uses of Regulatory Impact Assessment: A Meta-analysis of EU and UK Cases'. *Regulation & Governance*, 6: 23–45. https://doi.org/10.1111/j.1748-5991.2011.01123.x

Dunlop, C. A., Kamkhaji, J., Radaelli, C. M., Taffoni, G., and Wagemann, C. (2020). 'Does Consultation Count for Corruption? The Causal Relations in the EU-28'. *Journal of European Public Policy*, 27(11), 1718–1741. https://doi.org/10.1080/13501763.2020.1784984.

Livermore, M., and Revesz, R. (2021). *Reviving Rationality: Saving Our Cost-Benefit Analysis for the Sake of the Environment and Our Health*. Oxford University Press.

Pedersen, H. H., Binderkrantz, A. S., and Christiansen, P. M. (2014). 'Legislative Process in Denmark'. *Legislative Studies Quarterly*, 39: 199–225. https://doi.org/10.1111/lsq.12042.

Purnhagen, K. P., and Feindt, P. H. (2015). 'Better Regulatory Impact Assessment: Making Behavioural Insights Work for the Commission's New Better Regulation Strategy'. *European Journal of Risk Regulation*, 6(3), 361–368. www.jstor.org/stable/24769558.

Radaelli, , C. M. (2004). 'The Diffusion of Regulatory Impact Analysis: Best Practice or Lesson-drawing?'. *European Journal of Political Research*, 43: 723–747. https://doi.org/10.1111/j.0304-4130.2004.00172.x.

Revesz, R. L., and Livermore, M. A. (2008). *Retaking Rationality: How Cost-benefit Analysis Can Better Protect the Environment and Our Health*. Oxford University Press.

Rose-Ackerman, S. (2013). 'Precaution, Proportionality, and Cost/Benefit Analysis: False Analogies'. *European Journal of Risk Regulation*, 4(2), 281–286. www.jstor.org/stable/24323368.

Sunstein, C. R. (2001). 'Cost-Benefit Default Principles'. *Michigan Law Review*, 99(7), 1651–1723. https://doi.org/10.2307/1290477.

Sunstein, C. (2019) *The Cost-Benefit Revolution*. MIT Press.

Wegrich, K. (2015). 'Which Results? Better Regulation and Institutional Politics'. *European Journal of Risk Regulation*, 6(3), 369–371. www.jstor.org/stable/24769559.

Chapter 6 Regulatory Modalities, and Instruments and Techniques

Bemelmans-Videc, M.-L., Rist, R. C., and Vedung, E. O. (eds.). (2011). *Carrots, Sticks, and Sermons: Policy Instruments and Their Evaluation*. Vol. 1. Transaction, Routledge.

Lessing, L. (2009). *Code: And Other Laws of Cyberspace*. Basic Books.

Nemitz, P. (2018). 'Constitutional Democracy and Technology in the Age of Artificial Intelligence'. *Philosophical Transactions of the Royal Society A*, 376(2133), 20180089.

Thompson, G. (ed.). (1991). *Markets, Hierarchies and Networks: The Coordination of Social Life*. Sage.

Torfing, J. (2012). 'Governance Networks'. In D Levi-Faur (ed.), *The Oxford Handbook of Governance*. Oxford University Press, 99–112.

Chapter 7 Hybrid Instruments and Experimental Regulations

Ayres, I., and Braithwaite, J. (1992). *Responsive Regulation.* Oxford University Press.

Medzini, R. (2022). 'Enhanced Self-regulation: The Case of Facebook's Content Governance'. *New Media & Society* 24(10), 2227–2251.

Ogus, A. (1995). 'Rethinking Self-Regulation'. *Oxford Journal of Legal Studies,* 15, 97–108, https://doi.org/10.1093/ojls/15.1.97.

Rees, J. V. (1996). *Hostages of Each Other: The Transformation of Nuclear Safety since Three Mile Island.* University of Chicago Press.

Chapter 8 Regulatory Rules

Bevan, G., and Hood, C. (2006). 'What's Measured Is What Matters: Targets and Gaming in the English Public Health Care System'. *Public Administration,* 84, 517–538.

Black, J. (1998). 'Talking about Regulation'. *Public Law,* 77–105.

Busch, L. (2011). *Standards: Recipes for Reality.* MIT Press.

Ranchordás, S. (2022). 'Empathy in the Digital Administrative State'. *Duke Law Journal,* 71, 1341.

Raz, J. (1979). *The Authority of Law.* Oxford University Press.

Spinardi, G. (2019). 'Performance-based Design, Expertise Asymmetry, and Professionalism: Fire Safety Regulation in the Neoliberal Era'. *Regulation & Governance,* 13, 520–539.

Yeung, K. (2022). 'The New Public Analytics as an Emerging Paradigm in Public Sector Administration'. *Tilburg Law Review,* 27, 1–32.

Chapter 9 Regulatory Compliance, Public Enforcement and Private Certification

Ayres, I., and Braithwaite, J. (1992). *Responsive Regulation: Transcending the Deregulation Debate.* Oxford University Press.

Braithwaite, J., Walker, J., and Grabosky, P. (1987). 'An Enforcement Taxonomy of Regulatory Agencies.' *Law & Policy,* 9(3), 323–351.

Busch, L. (2011). 'The Private Governance of Food: Equitable Exchange or Bizarre Bazaar?'. *Agriculture and Human Values,* 28, 345–352.

European Commission. (2024). Regulatory Framework Proposal on Artificial Intelligence, https://digital-strategy.ec.europa.eu/en/policies/regulatory-framework-ai.

Grabosky, P. N., and Braithwaite, J. (1986). *Of Manners Gentle: Enforcement Strategies of Australian Business Regulatory Agencies.* Oxford University Press.

Hampton, P. (2005). *Reducing Administrative Burdens: Effective Inspection and Enforcement.* HM Treasury.

Hawkins, K. (1984). *Environment and Enforcement: Regulation and the Social Definition of Pollution.* Oxford University Press.

Hutter, B. M. (1997). *Compliance: Regulation and Environment.* Oxford University Press.

Kagan, R., and Scholtz, J. (1984). 'The Criminology of the Corporation and Regulatory Enforcement Strategies'. In J. Hawkins and J. Thomas (eds.), *Enforcing Regulation.* Kluwer-Nijhoff, 67–95.

Lipsky, M. (1980). *Street-level Bureaucracy: Dilemmas of the Individual in Public Service.* Russell Sage Foundation.

Yeung, K. (2004). *Securing Compliance.* Hart.

Chapter 10 Private Enforcement and Redress

Cane, P. (2002). *Responsibility in Law and Morality*. Bloomsbury/Hart.

Chevalier, E. (2020). 'Standing before French Administrative Courts and Environmental Protection: Not Specific Enough for an Effective Access to Justice?'. *Persona e Amministrazione*. 317(1). https://doi.org/10.14276/2610-9050.2207.

Garoupa, N., and Ginsburg, T. (2009). 'Guarding the Guardians: Judicial Councils and Judicial Independence'. *American Journal of Comparative Law*, 57(1), 103–134.

Issacharoff, S. (2007). 'Regulating after the Fact'. *DePaul Law Review*, 56, 375.

Loughlin, M. (2000). *Sword and the Scales*. Hart.

Oberdiek, J. (2017). *Imposing Risk: A Normative Framework*. Oxford University Press.

Yeung, K. (2013). 'Better Regulation, Administrative Sanctions and Constitutional Values'. *Legal Studies*, 33(2), 312–339.

(2019). *A Study of the Implications of Advanced Digital Technologies (including AI Systems) on the Concept of Responsibility within a Human Rghts Framework*. Council of Europe, MSI-AUT.

Chapter 11 Regulatory Legitimacy

Abbott, K. W., Levi-Faur, D., and Snidal, D. (2017). 'Theorizing Regulatory Intermediaries: The RIT Model'. *The Annals of the American Academy*, 670, 14–35. https://doi.org/10.1177/0002716216688272.

Allan, T. R. S. (1994). 'The Rule of Law'. in T. R. S. Allan (ed.), *Law, Liberty and Justice*. Oxford: Oxford University Press, 20–47.

Binderkrantz, A. S., Christiansen, P. M., and Pedersen, H. H. (2015). 'Interest Group Access'. *Governance*, 28: 95–112. https://doi.org/10.1111/gove.12089.

Bradford, A. (2019). *The Brussels Effect: How the European Union Rules the World*. Oxford University Press.

Braithwaite, J., and Drahos, P. (2000). *Global Business Regulation*. Oxford University Press.

Braun, C., and Busuioc, M. (2020). 'Stakeholder Engagement as a Conduit for Regulatory Legitimacy?'. *Journal of European Public Policy*, 27(11), 1599–1611, doi: 10.1080/13501763.2020.1817133.

Carpenter, D. (2010). *Reputation and Power: Organizational Image and Pharmaceutical Regulation at the FDA*. Princeton University Press.

Cashore, B. (2002). 'Legitimacy and the Privatization of Environmental Governance: How Non-State Market Driven (NSMD) Governance Systems Gain Rule Making Authority'. *Governance* 15, 503–529.

Cassese, S. (2005). 'Administrative Law without the State? The Challenge of Global Regulation'. *New York University Journal of International Law and Politics* 37, 663.

Curtin, D. (2009). *Executive Power in the European Union: Law, Practice, and Constitutionalism*. Oxford University Press.

Harlow, C., and Rawlings, R. (2007). 'Promoting Accountability in Multi-Level Governance: A Network Approach'. *European Law Journal* 13, 542.

Hyde, A. (1983). 'The Concept of Legitimation in the Sociology of Law'. *Wisconsin Law Review*, 379–476.

Jepperson, R. L. (1991). 'Institutions, Institutional Effects, and Institutionalism'. In W. W. Powell and P. J. DiMaggio (eds.), *The New Institutionalism in Organizational Analysis*. University of Chicago Press, 143–163.

Scott, C. (2000). 'Accountability in the Regulatory State'. *Journal of Law and Society*, 27, 38.

Schmidt, V. (2006). *Democracy in Europe: The EU and National Polities*. Oxford University Press.

Sunstein, C. (1990). *After the Rights Revolution: Reconceiving the Regulatory State*. Harvard University Press.

Thatcher, M. (2002). 'Regulation after Delegation: Independent Regulatory Agencies in Europe'. *Journal of European Public Policy*, 9, 954.

Tucker, R. C. (1968). 'The Theory of Charismatic Leadership'. *Daedalus*, 97 (3):731–756.

Tyler, T. R. (1990). *Why People Obey the Law*. Princeton University Press, Princeton.

Weber, M. ([1922] 1978). *Economy and Society: An Outline of Interpretive Sociology*. University of California Press.

(1948). 'Bureaucracy'. In H. H. Gerth and C. Wright Mills (eds.), *Max Weber, Essays in Sociology*. Routledge, 196–266.

(1964). *The Theory of Social and Economic Organization*. Edited by T.Parsons. Free Press.

Chapter 12 Regulatory Accountability

Albanese, R., Dacin, M. T., and Harris, I. C. (1997). 'Agents as Stewards'. *Academy of Management Review* 22(3): 609–611. doi: 10.5465/amr.1997.15868807.

Bovens, M. (1998). *The Quest for Responsibility: Accountability and Citizenship in Complex Organisations*. Cambridge University Press.

(2005). 'Public Accountability'. In E. Ferlie, L. Lynn and C. Pollitt (eds.), *The Oxford Handbook of Public Management*. Oxford University Press, 182–208.

(2007). 'Analysing and Assessing Accountability: A Conceptual Framework'. *European Law Journal*, 13(4), 447–468. https://doi.org/10.1111/j.1468-0386.2007.00378.x.

Brennan, N. M., and Solomon, J. (2008). 'Corporate Governance, Accountability and Mechanisms of Accountability: An Overview'. *Accounting, Auditing & Accountability Journal*, 21(7), 885–906. doi: 10.1108/09513570810907401.

Busuioc, E. M., and Lodge, M. (2016). 'The Reputational Basis of Public Accountability'. *Governance*, 29(2), 247–263. https://doi.org/10.1111/gove.12161.

Busuioc, M. (2013). *European Agencies: Law and Practices of Accountability*. Oxford University Press.

Davis, J. H., Schoorman, F. D., and Donaldson, L. (1997). 'The Distinctiveness of Agency Theory and Stewardship Theory (reply)'. *Academy of Management Review* 22(3), 611–613.

(2018). 'Toward a Stewardship Theory of Management'. In Alan E. Singer (ed.), *Business Ethics and Strategy*. Volumes I and II. Routledge, 473–500.

Gilad, S. (2008). 'Accountability or Expectations Management? The Role of the Ombudsman in Financial Regulation'. *Law & Policy*, 30(2), 227–253. https://doi.org/10.1111/j.1467-9930.2008.00275.x.

Grant, R. W., and Keohane, R. O. (2005). 'Accountability and Abuses of Power in World Politics'. *American Political Science Review*, 99, 29.

Kirkham, R. (2022). 'The Ombud as a Chameleon: A Story of Adaptation to Different Administrative Cultures'. In M. Hertogh et al. (eds.), *The Oxford Handbook of Administrative Justice*. Oxford University Press, 89–114.

Mashaw, J. L. (2006). 'Accountability and Institutional Design: Some Thoughts on the Grammar of Governance'. In M. W. Dowdle (ed.), *Public Accountability: Designs, Dilemmas and Experiences*. Cambridge University Press, 115–156.

Mulgan, R. (2003). *Holding Power to Account. Accountability in Modern Democracies*. Palgrave.

Nollkaemper, A. (2015). 'The Problem of Many Hands in International Law'. In A. Fabricotti (ed.), *The Political Economy of International Law: A European Perspective*. Edgar Elgar.

Otter, C. (2008). *The Victorian Eye: A Political History of Light and Vision in Britain, 1800–1910*. University of Chicago Press.

Schillemans, T., and Busuioc, M. (2015). 'Predicting Public Sector Accountability: From Agency Drift to Forum Drift'. *Journal of Public Administration Research and Theory*, 25(1), 191–215. https://doi.org/10.1093/jopart/muu024.

Schillemans, T., and Bjurstrøm, K. H. (2020). 'Trust and Verification: Balancing Agency and Stewardship Theory in the Governance of Agencies'. *International Public Management Journal*, 23(5), 650–676, doi: 10.1080/10967494.2018.1553807.

Thompson, D. F. (1980). 'Moral Responsibility of Public Officials: The Problem of Many Hands'. *American Political Science Review*, 74(4), 905–916.

Trebilcock, M. J., and Iacobucci, E. M. (2002). 'Privatization and Accountability'. *Harvard Law Review*, 116, 1422. https://doi.org/10.2307/1342731.

UK House of Lords. (2004). 'The Regulatory State: Ensuring its Accountability'. Report. https://publications.parliament.uk/pa/ld200304/ldselect/ldconst/68/68.pdf.

Conclusion

Bradford, A. (2020). *The Brussels Effect: How the European Union Rules the World*. Oxford University Press.

(2023). *Digital Empires: The Global Battle to Regulate Technology*. Oxford University Press.

Index

For EU product safety concerns, contact us at Calle de José Abascal, 56–1°,
28003 Madrid, Spain or eugpsr@cambridge.org.

www.ingramcontent.com/pod-product-compliance
Lightning Source LLC
LaVergne TN
LVHW062203200926
848484LV00006B/1311
* 9 7 8 1 0 0 9 3 7 9 0 1 4 *